LONELY PLANET PUBLICATIONS

NEIL WILSON
MARK BAKER

PRAGUE

CITY GUIDE

INTRODUCING PRAGUE

Interior of the Estates Theatre (p101), where Mozart's Don Giovanni *premiered in 1787*

Prague can be all things to all people. It's the equal of Paris in terms of beauty. The history goes back a millennium. And the beer? The best in Europe.

The 1989 Velvet Revolution that freed the Czechs from communism bequeathed to Europe a gem of a city to stand beside stalwarts like Rome, Amsterdam and London. Not surprisingly, visitors from around the world have come in droves, and on a hot summer day it can feel like you're sharing Charles Bridge with the rest of humanity. But even the crowds can't take away from the spectacle of a 14th-century stone bridge, a hilltop Gothic castle and a lovely, lazy river – the Vltava – that inspired one of the most hauntingly beautiful pieces of 19th-century classical music, Smetana's 'Moldau'.

Modern history buffs will be riveted by the ups and the downs of the 20th century here, from the country's founding in 1918 to the tragic Nazi occupation of WWII, the communist coup in 1948, the Warsaw Pact invasion of 1968, and finally the triumph of 1989 that brought hundreds of thousands of peaceful protesters onto the streets and sent playwright Václav Havel to Prague Castle.

Since 1989 it seems the changes have only become more frenetic. The city's arts and music scenes are thriving once again; the cultural calendar is packed with events and festivals, including the internationally renowned Prague Spring in May and early June. The standards of restaurants and hotels are much improved and unrecognisable from just a decade ago.

And if that's not enough to pique your interest, the beer is pretty good, too.

PRAGUE LIFE

It'll now cost you a whopping 50,000Kč fine to let your dog run off its leash, and dog owners are up in arms. Petrol prices may be rising, property values stagnating and the economy facing the possibility of its first prolonged slowdown since the 1989 Velvet Revolution, but one of the hotter topics at bars and cafés these days is the country's new animal law.

Supporters say the law protects both dogs from being struck down by cars and children from being bitten by aggressive animals, but at least a few suspicious Prague residents see a different motive: yet another chance for the cops to line their pockets with bribes. It's not unlike the 'points' system introduced a few years ago for driving infractions, they say. The result: the police now have more discretion than ever to levy 'fines', and road fatalities have never been higher.

A more likely explanation, though, is that the authorities are simply trying to get the city to clean up its act and pull it upmarket – to be more fitting of a major European tourist destination. There's been a growing sense since the Velvet Revolution first threw off the shackles 20 years ago that the pendulum had perhaps swung too far in the direction of lawlessness and that it was time to restore a sense of order.

The dog law has coincided with new rules on littering that could fine careless gum-chewers up to 30,000Kč for tossing gum onto the street. Smokers will have it equally tough disposing of cigarette butts. Even urinating in public, one of those peculiar Czech pastimes that was either refreshingly unabashed or downright disgusting (depending on how badly you had to go at the moment), is now against the law.

And speaking of going upmarket, the number of British stag parties appears to be dropping after several years of growth. You'll still see hordes of drunken mates on a weekend pre-nup bender, but not as frequently as you might have a couple of years ago. Economic worries in Britain and the ever-rising Czech crown apparently do have a silver lining.

Old Town Square (p87) bustles at dusk (as well as most other times of the day)

HIGHLIGHTS

1

HISTORY & ARCHITECTURE

In Prague you can soak up a thousand years of European history, laid out in a giant smorgasbord of architectural styles that ranges from soaring Gothic and voluptuous baroque to elegant Art Nouveau and that uniquely Czech take on architecture, Cubist.

2

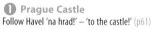

➊ Prague Castle
Follow Havel 'na hrad!' – 'to the castle!' (p61)

➋ Charles Bridge
At its best on a misty summer's morning (p75).

➌ Vyšehrad
Escape the crowds at Prague's other castle (p115).

➍ Prague Jewish Museum
A sombre reminder of a darker side of Prague's history (p96).

➎ Vinohrady
The district that brings on bouts of apartment-envy (p120).

➏ Municipal House
Art Nouveau for breakfast, lunch and dinner (p99).

1 Letná
Praguers and visitors alike love the views from this hilltop park (p131).

2 Wallenstein Garden
Now, *this* is what you call a *real* garden…(p79)

3 Vltava River
Take a paddle on a hired boat from Slav Island (p113).

OUTDOOR PRAGUE

When the sun comes out, Prague's countless parks and gardens – not to mention the Vltava and its islands – come into their own. Whether it's skating in Stromovka, hiking up Petřín or just lounging with a beer in Letná, don't forget to pack shades and sunscreen.

DRINKING

Prague is a drinker's town par excellence – the Czechs did invent lager, after all. From traditional pubs full of froth-tipped moustaches to cool cocktail bars where the staff are even more stylish than the clientele, Prague has the lot.

1 U zlatého tygra
Where Havel took Bill Clinton to experience a real Prague pub (p183).

2 U vystřeleného oka
Classic Žižkov pub, probably the most authentic in town (p186).

3 Letenský zameček (Letná beer garden)
Just the place to spend a lazy Sunday afternoon (p187).

ART & LITERATURE

From Kafka to Kundera, the Czechs have made a major contribution to 20th-century European literature. In the art world, 'artist-provocateur' David Černý keeps up the Czech tradition of creating challenging and controversial art that makes us smile at the same time.

❶ Veletržní Palace
Four floors of modern art in a magnificent functionalist building (p134).

❷ Franz Kafka Museum
Explore the claustrophobic and paranoid world of Kafka's novels (p79).

❸ Kafka's Grave
True Kafka fans can make a pilgrimage out to the Jewish Cemetery (p125).

❹ David Černý
Černý's witty works pop up all over Prague (p137).

❺ Franz Kafka Monument
Based on one of his stories, Kafka rides on an empty suit's shoulders (Map pp88–9).

4

5

MUSIC

Music is everywhere in Prague: from the great classical concert halls to the basement jazz joints; from the buskers lining Charles Bridge to the sounds of piano practice tinkling from an open window in a Malá Strana backstreet.

❶ Rudolfinum
Play 'spot the famous composer' among the statues lining the roof (p97).

❷ Dvořák's Tomb
The most famous Czech composer is buried at Vyšehrad Cemetery (p117).

❸ Buskers on Charles Bridge
A few coins in the hat gets you an open-air jazz gig (p75).

❹ Smetana Monument
Some consider Smetana superior to Dvořák – follow the debate at the Smetana museum (p100).

❺ Chapel of Mirrors
One of the prettiest concert venues in the city (p99).

❻ Smetana Hall, Municipal House
Stages the first performance of the annual Prague Spring festival (p99).

5

6

1 Bunkr Parukářka
Beer and industrial music in the depths of a nuclear bunker (p194).

2 Ecotechnical Museum
Who could resist a museum dedicated to sewage disposal? (p130)

3 Žižkov TV Tower
Futurist landmark covered in…crawling babies? (p128)

4 Cubist lamppost
Where else in the world has a Cubist lamppost? (p118)

OFFBEAT PRAGUE

One of the best bits about visiting Prague is wandering off the main streets to discover the sort of weird and wonderful stuff that you don't seem to find back home.

CONTENTS

THE AUTHORS

Neil Wilson

Neil first succumbed to the pleasures of Prague back in 1995, beguiled, like everyone else, by its ethereal beauty, but also drawn to the darker side of its hidden history. He has returned regularly for a fix of the world's finest beers and the chance to track down yet another obscure monument. Recently, Neil has worked on Lonely Planet's *Eastern Europe, Czech & Slovak Republics* and *Prague* guides. A full-time freelance writer since 1988, Neil has travelled on five continents and written around 50 travel and walking guides for various publishers. He is based in Edinburgh, Scotland. For more information see www.neil-wilson.com.

Neil was the coordinating author and wrote the Getting Started, Sports & Activities, Excursions, Transport and Directory chapters. He also cowrote the Neighbourhoods, Shopping, Eating, Drinking, Entertainment and Sleeping chapters.

NEIL'S TOP PRAGUE DAY

I'd start at Ebel Coffee House (p182) in the Týn Courtyard, relaxing with the papers over a cappuccino. After browsing the nearby Anagram (p146) and Big Ben (p146) bookshops, I'd cross the river to Malá Strana and wander through either the Wallenstein Garden (p79) or the Palace Gardens Beneath Prague Castle (p79).

For lunch I'd grab a riverside table at Hergetova Cihelna (p159), then take the funicular railway up Petřín (p84) for a garden stroll to Strahov Monastery (p69), followed by a visit to the Story of Prague Castle (p66) exhibit. Then I'd walk east through Letná Park to the Letenský sady beer garden (p187) for a Gambrinus with a view over the city.

Finally, I'd have dinner on the terrace at U zlaté studně (p158), followed by live jazz (and more beer) at U malého Glena (p197).

LONELY PLANET AUTHORS

Why is our travel information the best in the world? It's simple: our authors are passionate, dedicated travellers. They don't take freebies in exchange for positive coverage so you can be sure the advice you're given is impartial. They travel widely to all the popular spots, and off the beaten track. They don't research using just the internet or phone. They discover new places not included in any other guidebook. They personally visit thousands of hotels, restaurants, palaces, trails, galleries, temples and more. They speak with dozens of locals every day to make sure you get the kind of insider knowledge only a local could tell you. They take pride in getting all the details right, and in telling it how it is. Think you can do it? Find out how at **lonelyplanet.com**.

Mark Baker

Mark Baker is a journalist and freelance writer based in Prague. He first moved there in 1991 to cover the aftermath of the Velvet Revolution and wound up making a lifetime out of it. He was an editor at the *Prague Post* in its early days, was one of the original founders of the Globe Bookstore & Coffeehouse and also spent several years as an editor and correspondent at Prague-based Radio Free Europe/Radio Liberty. His articles have appeared in the *Wall Street Journal* and *National Geographic Traveler,* among others.

Mark wrote the Introducing Prague, Background and Architecture chapters, and cowrote the Neighbourhoods, Shopping, Eating, Drinking, Entertainment and Sleeping chapters.

PHOTOGRAPHER

Richard Nebesky

Richard was born in Prague's grungy Žižkov suburb, but surprisingly without a camera in hand. His father gave him his first point-and-shoot unit. Ever since, a camera has been with him on treks, ski adventures and cycling trips, and while researching Lonely Planet books around the globe. He has also worked for various magazines and travel guide publishers and on many social photography projects.

GETTING STARTED

Beyond booking accommodation, you can do as much or as little planning as you like – Prague is one of those places best explored at random, discovering hidden corners on your own. Getting around is easy, food is served all day (and half the night) and there are treats aplenty for budgets big or small. Just let serendipity be your guide!

WHEN TO GO

Prague caters for visitors all year round, so there's really no such thing as a bad time to visit. The city is at its prettiest in spring, when the many parks begin to bloom with flowers and the budding leaves on the trees are a glowing green.

The tourist crush is especially oppressive during Easter and Christmas through New Year, as well as in May (during the Prague Spring festival), June and September. Many Czechs go on holiday in July and August, when the weather can be uncomfortably hot – you'll probably want a hotel with air-con at this time of year. If you can put up with the cold and the periodic smog alerts, hotel space is plentiful in winter (outside Christmas to New Year), and the city looks gorgeous and mysterious under a mantle of snow.

FESTIVALS

Spring and autumn are the main festival seasons in Prague, as the big classical music events take place during these times. Other minor festivals and events are scattered throughout the year.

January

THREE KINGS' DAY (SVÁTEK TŘÍ KRÁLŮ)

6 January

Three Kings' Day, also known as Twelfth Night, marks the formal end of the Christmas season on 6 January. The Czechs celebrate it with carol-singing, bell-ringing and gifts to the poor.

ANNIVERSARY OF JAN PALACH'S DEATH

19 January

A gathering in Wenceslas Square commemorates the Charles University student who burned himself to death in 1969 in protest against the Soviet occupation (see the boxed text, p29).

February

MASOPUST

www.carnevale.cz

Street parties, fireworks, concerts and revelry mark the Czech version of carnival. Banned by the communists, this ancient tradition was first revived in Žižkov in 1993, and the rest of the city is now joining in. Celebrations start on a Friday before Shrove Tuesday (aka Mardi Gras), and end with a masked parade.

March

ST MATTHEW FAIR (MATĚJSKÁ POUŤ)

From the Feast of St Matthew (24 February) up to and including Easter weekend, the Výstaviště exhibition grounds (p130) fill up with roller coasters, fairground rides, ghost trains, shooting galleries and stalls selling candy floss and traditional heart-shaped cookies. The fair is open 2pm to 10pm Tuesday to Friday and 10am to 10pm Saturday and Sunday.

BIRTHDAY OF TOMÁŠ G MASARYK

7 March

The father figure and first president of Czechoslovakia is commemorated in a ceremony at Prague Castle.

EASTER MONDAY (PONDĚLÍ VELIKONOČNÍ)

In this mirthful rite of spring, Czech boys chase their favourite girls and swat them on the legs with willow switches decked with ribbons (you'll see them on sale everywhere); the girls respond with gifts of hand-painted eggs (likewise on sale), then everyone gets down to some serious partying. It's the culmination of several days of spring-cleaning, cooking and visiting family and friends.

ONE WORLD (JEDEN SVĚT)

www.oneworld.cz

This week-long film festival is dedicated to documentaries on the subject of human rights. Screenings are held at some of the smaller cinemas around town, including Kino Aero (p201).

FEBIOFEST

www.febiofest.cz

This international festival of film, TV and video features new works by international filmmakers. Shown throughout the Czech Republic and Slovakia.

April

BURNING OF THE WITCHES (PÁLENÍ ČARODĚJNIC) 30 April

This is the Czech version of a pre-Christian (pagan) festival for warding off evil, featuring the burning of brooms at Výstaviště (p130) and all-night, end-of-winter bonfire parties on Kampa island (p81) and in suburban backyards.

BOOKWORLD PRAGUE (SVĚT KNIHY)

www.bookworld.cz

This major international book festival is held at the Výstaviště exhibition grounds (p130). Though primarily an industry event, it's open to the general public and has author readings, book launches, exhibits, seminars and lectures, mostly in English.

May

LABOUR DAY (SVÁTEK PRÁCE) 1 May

Once sacred to the communists, the 1 May holiday is now just an opportunity for a picnic or a day in the country. To celebrate the arrival of spring, many couples lay flowers at the statue of the 19th-century romantic poet Karel Hynek Mácha (Map pp76–7), author of *Máj* (May), a poem about unrequited love. Former president Václav Havel has been known to pay homage here.

PRAGUE SPRING (PRAŽSKÉ JARO)

Running from 12 May to 3 June, this international music festival is Prague's most prestigious event, with classical music concerts held in theatres, churches and historic buildings. For details, see the boxed text, p202.

KHAMORO

www.khamoro.cz

This festival of Roma culture, with performances of traditional music and dance, exhibitions of art and photography, and a parade through Staré Město, is usually held in late May.

June

PRAGUE WRITERS' FESTIVAL

www.pwf.cz

An international meeting of writers from around the world, with public readings, lectures, discussions and bookshop events.

DANCE PRAGUE (TANEC PRAHA)

www.tanecpha.cz

International festival of modern dance held at theatres around Prague throughout June.

July

JAN HUS DAY (DEN JANA HUSA) 6 July

Celebrations are held to remember the burning at the stake of Bohemian religious reformer Jan Hus in 1415. They're kicked off with low-key gatherings and bell-ringing at Bethlehem Chapel (p101) the evening before.

August

FESTIVAL OF ITALIAN OPERA

www.opera.cz

Beginning sometime in late August and extending into September, this festival

ADVANCE PLANNING

Apart from booking flights and hotels well in advance in high season, Prague is not a city that asks you to do a great deal of forward planning.

If your main reason for visiting is to attend a major festival such as Prague Spring, check the festival website at least a month in advance, and book tickets for any performances you don't want to miss. If all you want to do is see some opera, listen to live jazz or catch a rock gig, take a look at websites such as www.prague.tv a week or two ahead to see what's on. Most opera and classical concert tickets are sold on the day or so before the performance.

We've mentioned in individual reviews where you might want to book a table at a particular restaurant. However, if you want somewhere special for, say, Valentine's Day, it's best to reserve a table a couple of weeks ahead.

HOW MUCH?

1L of petrol 33Kč

Bottled water (1.5L) 15Kč

Guardian newspaper 90Kč

Beer (0.5L) in tourist/nontourist pub 60Kč and up/30Kč

Pork & dumplings 100Kč to 150Kč

'Prague Drinking Team' T-shirt 200Kč to 400Kč (plus any remaining shreds of personal dignity)

Ticket to Laterna Magika 680Kč

Tour of Municipal House 160Kč

Cinema ticket 100Kč to 170Kč

Vintage car tour 980Kč

features the works of Verdi and other Italian composers performed at the Prague State Opera (p201) – your chance to see quality productions outside of the main opera season.

September

PRAGUE AUTUMN (PRAŽSKÝ PODZIM)

www.prazskypodzim.cz

This international festival of classical music is the autumn version of the renowned Prague Spring (p17). Most of the performances are held in Dvořák Hall at the Rudolfinum (p199).

October

INTERNATIONAL JAZZ FESTIVAL (MEZINÁRODNÍ JAZZOVÝ FESTIVAL)

www.jazzfestivalpraha.cz/jazz

Established in 1964, and based at the Reduta Jazz Club (p197), this two-week festival stretches from late October into early November, with a mix of Czech musicians and star performers from around the world.

December

CHRISTMAS-NEW YEAR (VÁNOCE-NOVÝ ROK)

From 24 December to 1 January many Czechs celebrate an extended family holiday. Revelling tourists engulf Prague, and a Christmas market is held in Old Town Square beneath a huge Christmas tree.

COSTS & MONEY

Gone are the days when Prague was a cheap destination. A rapidly growing tourism industry and an increasingly strong currency mean that the Czech capital now ranks alongside most Western European cities when it comes to quality hotels and restaurants.

You can expect to pay around €130 (US$200) a night for a double room in a midrange hotel, while luxury and boutique hotel rates can be in the €260 (US$400) range. Backpacker hostels typically charge around €15 (US$23) for a dorm bed. Dinner for two in a good Malá Strana restaurant can easily set you back €38 (US$60) per head with a bottle of wine, and the famously 'cheap' beer is now at least €2 (US$3) per half-litre in tourist bars.

The good news is that you can still find relatively inexpensive food and drink if you're prepared to venture off the beaten tourist trail – just a few blocks away from Old Town Square there are places where you can eat for under €11 (US$17) per person, and get that same beer for under €1 (US$1.50).

As for accommodation, search the internet for deals – many hotel websites offer special rates or weekend packages. Or consider visiting out of season: hotel rates can fall by up to 40% in winter.

INTERNET RESOURCES

Expats.cz (www.expats.cz) Community site for expats living in Prague: listings, articles, bar and restaurant reviews, forums etc.

Living Prague (www.livingprague.com) Insider guide to the city by a British expat who has lived there for more than a decade.

Prague City Hall (http://magistrat.praha-mesto.cz) Official website of the city council, with lots of useful background information.

Prague Daily Monitor (www.praguemonitor.com) News site with English translations of what's making headlines in Czech newspapers.

Prague Information Service (www.pis.cz) Official tourist information website.

Prague Public Transport (www.dpp.cz) Everything you ever wanted to know about Prague's metro, tram and bus services.

PragueTV (www.prague.tv) Useful listings site covering nightlife, cinema, restaurants etc.

All Praha (www.allpraha.com) Info for tourists and expats, with local listings (restaurants, bars, etc) reviewed by users.

HISTORY

AN UNFAMILIAR HISTORY

The great irony of a trip to Prague is that though the city is steeped in history, it's a history that is unfamiliar to many visitors. London, Paris and Rome can feel instantly recognisable because their stories and myths have played such an important part in the way that Western culture has traditionally been taught. Prague is not like that. A tour of Prague Castle, for example, reveals a bewildering array of Sigismunds, Bořislavs, Boleslavs and, especially, Václavs. If you're not a grad student in Slavic European history, you're not likely to recognise many of the names or grasp much of their significance. That's a shame. Not just because Czech history is filled with gripping characters and stories, but also because it's an integral part of European history as a whole.

Visitors may be surprised to learn, for example, that Prague, under Charles IV and subsequent rulers, was once the seat of the Holy Roman Empire. Not Nero's empire in Rome, of course, but the empire that had evolved by the 14th and 15th centuries into a network of Christian kingdoms and principalities. Prague, under Rudolf II, was also for a time the seat of the sprawling Habsburg Empire, with territories as far flung as modern-day Italy and Poland.

Indeed, the city was once so tied into what we now consider to be Western Europe that all it took was for two Catholic councillors and a secretary to be flung out of a window at Prague Castle in the 17th century to ignite a war – the Thirty Years' War – that would subsume the entire continent.

All this, of course, won't help you get through the Boleslavs and Václavs, but it should be enough to persuade you to look past those unpronounceable names and see the connections. A little knowledge can make a big difference and help make that slog through Prague Castle much more rewarding.

THE RECEIVED WISDOM

Before getting started, a few words are in order regarding how history has traditionally been taught and told in the Czech Republic. For decades now, under the communists and in the years since the Velvet Revolution, an orthodox version of history has held sway that tends to see the Czechs as victims in their own national drama. Czech history, in this view, is a straightforward narrative of a small but just nation struggling to emerge from under the thumb of much bigger and more powerful adversaries. These included, over the years, the hierarchy of the Catholic Church in Rome, the Habsburgs in Vienna, the Germans in more modern times and, most recently, the Russians. This theme still permeates popular attitudes and forms the subtext behind descriptive information presented at museums and exhibitions. It also forms the fodder for guidebooks and newspaper and magazine articles.

That's not to say it's false. In fact, there's much truth in it. The Czechs have endured long periods of war and hardship, suffering foreign invasions that were not of their choosing. It's

TIMELINE

500 BC–AD 400

Celtic tribes thrive in the territory of the modern-day Czech Republic, building settlements whose remains will later be discovered in and around Prague.

AD 500

Slavic tribes enter central Europe during the period of the Great Migration, forming settlements along the Vltava River. Recent excavations indicate that the largest of these may have been near Roztoky, northwest of Prague.

Early 600s

Princess Libuše, the fabled founder of the Přemysl dynasty, looks out over the Vltava valley and predicts that a great city will emerge there someday.

true that remarkable personalities, such as the religious reformer Jan Hus (see the boxed text, p23), were ultimately betrayed outside the country; indeed Czechoslovakia itself was in a sense betrayed by the West even before WWII. The Czechs also suffered greatly under both Nazism and a repressive, Soviet-style communism.

But this view of history tells only part of the story. The Czechs have always been closer to the centre of their own history – both in good ways and bad – than some of their history books would like to believe. Just as the communists could not have ruled so long without the active engagement of some Czechs (and the quiet acquiescence of many), so too did the Germans, Austrians, Catholics and others over the years join willing locals to do their bidding. This is part of 'Czech history', too.

It would also be misleading to characterise foreign influences as invariably negative. Prague, to its great benefit, has always been a cosmopolitan place – we need only look at a handful of architectural masterpieces to make the point. The Charles Bridge (p75) and parts of St Vitus Cathedral (p64) were designed by a German, Peter Parler. Many of the statues that line the bridge were sculpted by Austrians. The baroque masterpiece of St Nicholas Church (p79) in Malá Strana was the work of a father and son team from Bavaria; much of the rest of Malá Strana's baroque splendour was built by Italians. When President Tomáš Masaryk commissioned the renovation of Prague Castle (p61) in the 1920s, he selected a Slovenian, Jože Plečnik, as chief architect. The list could go on and on.

There are encouraging signs that this orthodox view is starting to give way to a more nuanced perspective. One example could be seen in a new history magazine that appeared on newsstands in 2008 with the intentionally provocative cover asking whether Jan Žižka – the revered Czech Hussite commander from the 15th century – was 'a hero or a traitor'. Though the title may have been aimed more at selling magazines than challenging historical dogma, it's hard to imagine such an article appearing even as recently as five or 10 years ago.

THE EARLY YEARS

There's been human habitation in and around Prague for some 600,000 years and permanent communities since around 4000 BC, but it's the Celts, who came to the area around 500 BC, that have aroused the most interest. The name 'Bohemia' for the western province of the Czech Republic derives from one of the most successful of the Celtic tribes, the Boii. Traces of Boii culture have been found as far away as southern Germany, leading some archaeologists to posit a relation between local Celts and those in France and possibly even further afield to the British Isles. It's also spurred playful speculation – more wishful thinking than historical fact – that the Czechs are actually the modern-day offspring of these historic warriors.

Celtic settlements have been unearthed in several parts of Prague. During the construction of metro line B in the 1980s, a large Celtic burial ground was discovered at Nové Butovice, and evidence of early iron furnaces has been found not far away in Jinonice. Some even think there was an early Celtic settlement where Prague Castle now stands, but there's no physical evidence to support the claim.

THE ARRIVAL OF THE SLAVS

It's unclear what prompted the great migration of peoples in the 6th and 7th centuries, but during this time large populations of Slavs began arriving in central Europe, driving out the

870s	26 August 1278	4 August 1306
Prince Bořivoj begins construction of Prague Castle on Hradčany to serve as the seat of his Přemysl dynasty – as it will for kings, emperors and presidents for centuries to come.	King Otakar II is thrashed by the Habsburgs at the Battle of Marchfeld (Moravské Pole in Czech) at the height of the Přemysl dynasty's influence.	The last Přemysl king, Wenceslas III, is murdered, leaving no male heir. The dynasty passes to John of Luxembourg, who will give Bohemia its greatest ruler, his son Charles IV.

Celts and pushing German tribes further to the west. The newcomers established several settlements along the Vltava, including one near the present site of Prague Castle and another upriver at Vyšehrad (p115).

Archaeologists working near the town of Roztoky, northwest of Prague, recently unearthed what may be the largest and oldest of these settlements, dating from the first decades of the 6th century.

THE MYTH OF LIBUŠE

Fittingly for a city that embraces so much mystery, the origins of Prague are shrouded in a fairy tale. Princess Libuše, the daughter of early ruler Krok, is said to have stood on a hill one day at the start of the 7th century and foretold of a glorious city that would one day become Prague. According to legend, Libuše needed a strong suitor who would yield sturdy heirs to the throne. Passing over a field of eligible bachelors, including some sickly looking royals, she selected a simple ploughman, Přemysl. She chose well. The Přemysl dynasty would go on to rule for several hundred years.

In the 9th century, the Přemysl prince, Bořivoj, selected an outcropping on Hradčany to build Prague Castle, the dynasty's seat and the locus of power in this part of the world ever since.

Christianity became the state religion under the rule of the pious Wenceslas (Václav in Czech), Duke of Bohemia (r c 925–929), now the chief patron saint of the Czech people. Wenceslas was the 'Good King Wenceslas' of the well-known Christmas carol, written in 1853 by English clergyman John Mason Neale. Neale, a scholar of European church history, had read about St Wenceslas's legendary piety, and based his carol on the story of the duke's page finding strength by following in the footsteps of his master. Wenceslas's conversion to Christianity is said to have angered his mother and his brother, Boleslav, who ended up killing the young king in a fit of jealousy.

In spite of the occasional fratricide, the Přemysls proved to be effective rulers, forging a genuine Slav alliance and governing Bohemia until the 14th century. Until the early 13th century, the Přemysl rulers were considered princes, but in 1212, the pope granted Otakar I the right to rule as a king. At one point, Přemysl lands stretched from modern-day Silesia (near the Czech–Polish border) to the Mediterranean Sea.

THE HOLY ROMAN EMPIRE

It's hard to imagine Prague will ever exceed the position it had in the 14th century, when for a time it became the seat of the Holy Roman Empire under King and later Emperor Charles IV (Karel IV).

The path to glory began predictably enough with the 1306 murder of Přemysl ruler Wenceslas III, leaving no male successor to the throne. Eventually, John of Luxembourg (Jan Lucemburský to the Czechs) assumed the Czech throne through his marriage to Wenceslas III's daughter Elyška, in 1310.

Under the enlightened rule of John's son, Charles IV, Prague grew into one of the continent's largest and most prosperous cities. It was at this time that the city assumed its handsome Gothic look. Charles commissioned both the bridge that now bears his name and St Vitus Cathedral, among other projects. He also established Charles University as the first university in central Europe.

26 August 1346

Charles IV becomes Bohemian king on the death of his father; later, he adds the honorific Holy Roman Emperor to his list of titles. Prague booms as the seat of the empire.

6 July 1415

Religious reformer Jan Hus is burned at the stake at Konstanz, Germany, for refusing to recant his criticisms of the Catholic Church. His death enrages supporters and enflames decades of religious strife.

30 July 1419

Angry Hussite supporters rush into the New Town Hall and toss several Catholic councillors out the window, introducing the word 'defenestration' to the world.

CZECH VERSION OF 'THE TROUBLES'

In contrast to the 14th century, the 15th century brought mostly hardship and war; much of the good of preceding years was undone in an orgy of religion-inspired violence and intolerance. This period saw the rise of the Church reformation movement led by Jan Hus (see the boxed text, opposite). Hus' intentions were admirable, but his movement ended up polarising the country.

In 1419, supporters of Hussite preacher Jan Želivský stormed Prague's New Town Hall on Wenceslas Square and tossed several Catholic councillors out of the windows. This act not only hardened attitudes on both sides but also introduced the word 'defenestration' (tossing someone from a window in order to do bodily harm) into the political lexicon.

The Hussites assumed control of Prague after the death of Holy Roman Emperor Wenceslas IV in 1419. This sparked the first anti-Hussite crusade, launched in 1420 by Holy Roman Emperor Sigismund. Hussite commander Jan Žižka successfully defended the city in the Battle of Vítkov Hill, but religious strife spilled into the countryside. The Hussites themselves were torn into warring factions: those wanting to make peace with the emperor and others wanting to fight to the end. The more radical Hussite faction, the Taborites, were ultimately defeated in battle at Lipany in 1434.

Following Sigismund's death, George of Poděbrady (Jiří z Poděbrad) ruled as Bohemia's one and only Hussite king, from 1452 to 1471, with the backing of the moderate Hussites known as the Utraquists. The damage, however, had been done, and once-prosperous Bohemia lay in ruin. The rest of the century was spent in an uneasy balance between the Protestant Czech citizenry and the Catholic nobility.

ENTER THE AUSTRIANS

Though it took time for the country to recover from the Hussite wars, the latter part of the 16th century is generally viewed as a second 'golden age' under Habsburg Emperor Rudolf II (the first being the reign of Charles IV in the 14th century). Austria's Habsburg dynasty generally gets a bad rap in Czech history books, largely because of the repressive means, including public executions, that the Habsburgs used to enforce their rule after the Czech defeat at Bílá Hora in 1620. But it's generally forgotten that it was the Czech nobility, in 1526, who invited the Habsburgs – in the person of Ferdinand I – to rule in the first place. Ferdinand endeared himself to the mostly Catholic nobility, but alienated large sections of Czech society.

His grandson Rudolf preferred Prague to Vienna and moved the seat of the Habsburg Empire here for the duration of his reign. Today Rudolf is generally viewed as something of a kook. It's true he used his patronage to support serious artists and scientists, including noted astronomers Tycho Brahe and Johannes Kepler, but he also had a soft spot for more esoteric pursuits such as soothsaying and alchemy. The English mathematician and occultist John Dee and his less well-regarded countryman Edward Kelly were just two of the noted mystics Rudolf retained at the castle in an eternal quest to turn base metals into gold. Rudolf was also a friend to Prague's large Jewish population, who enjoyed a great period of prosperity during his reign, despite being crowded into a tiny ghetto just north of the Old Town (see the boxed text, p25).

The end of Rudolf's reign in the early 17th century was marked by renewed strife between Protestants and Catholics, culminating in 1618 in what became known as the 'second defenestration of Prague'. A group of Protestant noblemen stormed into a chamber at Prague Castle and hurled

Early 15th century	1583	23 May 1618
The Hussite wars – pitting radical reformers against Catholics and, ultimately, different Hussite factions against each other – rage throughout Bohemia, laying waste to the country.	Habsburg Emperor Rudolf II moves the dynasty's seat from Vienna to Prague, ushering in a second golden age. It lasts only until Rudolf dies three decades later, when tensions between Protestants and Catholics start boiling over.	A Protestant mob pushes two Catholic councillors and their secretary from a window at Prague Castle. This 'second defenestration' pushes the Habsburgs into starting the Thirty Years' War.

JAN HUS

Jan Hus was the Czech lands' foremost – and one of Europe's earliest – Christian reformers, anticipating Martin Luther and the Lutheran reformation by more than a century.

Hus was born into a poor family in southern Bohemia in 1372. He studied at the Karolinum (Charles University) and eventually became dean of the philosophical faculty. Like many of his colleagues, Hus was inspired by the English philosopher and radical reformist theologian John Wycliffe. The latter's ideas on reforming the Roman Catholic priesthood meshed nicely with growing Czech resentment at the wealth and corruption of the clergy.

In 1391 Prague reformers founded the Bethlehem Chapel (p101), where sermons were given in Czech rather than Latin. Hus preached there for about 10 years while continuing his duties at the university. Hus' criticisms of the Catholic Church, particularly the practice of selling indulgences, endeared him to his followers but put him squarely in the pope's black book. The pope had Hus excommunicated in 1410, but he continued to preach. In 1415, he was invited to the Council of Constance to recant his views. He refused and was burned at the stake on 6 July 1415. An enormous statue of Hus stands in Old Town Square (p87).

two Catholic councillors and their secretary out the window. The men survived – legend has it they fell onto a dung heap that softened the blow. But the damage was done. The act sparked a decades-long war – the Thirty Years' War – that eventually consumed the whole of Europe and left Bohemia once again in tatters.

For the Czechs it was to get even worse. Following the second defenestration, the Czech nobility elected a German Protestant – Frederick V, Elector Palatine – to be their leader in a looming battle with the Habsburgs. Frederick's rule was dogged by poor morale, and most of the European powers sided with the Habsburgs. In the end, the Czechs were routed at the Battle of Bílá Hora (White Mountain; p142), on the western edge of Prague, on 8 November 1620. The fighting lasted less than two hours. The 'Winter King' (so called because he ruled Bohemia for just one winter) fled, and in 1621, the 27 nobles who had instigated the revolt were executed in Old Town Square.

The defeat slammed the door on Czech independence for three centuries. Czechs lost their privileges, rights and property, and almost even their national identity through enforced Catholicisation and Germanisation as part of the wider Counter-Reformation movement. During the Thirty Years' War, Saxons occupied Prague from 1631 to 1632, and the Swedes seized Hradčany and Malá Strana in 1648. Staré Město, though unconquered, suffered months of bombardment (the Old Town Tower on Charles Bridge still shows the scars of battle). Prague's population declined from 60,000 in 1620 to 24,600 in 1648. The Habsburgs moved their throne back to Vienna, reducing Prague to a provincial backwater.

REVIVAL OF THE CZECH NATION

Remarkably, Czech language and culture managed to hold on through the years of the Austrian occupation. As the Habsburgs eased their grip in the 19th century, Prague became the centre of the Czech National Revival. The revival found its initial expression not in politics – outright political activity was forbidden – but in Czech-language literature and drama. Important figures included linguists Josef Jungmann and Josef Dobrovský, and František Palacký, author of *Dějiny národu českého* (The History of the Czech Nation).

8 November 1620

Czech soldiers, united under Protestant leader Frederick V, Elector Palatine, lose a crucial battle at Bílá Hora, west of Prague, to Austrian Habsburg troops. The loss brings in 300 years of Austrian rule.

21 June 1621

Twenty-seven Czech noblemen are executed in Old Town Square for their part in instigating the anti-Habsburg revolt. Their severed heads are hung from the Old Town Tower on Charles Bridge.

29 October 1787

Wolfgang Amadeus Mozart, already far more popular in Prague than in Vienna, serves as conductor at the premiere of his opera *Don Giovanni*, staged at the Estates Theatre near Old Town Square.

While many of the countries in post-Napoleonic Europe were swept up in similar nationalist sentiments, social and economic factors gave the Czech revival particular strength. Educational reforms by Empress Maria Theresa (r 1740–80) had given even the poorest Czechs access to schooling, and a vocal middle class was emerging through the Industrial Revolution.

Prague joined in the 1848 democratic revolutions that swept Europe, and the city was first in line in the Austrian empire to rise in favour of reform. Yet like most of the others, Prague's revolution was soon crushed. In 1863, however, Czech speakers defeated the German speakers in Prague council elections and edged them out of power, though the shrinking German-language minority still wielded considerable power until the end of the century.

INDEPENDENCE AT LAST

For Czechs, WWI had a silver lining. The 1918 defeat of the Axis powers left the Austro-Hungarian Empire too weak to fight for its former holdings. Czech patriots Tomáš Garrigue Masaryk and Edvard Beneš had spent much of the war in the United States, where they lobbied ceaselessly with Czech and Slovak émigré communities for a joint Czech and Slovak state. The plea appealed especially to the idealistic American president, Woodrow Wilson, and his belief in the self-determination of peoples. The most workable solution appeared to be a single federal state of two equal republics, and this was spelled out in agreements signed in Cleveland, Ohio, in 1915 and Pittsburgh, Pennsylvania, in 1918 (both cities having large populations of Czechs and Slovaks).

As WWI drew to a close, Czechoslovakia declared its independence, with Allied support, on 28 October 1918. Prague became the capital, and the popular Masaryk, a writer and political philosopher, the republic's first president.

THE FIRST REPUBLIC & WORLD WAR II

Czechoslovakia in the two decades between independence and the 1939 Nazi invasion was a remarkably successful state. Even now Czechs consider the 'First Republic' another golden age of immense cultural and economic achievement.

Czechoslovakia's proximity to Nazi Germany and its sizable German minority in the Sudetenland border area, however, made it a tempting target for Adolf Hitler. Hitler correctly judged that neither Britain nor France had an appetite for war. At a conference in Munich in 1938, Hitler demanded that Germany be allowed to annex the Sudetenland. British Prime Minister Neville Chamberlain acquiesced, famously calling Germany's designs on Czechoslovakia a 'quarrel in a faraway country between people of whom we know nothing'.

On 15 March 1939 Germany occupied all of Bohemia and Moravia, declaring the region a 'protectorate', while Slovakia declared independence as a Nazi puppet state. During the war, Prague was spared significant physical damage, though the Nazis destroyed the Czech resistance – and killed thousands of innocent Czechs in retaliation for the assassination in Prague of SS general and Reichsprotektor Reinhard Heydrich by Czech patriots in 1942 (see the boxed text, p115).

Prague's pre-WWII Jewish community of around 40,000 was all but wiped out by the Nazis. Almost three-quarters of them, and 90% of all the Jews in Bohemia and Moravia, died of disease or starvation or were exterminated in camps from 1941 to 1944.

On 5 May 1945, with the war drawing to a close, the citizens of Prague staged an uprising against the Germans. The Red Army was advancing from the east and US troops had made it

3 July 1883

German-Jewish writer Franz Kafka is born just off Old Town Square. He'll go on to lead a double life: mild-mannered insurance clerk by day, harried father of the modern novel by night.

28 October 1918

A newly independent Czechoslovakia is proclaimed at the Municipal House (Obecní dům) in the final days of WWI. Crowds throng Wenceslas Square in jubilation.

1920s

The heyday of the First Republic, now seen as another golden age. Prague intellectuals are heavily influenced by modern movements in art, architecture, literature and photography.

THE JEWS OF PRAGUE

Prague's Jews first moved into a walled ghetto in about the 13th century, in response to directives from Rome that Jews and Christians should live separately. Subsequent centuries of repression and pogroms culminated in a threat from Ferdinand I (r 1526–64) to throw all the Jews out of Bohemia.

Official attitudes changed under Rudolf II at the end of the 16th century. Rudolf bestowed honour on the Jews and encouraged a flowering of Jewish intellectual life. Mordechai Maisel, the mayor of the ghetto at the time, became Rudolf's finance minister and the city's wealthiest citizen. Another major figure was Judah Loew ben Bezalel (Rabbi Loew), a prominent theologian, chief rabbi, student of the mystical teachings of the kabbalah and nowadays best known as the creator of the mystical creature, the Golem – a kind of proto-robot made from the mud of the Vltava River.

When they helped to repel the Swedes on Charles Bridge in 1648, the Jews won the favour of Ferdinand III to the extent that he had the ghetto enlarged. But a century later they were driven out of the city, only to be welcomed back when city residents missed their business.

In the 1780s Habsburg emperor Joseph II (r 1780–90) outlawed many forms of discrimination, and in the 19th century the Jews won the right to live where they wanted. Many chose to leave the ghetto for nicer parts of the city. At the end of the 19th century the city decided to clear the ghetto, which had become a slum. In place of the ancient buildings they built the beautiful Art Nouveau apartment houses found there today.

The ghetto, renamed Josefov in Joseph's honour, remained the spiritual heart of Prague's Jewish community, but that came to a brutal end with the Nazi occupation during WWII. Today the entire city is home to roughly 5000 Jews, a fraction of the community's former size.

as far as Plzeň (90km west of Prague), but were holding back from liberating the city in deference to their Soviet allies. The only help for Prague's lightly armed citizens came from Russian soldiers of the so-called Vlasov units, former POWs who had defected to the German side and now defected in turn to the Czech cause. Many people died in the uprising before the Germans pulled out on 8 May, having been granted free passage out in return for an agreement not to destroy more bridges and buildings. Most of Prague was thus liberated by its own citizens before the Red Army arrived on 9 May. Liberation Day is now celebrated on 8 May; under communism it was 9 May.

In 1945 Czechoslovakia was reconstituted as an independent state. One of its first acts was the expulsion of the remaining Sudeten Germans from the borderlands. By 1947, some 2.5 million ethnic Germans had been stripped of their Czechoslovak citizenship and forcibly expelled to Germany and Austria. Thousands died during the forced marches.

Despite a 1997 mutual apology for wartime misdeeds by the Czech Republic and Germany, the issue still brings emotions to the boil. Many Sudeten survivors feel their citizenship and property were taken illegally. Many Czechs, on the other hand, remain convinced that the Sudeten Germans forfeited their rights when they sought help from Nazi Germany, and that a formal apology by President Václav Havel in 1990 was unwarranted.

FROM THE NAZIS TO THE COMMUNISTS

For many Czechs, WWII had tarnished the image of the Western democracies for sanctioning Hitler's rise to power and the dismemberment of Czechoslovakia. Communist appeals for world peace and economic justice found a receptive ear in a war-torn country. In the first elections

30 September 1938

European powers, meeting in Munich, agree to Hitler's demand to annex Czechoslovakia's Sudetenland region. British PM Neville Chamberlain declares they have achieved 'peace in our time'.

15 March 1939

German soldiers cross the Czechoslovak frontier and occupy Bohemia and Moravia. Czechoslovak soldiers, ordered in advance not to resist, allow the Germans to enter without firing a shot.

27 May 1942

Czechoslovak patriots succeed in assassinating German Reichsprotektor Reinhard Heydrich. The men are later found hiding in a church in Nové Město. Trapped by Nazi soldiers, some take their own lives; the others are killed.

WHEN 'BIG BROTHER' WAS REAL LIFE

Twenty years on from the Velvet Revolution, it seems as if communism never happened. Prague has taken its place among Europe's colourful capitals, and on a sunny day it can feel like all is right with the world. But memories of a darker period still run deep. Anna Siskova, a Czechoslovak by birth, was a high school student in Bratislava in 1989 when communism fell. She now lives in Prague, where she works in communications for an international company. She told us a little bit about life with 'Big Brother'.

What's your strongest memory when you think back to communist times? Everything suddenly turns grey: grey streets, grey houses, shops that had identical goods all over Czechoslovakia no matter what city you lived in. I think about our family trips to the Black Sea. We went to Bulgaria, the only country easily accessible to citizens of the communist camp. To get to Yugoslavia, you needed a special grey passport. The Bulgarian coast was full of Hungarians, East Germans, Slovaks, Czechs and Poles. You could tell where someone was from by his or her swimsuit!

Do you remember where you were when you first heard about the Velvet Revolution? I remember exactly. It was 16 November, the day before. We were sent home from school early (normal procedure if there was a demonstration planned). We were told to go straight home and not to go to the centre. There was a student protest at the Ministry of Education and, surprisingly, state TV reported the students' complaints. On 17 November, when news came in from Prague, it was very surprising. I was excited. Older people kept saying we shouldn't be too enthusiastic – remember what happened with the Prague Spring? But I didn't care. I stood on the square every day. It was amazing.

Give us a feeling for how it was back then to live. How was it buying food or clothes? One of the best jobs was to work in a vegetable or a meat shop. If you knew someone from a *zelovoc* (fruit and veg shop), you could at least get bananas and tangerines. And clothes – everyone was wearing the same. There was no choice, and if the shops got something special – I remember once [there were] clothes from Greece – there was an enormous line in front. There was always some kind of shortage, though. When the paper factory burned down, there was no toilet paper in the whole country.

Is there anything from that period you really miss? What is worse now than it was then? People used to read more. They loved going to the theatre as they could always find some political hints in the plays. It was a strange atmosphere. I don't miss it, but it brings back nostalgic memories. As kids we were motivated to learn German and English, just so we could understand Austrian TV and radio, and English songs.

after the war, in 1946, the Communist Party of Czechoslovakia (KSČ) became the republic's dominant party, winning 36% of the popular vote.

As relations between wartime allies the US and the Soviet Union deteriorated, Soviet leader Josef Stalin tightened his grip on Eastern and Central Europe. In February 1948, with Stalin's blessing, Czechoslovak communists staged a bloodless coup, proclaiming a workers' state, with the government and economy to be organised along Soviet lines. KSČ leader Klement Gottwald announced the coup to euphoric crowds from the balcony of the Goltz-Kinský Palace (p92) on Old Town Square.

By the 1950s the initial enthusiasm had faded as communist economic policies nearly bankrupted the country and a wave of repression sent thousands to labour camps. In a series

5 May 1945

Prague residents begin an armed uprising against the Germans and liberate the city after three days of fighting. The Germans are given free passage out in exchange for agreeing not to destroy the city.

9 May 1945

The Soviet Army formally liberates the city, though most of the German soldiers are already defeated or gone. Under the communists, this will be recognised as the official day of liberation.

25 February 1948

Communists stage a bloodless coup. Party leader Klement Gottwald proclaims the news on Old Town Square. Crowds cheer, but the coup ultimately leads to four decades of oppressive communist rule.

READING UP ON CZECH HISTORY

Prague and the Czech Republic are not lacking in well-written historical accounts in English. The selection is particularly strong on books about the Nazi occupation and somewhat weaker about life under communism. Timothy Garton Ash's *The Magic Lantern* remains the gold standard for accounts in English of the Velvet Revolution.

- *Magic Prague* (Angelo Maria Ripellino, 1973) – Italian professor Ripellino breathes new life into historical figures through the ages in this inventive and highly entertaining blend of fact and fiction. With characters like Rudolf II, the Golem and Franz Kafka to work with, it's hard to see how he could miss. Out of print but possible to find used.
- *Prague: A Cultural History* (Richard Burton, 2003) – A beautifully written cultural history by an English professor obviously in love with Prague and its myths. The first chapter, 'How to Read Prague', is especially helpful for visitors. The chapters are arranged around stories and characters – both real and fictional – that have shaped the city.
- *Prague in Black and Gold* (Peter Demetz, 1998) – The first of two books by émigré Czech and literary historian Peter Demetz. This volume is a sweeping history of Demetz's hometown, with a keen eye for the absurd. It's a challenging read if you don't have a background in Czech or Central European history, but those who do will find it enriching.
- *Prague in Danger* (Peter Demetz, 2008) – Demetz's second (and more accessible) work is partly a classic history and partly a lively and moving chronicle of his own family – Demetz's mother was Jewish and died at Terezín. These personal remembrances are especially strong and give a first-hand feel for what life in Prague was like during the Nazi occupation. It's also a good general primer for historical markers like Reinhard Heydrich's assassination in 1942.
- *Prague in the Shadow of the Swastika* (Callum MacDonald and Jan Kaplan, 1995) – Part serious history and part powerful picture-book focusing on Prague during the Nazi occupation. Hard to find, but usually stocked by English booksellers in Prague, such as Big Ben Bookshop (p146).
- *So Many Heroes* (Alan Levy, 1980) – Gripping account of the 1968 Warsaw Pact invasion and the immediate aftermath through the eyes of an American journalist who witnessed it. Levy was eventually banned by the communists from living here and was allowed to return only in 1990. He served as editor-in-chief of the *Prague Post* until his death in 2004. Originally published under the title *Rowboat to Prague*.
- *The Coast of Bohemia* (Derek Sayer, 2000) – Broad historical treatment follows the rise of Czech national consciousness in the 19th century, through independence, the First Republic, WWII and the communist period. The title alludes to an oft-quoted line from Shakespeare's *The Winter's Tale*: 'Thou art perfect then, our ship hath touch'd upon the deserts of Bohemia?' – either proof of the Bard's appalling geography or a poetic reference to Bohemia's mythical seacoast.
- *The Killing of Reinhard Heydrich* (Callum MacDonald, 2007) – Absorbing account of the killing of Nazi Reichsprotektor Reinhard Heydrich in 1942 by Czech patriots who had parachuted in from Britain. The act remains highly controversial. The assassination helped burst the myth of Nazi invincibility, but resulted in reprisal attacks that cost thousands of lives.
- *The Magic Lantern: The Revolution of 1989 Witnessed in Warsaw, Budapest, Berlin, and Prague* (Timothy Garton Ash, 1993) – Some historians just seem to live right. Oxford professor Garton Ash had the professional and linguistic skills to interpret history as it was unfolding during the tumultuous months of 1989 – and the presence of mind to write it all down. Looks at the major anticommunist revolutions in Central Europe but is strong on the Velvet Revolution.
- *Under a Cruel Star: A Life in Prague 1941–1968* (Heda Margolius Kovály, 1997) – One of the few books to forge a link between the Nazi and communist periods. The author, Jewish and born in Prague, had the double misfortune of being sent to Terezín and Auschwitz during WWII, only to survive the war and marry an up-and-coming communist who was executed in the 1950s show trials. This remarkable book is unfortunately out of print and hard to find, but worth the effort.

20 November 1952

In a Soviet-style purge, communists accuse several of their own party functionaries, including General Secretary Rudolf Slánský, of treason. The prisoners are executed at Prague's Pankrác prison.

20–21 August 1968

Warsaw Pact forces, led by the Soviet Union, invade Czechoslovakia to put an end to reforms known as the Prague Spring. Reforming communist leader Alexander Dubček is replaced by hard-liner Gustáv Husák.

16 January 1969

Student Jan Palach immolates himself at the top of Wenceslas Square to protest the Warsaw Pact invasion. Thousands come to the square in the following days to mark his memory and attend his funeral.

of Stalin-style purges staged by the KSČ in the early '50s, many people, including top members of the party, were executed.

In the 1960s, Czechoslovakia enjoyed a gradual liberalisation under reformist party leader Alexander Dubček. The reforms reflected a popular desire for full democracy and an end to censorship – 'Socialism with a Human Face', as the party called it.

But Soviet leaders grew alarmed at the prospect of a democratic society within the Eastern Bloc and the potential domino effect on Poland and Hungary. The brief 'Prague Spring' was crushed by a Soviet-led Warsaw Pact invasion on the night of 20–21 August 1968. Prague was the major objective; Soviet forces, with the help of the Czechoslovak secret police, secured the airport for Soviet transport planes. At the end of the first day, 58 people died. Much of the fighting took place near the top of Wenceslas Square, where the façade of the National Museum still bears bullet scars.

In 1969 Dubček was replaced by the hard-line Gustáv Husák and exiled to the Slovak forestry department. About 14,000 party functionaries and another 280,000 members who refused to renounce their belief in 'Socialism with a Human Face' were expelled from the party and lost their jobs. Many other educated professionals became manual labourers and street cleaners.

In January 1977 a group of 243 writers, artists and other intellectuals signed a public demand for basic human rights, Charter 77, which became a focus for opponents of the regime. Prominent among them was the poet and playwright Václav Havel (see the boxed text, below).

VELVET REVOLUTION & DIVORCE

The year 1989 was a momentous one throughout Central and Eastern Europe. Czechoslovak communist officials watched nervously as one by one the neighbouring regimes toppled, cul-

PLAYWRIGHT-PRESIDENT VÁCLAV HAVEL

The Velvet Revolution produced at least one great name known around the world. Václav Havel – playwright, dissident and the country's first postcommunist president – was born on 5 October 1936, the son of a wealthy Prague businessman. His family's property was confiscated in the communist coup of 1948, and because of his bourgeois background, he was denied easy access to education. He nevertheless finished high school and studied for a time at university before landing a job as a stagehand at the Theatre on the Balustrade (p203). Nine years later he was its resident playwright.

His enthusiasm for the liberal reforms of the 'Prague Spring' and his signature on the Charter 77 declaration made him an enemy of the communist government. His works, which typically focused on the absurdities and dehumanisation of totalitarian bureaucracy, were banned and his passport seized. Altogether he spent some four years in jail for his activities on behalf of human rights.

The massive demonstrations of November 1989 thrust Havel into the limelight as a leading organiser of the noncommunist Civic Forum movement, which ultimately negotiated a peaceful transfer of power. Havel was swept into office as president shortly after, propelled by a wave of thousands of cheering demonstrators holding signs saying *Havel na hrad!* (Havel to the castle!)

In 2003, after two terms as president, Havel was replaced by former prime minister Václav Klaus. Since leaving office, Havel has finished at least two memoirs and recently returned to the stage as the author of a new and acclaimed play, *Odcházení* (Leaving).

1977

Life in Prague after 'normalisation' reaches a political and cultural nadir. Václav Havel and other dissidents sign Charter 77, a petition calling on Czechoslovakia to meet its international obligations on human rights.

17 November 1989

Police use violence to halt a student demonstration along Národní třída. The action shocks the nation, sparking days of demonstrations that culminate in the communists relinquishing power – soon to be called the Velvet Revolution.

12 March 1999

The Czech Republic formally enters the NATO military alliance along with Poland and Hungary. The move angers Russia in spite of assurances from NATO that the alliance is purely defensive.

STUDENT SACRIFICES

Throughout Czech history, from the time of Jan Hus to the Velvet Revolution, Prague's university students have not been afraid to stand up for what they believe. Many of them have even sacrificed their lives. Two student names that have gone down in 20th-century Czech history are Jan Opletal and Jan Palach.

On 28 October 1939, shortly after the start of WWII and on the 21st anniversary of Czechoslovak independence, Jan Opletal, a medical student, was shot and fatally wounded by police who were trying to break up an anti-Nazi rally. After his funeral, on 15 November, students took to the streets, defacing German street signs, chanting anti-German slogans, and taunting the police. The Nazi response was swift and brutal.

In the early hours of 17 November, now known as the 'Day of Students' Fight for Freedom and Democracy', the Nazis raided Prague's university dormitories and arrested around 1200 students before carting them off to various concentration camps. Some were executed and others died. Prague's universities were closed for the duration of WWII.

Thirty years after Opletal's death, on 16 January 1969, university student Jan Palach set himself on fire on the steps of the National Museum (Národní muzeum; p110) in protest against the Warsaw Pact invasion of Prague. He staggered down the steps in flames and collapsed on the pavement at the foot of the stairs. The following day around 200,000 people gathered in the square in his honour.

It was three days before he died, and his body was buried in the Olšany Cemetery (p128) in Žižkov. His grave became a focus for demonstrations and in 1974 his remains were exhumed and moved to his home village. By popular demand he was re-interred in Olšany Cemetery in 1990. A cross-shaped monument set into the pavement in front of the National Museum marks the spot where he fell.

The street in Staré Město called 17.listopadu (17 November; Map pp88–9) was named in honour of the students who suffered on 17 November 1939. Exactly 50 years later, on 17 November 1989, students marching along Národní třída in memory of that day were attacked and clubbed by police (there's a bronze memorial at the spot; see p111). The national outrage triggered by this event pushed the communist government toward its final collapse a few days later.

minating in the breeching of the Berlin Wall in early November. There was a growing sense of excitement within the population that the leadership would not be able to cling to power, but there was also palpable fear over how the transfer of power would take place.

On 17 November Prague's communist youth movement organised an officially sanctioned demonstration in memory of the students who were executed by the Nazis in 1939 (see the boxed text, above). But the peaceful crowd of 50,000 was cornered on Národní třída. Hundreds were beaten by police, and around 100 were arrested.

Czechs were electrified by this wanton police violence, and the following days saw nonstop demonstrations by students, artists and finally most of the population, peaking at a rally in Letná (p131) that drew some 750,000 people. Leading dissidents, with Havel at the forefront, formed an anticommunist coalition, which negotiated the government's resignation on 3 December. A 'government of national understanding' was formed with the communists as a minority. Havel was elected president by the Federal Assembly on 29 December. These events later became known as the Velvet Revolution because of their nonviolent nature.

Almost immediately after the revolution, problems arose between Czechs and Slovaks. The Slovaks had for a long time harboured grievances against the dominant Czechs, and many Slovaks dreamed of having their own state. The Czech side was deeply divided: some wanted to keep Czechoslovakia intact while others were willing to see the economically weaker Slovaks go their own way.

14 August 2002

Several city districts and the metro tunnels are inundated as the flooded Vltava River reaches its highest level in modern times. The damages cost several billion euros and spark redevelopment in hard-hit areas.

1 May 2004

The Czech Republic achieves its biggest foreign policy objective since the Velvet Revolution and joins the EU, along with several other former communist countries from Central and Eastern Europe.

15 February 2008

By a narrow margin, the Czech parliament re-elects conservative economist Vaclav Klaus to his second five-year term as President of the Czech Republic.

On 1 January 1993, amid much hand-wringing on both sides – especially from Havel, who refused to preside over the splitting up of the country – the Czechs and Slovaks peacefully divided into independent states.

POST-'89 PRAGUE

It would be impossible to summarise in a few paragraphs the changes that have taken place in the 20 years since the Velvet Revolution. The big-picture view is largely positive, though. The Czech Republic achieved its two major long-term foreign policy goals, joining the NATO military alliance in 1999 and the EU in 2004.

When it comes to local politics, the country continues to ride a knife-edge. Neither major centrist party, the right-leaning Civic Democratic Party (ODS) or the left-leaning Social Democrats (ČSSD), has been able cobble together a lasting consensus. In 2006, wrangling between the major parties left the country without a government for several months, leading local wags to declare the Czech Republic the world's largest nongovernmental organisation.

Havel finished 13 years as president in 2003 and was replaced by his rival, conservative Václav Klaus (formerly the prime minister). Klaus was re-elected to a second five-year term in 2008, though the president remains largely a figurehead.

In terms of the economy, Prague has prospered since the Velvet Revolution, becoming one of the biggest tourist draws on the continent. Unemployment is minimal, the shops are full and the façades that were crumbling a decade ago have been given facelifts.

It would be stretch, though, to say the economic transformation from communism to capitalism has gone off without a hitch. The complex process of selling off state-owned assets to private buyers was rife with corruption. And even now there's a lingering sense that wealth is concentrated in far too few hands and that while the communists may have lost the political game, they have prospered through their former positions and connections.

ARTS

Ask anyone outside the Czech Republic to name a famous Czech artist, musician or writer, and odds are he or she will come up with Alfons Mucha, Antonín Dvořák or Franz Kafka. But to the generation of Czechs that have grown up in the 20 years since the Velvet Revolution, these are names from the very distant past. Even relatively recent cultural icons like writers Milan Kundera or Ivan Klíma (both still alive and writing, by the way) seem out of touch with new realities. Václav Havel was only recently able to salvage his ageing reputation as a playwright with a hit play in 2008 – his first since 1989.

Enthused by romantic notions of the Czech National Revival, Art Nouveau or outdated notions of the noble dissident struggling against an oppressive communist regime, visitors to Prague all too often overlook the vibrant arts scene that has arisen here since 1989. Prague's major art galleries are complemented by dozens of small, independent and commercial galleries, where you can begin to appreciate the artistic energy that bubbles away beneath the city. And the many concert venues, jazz clubs and rock bars are fun, affordable and easily accessible.

MUSIC

Praguers have eclectic tastes, ranging from the ever-popular Mozart, who conducted the premier of *Don Giovanni* here in 1787, to Tom Waits, who sold out the Kongresové Centrum (Congress Centre) in a matter of hours for two concerts in July 2008.

The rock and pop scene has evolved greatly since 1989, when it was dominated by dissident-era rock bands and highly influential (but well past their prime) international acts like the Velvet Underground and the Rolling Stones. Those bands were soon drowned out by a flood of international acts and newer trends like electronic music, trance, techno, hip hop, rap, world and indie. One of the surprise bands to emerge in recent years has been Čechomor, which combines harmonies and Czech folk traditions in songs that are simple and yet hauntingly beautiful.

At the classical end of the musical spectrum, mezzo-soprano Magdalena Kožená (b 1973) is a leading light in the younger generation of opera singers. She has carved out a career as a major concert and recital artist – performing at the Salzburg, Glyndebourne and Edinburgh festivals, among others – and has recorded best-selling albums of Mozart arias, French opera and Bach's *St Matthew Passion*.

Classical

Classical music is hugely popular in Prague, and not only with the crowds of international aficionados who flock to the Prague Spring and Prague Autumn festivals – the Czechs themselves have always been keen fans. Under the Austro-Hungarian monarchy, Czechs were always considered to have discriminating tastes and even embraced Mozart's music long before the composer achieved any measure of respect in Vienna.

Distinctly Czech classical music first blossomed in the mid-19th century, when the National Revival saw the emergence of several great composers, who drew inspiration for their work from traditional Czech folk music. Bedřich Smetana (1824–84) incorporated folk motifs into his classic compositions. His best known works are *Prodaná nevěsta* (The Bartered Bride), *Dalibor a Libuše* (Dalibor and Libuše) and the six-part symphonic poem *Má vlast* (My Homeland), which contains his most famous composition outside the Czech Republic, *Vltava* (The Moldau).

Antonín Dvořák (1841–1904) is the best-known Czech composer internationally. He spent four years in the US, where he lectured on music and composed his famous *Symphony No 9, From the New World*, a copy of which was taken to the moon by Neil Armstrong in 1969. Among his other well-known works are two *Slavonic Dances* (1878 and 1881), the operas *Rusalka* and *Čert a Kača* (The Devil and Kate) and his religious masterpiece *Stabat Mater* (a 13th-century Latin hymn; the title means 'The Mother was Standing').

Moravian-born Leoš Janáček (1854–1928) is widely considered the leading Czech composer of the early modern period, though he was never as popular as Smetana and Dvořák in his native country. His discordant violin pieces are hard to listen to at first but mellow with familiarity. His better-known compositions include the tricky-to-pronounce-fast *The Cunning Little Vixen* and *Káťa Kabanová*, as well as the *Glagolská mše* (Glagolitic Mass) and *Taras Bulba*, based on Gogol's short story of the same name. Other well-known Czech composers include Josef Suk (1874–1935), Dvořák's son-in-law and author of the *Serenade for Strings* and the *Asrael Symphony*; and Bohuslav Martinů (1890–1959), famed for his opera *Julietta* and his *Symphony No 6*.

Among contemporary composers, the most widely known is probably Milan Slavický (b 1947), who teaches at the Prague Academy of Performing Arts. His most famous piece, *Requiem*, premiered in Prague in 2005. Other modern composers worth looking out for include Petr Eben (1929–2007), a survivor of the Buchenwald concentration camp during WWII who is known for his choral and organ music, and Marek Kopelent (b 1932), who made his name with avant-garde compositions in the 1950s and '60s.

Both locals and visitors can choose from a rich programme of concerts performed by Prague's three main resident orchestras: the Prague Symphony Orchestra (Symfonický orchestr hlavního města prahy; www.fok.cz); the Czech Philharmonic Orchestra (Ceska filharmonie; www.czechphilharmonic.cz); and the Czech National Symphony Orchestra (Český národní symfonický orchestr; www.cnso.cz).

Jazz

Jazz was already being played in Prague in the 1930s and retains a strong grip on the city. Czech musicians remained at the forefront of the European jazz scene until the communist takeover in 1948, when controls were imposed on performing and publishing jazz. Even so, in the late 1950s Prague Radio still had a permanent jazz orchestra, led by saxophonist Karel Krautgartner (1922–82).

Restrictions were gradually lifted in the 1960s. One of the top bands of this period was SH Quartet, which played for three years at Reduta, the city's first professional jazz club and still going strong (though no longer the centre of the jazz scene). Another leading band was Junior Trio, with Jan Hamr and brothers Miroslav and Allan Vitouš, all of whom left for the US after 1968. Hamr became prominent in American music circles as Jan Hammer and even composed the *Miami Vice* soundtrack (which sold some 4 million copies in the US alone).

Today, the scene is not quite as vibrant, but on any given night you can still catch a number of decent shows. One of the most outstanding musicians is Jiří Stivín, who produced two excellent albums in the 1970s with the band System Tandem and is regarded as one of the most innovative jazz musicians in Europe. Two others to watch for are Emil Viklický and Milan Svoboda.

Rock & Pop

The rock scene in Prague today is deeply divided into genres and subgenres, each with its own distinct fan base, groups and clubs. Electronic music, including techno and drum 'n' bass, is standard fare in many dance clubs. Other popular styles include indie rock (a catch-all for bands who don't fit a label), classic rock, revival, pop, folk rock, and even a budding Czech hip-hop scene.

Rock, in the form of American-style rock 'n' roll, took the country by storm in the 1950s. It was officially frowned upon but more or less tolerated. Even today, Czechs retain a fondness for '50s rockers like Elvis, Chuck Berry and Little Richard, and Czechs of all ages can still cut a rug much more skilfully than their American or Western European counterparts. Czech dancers like Roman Kolb regularly win world rock 'n' roll dance championships.

Popular music blossomed during the political thaw of the mid-1960s and Western influences from acts like the Beatles, Beach Boys and Rolling Stones were strongly felt. The 1967 hit single 'Želva' (Turtle) by the band Olympic bears the unmistakable traces of mid-decade Beatles. One of the biggest stars of that time was pop singer Marta Kubišová (b 1942). Banned by the communists for two decades after the 1968 Warsaw Pact invasion, she still occasionally performs in Prague; for many Czechs, her voice still captures something of the ill-fated optimism of the '68 period.

The 1968 Warsaw Pact invasion silenced the rock revolution. Many bands were prohibited from openly performing or recording. In their place, the authorities encouraged singers like Helena Vondráčková (b 1947) and Karel Gott (b 1939), who admittedly had beautiful voices but whose recordings lacked any originality. Many popular songs from those days, like Gott's classic 'Je jaka je' (She Is as She Is), are simply Czech covers of the most innocuous Western music of the day (in this case the Italian song 'Sereno è'). Vondráčková and Gott are still recording and remain highly popular. Most Czechs by now have forgiven them their collaboration during the 1970s and '80s, and their songs today invoke powerful feelings of nostalgia for what many now see as a simpler time.

Rock became heavily politicised during the 1980s and the run-up to the Velvet Revolution. Even the 'Velvet' part of the name owes a partial debt to rock music, in this case the American band the Velvet Underground, one of Havel's favourites and a strong influence on underground Czech bands at the time. Hardcore experimental bands like the Plastic People of the Universe were forced underground and developed huge cult followings. Another banned performer, Karel Kryl (1944–94), became an unofficial bard of the people, singing from his West German exile. His album *Bratříčku, Zavírej Vrátka* (O Brother, Shut the Door) came to symbolise the hopelessness that the Czechs felt during the Soviet invasion and the decades that followed.

The Velvet Revolution opened the door to a flood of influences from around the world. In the early days of Havel's presidency, rock icons who had inspired the revolution, like Frank Zappa, Mick Jagger and Lou Reed, were frequent visitors to the castle. Zappa was even referred to as the unofficial 'Culture Minister'. Early '90s Czech bands like rockers Lucie and Žlutý Pes soon gave way to a variety of sounds from the Nina Hagen–like screeching of early Lucie Bílá to the avant-garde chirping of Iva Bittová, in addition to a flood of mainstream Czech acts. The best of these included Psí Vojáci, Buty, Laura a Její Tygři, Už Jsme Doma, Support Lesbiens, and many more. Currently two of the most popular acts include hard rockers Kabát and the softer folk band Čechomor.

Prague has also become a more important concert venue for touring Western acts. In the first years after the Velvet Revolution, big names were few and far between, but did include the Rolling Stones (on several occasions), Pink Floyd, REM, U2, Bruce Springsteen and Guns N' Roses. Axl Rose legendarily opened his 1992 concert at Strahov stadium with the words, 'OK, you ex-commie bastards, it's time to rock and roll!' In recent years, everybody from Madonna to Green Day to Tom Waits has paid a visit, and every summer seems to bring a richer concert schedule.

LITERATURE

There's no shortage of new Czech literary talent. Names like Jáchym Topol, Petra Hůlová, Michal Viewegh, Magdaléna Platzová, Emil Hakl, Miloš Urban and Hana Androniková are already taking their places among the country's leading authors. They are pushing out the old-guard figures like Milan Kundera and Ivan Klíma, who are now seen as chroniclers of a very different age.

Increasingly, though, younger writers are looking outside the Czech Republic for themes and ideas. In the past, writers like Kundera or Klíma could ruminate for whole books on a character's internal motivations, but many newer writers are setting their novels further afield to win over readers hungry for adventure. One of the best recent titles, Hůlová's *Paměť mojí babičce* (Memories of My Grandmother; 2002), is set in Mongolia and tells of three generations of Mongolian women. Similarly, Platzová's *Sul, ovce a kamení* (Salt, Sheep and Stones; 2003) alternates between the Czech Republic and the Dalmatian coast. Another younger writer, Iva Pekárková, seems at home anywhere except the Czech Republic, placing stories in locations like New York, Thailand and India (see the boxed text, p37).

The bad news for English readers is that, with notable exceptions like Pekárková's *Truck Stop Rainbows*, Topol's stream-of-consciousness epic *City Sister Silver*, two titles by Michal

THE EXPAT CONTRIBUTION

Expat writers have had it rough in Prague. It's hard enough to be a successful writer, but thanks to the late American editor Alan Levy, expat scribes in Prague have laboured under almost unbearable levels of expectation. It was Levy who, writing in the first issue of the *Prague Post* in October 1991, coined the phrase that Prague was the 'Left Bank of the '90s'. He went on to write that future Isherwoods and Audens were already hard at work chronicling the course.

Yeah, right. In the first decade after Levy's pronouncement, it was easy enough to dismiss it as self-serving hype. It's true that Prague at the time was crawling with wannabe writers, but the actual combined published opus was thin indeed. With 20 years' hindsight, though, it's now possible to say the critics were maybe too quick to pounce. The Prague expat pond has actually spawned more than its fair share of decent writers. A partial list would include the following:

- Gary Shteyngart, a student at Charles University in the early 1990s and author of *The Russian Debutante's Handbook* (2003) and *Absurdistan* (2006), the former set partially in Prague in the aftermath of the Velvet Revolution.
- Jonathan Ledgard, a long-time Prague correspondent for *The Economist*, is the author of the acclaimed novel *Giraffe* (2006), based on the story of the slaughter of Central Europe's largest giraffe herd by the Czechoslovak secret police in 1975.
- Maarten Troost was a reporter in the early days of the *Prague Post* and the subsequent author of two hilarious titles: *The Sex Lives of Cannibals* (2004) and *Getting Stoned with the Savages* (2006) – books that could have been written about Prague but are actually about his later adventures in the South Pacific.
- Olen Steinhauer spent time here in the mid-'90s before decamping to Budapest to write five acclaimed Cold War spy thrillers. The fourth book, *Liberation Movements* (2006), opens in the Czech Republic, and shades of Prague can be seen throughout the series.
- Robert Eversz has lived off and on in Prague since 1992, and his 1998 novel *Gypsy Hearts* is set here. He's written several popular noir thrillers, including *Shooting Elvis* (1997), which explores America's obsession with celebrity culture.
- Arthur Phillips apparently never lived in Prague but still managed to write the best-known expat novel to come out of Eastern Europe, called simply *Prague* (2002) – though confusingly set in Budapest. Phillips does have a legit Prague connection, though: his short story 'Wenceslas Square' was printed in the 2003 anthology *Wild East: Stories from the Last Frontier*.

No discussion of expats would be complete without mentioning the growing genre of 'I Lived Here and This Is How It Was' books. Gene Deitch's *For the Love of Prague* is one of the most enjoyable. Deitch is a former Hollywood animator who moved to Prague in the late 1950s and worked on cartoons like *Tom and Jerry*, *Popeye* and *Krazy Kat* from behind the Iron Curtain. Douglas Lytle's *Pink Tanks and Velvet Hangovers* was written not long after the expat 'Golden Age' (from 1991 to 1995) and recounts the major events of the day filtered through the eyes of a young American journalist. One of the newest entries in the genre is Rachael Weiss's wide-eyed *Me, Myself and Prague*, the well-crafted story of an Australian woman who leaves the modern comforts of Sydney in 2005 to move to cold and cranky Prague. Not to spoil the ending, but she winds up loving it.

BOOKS FOR YOUR BACKPACK

Not much new Czech literature is available in translation, but there are still plenty of decent Czech writers available in English. Some of the best titles:

- *Bringing Up Girls in Bohemia* (Michal Viewegh, 1996) – Humorously captures the early years of newly capitalist Prague. The movie of the same name stars Czech actress Anna Geislerová and opens with Geislerová relaxing at the old Globe Bookstore & Coffeehouse in Holešovice – a classic intersection of art and real life.
- *Closely Watched Trains* (Bohumil Hrabal, 1965) – Hrabal's novella tells the story of a young man coming of age at a railway station during WWII. The screen adaptation won the Oscar for best foreign film in 1967.
- *City Sister Silver* (Jáchym Topol, 1994) – Translator Alex Zucker modestly describes this rambling, words-on-speed novel as 'the story of a young man trying to find his way in the messy landscape of post-communist Czechoslovakia'. Dense, deeply meaningful, and probably hard as hell to translate.
- *Daylight in the Nightclub Inferno* (edited by Elena Lappin, 1997) – Decent anthology of the best young Czech writers working in the years immediately after the Velvet Revolution. Includes selections from Jáchym Topol, Michal Viewegh, Daniela Fischerová and Michal Ajvaz, among others.
- *I Served the King of England* (Bohumil Hrabal, 1990) – Czechoslovakia's tortured history provided fodder for some brilliantly funny novels in Hrabal's capable hands. In this one, a vertically challenged waiter named Ditie rises, Švejk-like, to wealth and prominence under the German occupation, only to lose it all after the war.
- *Life with a Star* (Jiří Weil, 1949) – Jewish writer Weil survived the Nazi occupation by faking his own death and hiding out for the duration of the war. This highly moving account from that period tells the story of an ordinary bank clerk whose life is turned upside down when he's forced to wear the yellow star.
- *Mendelssohn is on the Roof* (Jiří Weil, 1960) – This classic from the Nazi occupation opens with an absurd account of SS workers ordered to remove a statue of the 'Jew composer' Mendelssohn from the Rudolfinum's roof. They can't figure out which one is him, so they pull down the statue with the biggest nose – which turns out to be Richard Wagner!
- *My Merry Mornings* (Ivan Klíma, 1986) – Klíma is a quietly powerful writer with an impressive collection of books from both the pre- and post-1989 period. Collections like *My Merry Mornings* or *My First Loves* capture the kind of quirky magic the city had before it was inundated with 'Prague Drinking Team' T-shirts.
- *Prague: A Traveler's Literary Companion* (edited by Paul Wilson, 1994) – Indispensable collection of excerpts and short stories from a range of Czech writers through the ages and conveniently organised according to districts of the city.
- *The Book of Laughter and Forgetting* (Milan Kundera, 1979) – Kundera wrote this poignant and very funny collection of thematically related short stories from his Paris exile in the 1970s. It immediately established his reputation as Central Europe's leading writer.
- *The Castle* (Franz Kafka, 1926) – Though Kafka was a quintessential Prague writer, very few of his books actually mention the city by name. *The Castle* is no exception. Poor K never makes it inside, and the novel ends 280 pages later in midsentence. A work of genius or simply frustrating? You decide.
- *The Good Soldier Švejk* (Jaroslav Hašek, 1923) – Hašek's WWI novel about an amiable Czech oaf who manages to avoid military service has fallen out of favour – Czechs resent the portrayal and foreigners don't get the humour. Still, for anyone with a fondness for the Austro-Hungarian monarchy, it's a must-read.
- *The Joke* (Milan Kundera, 1967) – Kundera's first novel was published in Czechoslovakia in 1967 in the brief thaw that preceded the Soviet invasion. It's a tragicomic love story of what happens when a spurned lover sends a dumb joke to his ideologically blinded girlfriend.
- *The Trial* (Franz Kafka, 1925) – 'Someone must have been telling lies about Josef K, for without having done anything wrong he was arrested one fine morning.' Kafka wrote these words in 1914, but they were eerily prophetic of the arrests of Czechs and Jews to come during WWII or of communist show trials after the war.
- *The Unbearable Lightness of Being* (Milan Kundera, 1984) – Kundera's best-known novel because of the 1988 movie starring Daniel Day-Lewis and Juliette Binoche. The novel's elixir of Prague during the 1968 invasion and a highly likeable womanising character named Tomáš combined to cement Kundera's genius rep in the 1980s. It's still highly readable.

Viewegh and a couple of anthologies, not much new literature has been published in English. Excerpts of Topol's second book, *Anděl* (Angel Station), can be found on the internet (www.postroadmag.com), but his third book, *Nemůžu se zastavit* (I Can't Stop), is unlikely to appear in English anytime soon.

It's not clear why international publishers are shunning new Czech literature. Maybe it's the fact that much of it isn't so different from modern literature anywhere else in the world.

Or maybe they feel that with communism out of the way, Czech literature lacks a big theme to define itself against. Whatever the reason, for the moment at least, non-Czech speakers will have to content themselves with classics from the communist era and earlier. Fortunately, these are still widely available and have held up remarkably well.

Kundera remains the undisputed champ of Czech literature and was even – grudgingly – awarded the Czech state prize for literature in 2007 for a new translation of his classic *The Unbearable Lightness of Being*. The word 'grudgingly' is in order because Czechs, perhaps unfairly, have never forgiven him for leaving his homeland in the mid-'70s just as they were suffering under the Russian occupation. For visitors to Prague, this book, along with *The Joke* and *The Book of Laughter and Forgetting*, remains the most rewarding (see the boxed text, opposite, for recommended titles). Kundera's later works, including 2007's *The Curtain*, tend toward drier, more clinical divinations of the novel and are best left to hardcore fans and grad students.

Other giants who came of age during the period from the Soviet-led invasion in 1968 to the Velvet Revolution include Ivan Klíma, Bohumil Hrabal, Josef Škvorecký and Václav Havel (as an essayist and playwright; see the boxed text, p28). Klíma, who survived the Terezín camp as a child and who still lives in Prague, is probably best known for his collections of bittersweet short stories of life in Prague in the 1970s and '80s like *My First Loves* and *My Merry Mornings*. He also wrote a series of very good novels after 1989 exploring the conflicting moral climate of post-Velvet Prague, including *Waiting for the Dark, Waiting for the Light* and *No Saints or Angels*.

Ask any Czech who their favourite author is: chances are the answer will be Bohumil Hrabal, and it's not hard to see why. Hrabal's writing captures what Czechs like best about their society and culture, including a keen wit, a sense of the absurd and a fondness for beer. He's also a great storyteller, and novels like *I Served the King of England* (which was made into a movie in 2006) and *The Little Town Where Time Stood Still* are both entertaining and insightful. Hrabal died in 1997 in classic Czech fashion – by falling from a window.

Josef Škvorecký emigrated to Canada shortly after the 1968 invasion and, like Kundera, his writing is dominated by themes of exile and memory. Look for *The Cowards, The Swell Season* and *The Engineer of Human Souls*.

No discussion of Czech literature would be complete without Franz Kafka, easily the best-known writer to have ever lived in Prague and author of the modern classics *The Trial* and *The Castle*. Though Kafka was German-speaking and Jewish, he's as thoroughly connected to the city as any Czech writer could be. Kafka was born just a stone's throw from the Old Town Square and rarely strayed more than a couple of hundred metres in any direction during the course of his short life (see the boxed text, p83). The Nazi occupation 15 years later wiped out any vestiges of Kafka's circle of German writers, which included his friend and publicist Max Brod and journalist Egon Erwin Kisch.

Kafka's Czech contemporary and easily his polar opposite was the pub scribe Jaroslav Hašek, author of the – in equal measures – loved and reviled *The Good Soldier Švejk*. For those who get the jokes, the book is a comic masterpiece of a bumbling, good-natured Czech named Švejk and his (intentional or not) efforts to avoid military service for Austria–Hungary during WWI. Czechs tend to bridle at the assertion that an idiot like Švejk could somehow embody any national characteristic. Admirers of the book, on the other hand, feel in this instance that perhaps the Czechs doth protest too much.

The Czech language is highly inflected, giving grammatically gifted writers ample ammo to build layers of meaning simply by playing with tenses and endings. The undisputed master of this is the interwar writer Karel Čapek, an essayist and author of several novels, including the science fiction *RUR (Rossum's Universal Robots)*, from where the English word 'robot' (from the Czech for 'labour') derives.

Czech contributions to literature are not limited to fiction. Czech poet Jaroslav Seifert (1901–86) won the Nobel Prize for Literature in 1984. The American publisher Catbird Press has come out with an excellent collection of his work in English, *The Poetry of Jaroslav Seifert*. The irony is that Seifert is not universally considered by Czechs to be their best poet. Depending on whom you ask, that distinction often belongs to poet-scientist Miroslav Holub (1923–98).

VISUAL ARTS

Ask about visual arts in Prague and many visitors will probably draw a blank, perhaps conjuring up some Art Nouveau images by Alfons Mucha (see the boxed text, p40). But the city has much more to offer than Mucha's sultry maidens. Prague has both a long tradition of avant-garde photography and a rich heritage of public sculpture, ranging from the baroque period to the present day. There is always something new and fascinating to see at the Veletržní Palace or in one of the private galleries around town.

Photography

Czech photographers have always been at the forefront of the medium. The earliest photographers, in the late 19th and early 20th centuries, worked in the pictorialist style, which viewed photography as a kind of extension of painting. Photographers were encouraged to use various shooting and printing techniques to introduce imprecision, much like an Impressionist painting.

It was after independence in 1918 and during the 1920s and '30s that early modern styles captured the Czech imagination. Local photographers seized on trends like Cubism, functionalism, Dadaism and Surrealism, turning out jarring abstracts that still look fresh today. Two of the best photographers from that time are František Drtikol and Jaroslav Rössler. Drtikol was a society portraitist who mainly shot nudes poised against dramatic, angular backdrops. Rössler spent several years in Paris, refining a style of powerful abstract imagery that draws on constructivist trends.

During communism photography was enlisted in the service of promoting the workers' state. Picture books from that time are comically filled with images of tractors, factories and housing projects. Serious photographers turned inward and intentionally chose subjects – like landscapes and still lifes – that were, at least superficially, devoid of political content.

Arguably the best Czech photographer from this period was Josef Sudek. During a career that spanned five decades until his death in the mid-'70s, Sudek turned his lens on the city of Prague to absolutely stunning effect. Sudek exhibitions are relatively rare, but collections of his photography are widely available at antiquarian bookshops around town.

Current Czech bad-boy photographer Jan Saudek (b 1935) continues to delight his fans (or appal his critics) with his dreamlike, hand-tinted prints that evoke images of utopia or dystopia – usually involving a nude or seminude woman or child. Saudek is unquestionably the best-known contemporary Czech photographer and his works are frequently on display, but the jury is still out on whether the pictures – especially those involving kids – don't transgress the boundaries.

Sculpture

Public sculpture has always played a prominent role in Prague, from the baroque saints that line the parapets of Charles Bridge to the monumental statue of Stalin that once faced the Old Town from atop Letná Hill (see the boxed texts, p80 and p93). More often than not, that role has been a political one.

In the baroque era, religious sculptures sprouted in public places; they included 'Marian columns' erected in gratitude to the Virgin Mary for protection against the plague or victory over anti-Catholic enemies. One such Marian column stood in Old Town Square from 1650 until 1918. The placing of the statue of St John of Nepomuk on Charles Bridge in 1683 was a conscious act of propaganda designed to create a new – and Catholic – Czech national hero who would displace the Protestant reformer Jan Hus. As such it was successful. John of Nepomuk was canonised in 1729, and the Nepomuk legend, invented by the Jesuits, has passed into the collective memory.

The period of the Czech National Revival saw Prague sculpture take a different tack: to raise public awareness of Czech traditions and culture. One of the most prolific sculptors of this period was Josef Václav Myslbek, whose famous statue of St Wenceslas, the Czech patron saint, dominates the upper end of Wenceslas Square (p105). He also created the four huge statues of the historic Czech characters Libuše, Přemysl, Šárka and Ctirad that grace the gardens in Vyšehrad fortress (p115).

CZECH RENEGADE WRITER IVA PEKÁRKOVÁ

Iva Pekárková (b 1963) is part of a generation of Czech writers who came of age as communism was ending but who had no intention of sticking around to see how it turned out. She left the country in 1985, spending some time in a refugee camp in Austria before finally winding up on the mean streets of New York, where she drove a cab. Placing her stories in settings as far away as India, Nigeria and Thailand, she projects strong female characters and draws energy from the clash of cultures. Her books include, in English, *Truck Stop Rainbows* (1992) and *Gimme the Money* (1996). She's won praise internationally for her tough subjects, but gets tweaked occasionally by Czech critics as not being 'Czech' enough. We caught up with Iva in London, where she lives these days, driving a cab and contemplating her next move.

So what are you working on? I've been living in London for two years now driving a minicab. (I just started a blog about it: http://pekarkova.blog.idnes.cz.) Meanwhile, I am getting ready to write a book about a phenomenon that's only come into focus the past few years: namely, the twisted relationships between older, and even very old, white women and young black men from Africa. If I do it right, it should be funny. I've just published a collection of short stories from London called *Love in London* (Láska v Londýně).

One might say Czech writers, these days, are grasping for original themes. Would you agree? The book business is actually exploding, with something like 50 to 80 new titles hitting the shelves each week. But booksellers and distributors haven't learned to distinguish between shit-lit and actual literature. No wonder readers get discouraged. When it comes to themes, I think it was Czech author Zuzana Brabcová who said, 10 years ago, [that] 'there were no stories in the Czech Republic'. I've taken a softer approach. I do believe there are stories, but they all seem to me to be recycled. All of the phenomena the Velvet Revolution brought and which Jáchym Topol calls 'the explosion of time' in his novel *City Sister Silver* – namely, chain stores, fashions, music, drugs and feminism – have been in the world for a long time, though they're still relatively new to us. They can be 'discovered' only within the context of the Czech Republic, and good writers always want to be discoverers. No wonder they are frustrated.

What's your favourite Czech book published in the past five years? That's tough. I like *Frišta* by journalist Petra Procházková, set in Afghanistan, Petra Hůlová's *Paměť mojí babičce*, set in Mongolia, and, thank god, one set in the Czech Republic: *Svatava Antošová's Dáma a švihadlo*, a tough, poetic, self-described 'killer-novel'.

Do you have a favourite author? I'm afraid it's still Bohumil Hrabal, though he's been dead a long time. Only a genius could squeeze wonderful and eventful stories out of a sleepy little village like Kersko.

Are there any new talents on the horizon? Petra Hůlová, though she's already been around a while.

The Art Nouveau sculptor Ladislav Šaloun was responsible for one of Prague's most iconic sculptures, the monument to Jan Hus that was unveiled in the Old Town Square (p87) in 1915 to commemorate the 500th anniversary of Hus being burned at the stake. The figure of Hus – standing firm and unmoving, while the events of history swirl around him – symbolised the Czech nation, which, three years later, would be fully independent for the first time in history. For three short years Hus stared across the square at the statue of the Virgin Mary – symbol of the Habsburg victory over the Czechs – until a mob toppled her soon after independence was declared in 1918. Šaloun's works also grace the façade of the Municipal House (p99), the Grand Hotel Evropa (see the boxed text, p112) and Prague City Hall (one block west of the Old Town Square on Mariánské náměstí). He created the bust of Antonín Dvořák that adorns the composer's tomb in Vyšehrad cemetery (p117).

Probably the most imposing and visible sculpture in Prague is the huge, mounted figure of Hussite hero Jan Žižka – reputedly the biggest equestrian statue in the world – that dominates the skyline above Žižkov, the city district named after him. Created by sculptor Bohumil Kafka (no relation to writer Franz) in 1950, it was originally intended to form part of the National Monument (p125) in memory of the Czechoslovak legions who had fought in WWI. It was instead hijacked by the communist government and made to serve as a political symbol of Czech workers and peasants.

The city's long tradition of politically charged sculpture continues today with the controversial and often wryly amusing works of David Černý (see the boxed texts, p39 and p137).

Painting

The luminously realistic 14th-century paintings of Magister Theodoricus, whose work hangs in the Chapel of the Holy Cross at Karlštejn Castle (p230) and in the Chapel of St Wenceslas in St Vitus Cathedral (p64), influenced art throughout Central Europe.

Another gem of Czech Gothic art is a late-14th-century altar panel by an artist known only as the Master of the Třeboň Altar; what remains of it is at the Convent of St Agnes (p95) in Prague's Old Town.

The Czech National Revival in the late 18th and 19th centuries witnessed the revival of a Czech style of realism, in particular by Mikuláš Aleš and father and son Antonín and Josef Mánes. Alfons Mucha is well known for his late-19th- and early-20th-century Art Nouveau posters, paintings and stained glass (see the boxed text, p104). Czech landscape painting developed in the works of Adolf Kosárek, followed by a wave of Impressionism and Symbolism in the hands of Antonín Slavíček, Max Švabinský and others.

In the early 20th century, Prague developed as a centre of avant-garde art, concentrated in a group of artists called Osma (the Eight). Prague was also a focus for Cubist painters, including Josef Čapek and the aptly named Bohumil Kubišta. The functionalist movement flourished between WWI and WWII in a group called Devětsíl, led by the critic and editor Karel Teige. Surrealists followed, including Zdeněk Rykr and Josef Šima.

Visual arts were driven underground during the Nazi occupation, and in the early years of the communist period painters were forced to work in the official Socialist Realist style, usually

ART TALK WITH GALLERY OWNER CAMILLE HUNT

Long-time expats and Prague residents French-Canadian Camille Hunt and Czech-American Katherine Kastner opened Hunt Kastner Artworks in 2005 after seeing a gap for a gallery focused on contemporary art and a growing need for professional representation of young Czech artists abroad. Camille filled us in on the contemporary art scene over lunch at Fraktal (p187), a couple of blocks from her gallery, found in an up-and-coming residential neighbourhood behind Letná Park.

What do you see as some of the main trends in Czech art? Do artists follow international fashions or are there also local developments? Generally, Czech art follows international trends. The art world has become a global village and influences are broadly shared. One local development we see in younger artists is mixing art with social activism. The 'Ladví' group of artists, for example, makes art by doing things like planting trees and fixing broken glass in the housing projects near Ladví in Prague 8 (www.ladviweb.ic.cz).

Who are some of the most exciting names in Czech art today? I would say Josef Bolf, a painter with strong, affective imagery about innocence and violence; Kryštof Kintera, who does sculpture and installation work on consumer society that forces us to reconsider our relation to everyday objects; and the Guma Guar artists' collective, who do political art, criticising the powers-that-be but with humour – always a good thing!

What's it like to run a gallery in Prague? What are some of the problems? It's great fun, and the public's reception has been gratifying. It's also challenging, as there isn't yet a developed market in this country for contemporary art. Most local collectors are focused on modern, not contemporary, art. Also, there are only a limited number of collectors interested in younger artists, and they're not used to buying through galleries. This is one of the reasons it's essential we participate in international art fairs.

What about prices? Are there any bargains to be had? Unfortunately, prices for contemporary art are not any lower here than anywhere else, especially as the Czech crown has been so strong.

Aside from your gallery, where are some good places to see contemporary art? The best galleries around town include Jiří Švestka (Map p106; Biskupský dvůr 6, Nové Město); the Rudolfinum (p97); Tranzit/Display (Map pp108–9; Dittrichova 9, Nové Město); NoD (Map pp88–9; Dlouhá 33, Staré Město); and Karlín Studios (Map pp126–7; Křižíková 34, Karlín).

You can see more contemporary Czech art at Hunt Kastner Artworks (Map pp132–3; ☎ 603 525 294; www.huntkastner.com; Kamenická 22, Letná; 🕒 1-6pm Tue-Fri, 2-6pm Sat or by appt; 🚊 1, 8, 15, 25, 26 to Kamenická).

DAVID ČERNÝ: ARTIST-PROVOCATEUR

Czech artist David Černý (b 1967) first made international headlines in 1991 when he painted Prague's memorial to the WWII Soviet tank crews bright pink (see the boxed text, p93). Since then he has cultivated a reputation as the *enfant terrible* of the Prague art scene – his works often turn into major media events, occasionally with police involved. Like others of his generation, he is virulently anticommunist. When the Rolling Stones played Prague in 2003, Keith Richards wore a Černý-designed T-shirt with the words 'Fuck the KSČM' (the initials of the Communist Party of Bohemia and Moravia).

Since the 'Pink Tank' episode, Černý has become internationally famous. He lived for a time in the US, and his art has been exhibited in New York, Chicago, Dresden, Berlin, Stockholm and London, among other places. Many of his works are on display in Prague (see the boxed text, p137).

He's also heavily involved in promoting cross-cultural links with artists abroad through his sprawling 'Meet Factory' (p137) artist-in-residency project in Smíchov. You can find more details on Černý's work and the Meet Factory on his website at www.davidcerny.cz.

depicting workers and peasants building the workers' state. Underground painters included Mikuláš Medek (whose abstract, Surrealist art was exhibited in out-of-the-way galleries) and Jiří Kolář, an outstanding graphic artist and poet whose name when pronounced sounds something like 'collage' – one of his favourite art forms.

CINEMA

For a small country with a minuscule box office, the Czech Republic has an active film industry, producing 15 to 20 features a year. Nearly all features receive some monetary support from the state and sponsors such as Czech TV, but it helps that Czechs are avid moviegoers. Hollywood films account for the majority of movie receipts, but Czech features still bring in around a quarter of the total box office.

Czechs were some of the earliest pioneers in movie-making, with the first Czech films – silent, American-style slapstick comedies – arriving at the end of the 19th century. Movie-making really took off during the interwar First Republic. American westerns were highly popular and even responsible for kicking off a Czech obsession with living in nature and the 'Wild West' that endures to this day. The first film ever to show full-frontal nudity was Gustav Machatý's *Exstace* (Ecstasy; 1932). Revealing it all was one Hedvige Kiesler, who went on to later stardom in Hollywood as Hedy Lamarr.

American films retained their popularity until the US entered WWII at the end of 1941 and the Nazis banned them. Even during the difficult years of the war, Czechs continued to go to the cinema, substituting American dramas and comedies with German ones. The communist coup in 1948 shifted the focus of movie-making from entertainment to education, and films were placed in the service of the state to foster the class consciousness of the workers. The result was predictable mediocrity that didn't end until the political thaw of the 1960s, when a younger generation from the Prague film academy, FAMU, crafted tragicomic films that slyly criticised the communists and garnered rave reviews around the world.

These 'New Wave' films, as they became known, took the world by storm. Czechoslovak films won the Oscar for Best Foreign Film twice in the 1960s, for Ján Kadár and Elmar Klos' *Little Shop on Main Street* (Obchod na korze) in 1965 and Jiří Menzel's *Closely Watched Trains* (Ostre sledované vlaky) in 1967. Miloš Forman was the acknowledged master of the New Wave, kicking off with the spare but absorbing *Black Peter* (Černý Petr) in 1963, and then creating classics like *Loves of a Blonde* (Lásky jedné plavovlásky; 1966) – which was nominated for an Oscar but didn't win – and *The Fireman's Ball* (Hoří, má panenko; 1967) before moving to the US after the Warsaw Pact invasion. Forman went on to win Oscars for Best Picture for *One Flew Over the Cuckoo's Nest* and *Amadeus*. Other prominent directors to emerge during the Czech New Wave included Ivan Passer, Věra Chytilová and Jan Němec, among others. Many of these directors' films are now available on DVD.

Since the Velvet Revolution, Czech directors have struggled to make meaningful films, given their tiny budgets and a constant flood of movies from the US. At the same time, they've had to endure nearly nonstop critical demands that their output meet the high standards for Czech

THE UNDERAPPRECIATED ALFONS MUCHA

Alfons Mucha (1860–1939) is probably the most famous visual artist to come out of the Czech lands, though his reputation within the Czech Republic is less exalted than it is abroad.

Mucha's life and career changed almost overnight after a chance meeting in a print shop led him to design a poster for famous actress Sarah Bernhardt, promoting her new play *Giselda*; you can see the original lithograph in the Mucha Museum (p104). The poster, with its tall, narrow format, muted colours, rich decoration and sensual beauty, created a sensation.

Mucha quickly became the most talked about artist in Paris. He signed a six-year contract with Bernhardt during which he created nine superb posters in what became known as *le style Mucha*. He also designed jewellery, costumes and stage sets, and went on to produce many more posters promoting, among other things, Job cigarette papers, Moët & Chandon champagne and tourism in Monaco and Monte Carlo.

Although firmly associated with Art Nouveau, Mucha himself claimed he did not belong to any one artistic movement, and saw his work as part of a natural evolution of Czech art. His commitment to the culture and tradition of his native land was expressed in the second half of his career, when he worked on the decoration of the Lord Mayor's Hall in Prague's Municipal House (p99), designed new stamps and banknotes and created a superb stained-glass window for St Vitus Cathedral (p64).

He devoted 18 years of his life (1910–28) to creating his *Slovanské epopej* (Slavic Epic), which he later donated to the Czech nation. The 20 monumental canvasses encompass a total area of around 0.5 sq km and depict events from Slavic history and myth. Although very different in style from his Paris posters, they retain the same mythic, romanticised quality, full of wild-eyed priests, medieval pageantry and battlefield carnage, all rendered in symbolic tints. In the artist's own words, 'black is the colour of bondage; blue is the past; yellow, the joyous present; orange, the glorious future'. (The *Slavic Epic* is on display in the town of Moravský Krumlov, near Brno, about 200km southeast of Prague.)

When the Nazis occupied Czechoslovakia in 1939, Mucha was one of the first to be arrested by the Gestapo. He was released but died a few days later, shortly before his 79th birthday. He is buried in the Slavín at Vyšehrad Cemetery (p117).

Mucha's granddaughter, Jarmila Plocková, uses elements of his paintings in her own works. Those interested can check out Art Décoratif (p146).

films set during the 1960s. Given the high expectations, the newer Czech directors have largely succeeded, settling for smaller, ensemble-driven films that focus on the hardships and moral ambiguities of life in a society rapidly transiting from communism to capitalism. If the Czech New Wave was mostly about making light of a bad situation, it wouldn't be a stretch to say today's films strive to make bad out of a comparatively light situation.

Films like David Ondříček's *Loners* (Samotáři), Jan Hřebejk's *Up and Down* (Horem pádem), Sasha Gedeon's *Return of the Idiot* (Návrat idiota), Bohdan Sláma's *Something Like Happiness* (Štěstí) and Petr Zelenka's *Wrong Way Up* (Příběhy obyčejného šílenství) are all very different, yet each explores the same familiar dark terrain of money, marital problems and shifting moral sands. Running against this grain has been director Jan Svěrák, who continues to make big-budget films that have attracted more international attention; he even took home the country's first Oscar since the 1960s, for the film *Kolja* in 1996.

In addition to Czech films, the country has managed to position itself as a lower-cost production centre for Hollywood films. Part of the pitch has been the excellent production facilities at Barrandov Studios, to the south of Smíchov. The effort has paid off, and dozens of big budget films – including *Mission: Impossible*, the James Bond film *Casino Royale* and the first two *Chronicles of Narnia* movies – have all been filmed here. Whether Prague can continue to lure big-time productions remains in doubt, however, as the Czech crown has appreciated and cheaper facilities in Hungary and Romania have opened up.

Animation and Fantasy

It's not surprising for a country with such a long tradition of puppetry that Czechs would also excel at animation. The centre for much of this activity was Prague's famed Krátký Film studios.

Czechs are especially well known in Central and Eastern Europe for animated films and shorts aimed at kids; the most popular character is doubtless 'Krtek', the little mole, created by animator Zdeněk Miler in the 1950s. You'll recognise Krtek puppets in shops by his big white eyes, red nose, and three strands of hair on his head. Krtek has starred in dozens of films over the years, starting with the 1957 classic *How the Mole Got His Trousers* (Jak krtek ke kalhotkám přišel).

Czech painter and illustrator Jiří Trnka won worldwide recognition for his evocative puppet animation films, beginning in 1946 with *The Czech Year* and continuing until his death in 1969. His best works include a parody of American westerns called *Song of the Prairie*, *The Emperor's Nightingale* (narrated by Boris Karloff in a 1951American version), *The Good Soldier Švejk* and, finally, 1965's *The Hand* – a highly politicised work illustrating the struggle of the artist against totalitarian authority, portrayed by a simple, white-gloved hand. That film was initially tolerated by the government but banned from theatres shortly after Trnka's death. It wasn't rereleased until after 1989.

Czech Jan Švankmajer is celebrated for his bizarre, surrealist animation work and stop-motion feature films, including his 1988 version of *Alice in Wonderland*, called *Alice* (Něco z Alenky), and the 1994 classic, *Faust* (Lekce Faust). His 1996 *Conspirators of Pleasure* (Spiklenci slasti) is an over-the-top take on fetishism and self-gratification. There's no dialogue, making it accessible (if that's the right word) in any language.

THEATRE

Theatre in Prague remains a popular and vital art form, in spite of rising competition from the internet, film and TV. Openings for key performances, such as Tom Stoppard's riveting play *Rock 'n' Roll* at the National Theatre (Národní divadlo; p201) in 2007 or Václav Havel's acclaimed *Odcházení* (Leaving) at Divadlo Archa in 2008, are often sold out months in advance and duly debated in the papers and by the public for weeks after.

In addition to the main venues, including the National Theatre and the Estates Theatre (Stavovské divadlo; p199), there are dozens of smaller theatres scattered around the centre and in nearly every one of the city's neighbourhoods and districts. Unfortunately for non-Czech speakers, much of the action remains inaccessible. Occasionally, big theatrical events will be supertitled in English, but the bread and butter of Czech drama is performed in Czech only. Two theatres, Archa and the Švandovo divadlo in Smíchov (p203), are committed to English-friendly performances and occasionally host English drama in the original language. Additionally, the annual Fringe Festival, held at the end of May and early June, brings a week of nonstop drama, comedy and sketch performances, much of it in English.

Theatre has always played a strong role in the Czechs' national consciousness, both as a way of promoting linguistic development and defending the fledgling culture against the dominant Habsburg, German and, later, communist influences. Czech-language (as opposed to German) drama found an early home in the late 18th century at the Nostitz Theatre, now the Estates Theatre. Historical plays with a nationalist subtext flourished during the 19th century as part of the Czech National Revival. The decade-long construction of the National Theatre and its opening in 1881 was considered a watershed in Czech history. Tragically, the theatre burned down shortly after opening but was completely rebuilt following a public outcry just two years later.

Drama flourished in the early years of independent Czechoslovakia, but suffered under the Nazi occupation, when many Czech-language theatres were closed or converted into German theatres. Under communism, classical performances were of a high quality, but the modern scene was stifled. Exceptions included the pantomime of the Cerné divadlo (Black Theatre) and the ultramodern Laterna Magika (Magic Lantern), founded by Alfréd Radok and still going strong.

Many fine plays during this period, including those by Havel, were not performed locally because of their antigovernment tone, but appeared in the West. In the mid-1960s, free expression was briefly explored in Prague's Theatre on the Balustrade (Divadlo na zábradlí; p203), with works by Havel, Ladislav Fialka and Milan Uhde, and performances by the comedy duo of Jiří Suchý and Jiří Šlitr. The centrality of theatre to Czech life was confirmed in 1989 during the Velvet Revolution, when Havel and his Civic Forum movement chose to base themselves at the Laterna Magika for their epic negotiations to push the communists from power.

While theatre remains a vital art form and is well attended, there are concerns for its future as prices for performances rise and cultural budgets remain under pressure. One of the main issues facing the city government is how to finance cultural establishments, and many in City Hall are

GREAT CZECH FILMS

- *Amadeus* (1985) – Until the Velvet Revolution, the biggest Hollywood production to be filmed here. Director Miloš Forman chose Prague for his Oscar-winning tale of composer Wolfgang Amadeus Mozart because it looked more like '18th-century Vienna' than Vienna – he even got to film inside the Estates Theatre, where *Don Giovanni* premiered in 1787.
- *Beauty in Trouble* (Kráska v nesnázích; 2006) – By acclaimed director Jan Hřebejk, who holds a mirror up to Czech society, showing it warts and all. Czech actress Anna Geislerová plays a woman whose life collapses after the 2002 Prague floods and who takes up a hesitant relationship with a wealthy Czech émigré living in Italy.
- *Black Peter* (Černý Petr; 1963) – This early Miloš Forman film wowed the New York critics on its debut with its cinematic illusions to the French New Wave and its slow but mesmerising teenage-boy-comes-of-age storyline. Also called *Peter and Pavla*.
- *Bony a Klíd* (1987) – Vít Olmer's communist-era classic looks at Prague in the pre–Velvet Revolution years, when a corrupt secret police and organised crime were one and the same. Banned on release, it was widely circulated underground on video and features arguably the best-ever use of a Frankie Goes to Hollywood soundtrack.
- *Closely Watched Trains* (Ostre sledované vlaky; 1966) – Jiří Menzel's adaptation of Bohumil Hrabal's comic WWII classic won an Oscar in 1967 and put the Czech New Wave on the international radar screen. Watch for young Miloš gently broaching the subject of premature ejaculation with an older woman as she lovingly strokes a goose's neck.
- *Cosy Dens* (Pelíšky; 1999) – The story of two neighbours on the eve of the 1968 Warsaw Pact invasion with radically differing political views. Czech directors have yet to make the definitive film about communism, but this attempt – sad and funny in equal measures – comes close.
- *Czech Dream* (Český sen; 2004) – Arguably the finest Czech documentary in recent years. Two local wags fake the opening of a new hypermarket, handing out flyers promising the lowest prices ever, and then film the result. The ending is both predictable and sad, an allegory of the newly capitalist Czech Republic.
- *Divided We Fall* (Musíme si pomáhat; 2000) – Jan Hřebejk and Petr Jarchovský's comic but unsparing view of the German occupation and the Czechs who collaborated. A couple hides a Jewish refugee in their house and must take convoluted steps to conceal their actions – including publicly embracing the Nazis.
- *Kolya* (Kolja; 1996) – Jan Svěrák's Oscar-winning tale of an ageing Czech bachelor and a cute Russian kid was originally cheered for helping salvage Czech films' international reputation. It hasn't worn well with time and is now considered syrupy. Still worth a look for the sumptuous shots of what was intended to be prerevolutionary Prague.
- *Loners* (Samotáři; 2000) – David Ondříček's hugely influential film set the standard for the ensemble-driven, life-of-a-20-something chronicles that have become the staple of post–Velvet Revolution Czech cinema.
- *Loves of a Blonde* (Lásky jedné plavovlásky; 1965) – Miloš Forman's bittersweet love story of a naive girl from a small factory town and her more sophisticated Prague beau. Arguably Forman's finest film, effortlessly capturing both the innocence and the hopelessness of those grey days of the mid-1960s.
- *Panel Story* (Panelstory; 1979) – Věra Chytilová's classic from communist times about young families who buy apartments in the new high-rise apartment blocks going up all over town, only to discover how bad they are. It's mesmerising from the opening shot on.
- *Something Like Happiness* (Štěstí; 2005) – Bohdan Sláma's bleak film is similar in tone to *Beauty in Trouble* and also stars Geislerova, but this time around she plays an emotionally disturbed mother on the verge of a breakdown in the northern city of Most. The movie is redeemed by level-headed Monika, played by Czech actress Tatiana Vilhelmová.
- *The Ride* (Jízda; 1994) – Hugely influential Czech road movie starring a young Geislerová, who hitchhikes her way to hopeful freedom. Captured something of the optimism and spirit of those early postrevolutionary years.
- *Up and Down* (Horem pádem; 2004) – Director Jan Hřebejk's highly regarded film is one of several in recent years that takes a hard look at the new realities of post–Velvet Revolution Prague, where money talks and age-old hatreds are given more-or-less free rein.

calling for substantial cuts to subsidies. Former president and playwright Václav Havel took the controversial step in 2008 of calling on Prague residents not to support the ruling right-of-centre Civic Democratic Party (ODS) because of the party's position on cultural funding.

Havel's play, *Odcházení*, his first major dramatic work since 1989, opened to nearly universal acclaim in May 2008. It's a parody of life in postcommunist Prague, involving a compromised politician, Vlastík Klein, who bears at least a superficial resemblance to Havel's political rival, President Václav Klaus (even having the same initials). Havel wrote the female lead for his second and current wife Daša, but she fell ill shortly before the play's premiere and was not able to perform. An English version of the play was being readied for debuts in London and New York.

In addition to traditional drama, Czechs have a long history of puppet and marionette theatre going back to the Middle Ages. A major figure of this art form was Matej Kopecký (1775–1847). Marionette theatres opened in Prague and Plzeň in the early 20th century. Josef Skupa's legendary Spejbl and Hurvínek (a Czech version of 'Punch and Judy') attracted large crowds then, and still does.

ENVIRONMENT & PLANNING

Prague has gone a long way towards improving the quality of its air: restricting coal burning within the city, capping factory emissions, and pulling ageing lorries, coaches and cars off the streets. Still, much of this good work has been undercut by a massive increase in automobiles on roadways. The authorities are now in the midst of building an ambitious ring-road system to reroute long-haul traffic around the city, and are even considering introducing a London-style congestion fee to limit the number of drivers in the centre.

Sprawl remains a potentially more vexing problem. The Velvet Revolution sparked a 20-year building boom that shows no sign of letting up. Every year sees thousands of acres of orchards and farmland paved over to make way for new housing developments and shopping centres. These in turn create new traffic patterns and problems of their own. Attempts by the city to limit or plan development have so far had only limited success.

THE LAND

Prague's Old Town (Staré Město) and Malá Strana – along with the districts of Smíchov to the south and Karlín and Holešovice to the east and north – sit along a low-lying bend of the Vltava River, the longest river in the Czech Republic. The position leaves the districts prone to flooding, and over the years the city has seen a series of serious floods, beginning with the deluge of 1342, which wiped out Judith Bridge, precursor to Charles Bridge.

Until relatively recently, the flood of 1890, which broke away part of Charles Bridge, was considered an insuperable deluge, but the devastating flood of 2002 was worse. Heavy rains swelled the Vltava's tributaries and caused officials to make the fateful error of opening levees upriver to release the pressure. The result was a wall of water that cascaded into the city on 13 August 2002, inundating Malá Strana as well as Smíchov, Karlín, Holešovice and the Prague Zoo at Troja.

The surface of the Old Town was spared destruction by last-minute metal barriers that were erected along the banks, though the groundwater rose to nearly street level, flooding out the old Gothic cellars. Some 19 people were killed and many of the zoo's animals were drowned or intentionally destroyed to put them out of their misery. The damage was estimated at €2.4 billion. The flood had a silver lining for formerly industrial districts like Smíchov, Karlín and Holešovice, though – hundreds of millions of crowns in flood relief and development money have been channelled into the districts, transforming them from borderline slums into highly desirable residential neighbourhoods.

The city centre is surrounded on three sides by high hills: Petřín and Hradčany to the west, Letná to the north and the Žižkov bluff to the east. This creates some lovely vistas, but in practical terms restricts the number of roads and access ways that can be built and forces traffic onto a few very heavily congested trunk roads. It's also hampered efforts to promote cycling. While much of the Old Town is flat, the hills present considerable obstacles for potential bicycle commuters coming in from the western, northern and eastern sides.

GREEN PRAGUE

When it comes to large-scale recycling, sustainable energy and organic farming, the Czech Republic still lags far behind Germany, the UK and Scandinavia. All the same, Czech industry has cleaned up its act considerably since the fall of communism, with the annual production of greenhouse gases falling to a fraction of pre-1989 levels.

Czechs have been recycling waste for a long time; you'll find large bins for glass, plastics and papers all over Prague. Most glass bottles are recyclable, and the prices of many bottled drinks – beer, too – include a deposit refundable at supermarkets.

Property developers are finally seeing the economic and marketing potential in making sustainable buildings, and several new projects now tout their 'greenness'. Two developments on opposite sides of the city – the Park, next to the Chodov metro station in the south, and the River City-Amazon Court development in Karlín – are being touted as pioneers in 'green' architecture.

One intractable problem that bedevils green planners is what to do about the *paneláky* – the high-rise public-housing projects that ring the city and are home to a majority of Prague's population. The projects are notoriously environmentally unfriendly, allowing residents to bake in the summer while leaking valuable heat in the winter. Many of them are now being fixed up with the help of public funding and mortgage financing.

URBAN PLANNING & DEVELOPMENT

Since the 1989 Velvet Revolution, city authorities have tried to strike a balance between promoting economic growth while preserving green areas that surround the city and contribute greatly to the quality of life.

The jury is still out as to whether they've succeeded, but the consensus is they've not done enough. Critics point to the recent explosion in hypermarket shopping complexes that ring the outskirts in all directions. The pattern has been the same nearly everywhere, with developers buying up large tracts of land – usually near metro terminuses – and then constructing mixed-use commercial and residential zones, drawing shoppers and commuters to areas that just a few years ago were farmers' fields. The full impact is not yet clear, but there's concern that the new developments are siphoning off money and vitality from the centre.

To be sure, city authorities inherited a highly dysfunctional planning system from the previous communist government. The roadways and retail spaces were woefully inadequate. One need only look at the city's main highway, the *magistrála,* that ploughs through the heart of the city and severs the National Museum (p110) from the rest of Wenceslas Square, to see how poor the planning was during those times.

Along with this boom in private development, the city has embarked on the largest public-works build-up in its history, the centrepiece of which will be an enormous ring-road system of roads, bridges and tunnels that will allow traffic to bypass the city centre. Crews in late 2007 broke ground on the Blanka Tunnel (Prague's 'Big Ditch'), which will eventually run from the district of Břevnov in Prague 6 all the way to near the Prague Zoo in Troja, including stretches below Letná and Stromovka parks. At a cost of €800 million, it's one of the most expensive construction projects in the EU. The tunnel is scheduled to be finished in 2010. In addition, authorities have announced plans to build a rail link between the centre and Prague Airport and have committed themselves to a massive expansion of the metro system until the year 2100, including starting construction of a new D line in 2010. The year 2008 saw the opening of three new metro stations along the northern portion of the C line, which now runs all the way to – what else? – a major shopping centre at Letňany.

Plans by Czech Rail, the public railway authority, to upgrade stations and improve services have languished, though. Major renovations set for both the main station, Hlavní nádraží, and the chief station servicing key destinations like Budapest, Vienna and Berlin, Nádraží Holešovice, are proceeding slowly, and both are likely to remain eyesores for years to come. In an apparent literary in-joke, the wags at Czech Rail in 2007 formally renamed Nádraží Holešovice as 'Nádraží Franze Kafky' (Franz Kafka Station), unfortunately linking Kafka's name to one of the most decrepit train stations in the country. (Thanks, guys!)

Meanwhile, work is continuing on long-overdue repairs to Charles Bridge. Sections of the bridge are likely to remain closed to visitors, though the span itself remains open across its length.

GOVERNMENT & POLITICS

As capital of the Czech Republic, Prague is the seat of the government, parliament and the presidency. The city itself is governed separately. The mayor is Pavel Bém (b 1963), a trained medical doctor and one of the most popular politicians in the country. Bém has worked hard

(Continued on page 53

ARCHITECTURE

Modern art on display at the functionalist Veletržní Palace (p134), Holešovice

ARCHITECTURE

Prague is a living textbook of a thousand years of European architecture. The city's historic core escaped significant damage in WWII, so it records a millennium of continuous urban development, with baroque façades encasing Gothic houses perched on top of Romanesque cellars – all following a street plan that emerged in the 11th century. Much of it is protected as a Unesco World Heritage site.

ROMANESQUE

The oldest surviving buildings in Prague date back to the Přemysl dynasty. In the crypt of St Vitus Cathedral (Katedrála sv Vita; p64) are the remains of the Rotunda of St Vitus, built for Duke Wenceslas (the 'Good King Wenceslas' of Christmas-carol fame) in the early 10th century.

Several stone Romanesque rotundas (circular churches from the 10th to 12th centuries) survive intact in Prague, though most have been incorporated into larger churches. Examples include the Rotunda of St Longinus (early 12th century; p113) in Nové Město, the Rotunda of the Holy Cross (mid-12th century; p102) in Staré Město, and the Rotunda of St Martin (late 11th century; p117) at Vyšehrad. Prague's finest Romanesque structure is the Basilica of St George (p66) at Prague Castle. Although its exterior is hidden behind an elaborate 17th century baroque façade, the interior exhibits the heavy walls, plain columns and barrel-vaulted ceilings that typify Romanesque.

GOTHIC

Gothic style flourished in Prague from the 13th to the 16th centuries. It represented not just a new aesthetic but a design revolution that allowed architects to build thinner walls and higher vaults. Gothic architecture is characterised by tall, pointed arches, ribbed vaults and columns, external flying buttresses and tall, narrow windows with intricate tracery supporting great expanses of stained glass.

Czech Gothic architecture flourished during the rule of Charles IV, especially in the hands of German architect Peter Parler (Petr Parléř), best known for the eastern part of St Vitus Cathedral (p64)

The Romanesque Basilica of St George, Prague Castle

The Gothic interior of St Vitus Cathedral, Prague Castle

Detail of the fountain at the Renaissance Summer Palace, Royal Garden, Prague Castle

at Prague Castle. Begun by Matthias of Arras (Matyáš z Arrasu) in 1344, work continued under Parler until his death in 1399. Parler was also responsible for the Gothic design of the Charles Bridge (p75), the Old Town Bridge Tower (p98), the Church of Our Lady of the Snows (p105) and the Cathedral of St Barbara (p239) in Kutná Hora.

Another master builder was Benedikt Rejt, whose finest legacy is the petal-shaped vaulting of Vladislav Hall (1487–1500; p64) in the Old Royal Palace at Prague Castle. Its flowing, intertwined ribs are a beautiful example of late Gothic craftsmanship.

RENAISSANCE

When the Habsburgs assumed the Bohemian throne in the early 16th century, they invited Italian architects to Prague to help create a royal city worthy of their status. The Italians brought a new enthusiasm for classical forms, an obsession with grace and symmetry and a taste for exuberant decoration.

The mix of local and Italian styles gave rise to a distinctive 'Bohemian Renaissance', featuring heavy, ornamental stucco decoration and paintings of historical or mythical scenes. The technique of *sgraffito* – from the Italian word 'to scrape' – was often used, creating patterns and pictures by scraping through an outer layer of pale plaster to reveal a darker surface underneath.

The Summer Palace (Letohrádek; 1538–60; p63), or Belvedere, found in the gardens to the north of Prague Castle, was built for Queen Anna, the consort of Prague's first Habsburg ruler Ferdinand I. It is almost pure Italian Renaissance, with features that will remind some of Brunelleschi's work in Florence.

Other examples of Renaissance buildings are the Ball-Game House (Míčovna; 1569; p63) in Prague Castle; the Schwarzenberg Palace (1546–67; p68) in Hradčany, with its striking Venetian-style *sgraffito* decoration; the House at the Minute (Dům U minuty; 1546–1610; p92) in Staré Město; and the Star Summer Palace (Hvězda; 1556; p142).

BAROQUE

St Nicholas Church, Malá Strana

In the aftermath of the Thirty Years' War (1618–48), the triumphant Habsburg Empire embarked on a campaign to rebuild and re-Catholicise the Czech lands. The ornate baroque style, with its marble columns, florid sculpture, frescoed ceilings and rich ornamentation, was consciously used by the Catholic Church as an instrument of propaganda. By the 18th century a distinctly Czech baroque style had emerged. Its best-known practitioners were the Bavarian father and son Kristof and Kilian Ignatz Dientzenhofer and the Italian Giovanni Santini.

The most impressive example of Prague baroque is the Dientzenhofers' St Nicholas Church in Malá Strana (1704–55; p79). Its massive green dome dominates Malá Strana in a fitting symbol of the Catholic Church's dominance over 18th-century Prague. Visitors enter through the western door at the foot of an undulating, tripartite façade decorated with the figures of saints, into a fantasy palace of pale pink, green and gold, where a profusion of pilasters, arches and saintly statues leads your eye upward to the luminous gleam of the dome. The magnificent fresco that adorns the ceiling of the nave depicts the apotheosis of St Nicholas, and portrays the saint performing acts such as rescuing shipwrecked sailors, saving three unjustly condemned men, and saving women from prostitution by throwing them bags of gold.

The final flourish of late baroque was rococo, a sort of 'baroque on steroids' featuring even more elaborate decoration. The Goltz-Kinský Palace (1755–65; p92), overlooking Old Town Square, has a rococo façade.

NEOCLASSICAL

After the exuberance of the 17th and 18th centuries, the architecture of the 19th century was comparatively dull. There was a feeling among architects that baroque and rococo had taken pure decoration as far as it could go and there was a need to simplify styles. They looked to classical Greece and Rome, where the buildings were prized for their restraint, symmetry and formal elegance. In practice, that meant stern façades, heavy columns and the conscious use of classical elements like triangular pediments above doors and windows.

Prague at the time was under the thumb of Habsburg Vienna, where neoclassical was perfectly in tune with the conservative tastes of Emperor Franz Josef I. It survives in hundreds of buildings across the city. As you walk around and admire the architecture, don't be fooled by appearances. If a building has lots of faux columns and rows of identical windows – and looks a little, well, *boring* – chances are that it's 19th-century neoclassical.

Neoclassical and other 'historicist' styles are closely associated with the 19th-century Czech National Revival. The National Theatre (Národní divadlo; 1888; p112) and National Museum (Národní muzeum; 1891; p110) were both built in neo-Renaissance style. The buildings are noteworthy not so much for the quality of the architecture – many critics would call them ponderous – but for what they represented: the chance for Czechs to show they were the equals of their Viennese overlords.

The 19th-century neogothic revival may have been the most successful style ever adopted here. In the 1880s and '90s, officials ordered the construction of dozens of faux neogothic spires – including those atop the Powder Gate (Prašná brána) and the Jindřišská Tower (Jindřišská věž) – lending Prague the nickname 'City of a Hundred Spires'.

ART NOUVEAU

As the 19th century drew to a close, Czech architects began to tire of the relentlessly linear neoclassical façades and the pompous, retrograde style of imperial Vienna. They were looking for something new and found inspiration in Paris with Art Nouveau and its flowing lines and emphasis on beauty.

Art Nouveau was frequently applied to upmarket hotels, including the Hotel Central (1899–1901; Map p106) on Hybernská in Nové Město, whose façade is decorated with stuccoed foliage, ornate lamps and a concrete cornice beneath a decorated gable. The more-famous Grand Hotel Evropa (1906; p112) on Wenceslas Square is even grander and more ornate (on the outside at least; the accommodation inside leaves a lot to be desired), while the Hotel Paříž (1904; Map pp88–9) on U Obecního Domu in Staré Město has retained its interior as well as exterior splendour.

The city's finest expression of Art Nouveau is the magnificent Municipal House (Obecní dům; 1906–12; p99). Every aspect of the building's decoration was designed by leading Czech artists of the time, most famously Alfons Mucha (see the boxed text, p40), who decorated the Lord Mayor's Hall.

CUBIST

In a period of just 10 years (1910–20), barely half a dozen architects bequeathed to Prague a unique legacy of buildings – mostly private homes and apartment blocks – that were influenced by the Cubist art movement. The Cubist style spurned the regular lines of traditional architecture and the sinuous forms of Art Nouveau in favour of triangular, polygonal and pyramidal forms, emphasising diagonals rather than horizontals and verticals and achieving a jagged, almost crystalline effect.

Some of Prague's finest Cubist houses (Map p116) were designed by Josef Chochol in 1912–14 and can be seen in the neighbourhood below the Vyšehrad fortress: check out Villa Libušina at the corner

Cubist house on Rašínovo nábřeží, Vyšehrad

top picks

ROMANESQUE

- Basilica of St George (p66)
- Rotunda of St Martin (p117)
- Rotunda of St Longinus (p113)

GOTHIC

- St Vitus Cathedral (p64)
- Vladislav Hall (p64)
- Charles Bridge (p75)

RENAISSANCE

- Summer Palace (p63)
- Schwarzenberg Palace (p68)
- House at the Minute (p92)

BAROQUE

- St Nicholas Church, Malá Strana (p79)
- Loreta (p69)
- Goltz-Kinský Palace (p92)

NEOCLASSICAL

- National Theatre (p112)
- National Museum (p110)
- Rudolfinum (p97)

ART NOUVEAU

- Municipal House (p99)
- Grand Hotel Evropa (p112)
- Hotel Paříž (Map pp88–9)

CUBIST

- Houses below Vyšehrad Castle (Map p116)
- House of the Black Madonna (p100)
- Bank of Czechoslovak Legions (Map p106)

FUNCTIONALIST

- Baťa shoe store (p149)
- Villa Müller (p141)
- Veletržní Palace (p134)

COMMUNIST

- Hotel Crowne Plaza (p131)
- Kotva department store (Map pp88–9)
- Žižkov TV Tower (p128)

POST-1989

- Dancing Building (p113)
- Former Holešovice brewery (Map pp132–3)
- Nový Smíchov shopping centre & adjoining office complexes (p151)

Art Nouveau detail, Municipal House, Staré Město

of Vnislavova and Rašínovo nábřeží, the houses at Rašínovo nábřeží 6–10 and the apartment block at Neklanova 30. Other appealing examples include the House of the Black Madonna (Dům U černé Matky Boží; 1912; p100) in Staré Město (which houses the Museum of Czech Cubism) and the twin houses (Map pp70–1) at Tychonova 4–6 in Hradčany, all by Josef Gočár, and a 1921 apartment block (Mapp88–9) created by Otakar Novotný at Elišky Krásnohorské 10–14 in Staré Město.

After WWI, Cubism evolved into another unique Prague style as architects such as Pavel Janák and Josef Gočár added colour and decorative elements to their angular façades in another attempt to define a Czech national style. The more rounded forms that characterise these buildings led to the name 'rondocubism'. This short-lived style is seen in Janák's monumental Adria Palace (1922–25; p111) on Národní třída and in the tall, narrow apartment building at Jungmannovo náměstí 4, but its finest expression is seen in Gočár's Bank of Czechoslovak Legions (Legiobank; 1921–23; Map p106) at Na Poříčí 24, with its hypnotic alternation of rounded and right-angled features.

During this period, Cubist designs were extended into both the field of decorative arts – examples of Cubist furniture, ceramics and glassware can be seen in the Museum of Decorative Arts (p95) and the Museum of Czech Cubism (p100) – and the more mundane domain of street fixtures. Prague must be the only city in the world with a Cubist lamppost (Map pp108–9). Even Franz Kafka's tombstone (see p125), designed by Leopold Ehrmann in 1924, evokes the Cubist style in its crystalline prismatic pillar.

FUNCTIONALIST

The early modern mantra that 'form follows function' found a receptive following in the generation of architects that came of age in the 1920s and '30s. Functionalism – similar to Germany's Bauhaus school – appealed to architects precisely because it rejected everything that came before it. Cubism, and especially rondocubism, suddenly seemed overly decorative and more concerned with a building's aesthetics than its function.

In Czechoslovakia, Brno emerged as the centre of functionalist architecture; still, Prague has its share of smart-looking modern boxes, easily identified by their horizontal windowpane fronts and flat roofs. At their best, functionalist buildings enjoy the virtues of simplicity and symmetry.

Functionalism works best on a smaller scale in villas and small apartment blocks, but one successful functionalist building in the centre is the Baťa shoe store (1929; p149) on Wenceslas Square. Its seven-storey façade consists almost entirely of glass and still radiates a kind of infectious, flappers-and-Great-Gatsby modernism.

Functionalist fans will want to see Adolf Loos' Villa Müller (1930; p141) in the western suburb of Střešovice. Loos built the house in 1930 for industrialist František Müller and his wife, choosing a spare minimalist design and then filling the interior with sumptuous travertine marble and exotic hardwoods.

COMMUNIST

Ask your average Czech if the communist period produced anything of architectural value, and you'll get a belly laugh. The communists are uniformly derided for building hideous housing projects (called *paneláky* because they were built from pre-fab panels) and hundreds of schools, hospitals and institutes from a handful of cookie-cutter designs that are indistinguishable from one another, down to the same cheap, pale-green linoleum.

With the passage of time, though, some critics are starting to soften their views, and slowly an appreciation for the period is beginning to take root. It's not that the buildings are good, but at least they're bad in an interesting way.

In the early years after WWII, Czechoslovak architects were forced to design in the bombastic Stalinist, Socialist Realist style. The best of these is the former Hotel International (now the Hotel Crowne Plaza; 1954; p131) in Dejvice.

The mid-'70s apparently spurred a contest to see who could build the most dysfunctional department store. Both the Máj building (now Tesco; 1975; Map pp108–9), in Nové Město, and Kotva (1975; Map pp88–9), on the edge of Staré Město, opened the same year, and exhibited different tendencies of the then-popular 'brutalist' style. Tesco faintly resembles a mini Centre Pompidou, with its metal-and-glass façade consciously exposing the building's pipes and ducts. Kotva, built from giant hexagons perched on rough-hewn concrete posts, is closer to Prince Charles' carbuncles and wouldn't look amiss in a British Midlands town centre from the 1970s. Tellingly, both buildings have been granted protected landmark status.

The Žižkov TV Tower (p128) dates from the end of the communist period. Its sheer scale dwarfs everything around – a metaphor for a communist system totally out of sync with the city. Surprisingly, it's worn well and locals point with some pride to a structure that pushes the extremes of ugliness to achieve something close to beauty.

POST-1989

Architectural purists are aghast by what has been designed and built since 1989. They point to hundreds of shopping-centre complexes, hypermarkets and McMansions that have sprung up on the outskirts of the city in all directions.

That said, it hasn't been a total loss. Arguably the most interesting structure of the post–Velvet Revolution period has been the so-called Dancing Building (1992–96; p113) on Rašínovo nábřeží in Nové Město, designed by Czech-based Croatian architect Vlado Milunić and American architect Frank Gehry. Built on a gap site created by a stray Allied bomb in WWII, it's a bold work whose curves seem tailor-made for guidebooks and tourist brochures. The building's resemblance to a pair of dancers soon saw it acquire the nickname 'Fred and Ginger', after the legendary dancing duo of Astaire and Rogers.

Some of the best new commercial architecture is happening in former industrial districts like Smíchov, Karlín and Holešovice. One of the most innovative of these 'lifestyle' office-and-residential complexes is in Holešovice, where developers are rehabbing the former Holešovice brewery (Map pp132–3).

The future of architecture came to Prague in 2007 in the form of Czech-émigré architect Jan Kaplický's controversial proposal to build a new national library near Letná Park. Kaplický and his London-based firm, Future Systems, are renowned for their wavy-lined, organic, 'blob'-style architecture. The nine-storey building has been described as a 'biomorphic sea creature' (local wags call it 'the octopus'). At the time of research, however, it wasn't clear whether the building would ever be built.

The Dancing Building, Nové Město

(Continued from page 44)

to clean up the city's image, including once famously posing as an Italian tourist in a taxi to see whether he would get ripped off. He did.

The national government is plagued by near constant instability, resulting from the fact that neither of the large centrist parties, the centre-right Civic Democratic Party (ODS) or the centre-left Social Democrats (ČSSD), will form a government with the main Communist party, the KSČM. In practice, that means fragile coalitions have to be stitched together with the two remaining smaller parties, the Christian Democrats (KDU-ČSL) and the Greens (SZ). The current coalition – always rumoured on the verge of toppling – links the ODS, KDU-ČSL and the Greens.

President Václav Klaus won re-election to a second five-year term in February 2008. Klaus, a noted sceptic of the EU and vocal critic of efforts to slow global warming, remains a highly polarising figure. His high-profile critiques of environmental efforts to cap greenhouse gases have made him the darling of the conservative think-tank crowd but have embarrassed many Czechs who see climate change as a serious issue.

MEDIA

Czechs are newspaper junkies, and you'll see people with their noses buried in the latest rag in bars, on trams, on park benches, and even walking on the street. Sadly, the overall standard of newspaper journalism today is low compared with the interwar years, any lingering tradition of quality investigative reporting having been thoroughly stamped out during the communist era.

There are five major national dailies; most are now in the hands of German and Swiss media magnates. The biggest seller is the tabloid *Blesk*, controlled by the Swiss Ringier group. Also popular are the centre-right *Mladá fronta DNES* and the former communist paper, the left-leaning *Právo*. In addition to the dailies, free papers handed out each morning at tram and metro stations, such as the ever-popular *Metro* or the more recent *24hodin* (24 Hours), have made huge inroads in readership. These are generally of execrable quality, though, and have helped encourage newspaper standards ever further downward.

As far as English-language media go, the venerable *Prague Post* (now in its 17th year) continues to publish in spite of rumours that it's on its last legs. The quality of the writing ebbs

TOP MEDIA WEBSITES

Leading Czech dailies:

- *Blesk* (www.blesk.cz, in Czech only)
- *Lidové noviny* (www.lidovky.cz, in Czech only)
- *Mladá fronta DNES* (http://zpravy.idnes.cz/mfdnes.asp, in Czech only)
- *Právo* (http://pravo.novinky.cz, in Czech only)

English-language media:

- *aktuálně.cz* (http://aktualne.centrum.cz/czechnews) – Overview of politics and economics published in conjunction with the Czech online newspaper.
- *Czech Business Weekly* (www.cbw.cz)
- *Czech Happenings* (www.ceskenoviny.cz/news) – English-language news magazine operated by the Czech News Agency, CTK.
- *The New Presence* (www.new-presence.cz)
- *Prague Post* (www.praguepost.com)
- *Prague Daily Monitor* (www.praguemonitor.com)
- Radio Prague (www.radio.cz) – Useful translations of news and cultural features broadcast by the international service of Czech radio.
- *Provokátor* (http://provokator.org) – Online 'zine, strong on the club scene, music and lifestyle. Excellent online timetable for club bookings.
- *Think Again* (www.thinkagain.cz) – Latest incarnation of what must be the longest-running alternative magazine in post–Velvet Revolution Prague. Fun and often witty articles on alternative culture, fashion and happenings.

CZECH TONGUE TWISTERS

Forget Sally's seashells or Peter Piper's pickled peppers. With a language in which vowels appear to be optional, Czechs have a tradition of world-beating tongue twisters. Practise these a few times if you want to impress your Czech hosts:

- Strč prst skrz krk (literally, 'Put your finger through your throat')
- Třistatřicettři stříbrných stříkaček stříkalo přes třistatřicettři stříbrných střech (Three-hundred-thirty-three silver sprinklers were spraying over 333 silver roofs)
- Šel pštros s pštrosáčaty pštrosí ulicí (The ostrich went with its baby ostriches through Ostrich Street)

If you're really good, try this one (courtesy of Wikipedia – though we've never heard anyone attempt it):

- Prd krt skrz drn, zprv zhlt hrst zrn (A mole farted through the grass, having swallowed a handful of grain)

and flows depending on the staff, but the tabloid insert *Night and Day* remains an excellent weekly guide to restaurants, movies, happenings, concerts and galleries. Competing with the *Prague Post* in the internet space is the *Prague Daily Monitor*, a lively mix of original stories, supplemented by translations from Czech papers, wire-service pickups, and links to other news sources, including local blogs. *The New Presence* is a quarterly English translation of the Czech *Nová přítomnost*, with features on current affairs, politics and business; on the serious business side, the *Czech Business Weekly* is a comprehensive look at economic issues, real estate, stock trading and other pursuits that make the country tick.

The situation is bleaker when it comes to 'zines. Over the years, Prague has supported dozens of English-language start-ups, alternative weeklies and general rant rags, but their number has dwindled in recent years. This probably reflects the shift in the expat community from slackers to older professionals and the influence of the internet, which makes printing on dead trees seem increasingly old-fashioned. One that's still holding on is the cheeky bimonthly *Think Again*, available around town in bars and coffee shops.

LANGUAGE

The Czech language is strongly bound up with the country's cultural and ethnic identity. Czech was squelched for centuries in favour of German during the Habsburg occupation and re-emerged as a literary language only in the 19th century. By the end of that century the number of Czech speakers in the city exceeded German speakers, and by 1939, when the Nazis rolled in, German speakers were a distinct minority (though Prague was still technically bilingual). During the war the Nazis attempted to reinstall German as the leading language, and after WWII, the Russians took their turn at cultural hegemony, making classes in learning Russian compulsory in schools.

Against this backdrop of struggle for linguistic supremacy, it's not surprising that Czechs sometimes appear unwilling to simply chuck it all and just speak English. That said, you're unlikely to have any major problem in central Prague, where residents are accustomed to fielding basic queries in English. The situation changes outside the centre or in the rest of the country. In general, younger people can muster a bit of English. Older people usually know some German.

Czechs take a perverse pride in the difficulty of their tongue. Even compared with other Slavic languages like Polish and Russian, Czech is usually considered a notch harder. To give you an idea, nouns have four genders (masculine inanimate, masculine animate, feminine and neuter) and each is declined differently depending on its position in a sentence. If you assume around a dozen different noun types and at least half a dozen possible endings for each, you've got over 70 possible spellings – and that's just nouns. It's no wonder that even the most well-meaning visitor eventually shrugs his or her shoulders and falls back on the standard *Mluvíte anglicky?* (Do you speak English?)

For more information, see the Language chapter, p257.

NEIGHBOURHOODS

top picks

NEIGHBOURHOODS

The Vltava River sidles through the centre of Prague like a giant question mark, with the city centre straddling its lower half. There is little method in Prague's haphazard sprawl – it's a city that has grown organically from its medieval roots, snagging villages and swallowing suburbs as it spread out into the wooded hills of central Bohemia.

'Prague is a city that has grown organically from its medieval roots, spreading out into the wooded hills of central Bohemia.'

The oldest parts of Prague cluster tightly just south of the river bend – Charles Bridge, the original crossing point on the Vltava, is the seed from which the city spread. At its western end is Malá Strana (Little Quarter), Prague's Left Bank: a banquet of beautiful baroque buildings interlaced with hidden gardens, its cobbled streets and squares lined with appealing bars, restaurants and cafés. The main sights here are the historic delights of St Nicholas Church and the Wallenstein Gardens, and more modern spots like the Franz Kafka Museum and John Lennon Wall.

Nerudova street leads uphill from Malá Strana's main square to Hradčany, the medieval castle district, dominated by the spires of St Vitus Cathedral, a landmark visible from most parts of the city. Visitors crowd the castle precincts and jostle for position at the midday changing of the guard, but elsewhere this is rather a peaceful part of town, with many quiet lanes to explore.

From the eastern end of Charles Bridge, tourist-thronged Karlova street leads to Old Town Square, the heart of medieval Staré Město (Old Town). Bounded by the river on one side and the line of the old city walls (along Revoluční, Na Příkopě and Národní třída) on the other, Staré Město is where you'll find many of Prague's most popular attractions, including the Old Town Hall, Astronomical Clock, Municipal House and Jewish Museum, as well as major concert and opera venues like the Rudolfinum and Estates Theatre.

Wrapped around Staré Město to the south and east, and bounded by the busy traffic artery of Wilsonova, is Nové Město (New Town) – this being Prague, 'new' means 14th-century. Its focal point is the kilometre-long boulevard of Wenceslas Square, and it's where you'll find the Mucha Museum, the National Museum, the National Theatre and many of Prague's more modern hotels and restaurants. At its southern end is the ancient citadel of Vyšehrad, perched on a crag high above the eastern bank of the river.

Beyond the centre lie mostly 19th- and 20th-century suburbs, just a five- or 10-minute tram or metro ride away. To the east lies elegant Vinohrady, with its leafy avenues and cool cafés, which are beginning to spill further east into Vršovice. To their north are grungy Žižkov, famed for its prominent TV Tower and down-to-earth pubs and clubs, and rapidly redeveloping Karlín. The latter two are separated by Vítkov Hill, another prominent landmark, topped by the boxy National Monument and the giant equestrian statue of Jan Žižka.

Back on the west side of the river, to the north of Hradčany, lie the up-and-coming suburbs of Holešovice, Bubeneč and Dejvice. Apart from the Veletržní Palace art gallery and the open green spaces of Letná and Stromovka there are not too many sights here, but there are plenty of worthwhile restaurants, bars and clubs. The same can be said of the formerly industrial district Smíchov, to the south of Malá Strana.

Finally, we have gathered together a grab-bag of outlying attractions under the heading Outer Neighbourhoods, taking in districts such as Troja, home to Prague Zoo; Střešovice, with its Public Transport Museum; and Zbraslav, where a centuries-old chateau now houses an outpost of the National Gallery.

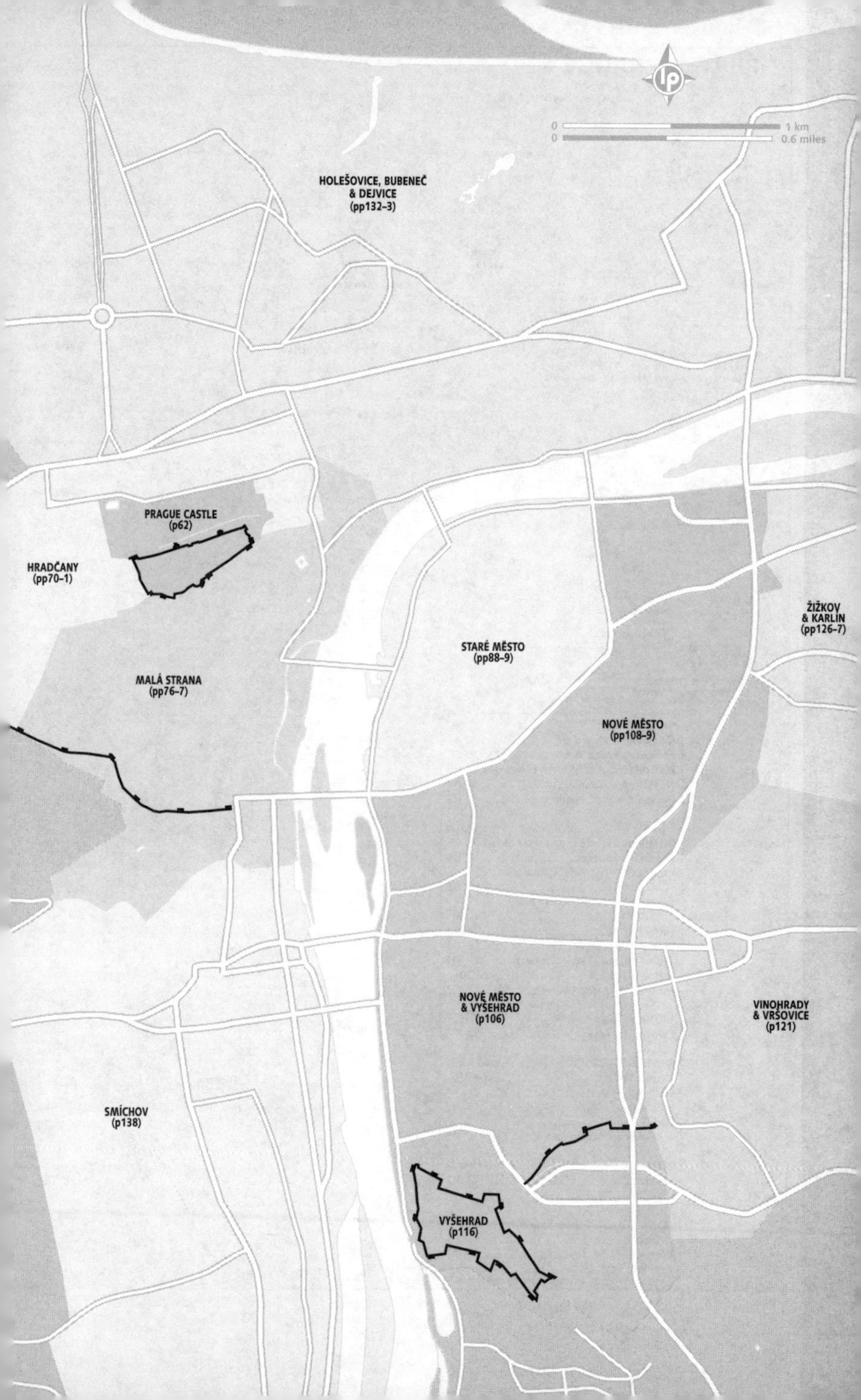

0 1 km
0 0.6 miles
HOLEŠOVICE, BUBENEČ & DEJVICE (pp132–3)
PRAGUE CASTLE (p62)
HRADČANY (pp70–1)
STARÉ MĚSTO (pp88–9)
ŽIŽKOV & KARLÍN (pp126–7)
MALÁ STRANA (pp76–7)
NOVÉ MĚSTO (pp108–9)
NOVÉ MĚSTO & VYŠEHRAD (p106)
VINOHRADY & VRŠOVICE (p121)
SMÍCHOV (p138)
VYŠEHRAD (p116)

GREATER PRAGUE

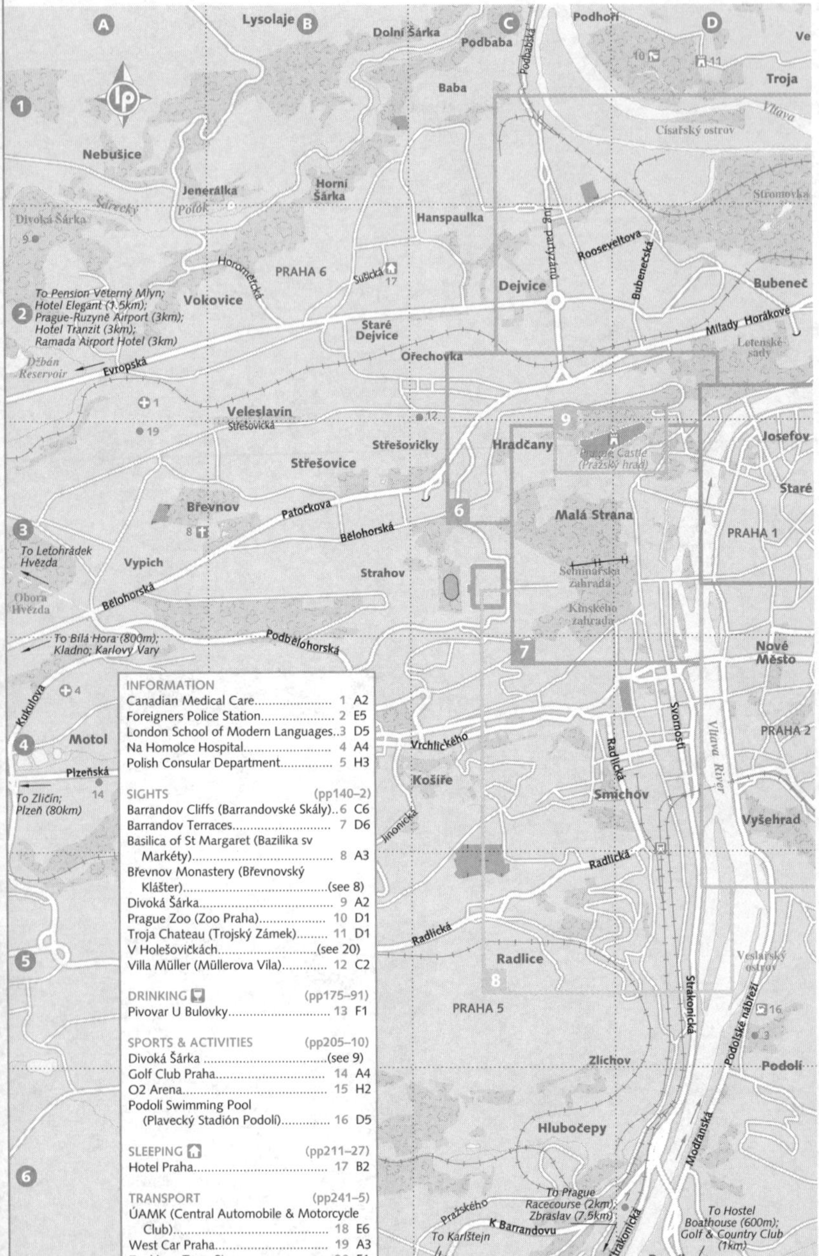

INFORMATION

Canadian Medical Care	1	A2
Foreigners Police Station	2	E5
London School of Modern Languages	3	D5
Na Homolce Hospital	4	A4
Polish Consular Department	5	H3

SIGHTS (pp140–2)

Barrandov Cliffs (Barrandovské Skály)	6	C6
Barrandov Terraces	7	D6
Basilica of St Margaret (Bazilika sv Markéty)	8	A3
Břevnov Monastery (Břevnovský Klášter)	(see 8)	
Divoká Šárka	9	A2
Prague Zoo (Zoo Praha)	10	D1
Troja Chateau (Trojský Zámek)	11	D1
V Holešovičkách	(see 20)	
Villa Müller (Müllerova Vila)	12	C2

DRINKING (pp175–91)

Pivovar U Bulovky	13	F1

SPORTS & ACTIVITIES (pp205–10)

Divoká Šárka	(see 9)	
Golf Club Praha	14	A4
O2 Arena	15	H2
Podolí Swimming Pool (Plavecký Stadión Podolí)	16	D5

SLEEPING (pp211–27)

Hotel Praha	17	B2

TRANSPORT (pp241–5)

ÚAMK (Central Automobile & Motorcycle Club)	18	E6
West Car Praha	19	A3
Zenklova Tram Stop	20	F1

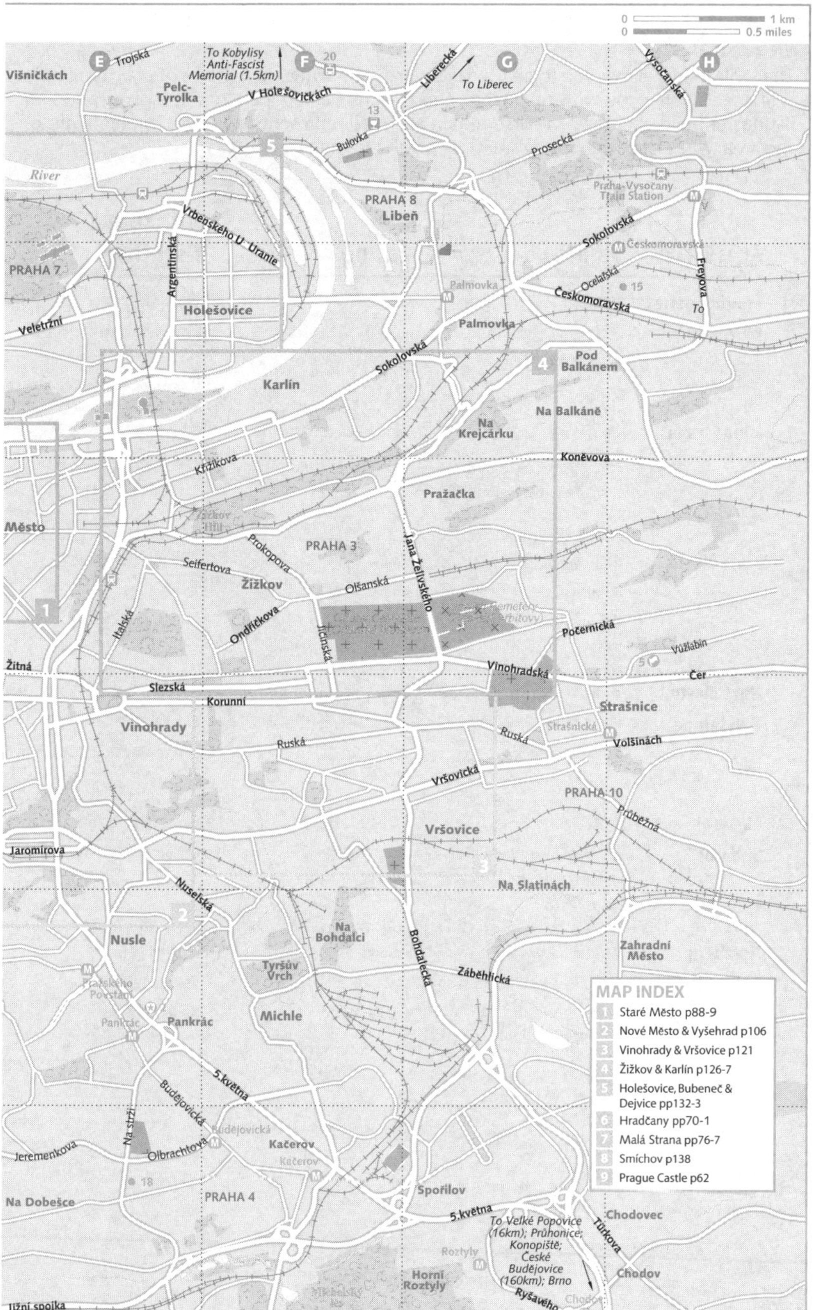
0 1 km
0 0.5 miles
E
F
G
H
Trojská
To Kobylisy Anti-Fascist Memorial (1.5km)
To Liberec
Višničkách
Pelc-Tyrolka
V Holešovičkách
Liberecká
Vysočanská
Bulovka
Prosecká
River
Praha-Vysočany Train Station
PRAHA 8
Libeň
Vrbenského
U Uranie
Sokolovská
Českomoravská
PRAHA 7
Argentinská
Palmovka
Ocelářská
Freyova
Holešovice
Českomoravská
To
Veletržní
Palmovka
Sokolovská
Pod Balkánem
Karlín
Na Balkáně
Na Krejcárku
Křižíkova
Koněvova
Pražačka
Město
PRAHA 3
Jana Želivského
Prokopova
Seifertova
Žižkov
Olšanská
Italská
Ondříčkova
Jičínská
Počernická
Vinohradská
Vúžlabin
Žitná
Čer
Slezská
Korunní
Strašnice
Vinohrady
Ruská
Strašnická
Ruská
Volšinách
Vršovická
PRAHA 10
Průběžná
Vršovice
Jaromírova
Na Slatinách
Nuselská
Na Bohdalci
Bohdalecká
Nusle
Zahradní Město
Tyršův Vrch
Záběhlická
Pražského Povstání
Pankrác
Pankrác
Michle
5.května
Budějovická
Na strži
Budějovická
Jeremenkova
Olbrachtova
Kačerov
Kačerov
Na Dobešce
PRAHA 4
Spořilov
5.května
To Velké Popovice (16km); Průhonice; Konopiště; České Budějovice (160km); Brno
Chodovec
Türkova
Roztyly
Horní Roztyly
Chodov
Ryšavého
Jižní spojka
Chodov
MAP INDEX
1 Staré Město p88-9
2 Nové Město & Vyšehrad p106
3 Vinohrady & Vršovice p121
4 Žižkov & Karlín p126-7
5 Holešovice, Bubeneč & Dejvice pp132-3
6 Hradčany pp70-1
7 Malá Strana pp76-7
8 Smíchov p138
9 Prague Castle p62

ITINERARY BUILDER

The table below allows you to plan a day's worth of activities in any area of the city. Simply select which area you wish to explore, and then mix and match from the corresponding listings to build your day. The first item in each cell represents a well-known highlight of the area, while the other items are more off-the-beaten-track gems.

AREA / ACTIVITIES	Sights	Eating	Drinking & Nightlife
Prague Castle & Hradčany	St Vitus Cathedral (p64) Story of Prague Castle (p66) Strahov Library (p69)	Víkarka (p157) Malý Buddha (p158) U zlaté hrušky (p157)	Lobkowicz Palace Café (p180) Pivnice U černého vola (p180) U zavěšenýho kafé (p179)
Malá Strana	Charles Bridge (p75) Wallenstein Garden (p79) Franz Kafka Museum (p79)	Hergetová cihelná (p159) La Cantina (p159) U malé velryby (p159)	U malého Glena (p197) Klub Újezd (p180) St Nicholas Café (p180)
Staré Město	Old Town Square (p87) Municipal House (p99) Prague Jewish Museum (p96)	Kolkovna (p162) Angel (p161) Lehká hlava (p163)	U zlatého tygra (p183) Kozička (p182) Čili Bar (p183)
Nové Město & Vyšehrad	Wenceslas Square (p105) Mucha Museum (p104) Vyšehrad (p115)	Kogo (p164) Karavanseráj (p165) Oliva (p164)	Bokovka (p184) Pivovarský dům (p179) Lucerna Music Bar (p198)
Eastern Suburbs	TV Tower (p128) National Monument (p125) Vinohrady Walking Tour (p120)	Ambiente (p167) Mozaika (p167) Café FX (p168)	Caffé Kaaba (p185) Corner Bar & Bistro (p186) Palác Akropolis (p198)
Northern Suburbs	Veletržní Palace (p134) National Technical Museum (p133) Stromovka (p133)	Da Emanuel (p170) La Crêperie (p172) Capua (p171)	Cross Club (p194) Fraktal (p187) Andaluský pes (p189)

PRAGUE CASTLE

Eating p157; Drinking p179

Prague Castle – Pražský hrad, or just *hrad* to Czechs – is Prague's most popular attraction. According to *Guinness World Records,* it's the largest ancient castle in the world: 570m long, an average of 128m wide and covering a total area bigger than seven football fields.

Its history begins in the 9th century when Prince Bořivoj founded a fortified settlement here. It grew haphazardly as rulers made their own additions, creating an eclectic mixture of architectural styles. The castle has always been the seat of Czech rulers as well as the official residence of the head of state, although the Czech Republic's first president, Václav Havel, chose to live in his own house on the outskirts of the city.

Prague Castle has seen four major reconstructions, from that of Prince Soběslav in the 12th century to a classical face-lift under Empress Maria Theresa (r 1740–80). In the 1920s President Masaryk hired a Slovene architect, Jože Plečnik, to renovate the castle; his changes created some of its most memorable features and made the complex more tourist-friendly.

We've organised this section starting with the castle's main entrance at the western end, then moving through the various courtyards and sights before exiting at the eastern end. You'll need at least two hours to see the main sights, and all day if you want to visit everything.

The following areas are wheelchair-accessible: the main entrance to St Vitus Cathedral, the Old Royal Palace, Vladislav Hall, the Basilica of St George, Ball-Game House, Prague Castle Gallery and the castle gardens. There's a wheelchair-accessible toilet to the right of the cathedral entrance.

Tickets & Opening Hours

You can wander freely through the castle grounds (5am-midnight Apr-Oct, 6am-11pm Nov-Mar), the castle gardens (10am-6pm Apr & Oct, to 7pm May & Sep, to 9pm Jul & Aug, closed Nov-Mar) and St Vitus Cathedral without a ticket, but you'll need one for all the main historic buildings (9am-6pm Apr-Oct, to 4pm Nov-Mar).

There are six different tickets (each valid for two days), which allow entry to various combinations of sights (see the boxed text, p66); you can buy tickets at either of two information centres (Map p62; 224 373 368, 224 372 423; www.hrad.cz; 9am-6pm Apr-Oct, to 4pm Nov-Mar) in the Second and Third Courtyards, or from ticket offices at the entrances to Golden Lane, the Old Royal Palace and the Story of Prague Castle exhibition.

Concession prices are for those aged seven to 16, students and disabled visitors; children aged six or under get in free. The family ticket is valid for two adults and any children aged 16 or under. Taking photographs indoors will cost you an extra 50Kč, and the use of a flash or tripod is not allowed.

Tickets listed here do not include admission to other art galleries and museums within the castle grounds; those admission costs are listed in the individual reviews.

One-hour guided tours are available in Czech (200Kč for up to four people, plus 50Kč per additional person), and in English, French, German, Italian, Russian and Spanish (400Kč, plus 100Kč per additional person) Tuesday to Sunday. Alternatively you can rent an audio guide (150Kč for two hours) from the information centres.

There's a post office (8am-7pm Mon-Fri, 10am-7pm Sat), currency exchange (8.10am-6.10pm) and ATM next to the information centre in the Third Courtyard, and another ATM and currency exchange inside the information centre in the Second Courtyard. You can buy tickets for concerts and other special events at the ticket office (224 373 483; 9am-5pm Apr-Oct, to 4pm Nov-Mar) in the Chapel of the Holy Cross in the Second Courtyard.

FIRST COURTYARD

The First Courtyard lies beyond the castle's main gate on Hradčany Square (Hradčanské náměstí), flanked by huge, baroque statues of battling Titans (1767–70) that dwarf the castle guards standing beneath them. After the fall of communism in 1989 then-president Václav Havel hired his old pal Theodor Pistek, the costume designer on the film *Amadeus* (1984), to replace their communist-era khaki uniforms with the stylish pale-blue kit they now wear, which harks back to the army of the first Czechoslovak Republic of 1918–38.

The changing of the guard takes place every hour on the hour, but the longest and most

PRAGUE CASTLE

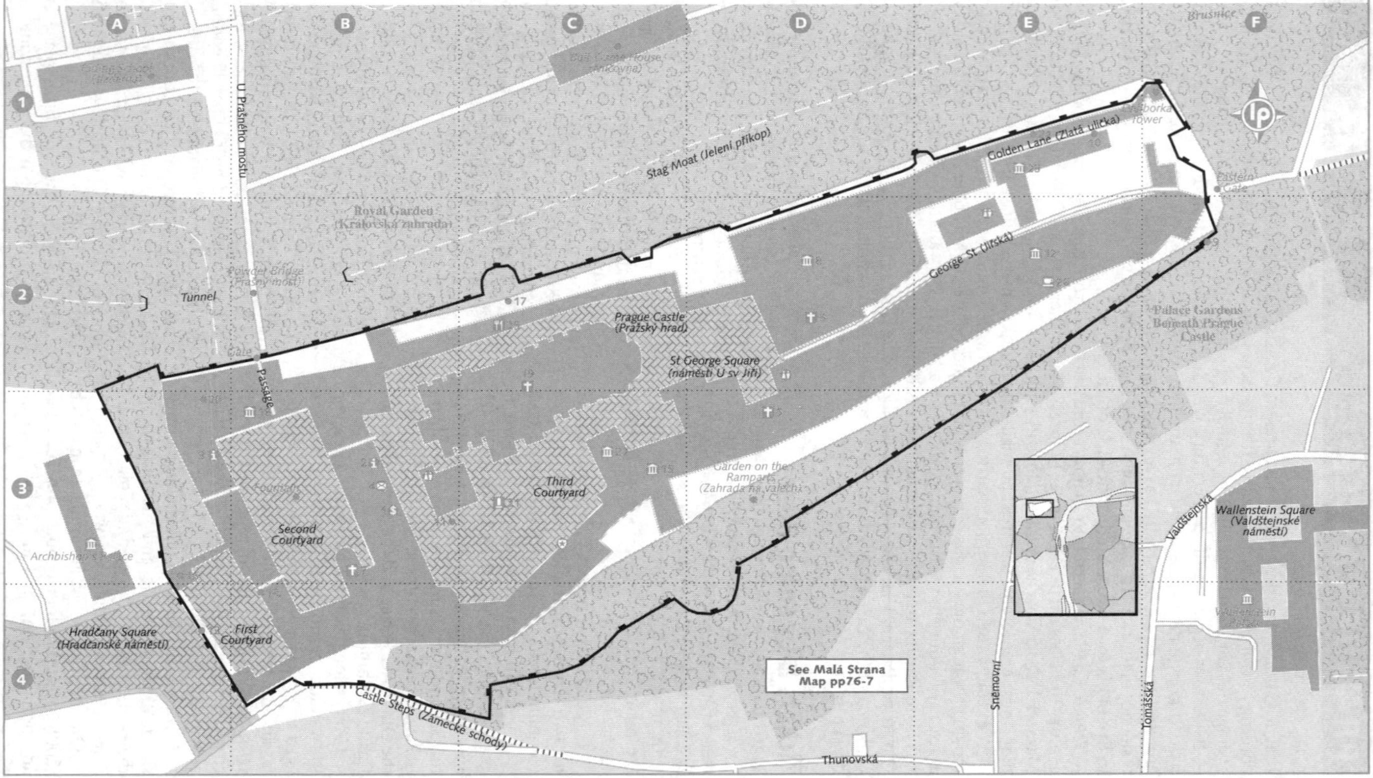

PRAGUE CASTLE

INFORMATION		
Currency Exchange & ATM	1	B3
Information Centre	2	B3
Information Centre & ATM	3	A3
Post Office	4	B3
Ticket Office	(see 7)	
SIGHTS & ACTIVITIES (pp61–7)		
All Saints' Chapel (Kaple Všech Svatých)	5	D3
Basilica of St George (Bazilika Sv Jiří)	6	D2
Chapel of the Holy Cross (Kaple Sv Kríže)	7	B3
Convent of St George (Klášter Sv Jiří)	8	D2
Entrance to Palace Gardens Below Prague Castle	9	F2
Golden Lane (Zlatá Ulička)	10	E1
Granite Monolith	11	B3
Lobkowicz Palace	12	E2
Main Gate	13	A4
Matthias Gate (Matyášova Brána)	14	B4
Old Royal Palace (Starý Královský Palác)	15	C3
Plečník Hall (Plečníkova Síň)	16	A3
Powder Tower (Prašná Věž)	17	C2
Prague Castle Picture Gallery (Obrazárna Pražského Hradu)	18	B3
Rudolph Gallery (Rudolfova Galerie)	(see 20)	
St Vitus Cathedral (Katedrala Sv Víta)	19	C2
Spanish Hall (Španelský Sál)	20	A3
Statue of St George & the Dragon	21	C3
Story of Prague Castle	22	C3
Toy Museum	23	E1
Zlatá Ulička 22 (Kafka's Sister's Cottage)	24	E1
EATING (pp153–73)		
Vikárka	25	C2
DRINKING (pp175–91)		
Lobkowicz Palace Café	26	E2

impressive display is at noon, when banners are exchanged while a brass band plays a fanfare from the windows of the Plečnik Hall (Plečnikova síň), which overlooks the First Courtyard.

This impressive hall, which opens off the left side of the baroque Matthias Gate (Matyášova brána; 1614), was created by Slovenian architect Jože Plečnik as part of the 1920s restoration of the castle; the pointy flagpoles in the First Courtyard are also Plečnik's. As you pass through the gate, note the contrast between the gilded baroque staircase to your right and the Doric simplicity of Plečnik's stair to the left.

SECOND COURTYARD

You pass through the Matthias Gate into the Second Courtyard, centred on a baroque fountain and a 17th-century well with beautiful Renaissance latticework. On the right, the Chapel of the Holy Cross (kaple sv Kříže; 1763) was once the treasury of St Vitus Cathedral; today it houses the castle's box office and souvenir shop.

The magnificent Spanish Hall (Španělský sál) and Rudolph Gallery (Rudolfova galerie) in the northern wing of the courtyard are reserved for state receptions and special concerts; they are open to the public just two days a year, usually on the first Saturdays after Liberation Day (8 May) and Republic Day (28 October).

PRAGUE CASTLE GALLERY Map p62

Obrazárna pražského hradu; ☎ 224 373 531; www.obrazarna-hradu.cz; Pražský hrad, II. nádvoří; adult/concession 150/80Kč, 4-6pm Mon admission free; 9am-6pm Apr-Oct, to 4pm Nov-Mar; 22, 23

The same Swedish army that looted the famous bronzes in the Wallenstein Garden (p79) in 1648 also nicked Rudolf II's art treasures. This exhibition of 16th- to 18th-century European art, housed in the beautiful Renaissance stables at the northern end of the Second Courtyard, is based on the Habsburg collection that was begun in 1650 to replace the lost paintings; it includes works by Cranach, Holbein, Rubens, Tintoretto and Titian.

ROYAL GARDEN Map p62

The gate on the northern side of the Second Courtyard leads to the Powder Bridge (Prašný most; 1540), which spans the Stag Moat (Jelení příkop) and leads to the Royal Garden (Královská zahrada), which started life as a Renaissance garden built by Ferdinand I in 1534. The most beautiful of the garden's buildings is the Ball-Game House (Míčovna; 1569; Map pp70–1), a masterpiece of Renaissance *sgraffito* where the Habsburgs once played a primitive version of badminton. To the east is the Summer Palace Letohrádek; 1538-60; Map pp70–1), or Belvedere, the most authentic Italian Renaissance building outside Italy, and to the west the former Riding School (Jízdárna; 1695; Map pp70–1). All three are used as venues for temporary exhibitions of modern art.

A footpath to the west of the Powder Bridge (on the castle side) leads down into the Stag Moat, and doubles back through a modern (and rather Freudian) red-brick tunnel beneath the bridge. If you then follow the path east along the moat you'll eventually end up at a busy road that leads down to Malostranská metro station. A gate on the outer wall of the castle, overlooking the moat, leads to a nuclear shelter started by the communists in the 1950s but never

TRANSPORT: PRAGUE CASTLE

Metro The nearest metro station is Malostranská, but from here it's a stiff climb up the Old Castle Steps to the eastern end of the castle. Hradčanská station is about 10 minutes' walk north of the castle, but it's an easy, level walk.

Tram Take lines 22 or 23 from Národní třída on the southern edge of Staré Město, Malostranská náměstí in Malá Strana, or Malostranská metro station to the Pražský hrad stop. If you want to explore Hradčany first, stay on the tram until Pohořelec, the second stop after.

completed; its tunnels run beneath most of the castle.

THIRD COURTYARD

As you pass through the passage on the eastern side of the Second Courtyard, the huge western façade of St Vitus Cathedral soars directly above you; to its south (to the right as you enter) lies the Third Courtyard. At its entrance you'll see a 16m-tall granite monolith dedicated to the victims of WWI, designed by Jože Plečnik in 1928, and a copy of a 14th-century bronze figure of St George slaying the dragon; the original is on display in the Story of Prague Castle exhibition.

The courtyard is dominated by the southern façade of St Vitus Cathedral, with its grand centrepiece the Golden Gate (Zlatá brána), an elegant, triple-arched Gothic porch designed by Peter Parler. Above it is a mosaic of the Last Judgment (1370–71) – on the left, the godly rise from their tombs and are raised into Heaven by angels; on the right, sinners are cast down into Hell by demons; and in the centre, Christ reigns in glory with six Czech saints – Procopius, Sigismund, Vitus, Wenceslas, Ludmila and Adalbert – below. Beneath them, on either side of the central arch, Charles IV and his wife kneel in prayer.

To the left of the gate is the Great Tower, which was left unfinished by Parler's sons in the 15th century; its soaring Gothic lines are capped by a Renaissance gallery added in the late 16th century and a bulging spire that dates from the 1770s.

OLD ROYAL PALACE Map p62

Starý královský palác; admission Prague Castle tour tickets only; 🕑 9am-6pm Apr-Oct, to 4pm Nov-Mar

The Old Royal Palace at the courtyard's eastern end is one of the oldest parts of the castle, dating from 1135. It was originally used only by Czech princesses, but from the 13th to the 16th centuries it was the king's own palace.

At its heart is the Vladislav Hall (Vladislavský sál), famous for its beautiful, late-Gothic vaulted ceiling (1493–1502) designed by Benedikt Rejt. Though around 500 years old, the flowing, interwoven lines of the vaults have an almost Art Nouveau feel, in contrast to the rectilinear form of the Renaissance windows. The vast hall was used for banquets, councils and coronations, and for indoor jousting tournaments – hence the Riders' Staircase (Jezdecké schody) on the northern side, designed to admit a knight on horseback. All the presidents of the republic have been sworn in here.

A door in the hall's southwestern corner leads to the former offices of the Bohemian Chancellery (České kanceláře). On 23 May 1618, in the second room, Protestant nobles rebelling against the Bohemian estates and the Habsburg emperor threw two of his councillors and their secretary out of the window. They survived, as their fall was broken by the dung-filled moat, but this Second Defenestration of Prague sparked off the Thirty Years' War (see p23).

At the eastern end of the Vladislav Hall you'll come to a balcony that overlooks All Saints' Chapel (kaple Všech svatých); a door to the right leads you to a terrace with great views across the city. To the right of the Riders' Staircase you'll spot an unusual Renaissance doorway framed by twisted columns that leads to the Diet (Sněmovna), or Assembly Hall, which displays another beautifully vaulted ceiling. To the left, a spiral staircase leads you up to the New Land Rolls Room (Říšská dvorská kancelář), the old repository for land titles, where the walls are covered with the clerks' coats of arms.

ST VITUS CATHEDRAL Map p62

Katedrála sv Víta; ☎ 257 531 622; www.katedralapraha.cz; Pražský hrad, III. nádvoří; admission free; 🕑 9am-5pm Mon-Sat & noon-5pm Sun Mar-Oct, 9am-4pm Mon-Sat & noon-4pm Nov-Feb

At first glance the western façade of St Vitus Cathedral, which looms above the entrance to the Third Courtyard, appears impressively Gothic, but in fact the triple doorway dates only from 1953, one of the last parts of the church to be completed. The cathedral's foundation stone was laid in 1344 by Emperor Charles IV, on the site of a 10th-century Romanesque rotunda built by Duke Wenceslas.

Charles' original architect, Matthias of Arras (Matyáš z Arrasu), began work in 1344 on the choir in the French Gothic style, but died eight years later. His German successor, Peter Parler – a veteran of Cologne's cathedral – completed most of the eastern part of the cathedral in a freer, late-Gothic style before he died in 1399. Renaissance and baroque details were added over the following centuries, but it was only in 1861 during the Czech National Revival that a concerted effort was made to finish the cathedral – everything between the western door and the crossing was built during the late 19th and early 20th centuries. It was finally consecrated in 1929.

Inside, the nave is flooded with colour from beautiful stained-glass windows created by eminent Czech artists of the early 20th century – note the one by Art Nouveau artist Alfons Mucha (see the boxed text, p40) in the third chapel on the northern side, to the left as you enter, which depicts the lives of Sts Cyril and Methodius (1909). Nearby is a wooden sculpture of the crucifixion (1899) by František Bílek.

Walk up to the crossing, where the nave and transept meet, which is dominated by the huge and colourful south window (1938) by Max Švabinský, depicting the Last Judgment – note the fires of Hell burning brightly in the lower right-hand corner. In the north transept, beneath the baroque organ, are three carved wooden doors decorated with reliefs of Bohemian saints, including St Vitus being tortured in a cauldron of boiling oil. Look on the left-hand door for the martyrdom of St Wenceslas. He is down on one knee, clinging to a lion's-head door handle, while his treacherous brother Boleslav drives a spear into his back. You can see that very door handle on the other side of the church – it's now the door to the Chapel of St Wenceslas.

Just to the right of the south transept is the entrance to the 96m-tall Great Tower (🕑 last entry 4.15pm Apr-Oct, closed during bad weather). You can climb the 297 slightly claustrophobic steps to the top for excellent views, and you also get a close look at the clockworks (1597). The tower's Sigismund Bell, made by Tomáš Jaroš in 1549, is the largest bell in the Czech Republic.

The eastern end of the cathedral is capped with graceful late-Gothic vaulting dating from the 14th century. In the centre lies the ornate Royal Mausoleum (1571–89) with its cold marble effigies of Ferdinand I, his wife Anna Jagellonská and their son Maximilián II. On the ambulatory's northern side, just beyond the old sacristy and the confessional booths, a wooden relief (1630) by Caspar Bechterle shows Protestant Frederick of the Palatinate (in his horse-drawn coach) legging it out of Prague after the Catholic victory at the battle of Bílá Hora.

As you round the far end of the ambulatory you pass the tomb of St Vitus – as well as being a patron saint of Bohemia, Vitus is a patron of actors, entertainers and dancers, and is said to protect against lightning, dog bites and oversleeping. The brass crosiers set in the floor nearby mark the tombs of bishops. Further round you reach the spectacular, baroque silver tomb of St John of Nepomuk, its draped canopy supported by a squadron of chubby silver angels (the tomb contains two tonnes of silver in all).

The nearby Chapel of St Mary Magdalene contains the grave slabs of Matthias of Arras and Peter Parler. Beyond is the ornate, late-Gothic Royal Oratory, a fancy balcony with ribbed vaulting carved to look like tree branches.

In the corner of the neighbouring Chapel of the Holy Rood, stairs lead down to the crypt, where you can see the remains of earlier churches that stood on the site of the cathedral, including an 11th-century Romanesque basilica. Beyond, you can crowd around the entrance to the Royal Crypt to see the marble sarcophagi (dating only from the 1930s), which contain the remains of Czech rulers including Charles IV, Wenceslas IV, George of Poděbrady (Jiří z Poděbrad) and Rudolf II.

The biggest and most beautiful of the cathedral's numerous side chapels is Parler's Chapel of St Wenceslas. Its walls are adorned with gilded panels containing polished slabs of semiprecious stones. Wall paintings from the early 16th century depict scenes from the life of the Czechs' patron saint, while even older frescoes show scenes from the life of Christ. On the southern side of the chapel a small door – locked with seven locks – hides a staircase leading to the Coronation Chamber above the Golden Gate, where the Bohemian crown jewels are kept (you can see replicas in the Story of Prague Castle exhibition; see p66).

PRAGUE CASTLE TICKETS

Prague Castle – long tour (adult/concession/family 350/175/500Kč) Includes Old Royal Palace, Story of Prague Castle, Basilica of St George, Convent of St George, Powder Tower, Golden Lane and Daliborka, Prague Castle Gallery.

Prague Castle – short tour (adult/concession/family 250/120/300Kč) Includes Old Royal Palace, Story of Prague Castle, Basilica of St George, Golden Lane and Daliborka.

Story of Prague Castle (adult/concession/family 140/70/200Kč) Admission to Story of Prague Castle exhibition only.

Prague Castle Gallery (adult/concession/family 150/80/200Kč) Admission to Prague Castle Gallery only.

Convent of St George (adult/concession/family 150/80/200Kč) Admission to Convent of St George only.

Powder Tower (adult/concession/family 50/25/70Kč) Admission to Powder Tower only.

STORY OF PRAGUE CASTLE Map p62

☎ 224 373 102; www.pribeh-hradu.cz; admission included in Prague Castle tour ticket, or adult/child 140/70Kč; ⏲ 9am-6pm Apr-Oct, to 4pm Nov-Mar

Housed in the Gothic vaults beneath the Old Royal Palace, this huge and impressive collection of artefacts is the most interesting exhibit in the entire castle. It traces 1000 years of the castle's history, from the building of the first wooden palisade to the present day – illustrated by large models of the castle at various stages in its development – and exhibits precious items such as the helmet and chain mail worn by St Wenceslas, illuminated manuscripts, and replicas of the Bohemian crown jewels, including the gold crown of St Wenceslas, which was made for Charles IV in 1346 from the gold of the original Přemysl crown (for more on the Přemysl dynasty see p21).

Anyone with a serious interest in Prague Castle should visit here first, as orientation. If you don't have a Prague Castle tour ticket, you can buy individual tickets at the entrance to the exhibit (cash only).

ST GEORGE SQUARE

St George Square (Jiřské náměstí), the plaza to the east of the cathedral, lies at the heart of the castle complex.

BASILICA OF ST GEORGE Map p62

Bazilika sv Jiří; Jiřské náměstí; admission with Prague Castle tour ticket; ⏲ 9am-6pm Apr-Oct, to 4pm Nov-Mar

The striking, brick-red, early-baroque façade that dominates the square conceals the Czech Republic's best-preserved Romanesque church, established in the 10th century by Vratislav I (the father of St Wenceslas). What you see today is mostly the result of restorations made between 1887 and 1908.

The austerity of the Romanesque nave is relieved by a baroque double staircase leading to the apse, where fragments of 12th-century frescoes survive. In front of the stairs lie the tombs of Prince Boleslav II (d 997; on the left) and Prince Vratislav I (d 921), the church's founder. The arch beneath the stairs allows a glimpse of the 12th-century crypt; Přemysl kings (see p21) are buried here and in the nave.

The tiny baroque chapel beside the entrance is dedicated to St John of Nepomuk (his tomb lies in St Vitus Cathedral; see p65).

CONVENT OF ST GEORGE Map p62

Klášter sv Jiří; ☎ 257 531 644; www.ngprague.cz; Jiřské náměstí 33; admission with Prague Castle long tour ticket, or adult/concession 150/80Kč; ⏲ 10am-6pm Tue-Sun

The very ordinary-looking building to the left of the basilica was Bohemia's first convent, established in 973 by Boleslav II. Closed and converted to an army barracks in 1782, it now a houses a branch of the National Gallery, featuring a collection of 19th-century Bohemian art. Highlights include the Art Nouveau sculpture of Josef Myslbek, Stanislav Sucharda and Bohumil Kafka; the glowing portraits by Josef Mánes; and the forest landscapes by Július Mařák.

POWDER TOWER Map p62

Prašná věž; admission with Prague Castle long tour ticket; ⏲ 9am-6pm Apr-Oct, to 4pm Nov-Mar

A passage to the north of St Vitus Cathedral leads to the Powder Tower (also called Mihulka), which was built at the end of the 15th century as part of the castle's defences. Later it became the workshop of the cannon- and bell-maker Tomáš Jaroš, who cast the bells for St Vitus Cathedral. Alchemists employed by Rudolf II also worked here. Today the 1st floor houses a rather dull exhibition about the castle's military history.

GEORGE STREET

George St (Jiřská) runs from the Basilica of St George to the castle's eastern gate.

GOLDEN LANE Map p62

Zlatá ulička; admission with Prague Castle tour ticket; 9am-6pm Apr-Oct, to 4pm Nov-Mar

Golden Lane is a picturesque, cobbled alley running along the northern wall of the castle. Its tiny, colourful cottages were built in the 16th century for the sharpshooters of the castle guard, but were later used by goldsmiths. In the 18th and 19th centuries they were occupied by squatters, and then by artists, including the writer Franz Kafka (who stayed at his sister's house at No 22 from 1916 to 1917) and the Nobel-laureate poet Jaroslav Seifert. Today, the lane is an overcrowded tourist trap lined with craft and souvenir shops.

At its eastern end is the Daliborka, a round tower named after the knight Dalibor of Kozojedy, imprisoned here in 1498 for supporting a peasant rebellion, and later executed. During his imprisonment, according to an old tale, he played a violin that could be heard throughout the castle. Composer Bedřich Smetana (see p31) based his 1868 opera *Dalibor* on the tale. More interesting than the small display of torture instruments in the tower is the modern bronze sculpture *Parable with a Skull*, by Jaroslav Róna (who also created the Franz Kafka Monument in Josefov; Map pp88–9). Supposedly inspired by one of Kafka's characters, it shows a prostrate human figure bearing a giant skull on its back (you can still see homeless people in Prague begging in this traditional but submissive and rather despairing posture).

LOBKOWICZ PALACE Map p62

Lobkovický palác; 233 312 925; www.lobkowiczevents.cz/palace; Jiřská 3; adult/concession/family 275/175/690Kč; 10.30am-6pm

Built in the 16th century, this palace has been home to the aristocratic Lobkowicz family for around 400 years. Confiscated by the Nazis in WWII, and again by the communists in 1948, it was finally returned in 2002 to William Lobkowicz, an American property developer and grandson of Maximilian, the 10th Prince Lobkowicz, who fled to the USA in 1939. It was opened to the public as a private museum in 2007.

You tour the main exhibition, known as the Princely Collections, with an audio guide dictated by William and his family – this personal connection really brings the displays to life, and makes the palace one of the castle's most interesting attractions. Highlights include paintings by Cranach, Breughel the Elder, Canaletto and Piranesi, original musical scores annotated by Mozart, Beethoven and Haydn (the 7th prince was a great patron of music – Beethoven dedicated three symphonies to him), and an impressive collection of musical instruments. But it's the personal touches that make an impression, like the 16th-century portrait of a Lobkowicz ancestor wearing a ring that William's mother still wears today, and an old photo album with a picture of a favourite family dog smoking a pipe.

The palace has an excellent café (p180), and stages concerts of classical music at 1pm each day (390Kč; www.praguecastleconcert.cz).

TOY MUSEUM Map p62

Muzeum hraček; 224 372 294; Jiřská 6; adult/concession/family 60/30/120Kč; 9.30am-5.30pm

In the tower of the Burgrave's Palace (Nejvyšší Purkrabství), across the street from the Lobkowicz Palace, is the second-largest toy museum in the world. It's an amazing collection – with some artefacts dating back to ancient Greece – but a bit frustrating for the kids as most displays are hands-off. Toys range from model trains and teddy bears to Victorian dolls, Action Men and the definitive Barbie collection.

GARDEN ON THE RAMPARTS

At the castle's eastern gate, you can either descend the Old Castle Steps to Malostranská metro station (Map pp70–1) or turn sharp right and wander back to Hradčanské náměstí through the Garden on the Ramparts (Zahrada na valech; Apr-Oct only). The terrace garden offers superb views across the roof-tops of Malá Strana and permits a peek into the back garden of the British embassy.

Alternatively, you can descend to Malá Strana through the terraced Palace Gardens beneath Prague Castle (Palácové zahrady pod Pražským hradem; p79).

HRADČANY

Eating p157; Drinking p179; Shopping p144; Sleeping p213

Hradčany is the attractive and peaceful residential area stretching west from Prague Castle to Strahov Monastery. It became a town in its own right in 1320, and twice suffered heavy damage – once in the Hussite wars and again in the Great Fire of 1541 – before becoming a borough of Prague in 1598. After this, the Habsburg nobility built many palaces here in the hope of cementing their influence with the rulers in Prague Castle.

HRADČANY SQUARE

Hradčany Square (Hradčanské náměstí), facing the castle entrance, has retained its shape since the Middle Ages, with a central plague column by Ferdinand Brokoff (1726) and several former canons' residences (Nos 6 to 12) with richly decorated façades. At No 16 is the rococo Archbishop's Palace (Arcibiskupský palác), bought by Archbishop Antonín Brus of Mohelnice in 1562, and the seat of archbishops ever since; the exterior was given a rococo makeover between 1763 and 1765 (it's open to the public only on the day before Good Friday).

A statue of Tomáš Masaryk, first president of the Czechoslovak Republic, watches over the entrance to the castle.

SCHWARZENBERG PALACE Map pp70–1

Schwarzenberský palác; ☎ 224 810 758; www.ngprague.cz; Hradčanské náměstí 2; adult/child 150/80Kč; 10am-6pm Tue-Sun; 22, 23

Sporting a beautifully preserved façade of black-and-white Renaissance *sgraffito*, the newly renovated Schwarzenberg Palace houses the National Gallery's collection of baroque art. Sadly, a lot of the paintings are poorly lit and suffer from reflections from nearby windows – a shame, as the inside of the palace itself is far less impressive than the outside, and the collection is really only of interest to art aficionados.

The ground floor is given over to two masters of baroque sculpture, Matthias Braun and Maximilian Brokof, whose overwrought figures appear to have been caught in a hurricane, such is the liveliness of their billowing robes. The highlights of the 1st floor are the moody 16th-century portraits by Petr Brandl and Jan Kupecký, while the top floor boasts a display of engravings by Albrecht Dürer.

STERNBERG PALACE Map pp70–1

Šternberský palác; ☎ 233 090 570; www.ngprague.cz; Hradčanské náměstí 15; adult/child 150/80Kč; 10am-6pm Tue-Sun; 22, 23

Tucked behind the Archbishop's Palace is the baroque Sternberg Palace, home to the National Gallery's collection of 14th- to 18th-century European art, including works by Goya and Rembrandt. Fans of medieval altarpieces will be in heaven; there are also several Rubens, some Rembrandt and Breughel, and a large collection of Bohemian miniatures. Pride of the gallery is the glowing *Feast of the Rosary* by Albrecht Dürer, an artist better known for his engravings. Painted in Venice in 1505 as an altarpiece for the church of San Bartolomeo, it was brought to Prague by Rudolf II; in the background, beneath the tree on the right, is the figure of the artist himself. For a bit of grotesque realism, it's worth a trip to the back of the 1st floor to see the 16th-century Dutch painting *The Tearful Bride*.

LORETA SQUARE

From Hradčany Square it's a short walk west to Loreta Square (Loretánské náměstí), created early in the 18th century when the imposing Černín Palace was built. At the northern end of the square is the Capuchin Monastery (1600–02), which is Bohemia's oldest working monastery.

ČERNÍN PALACE Map pp70–1

Černínský palác; Loretánské náměstí; closed to the public

The late-17th-century early-baroque palace facing the Loreta boasts Prague's largest monumental façade. This imposing building has housed the foreign ministry since the creation of Czechoslovakia in 1918, except during WWII when it served as the headquarters of the Nazi Reichsprotektor,

TRANSPORT: HRADČANY

Tram Lines 22 and 23 stop at Pohořelec, at the western end of Hradčany.

top picks

IT'S FREE

- Charles Bridge (p75)
- National Museum (p110) on the first Monday of the month
- Prague Castle (p61) grounds and gardens
- Nave of St Vitus Cathedral (p64)
- Letná (p131) and Stromovka (p133)

and is where the documents that dissolved the Warsaw Pact were signed in 1991.

In 1948, Jan Masaryk – son of the Czechoslovak Republic's founding father, Tomáš Masaryk, and the only noncommunist in the new Soviet-backed government – fell to his death from one of the upper windows. Did he fall, or was he pushed? (See p22 and p22.)

LORETA Map pp70–1

☎ 220 516 740; Loretánské náměstí 7; adult/concession 110/90Kč; 9am-12.15pm & 1-4.30pm; 22, 23

The square's main attraction is the Loreta, a baroque place of pilgrimage founded by Benigna Kateřina Lobkowicz in 1626, and designed as a replica of the supposed Santa Casa (Sacred House; the home of the Virgin Mary). Above the entrance 27 bells, made in Amsterdam in the 17th century, play 'We Greet Thee a Thousand Times' on the hour. Legend says that the original Santa Casa was carried by angels to the Italian town of Loreto as the Turks were advancing on Nazareth. The duplicate Santa Casa, with fragments of its original frescoes, is in the centre of the courtyard.

Behind the Santa Casa is the Church of the Nativity of Our Lord (kostel Narození Páně), built in 1737 to a design by Kristof Dientzenhofer (see p48). The claustrophobic interior includes two skeletons – of the Spanish saints Felicissima and Marcia – dressed in aristocratic clothing with wax masks concealing their skulls.

At the corner of the courtyard is the unusual Chapel of Our Lady of Sorrows (kaple Panny Marie Bolestné), featuring a crucified bearded lady. She was St Starosta, pious daughter of a Portuguese king who promised her to the king of Sicily against her wishes. After a night of tearful prayers she awoke with a beard, the wedding was called off, and her father had her crucified. She was later made patron saint of the needy and the godforsaken.

The church's treasury (1st floor) has been ransacked several times over the centuries, but it remains a bastion of over-the-top religious bling centred on the 90cm-tall Prague Sun (Pražské slunce), made of solid silver and gold and studded with 6222 diamonds.

Photography is not allowed, and the rule is enforced with a 1000Kč fine.

STRAHOV MONASTERY

In 1140 Vladislav II founded Strahov Monastery (Strahovský klášter; Map pp70–1) for the Premonstratensian order. The present monastery buildings, completed in the 17th and 18th centuries, functioned until the communist government closed them down and imprisoned most of the monks; they returned in 1990.

Inside the main gate is the 1612 Church of St Roch (kostel sv Rocha), which is now an art gallery, and the Church of the Assumption of Our Lady (kostel Nanebevzetí Panny Marie), built in 1143 and heavily decorated in the 18th century in the baroque style; Mozart is said to have played the organ here.

MINIATURE MUSEUM Map pp70–1

Muzeum miniatur; ☎ 233 352 371; www.muzeumminiatur.com; Strahovské II.nádvoří; adult/child 50/20Kč; 9am-5pm; 22, 23

The 'write your name on a grain of rice' movement may have undermined the respectability of miniature artists, but Siberian technician Anatoly Konyenko will restore your faith with his microscopic creations. Konyenko once used to manufacture tools for eye microsurgery, but these days he'd rather spend 7½ years crafting a pair of golden horseshoes for a flea. See those, as well as the world's smallest book and strangely beautiful silhouettes of cars on the leg of a mosquito. Weird but fascinating.

STRAHOV LIBRARY Map pp70–1

Strahovská knihovna; ☎ 233 107 718; www.strahovskyklaster.cz; Strahovské I.nádvoří; adult/concession 80/50Kč; 9am-noon & 1-5pm; 22, 23

The biggest attraction of Strahov Monastery is the Strahov Library, the largest monastic library in the country, with two magnificent baroque halls. You can peek through the doors but, sadly, you can't go

HRADČANY

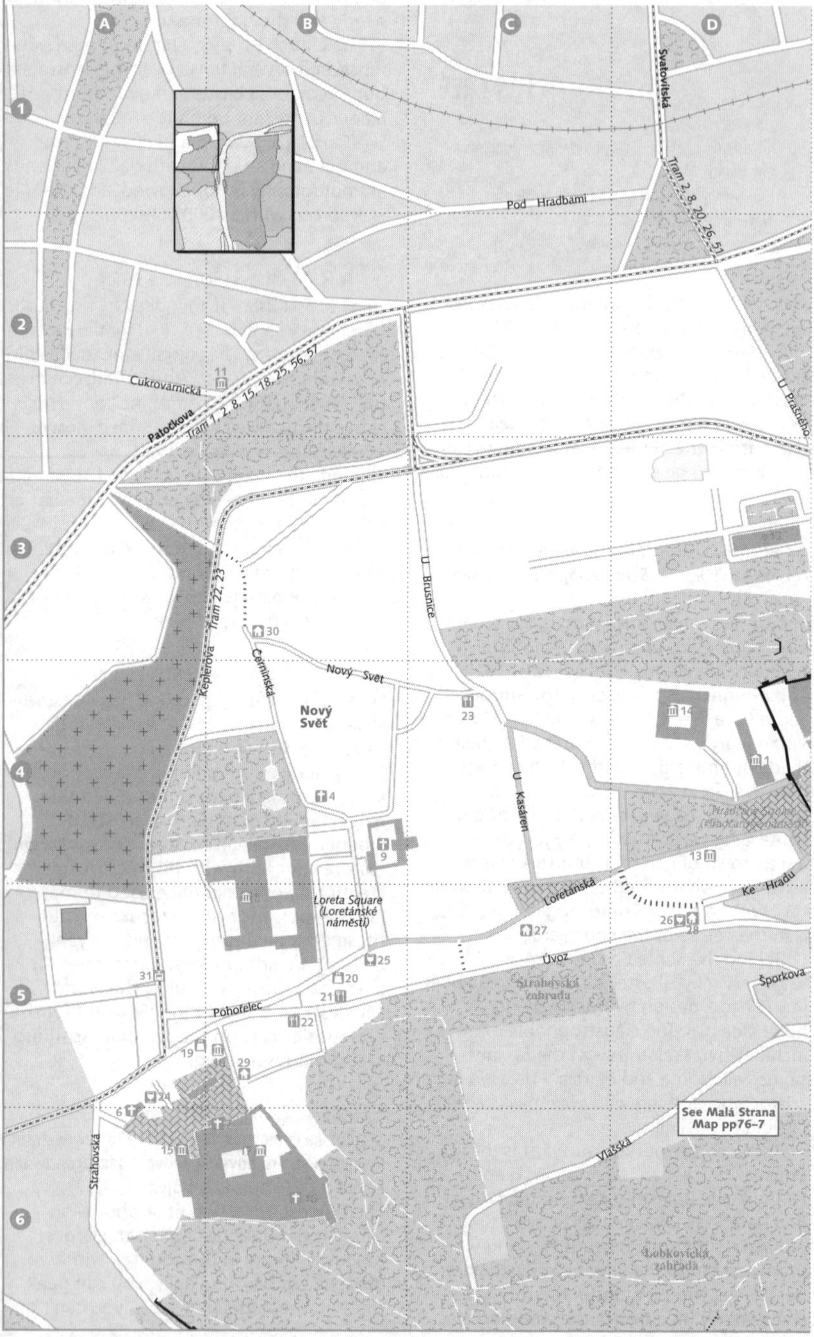
A
B
C
D
1
2
3
4
5
6
Svatovítská
Tram 2, 8, 20, 26, 51
Pod Hradbami
Cukrovarnická
Patočkova
Tram 1, 2, 8, 15, 18, 25, 56, 57
U Prašného
Keplerova
Tram 22, 23
U Brusnice
Černínská
Nový Svět
Nový Svět
U Kasáren
Loreta Square
(Loretánské náměstí)
Loretánská
Ke Hradu
Úvoz
Pohořelec
Strahovská zahrada
Šporkova
Strahovská
Vlašská
See Malá Strana Map pp76–7
Lobkovická zahrada
1
4
6
9
11
13
14
15
19
20
21
22
23
24
25
26
27
28
29
30
31

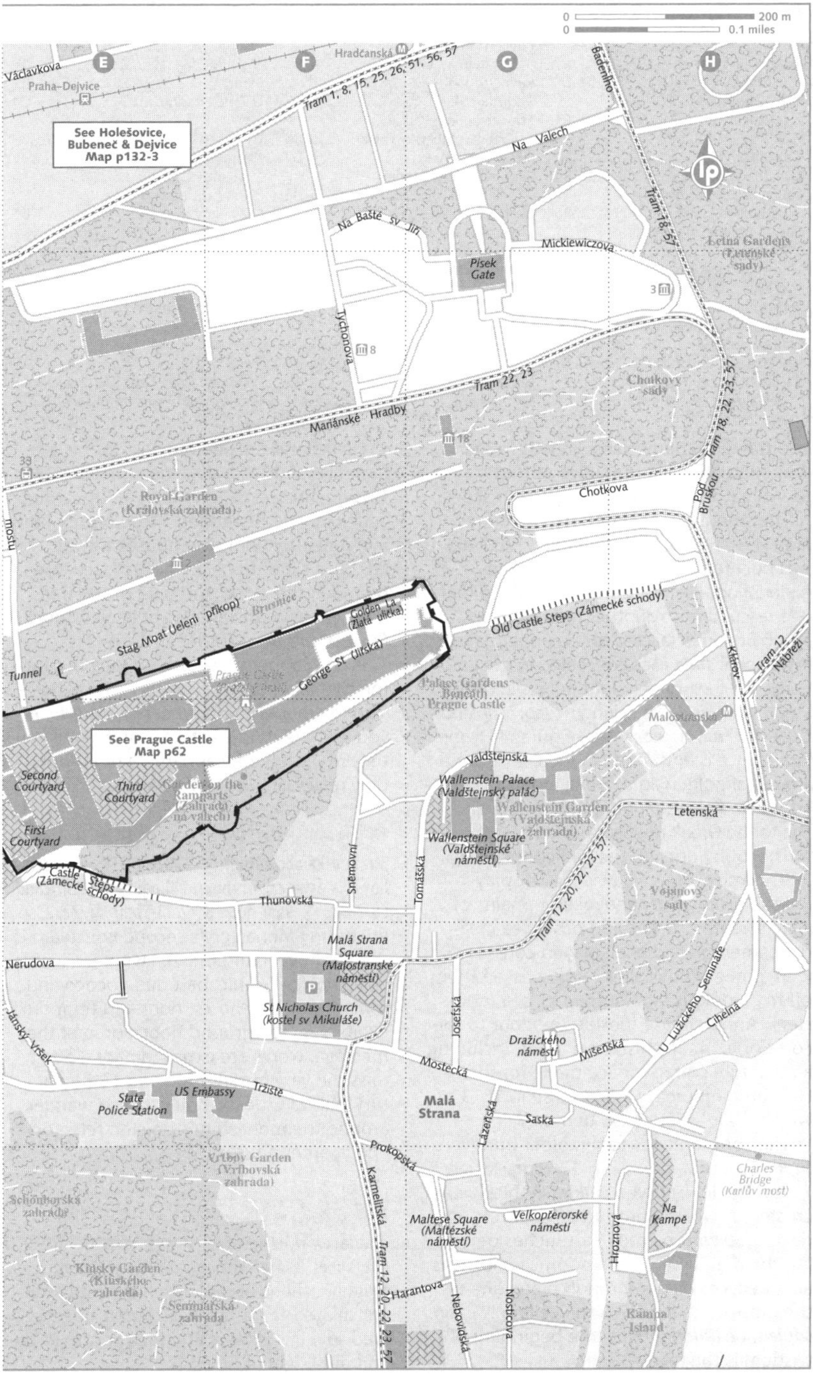
0 200 m
0 0.1 miles
E
F
G
H
Václavkova
Praha–Dejvice
Hradčanská
Tram 1, 8, 15, 25, 26, 51, 56, 57
Badeniho
See Holešovice, Bubeneč & Dejvice Map p132-3
Na Valech
Tram 18, 57
Na Baště sv Jiří
Mickiewiczova
Písek Gate
Letná Gardens (Letenské sady)
3
Tychonova
8
Tram 22, 23
Chotkovy sady
Mariánské Hradby
18
Tram 18, 22, 23, 57
33
Royal Garden (Královská zahrada)
Pod Bruskou
Chotkova
mostu
Stag Moat (Jelení příkop)
Bruslnice
Golden La (Zlatá ulička)
Old Castle Steps (Zámecké schody)
George St (Jiřská)
Tunnel
Prague Castle
Palace Gardens Beneath Prague Castle
Klárov
Tram 12
Nábřeží
Malostranská
See Prague Castle Map p62
Valdštejnská
Second Courtyard
Third Courtyard
Gardens on the Ramparts (Zahrada na valech)
Wallenstein Palace (Valdštejnský palác)
Wallenstein Garden (Valdštejnská zahrada)
Letenská
First Courtyard
Wallenstein Square (Valdštejnské náměstí)
Sněmovní
Tomášská
Tram 12, 20, 22, 23, 57
Castle Steps (Zámecké schody)
Thunovská
Vojanovy sady
Malá Strana Square (Malostranské náměstí)
Nerudova
U Lužického Semináře
P
St Nicholas Church (kostel sv Mikuláše)
Josefská
Jánský Vršek
Cihelná
Dražického náměstí
Míšeňská
Mostecká
State Police Station
US Embassy
Tržiště
Malá Strana
Lázeňská
Saská
Prokopská
Charles Bridge (Karlův most)
Vrtbov Garden (Vrtbovská zahrada)
Schönbornská zahrada
Karmelitská
Na Kampě
Maltese Square (Maltézské náměstí)
Velkopřerorské náměstí
Hroznová
Kinský Garden (Kinského zahrada)
Harantova
Seminářská zahrada
Tram 12, 20, 22, 23, 57
Nebovidská
Nosticova
Kampa Island

HRADČANY

SIGHTS & ACTIVITIES

Archbishop's Palace (Arcibiskupský Palác)	1	D4
Ball-Game House (Míčovna)	2	E3
Bílek Villa (Bílkova Vila)	3	H2
Capuchin Monastery	4	B4
Černín Palace (Černinský Palác)	5	B5
Church of St Roch (Kostel sv Rocha)	6	A6
Church of the Assumption of Our Lady (Kostel Nanebevzetí Panny Marie)	7	B6
Cubist Houses	8	F2
Loreta	9	B4
Miniature Museum (Muzeum Miniatur)	10	B5
Public Transport Museum	11	B2
Riding School (Jízdárna)	12	D3
Schwarzenberg Palace (Schwarzenberský Palác)	13	D4
Sternberg Palace	14	D4
Strahov Library (Strahovská Knihovna)	15	A6
Strahov Monastery (Strahovský Klášter)	16	B6
Strahov Picture Gallery (Strahovská Obrazárna)	17	B6
Summer Palace (Letohrádek)	18	G2

SHOPPING (pp143–51)

Antique Music Instruments	19	A5
Houpací Kůň	20	B5
Icon Gallery	(see 19)	

EATING (pp153–73)

Malý Buddha	21	B5
Saté	22	B5
U Zlaté Hrušky	23	C4

DRINKING (pp175–91)

Klášterní pivovar Strahov	24	A5
Pivnice U Černého Vola	25	B5
U Zvěšenýho Kafe	26	D5

SLEEPING (pp211–27)

Domus Henrici	27	C5
Hotel U Krále Karla	28	D5
Residence Monastery	29	B5
Romantik Hotel U Raka	30	B3

TRANSPORT (pp241–5)

Pohořelec Tram Stop	31	A5
Pražský Hrad Tram Stop	32	E2

into the halls themselves – it was found that fluctuations in humidity caused by visitors' breath was endangering the frescoes.

The stunning interior of the two-storey-high Philosophy Hall (Filozofický sál; 1780–97) was built to fit around the carved and gilded, floor-to-ceiling walnut shelving that was rescued from another monastery in South Bohemia (access to the upper gallery is via spiral staircases concealed in the corners). The feeling of height here is accentuated by a grandiose ceiling fresco, *Mankind's Quest for True Wisdom* – the figure of Divine Providence is enthroned in the centre amid a burst of golden light, while around the edges are figures ranging from Adam and Eve to the Greek philosophers.

The lobby outside the hall contains an 18th-century Cabinet of Curiosities, displaying the grotesquely shrivelled remains of sharks, skates, turtles and other sea creatures; these flayed and splayed corpses were prepared by sailors, who passed them off to credulous landlubbers as 'sea monsters'. Another case (beside the door to the corridor) contains historical items, including a miniature coffee service made for the Habsburg empress Marie Louise in 1813, which fits into four false books.

The corridor leads to the older but even more beautiful Theology Hall (Teologiský sál; 1679). The low, curved ceiling is thickly encrusted in ornate baroque stuccowork, and decorated with painted cartouches depicting the theme of 'True Wisdom', which was acquired, of course, through piety; one of the mottoes that adorns the ceiling is *initio sapientiae timor domini:* 'the beginning of wisdom is the fear of God'.

On a stand outside the hall door is a facsimile of the library's most prized possession, the Strahov Evangeliary, a 9th-century codex in a gem-studded 12th-century binding. A nearby bookcase houses the Xyloteka (1825), a set of booklike boxes, each one bound in the wood and bark of the tree it describes, with samples of leaves, roots, flowers and fruits inside.

In the connecting corridor, look out for the two long, brown, leathery things beside the model ship and narwhal tusk – if you ask, the prudish attendant will tell you they're preserved elephants' trunks, but they're actually whales' penises.

STRAHOV PICTURE GALLERY Map pp70–1

Strahovská obrazárna; ☎ 220 517 278; www.strahovskyklaster.cz; Strahovské II.nádvoří; adult/child 60/30Kč; 9am-noon & 12.30-5pm; 22, 23

In Strahov Monastery's second courtyard is the Strahov Picture Gallery, with a valuable collection of Gothic, baroque, rococo and romantic art on the 1st floor and temporary exhibits on the ground floor. Some of the medieval works are extraordinary – don't miss the very modern-looking 14th-century Jihlava Crucifix. You can also wander around the monastery's cloister, refectory and chapter house.

PÍSEK GATE

The area northeast of Prague Castle around the Písek Gate (see opposite) is a quiet, leafy neighbourhood of expensive villas and foreign consulates. It's a bit of a tourist no-man's-land, and few visitors find their way to its one and only sight of note.

BÍLEK VILLA Map pp70–1

Bílkova vila; ☎ 224 322 021; Mickiewiczova 1; adult/child 50/30Kč; 10am-6pm Tue-Sun; 18, 22, 23

This striking red-brick villa, designed by sculptor František Bílek in 1912 as his own home, houses a museum of his unconventional stone and wood reliefs, furniture and graphics. It was closed for renovation at the time of research, but should reopen in summer 2009.

HRADČANY

Walking Tour

1 Písek Gate As you leave the top of the escalators in Hradčanská metro station, turn right and head for the stairway in the right-hand corner marked 'Pražský hrad'. At street level turn right, and then go right again through the gap in the building. This leads to the street called K Brusce – head for the stone portal of the Písek Gate (Písecká brána) that you'll see straight ahead. The baroque gateway, decorated with carved military emblems, was built by Giovanni Battisti for Charles VI in 1721 as part of Prague's new fortifications; the streets on either side still follow the outlines of the bastions of sv Jiří (St George) to the right and sv Ludmila to the left. A century later, in 1821, the gate became the terminus of Prague's first horse-drawn railway.

2 Cubist houses Bear right past the gate, then turn right on U Písecké Brány, and then left at the end onto Tychonova. Here you will pass two attractive Cubist houses designed by Josef Gočár.

3 Summer Palace When you reach Mariánské Hradby (the street with the tram lines), cross it and enter the Royal Garden (Královská zahrada; p63) beside the beautiful, Renaissance Summer Palace (Letohrádek; p63). (The gardens are open from April to October only; at other times of the year you'll have to go right along Mariánské Hradby and enter Prague Castle via U Prašného mostu.)

4 Ball-Game House Turn right beyond the Letohrádek, continuing past the equally stunning Ball-Game House (Míčovna; p63), and follow the upper rim of the Stag Moat (Jelení příkop) to the western end of the gardens.

5 Powder Bridge Go through the gate and turn left to enter the Second Courtyard of Prague Castle (p61) via the Powder Bridge (Prašná most); that's powder as in gunpowder, not a reference to poor-quality construction. Visit the castle if you wish, but for the moment we'll leave the courtyard via the first gate on the right, which leads past a window giving a glimpse into the ruins of a Romanesque chapel, and into Hradčany Square.

6 Hradčany Square Now watched over by a statue of Tomáš Masaryk, the first president of Czechoslovakia, Hradčany Square (Hradčanské náměstí; p68) was once the social heart of the aristocratic quarter of Hradčany. On the southern side of the square is the extravagant Renaissance status symbol of the Schwarzenberg Palace (Schwarzenberský palác; p68). On the northern side you can see the rococo Archbishop's Palace (Arcibiskupský palác) and the *sgrafitto*-covered Martinic Palace (Martinický palác), which served as Hradčany's town hall. More recently the palace was used as Mozart's house in the film *Amadeus*.

7 Church of St John Nepomuk At the far end of the square, bear right on the narrow cobbled street of Kanovnická, and pass the pretty little Church of St John Nepomuk (kostel sv Jan Nepomucký), built in 1729 by the king of Prague baroque, Kilian Dientzenhofer. Take the first lane on the left downhill from the church.

8 Nový Svět The lane is called Nový Svět (New World) and is a picturesque cluster of little cottages once inhabited by court artisans and tradesmen, a far cry from the fancy palaces at the top of the hill. No 1 Nový Svět was the humble home of court astronomer Tycho Brahe and, after 1600, his successor Johannes Kepler; the atmospheric restaurant U zlaté hrušky (p157) is just next door. Continue downhill to where Nový Svět ends in a leafy hollow occupied by the Romantik Hotel U Raka (p213).

9 Loreta Turn left and climb slowly up Černínská to the pretty square in front of the extravagantly baroque Loreta (p69), a shrine to the Virgin Mary and a hugely popular place of pilgrimage for Roman Catholics. Opposite is the imposing 150m-long façade of the Černín Palace (Černínský palác; p68), dating from 1692.

10 Strahov Monastery At the southern end of the square turn right into Pohořelec and continue to the far western side. A little alley at No 9 leads into the courtyard of Strahov Monastery (Strahovský klášter; p69), where you

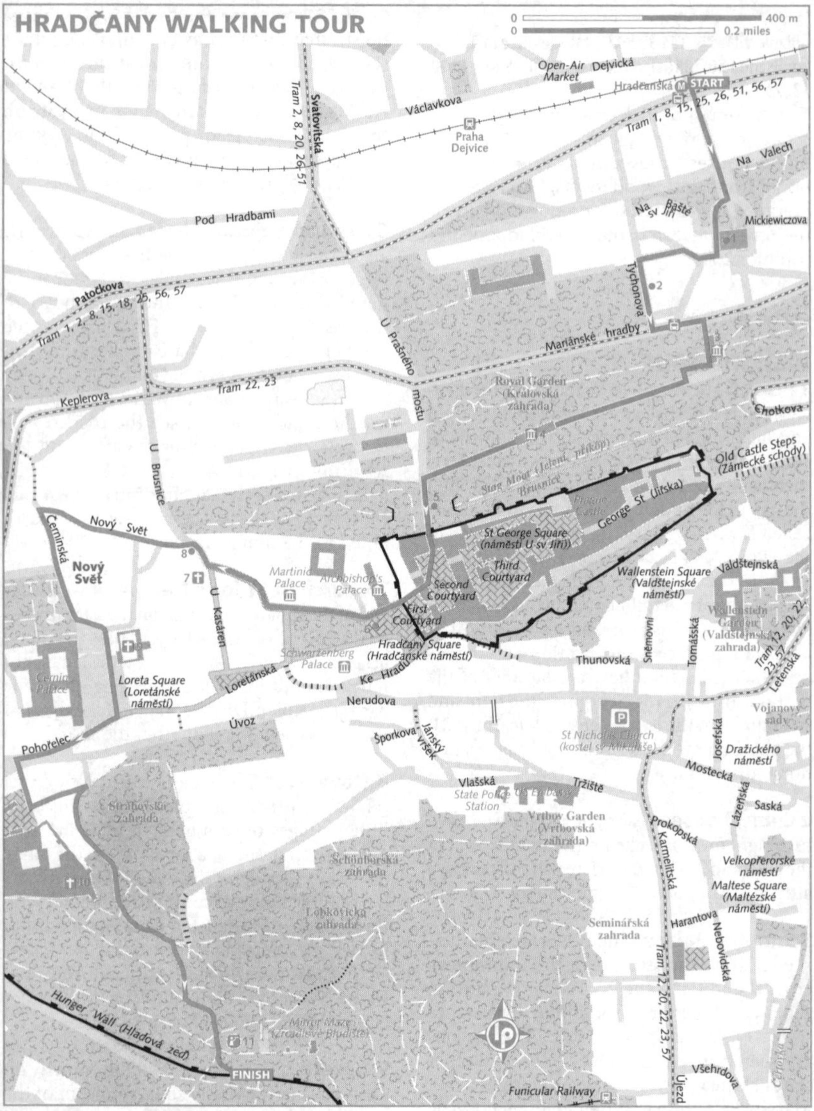

WALK FACTS

Start Hradčanská metro station
End Petřín Hill (tram 12, 20, 22, 23 or funicular)
Distance 2.5km
Time One hour
Exertion Easy
Fuel stop U zlaté hrušky

can visit the library before going through the gate at the eastern end of the courtyard into the gardens above Malá Strana.

11 Petřín Lookout Tower Turn right on the footpath here (signposted 'Rozhledna & Bludiště') and finish the walk with a stroll along to the Petřín Lookout Tower (Petřínská rozhledna; p84).

MALÁ STRANA

Eating p158; Drinking p180; Shopping p145; Sleeping p214

Almost too picturesque for its own good, the baroque district of Malá Strana (Little Quarter) tumbles down the hillside between Prague Castle and the river. The focal point of the neighbourhood is Malostranské náměstí, a square dominated by the soaring green dome of St Nicholas Church. To its north is a maze of palaces and gardens, home to government offices and foreign embassies; to the south are parks and gardens straggling along the banks of the Vltava before merging into the more commercialised streets of Smíchov (p137).

Once you get away from the crowded pavements of Mostecká and Nerudova – the main tourist route between Charles Bridge and the castle – there are cobbled backstreets to explore, with historic hidden gardens hidden (see the Walking Tour, p85), quaint and colourful house signs perched above doorways, and countless little bars and cafés where you can while away an afternoon.

Having started life as a market settlement in the 8th or 9th century, Přemysl Otakar II granted Malá Strana town status in 1257. The district was almost destroyed on two separate occasions: during battles between the Hussites and the Prague Castle garrison in 1419, and then in the Great Fire of 1541. Following this massive devastation Renaissance buildings and palaces sprang up, followed by the many baroque churches and palaces that lend Malá Strana much of its charm.

PRAGUE CASTLE TO CHARLES BRIDGE

Following the tourist crowds downhill from the castle via Ke Hradu, you soon arrive at Nerudova, architecturally the most important street in Malá Strana; most of its old Renaissance façades were 'baroquefied' in the 18th century. It's named after the Czech poet Jan Neruda (famous for his short stories, *Tales of Malá Strana*), who lived at the House of the Two Suns (dům U dvou slunců; Nerudova 47) from 1845 to 1857.

The House of the Golden Horseshoe (dům U zlaté podkovy; Nerudova 34) is named after the relief of St Wenceslas above the doorway – his horse was said to be shod with gold. From 1765 Josef of Bretfeld made his Bretfeld Palace (Nerudova 33) a social hotspot, entertaining Mozart and Casanova. The baroque Church of Our Lady of Unceasing Succour (kostel Panny Marie ustavičné pomoci; Nerudova 24) was a theatre from 1834 to 1837, and staged Czech plays during the Czech National Revival.

Most of the buildings bear house signs. Built in 1566, St John of Nepomuk (Nerudova 18) is adorned with the image of one of Bohemia's patron saints, while the House at the Three Fiddles (dům U tří houslíček; Nerudova 12), a Gothic building rebuilt in Renaissance style during the 17th century, once belonged to a family of violin makers.

Malostranské náměstí (Map pp76–7), Malá Strana's main square, is divided into an upper and lower part by St Nicholas Church (p79), the district's most distinctive landmark. The square has been the hub of Malá Strana since the 10th century, though it lost some of its character when Karmelitská street was widened early in the 20th century, and a little more when Prague's first Starbucks opened here in 2008. Today, it's a mixture of official buildings and touristy restaurants, with a tram line through the middle of the lower square.

The nightclub and bar at No 21, Malostranská beseda (see p198), was once the old town hall. Here in 1575 non-Catholic nobles wrote the so-called České Konfese (Czech Confession), a pioneering demand for religious tolerance addressed to the Habsburg emperor and eventually passed into Czech law by Rudolf II in 1609. On 22 May 1618 Czech nobles gathered at the Smiřický Palace (Malostranské náměstí 18) to plot a rebellion against the Habsburg rulers – the next day they flung two Habsburg councillors out of a window in Prague Castle.

CHARLES BRIDGE Map pp76–7 & pp88–9

Karlův most

Strolling across Charles Bridge is everybody's favourite Prague activity. However, by 9am it's a 500m-long fairground, with an army of tourists squeezing through a gauntlet of hawkers and buskers beneath the impassive gaze of the baroque statues that line the parapets (see the boxed text, p80). If you want to experience the bridge at its most atmospheric try to visit it at dawn.

In 1357 Charles IV commissioned Peter Parler (the architect of St Vitus Cathedral) to replace the 12th-century Judith Bridge, which had been washed away by floods in 1342. (You can see the only surviving arch of the Judith Bridge by taking a boat trip with Prague Venice; see p251.)

The new bridge was completed around 1400, and took Charles' name only in the

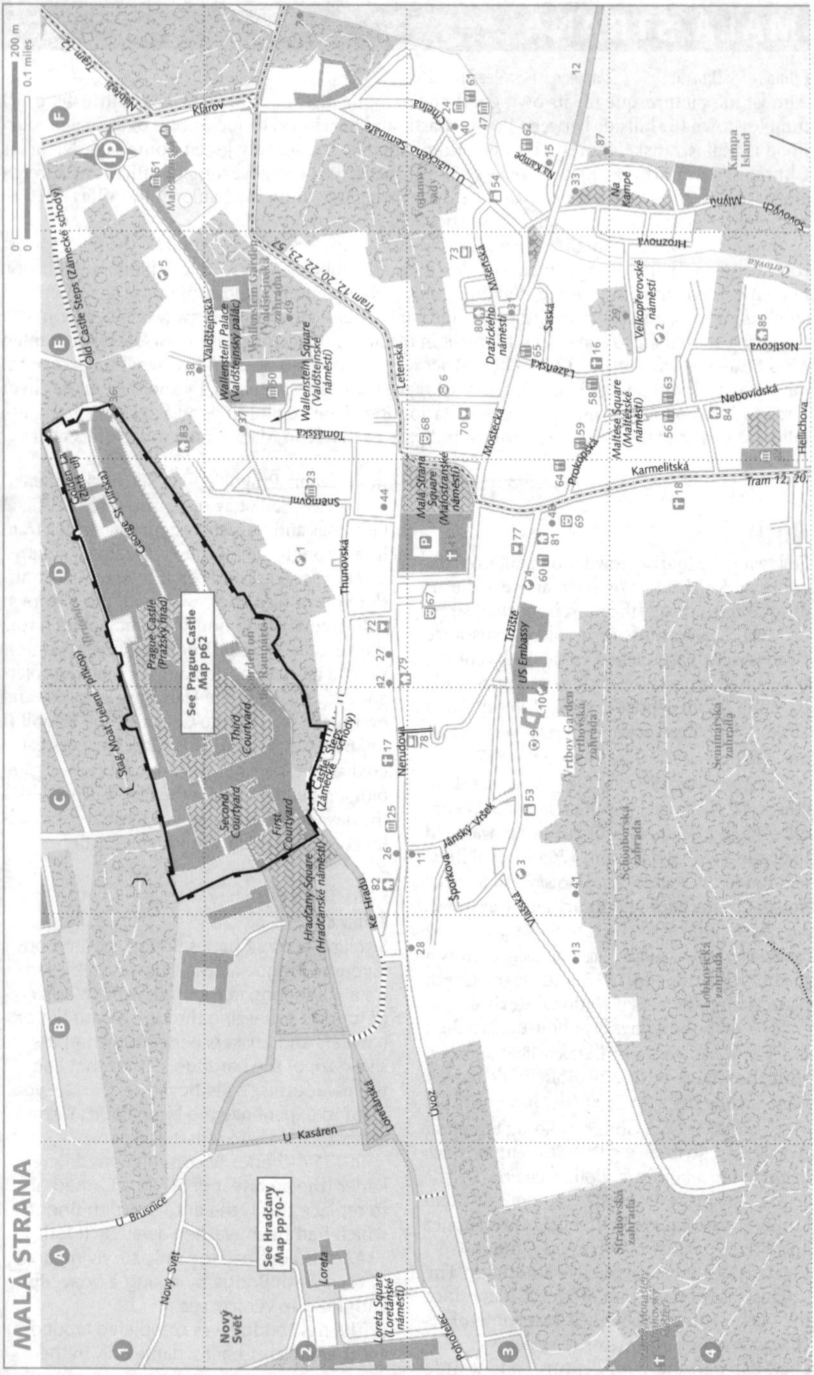

MALÁ STRANA
See Hradčany Map pp70-1
See Prague Castle Map p62
Nový Svět
Loreta
Loreta Square (Loretánské náměstí)
U Brusnice
U Kasáren
Loretánská
Pohořelec
Úvoz
Ke Hradu
Hradčany Square (Hradčanské náměstí)
First Courtyard
Second Courtyard
Third Courtyard
Prague Castle (Pražský hrad)
Stag Moat (Jelení příkop)
Golden La (Zlatá ulička)
George St (Jiřská)
Garden on the Ramparts
Castle Steps (Zámecké schody)
Old Castle Steps (Zámecké schody)
Nerudova
Thunovská
Sněmovní
Tomášská
Valdštejnská
Wallenstein Palace (Valdštejnský palác)
Wallenstein Garden (Valdštejnská zahrada)
Wallenstein Square (Valdštejnské náměstí)
Letenská
Tram 12, 20, 22, 23, 57
Klárov
Nábřeží
Tram 12
Malostranská
U Lužického Semináře
Cihelná
Vojanovy sady
Malá Strana Square (Malostranské náměstí)
Mostecká
Dražického náměstí
Míšeňská
Saská
Lázeňská
Na Kampě
Kampa Island
Hroznová
Mlýnská
Sovových
Čertovka
Velkopřevorské náměstí
Maltese Square (Maltézské náměstí)
Nebovidská
Nostická
Prokopská
Karmelitská
Tram 12, 20
Hellichova
Tržiště
US Embassy
Šporkova
Jánský Vršek
Vlašská
Vrtbov Garden (Vrtbovská zahrada)
Schönbornská zahrada
Seminářská zahrada
Lobkovická zahrada
Strahovská zahrada
200 m
0.1 miles

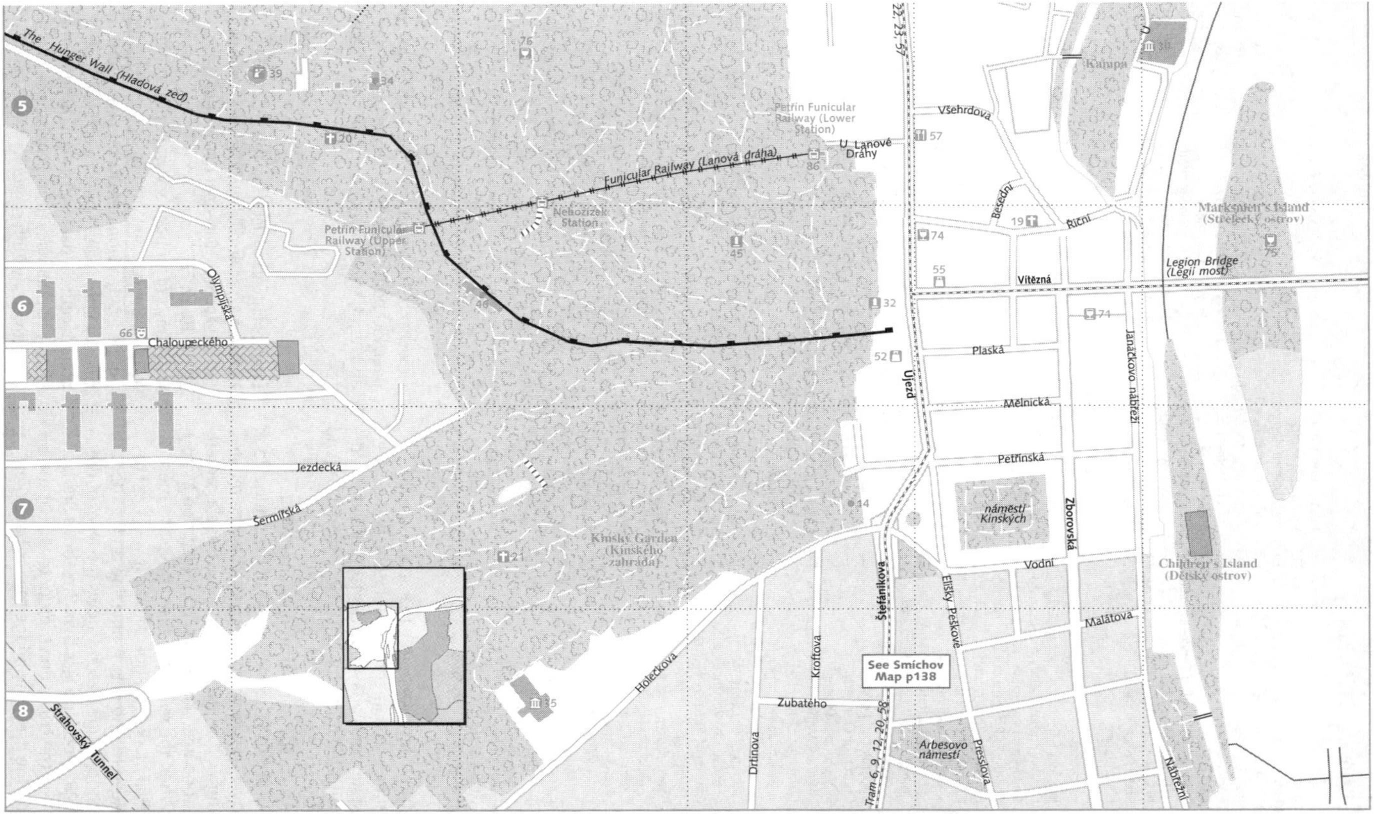
The Hunger Wall (Hladová zeď)
39
34
76
20
Petřín Funicular Railway (Lower Station)
U Lanové Dráhy
86
Funicular Railway (Lanová dráha)
Nebozízek Station
Petřín Funicular Railway (Upper Station)
45
46
Olympijská
66
Chaloupeckého
Jezdecká
Šermířská
Kinský Garden (Kinského zahrada)
21
35
Strahovský Tunnel
Holečkova
22, 23, 57
Všehrdova
57
Besední
19
Říční
74
55
Vítězná
32
52
Újezd
Plaská
Mělnická
Petřínská
14
náměstí Kinských
Zborovská
Vodní
Janáčkovo nábřeží
Kampa
30
U
Marksmen's Island (Střelecký ostrov)
75
Legion Bridge (Legií most)
Children's Island (Dětský ostrov)
Malátova
Štefánikova
Elišky Peškové
Kroftova
Zubatého
Drtinova
See Smíchov Map p138
Tram 6, 9, 12, 20, 58
Arbesovo náměstí
Presslova
Nábřežní
5
6
7
8

MALÁ STRANA

INFORMATION

British Embassy 1 D2
French Embassy 2 E4
German Embassy 3 C3
Irish Embassy 4 D3
Polish Embassy 5 E1
Post Office 6 E3
Prague Information Service (see 31)
Prague Venice 7 F2
Prague Venice 8 E3
State Police Station 9 C3
US Embassy 10 C3

SIGHTS & ACTIVITIES (pp75–86)

Bretfeld Palace 11 C3
Charles Bridge (Karlův most) 12 F3
Children's Playground 13 B3
Children's Playground 14 D7
Children's Playground 15 F3
Church of Our Lady Below the Chain (Kostel Panny Marie pod Řetězem) 16 E3
Church of Our Lady of Unceasing Succour (Kostel Panny Marie Ustavičné Pomoci) 17 C2
Church of Our Lady Victorious (Kostel Panny Marie Vítězné) 18 D4
Church of St John at the Laundry (Kostel sv Jana na Prádle) 19 E6
Church of St Lawrence (Kostel sv Vavřince) 20 B5
Church of St Michael (Kostel sv Michala) 21 C7
Czech Museum of Music (České Muzeum Hudby) 22 E4
Czech Parliament House (Sněmovna) 23 D2
Franz Kafka Museum (Muzeum Franzy Kafky) 24 F3
Historical Pharmacy Exhibition 25 C2
House of the Golden Horseshoe 26 C2
House of the Three Fiddles 27 D2
House of the Two Suns 28 B3
John Lennon Wall 29 E4
Kampa Museum (Muzeum Kampa) 30 F5
Malá Strana Bridge Tower 31 E3
Memorial to the Victims of Communism 32 D6
Metal Plaque 33 F3
Mirror Maze (Zrcadlové Bludiště) 34 B5
Musaion 35 C8
Museum of the Infant Jesus of Prague (Muzeum Pražského Jezulátka) (see 18)
Palace Gardens Beneath Prague Castle Entrance 36 E1
Palace Gardens Beneath Prague Castle Entrance 37 E2
Palace Gardens Beneath Prague Castle Entrance 38 E1
Petřín Funicular Railway (Lower Station) (see 86)
Petřín Lookout Tower 39 B5
Proudy (Streams) - David Černý Sculpture 40 F3
Quo Vadis - David Černý Sculpture 41 C3
St John of Nepomuk House 42 D2
St Nicholas Church (Kostel sv Mikuláše) 43 D3
Smiřický Palace 44 D2
Statue of Karel Hynek Mácha 45 D6
Štefánik Observatory 46 C6
Tržiště 15 (Kafka's Home 1917) (see 10)
Václav Havel Library 47 F3
Vrtbov Garden Entrance 48 D3
Wallenstein Garden (Valdštejnská Zahrada) 49 E2
Wallenstein Palace (Valdštejnský Palác) 50 E2
Wallenstein Riding School (Valdštejnská Jízdárna) 51 F1

SHOPPING (pp143–51)

Capriccio 52 D6
Pavla & Olga 53 C3
Shakespeare & Sons 54 F3
Vetešnictví 55 E6

EATING (pp153–73)

Café de Paris 56 E4
Café Savoy (see 71)
Cantina 57 E5
Cukrkávalimonáda 58 E3
El Centro 59 E3
Gitanes 60 D3
Hergetova Cihelna 61 F3
Kampa Park 62 F3
U Malé Velryby 63 E4
U Maltézských Rytířů 64 D3
U Zlaté Studně (see 83)
Vacek Bio-Market 65 E3

ENTERTAINMENT (pp193–203)

Klub 007 Strahov 66 A6
Liechtenstein Palace 67 D3
Malostranská Beseda 68 E3
U Malého Glena 69 D3

DRINKING (pp175–91)

Blue Light 70 E3
Café Savoy 71 E6
Hostinec U Kocoura 72 D2
Kafíčko 73 E3
Klub Újezd 74 E6
Letní Bar 75 F6
Petřínské Terasy 76 C5
St Nicholas Café 77 D3
U Zeleného Čaje 78 C3

SLEEPING (pp211–27)

Castle Steps 79 D2
Charles Bridge B&B 80 E3
Hotel Aria 81 D3
Hotel Neruda 82 C2
Hotel U Zlaté Studně 83 E1
Mandarin Oriental 84 E4
Pension Dientzenhofer 85 E4

TRANSPORT (pp241–5)

Petřín Funicular Railway (Lower Station) 86 D5
PPS Boat Landing 87 F3

19th century – before that it was known simply as Kamenný most (Stone Bridge). Despite occasional flood damage, it withstood wheeled traffic for 600 years – thanks, legend says, to eggs mixed into the mortar – until it was made pedestrian-only after WWII.

At the Staré Město end of the bridge, look over the downstream parapet at the retaining wall on the right and you'll see a carved stone head known as Bradáč (Bearded Man). When the river level rose above this medieval marker, Praguers knew it was time to head for the hills. A blue line on the modern flood gauge nearby shows the level of the 2002 flood, no less than 2m above Bradáč!

In the crush, don't forget to look at the bridge itself (the bridge towers have great views) and the grand vistas up and down the river. Pickpocket gangs work the bridge day and night, so keep your purse or wallet safe.

HISTORICAL PHARMACY EXHIBITION

Map pp76–7

Expozice historických lékáren; ☎ 257 531 502; Nerudova 32; adult/child 40/20Kč; 11am-6pm Tue-Sun Apr-Sep, 10am-5pm Tue-Sun Oct-Mar; 12, 20, 22, 23

Hradčany's first pharmacy was opened here in 1749; the building, known as U zlatého lva (At the Golden Lion) retains original 19th-century fittings and houses a collection of pharmaceutical paraphernalia illustrating the history of pharmacy from Renaissance times up to the early 20th century.

MALÁ STRANA BRIDGE TOWER
Map pp76–7

Malostranská mostecká věž; ☎ 257 530 487; Charles Bridge; adult/child 70/50Kč; 🕒 10am-6pm Apr-Oct; 🚊 12, 20, 22, 23

There are actually two towers at the Malá Strana end of Charles Bridge. The lower one was originally part of the long-gone 12th-century Judith Bridge (p75), while the taller one was built in the mid-15th century in imitation of the Staré Město tower (see p98). The taller tower is open to the public and houses an exhibit on the history of Charles Bridge, though like its Staré Město counterpart the main attraction is the view from the top.

ST NICHOLAS CHURCH Map pp76–7

Kostel sv Mikuláše; ☎ 257 534 215; www.psalterium.cz; Malostranská náměstí 38; adult/child under 10yr 70Kč/free; 🕒 9am-5pm Mar-Oct, to 4pm Nov-Feb; 🚊 12, 20, 22, 23

Malá Strana is dominated by the huge green cupola of St Nicholas Church, one of Central Europe's finest baroque buildings. (Don't confuse it with the other Church of St Nicholas on Old Town Square, p91.) It was begun by famed German baroque architect Kristof Dientzenhofer (see p48); his son Kilian continued the work and Anselmo Lurago finished the job in 1755.

On the ceiling, Johann Kracker's 1770 *Apotheosis of St Nicholas* is Europe's largest fresco (clever trompe l'oeil technique has made the painting merge almost seamlessly with the architecture). In the first chapel on the left is a mural by Karel Škréta, which includes the church official who kept track of the artist as he worked; he is looking out through a window in the upper corner.

Mozart himself tickled the ivories on the 2500-pipe organ in 1787, and was honoured with a requiem Mass here (14 December 1791). Take the stairs up to the gallery to see Škréta's gloomy 17th-century Passion Cycle paintings and the scratchings of bored 1820s tourists and wannabe Franz Kafkas on the balustrade.

TRANSPORT: MALÁ STRANA

Metro Malostranská metro station is in northern Malá Strana, about five minutes' walk from Malostranské náměstí.

Tram Lines 12, 20, 22 and 23 run along Újezd and through Malostranské náměstí.

NORTHERN MALÁ STRANA

From the northern side of Malostranské náměstí, Thunovská and the Castle Steps (Zámecké schody) lead up to the castle. At the eastern end of Thunovská, on Sněmovní, is the Czech Parliament House (Sněmovna), seat of the lower house of parliament, once home to the national assembly that deposed the Habsburgs from the Czech throne on 14 November 1918.

FRANZ KAFKA MUSEUM Map pp76–7

Muzeum Franzy Kafky; ☎ 257 535 507; www.kafkamuseum.cz; Hergetova Cíhelná, Cihelná 2b; adult/child 120/60Kč; 🕒 10am-6pm; 🚊 12, 20, 22, 23

This much-hyped exhibition on the life and work of Prague's most famous literary son opened here in 2005, after six years in Barcelona and New York. Entitled 'City of K', it explores the intimate relationship between the writer and the city that shaped him through the use of original letters, photographs, quotations, period newspapers and publications, and video and sound installations. Does it vividly portray the claustrophobic bureaucracy and atmosphere of brooding menace that characterised Kafka's world? Or is it a load of pretentious bollocks? You decide.

Outside the museum stands one of David Černý's amusing and controversial sculptures, Proudy (Streams; see p137).

PALACE GARDENS BENEATH PRAGUE CASTLE Map pp76–7

Palácové zahrady pod Pražským hradem; ☎ 257 010 401; Valdštejnské náměstí 3, Valdštejnská 12-14; adult/child 95/65Kč; 🕒 10am-9pm Jun & Jul, to 8pm Aug, to 7pm May & Sep, to 6pm Apr & Oct; 🚊 12, 20, 22, 23

These beautiful, terraced gardens on the steep southern slopes of the castle hill date from the 17th and 18th centuries, when they were created for the owners of the adjoining palaces. They were restored in the 1990s and contain a Renaissance loggia with frescoes of Pompeii and a baroque portal with sundial that cleverly catches the sunlight reflected off the water in a triton fountain.

There are two entrances on Valdštejnska street: one opposite the Wallenstein Palace, and one next to the Palffy Palace Restaurant. There's also one at the top of the hill in the Garden on the Ramparts at Prague Castle.

CHARLES BRIDGE STATUES

The first monument erected on the bridge was the crucifix near the eastern end, in 1657. The first statue – the Jesuits' 1683 tribute to St John of Nepomuk – inspired other Catholic orders, and over the next 30 years a score more went up, like ecclesiastical billboards. New ones were added in the mid-19th century, and one (plus replacements for some lost to floods) in the 20th. As most of the statues were carved from soft sandstone, several weathered originals have been replaced with copies. Some originals are housed in the Casemates (p115) at Vyšehrad; others are in the Lapidárium (p131) in Holešovice.

Starting from the western (Malá Strana) end, with odd numbers on your left and even ones on your right, the statues that line the bridge are as follows:

1 Sts Cosmas & Damian (1709) Charitable 3rd-century physician brothers.

2 St Wenceslas (sv Václav; 1858) Patron saint of Bohemia.

3 St Vitus (sv Víta; 1714) Patron saint of Prague (and of dogs, dancers, actors and comedians).

4 Sts John of Matha & Félix de Valois (1714) 12th-century French founders of the Trinitarian order, whose mission was the ransom of enslaved Christians (represented by a Tatar standing guard over a group of them), with St Ivo (No 30).

5 St Philip Benizi (sv Benicius; 1714) Miracle worker and healer.

6 St Adalbert (sv Vojtěch; 1709) Prague's first Czech bishop, canonised in the 10th century. Replica.

7 St Cajetan (1709) Italian founder of the Theatine order in the 15th century.

8 The Vision of St Luitgard (1710) Agreed by many to be the finest piece on the bridge, in which Christ appears to the blind saint and allows her to kiss his wounds.

9 St Augustine (1708) Reformed hedonist, famous for his *Confessions,* theological fountainhead of the Reformation. Also, patron saint of brewers. Replica.

10 St Nicholas of Tolentino (1706) Patron of Holy Souls. Replica.

11 St Jude Thaddaeus (1708) Apostle and patron saint of hopeless causes. Further on the right, beyond the railing, is a column with a statue of the eponymous hero of the 11th-century epic poem *Song of Roland* (Bruncvík).

12 St Vincent Ferrer (1712) A 14th-century Spanish priest, shown with St Procopius, Hussite warrior-priest.

13 St Anthony of Padua (1707) The 13th-century Portuguese disciple of St Francis of Assisi.

14 St Francis Seraphinus (1855) Patron of the poor and abandoned.

WALLENSTEIN GARDEN Map pp76–7

Valdštejnská zahrada; Letenská 10; admission free; 10am-6pm Apr-Oct; M Malostranská

This huge, walled garden lurks behind the Wallenstein Palace, an oasis of peace amid the bustle of Malá Strana streets. Its finest feature is the huge loggia decorated with scenes from the Trojan Wars, flanked to one side by an aviary with a pair of Eagle Owls, and an enormous fake stalactite grotto – see how many hidden animals and grotesque faces you can spot. The bronze statues of Greek gods lining the avenue opposite the loggia are copies – the originals were carted away by marauding Swedes in 1648 and now stand outside the royal palace of Drottningholm near Stockholm.

At the eastern end of the garden is an ornamental pond, home to some seriously large carp, and the Wallenstein Riding School (Valdštejnská jízdárna; ☎ 257 073 136; Valdštejnská 3; adult/child 150/80Kč; 10am-6pm Tue-Sun), which hosts changing exhibitions of modern art. Enter the garden on Letenská (beside Malostranská metro station) or via the Wallenstein Palace (see the walking tour on p85).

WALLENSTEIN PALACE Map pp76–7

Valdštejnský palác; ☎ 257 071 111; Valdštejnské náměstí 4; admission free; 10am-5pm Sat & Sun Apr-Oct, to 4pm Sat & Sun Nov-Mar; 12, 20, 22, 23

The small Wallenstein Square (Valdštejnské náměstí), northeast of Malá Strana Square, is dominated by the monumental 1630 palace of Albrecht of Wallenstein, general of the Habsburg armies, who financed the construction with the confiscated properties of Protestant nobles he defeated at the Battle of (White Mountain) in 1620. It now houses the Senate of the Czech Republic, but you can visit some rooms on weekends. The ceiling fresco in the Baroque Hall shows Wallenstein as a warrior at the reins of a chariot, while the unusual oval Audience Hall has a fresco of Vulcan at work in his forge.

15 St John of Nepomuk (1683) Bronze. Patron saint of Czechs. According to the legend on base of the statue, Wenceslas IV had him trussed up in armour and thrown off the bridge in 1393 for refusing to divulge the queen's confessions (he was her priest), though the real reason had to do with the bitter conflict between church and state; the stars in his halo allegedly followed his corpse down the river. Tradition says that if you rub the bronze plaque, you will one day return to Prague. A bronze cross set in the parapet between statues 17 and 19 marks where he was thrown off.

16 St Wenceslas as a boy (c 1730) With his grandmother and guardian St Ludmilla, patroness of Bohemia.

17 St Wenceslas (1853) With St Sigismund, son of Charles IV, and St Norbert, 12th-century German founder of the Premonstratensian order.

18 St Francis Borgia (1710) A 16th-century Spanish priest.

19 St John the Baptist (1857) By Josef Max.

20 St Christopher (1857) Patron saint of travellers.

21 Sts Cyril & Methodius (1938) The newest statue. These two introduced Christianity and a written script (Cyrillic) to the Slavs in the 9th century.

22 St Francis Xavier (1711) A 16th-century Spanish missionary celebrated for his work in the Orient. Replica.

23 St Anne with Madonna & Child (1707) St Anne is the mother of the Virgin Mary.

24 St Joseph (1854) Husband of the Virgin Mary.

25 Crucifix (1657) Gilded bronze. With an invocation in Hebrew saying 'holy, holy, holy Lord' (funded by the fine of a Jew who had mocked it in 1696); the stone figures date from 1861.

26 Pietá (1859) Mary holding the body of Christ following the crucifixion.

27 Madonna with St Dominic (1709) Spanish founder of the Dominicans, with St Thomas Aquinas. Replica.

28 Sts Barbara, Margaret & Elizabeth (1707) St Barbara, 2nd-century patron saint of miners; St Margaret, 3rd- or 4th-century patron saint of expectant mothers; and St Elizabeth, a 13th-century Slovak princess who renounced the good life to serve the poor.

29 Madonna with St Bernard (1709) Founder of the Cistercian order in the 12th century. Replica.

30 St Ivo of Kermartin (1711) A 13th-century Breton, patron saint of lawyers and orphans. Replica.

VÁCLAV HAVEL LIBRARY Map pp76–7

Knihovna Václava Havla; ☎ 222 220 112; Cihelná 2b; www.vaclavhavel-knihovna.org; adult/child 80/40Kč; 10am-6pm Tue-Sun; 12, 20, 22, 23

This exhibition, next door to the Franz Kafka Museum, charts the life and work of the Czech Republic's first playwright-president: writer, dramatist and political dissident Václav Havel, who led the country from 1989 to 2003, through the aftermath of communism and the Velvet Divorce. Featured are displays of documents, photographs, original writings and a reconstruction of Havel's presidential office in Prague Castle.

SOUTHERN MALÁ STRANA

The southern part of Malá Strana centres on pretty Maltese Square (Maltézské náměstí; Map pp76–7), which takes its name from the Knights of Malta who, in 1169, established a monastery beside the austere, early-Gothic towers of the Church of Our Lady Below the Chain (kostel Panny Marie pod řetězem). The knights were charged with protecting the bridge across the river – the chain refers to the barrier they used.

To the east of the square is Kampa (Map pp76–7), an 'island' created by the Čertovka (Devil's Stream) – the most peaceful and picturesque part of Malá Strana. In the 13th century Prague's first mill, the Sovovský mlýn (now Kampa Museum), was built here, and other mills followed. Kampa was once farmland (the name Kampa comes from campus, Latin for 'field'), but the island was settled in the 16th century after being raised above flood level. In 1939 the river was so low that it was again joined to the mainland, and coins and jewellery were found in the dry channel.

The area where the Čertovka passes under Charles Bridge is sometimes called Prague's Venice – the channel is often crowded with dinky tour boats. Cafés beckon from Na Kampě, the small square south of the bridge, though the summer sun is fierce here. Kampa's southern end, beyond the square, is a pleasant wooded park with views across to Staré Město.

Near the southern end of Kampa on the mainland lies one of Malá Strana's oldest Gothic buildings, the Church of St John at the Laundry (kostel sv Jana na prádle; Map pp76–7), built in 1142 as a local parish church. Inside are the remains of 14th-century frescoes.

Marksmen's Island (Střelecký ostrov; Map pp76–7), just south of Kampa, is crossed by the Legion Bridge (Legií most). The island's name originates in its use in the 16th century as a cannon and rifle target for the Prague garrison. During summer it has an open-air bar and cinema (see the boxed text, p188), and there's a little beach at the northern end. Take the steps going down from Legion Bridge to get there.

CHILDREN'S ISLAND Map pp76–7

Dětský ostrov; access from Nábřežní; admission free; 24hr; M Anděl

Prague's smallest island offers a leafy respite from the hustle and bustle of the city, with a selection of swings, slides, climbing frames and sandpits to keep the kids busy, as well as a rope swing, skateboard ramp, mini football pitch, netball court, and lots of open space for older siblings to run wild. There are plenty of benches to take the strain off weary parental legs, and a decent bar and restaurant at the southern end.

JOHN LENNON WALL Map pp76–7

Velkopřevorské náměstí; 12, 20, 22, 23

After his murder on 8 December 1980 John Lennon became a pacifist hero for many young Czechs. An image of Lennon was painted on a wall in a secluded square opposite the French Embassy (there is a niche on the wall that looks like a tombstone), along with political graffiti and Beatles lyrics. Despite repeated coats of whitewash, the secret police never managed to keep it clean for long, and the Lennon Wall became a political focus for Prague youth (most Western pop music was banned by the communists, and some Czech musicians were even jailed for playing it).

Post-1989 weathering and lightweight graffiti ate away at the political messages and images, until little remained of Lennon but his eyes, but visiting tourists began making their own contributions. The wall is the property of the Knights of Malta, and they have repainted it several times, but it soon gets covered with more Lennon images, peace messages and inconsequential tourist graffiti. In recent years the Knights have bowed to the inevitable and now don't bother to whitewash it any more.

KAMPA MUSEUM Map pp76–7

Muzeum Kampa; ☎ 257 286 147; www.museumkampa.cz; U Sovových Mlýnů 2; admission to permanent exhibition only adult/concession 120/60Kč, to permanent & temporary exhibitions 180/90Kč; 10am-6pm; 12, 20, 22, 23

Housed in a renovated mill building, this gallery is devoted to 20th-century and contemporary art from Central Europe. The highlights of the permanent exhibition are extensive collections of bronzes by Cubist sculptor Otto Gutfreund and paintings by František Kupka, a pioneer of abstract art. The most impressive canvas is Kupka's *Cathedral*, a pleated mass of blue and red diagonals suggesting a curtain with a glimpse of darkness beyond. Free admission on the first Wednesday of each month.

CZECH MUSEUM OF MUSIC Map pp76–7

České muzeum hudby; ☎ 257 257 777; www.nm.cz; Karmelitská 2/4; adult/concession 100/50Kč; 10am-6pm Wed-Mon; 12, 20, 22, 23

A 17th-century baroque monastery building with an impressive central atrium makes a beautiful setting for the new Museum of Music. The museum's permanent exhibition, entitled 'Man–Instrument–Music', explores the relationship between human beings and musical instruments through the ages, and showcases an incredible collection of violins, guitars, lutes, trumpets, flutes and harmonicas – all set to music, of course.

MUSEUM OF THE INFANT JESUS OF PRAGUE Map pp76–7

Muzeum Pražského Jezulátka; ☎ 257 533 646; www.pragjesu.info; Karmelitská 9; admission free; church 8.30am-6pm Mon-Sat & 8.30am-8pm Sun, museum 9.30am-5.30pm Mon-Sat & 1-6pm Sun, closed 1 Jan, 25 & 26 Dec & Easter Mon; 12, 20, 22, 23

The Church of Our Lady Victorious (kostel Panny Marie Vítězné), built in 1613, has on its central altar a 47cm-tall waxwork figure of the baby Jesus, brought from Spain in 1628. Known as the Infant Jesus of Prague (Pražské Jezulátko), it is said to have protected Prague from the plague and from the destruction of the Thirty Years' War. An 18th-century

KAFKA'S PRAGUE

Although he wrote his works in German, Franz Kafka (1883–1924) was very much a son of the Czech capital. He lived in Prague all his life, haunting the city and being haunted by it, both hating it and needing it. His novel *The Trial* can be seen as a metaphysical geography of Staré Město, whose maze of alleys and passageways break down the usual boundaries between outer streets and inner courtyards, between public and private, new and old, real and imaginary.

For most of his life Kafka lived close to Old Town Square, growing up and going to school, working and meeting friends; his own words were: 'this narrow circle encompasses my entire life'. Many guidebooks and walking tours claim to show you 'Kafka's Prague', but any familiarity with his work soon shows that such a place existed only in Kafka's mind. So rather than describe some arbitrary walking trail, we have listed the various places associated with the writer's life in chronological order, so you can wander between them by whichever route you like, as Kafka would have done himself.

- U Radnice 5 (Map pp88–9; 1883–88) is where Kafka was born on 3 July 1883 in an apartment beside the St Nicholas Church; all that remains of the original building is the stone portal. It now houses a Kafka Exhibition, in reality a thinly disguised souvenir shop.
- Celetná 2 (Map pp88–9; 1888–89), 'The Sixt House', was Kafka's childhood home for a brief period.
- House at the Minute (dům U minuty; Map pp88–9; 1889–96) is where Kafka lived as a schoolboy, in the Renaissance corner building that's now part of the Old Town Hall. In a letter he recalled attending primary school in Masná street, and being dragged reluctantly across the square each day by the family cook, whose duty it was to deposit him in class.
- Goltz-Kinský Palace (Map pp88–9) is where Kafka attended high school, at the Old Town State Gymnasium, on the 2nd floor of the palace, between 1893 and 1901. For a time his father ran a clothing shop on the ground floor there, in premises now occupied by the Kafka Bookshop.
- Celetná 3 (Map pp88–9; 1896–1907), known as House at the Three Kings, is where Kafka first had a room to himself, and where he wrote his first story. His bedroom window looked out onto the Church of Our Lady Before Týn.
- Assicurazioni Generali (Map pp108–9; 1907–8) was the Italian insurance firm, located at No 19 Wenceslas Square, where Kafka took his first job, as an insurance clerk, after earning a law degree from Charles University in 1906. Long hours, poor pay and bureaucratic boredom took its toll, and he quit after only nine months.
- Workers' Accident Insurance Co (Map pp88–9), an office at Na Poříčí 7 in Nové Město, is where Kafka toiled on the 5th floor for 14 years, from 1908 until his retirement (due to ill health) in 1922.
- U Jednorožce (At the Unicorn; Map pp88–9), a house on the southern side of Old Town Square at No 17, was owned by Otto Fanta and his wife Berta, who hosted a regular literary salon popular with fashionable European thinkers of the time, including Kafka and fellow writers Max Brod (Kafka's friend and biographer), Franz Werfel and Egon Erwin Kisch.
- Pařížská 36 (Map pp88–9; 1907–13), in an apartment overlooking the river beside the Čech Bridge (Čechův most), was where Kafka wrote *The Judgement* and began work on *Metamorphosis*. (The building no longer exists.)
- Pařížská 1 (Map pp88–9; 1913–14), a luxurious top-floor apartment in the Oppelt House, across from the Church of St Nicholas, was the last place Kafka lived with his parents – and the setting for his horrific parable *Metamorphosis*.
- Bílkova 22 (Map pp88–9; 1914–15) was where, at the age of 31, Kafka lived in a flat after moving out of his parental home for the first time, and where he began work on *The Trial*.
- Dlouhá 16 (Map pp88–9; 1915–17) was where Kafka rented a place of his own, at the narrow corner with Masná. He moved around a lot in the next few years, visiting Berlin and Vienna, and visiting with his parents at the Oppelt House when he returned to Prague.
- Zlatá ulička 22 (Map p62) was Kafka's sister's rented cottage in the castle grounds. During the winter of 1916–17 Kafka stayed here to escape the noise and distraction of his Old Town flat, and produced more than a dozen stories.
- Tržiště 15 (Map pp76–7; 1917), the Schönborn Palace in Malá Strana (now the US Embassy), was where Kafka took a flat for a few months. He was happy here for a while until he suffered a lung haemorrhage, a symptom of the tuberculosis that would eventually kill him. He spent the rest of his life either seeking medical treatments or staying with his parents, and died in Vienna on 3 June 1924. He was buried in the Jewish Cemetery in Žižkov (see p125).

German prior, ES Stephano, wrote about the miracles, kicking off what eventually became a worldwide cult; today the statue is visited by a steady stream of pilgrims, especially from Italy, Spain and Latin America. It was traditional to dress the figure in beautiful robes, and over the years various benefactors donated richly embroidered dresses. Today the Infant's wardrobe consists of more than 70 costumes donated from all over the world; these are changed regularly in accordance with a religious calendar.

At the back of the church is the museum, displaying a selection of the frocks used to dress the Infant; shops in the street nearby sell copies of the wax figure. Looking at all this, you can't help thinking about the Second Commandment ('Thou shalt not make unto thee any graven image…') and the objectives of the Reformation. Jan Hus must be spinning in his grave.

VRTBOV GARDEN Map pp76–7

Vrtbovská zahrada; ☎ 257 531 480; www.vrtbovska.cz; Karmelitská 25; adult/concession 45/30Kč; 10am-6pm Apr-Oct; 12, 20, 22, 23

This 'secret garden', hidden along an alley at the corner of Tržiště and Karmelitská, was built in 1720 for the Earl of Vrtba, the senior chancellor of Prague Castle. It's a formal baroque garden, climbing steeply up the hillside to a terrace graced with baroque statues of Roman mythological figures by Matthias Braun – see if you can spot Vulcan, Diana and Mars. Below the terrace (on the right, looking down) is a tiny studio once used by Czech painter Mikuláš Aleš, and above is a little lookout with good views of Prague Castle and Malá Strana.

PETŘÍN

This 318m-high hill is one of Prague's largest green spaces. It's great for quiet, tree-shaded walks and fine views over the 'City of a Hundred Spires'. There were once vineyards here, and a quarry that provided the stone for most of Prague's Romanesque and Gothic buildings.

Petřín is easily accessible on foot from Strahov Monastery (p69), or you can ride the funicular railway (lanová draha) from Újezd up to the top. You can also get off two-thirds of the way up at Nebozízek.

In the peaceful Kinský Garden (Kinského zahrada), on the southern side of Petřín, is the 18th-century wooden Church of St Michael (kostel sv Michala), transferred here, log by log, from the village of Medveďov in Ukraine. Such structures are rare in Bohemia, though still common in Ukraine and northeastern Slovakia.

MEMORIAL TO THE VICTIMS OF COMMUNISM Map pp76–7

Památník obětem komunismu; cnr Újezd & Vítězná; 6, 9, 12, 20, 22, 23

This striking sculptural group consists of several ragged human figures (controversially, all are male) in progressive stages of disintegration, descending a staggered slope. A bronze strip inlaid into the ground in front of them records the terrible human toll of the communist era – 205,486 arrested; 170,938 driven into exile; 248 executed; 4500 who died in prison; and 327 shot while trying to escape across the border.

MIRROR MAZE Map pp76–7

Zrcadlové bludiště; adult/child 70/50Kč; 10am-10pm May-Aug, 10am-8pm Sep, 10am-7pm Apr, 10am-6pm Oct, 10am-5pm Sat & Sun Nov-Mar; funicular railway

Below the lookout tower (below) is the Mirror Maze, also built for the 1891 Prague Exposition. As well as the maze, which is good for a laugh, there's a diorama of the 1648 battle between Praguers and Swedes on Charles Bridge. Opposite is the Church of St Lawrence (kostel sv Vavřince), which contains a ceiling fresco depicting the founding of the church in 991 at a pagan site with a sacred flame.

MUSAION Map pp76–7

☎ 257 325 766; Kinského zahrada 98; adult/child 80/40Kč; 10am-5pm Tue-Sun May-Sep, 9am-5pm Tue-Sun Oct-Apr; 6, 9, 12, 20

This renovated summer palace houses the National Museum's ethnographic collection, with exhibits covering traditional Czech folk culture and art, including music, costume, farming methods and handicrafts. There are regular folk concerts and workshops demonstrating traditional crafts such as blacksmithing and woodcarving; in the summer months there's a garden café.

PETŘÍN FUNICULAR RAILWAY Map pp76–7

Lanová draha na Petřín; ☎ 800 19 18 17; www.dpp.cz; adult/child 26/13Kč; 9am-11.30pm Apr-Oct, 9am-11.20pm Nov-Mar; 12, 20, 22, 23

First opened in 1891, Prague's little funicular railway now uses modern coaches that trundle back and forth on 510m of track, saving visitors a climb up Petřín hill. It runs every 10 minutes (every 15 minutes November to March) from Újezd to the Petřín Lookout Tower, with a stop at Nebozízek. Ordinary 26Kč transfer tickets, valid on tram and metro, are valid on the funicular, too.

PETŘÍN LOOKOUT TOWER Map pp76–7

Petřínská rozhledna; ☎ 257 320 112; adult/child 70/50Kč; 10am-10pm May-Aug, to 8pm Sep, to 7pm Apr, to 6pm Oct, to 5pm Sat & Sun Nov-Mar; funicular railway

The summit of Petřín is topped off with a 62m-tall Eiffel Tower lookalike built in 1891 for the Prague Exposition. You can climb its 299 steps for some of the best views in Prague – on clear days you can see the forests of Central Bohemia to the southwest. (There's also a lift.) On the way to the tower you cross the Hunger Wall (Hladová zeď), running from Újezd to Strahov. These fortifications were built in 1362 under Charles IV, and are so named because they were built by the poor of the city in return for food – an early job-creation scheme.

ŠTEFÁNIK OBSERVATORY Map pp76–7

Štefánikova hvězdárna; ☎ 257 320 540; www.observatory.cz; adult/child 40/30Kč; hours vary, see website; funicular railway

Just south of the funicular's top station is this 'people's observatory', opened in 1928 to further public awareness of astronomy and other sciences. There are exhibitions on astronomy, but the main attraction is the double Zeiss astrograph telescope, which also dates from 1928 and allows observation of the sun and sunspots. On clear nights you can observe the moon, stars and planets.

MALÁ STRANA GARDENS Walking Tour

1 Prague Castle Lookout Begin at the lookout just outside the eastern entrance to Prague Castle, which offers a fine view over the rooftops of Malá Strana. On the steep slope directly below are the gardens belonging to the 18th-century aristocratic palaces ranged along Valdštejnská street, now restored and open to the public.

2 Palace Gardens beneath Prague Castle Go through the gate into the Garden on the Ramparts (Zahrada na valech; p67) and find the entrance to the Palace Gardens beneath Prague Castle (Palácové zahrady pod Pražským hradem; p79). Note that there is an admission fee, and the gardens are open only from April to October; in winter, begin this walking tour from Malostranská metro station and walk southwest along Valdštejnská to the Wallenstein Palace.

3 Wallenstein Garden After you have explored the palace gardens, exit via the main gate on Valdštejnská and turn right. When you reach Wallenstein Square (Valdštejnské náměstí), turn left into the main entrance to the Wallenstein Palace (Valdštejnský palác; p80) and go through the courtyard into the peace of the Wallenstein Garden (Valdštejnská zahrada; p79). Head for the northeastern corner, to the right of the big fishpond, and leave through the gate beside Malostranská metro station (if it's closed, go back along the southern wall and exit through the gate on Letenská).

4 Vojan Gardens Turn right on Klárov, go straight across the junction with the tram line, and continue along U Lužického Semináře. Just past the Černý Orel restaurant, a gate on the right gives access to the Vojan Gardens (Vojanovy sady), the poor relation of Malá Strana's many parks. Less manicured but more peaceful than the others, it's a public park where local folk take a breather with the kids or sit in the sun on the benches. If you're feeling hungry, the riverside terrace of Hergetova Cihelna (p159) is a great place for lunch.

5 Na Kampě Continue along U Lužického Semináře, and when the street narrows bear left across the little bridge over the Čertovka (Devil's Stream) onto the island called Kampa (p81). Pass under Charles Bridge and emerge into the picturesque little square of Na Kampě. To your left, at about waist height on the wall to the left of the little gallery under the stairs, is a small memorial plaque that reads *Výska vody 4.září 1890* (height of waters, 4 September 1890), marking the level reached by the floodwaters of 1890. Directly above it – above head height – is another marking the height of the 2002 floods. (There are several similar plaques around Kampa.) By the way, fans of the Tom Cruise film *Mission: Impossible* might recognise this little square – many of the night scenes in the movie were shot here.

6 Kampa Museum Head on through the square and into the leafy riverside park known simply as Kampa (from the Latin campus, meaning 'field'); one of the city's favourite chill-out zones, it's usually littered with lounging bodies in summer. If the mood strikes, go for a wander through the modern art collections of the Kampa Museum (p82), housed in a restored mill complex on the edge of the river.

7 John Lennon Wall Double back north and, as soon as you reach the cobblestones before Na Kampě, bear left along Hroznová, a backstreet that leads to a little bridge over the Čertovka beside Prague's most photographed water wheel. The bridge leads onto a tiny cobbled square with the John Lennon Wall (p82) on one side and the

MALÁ STRANA GARDENS WALKING TOUR

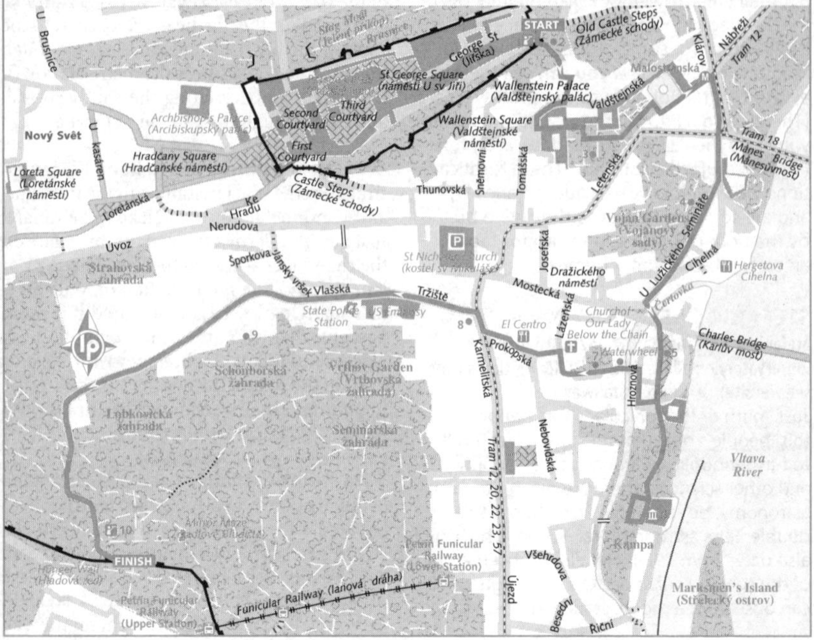

baroque palace that houses the French embassy on the other. The far end of the square curves right, past the severe Gothic towers of the Church of Our Lady Below the Chain (kostel Panny Marie pod řetězem; p81). Just beyond the church, on the right, is the embassy of the Knights of Malta, which featured in the movie *Amadeus* as the house of Salieri. Turn left opposite the church and bear right along Prokopská; if you fancy a drink – and you may well do by now – El Centro (p160) is on your right. At the end of Prokopská, cross busy Karmelitská and turn right.

8 Vrtbov Garden Just past the bar called U malého Glena is an alley on your left that leads to the Vrtbov Garden (Vrtbovská zahrada; p84), one of Malá Strana's least visited but most beautiful gardens. After visiting the garden, turn left along Tržiště and its continuation Vlašská, passing in turn the Irish, US and German embassies.

9 Quo Vadis A few hundred metres beyond the German embassy there's a little park and playground on the left; leave the street and turn left along the dirt track beyond the wall at the far end of the playground, and you'll be able to peek into the back garden of the German embassy to see David Černý's famous sculpture *Quo Vadis* – a Trabant car perched on four human legs. It's a memorial to the East German asylum seekers who sought refuge here in 1989 during the final death throes of the communist era (for more on David Černý, see the boxed texts, p39 and p137).

10 Petřín Lookout Tower Follow Vlašská to its end and climb the steps that lead up to the top of Petřín Hill and finish your walk at the Petřín Lookout Tower (Petřínská rozhledna; p84). From here you can take the Petřín Funicular Railway (p84) back down to Újezd or slowly wander down one of the many footpaths.

WALK FACTS

Start Prague Castle (tram 22, 23 or metro Malostranská)

End Petřín Hill (tram 12, 20, 22, 23 or funicular)

Distance 4km

Time Two hours

Exertion Moderate

Fuel stops Hergetova Cihelna, El Centro

STARÉ MĚSTO

Eating p160; Drinking p181; Shopping p145; Sleeping p216

Staré Město – meaning 'Old Town' – is the historic heart of medieval Prague, centred on one of Europe's most spectacular town squares. Its origins date back to the 10th century, when a marketplace and settlement grew up on the east bank of the river. In the 12th century this was linked to the castle district by Judith Bridge, the forerunner of Charles Bridge, and in 1231 Wenceslas I honoured it with a town charter and the beginnings of a fortification.

The town walls are long gone, but their line can still be traced along the streets Národní třída, Na Příkopě (which means 'on the moat') and Revoluční, and the Old Town's main gate – the Powder Gate – still survives.

Staré Město shared in the boom when Charles IV gave Prague a Gothic face befitting its new status as capital of the Holy Roman Empire. He founded Charles University in 1348 and commissioned Charles Bridge in 1357. When Emperor Joseph II united Prague's towns into a single city in 1784 the Old Town Hall (Staroměstská radnice) became its seat of government.

In an attempt to escape the frequent floods caused by the Vltava River, the level of the town was gradually raised. Beginning in the 13th century, new houses were simply built on top of older ones (many of Staré Město's Gothic buildings have Romanesque basements). A huge fire in 1689 created space for an orgy of rebuilding during the Catholic Counter-Reformation of the 17th and 18th centuries, giving this originally Gothic district a baroque makeover.

The only intrusions into Staré Město's medieval maze of a street plan have been the appropriation of a huge block in the west for the Jesuits' massive college, the Klementinum, in the 16th and 17th centuries, and the slum clearance of Josefov, the Jewish quarter, at the end of the 19th century.

At the centre of everything is Old Town Square (Staroměstské náměstí). If the labyrinth of narrow streets around the square can be said to have a 'main drag' it's the so-called Royal Way, the ancient coronation route to Prague Castle, running from the Powder Gate along Celetná to Old Town Square and Little Square (Malé náměstí), then along Karlova and across Charles Bridge.

OLD TOWN SQUARE

One of Europe's biggest and most beautiful urban spaces, the Old Town Square (Staroměstské náměstí, or Staromák for short) has been Prague's principal public square since the 10th century, and was its main marketplace until the beginning of the 20th century.

Despite the swarms of tourists, crowded pavement cafés and over-the-top commercialism, it's impossible not to enjoy the spectacle: tour leaders thrusting through crowds, umbrellas borne aloft like battle standards, with clients straggling behind like a gaggle of ducklings; students dressed as frogs and chickens handing out flyers for a drama production; middle-aged couples in matching, too-short shorts and sensible shoes, frowning at pink-haired, leather-clad punks with too many piercings; gangs of red-faced lads in football shirts slopping beer and ice cream on the cobblestones; and a bored-looking guy with a placard advertising a museum of torture instruments.

There are busking jazz bands and alfresco concerts, political meetings and fashion shows, plus Christmas and Easter markets, all watched over by Ladislav Šaloun's brooding Art Nouveau statue of Jan Hus (see the boxed text, p23). It was unveiled on 6 July 1915, the 500th anniversary of Hus' death at the stake.

The brass strip on the ground nearby is the so-called Prague Meridian. Until 1915 the square's main feature was a 17th-century plague column (see the boxed text, p93), whose shadow used to cross the meridian at high noon.

CHURCH OF OUR LADY BEFORE TÝN

Map pp88–9

Kostel Panny Marie před Týnem; Staroměstské náměstí; admission free; 10am-1pm & 3-5pm Tue-Sat; M Staroměstská

The distinctive, spiky-topped Týn Church is early Gothic, though it takes some imagination to visualise the original in its entirety because it's partly hidden behind the four-storey Týn School (not a Habsburg plot to obscure this 15th-century Hussite stronghold, but almost contemporaneous with it). The church's name originates from the Týn Courtyard (p94) behind the church.

Though Gothic on the outside, the church's interior is smothered in heavy baroque. Two of the most interesting features

STARÉ MĚSTO

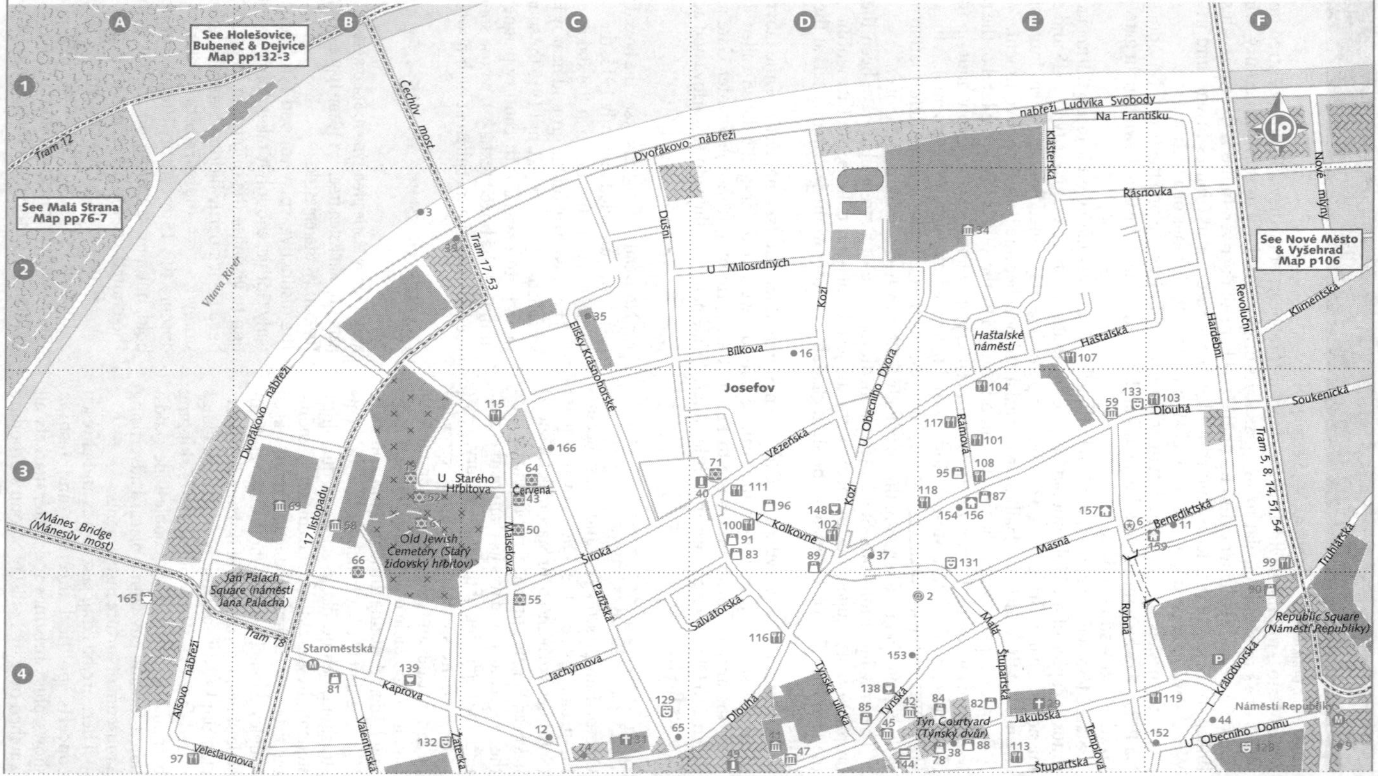
0 200 m
0 0.1 miles
See Holešovice, Bubeneč & Dejvice Map pp132-3
See Malá Strana Map pp76-7
See Nové Město & Vyšehrad Map p106
Vltava River
Tram 12
Čechův most
Tram 17, 53
Mánes Bridge (Mánesův most)
Dvořákovo nábřeží
nábřeží Ludvíka Svobody
Na Františku
Klášterská
Řásnovka
Nové mlýny
Revoluční
Klimentská
Hardební
Haštalská
Haštalské náměstí
Soukenická
Dlouhá
Tram 5, 8, 14, 51, 54
Truhlářská
Republic Square (Náměstí Republiky)
Králodvorská
Náměstí Republiky
U Obecního Domu
Benediktská
Rybná
Masná
Templová
Jakubská
Štupartská
Malá Štupartská
Týn Courtyard (Týnský dvůr)
Týnská
Týnská ulička
Dušní
U Milosrdných
Kozí
Bílkova
U Obecního Dvora
Josefov
Rámová
Vězeňská
V Kolkovně
Eliščy Krásnohorské
Široká
Pařížská
Salvátorská
Jáchymova
U Starého Hřbitova
Červená
Maiselova
Old Jewish Cemetery (Starý židovský hřbitov)
17 listopadu
Jan Palach Square (náměstí Jana Palacha)
Tram 18
Staroměstská
Kaprova
Valentinská
Žatecká
Alšovo nábřeží
Veleslavínova

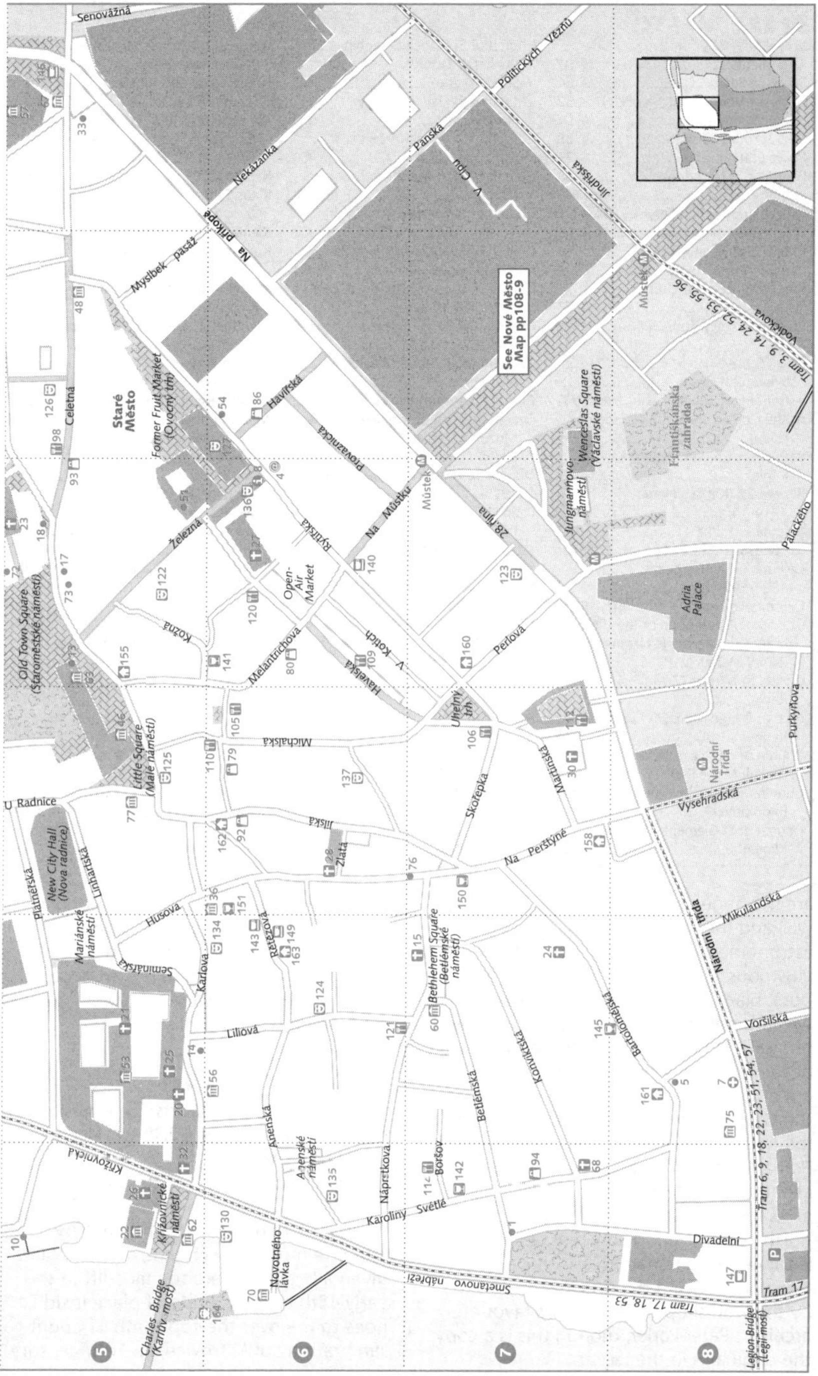
Senovážná
Politických Vězňů
Nekázanka
Panská
V Cípu
Jindřišská
Na příkopě
Mysbek pasáž
See Nové Město Map pp108-9
Můstek
Tram 3, 9, 14, 24, 52, 53, 55, 56
Vodičkova
Staré Město
Celetná
Former Fruit Market (Ovocný trh)
Havířská
Provaznická
Wenceslas Square (Václavské náměstí)
Jungmannovo náměstí
Františkánská zahrada
Železná
Na Můstku
Rytířská
Open-Air Market
28.října
Palackého
Old Town Square (Staroměstské náměstí)
Kožná
Melantrichova
V Kotcích
Havelská
Perlová
Adria Palace
Uhelný trh
Michalská
Little Square (Malé náměstí)
U Radnice
New City Hall (Nová radnice)
Linhartská
Platnéřská
Jilská
Skořepka
Martinská
Národní Třída
Purkyňova
Vyšehradská
Zlatá
Na Perštýně
Husova
Mariánské náměstí
Karlova
Řetězová
Bethlehem Square (Betlémské náměstí)
Národní třída
Mikulandská
Seminářská
Liliová
Konviktská
Bartolomějská
Voršilská
Anenská
Betlémská
Křižovnická
Anenské náměstí
Náprstkova
Boršov
Karoliny Světlé
Tram 6, 9, 18, 22, 23, 51, 54, 57
Křižovnické náměstí
Divadelní
Novotného lávka
Smetanovo nábřeží
Tram 17, 18, 53
Tram 17
Charles Bridge (Karlův most)
Legion Bridge (Legií most)

STARÉ MĚSTO

INFORMATION

Apartments.cz.............................1 A7
Bohemia Bagel.............................2 E4
Evropská Vodní Doprava (EVD)...3 B2
Internet Centre.............................4 D6
Lost & Found Office.....................5 B8
Police Station...............................6 E3
Polyclinic at Národní....................7 B8
Pragotur.............................(see 63)
Prague Information Service.....(see 63)
Prague Information Service.........8 D6
Prague Sightseeing Tours.............9 F4
Prague Venice.............................10 A5
Prague Wheelchair Users Organisation.............................11 F3
Precious Legacy Tours.................12 C4

SIGHTS & ACTIVITIES (pp87–103)

Astronomical Clock.......................13 D5
Astronomical Tower..............(see 53)
At the Golden Snake (U Zlatého Hada)..............................14 B5
Bethlehem Chapel (Betlémská Kaple)..............................15 B7
Bílkova 22 (Kafka's Home 1914-15)..............................16 D2
Celetná 2 (Kafka's Home 1888-89)..............................17 D5
Celetná 3 (Kafka's Home 1896-1907)..............................18 D5
Ceremonial Hall (Obradní Síň)...19 B3
Chapel of Assumption of the Virgin Mary (Vlašska Kaple Nanebevzetí Panny Marie)..............................20 B5
Chapel of Mirrors (Zrcadlová Kaple)..............................21 B5
Charles Bridge Museum (Muzeum Karlova Mostu)..............................22 A5
Church of Our Lady Before Týn Kostel (Panny Marie Před Týnem)...23 D5
Church of St Bartholomew (Kostel sv Bartoloměje)..............................24 B7
Church of St Clement (Kostel sv Klimenta)..............................25 B5
Church of St Francis Seraphinus (Kostel sv Františka Serafinského)..............................26 A5
Church of St Gall (Kostel sv Havla)..............................27 D6
Church of St Giles (Kostel sv Jiljí)..............................28 C6
Church of St James (Kostel sv Jakuba)..............................29 E4
Church of St Martin in the Wall (Kostel sv Martin ve Zdi).....30 C7
Church of St Nicholas (Kostel sv Mikuláše)..............................31 C4
Church of the Holy Saviour (Kostel Nejsvětějšího Spasitele).......32 A5
Commercial Bank (Komerční Banka)..............................33 F5
Convent of St Agnes (Klášter sv Anežky)..............................34 E2
Cubist Apartment Block..........35 C2
Czech Museum of Fine Arts (České Muzeum Výtvarných Umění)..............................36 C6
Dlouhá 16 (Kafka's Home 1915-17)..............................37 D3
Dům U Černého Medvěda (House at the Black Bear)..............................38 E4
Estates Theatre (Stavovské Divadlo)..........................(see 127)
Former Site of Pařížská 36 (Kafka's Home 1907-13)..............................39 B2
Franz Kafka Monument..........40 D3
Galerie Rudolfinum..............(see 69)
Goltz-Kinský Palace (Palác Kinských)..............................41 D4
Granovsky Palace..............................42 D4
High Synagogue (Vysoká Synagóga)..............................43 C3
Hotel Paříž..............................44 F4
House at the Golden Ring (Dům U Zlatého Prstenu)..............................45 D4
House at the Minute (Dům U Minuty, Kafka's Home 1889-96)..............................46 C5
House at the Stone Bell (Dům U Kamenného Zvonu)..............................47 D4
House of the Black Madonna (Dům U Černé Matky Boží)..............................48 E5
Jan Hus Statue..............................49 D4
Jewish Town Hall (Židovská Radnice)..............................50 C3
Karolinum (Univerzita Karlova)..51 D5
Klaus Synagogue (Klauzová Synagóga)..............................52 B3
Klementinum..............................53 B5
Kolowrat Theatre (Divadlo Kolowrat)..............................54 E6
Maisel Synagogue (Maiselova Synagóga)..............................55 C4
Marionette Museum (Muzeum Loutek)..............................56 B6
Municipal House (Obecní Dům)..57 F5
Museum of Czech Cubism (Muzeum Českého Kubismu) ....(see 48)
Museum of Decorative Arts (Umělecko-Průmyslové Muzeum)..............................58 B3
NoD Gallery..............................59 E3
Náprstek Museum (Náprstkovo Muzeum)..............................60 B7
Old Jewish Cemetery (Starý Židovský Hřbitov)..............................61 B3
Old Town Bridge Tower (Staroměstska Mostecká Věž)..............................62 A5
Old Town Hall (Staroměstska Radnice)..............................63 D5
Old-New Synagogue (Staronová Synagóga)..............................64 C3
Pařížská 1 (Former Kafka Family Home)..............................65 C4
Pinkas Synagogue (Pinkasova Synagóga)..............................66 B3
Powder Gate (Prašná Brána)......67 F5
Rotunda of the Holy Cross (Kaple sv Kříže)..............................68 A7
Rudolfinum..............................69 B3
Smetana Museum (Muzeum Bedřicha Smetany)..............................70 A6

are the huge rococo altar on the northern wall and the tomb of Tycho Brahe, the Danish astronomer who was one of Rudolf II's most illustrious 'consultants' (he died in 1601 of a burst bladder following a royal piss-up – he was too polite to leave the table to relieve himself). On the inside of the southern wall of the church are two small windows – they are now blocked off, but once opened into the church from rooms in the neighbouring house at Celetná 3, where the teenage Franz Kafka once lived (from 1896 to 1907; see the boxed text, p83).

As for the exterior of the church, the north portal overlooking Týnská ulička is topped by a remarkable 14th-century tympanum showing the Crucifixion, carved by the workshop of Charles IV's favourite architect Peter Parler, though this is a copy; the original is in the Lapidárium (p131).

The entrance to the church is along a passage from the square, through the second (from the left) of the Týn School's four arches. The Týn Church is an occasional concert venue and has a very grand-sounding pipe organ.

CHURCH OF ST JAMES Map pp88–9

Kostel sv Jakuba; Malá Štupartská 6; admission free; 9.30am-12.30pm & 2.30-4pm Mon-Sat; M Staroměstská

The great Gothic mass of the Church of St James, located to the east of Týn Courtyard, began in the 14th century as a Minorite monastery church, and was later given a beautiful baroque face-lift in the early 18th century. Pride of place inside goes to the over-the-top tomb of Count Jan Vratislav of Mitrovice, an 18th-century

STARÉ MĚSTO

Spanish Synagogue (Spanělská Synagóga)........ 71 D3
Týn School........ 72 D5
U Jednorožce (At the Unicorn).. 73 D5
U Radnice 5 (Kafka's Birthplace)........ 74 C4
Viola Building........ 75 B8
Viselec (Hanging Out) – David Černý Sculpture........ 76 C7
VJ Rott Building........ 77 C5

SHOPPING (pp143–51)
Anagram........ 78 E4
Art Deco Galerie........ 79 C6
Art Décoratif........ 80 D6
Arzenal........ 81 B4
Big Ben........ 82 E4
Bohème........ 83 D3
Botanicus........ 84 E4
Bríc á Brac........ 85 D4
Frey Wille........ 86 E6
Granát Turnov........ 87 E3
Keramika v Ungeltu........ 88 E4
Klara Nademlýnská........ 89 D3
Kotva........ 90 F4
Kubista........(see 48)
Le Patio Lifestyle........ 91 D3
Maximum Undergound........ 92 C6
Modernista........ 93 D5
Pavla & Olga........ 94 A7
Qubus........ 95 E3
TEG........ 96 D3

EATING (pp153–73)
Allegro........ 97 A4
Ambiente Pasta Fresca........ 98 E5
Ambiente Pizza Nuova........ 99 F3
Angel........ 100 D3
Ariana........ 101 E3
Bakeshop Praha........ 102 D3
Beas Vegetarian Dhaba........(see 153)
Casa Argentina........ 103 F3
Chez Marcel........ 104 E3
Country Life........ 105 C6
Culinaria........ 106 C7
Dahab........ 107 E2
DaNico........ 108 E3
Havelská Open-Air Market .. 109 D6
Khajuraho........ 110 C6
Kolkovna........ 111 D3
Káva Káva Káva........ 112 C7
La Provence........ 113 E4
Lehká Hlava........ 114 A7
Les Moules........ 115 C3
Michelské Pekářství........ 116 D4
Orange Moon........ 117 E3
Rasoi........ 118 E3
Red, Hot & Blues........ 119 F4
Siam-I-San........(see 81)
U Zavoje........ 120 D6
V Zátiší........ 121 B6

ENTERTAINMENT (pp193–203)
Agharta Jazz Centrum........ 122 D5
Batalion........ 123 D7
Blues Sklep........ 124 B6
Bohemia Ticket International (BTI)........ 125 C5
Celetná Theatre (Divadlo v Celetné)........ 126 E5
Church of St Francis........(see 34)
Dvořák Hall (Dvořakova Sín) (see 69)
Estates Theatre (Stavovské Divadlo)........ 127 E6
Estates Theatre Box Office....(see 54)
FOK Box Office........ 128 F4
Image Theatre........ 129 C4
Karlovy Lázně........ 130 A6
M1 Secret Lounge........ 131 E3
National Marionette Theatre (Narodní Divadlo Marionet)........ 132 B4
Prague Spring Box Office......(see 69)
Roxy........ 133 E3
Smetana Hall........(see 57)
Ta Fantastika........ 134 B6
Theatre on the Balustrade (Divadlo Na Zábradlí)........ 135 A6
Ticketcentrum........ 136 D6
USP Jazz Lounge........ 137 C6

DRINKING (pp175–91)
Bar & Books........ 138 D4
Bodeguita del Medio........ 139 B4
Café Café........ 140 D6
Čili Bar........ 141 D6
Duende........ 142 A7
Ebel Coffee House........ 143 B6
Ebel Coffee House........ 144 D4
Friends........ 145 B8
Grand Café Orient........(see 48)
Káva Káva Káva........(see 112)
Kavárna Obecní Dům........ 146 F5
Kavárna Slavia........ 147 A8
Kozička........ 148 D3
Literarni Kavarna Retezova........ 149 B6
Monarch Vinný Sklep........ 150 C7
Municipal House Café........(see 57)
U Medvídků........(see 158)
U Zlatého Tygra........ 151 C6

SPORTS & ACTIVITIES (pp205–10)
City Bike........ 152 F4
Fitness Týn........ 153 D4
Praha Bike........ 154 E3

SLEEPING (pp211–27)
Apostolic Residence........ 155 D5
Hotel Antik........ 156 E3
Hotel Josef........ 157 E3
Hotel U Medvídků........ 158 C7
Old Prague Hostel........ 159 F3
Perla Hotel........ 160 D7
Residence Karolina........ 161 B8
Savic Hotel........ 162 C6
U Zeleného Věnce........ 163 B6

TRANSPORT (pp241–5)
Boat Hire........ 164 A6
Boat Hire........ 165 A4
Europcar........ 166 C3

lord chancellor of Bohemia, found in the northern aisle.

In the midst of the gilt and stucco is a grisly memento: on the inside of the western wall (look up to the right as you enter) hangs a shrivelled human arm. Legend claims that when a thief tried to steal the jewels from the statue of the Virgin around the year 1400, the Virgin grabbed his wrist in such an iron grip that his arm had to be lopped off. (The truth may not be far behind: the church was a favourite of the guild of butchers, who may have administered their own justice.)

It's well worth a visit to enjoy St James' splendid pipe organ and famous acoustics. Recitals – free ones at 10.30am or 11am after Sunday Mass – and occasional concerts are not always advertised by ticket agencies, so check the noticeboard outside.

CHURCH OF ST NICHOLAS Map pp88–9

Kostel sv Mikuláše; Staroměstské náměstí; admission free; noon-4pm Mon, 10am-4pm Tue-Sat, noon-3pm Sun; M Staroměstská

The baroque wedding cake in the northwestern corner of Old Town Square is the Church of St Nicholas, built in the 1730s by Kilian Dientzenhofer (not to be confused with at least two other St Nicholas churches in Prague, including the Dientzenhofers' masterwork in Malá Strana; see p79). Considerable grandeur has been worked into a very tight space; originally the church was wedged behind the Old Town Hall's northern wing (destroyed in 1945). Chamber concerts are often held beneath its stucco decorations, a visually splendid (though acoustically mediocre) setting.

TRANSPORT: STARÉ MĚSTO

Metro Staroměstská station is a few minutes' walk northwest of Old Town Square, and Můstek station is five minutes' walk to the south.

Tram No trams run close to Old Town Square. Trams 17 and 18 run along the western edge of Staré Město near the river, while lines 5, 8 and 14 stop at Republic Square (náměstí Republiky), across the street from the Municipal House (Obecní dům). Trams 6, 9, 18, 21, 22 and 23 run along Národní třída on the southern edge of Staré Město.

GOLTZ-KINSKÝ PALACE Map pp88–9

Palác Kinských; ☎ 224 810 758; Staroměstské náměstí 12; adult/child 100/50Kč; 🕑 10am-6pm Tue-Sun; Ⓜ Staroměstská

Fronting the late-baroque Goltz-Kinský Palace is probably Prague's finest rococo façade, finished in 1765 by the redoubtable Kilian Dientzenhofer (see p48). Alfred Nobel, the Swedish inventor of dynamite, once stayed here; his crush on pacifist Bertha Kinský may have influenced him to establish the Nobel Peace Prize. Many living Praguers have a darker memory of the place, for it was from its balcony in February 1948 that Klement Gottwald proclaimed communist rule in Czechoslovakia.

There are Kafka connections here, too – young Franz once attended a school around the back of the building, and his father ran a shop in the premises now occupied by the Kafka Bookshop (see the boxed text, p83).

Today, the palace is home to a branch of the National Gallery, housing a collection of 17th- to 20th-century Czech landscape art and temporary art exhibitions.

HOUSE AT THE GOLDEN RING Map pp88–9

Dům U zlatého prstenu; ☎ 224 827 022; Týnská 6; adult/child 120/60Kč; 🕑 10am-6pm Tue-Sun; Ⓜ Staroměstská

The restored Renaissance House at the Golden Ring, located at the corner of Týnská just outside the western entrance to Týn courtyard, contains another branch of the Prague City Gallery; the original painted ceiling beams can still be seen in some of the rooms. It was closed for reconstruction work at the time of research, but was due to reopen soon with a collection of Central European art from the second half of the 20th century.

HOUSE AT THE STONE BELL Map pp88–9

Dům U kamenného zvonu; ☎ 224 827 526; Staroměstské náměstí 13; adult/child 120/60Kč; 🕑 10am-6pm Tue-Sun; Ⓜ Staroměstská

Next door to the Goltz-Kinský Palace is this elegant medieval building, its 14th-century Gothic dignity rescued from a second-rate baroque renovation. During restoration in the 1980s the stucco façade was stripped away to reveal the original stonework; the eponymous stone bell is on the building's corner. Inside, two restored Gothic chapels now serve as branches of the Prague City Gallery (with changing exhibits of modern art) and as chamber-concert venues.

OLD TOWN HALL Map pp88–9

Staroměstská radnice; ☎ 12444; Staroměstské náměstí 1; separate tickets for guided tour & admission to tower, each adult/child 70/50Kč; 🕑 11am-6pm Mon, 9am-6pm Tue-Sun Apr-Oct, 9am-5pm Tue-Sat, 11am-5pm Sun Nov-Mar; Ⓜ Staroměstská

Prague's Old Town Hall, founded in 1338, is a hotchpotch of medieval buildings acquired piecemeal over the centuries, presided over by a tall Gothic tower with a splendid Astronomical Clock (see the boxed text, p94). The main entrance is to the left of the clock; beyond that is the House at the Minute (dům U minuty), an arcaded building covered with Renaissance *sgraffito* – Franz Kafka lived here (1889–96) as a child just before the building was bought by the town council.

As well as housing the Old Town's main tourist information office, the town hall has several historic attractions, and hosts art exhibitions (adult/concession 60/40Kč) on the ground floor and the 2nd floor. The guided tour takes you through the council chamber and assembly room, with beautiful mosaics dating from the 1930s, before visiting the Gothic chapel and taking a look at the inner workings of the 12 apostles who parade above the Astronomical Clock every hour. The tour is rounded off with a trip through the Romanesque and Gothic cellars beneath the building. However, the town hall's best feature is the view from the 60m-tall tower, which is well worth the climb (there's also a lift).

The area outside the town hall is one of the most crowded corners of Old Town Square, especially during the hourly show put on by the Astronomical Clock. Around the corner to the right, a plaque on the building's eastern face lists the 27 Protestant nobles who were beheaded

THE MISSING MONUMENTS

Prague witnessed several profound changes of political regime during the 20th century: from Habsburg Empire to independent Czechoslovak Republic in 1918; to Nazi Protectorate from 1938 to 1945; to communist state in 1948; and back to democratic republic in 1989.

Each change was accompanied by widespread renaming of city streets and squares to reflect the heroes of the new regime. The square in front of the Rudolfinum in Staré Město, for example, has been known variously as Smetanovo náměstí (Smetana Square; 1918–39); Mozartplatz (Mozart Square; 1939–45); náměstí Krasnoarmějců (Red Army Square; 1948–89); and náměstí Jana Palacha (Jan Palach Square; 1989–present).

This renaming was often followed by the removal of monuments erected by the previous regime. Here are four of Prague's most prominent 'missing monuments'.

The Missing Virgin

If you look at the ground in Old Town Square (Staroměstské náměstí; Map pp88–9) about 50m south of the Jan Hus monument, you'll see a circular stone slab set among the cobblestones at the far end of the brass strip marking the Prague Meridian (p87). This was the site of a Marian column (a pillar bearing a statue of the Virgin Mary), erected in 1650 in celebration of the Habsburg victory over the Swedes in 1648. It was surrounded by figures of angels crushing and beating down demons – a rather unsubtle symbol of a resurgent Catholic Church defeating the Protestant Reformation.

The column was toppled by a mob – who saw it as a symbol of Habsburg repression – on 3 November 1918, five days after the declaration of Czechoslovak independence. Its remains can be seen in the Lapidárium (p131).

The Missing General

A prominent victim of the change of regime in 1918 was the statue of Field Marshal Václav Radecký (1766–1858) – or Count Josef Radetzky, to give him his Austrian name – that once stood in the lower part of Malá Strana Square (Malostranské náměstí; Map pp76–7); it is now in the Lapidárium (p131). Although Radecký was a Czech, his fame derived from leading the Habsburg armies to victory against Napoleon and crushing the Italians at the battles of Custoza and Novara. (Composer Johann Strauss the Elder wrote the *Radetzky March* in his honour.) The Starbucks coffee shop here was once called the Radetzky Café.

The Missing Dictator

If you stand on Old Town Square (Map pp88–9) and look north along the arrow-straight avenue of Pařížská you will see, on a huge terrace at the far side of Čechův most, a giant metronome. If the monumental setting seems out of scale that's because the terrace was designed to accommodate the world's biggest statue of Stalin. Unveiled in 1955 – two years after Stalin's death – the 30m-high, 14,000-tonne colossus showed Uncle Joe at the head of two lines of communist heroes, Czech on one side, Soviet on the other. Cynical Praguers used to constant food shortages quickly nicknamed it *fronta na maso* (the meat queue).

The monument was dynamited in 1962, in deference to Khrushchev's attempt to airbrush Stalin out of history. The demolition crew was instructed, 'it must go quickly, there mustn't be much of a bang, and it should be seen by as few people as possible'. The Museum of Communism (p107) has a superb photo of the monument – and of its destruction.

The Missing Tank

Kinský Square (náměstí Kinských; Map pp76–7), at the southern edge of Malá Strana, was until 1989 known as náměstí Sovětských tankistů (Soviet Tank Crews Square), named in memory of the Soviet soldiers who 'liberated' Prague on 9 May 1945. For many years a Soviet T-34 tank – allegedly the first to enter the city – squatted menacingly atop a pedestal here (in fact it was a later Soviet 'gift').

In 1991 artist David Černý (p39) decided that the tank was an inappropriate monument to the Soviet soldiers and painted it bright pink. The authorities had it painted green again, and charged Černý with a crime against the state. This infuriated many parliamentarians, 12 of whom repainted the tank pink. Their parliamentary immunity saved them from arrest and secured Černý's release.

After complaints from the Soviet Union the tank was removed. Its former setting is now occupied by a circular fountain surrounded by park benches; the vast granite slab in the centre is split by a jagged fracture, perhaps symbolic of a break with the past. The tank still exists, and is still pink – it's at the Military Museum in Lešany, near Týnec nad Sázavou, 30km south of Prague.

THE ASTRONOMICAL CLOCK

The Old Town Hall tower was given a clock in 1410 by the master clockmaker Mikuláš of Kadaně; this was improved in 1490 by one Master Hanuš, producing the mechanical marvel you see today. Legend has it that Hanuš was afterwards blinded so he could not duplicate the work elsewhere, and in revenge crawled up into the clock and disabled it. (Documents from the time suggest that he carried on as clock-master for years – unblinded – although the clock apparently didn't work properly until it was repaired in about 1570.)

Four figures beside the clock represent the deepest civic anxieties of 15th-century Praguers: Vanity (with a mirror), Greed (with his money bag; originally a Jewish moneylender, but cosmetically altered after WWII), Death and Pagan Invasion (represented by a Turk). The four figures below these are the Chronicler, Angel, Astronomer and Philosopher.

On the hour, Death rings a bell and inverts his hourglass, and the 12 Apostles parade past the windows above the clock, nodding to the crowd. On the left side are Paul (with a sword and a book), Thomas (lance), Jude (book), Simon (saw), Bartholomew (book) and Barnabas (parchment); on the right side are Peter (with a key), Matthew (axe), John (snake), Andrew (cross), Philip (cross) and James (mallet). At the end, a cock crows and the hour is rung.

On the upper face, the disk in the middle of the fixed part depicts the world known at the time – with Prague at the centre, of course. The gold sun traces a circle through the blue zone of day, the brown zone of dusk (*Crepusculum* in Latin) in the west *(Occasus)*, the black disc of night, and dawn *(Aurora)* in the east *(Ortus)*. From this the hours of sunrise and sunset can be read. The curved lines with black Arabic numerals are part of an astrological 'star clock'.

The sun arm points to the hour (without any daylight-saving time adjustment) on the Roman-numeral ring; the top XII is noon and the bottom XII is midnight. The outer ring, with Gothic numerals, reads traditional 24-hour Bohemian time, counted from sunset; the number 24 is always opposite the sunset hour on the fixed (inner) face.

The moon, with its phases shown, also traces a path through the zones of day and night, riding on the offset moving ring. On the ring you can also read which houses of the zodiac the sun and moon are in. The hand with a little star at the end of it indicates sidereal (stellar) time.

The calendar wheel beneath all this astronomical wizardry, with 12 seasonal scenes celebrating rural Bohemian life, is a duplicate of one painted in 1866 by the Czech Revivalist Josef Mánes. You can have a close look at the beautiful original in the Prague City Museum (p105). Most of the dates around the calendar wheel are marked with the names of their associated saints; 6 July honours Jan Hus.

here in 1621 after the Battle of Bílá Hora; white crosses on the ground mark where the deed was done. Another plaque commemorates a critical WWII victory by Red Army and Czechoslovak units at Dukla Pass in Slovakia, and yet another the Czech partisans who died during the Prague Rising on 8 May 1945. If you look at the neogothic eastern gable, you can see that its right-hand edge is ragged – the wing that once extended north from here was blown up by the Nazis in 1945, on the day before the Soviet army marched into the city.

TÝN COURTYARD Map pp88–9

Týnský dvůr; entrances on Malá Štupartská & Týnská ulička; admission free; 24hr; M Staroměstská

This picturesque courtyard tucked behind the Church of Our Lady Before Týn was originally a sort of medieval caravanserai – a fortified hotel, trading centre and customs office for visiting foreign merchants. First established as long ago as the 11th century, it's still often called by its German name, Ungelt ('customs duty'), and was busiest and most prosperous during the reign of Charles IV. Now attractively renovated, the courtyard houses shops, restaurants and hotels.

In the northwest corner is the 16th-century Granovsky Palace, with an elegant Renaissance loggia, and *sgraffito* and painted decoration depicting biblical and mythological scenes. Across the yard, to the right of the V Ungeltu shop, is dům U černého medvěda (House at the Black Bear), whose baroque façade is adorned with a statue of St John of Nepomuk above the door and a bear in chains on the corner, a reminder of the kind of 'entertainment' that once took place here.

JOSEFOV

Half-a-dozen historic synagogues, a town hall and the Old Jewish Cemetery are all that survive of the once-thriving Jewish quarter of Josefov – the slice of Staré Město bounded by Kaprova, Dlouhá and Kozí. Most of the district's buildings were demolished around the turn of the 20th century, when massive redevelopment saw the old slums replaced with expensive new apartments.

When the ghetto was cleared at the turn of the 20th century, the broad boulevard of

Pařížská třída (Paris Ave) was driven in a straight line through the heart of the old slums. This was a time of widespread infatuation with the French Art Nouveau style, and the avenue and its side streets were lined with elegant apartment buildings adorned with stained glass and sculptural flourishes. In recent years Pařížská has become a glitzy shopping strand, studded with expensive brand names such as Dior, Louis Vuitton and Fabergé.

Jan Palach Square (náměstí Jana Palacha; Map pp88–9) is named after the young Charles University student who in January 1969 set himself alight in Wenceslas Square in protest against the Soviet invasion (see the boxed text, p29). On the eastern side of the square, beside the entrance to the philosophy faculty building where Palach was a student, is a bronze memorial plaque with a ghostly death mask.

Presiding over the square is the Rudolfinum, home to the Czech Philharmonic Orchestra. This and the National Theatre, both designed by architects Josef Schulz and Josef Zítek, are considered Prague's finest neo-Renaissance buildings. Completed in 1884, the Rudolfinum served between the wars as the seat of the Czechoslovak parliament, and during WWII as the administrative offices of the occupying Nazis (see the boxed text, below).

CONVENT OF ST AGNES Map pp88–9

Klášter sv Anežky; ☎ 224 810 628; www.ngprague.cz; U Milosrdných 17; adult/child 150/80Kč; 10am-6pm Tue-Sun; 5, 8, 14

In the northeastern corner of Staré Město is the former Convent of St Agnes, Prague's oldest surviving Gothic building. The 1st-floor rooms hold the National Gallery's permanent collection of medieval art (1200–1550) from Bohemia and Central Europe.

In 1234 the Franciscan Order of the Poor Clares was founded by Přemysl king Wenceslas I, who made his sister Anežka (Agnes) its first abbess. Agnes was beatified in the 19th century and, with hardly accidental timing, Pope John Paul II canonised her as St Agnes of Bohemia just weeks before the revolutionary events of November 1989.

In the 16th century the buildings were handed over to the Dominicans, and after Joseph II dissolved the monasteries, they became a squatters' paradise. It is only since the 1980s that the convent complex has been restored and renovated. In addition to the 13th-century cloister, you can visit the French Gothic Church of the Holy Saviour, which contains the tombs of St Agnes and of Wenceslas I's Queen Cunegund. Alongside this is the smaller Church of St Francis, where Wenceslas I is buried; part of its ruined nave now serves as a chilly concert hall.

The gallery is fully wheelchair accessible, and the ground-floor cloister has a tactile presentation of 12 casts of medieval sculptures with explanatory text in Braille.

MUSEUM OF DECORATIVE ARTS

Map pp88–9

Umělecko-průmyslové muzeum; ☎ 251 093 111; www.upm.cz; 17.listopadu 2; permanent collection adult/child 80/40Kč, temporary exhibitions 80/40Kč, combined 120/70Kč; 10am-7pm Tue, to 6pm Wed-Sun; M Staroměstská

This museum opened in 1900 as part of a European movement to encourage a return to the aesthetic values sacrificed to the Industrial Revolution. Its four halls are a feast for the eyes, full of 16th- to 19th-century artefacts such as furniture, tapestries, porcelain and a fabulous collection of glasswork.

MENDELSSOHN IS ON THE ROOF

The roof of the Rudolfinum (p97) is decorated with statues of famous composers. It housed the German administration during WWII, when the Nazi authorities ordered that the statue of Felix Mendelssohn – who was Jewish – should be removed.

In *Mendelssohn is on the Roof*, a darkly comic novella about life in wartime Prague, the Jewish writer Jiří Weil weaves a wryly amusing story around this true-life event. The two Czech labourers given the task of removing the statue can't tell which of the two dozen or so figures is Mendelssohn – they all look the same, as far as they can tell. Their Czech boss, remembering his lectures in 'racial science', tells them that Jews have big noses. 'Whichever one has the biggest conk, that's the Jew.'

So the workmen single out the statue with the biggest nose – 'Look! That one over there with the beret. None of the others has a nose like his' – then sling a noose around its neck and start to haul it over. As their boss walks across to check on their progress, he gapes in horror as they start to topple the figure of the only composer on the roof that he does recognise – Richard Wagner.

The neo-Renaissance building is itself a work of art, the façade decorated with reliefs representing the various decorative arts and the Bohemian towns famous for them. The staircase leading up from the entrance hall to the main exhibition on the 2nd floor is beautifully decorated with colourful ceramics, stained-glass windows and frescoes representing graphic arts, metalworking, ceramics, glass-making and goldsmithing. It leads to the ornate Votive Hall, which houses the Karlštejn Treasure, a hoard of 14th-century silver found hidden in the walls of Karlštejn Castle (see p230) in the 19th century.

To the right is a textiles exhibit and a fascinating collection of clocks, watches, sundials and astronomical devices, but the good stuff is to the left in the glass and ceramics hall – exquisite baroque glassware, a fine collection of Meissen porcelain and a range of Czech glass, ceramics and furniture in Cubist, Art Nouveau and Art Deco styles, the best pieces being by Josef Gočár and Pavel Janák. The graphic arts section has some fine Art Nouveau posters, and the gold and jewellery exhibit contains some real curiosities – amid the Bohemian garnet brooches, 14th-century chalices, diamond-studded monstrances and Art Nouveau silverware you will find a Chinese rhino-horn vase in a silver mount, a delicate nautilus shell engraved with battle scenes, and a silver watchcase in the shape of a skull.

Labels are in Czech, but detailed English and French texts are available in each room. What you see is only a fraction of the collection; other bits appear now and then in single-theme exhibitions.

PRAGUE JEWISH MUSEUM Map pp88–9

Židovské muzeum Praha; ☎ 222 317 191; www.jewishmuseum.cz; Reservation Centre, U Starého Hřbitova 3a; ordinary ticket adult/child 300/200Kč, combined ticket 480/320Kč; 9am-6pm Sun-Fri Apr-Oct, to 4.30pm Sun-Fri Nov-Mar, closed on Jewish hols; Ⓜ Staroměstská

In one of the most grotesquely ironic acts of WWII, the Nazis took over the management of the Prague Jewish Museum – first established in 1906 to preserve artefacts from synagogues that were demolished during the slum clearances in Josefov around the turn of the 20th century – with the intention of creating a 'museum of an extinct race'. They shipped in materials and objects from destroyed Jewish communities throughout Bohemia and Moravia, helping to amass what is probably the world's biggest collection of sacred Jewish artefacts and a moving memorial to seven centuries of oppression.

The museum consists of six Jewish monuments clustered together in Josefov: the Maisel Synagogue; the Pinkas Synagogue; the Spanish Synagogue; the Klaus Synagogue; the Ceremonial Hall; and the Old Jewish Cemetery. There is also the Old-New Synagogue, which is still used for religious services, and requires a separate ticket or additional fee. If you are pressed for time, the highlights are the Old-New Synagogue and the Old Jewish Cemetery.

An ordinary ticket gives admission to all six main monuments; a combined ticket includes the Old-New Synagogue as well. Admission to the Old-New Synagogue alone costs 200/140Kč. You can buy tickets at the Reservation Centre (see address preceding), the Pinkas Synagogue, the Spanish Synagogue and the shop opposite the entrance to the Old-New Synagogue. Queues tend to be shortest at the Spanish Synagogue.

Completed around 1270, the Old-New Synagogue (Staronová synagóga; Červená 2) is Europe's oldest working synagogue and one of Prague's earliest Gothic buildings. You step down into it because it predates the raising of Staré Město's street level in medieval times to guard against floods. Men must cover their heads (a hat or bandanna will do; paper yarmulkes are handed out at the entrance). Around the central chamber are an entry hall, a winter prayer hall and the room from which women watch the men-only services. The interior, with a pulpit surrounded by a 15th-century wrought-iron grill, looks much as it would have 500 years ago. The 17th-century scriptures on the walls were recovered from beneath a later 'restoration'. On the eastern wall is the Holy Ark that holds the Torah scrolls. In a glass case at the rear, little light bulbs beside the names of the prominent deceased are lit on their death days.

With its steep roof and Gothic gables, this looks like a place with secrets, and at least one version of the Golem legend ends here. Left alone on the Sabbath, the creature runs amok; Rabbi Loew rushes out in the middle of a service, removes its magic talisman and carries the lifeless body into the synagogue's attic, where some insist it still lies.

Across the narrow street is the elegant 16th-century High Synagogue (Vysoká synagóga), so-called because its prayer hall (closed to the public) is upstairs. Around the corner is the Jewish Town Hall (Židovská radnice), also closed to the public, built by Mordechai Maisel in 1586 and given its rococo façade in the 18th century. It has a clock tower with one Hebrew face where the hands, like the Hebrew script, run 'backwards'.

The handsome Pinkas Synagogue (Pinkasova synagóga; Široká 3) was built in 1535 and used for worship until 1941. After WWII it was converted into a memorial, with wall after wall inscribed with the names, birth dates, and dates of disappearance of the 77,297 Czech victims of the Nazis. It also has a collection of paintings and drawings by children held in the Terezín concentration camp (see p234) during WWII.

The Pinkas Synagogue contains the entrance to the Old Jewish Cemetery (Starý židovský hřbitov; entrance on Široká), Europe's oldest surviving Jewish graveyard. Founded in the early 15th century, it has a palpable atmosphere of mourning even after two centuries of disuse (it was closed in 1787); however, remember that this is one of Prague's most popular sights, so if you're hoping to have a moment of quiet contemplation you'll probably be disappointed. Around 12,000 crumbling stones (some brought from other, long-gone cemeteries) are heaped together, but beneath them are perhaps 100,000 graves, piled in layers because of the lack of space.

The most prominent graves, marked by pairs of marble tablets with a 'roof' between them, are near the main gate; they include those of Mordechai Maisel and Rabbi Loew. The oldest stone (now replaced by a replica) is that of Avigdor Karo, a chief rabbi and court poet to Wenceslas IV, who died in 1439. Most stones bear the name of the deceased and his or her father, the date of death (and sometimes of burial), and poetic texts. Elaborate markers from the 17th and 18th centuries are carved with bas-reliefs, some of them indicating the deceased's occupation – look out for a pair of hands marking the grave of a pianist.

Since the cemetery was closed, Jewish burials have taken place at the Jewish Cemetery (p125) in Žižkov. There are remnants of another old Jewish burial ground at the foot of the TV Tower in Žižkov (see p128).

You exit the cemetery through a gate between the Klaus Synagogue and the Ceremonial Hall (Obřadní síň), both of which house exhibitions on Jewish forms of worship, family ceremonies and traditions such as birth, circumcision, bar mitzvah and marriage.

A block to the southeast lies the neo-gothic Maisel Synagogue (Maiselova synagóga; Maiselova 10), which replaced a Renaissance original built by Mordechai Maisel, mayor of the Jewish community, in 1592. It houses an exhibit on the history of the Jews in Bohemia and Moravia from the 10th to the 18th centuries, with displays of ceremonial silver, textiles, prints and books.

Finally, about two blocks east of the Maisel is the Spanish Synagogue (Španělská synagóga; Vězeňská 1). Named after its striking Moorish interior and dating from 1868, its exhibit continues the story of the Jews in the Czech Republic from emancipation to the present day.

RUDOLFINUM Map pp88–9

☎ 227 059 270; www.rudolfinum.cz; Alšovo nábřeží 12; 🚊 17, 18

This complex of concert halls and offices built in neo-Renaissance style in the late 19th century is the home turf of the Czech Philharmonic Orchestra – the impressive Dvořák Hall, its stage dominated by a vast organ, is one of the main concert venues for the Prague Spring festival (see the boxed text, p202). The building served as the seat of the Czechoslovak parliament from 1918 to 1938.

The northern part of the complex (entrance facing the river) houses the Galerie Rudolfinum (☎ 227 059 205; www.galerierudolfinum.cz; adult/child 120/60Kč; 🕑 10am-6pm Tue-Sun), a gallery that specialises in changing exhibitions of contemporary art. There's also a sumptuous café with tables ranged amid the Corinthian splendour of the Column Hall.

ALONG THE ROYAL WAY

The Royal Way (Královská cesta) was the ancient processional route followed by Czech kings on their way to St Vitus Cathedral for coronation. The route leads from the Powder Gate (Prašná brána; p100) along Celetná, through Old Town Square and Little Square (Malé náměstí), along Karlova and across Charles Bridge to Malá Strana Square (Malostranské náměstí), before climbing up Nerudova to the castle. The only procession that makes its way along these streets today is the daily crush of tourists shouldering their way through a gauntlet of gaudy souvenir shops and bored-looking leaflet touts. For a less crowded alternative route, see the Walking Tour on p102.

Celetná, leading from the Powder Gate to Old Town Square, is an open-air museum of pastel-painted baroque façades covering Gothic frames resting on Romanesque foundations, deliberately buried to raise Staré Město above the floods of the Vltava River. But the most interesting building – Josef Gočár's delightful House of the Black Madonna (dům U černé Matky Boží), now the Museum of Czech Cubism (p100) – dates only from 1912.

Little Square (Malé náměstí; Map pp88–9), the southwestern extension of Old Town Square, has a Renaissance fountain with a 16th-century wrought-iron grill. Here several fine baroque and neo-Renaissance exteriors adorn some of Staré Město's oldest structures. The most colourful is the VJ Rott Building (1890), decorated with wall paintings by Mikulaš Aleš.

A dog-leg from the southwestern corner of the square leads to narrow, cobbled Karlova (Charles St; Map pp88–9), which continues as far as Charles Bridge – this section is often choked with tourist crowds. On the corner of Liliová is the house called At the Golden Snake (U zlatého hada), the site of Prague's first coffee house, opened in 1708 by an Armenian named Deomatus Damajan.

Karlova sidles along the massive southern wall of the Klementinum (right) before emerging at the riverside on Křižovnické náměstí. On the north side of the square is the 17th-century Church of St Francis Seraphinus (kostel sv Františka Serafínského), its dome decorated with a fresco of the Last Judgment. It belongs to the Order of Knights of the Cross, the only Bohemian order of Crusaders still in existence.

Just south of the bridge, at the site of the former Old Town mill, is Novotného lávka (Map pp88–9), a riverside terrace full of sunny, overpriced *vinárny* (wine bars) with great views of the bridge and castle, its far end dominated by a statue of composer Bedřich Smetana.

CHARLES BRIDGE MUSEUM Map pp88–9

Muzeum Karlova mostu; ☎ 739 309 551; www.muzeumkarlovamostu.cz; Křižovnické náměstí 3; adult/concession 150/100Kč; 🕑 10am-8pm Apr-Oct, to 6pm Nov-Mar; Ⓜ Staroměstská

Founded in the 13th century, the Order of the Knights of the Cross with the Red Star were the guardians of Judith Bridge (and its successor Charles Bridge), with their 'mother house' at the Church of St Francis Seraphinus on Křižovnické náměstí. This new museum, housed in the order's headquarters, covers the history of Prague's most famous landmark, with displays on ancient bridge-building techniques, masonry and carpentry, and models of both Judith and Charles Bridges. In Room 16 you can descend into the foundations of the building to see some of the original stonework of Judith Bridge (dating from 1172), but perhaps the most impressive exhibits are the old photographs of flood damage to Charles Bridge in 1890, when three arches collapsed and were swept away.

OLD TOWN BRIDGE TOWER Map pp88–9

Staroměstská mostecká věž; Charles Bridge; adult/child 70/50Kč; 🕑 10am-10pm May-Sep, to 7pm Apr & Oct, to 6pm Mar, to 5pm Nov-Feb; Ⓜ Staroměstská

Perched at the eastern end of Charles Bridge, this elegant late-14th-century tower was built not only as a fortification but also as a triumphal arch marking the entrance to the Old Town. Like the bridge itself, it was designed by Peter Parler and incorporates many symbolic elements. Here, at the end of the Thirty Years' War, an invading Swedish army was finally repulsed by a band of students and Jewish ghetto residents.

On the 1st floor there's a small exhibition and a video explaining the astronomical and astrological symbolism of Charles Bridge and the bridge tower, while the 2nd floor has a display of photographs recording the restoration of the tower's east face, completed in 2007. The main justification for paying the admission fee, however, is the amazing view from the top of the tower.

CZECH MUSEUM OF FINE ARTS Map pp88–9

České muzeum výtvarných umění; ☎ 222 220 218; www.cmvu.cz; Husova 19-21; adult/child 50/20Kč; 🕑 10am-6pm Tue-Sun; Ⓜ Staroměstská

Housed in three beautifully restored Romanesque and Gothic buildings, this often-overlooked little gallery stages temporary exhibitions of 20th-century and contemporary art, though it's worth the admission fee just for a look at the architecture.

KLEMENTINUM Map pp88–9

☎ 222 220 879; www.klementinum.cz; entrances to courtyards on Křížovnická, Karlova & Mariánské náměstí; Ⓜ Staroměstská

When the Habsburg emperor Ferdinand I invited the Jesuits to Prague in 1556 to boost the power of the Roman Catholic Church in Bohemia, they selected one of the city's choicest pieces of real estate and in 1587 set to work on the Church of the Holy Saviour (kostel Nejsvětějšího Spasitele), Prague's flagship of the Counter-Reformation. The western façade faces Charles Bridge, its sooty stone saints glaring down at the traffic jam of trams and tourists on Křížovnické náměstí.

After gradually buying up most of the adjacent neighbourhood, the Jesuits started building their college, the Klementinum, in 1653. By the time of its completion a century later it was the largest building in the city after Prague Castle. When the Jesuits fell out with the pope in 1773, it became part of Charles University.

The Klementinum today is a vast complex of beautiful baroque and rococo halls, now occupied by the Czech National Library. Most of the buildings are closed to the public, but you can take a 50-minute guided tour of the baroque Library Hall & Astronomical Tower and the Chapel of Mirrors (adult/child 220/140Kč; 10am-7pm, hourly Mon-Thu, every 30min Fri-Sun). The chapel dates from the 1720s and is an ornate confection of gilded stucco, marbled columns, fancy frescoes and ceiling mirrors – think baroque on steroids. Concerts of classical music are held here daily (tickets are available at most ticket agencies).

There are two other interesting churches in the Klementinum. The Church of St Clement (kostel sv Klimenta; services 8.30am & 10am Sun), lavishly redecorated in the baroque style from 1711 to 1715 to plans by Kilian Dientzenhofer, is now a Greek Catholic chapel. Conservatively dressed visitors are welcome to attend the services. And then there's the elliptical, Italian Chapel of the Assumption of the Virgin Mary (Vlašská kaple Nanebevzetí Panny Marie), built in 1600 for the Italian artisans who worked on the Klementinum (it's still technically the property of the Italian government).

MARIONETTE MUSEUM Map pp88–9

Muzeum loutek; 222 228 511; www.puppetart.com; Karlova 12; adult/child 100/50Kč; noon-8pm; 17, 18

Rooms peopled with a multitude of authentic, colourful marionettes illustrate the evolution of this wonderful Czech tradition from the late-17th to early-19th centuries. The star attractions are the Czech children's favourites, Spejbl and Hurvínek – kids and adults alike can enjoy the Czech equivalent of Punch and Judy at the Spejbl & Hurvínek Theatre (p203).

MUNICIPAL HOUSE Map pp88–9

Obecní dům; 222 002 101; www.obecni-dum.cz; náměstí Republiky 5; guided tours adult/child 160/110Kč; bldg 7.30am-11pm, information centre 10am-7pm; M Náměstí Republiky

Prague's most exuberant and sensual building stands on the site of the Royal Court, seat of Bohemia's kings from 1383 to 1483 (when Vladislav II moved to Prague Castle), which was demolished at the end of the 19th century. Between 1906 and 1912 the Municipal House was built in its place – a lavish joint effort by around 30 leading artists of the day, creating a cultural centre that was the architectural climax of the Czech National Revival. Restored in the 1990s after decades of neglect during the communist era, the entire building was a labour of love, every detail of design and decoration carefully considered, every painting and sculpture loaded with symbolism.

The mosaic above the entrance, *Homage to Prague*, is set between sculptures representing the oppression and rebirth of the Czech people; other sculptures ranged along the top of the façade represent history, literature, painting, music and architecture. You pass beneath a wrought-iron and stained-glass canopy into an interior that is Art Nouveau down to the doorknobs (you can look around the lobby and the downstairs bar for free). The restaurant and the *kavárna* (café; see the boxed text, p181) flanking the entrance are like walk-in museums of Art Nouveau design.

Upstairs are half a dozen sumptuously decorated halls and assembly rooms that you can visit by guided tour (90 minutes, three or four per day), which can be booked at the building's information centre (through the main entrance, and around to the left of the stairs).

First stop on the tour is Smetana Hall, Prague's biggest concert hall, with seating for 1200 ranged beneath an Art Nouveau glass dome. The stage is framed by sculptures representing the Vyšehrad legend (to the right) and Slavonic dances (to the left).

Several impressive official apartments follow, but the highlight of the tour is the octagonal Lord Mayor's Hall (Primatorský sál), whose windows overlook the main entrance.

Every aspect of its decoration was designed by Alfons Mucha, who also painted the superbly moody murals that adorn the walls and ceiling. Above you is an allegory of *Slavic Concord*, with intertwined figures representing the various Slavic peoples watched over by the Czech eagle. Figures from Czech history and mythology, representing the civic virtues, occupy the spaces between the eight arches, including Jan Hus as *Spravedlnost* (justice), Jan Žižka as *Bojovnost* (military prowess) and the Chodové (medieval Bohemian border guards) as beady-eyed *Ostražitost* (vigilance).

On 28 October 1918 an independent Czechoslovak Republic was declared in Smetana Hall, and in November 1989 meetings took place here between Civic Forum and the Jakeš regime. The Prague Spring (Pražské jaro) music festival (see the boxed text, p202) always opens on 12 May, the anniversary of Smetana's death, with a procession from Vyšehrad to the Municipal House followed by a gala performance of his symphonic cycle *Má Vlast* (My Country) in Smetana Hall.

MUSEUM OF CZECH CUBISM Map pp88–9

Muzeum Českého kubismu; ☎ 224 211 746; Ovocný trh 19; adult/child 100/50Kč; 10am-6pm Tue-Sun; M Náměstí Republiky

Though dating from 1912, Josef Gočár's House of the Black Madonna (dům U černé Matky Boží) – Prague's first and finest example of Cubist architecture – still looks modern and dynamic. It now houses three floors of remarkable Cubist paintings and sculpture, as well as furniture, ceramics and glassware in Cubist designs.

POWDER GATE Map pp88–9

Prašná brána; ☎ 724 063 723; Na Příkopě; adult/child 70/50Kč; 10am-6pm mid-Mar–Oct; M Náměstí Republiky

The 65m-tall Powder Gate was begun in 1475 on the site of one of Staré Město's original 13 gates. Built during the reign of King Vladislav II Jagiello as a ceremonial entrance to the city, it was left unfinished after the king moved from the neighbouring Royal Court to Prague Castle in 1483. The name comes from its use as a gunpowder magazine in the 18th century. Josef Mocker rebuilt and decorated it and put up a steeple between 1875 and 1886, giving it its neogothic icing.

The tower houses exhibitions on the history of the Royal Court (see Municipal House, p99) and the towers that once punctuated Prague's town walls, but the main attraction is the view from the top.

SMETANA MUSEUM Map pp88–9

Muzeum Bedřicha Smetany; ☎ 222 220 082; Novotného lávka 1; adult/child 50/25Kč; 10am-noon & 12.30-5pm Wed-Mon; M Staroměstská

This small museum is devoted to Bedřich Smetana, Bohemia's favourite composer. It isn't that interesting unless you're a Smetana fan, and has only limited labelling in English, but there's a good exhibit on popular culture's feverish response to Smetana's opera *The Bartered Bride* – it seems Smetana was the Andrew Lloyd Webber of his day.

HAVELSKÉ MĚSTO

In about 1230 a market district named Havelské Město (St Gall's Town; Map pp88–9), named after the 7th-century Irish monk who helped introduce Christianity to Europe, was laid out for the pleasure of the German merchants invited to Prague by Wenceslas I.

Modern-day Rytířská and Havelská streets were at that time a single plaza surrounded by arcaded merchants' houses. Specialist markets included those for coal (Uhelný trh) at the western end of the plaza and for fruit (Ovocný trh) at the eastern end. In the 15th century an island of stalls was built down the middle.

All that remains of St Gall's market today is the touristy open-air market on Havelská and the clothes hawkers in adjacent V Kotcích. Though no match for the original, it's still Prague's most central open-air market.

At the eastern end of Havelská is the Church of St Gall (kostel sv Havla), as old as St Gall's Town itself, where Jan Hus and his predecessors preached religious reform. The Carmelites took possession of it in 1627, and in 1723 added its shapely baroque façade. The Czech baroque painter Karel Škréta (1610–74) is buried in the church.

Near the former Uhelný trh (coal market) is the plain, 12th-century Church of St Martin in the Wall (kostel sv Martin ve zdi), a parish church enlarged and Gothicised in the 14th century. The name comes from its having had the Old Town wall built right around it. In 1414 the church was the site of the first-ever Hussite communion service *sub utraque specie* (with both bread and wine), from which the name 'Utraquist' derives.

KAROLINUM Map pp88–9

Univerzita Karlova; ☎ 224 491 250; www.cuni.cz/ukeng-4.html; Ovocný trh 3; Ⓜ Můstek

Central Europe's oldest university, founded by Charles IV in 1348, was originally housed in the so-called Rotlev House. With Protestantism and Czech nationalism on the rise, the reforming preacher Jan Hus became Charles University's rector in 1402 and soon persuaded Wenceslas IV to slash the voting rights of the university's German students – thousands of them left Bohemia when this was announced.

The facilities of the ever-expanding university were concentrated here in 1611, and by the 18th century the old burgher's house had grown into a sizeable complex known as the Karolinum. After the Battle of Bílá Hora (1620) it was handed over to the Jesuits, who gave it a baroque makeover; when they were booted out in 1773 the university took it back. Charles University now has faculties all over Prague, and the Karolinum today houses only some faculty offices, the University Club and a ceremonial hall. It is open to the public only on 'open doors' days (details from tourist information offices).

Among pre-university Gothic survivals is the Chapel of Sts Cosmas & Damian (kaple sv Kosmas a Damian), with its extraordinary oriel window protruding from the southern wall. Built around 1370, it was renovated in 1881 by Josef Mocker.

ESTATES THEATRE Map pp88–9

Stavovské divadlo; ☎ 224 215 001; www.narodni-divadlo.cz; Ovocný trh 1; Ⓜ Náměstí Republiky

Beside the Karolinum is Prague's oldest theatre and finest neoclassical building, the Estates Theatre, where the premiere of Mozart's *Don Giovanni* was performed on 29 October 1787, with the maestro himself conducting. Opened in 1783 as the Nostitz Theatre (after its founder, Count Anton von Nostitz-Rieneck), it was patronised by upper-class German citizens and thus came to be called the Estates Theatre – the Estates being the traditional nobility.

After WWII it was renamed the Tylovo divadlo (Tyl Theatre) in honour of the 19th-century Czech playwright Josef Kajetán Tyl. One of his claims to fame is the Czech national anthem, *Kde domov můj?* (Where is My Home?), which came from one of his plays. In the early 1990s the theatre's name reverted to Estates Theatre. Around the corner is the 17th-century Kolowrat Theatre (Ovocný trh 6), now also a National Theatre venue. See also p199 for more information on classical-music venues.

SOUTHWESTERN STARÉ MĚSTO

The meandering lanes and passageways between Karlova and Národní třída are Prague's best territory for aimless wandering. When the crowds thin out late in the day, this area can cast such a spell that it's quite a surprise to emerge from its peaceful backstreets into the bustle of the 21st century.

The charm goes a bit cold along Bartolomějská, however, and not just because it is lined with police offices. Before November 1989 this block was occupied by the StB (Státní bezpečnost, or State Security), the hated secret police. Older Czechs are still understandably twitchy about police of any kind and it's a common suspicion that a few former StB officers are still around, just wearing new uniforms.

Backing onto Bartoloměјská is an old convent and the once-lovely 18th-century Church of St Bartholomew (kostel sv Bartoloměje), for a time part of the StB complex but now returned to the Franciscans. The area boasts a couple more historic churches in the shape of the Bethlehem Chapel and the Rotunda of the Holy Cross.

BETHLEHEM CHAPEL Map pp108–9

Betlémská kaple; ☎ 224 248 595; Betlémské náměstí 3; adult/child 50/30Kč; 🕑 10am-6.30pm Tue-Sun Apr-Oct, to 5.30pm Tue-Sun Nov-Mar; 🚊 6, 9, 18, 21, 22, 23

The Bethlehem Chapel is one of Prague's most important churches, being the true birthplace of the Hussite cause. In 1391, Reformist Praguers won permission to build a church where services could be held in Czech instead of Latin, and proceeded to construct the biggest chapel Bohemia had ever seen, able to hold 3000 worshippers. Architecturally it was a radical departure, with a simple square hall focused on the pulpit rather than the altar. Jan Hus preached here from 1402 to 1412, marking the emergence of the Reform movement from the sanctuary of the Karolinum (where he was rector).

In the 18th century the chapel was torn down. Remnants were discovered around 1920, and from 1948 to 1954 – because Hussitism had official blessing as an ancient form of communism – the whole thing was painstakingly reconstructed in its original form, based on old drawings, descriptions, and traces of the original work. It's now a national cultural monument.

Only the southern wall of the chapel is brand new. You can still see some original parts in the eastern wall: the pulpit door, several windows and the door to the preacher's quarters. These quarters, including the rooms used by Hus and others, are also original; they are now used for exhibits. The wall paintings are modern, and are based on old Hussite tracts. The indoor well predates the chapel.

The chapel has an English text available at the door. Every year on the night of 5 July, the eve of Hus' burning at the stake in 1415, a commemorative celebration is held here, with speeches and bell-ringing.

CHURCH OF ST GILES Map pp88–9

Kostel sv Jiljí; cnr Zlatá & Husova; 🚋 6, 9, 18, 21, 22, 23

With stocky Romanesque columns, tall Gothic windows, and an exuberant baroque interior, the Church of St Giles – founded in 1371 – is a good place to ponder the architectural development of Prague's religious buildings. The proto-Hussite reformer Jan Milíč of Kroměříž preached here before the Bethlehem Chapel was built. The Dominicans gained possession during the Counter-Reformation, built a cloister next door and 'baroquefied' it in the 1730s. Václav Reiner, the Czech painter who created the ceiling frescoes, is buried here.

NÁPRSTEK MUSEUM Map pp108–9

Náprstkovo muzeum; ☎ 224 497 500; www.aconet.cz/npm; Betlémské náměstí 1; adult/child 80/40Kč; 🕒 9am-5.30pm Tue-Sun; 🚋 6, 9, 18, 21, 22, 23

The small Náprstek Museum houses an ethnographical collection of Asian, African and American cultures, founded by Vojta Náprstek, a 19th-century industrialist with a passion for both anthropology and modern technology (his technology exhibits are now part of the National Technical Museum in Holešovice; p133).

ROTUNDA OF THE HOLY CROSS

Map pp108–9

Kaple sv kříže; Konviktská; 🕒 services 5pm Sun & Tue, in English 5.30pm 1st Mon of each month; 🚋 6, 9, 18, 21, 22, 23

This tiny Romanesque rotunda is one of Prague's oldest buildings, starting out as a parish church in about 1100. Saved from demolition and restored in the 1860s by a collective of Czech artists, it still has the remnants of some 600-year-old wall frescoes, though you will have to attend Mass to see them.

NOT QUITE THE ROYAL WAY

Walking Tour

1 Republic Square At Republic Square (náměstí Republiky), three ages of Prague architecture face each other across the intersection of Na Příkopě and Celetná – the sooty Gothic tracery of the Powder Gate (Prašná brána; p100), the elegant Art Nouveau convolutions of the Municipal House (Obecní dům; p99), and the stern functionalist façades of the Czech National Bank (Česká národní banka) and the Commercial Bank (Komerční banka). As you look west along Celetná you'll see the tower of the Old Town Hall framed at the end of the street like a target in a gun-sight; set off towards it.

2 House of the Black Madonna In addition to the many souvenir shops, Celetná is lined with many interesting buildings. As you reach the open space of Ovocný trh you'll see an unusual, origami-like façade on the left. It belongs to the House of the Black Madonna (dům U černé Matky Boží), one of Prague's finest examples of Cubist architecture, and home of the Museum of Czech Cubism (p100).

3 Celetná Theatre A little further along Celetná, turn right into the passage at No 17, which leads to a peaceful little courtyard beside the Celetná Theatre (divadlo v Celetné; p202). Head up the stairs to Café Gaspar Kasper if you fancy a coffee or a cold beer.

4 Church of St James The passage on the far side of the courtyard leads out onto Štupartská; go straight ahead along Malá Štupartská for a look at the baroque sculptures adorning the façade of the Church of St James (kostel sv Jakuba; p90). If it's open, go inside for a peek at its gloomy, gilded splendour and the grisly exhibit hanging next to the door.

5 Týn Courtyard Retrace your steps for a few metres and turn right through the cobbled passage just beyond Big Ben Bookshop to enter the Týn Courtyard (Týnský dvůr; p94). This lovely little square is lined with posh shops, good restaurants and a Renaissance loggia,

NOT QUITE THE ROYAL WAY

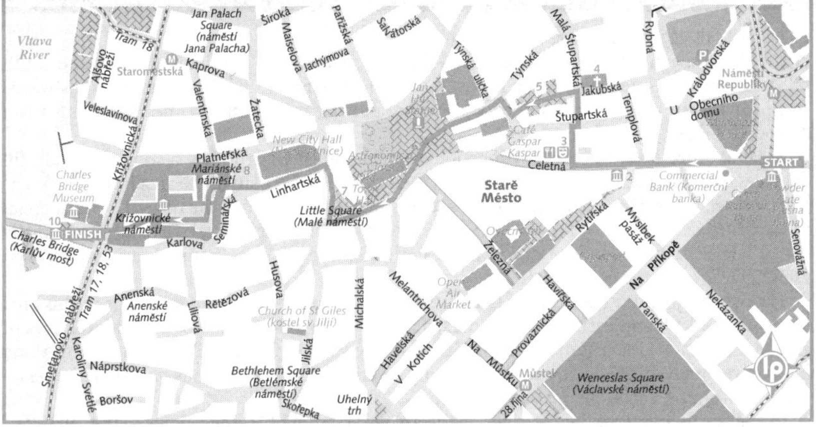

WALK FACTS

Start Republic Square (metro Náměstí Republiky)
End Charles Bridge (tram 17, 18)
Distance 1.5km
Time 45 minutes
Exertion Easy
Fuel stop Café Gaspar Kasper

and has a fine view of the twin steeples of the Church of Our Lady Before Týn (kostel Panny Marie před Týnem; p87). Exit at the far end of the courtyard and go along the narrow alley to the right of the church, stopping to look up at the semicircular tympanum above the northern door, decorated with a superb Gothic relief of the Last Judgment.

6 Old Town Square You emerge from the alley into the melee of Old Town Square (Staroměstské náměstí; p87), dominated by the brooding statue of Jan Hus and the Gothic tower of the Old Town Hall (Staroměstská Radnice; p92). If you've timed it right, you'll be able to join the crowd at the foot of the tower to watch a performance by the Astronomical Clock (see the boxed text, p94) set into the tower wall.

7 Little Square Continue past the clock and the *sgraffito*-clad House at the Minute (dům U minuty) to reach Little Square (Malé náměstí). To your left you'll see the beautiful baroque shop called U zlaté koruny (At the Golden Crown); it was once a pharmacy (you can still see the original fittings) but now houses a jewellery shop. Ahead is the neo-Renaissance façade of the VJ Rott Building, decorated with colourful murals by Mikuláś Ales. You'll see the main tourist throng bearing left into Karlova, but bear right towards the opposite end of the square and then turn left into Linhartská.

8 Virgin Mary Square This leads to the quieter space of Virgin Mary Square (Mariánské náměstí), dominated by New City Hall (Nova radnice), seat of Prague's city council. The façade is framed by brooding Art Nouveau statues by Ladislav Šaloun, the same chap who created the Jan Hus Monument in Old Town Square, and decorated with red and yellow flags, Prague's municipal colours.

9 Klementinum Facing City Hall across the square is the main gate of the Klementinum (p98). Go through the gate into the courtyard and turn left; on your right is the entrance to the Chapel of Mirrors (Zrcadlová kaple), where classical concerts are held daily. Continue past the chapel and through the triple arch, then turn right and continue through the quiet courtyards (look up to your right to spot a modern sculpture of a child with a paper plane perched on a ledge).

10 Old Town Bridge Tower At the far end of the Klementinum courtyards you emerge again into the bustling traffic and tourist crowds of Křížovnické náměstí. End your walk by climbing up the Old Town Bridge Tower (Staroměstská mostecká věž; p98) for a view over Prague's most famous bridge, before visiting the nearby Charles Bridge Museum (p98).

NOVÉ MĚSTO & VYŠEHRAD

Eating p163; Drinking p183; Shopping p148; Sleeping p218

Nové Město means 'New Town', although this crescent-shaped district to the east and south of Staré Město was new only when it was founded by Charles IV in 1348. It extends eastwards from Revoluční and Na Příkopě to Wilsonova and the main railway line, and south from Národní třída to Vyšehrad.

Most of Nové Město's outer fortifications were demolished in 1875 – a section of wall still survives in the south, facing Vyšehrad – but the original street plan of the area has been essentially preserved, with three large market squares that once provided the district's commercial focus: Senovážné náměstí (Hay Market Square), Wenceslas Square (Václavské náměstí; originally called Koňský trh, or Horse Market) and Charles Square (Karlovo náměstí; originally called Dobytčí trh, or Cattle Market).

Though originally a medieval neighbourhood, most of the surviving buildings in this area are from the 19th and early 20th centuries, many of them among the city's finest examples of Art Nouveau, neo-Renaissance, Czech National Revival and functionalist architecture. Many blocks are honeycombed with pedestrian-only arcades – Prague's famous *pasážy* (passages) – lined with shops, cafés, cinemas and theatres.

In the south, overlooking the river, is the ancient citadel of Vyšehrad. Since the 1920s the old fortress has been a quiet park, with splendid panoramas of the Vltava Valley. It retains a fond place in Czech hearts and is a popular destination for weekend family outings – take along a picnic and find a quiet spot among the trees, or on the battlements with a view over the river.

NORTHERN NOVÉ MĚSTO

The northern part of Nové Město stretches from the Vltava River down to Wenceslas Square. The area is mostly rather nondescript, but there are a few gems hidden away among the bland façades.

JINDŘIŠSKÁ TOWER Map pp108–9

Jindřišská věž; ☎ 224 232 429; www.jindrisskavez.cz; Jindřišská 1; adult/child 75/25Kč; 🕑 9am-7pm Mon-Fri, 10am-7pm Sat & Sun; 🚊 3, 9, 14, 24

This Gothic bell tower, dating from the 15th century but rebuilt in the Gothic style in the 1870s, dominates the end of Jindřišská, a busy street running northeast from Wenceslas Square. Having stood idle for decades, the tower was renovated and reopened in 2002 as a tourist attraction, complete with exhibition space, shop, café and restaurant, and a lookout gallery on the 10th floor.

JUBILEE SYNAGOGUE Map pp108–9

Jubilejní synagóga; ☎ 222 319 002; Jeruzalémská 7; admission 50Kč; 🕑 1-5pm Sun-Fri Apr-Oct, closed on Jewish hols; Ⓜ Hlavní Nádraží

The colourful Moorish façade of the Jubilee Synagogue, also called the Velká synagóga (Great Synagogue), dates from 1906. Note the names of the donors on the stained-glass windows, and the grand organ above the entrance.

MUCHA MUSEUM Map pp108–9

Muchovo muzeum; ☎ 221 451 333; www.mucha.cz; Panská 7; adult/child 120/60Kč; 🕑 10am-6pm; Ⓜ Můstek

This fascinating (and busy) museum features the sensuous Art Nouveau posters, paintings and decorative panels of Alfons Mucha (1860–1939), as well as many sketches, photographs and other memorabilia. The exhibits include countless artworks showing Mucha's trademark Slavic maidens with flowing hair and piercing blue eyes, bearing symbolic garlands and linden boughs; photos of the artist's Paris studio, one of which shows a trouserless Gaugin playing the harmonium; a powerful canvas entitled *Old Woman in Winter;* and the original of the 1894 poster of actress Sarah Bernhardt as Giselda, which shot him to international fame. The fascinating 30-minute video documentary about Mucha's life is well worth watching, and helps to put his achievements in perspective. For more information on Mucha see the boxed text, p40.

POSTAL MUSEUM Map p106

Poštovní muzeum; ☎ 222 312 006; Nové Mlýny 2; adult/child 25/10Kč; 🕑 9am-noon & 1-5pm Tue-Sun; 🚊 5, 18, 14

Philatelists will love this tiny museum with its letter boxes, mail coach and drawers of old postage stamps, including a rare Penny

Black. Look for the beautiful stamps created in the early 20th century by Czech artists Josef Navrátil and Alfons Mucha.

Across the street is the Petrská Waterworks Tower (Petrská vodárenská věž), which was built about 1660 on the site of earlier wooden ones. From here, wooden pipes once carried river water to buildings in Nové Město.

PRAGUE CITY MUSEUM Map p106

Muzeum hlavního města Prahy; ☎ 224 816 773; www.muzeumprahy.cz; Na Poříčí 52; adult/child 100/40Kč, 1st Thu of each month 1Kč; 9am-6pm Tue-Sun, to 8pm 1st Thu of each month; Ⓜ Florenc

This excellent museum, opened in 1898, is devoted to the history of Prague from prehistoric times to the 20th century. Among the many intriguing exhibits are the brown silk funeral cap and slippers worn by astronomer Tycho Brahe when he was interred in the Týn Church in 1601 (they were removed from his corpse in 1901) and the Astronomical Clock's original 1866 calendar wheel with Josef Mánes' beautiful painted panels representing the months – that's January at the top, toasting his toes by the fire, and August near the bottom, sickle in hand, harvesting the corn.

But what everybody comes to see is Antonín Langweil's astonishing 1:480 scale model of Prague as it looked between 1826 and 1834. The display is most rewarding after you get to know Prague a bit, as you can spot the changes – look at St Vitus Cathedral, for example, still only half-finished.

Most labels are in English as well as Czech, but you'll need the English text (available at the ticket desk) for Room I (prehistory to medieval).

PRAGUE MAIN TRAIN STATION

Map pp108–9

Praha hlavní nádraží; Wilsonova; closed 12.40-3.15am; Ⓜ Hlavní Nádraží

What? The train station is actually a tourist attraction? Perhaps not all of it, but it's worth going to the top floor for a look at the grimy, soot-blackened splendour of the original Art Nouveau building designed by Josef Fanta and built between 1901 and 1909. The domed interior is adorned with a mosaic of two nubile ladies, the words *Praga: mater urbium* (Prague, Mother of Cities) and the date '28.října r:1918' (28 October 1918, Czechoslovakia's Independence Day).

WENCESLAS SQUARE & AROUND

Originally a medieval horse market, and more a broad, sloping boulevard than a typical city square, Wenceslas Square (Václavské náměstí, also called Václavák) got its present name during the nationalist revival of the mid-19th century. Since then it has witnessed a great deal of Czech history – a giant Mass was held here during the revolutionary upheavals of 1848; in 1918 the creation of the new Czechoslovak Republic was celebrated here; and in 1989 the fall of communism was announced here.

Following the police attack on a student demonstration on 17 November 1989 (see the boxed text, p29), angry citizens gathered in Wenceslas Square by the thousands night after night. A week later, in a stunning mirror image of Klement Gottwald's 1948 proclamation of communist rule in Old Town Square, Alexander Dubček and Václav Havel stepped onto the balcony of the Melantrich Building to a thunderous and tearful ovation, and proclaimed the end of communism in Czechoslovakia.

At the southern end of the square is Josef Myslbek's muscular equestrian statue of St Wenceslas (sv Václav; Map pp108–9), the 10th-century pacifist Duke of Bohemia and the 'Good King Wenceslas' of Christmas carol fame (he was never a king, only a prince, but was widely regarded as being a good man). Flanked by other patron saints of Bohemia – Prokop, Adalbert, Agnes and Ludmila – he has been plastered with posters and bunting at every one of the square's historical moments. Near the statue, a small memorial to the victims of communism bears photographs and handwritten epitaphs to Jan Palach and other anticommunist rebels.

In contrast to the solemnity of this shrine, the square around it has become a monument to capitalism, a gaudy gallery of cafés, fast-food outlets, expensive shops, greedy cabbies and pricey hotels, haunted at night by drunken British stag parties, prostitutes and strip club touts.

CHURCH OF OUR LADY OF THE SNOWS

Map pp108–9

Kostel Panny Marie sněžné; Jungmannovo náměstí 18; Ⓜ Můstek

The most sublime attraction in the neighbourhood is this Gothic church at the northern end of Wenceslas Square. It was begun in the 14th century by Charles IV but only the chancel was ever completed, which

NOVÉ MĚSTO & VYŠEHRAD

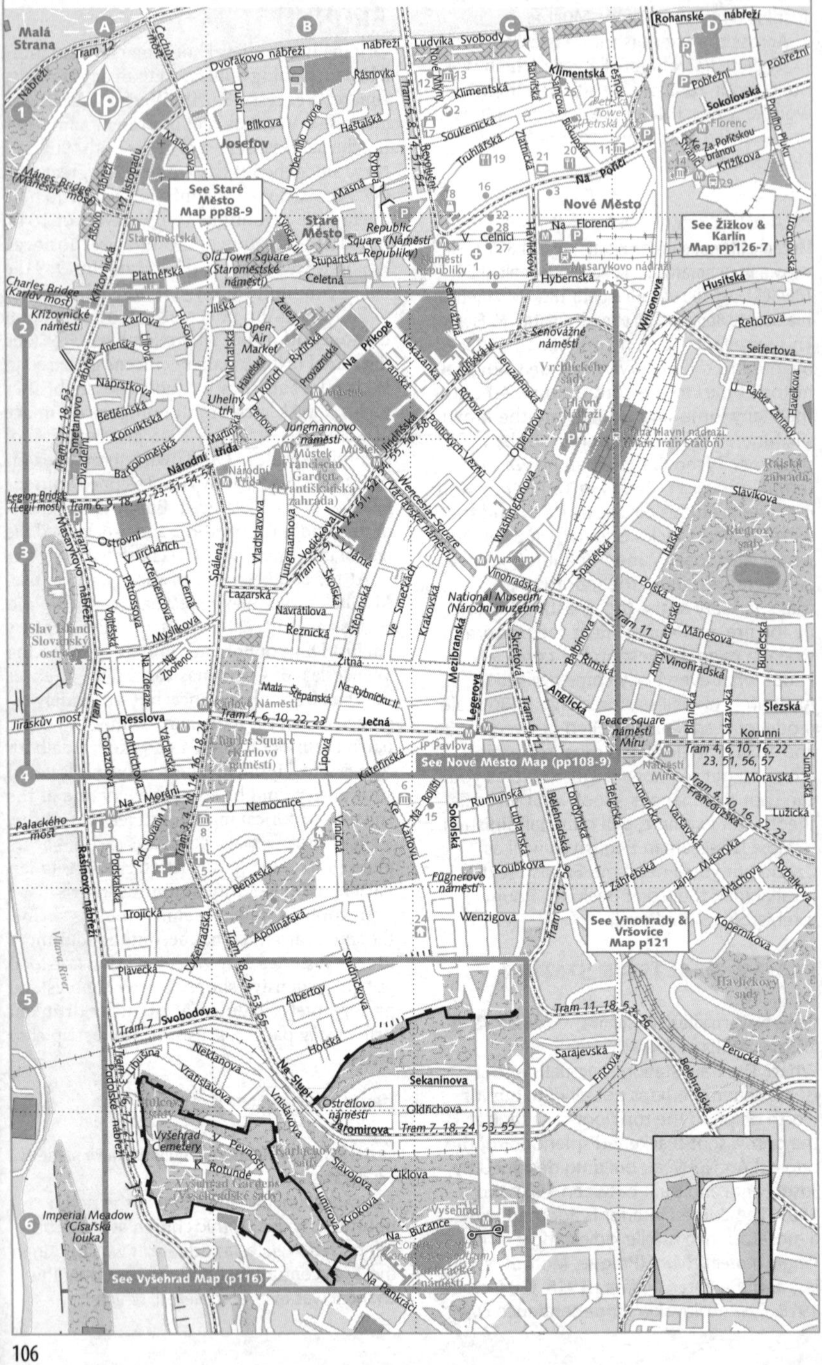

NOVÉ MĚSTO & VYŠEHRAD

INFORMATION
American Dental Associates........1 C2
Australian Consulate..................2 C1

SIGHTS & ACTIVITIES (pp104–19)
Bank of Czechoslovak Legions....3 C1
Charles University Botanical Garden (Botanická Zahrada Univerzity Karlovy)................................4 B5
Church of St John of Nepomuk on the Rock (Kostel Sv Jana Nepomuckého na Skalce).......5 A4
Dvořák Museum (Muzeum Antonina Dvořáka)................6 B4
Emmaus Monastery (Klášter Emauzy)...............................7 A4
Faust House (Faustův Dům)........8 A4
František Palacký Memorial........9 A4
Hotel Central...........................10 C2
Jiří Švestka..............................11 D1
Petrská Waterworks Tower (Petrská Vodárenská Věž).....12 C1
Postal Museum (Poštovní Muzeum)............................13 C1
Prague City Museum (Muzeum Hlavního Města Prahy)..........14 D1
U Kalicha...............................15 C4
Vila Amerika...........................(see 6)
Workers' Accident Insurance Co (Kafka's Workplace 1908-22)............................16 C1

SHOPPING (pp143–51)
Galerie České Plastiky.............17 C1
Palladium Praha Shopping Centre................................18 C1

EATING (pp153–73)
Albio..19 C1
Siam Orchid..............................20 C1

DRINKING (pp175–91)
Café Imperial...........................21 C1

SPORTS & ACTIVITIES (pp205–10)
Sportcentrum YMCA................22 C1

SLEEPING (pp211–27)
Alfa Tourist Service..................23 C2
Hostel U Melounu....................24 C5
Hotel 16 U Sv Kateřiny............25 B4

TRANSPORT (pp241–5)
Avis...26 C1
ČD Travel................................27 C2
Cedaz Minibus Stop................(see 28)
Czech Airlines (ČSA)................28 C2
Florenc Bus Station..................29 D1
Student Agency......................(see 29)
Touring Bohemia/ Eurolines............................(see 29)

accounts for its proportions – seemingly taller than it is long. Charles had intended it to be the grandest church in Prague; the nave is higher than that of St Vitus Cathedral, and the altar is the city's tallest. It was a Hussite stronghold, ringing with the sermons of Jan Želivský, who led the 1419 defenestration that touched off the Hussite Wars.

The church is approached through an arch in the Austrian Cultural Institute on Jungmannovo náměstí, but you can get a good view of the exterior from the neighbouring Franciscan Garden (see p118). Beside the church is the Chapel of the Pasov Virgin, now a venue for temporary art exhibitions.

LUCERNA PALACE Map pp108–9

Palác Lucerna; Vodičkova 36; 3, 9, 14, 24
The most elegant of Nové Město's many shopping arcades runs beneath the Art Nouveau Lucerna Palace (1920), between Štěpánská and Vodičkova streets. The complex was designed by Václav Havel (grandfather of the expresident), and is still partially owned by the family. It includes theatres, a cinema, shops, a rock club and several cafés and restaurants. In the marbled atrium hangs artist David Černý's sculpture Horse, a wryly amusing counterpart to the equestrian statue of St Wenceslas in Wenceslas Square. Here St Wenceslas sits astride a horse that is decidedly dead; Černý never comments on the meaning of his works, but it's safe to assume that this Wenceslas (Václav in Czech) is a reference to Václav Klaus, former prime minister and now president of the Czech Republic.

The neighbouring Novák Arcade, connected to the Lucerna and riddled by a maze of passages, has one of Prague's finest Art Nouveau façades (overlooking Vodičkova), complete with mosaics of country life.

MUSEUM OF COMMUNISM Map pp108–9

Muzeum komunismu; 224 212 966; www.muzeumkomunismu.cz; Na Příkopě 10; adult/child 180/140Kč; 9am-9pm; M Můstek
It's difficult to think of a more ironic site for a museum of communism – it occupies part of an 18th-century aristocrat's palace, stuck between a casino on one side and a McDonald's burger restaurant on the other. Put together by an American expat and his Czech partner, the museum tells the story of Czechoslovakia's years behind the Iron Curtain in photos, words and a fascinating and varied collection of…well, stuff. The empty shops, corruption, fear and double-speak of life in socialist Czechoslovakia are well conveyed, and there are rare photos of the Stalin monument that once stood on Letná terrace – and its spectacular destruction. Be sure to watch the video about protests leading up to the Velvet Revolution: you'll never think of it as a pushover again.

NA PŘÍKOPĚ Map pp108–9

Na Příkopě (On the Moat), along with Revoluční (Revolution), 28.října (28 October 1918; Czechoslovak Independence Day) and Národní třída (National Ave), follows the line of the moat that once ran along the foot of Staré Město's city walls (the moat was filled in at the end of the 18th century).

NOVÉ MĚSTO

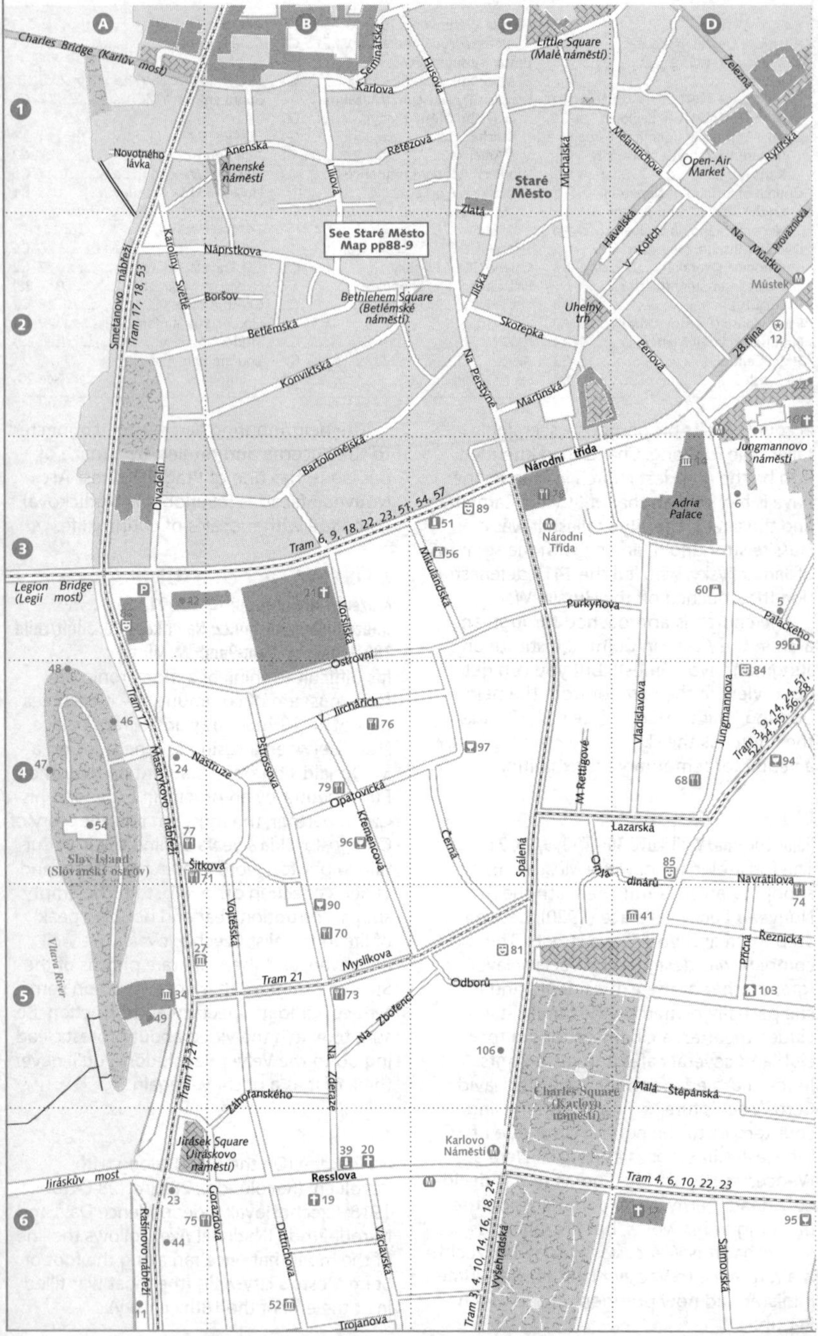
A
B
C
D
1
2
3
4
5
6
Charles Bridge (Karlův most)
Seminářská
Karlova
Husova
Little Square
(Malé náměstí)
Železná
Melantrichova
Rytířská
Open-Air
Market
Novotného
lávka
Anenská
Anenské
náměstí
Řetězová
Liliová
Staré
Město
Michalská
Zlatá
Havelská
V Kotcích
Na Můstku
Provaznická
Můstek
Smetanovo nábřeží
Tram 17, 18, 53
Karoliny Světlé
Náprstkova
See Staré Město
Map pp88-9
Boršov
Bethlehem Square
(Betlémské
náměstí)
Jilská
Uhelný
trh
Skořepka
Perlová
28.října
12
Betlémská
Konviktská
Na Perštýně
Martinská
Bartolomějská
Divadelní
Národní třída
Jungmannovo
náměstí
1
14
Adria
Palace
6
Tram 6, 9, 18, 22, 23, 51, 54, 57
89
78
51
56
Národní
Třída
Mikulandská
Legion Bridge
(Legií most)
P
42
21
Voršilská
Purkyňova
60
5
Palackého
99
Ostrovní
84
48
Tram 17
V Jirchářích
46
76
Vladislavova
Jungmannova
Tram 3, 9, 14, 24, 51, 52, 54, 55, 56, 58
97
94
47
Masarykovo nábřeží
24
Náplavka
Pštrossova
M. Rettigové
79
Opatovická
68
54
77
Křemencova
Lazarská
Černá
96
Spálená
Slav Island
(Slovanský ostrov)
Šitkova
71
Ostrovní
Ve Smečkách
85
dinárů
Navrátilova
74
90
Vojtěšská
70
41
Řeznická
27
Vltava River
81
Myslíkova
Příčná
Tram 21
Odborů
5
34
73
103
49
Na Zbořenci
106
Tram 17, 21
Na Zderaze
Charles Square
(Karlovo
náměstí)
Malá Štěpánská
Zahořanského
Jirásek Square
(Jiráskovo
náměstí)
Karlovo
Náměstí
39
20
Jiráskův most
Resslova
Tram 4, 6, 10, 22, 23
23
19
Gorazdova
17
Rašínovo nábřeží
75
95
44
Dittrichova
Václavská
Vyšehradská
Tram 3, 4, 10, 14, 16, 18, 24
Salmovská
11
52
Trojanova

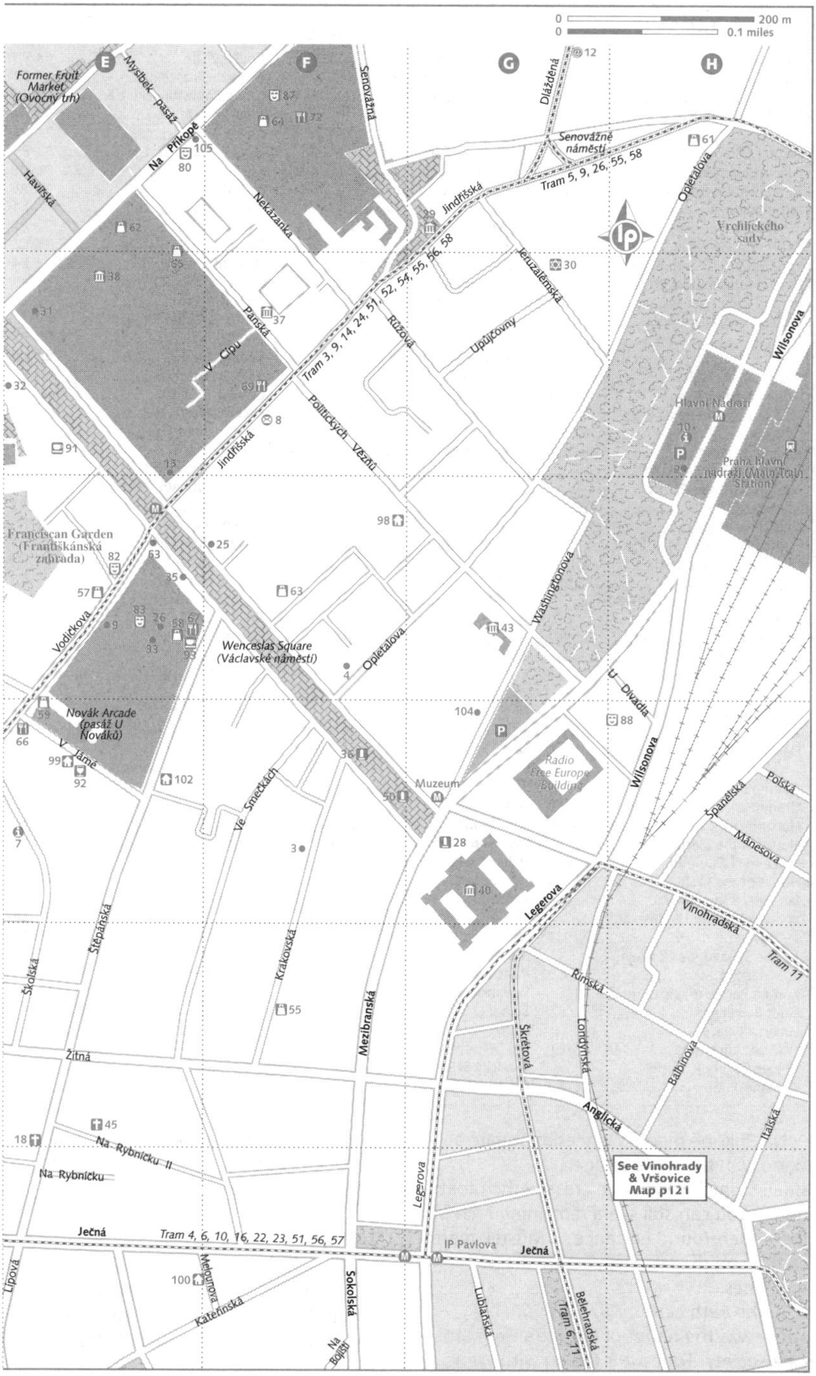
0 200 m
0 0.1 miles
E
F
G
H
Former Fruit Market (Ovocný trh)
Myslbek pasáž
Na Příkopě
Havířská
Senovážná
Dlážděná
Senovážné náměstí
Tram 5, 9, 26, 55, 58
Jindřišská
Nekázanka
Opletalova
Vrchlického sady
Jeruzalémská
Panská
V Cípu
Tram 3, 9, 14, 24, 51, 52, 54, 55, 56, 58
Růžová
Senovážná
Politických Vězňů
Hlavní Nádraží
Praha hlavní nádraží (Main Train Station)
Wilsonova
Franciscan Garden (Františkánská zahrada)
Vodičkova
Washingtonova
Wenceslas Square (Václavské náměstí)
Opletalova
U Divadla
Novák Arcade (pasáž U Nováků)
V Jámě
Radio Free Europe Building
Muzeum
Ve Smečkách
Wilsonova
Španělská
Polská
Mánesova
Legerova
Vinohradská
Tram 11
Římská
Štěpánská
Školská
Krakovská
Mezibranská
Škrétova
Londýnská
Balbínova
Žitná
Anglická
Italská
Na Rybníčku II
Na Rybníčku
See Vinohrady & Vršovice Map p121
Legerova
Ječná
Tram 4, 6, 10, 16, 22, 23, 51, 56, 57
IP Pavlova
Ječná
Lípová
Melounova
Kateřinská
Sokolská
Na Bojišti
Ljubljaňská
Tram 6, 11
Bělehradská

NOVÉ MĚSTO

INFORMATION

Austrian Cultural Institute........... 1 D2
AVE Travel.................................. 2 H2
Czech Blind United.......................3 F4
DHL..4 F3
District Clinic (24hr Pharmacy)....5 D3
Globe Bookstore & Café.........(see 70)
Happy House Rentals................ 6 D3
Information-Advisory Centre of Charles University (IPC)..........7 E4
Main Post Office..........................8 F2
Prague Card Change Office.........9 E3
Prague Information Service....... 10 H2
Prague Passenger Shipping....... 11 A6
Praha 1 Police Station............... 12 D2
Spika..13 G1

SIGHTS & ACTIVITIES (pp104–15)

Adria Palace...............................14 D3
Assicurazioni Generali (Kafka's Workplace 1907-08).............15 E2
Baťa Shoe Store.......................(see 32)
Church of Our Lady of the Snows (Kostel Panny Marie Sněžné).......................16 D2
Church of St Ignatius (Kostel sv Ignáce)..................17 D6
Church of St Stephen (Kostel sv Štěpána)................18 E5
Church of St Wenceslas in Zderaz (Kostel sv Václava na Zderaza).............................. 19 B6
Church of Sts Cyril & Methodius (Kostel sv Cyril a Metoděj)....20 B6
Convent of St Ursula (Klášter sv Voršila)............... 21 B3
Cubist Lamppost...................... 22 D2
Dancing Buidling (Tančící Dům)..23 A6
Goethe Institute....................... 24 A4
Grand Hotel Evropa..................25 F3
Horse-David Černý Sculpture....26 E3
House of the Black Rose (Dům U Černé Růže)..........(see 62)
House of the Hlahol Choir........ 27 A5
Jan Palach Memorial................ 28 G4
Jindřišská Tower (Jindřišská Věž).. 29 G1
Jubilee Synagogue (Jubilejní Synagóga)........................... 30 G2
Koruna Palace (Palác Koruna)...31 E2
Lindt Building............................32 E2
Lucerna Palace (Palác Lucerna)..................... 33 E3
Mánes Gallery (Galerie Mánes)................................ 34 A5
Melantrich Building...................35 E3
Memorial to Victims of Communism........................ 36 F4
Mucha Museum (Muchovo Muzeum)...............................37 F2
Museum of Communism (Muzeum Komunismu)..........38 E2
National Memorial to the Victims of Post-Heydrich Terror (Národní Památník Obětí Heydrichiády).......................39 B6
National Museum (Národní Muzeum)............................ 40 G4
National Theatre-Národni divadlo..............................(see 86)
New Town Hall (Novoměstská Radnice)........ 41 D5
Nová Scéna................................42 A3
Peček Palace (Pačkův Palác).......................43 G3
Rašínovo Nábřeží 78 (Václav Havel's Old Flat).......44 A6
Rotunda of St Longinus (Rotunda sv Longina)...........45 E5
Rowboat Hire........................... 46 A4
Rowboat Hire........................... 47 A4
Rowboat Hire........................... 48 A4
Šitovská Věž............................. 49 A5
St Wenceslas (sv Václav) Statue................ 50 F4
Student Memorial.....................51 C3
Tranzit/Display Gallery.............52 B6
Wiehl House (Wiehlův dům).....................53 E3
ofín... 54 A4

SHOPPING (pp143–51)

Baťa...(see 32)
Bazar...55 F5
Belda Jewellery........................ 56 C3
Bontonland.............................(see 31)
Foto Škoda................................57 E3
Globe Bookstore & Café.........(see 70)
Helena Fejková Gallery.............58 E3
Jan Pazdera...............................59 E4
Kanzelsberger........................(see 32)
Kiwi.. 60 D3
Manufactura Abram Kelly......... 61 H1
Moser..62 E1
Palác Knih Neo Luxor................63 F3
Slovanský Dům..........................64 F1
Zerba.. 65 E2

EATING (pp153–73)

Branický Sklípek........................ 66 E4
Cellarius....................................67 E3
Country Life............................. 68 D4
Fruits de France........................ 69 F2
Globe Bookstore & Café........... 70 B5
Karavanseráj............................. 71 A4
Kogo..72 F1
Lemon Leaf............................... 73 B5
Miyabi....................................... 74 D5
Na Rybářně............................... 75 A6
Pizzeria Kmotra......................... 76 B4
Suterén..................................... 77 A4
Tesco... 78 C3
U Matěje Kotrby........................ 79 B4

ENTERTAINMENT (pp193–203)

Bohemia Ticket International (BTI).. 80 E1
Kino MAT................................. 81 C5
Kino Světozor............................ 82 E3
Laterna Magika........................(see 42)
Lucerna Music Bar.................... 83 E3
Metropolitan Jazz Club............. 84 D4
Minor Theatre (Divadlo Minor).......................85 D4
National Theatre-Národni divadlo...................................... 86 A3
Palace Cinemas.........................87 F1
Prague State Opera (Státní Opera Praha)............. 88 H4
Reduta Jazz Club...................... 89 C3
Reduta Theatre........................(see 89)
Rock Café................................(see 89)
Ticketpro.................................(see 83)

DRINKING (pp175–91)

Bokovka.................................... 90 B5
Dobrá Čajovna.......................... 91 E2
Jáma... 92 E4
Kavárna Lucerna....................(see 26)
Kávovarna................................. 93 E3
Novoméstský Pivovar............... 94 D4
Pivovarský Dům........................ 95 D6
U Fleků..................................... 96 B4
Velryba...................................... 97 C4

SLEEPING (pp211–27)

Hotel Yasmin............................. 98 F3
Icon Hotel 99 E4
Miss Sophie's........................... 100 E6
Penzión U Šuterů..................... 101 D3
Radisson SAS Alcron Hotel...... 102 E4
Suitehome Residence.............. 103 D5

TRANSPORT (pp241–5)

A-Rent Car/Thrifty................. 104 G4
Čedok...................................... 105 E1
Hertz....................................... 106 C5

Na Příkopě meets Wenceslas Square at Na Můstku (On the Little Bridge; Map pp108–9). A small stone bridge once crossed the moat here – you can still see a remaining arch in the underground entrance to Můstek metro station, on the left just past the ticket machines.

In the 19th century this fashionable street was the haunt of Prague's German café society. Today it is (along with Wenceslas Square and Pařížská) the city's main upmarket shopping precinct, lined with banks, shopping malls and tourist cafés.

NATIONAL MUSEUM Map pp108–9

Národní muzeum; ☎ 224 497 111; www.nm.cz; adult/child 120/70Kč, admission free 1st Mon of each month; 10am-6pm May-Sep, 9am-5pm Oct-Apr, closed 1st Tue of month; Ⓜ Muzeum

Looming above Wenceslas Square is the neo-Renaissance bulk of the National Museum, designed in the 1880s by Josef Schulz as an architectural symbol of the Czech National Revival.

The main displays of rocks, fossils and stuffed animals have a rather old-fashioned feel – serried ranks of glass display cabinets arranged on creaking parquet floors – but even if trilobites and taxidermy are not your thing it's still worth a visit just to enjoy the marbled splendour of the interior and the views down Wenceslas Square. The opulent main staircase is an extravaganza of polished limestone and serpentine, lined with paintings of Bohemian castles and medallions of kings and emperors. The domed pantheon, with four huge lunette paintings of (strangely womanless) Czech legend and history by František Ženíšek and Václav Brožík, houses bronze busts and statues of the great and the good of Czech art and science.

The light-coloured areas on the façade of the museum are patched-up bullet holes. In 1968 Warsaw Pact troops apparently mistook the museum for the former National Assembly or the radio station, and raked it with gunfire. It's also here where you'll find a cross-shaped memorial set into the pavement, to the left of the fountain in front of the museum, that marks the spot where Jan Palach fell (see the boxed text, p29).

The museum building is badly in need of a face-lift, and in 2011 it will close for five years to allow for major renovation.

NÁRODNÍ TŘÍDA Map pp108–9

Národní třída (National Ave) is central Prague's 'high street', a stately row of mid-range shops and grand public buildings, notably the National Theatre at the Vltava River end.

Fronting Jungmannovo náměstí, at the eastern end, is an imitation Venetian palace known as the Adria Palace. Its distinctive, chunky architectural style, dating from the 1920s, is known as 'rondocubism'. Note how the alternating angular and rounded window pediments echo similar features in neoclassical baroque buildings such as the Černin Palace (p68).

Beneath it is the Adria Theatre, birthplace of Laterna Magika and meeting place of Civic Forum in the heady days of the Velvet Revolution. From here, Dubček and Havel walked to the Lucerna Palace and their 24 November 1989 appearance on the balcony of the Melantrich Building. Wander through the arcade for a look at the lovely marble, glass and brass decoration; the main atrium has a 24-hour clock from the 1920s, flanked by sculptures depicting the signs of the zodiac. It was once the entrance to the offices of the Adriatica insurance company (hence the building's name).

Along the street, inside the arcade near No 16, is a bronze plaque on the wall with a cluster of hands making the peace sign and the date '17.11.89', in memory of students beaten up by police on that date (see the boxed text, p29).

West of Voršilská, the lemon-yellow walls of the Convent of St Ursula (klášter sv Voršila) frame a pink church, which has a lush baroque interior that includes a battalion of Apostle statues. Out front is the figure of St John of Nepomuk, and in the façade's lower-right niche is a statue of St Agatha holding her severed breasts – one of the more gruesome images in Catholic hagiography.

Across the road at No 7 is the Art Nouveau façade (by Osvald Polívka) of the Viola Building (Map pp88–9), former home of the Prague Insurance Co, with the huge letters 'PRAHA' entwined around five circular windows, and mosaics spelling out *život, kapitál, důchod, věno* and *pojišťuje* (life, capital, income, dowry and insurance). The building next door, a former publishing house, is also a Polívka design.

On the southern side at No 4, looking like it has been built out of old TV screens, is the Nová Scéna (1983), the 'New National Theatre' building, now home of Laterna Magika (see p202).

TRANSPORT: NOVÉ MĚSTO

Metro The city's three metro lines all intersect in Nové Město, at Muzeum and Můstek stations at the eastern and western ends (respectively) of Wenceslas Square, and at Florenc station in northern Nové Město, while Karlovo náměstí station on Line B serves southern Nové Město.

Tram Cutting across the middle of Wenceslas Square, trams 3, 9, 14 and 24 run along Vodičkova and Jindřišská. Lines 17 and 21 run along the river embankment in the west.

top picks

ARCHITECTURE

Despite the parade of garish ads and globalised brand names, Wenceslas Square still manages some architectural dignity, having retained some of the city's finest early-20th-century buildings. Here are the edited highlights, starting at the southern (uphill) end and working down, with even numbers on the western (left) side:

- No 25 Grand Hotel Evropa (1906) is perhaps the most beautiful building on the square, Art Nouveau inside and out; have a peep at the French restaurant at the rear of the ground floor, and at the 2nd-floor atrium.
- No 36 Melantrich Building (1914), now a Marks & Spencer; the balcony overlooking the Tramvaj Café is where Havel and Dubček appeared to announce the end of communist rule in November 1989.
- No 34 Wiehl House (Wiehlův dům; 1896) has a gorgeous façade decorated with neo-Renaissance murals by top Czech artist Mikuláš Aleš and others; it's named after its designer, Antonín Wiehl.
- No 6 Baťa shoe store (1929) is a functionalist masterpiece, designed by Ludvík Kysela for Tomáš Baťa, art patron, progressive industrialist and founder of the worldwide shoe empire.
- No 4 Lindt Building (1927) was also designed by Ludvík Kysela, and is one of the republic's earliest functionalist buildings.
- No 1 Koruna Palace (1914), with an Art Nouveau design by Antonín Pfeiffer, has a tower topped with a crown of pearls; note its tiny but charming façade around the corner on Na Příkopě.

Finally, facing the Vltava near Smetanovo nábřeží is the National Theatre (Národní divadlo), neo-Renaissance flagship of the Czech National Revival and one of Prague's most impressive buildings. Funded entirely by private donations and decorated inside and out by a roll call of prominent Czech artists, architect Josef Zítek's masterpiece burned down within weeks of its 1881 opening but, incredibly, was funded again and restored under Josef Schulz in less than two years. It's now used mainly for ballet and opera performances (see p201).

Across from the theatre is the Kavárna Slavia (see the boxed text, p181), known for its Art Deco interior and river views, once *the* place to be seen or to grab an after-theatre meal. Now renovated, it's once again the place to be seen – though mainly by other tourists.

PEČEK PALACE Map pp108–9

Pečkův palác; Politických Vězňů 20; closed to the public; Ⓜ Muzeum

This gloomy neo-Renaissance palace served as the wartime headquarters of the Gestapo. A memorial on the corner of the building honours the many Czechs who were tortured and executed in the basement detention cells. Today, it is home to the Ministry of Trade & Industry.

ALONG THE RIVER

The Nové Město riverfront, stretching south from the National Theatre to Vyšehrad, is lined with some of Prague's grandest 19th- and early-20th-century architecture – it's a great place for an evening stroll, when the setting sun gilds the façades with a beautiful golden light.

Masarykovo nábřeží (Masaryk Embankment; Map pp108–9) sports a series of stunning Art Nouveau buildings. At No 32 is the duck-egg green Goethe Institute, once the East German embassy, while No 26 is a beautiful apartment building with owls perched in the decorative foliage that twines around the door, dogs peeking from the balconies on the 5th floor, and birds perched atop the balustrade.

No 16 is the House of the Hlahol Choir, built in 1906 by Josef Fanta for a patriotic choral society associated with the Czech National Revival. It's decorated with elaborate musical motifs topped by a giant mosaic depicting *Music* – the motto beneath translates as 'Let the song reach the heart; let the heart reach the homeland'.

At the next bridge is Jirásek Square (Jiráskovo náměstí), dedicated to writer Alois Jirásek (1851–1930), author of *Old Czech Legends* (studied by all Czech schoolchildren) and an influential figure in the drive towards Czechoslovak independence. His statue is overlooked by the famous Dancing Building.

A little further along the riverbank is Rašínovo nábřeží 78, an apartment building designed by the grandfather of ex-president Václav Havel – this was where Havel first chose to live (in preference to Prague Castle) after being elected as president in December 1989, surely the world's least pompous presidential residence.

Two blocks south, sitting on Palackého náměstí, is Stanislav Sucharda's extraordinary Art Nouveau František Palacký Memorial (Map p106); a swarm of haunted bronze figures (allegories of the writer's imagination) swirling around a stodgy statue of the 19th-century historian and giant of the Czech National Revival.

DANCING BUILDING Map pp108–9

Tančící dům; Rašínovo nábřeží 80; 17, 21

The junction where Resslova meets the river at Rašínovo nábřeží is dominated by the Dancing Building, built in 1996 by architects Vlado Milunić and Frank Gehry. The curved lines of the narrow-waisted glass tower clutched against its more upright and formal partner led to it being christened the 'Fred & Ginger Building', after legendary dancing duo Fred Astaire and Ginger Rogers. It's surprising how well it fits in with its ageing neighbours.

MÁNES GALLERY Map pp108–9

Galerie Mánes; 224 930 754; www.nadace-cfu.cz; Masarykovo nábřeží 1; adult/child 60/30Kč; 10am-6pm Tue-Sun; 17, 21

Spanning a branch of the river beneath a 15th-century water tower is the Mánes Building (1927–30), which houses an art gallery founded in the 1920s by a group of artists, headed by painter Josef Mánes, as an alternative to the Czech Academy of Arts. It is still one of Prague's best venues for viewing contemporary art, with a lively programme of changing exhibitions. The building itself, designed by Otakar Novotný, is considered a masterpiece of functionalist architecture.

SLAV ISLAND Map pp108–9

Slovanský ostrov; Masarykovo nábřeží; 17, 21

This island is a sleepy, dog-eared sandbank with pleasant gardens, river views and several jetties where you can hire rowing boats. Its banks were reinforced with stone in 1784, and a spa and a dye works were built in the early part of the following century. Bohemia's first train had a demonstration run here in 1841, roaring down the island at a rattling 11km/h. In 1925 the island was named after the Slav conventions that had taken place here since 1848.

top picks

FOR CHILDREN

- Boat trips (p251)
- Children's Island (p82)
- Mirror Maze (p84)
- National Technical Museum (p133)
- Prague Zoo (p140)

In the middle stands Žofín, a 19th-century cultural centre that has been restored and opened as a restaurant and social venue. At the southern end is Šitovská věž, a 15th-century water tower (once part of a mill) with an 18th-century onion-dome roof.

CHARLES SQUARE & AROUND

With an area of more than seven hectares, Charles Square (Karlovo náměstí; Map pp108–9) is the city's biggest square; it's more like a small park, really. Presiding over it is the Church of St Ignatius (kostel sv Ignáce), a 1660s baroque *tour de force* designed for the Jesuits by Carlo Lurago.

The baroque palace found at the southern end of the square belongs to Charles University. It's known as Faust House (Faustův dům; Map p106) because, according to a popular story, this house was where Mephisto took Dr Faust away to hell through a hole in the ceiling, and because of associations with Rudolf II's English court alchemist, Edward Kelley, who toiled here in the 16th century trying to convert lead into gold.

Resslova runs west from Karlovo náměstí to the river. Halfway along is the baroque Church of Sts Cyril & Methodius, a 1730s work by Kilian Dientzenhofer and Paul Bayer. The crypt now houses the moving National Memorial to the Victims of Post-Heydrich Terror.

On the other side of Resslova you'll find the 14th-century Gothic Church of St Wenceslas in Zderaz, the former parish church of Zderaz, a village that predates Nové Město. On its western side are parts of a wall and windows from its 12th-century Romanesque predecessor.

The area to the east of Karlovo náměstí is occupied by Charles University's medical faculty, and is full of hospitals and clinics. Halfway between Žitná and Ječná on Štěpánská is the 14th-century Church of St Stephen (kostel sv Štěpána). Behind it on Na Rybníčku II is one of Prague's three surviving Romanesque rotundas, the Rotunda of St Longinus (rotunda sv Longina), built in the early 12th century.

CHARLES UNIVERSITY BOTANICAL GARDEN Map p106

Botanická zahrada Univerzity Karlovy; 221 953 142; Viničná 7; admission to garden free, to glasshouses adult/child 50/25Kč; 10am-6pm Mar-Nov, to 5pm Dec-Feb; 18, 24

Just south of Karlovo náměstí (main entrance on Na Slupi) is Charles University's botanical garden. Founded in 1775 and moved from

Smíchov to its present site in 1898, it's the country's oldest botanical garden. The steep, hillside garden concentrates on Central European flora and is especially pretty in spring.

CHURCH OF THE ASSUMPTION OF THE VIRGIN MARY & CHARLEMAGNE

Map p116

Kostel Nanebevzetí Panny Marie a Karla Velikého; Ke Karlovu; 10am-5pm Mon-Sat; 6, 11 to Bělehradská or M IP Pavlova

At the southern end of Ke Karlovu is a little church with a big name, founded by Charles IV in 1350 and modelled on Charlemagne's burial chapel in Aachen. In the 16th century it acquired its fabulous ribbed vault, the revolutionary unsupported span of which was attributed by some to witchcraft.

From the terrace beyond the church you can see some of Nové Město's original fortifications, and look out towards ancient Vyšehrad and the modern Nusle Bridge (Nuselský most), which vaults across the valley of the Botič creek, with six lanes of traffic on top and the metro inside.

DVOŘÁK MUSEUM Map p106

Muzeum Antonína Dvořáka; 224 923 363; www.nm.cz; Ke Karlovu 20; adult/child 50/25Kč; 10am-1.30pm & 2-5.30pm Tue-Sun Apr-Sep, 9.30am-1.30pm & 2-5pm Tue-Sun Oct-Mar; M IP Pavlova

The most striking building in the drab neighbourhood south of Ječná is the energetically baroque Vila Amerika, a 1720s, French-style summer house designed by (you guessed it) Kilian Dientzenhofer. It's one of the city's finest baroque buildings, and now houses a museum dedicated to the composer Antonín Dvořák. Special concerts of Dvořák's music are staged here.

EMMAUS MONASTERY Map p106

Klášter Emauzy; Vyšehradská 49; 8am-6pm Mon-Fri, services noon Mon-Fri, 10am Sun; 18, 24

Founded for a Slavonic Benedictine order at the request of Charles IV, and originally called Na Slovanech, the Emmaus Monastery dates from 1372. During WWII the monastery was seized by the Gestapo and the monks were sent to Dachau concentration camp, then in February 1945 it was almost destroyed by a stray Allied fire-bomb. Some monks returned after the war, but the reprieve was short-lived: in 1950 the communists closed down the monastery, and tortured the prior to death. It was finally restored to the Benedictine order in 1990, and reconstruction has been going on ever since.

The monastery's Gothic Church of Our Lady (kostel Panny Marie), badly damaged by the 1945 bombing, reopened in 2003, though the swooping, twin spires were added back in the 1960s. The atmospheric Gothic cloisters have some fine, but faded, original frescoes dating from the 14th century, salted with bits of pagan symbolism.

Across Vyšehradská is the baroque Church of St John of Nepomuk on the Rock (kostel sv Jana Nepomuckého na Skalce), built in 1739 and one of the city's most beautiful Dientzenhofer churches.

NATIONAL MEMORIAL TO THE VICTIMS OF POST-HEYDRICH TERROR Map pp108–9

Národní památník obětí Heydrichiády; 224 920 686; Resslova 9; adult/child 50/20Kč; 10am-5pm Tue-Sun Mar-Oct, to 4pm Tue-Sun Nov-Feb; M Karlovo Náměstí

In 1942 seven Czech paratroopers who were involved in the assassination of Reichsprotektor Reinhard Heydrich (see the boxed text, opposite) hid in the crypt of the Church of Sts Cyril & Methodius for three weeks after the killing, until their hiding place was betrayed by the Czech traitor Karel Čurda. The Germans besieged the church, first attempting to smoke the paratroopers out and then flooding the church with fire hoses. Three paratroopers were killed in the ensuing fight; the other four took their own lives rather than surrender to the Germans.

The crypt now houses a moving memorial to the men, with an exhibit and video about Nazi persecution of the Czechs. In the crypt itself you can still see the bullet marks and shrapnel scars on the walls, and signs of the paratroopers' last desperate efforts to dig an escape tunnel to the sewer under the street. On the Resslova side of the church, the narrow gap in the wall of the crypt where the Germans inserted their fire hoses is still pitted with bullet marks.

NEW TOWN HALL Map pp108–9

Novoměstská radnice; 224 948 229; www.novomestskaradnice.cz; Karlovo náměstí 23; adult/child 40/20Kč; 10am-6pm Tue-Sun May-Sep; M Karlovo Náměstí

The historical focus of Charles Square is the New Town Hall, built in the late 14th century when the New Town was still new. From the window of the main hall (the tower was not built until 1456), two of Wenceslas IV's Catholic councillors were flung to their deaths in 1419 by followers of the Hussite preacher Jan Želivský, giving 'defenestration' (throwing out of a window) a lasting political meaning and sparking off the Hussite Wars. (This tactic was repeated at Prague Castle in 1618.) You can visit the Gothic Hall of Justice, which was the site of the defenestration, and climb the 221 steps to the top of the tower.

U KALICHA Map p106

☎ 224 912 557; www.ukalicha.cz; Na Bojišti 12; 11am-11pm; M IP Pavlova

A few blocks east of Karlovo náměstí is the pub U kalicha (At the Chalice). This is where the eponymous antihero was arrested at the beginning of Jaroslav Hašek's comic novel of WWI, *The Good Soldier Švejk* (which Hašek cranked out in instalments from his own local pub). The pub is milking the connection for all it's worth – it's an essential port of call for Švejk fans, but the rest of us can find cheaper beer and dumplings elsewhere.

VYŠEHRAD

Legend has it that Vyšehrad (High Castle) is the place where Prague was born. According to myth the wise chieftain Krok built a castle here in the 7th century, and Libuše, the cleverest of his three daughters, prophesied that a great city would rise here. Taking as her king a ploughman named Přemysl, she founded both the city of Prague and the Přemysl dynasty.

Archaeologists have discovered that various early Slavonic tribes set up camp at Vyšehrad, a crag above the Vltava River south of the Nusle Valley. The site may have been permanently settled as early as the 9th century, and Boleslav II (r 972–99) may have lived here for a time. By the mid-11th century there was a fortified settlement, and Vratislav II (r 1061–92) moved his court here from Hradčany, beefing up the walls and adding a castle, the Basilica of St Lawrence, the original Church of Sts Peter & Paul and the Rotunda of St Martin. His successors stayed until 1140, when Vladislav II returned to Hradčany.

Vyšehrad then faded into the background until Charles IV, aware of its symbolic importance, repaired the walls and joined them to those of his new town, Nové Město. He built a small palace and decreed that the coronations of Bohemian kings should begin with a procession from here to Hradčany.

Nearly everything there was wiped out during the Hussite Wars. The fortress remained a ruin – except for a ramshackle township of artisans and traders – until after the Thirty Years' War, when Leopold I refortified it.

The Czech National Revival generated new interest in Vyšehrad as a symbol of Czech history. Painters painted it, poets sang about the old days, and Smetana set his patriotic opera *Libuše* here. In 1866 many of the old fortifications were dismantled, various buildings were restored, and the parish graveyard was converted into a national memorial cemetery. Today it is a peaceful green park with great views across the river, the haunt of old ladies walking their dogs, mothers playing with their children on the lawns, and young lovers canoodling on park benches.

BRICK GATE & CASEMATES Map p116

Vratislavova; 9.30am-6pm Apr-Oct, to 5pm Nov-Mar; M Vyšehrad

At the 19th-century Brick Gate (Cihelná brána; admission 10Kč) on the northern side of the fortress you can see an exhibit explaining the history of Vyšehrad and Prague's other fortifications. Here you will also find the entrance

THE HEYDRICH ASSASSINATION

In 1941, in response to a series of crippling strikes and sabotage operations by the Czech resistance movement, the German government appointed SS general Reinhard Heydrich, an antisubversion specialist, as Reichsprotektor of Bohemia and Moravia. Heydrich immediately cracked down on resistance activities with a vengeance.

In a move designed to support the resistance and boost Czech morale, Britain secretly trained a team of Czechoslovak paratroopers for an attempt to assassinate Heydrich. Astonishingly, it succeeded. On 27 May 1942, two paratroopers, Jan Kubiš and Jozef Gabčík, attacked Heydrich as he rode in his official car through the city's Libeň district (see p142) – he later died of his wounds. The assassins and five co-conspirators fled but were betrayed in their hiding place in the Church of Sts Cyril & Methodius (see opposite); all seven died in the ensuing siege.

The Nazis reacted with a frenzied wave of terror, which included the annihilation of two entire Czech villages, Lidice and Ležáky (see p234 for more on the grim fate of Lidice) and the shattering of the underground movement.

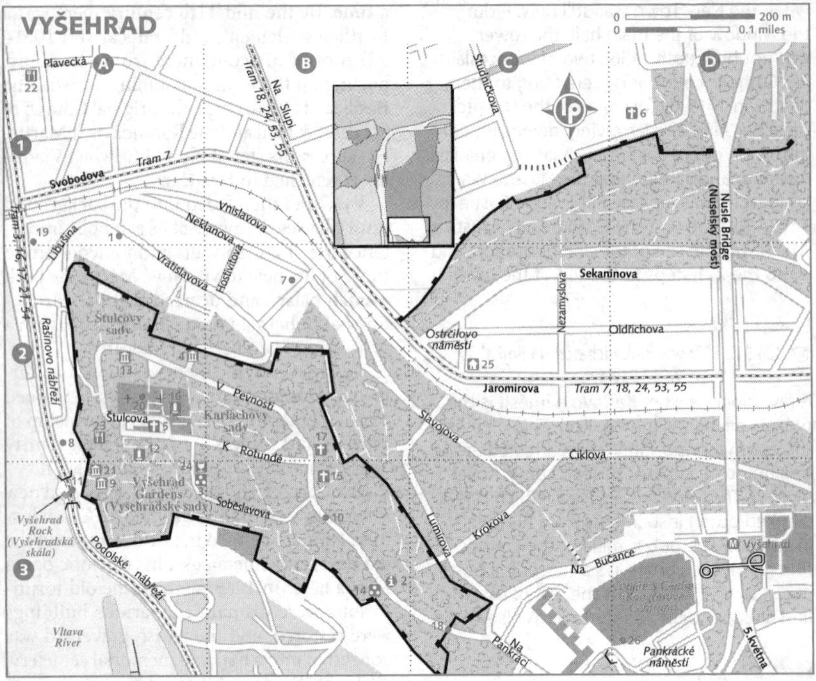

VYŠEHRAD

INFORMATION
Institute for Language & Preparatory Studies.................1 A1
Vyšehrad Information Office.................2 B3

SIGHTS & ACTIVITIES (pp115–18)
Basilica of St Lawrence (Bazilika sv Vavřince).............3 A3
Brick Gate (Cihelná Brána).....................4 A2
Casemates (Kasematy).............(see 4)
Church of Sts Peter & Paul (Kostel sv Petra a Pavla)..........5 A2
Church of the Assumption of the Virgin Mary & Charlemagne (Kostel Nanebevzetí Panny Marie a Karla Velikého)..............6 D1
Church of the Beheading of John the Baptist (Kostelík Stětí sv Jana Křtitele)..........(see 17)
Cubist Apartment Block.............7 B2
Cubist Houses.....................8 A2
Gothic Cellar (Gotický Sklep)......9 A3
Leopold Gate (Leopoldova Brána).................10 B3
Libuše's Bath.....................11 A3
Myslbek Statues.....................12 A2
New Provost's House (Nové Proboštství).................13 A2
Peak Gate (Špička Brána).........14 B3
Rotunda of St Martin...............15 B3
Royal Palace.......................(see 21)
Slavín..............................16 A2
St Mary Chapel in the Ramparts (Kaple Panny Marie v Hradbách).......................17 B2
Tábor Gate (Táborská Brána).... 18 C3
Villa Libušina (Cubist House).....19 A1
Vyšehrad Cemetery.................20 A2
Vyšehrad Gallery (Galerie Vyšehrad).......................21 A3

EATING (pp153–73)
Oliva..............................22 A1
Rio's Vyšehrad.....................23 A2
U Neklana.........................(see 7)

DRINKING (pp175–91)
Občerstvení U Okénka............24 A3

SLEEPING (pp211–27)
Hotel Union.........................25 C2

TRANSPORT (pp241–5)
CS-Czechocar.......................26 D3

to the Casemates (adult/child 30/20Kč), a system of vaulted brick tunnels beneath the ramparts. The largest of these is the barrel-vaulted Gorlice Hall, which served as an air-raid shelter and potato store during WWII. It now houses six of the original baroque statues from Charles Bridge, including *St Ludmila with the Young St Wenceslas* by Matthias Braun (the other originals are in the Lapidárium; see p131), as well as temporary art exhibitions in summer. The Casemates ticket also gives admission to the Gothic Cellar (see opposite).

CHURCH OF STS PETER & PAUL

Map p116

Kostel sv Petra a Pavla; ☎ 249 113 353; K Rotundě 10; adult/child 10/5Kč; 9am-noon & 1-5pm Wed-Mon; Ⓜ Vyšehrad

Vratislav II's Church of Sts Peter & Paul has been built and rebuilt over the centuries, culminating in a neogothic work-over by Josef Mocker in the 1880s. The twin steeples, a distinctive feature of the Vyšehrad skyline, were added in 1903. The interior is a swirling acid trip of colourful Art Nouveau frescoes, painted in the 1920s by various Czech artists.

GOTHIC CELLAR Map p116

Gotický sklep; Vyšehradský sady; adult/child 30/20Kč; 9.30am-6pm Apr-Oct, to 5pm Nov-Mar; M Vyšehrad

The restored Gothic cellars that once lay beneath Charles IV's palace (now gone) house an exhibition dedicated to the history and legend of Vyšehrad. It is packed with archaeological finds and religious relics associated with life on the fortress from 3800 BC until the present day.

ROTUNDA OF ST MARTIN Map p116

Rotunda sv Martina; V Pevnosti; closed to the public; M Vyšehrad

Vratislav II's little chapel, the 11th-century Rotunda of St Martin, is Prague's oldest surviving building. In the 18th century it was used as a powder magazine. The door and frescoes date from a renovation made about 1880.

Nearby are a 1714 plague column and the baroque St Mary Chapel in the Ramparts (kaple Panny Marie v hradbách), dating from about 1750, and behind them the remains of the 14th-century Church of the Beheading of St John the Baptist (kostelík Stětí sv Jana Křtitele).

VYŠEHRAD CITADEL Map p116

241 410 348; www.praha-vysehrad.cz; V Pevnosti 5; admission free; grounds 24hr, information office 9.30am-6pm Apr-Oct, to 5pm Nov-Mar; M Vyšehrad

The main entrance to the citadel is through the Tábor Gate (Táborská brána) at the southeastern end. On the other side of the brick ramparts and ditch are the scant remnants of the Gothic Peak Gate (Špička brána), a fragment of arch that is now part of the information office – all that remains of Charles IV's 14th-century fortifications. Beyond that lies the grand, 17th-century Leopold Gate (Leopoldova brána), the most elegant of the fortress gates.

It's possible to walk around most of the battlements, with grand views over the river and city. Beside the southwestern bastion are the foundations of a small royal palace built by Charles IV but dismantled in 1655. Perched on the bastion itself is the Vyšehrad Gallery (galérie Vyšehrad; admission 10Kč; same as information office), which holds temporary exhibitions. Below the bastion are some ruined guard towers poetically named Libuše's Bath. You can also examine the foundations of the 11th-century Romanesque Basilica of St Lawrence (bazilika sv Vavřince; admission 5Kč; 11am-5pm Mon-Fri, 11.30am-4pm Sat & Sun). Ask for the key at the snack bar next door.

South of the Church of Sts Peter & Paul lie the Vyšehrad Gardens (Vyšehradské sady), with four imposing statues by Josef Myslbek based on Czech legends. Prague's founders Libuše and Přemysl are in the northwestern corner; in the southeast are Šárka and Ctirad (see p130). On Sundays in May, June and August, open-air concerts are held here at 2.30pm, with anything from jazz to oompah bands to chamber music.

In the northwestern corner is the former New Provost's House (Nové proboštství), built in 1874. In the adjacent park, Štulcovy sady, there is an open-air Summer Theatre (Letní scéna) where you can catch a concert or cultural show at 6pm on most Thursdays or the odd children's performance on Tuesday afternoon (usually around 2pm).

The information centre sells a map and guide to Vyšehrad's buildings in English, German, French and Italian.

TRANSPORT: VYŠEHRAD

Metro Vyšehrad metro station (on line C) is five minutes' walk east of the citadel, past the Congress Centre (Kongresové centrum).

Tram Lines 17 and 21 run along the riverbank below the citadel; trams 7, 18 and 24 run along the Nusle Valley to its east. From the tram stop on either line, it's a steep climb up to the citadel.

VYŠEHRAD CEMETERY Map p116

Vyšehradský hřbitov; 249 198 815; K Rotundě 10; admission free; 8am-7pm May-Sep, to 6pm Mar, Apr & Oct, to 5pm Nov-Feb; M Vyšehrad

For Czechs, the Vyšehrad Cemetery is the hill's main attraction. In the late 19th century the parish graveyard was made into a memorial cemetery for famous figures of Czech culture, with a graceful, neo-Renaissance arcade running along the northern and western sides. For the real heroes, an elaborate pantheon called the Slavín (loosely, 'Hall of Fame'), designed by Antonín Wiehl, was added at the eastern end in 1894; its 50-odd occupants include painter Alfons Mucha, sculptor Josef Myslbek and architect Josef Gočár. The motto reads *Ač Zemeřeli Ještě Mluví* (Though dead, they still speak).

The 600 or so graves in the rest of the cemetery include those of composers Smetana and Dvořák and writers Karel Čapek, Jan Neruda and Božena Němcová; there's a directory of famous names at the entrance. One word that you will see all over the place is *rodina* – it means 'family'.

Many of the tombs and headstones are themselves works of art – Dvořák's is a sculpture by Ladislav Šaloun, the Art Nouveau sculptor who created the Jan Hus monument in Old Town Square. To find it from the gate beside the church, head straight across to the colonnade on the far side, and turn left; it's the fifth tomb on your right. To find Smetana's grave, go to the Slavín and stand facing the monument; it's the pale-grey obelisk to your right.

The annual Prague Spring music festival (see the boxed text, p202) kicks off on 12 May, the anniversary of Smetana's death, with a procession from his grave at Vyšehrad to the Municipal House (p99).

AROUND WENCESLAS SQUARE

Walking Tour

1 National Museum Begin at the steps in front of the neo-Renaissance National Museum (Národní muzeum; p110), which dominates the upper end of Wenceslas Square (Václavské náměstí). From the steps you have a grand view down the square, a focal point of Czech history since the 19th century. At the foot of the steps is a pavement memorial to student Jan Palach (see the boxed text, p29).

2 Statue of St Wenceslas Cross the busy traffic artery of Mezibranská to Prague's famous landmark, the equestrian statue of St Wenceslas (sv Václav), the 10th-century 'Good King Wenceslas' of Christmas-carol fame.

3 Memorial to the Victims of Communism A flower bed a short distance downhill from the statue contains a modest memorial to those who died for their resistance to communism (see also p84). Around the anniversary of Jan Palach's death (19 January) the memorial is surrounded by votive candles, flowers and photographs.

4 Grand Hotel Evropa Wander down the middle of the square, admiring the grand buildings on either side. The finest is the 1906 Art Nouveau Grand Hotel Evropa (p112) at No 25, about halfway down on the right.

5 Melantrich Building Across the street at No 36 is the Melantrich Building, from whose balcony the death of Czech communism was pronounced by Alexander Dubček and Václav Havel on 24 November 1989 (it now houses a Marks & Spencer store).

6 Lucerna Palace Turn left into Pasáž Rokoko, a glittering, mirror-lined Art Deco shopping arcade directly across the street from the Grand Hotel Evropa. It leads to the central atrium of the Lucerna Palace (palác Lucerna; p107), dominated by David Černý's Horse, an ironic twist on the St Wenceslas statue in the square outside (it helps to know that the first prime minister of the Czech Republic was also a Václav). For more on David Černý, see the boxed texts, p39 and p137. Turn right beneath the dead horse (you'll see when you get there), and follow the passage to Vodičkova. Bear right across the street and enter the Světozor arcade. Up ahead you'll see a beautiful stained-glass window dating from the late 1940s – it's actually an advertisement for Tesla Radio, an old Czech electronics company.

7 Franciscan Garden At the far end of the Světozor arcade, turn left into the Franciscan Garden (Františkánská zahrada), a hidden oasis of peace and greenery dominated by the soaring nave of the Church of Our Lady of the Snows. Make your way to the far northern corner of the garden, diagonally opposite from where you came in, and you'll find an exit to Jungmann Square (Jungmannovo náměstí).

8 Church of Our Lady of the Snows Go past the arch leading to the Church of Our Lady of the Snows (kostel Panny Marie sněžné; p105), an old Gothic church and former Hussite stronghold, and turn right.

9 Cubist lamppost Keep to the right of the Lancôme shop, and you will come to what

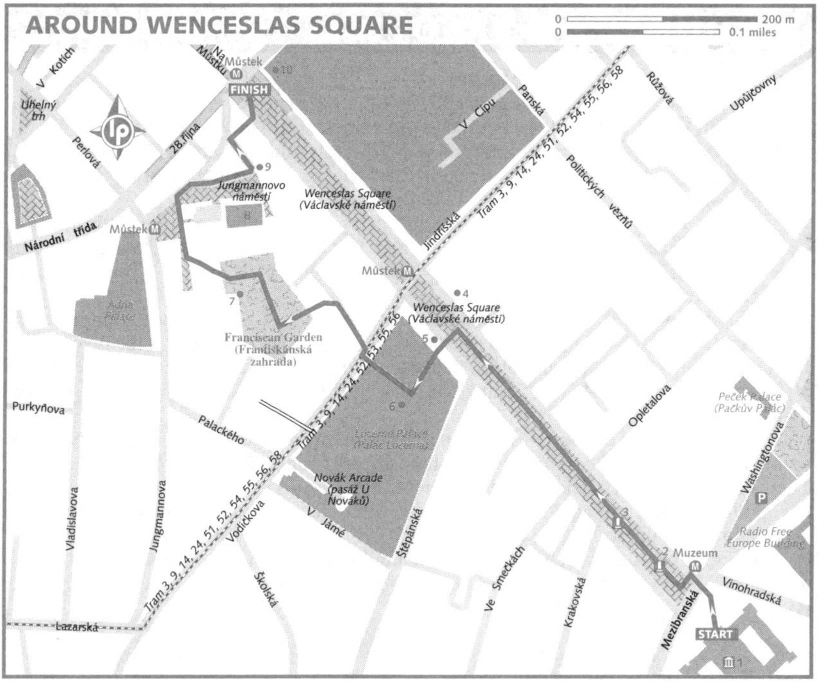

WALK FACTS

Start National Museum (metro Muzeum)

End Na Můstku (metro Můstek)

Distance 1.5km

Time 45 minutes

Exertion Easy

Fuel stops Various cafés around Nové Město

must be the only Cubist lamppost in the entire world, dating from 1915. Turn left here and then duck right through the short Lindt arcade and you will emerge at the foot of Wenceslas Square.

10 Koruna Palác Across the street, on the cornet with Na Příkopě, is the Art Nouveau Koruna Palác (Crown Palace) – look up and you will see the corner tower with the crown of pearls that gives the building its name. From here you can head right along Na Příkopě to the Municipal House and the beginning of the Not Quite the Royal Way walking tour (p102), or retire to one of the many nearby bars and cafés.

VINOHRADY & VRŠOVICE

Eating p166; Drinking p184; Shopping p149; Sleeping p219

Upscale Vinohrady is one of the few parts of Prague that has a consistent personality throughout. In Vinohrady's case, that would be bourgeois. An address in an early 20th-century townhouse on one of Vinohrady's leafy streets marks one as upwardly mobile, enjoying the good life, and perhaps eyeing a move someday to a villa in Střešovice or the nether reaches of Dejvice (in Prague terms, the sign that one's really arrived).

The name Vinohrady means 'vineyards' and refers to the vines that were cultivated here in centuries past; as recently as 200 years ago there was little urbanisation. There is still some wine cultivation in the area and even a lovely, restored wooden gazebo where you can sample some of the local product (p186).

Vinohrady's physical and commercial heart is Peace Square (náměstí Míru), dominated by the neogothic Church of St Ludmilla (kostel sv Ludmily). Right behind it is the neo-Renaissance National House (Národní dům), holding exhibitions and concerts. On the north side of the square is the Vinohrady Theatre (divadlo na Vinohradech), built in 1909, a popular drama venue.

For visitors, there are not many traditional sights, but it's a great place to ramble. The streets to the right or left of the main avenue, Vinohradská, are filled with small cafés and restaurants. There are plenty of parks and at least one terrific open-air beer garden (p184). It's also become the unofficial centre of Prague's gay community, with small bars tucked here and there, as well as the home of mammoth dance club Valentino (p196) in the former Radio Palác complex.

Vršovice is not quite as sophisticated, yet it's hoping a little of Vinohrady's polish might rub off. The area along Francouzská, where it meets Moskevká, including Voroněžská and Krymská, is rapidly gentrifying, and worth a look.

CHURCH OF THE MOST SACRED HEART OF OUR LORD Map p121

Kostel Nejsvětějšího Srdce Páně; náměstí Jiřího z Poděbrad 19; services 8am & 6pm Mon-Sat, 7am, 9am, 11am & 6pm Sun; M Jiřího z Poděbrad

This church was built in 1932 and is one of Prague's most original and unusual pieces of 20th-century architecture. It's the work of Jože Plečnik, the Slovenian architect who also raised a few eyebrows with his additions to Prague Castle. Inspired by Egyptian temples and early Christian basilicas, the glazed-brick building sports a massive, tombstone-like bell tower pierced by a circular glass clock-window.

TRANSPORT: VINOHRADY & VRŠOVICE

Metro Line A runs east through Vinohrady starting at Náměstí Miru station.

Tram Line 11 runs east along Vinohradská and south down Bělehradská; lines 10 and 16 run east along Korunní; lines 4, 22 and 23 run east along Francouská, turning south to meet up with lines 6, 7 and 24, which also run east along Vršovická.

VINOHRADY & VRŠOVICE Walking Tour

This walk (see Map p123) covers a lot of ground but thankfully has few hills. It meanders along some of Prague's nicest residential streets, allowing you to indulge your inner real estate agent for a moment. In the first years after the 1989 revolution, apartments in Vinohrady were going for a song; now they fetch prices that would not be out of place in Paris or London. You could plan a midmorning start, with a light lunch at Viniční Altán or a bigger meal at Mozaika, or an early afternoon start and wind up with a beer at the Riegrovy sady beer garden.

1 Peace Square (náměstí Míru) Known affectionately to Czechs as 'Mirák' – a diminutive form of 'Míru' – this leafy square is the lively heart of Vinohrady. The name still has faint echoes of communist times, when everything was labelled 'Peace' this or 'Peace' that. After 1989, there was talk of scrapping the name. In the end, though, Prague residents decided they didn't mind, and the 'Peace' stayed.

2 Americká Leave the square via Americká, a quiet residential street leading south. It's hard to believe now, but by the time of the Velvet Revolution this street was badly rundown; several apartment houses were even abandoned.

VINOHRADY & VRŠOVICE

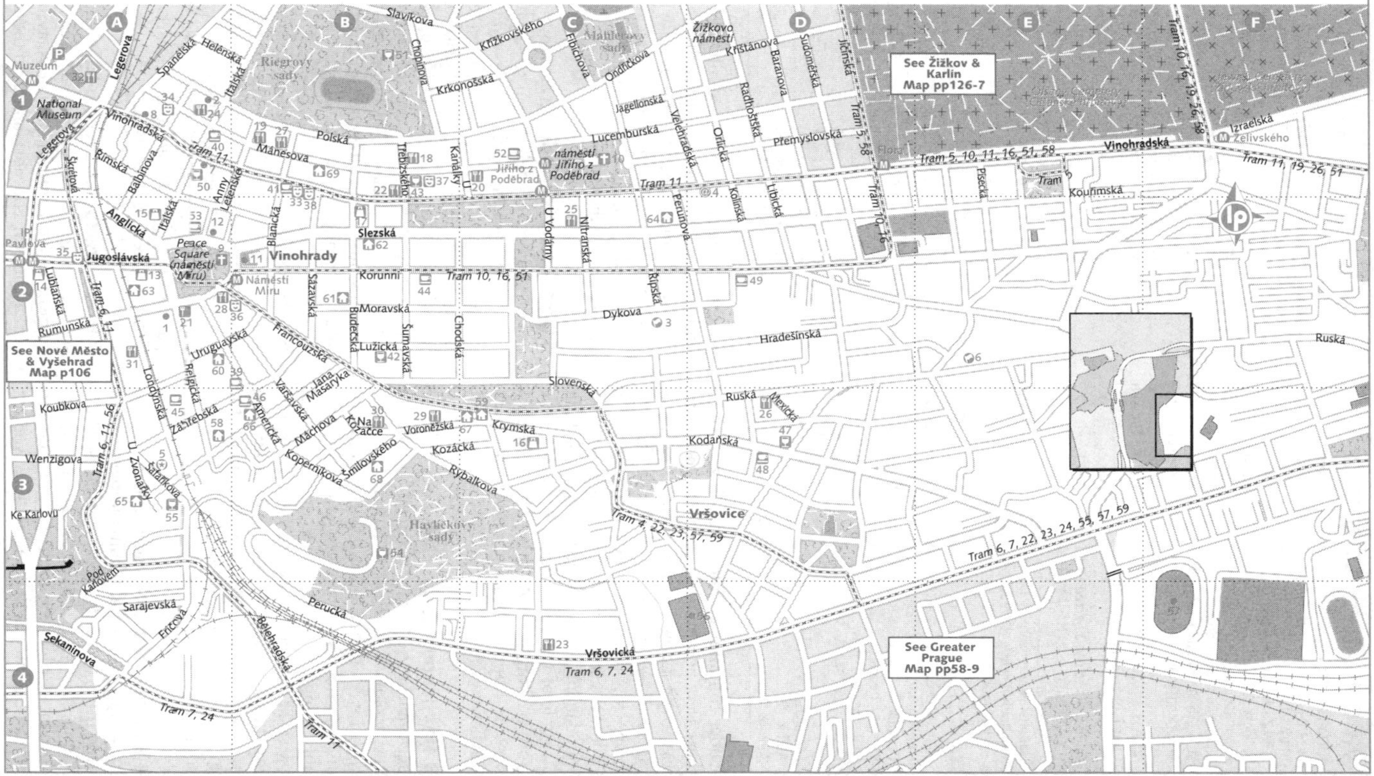

VINOHRADY & VRŠOVICE

Under communism, older buildings such as these were poorly maintained and the vogue was to get a new place in a high-rise housing estate – a *panelák* – on the outskirts of town. Now the trend is exactly the opposite. Follow the street and walk through the small roundabout, marked by an ugly fountain built a couple of years ago chiefly to keep people from parking here. At this point Americká become Koperníkova and ends at the park Havlíčkovy sady.

3 Havlíčkovy sady This rocky hillside park marks the border between Vinohrady and Vršovice and is particularly popular with lovers (since it's relatively secluded) and mothers with strollers (which is arguably a logical consequence of the 'lovers' part). There's no prescribed walk for exploring the park – just choose the most inviting path leading vaguely downhill. Look for signs to the wine garden and gazebo Viniční Altán (p186).

4 Viniční Altán At this stage you're likely to have one of those light-bulb moments when everything suddenly seems clear: this is how Vinohrady ('vineyards') got its name. Open-air wine gardens are a rarity in Prague and none are as nice as this one, with its wooden gazebo overlooking a terraced hillside lined with grape vines. The wine list includes bottles from around the world, but go with a local vintage. On the food side, the choices are limited to salads and sausages – mostly to accompany the beverages.

5 U Havlíčkových Sadů Retrace your steps as best you can through the park, back to the street that lines the park, U Havlíčkových Sadů. Follow this to the right, then make a left at the end of the street onto Rybalkova. Follow Rybalkova, passing the street Voroněžská, which leads down into Vršovice, and continue on to Máchova. At Máchova turn right, crossing busy Francouzská onto Šumavská, and then make a right at Lužická.

6 Lužická This is another classic, tree-lined Vinohrady street, filled with handsome apartment houses and rapidly rising housing valuations – which is just the way the locals like it. Lužická empties out into a small park. Cut straight ahead through park, and onto the street Hradešínská.

7 Hradešínská This street and the one that parallels it to the right, Na Šafránce, have some of the most beautiful private villas in this part of the city. The most famous of these is at

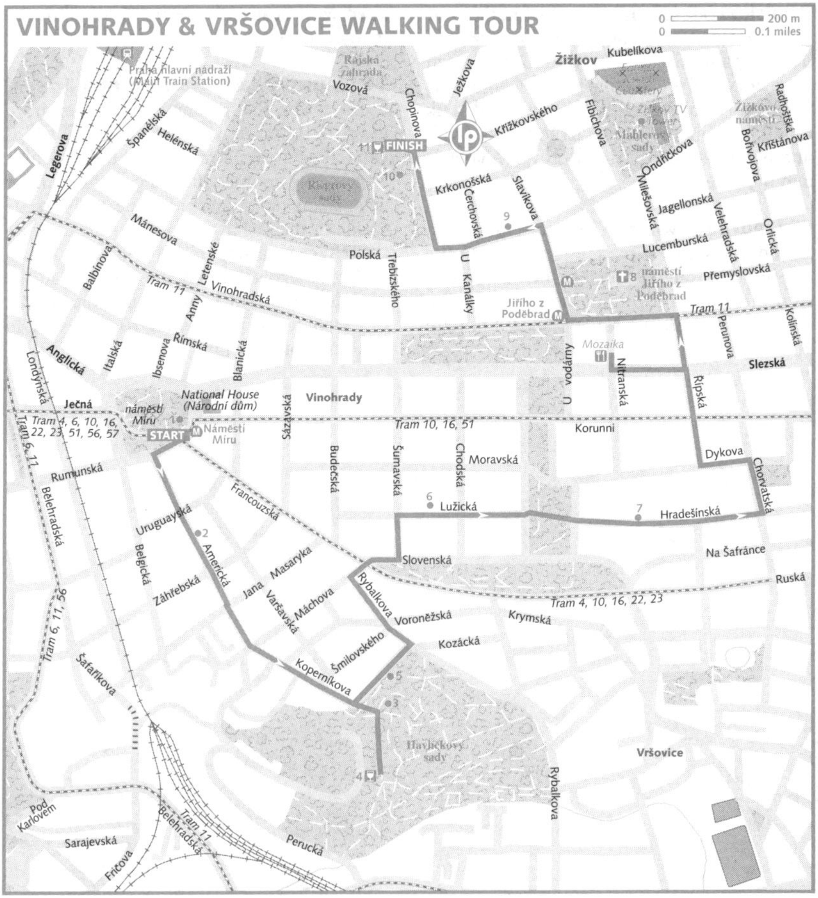

WALK FACTS

Start Peace Square (metro Náměstí Míru or tram 4, 10, 16, 22, 23)
End Riegrovy sady beer garden (metro Jiřího z Poděbrad or tram 11)
Distance 4km to 5km
Time Two to three hours
Exertion Moderate
Fuel stops Viniční Altán, Mozaika, Riegrovy sady beer garden

Hradešínská 6, the family home of early modern Czech architect Jan Kotěra, built in 1908. Turn left at Chorvatská and left again onto Dykova, then right onto Řípská, with a dead-on view of Žižkov's TV Tower (p128) in the background. If it's mealtime, walk one more block to the left to Nitranská to Mozaika (p167), one of the best newer restaurants in the city. At lunch you probably won't have to book ahead, but it can get crowded at dinner.

8 Church of the Most Sacred Heart of Our Lord Řípská takes you eventually to Vinohradská and náměstí Jiřího z Poděbrad, defined by the imposing dark-red brickwork and enormous clock of one of the city's most controversial churches (p120), the work of the modern Slovene master Jože Plečnik. Unless it's Sunday around Mass time, you're unlikely to get a glimpse inside, but walk around to the front entrance just in case the door is open. To continue the walk, find the street Slavíkova that runs past the church's front entrance and follow it to the right, arriving at Polská.

9 Polská Walk left onto Polská for another row of handsome townhouses in various states of disrepair and renovation. About 200m down the road, you'll see the small street Chopinova, which runs to the right. Take this and walk uphill, passing the streets Krkonošská (with another great view of the Žižkov TV Tower) and then Na Švíhance.

10 Riegrovy sady You'll see the entrance to Vinohrady's largest park, Riegrovy sady, to the left, just opposite Na Švíhance. Before dipping into the park you might want to meander down Krkonošská or Na Švíhance. Both are lined with beautifully restored townhouses, many with Art Nouveau façades.

11 Riegrovy sady beer garden The entrance to the beer garden is about 50m from the park entrance; you'll see it to the left as you follow the walkway in. End the walk here or continue another 100m along the path for an amazing panorama of Prague, with Prague Castle in the distance. To return to the centre, retrace your steps to the Jiřího z Poděbrad metro. Alternatively, follow the path in the park downhill, which takes you to the bottom of Vinohradská, from where you can walk to the centre or take tram 11.

ŽIŽKOV & KARLÍN

Eating p168; Drinking p186; Sleeping p221

Named after the one-eyed Hussite hero, Jan Žižka, who defeated the Holy Roman Emperor Sigismund here in 1420, Žižkov was one of Prague's earliest industrial suburbs. It has long had a reputation as a rough-and-ready, working-class neighbourhood, and was full of left-wing revolutionary fervour well before the communist takeover of 1948 – in fact, Žižkov was an independent municipality from 1881 till 1922 and was widely known as the 'people's republic of Žižkov'.

Today it is one of Prague's liveliest districts, with more bars per capita than any other part of Prague (or indeed, it is claimed, any other part of Europe). It's still pretty rough around the edges and much of the district is still grimy and run-down, but the streets near the city centre are slowly getting a face-lift as gentrification creeps in – the upper part of the district is already being referred to in estate agents' adverts as 'Lower Vinohrady'.

The district is dominated by two prominent hilltop landmarks – the communist-vintage TV Tower and the National Monument. The latter sits atop Žižkov Hill, originally known as Vítkov. The famous Battle of Vítkov took place in July 1420 on the long, narrow ridge that separates the Žižkov and Karlín districts. A colossal statue of Jan Žižka (Map pp126–7), the victorious Hussite general, was erected here in 1950, commanding superb views across Staré Město to Prague Castle.

The mostly residential suburb of Karlín lies to the north of Žižkov, squeezed between Žižkov Hill and the Vltava River. It was devastated by the floods of 2002, and since then has been undergoing massive redevelopment, with new glass-and-steel office complexes rising along the banks of the river. The older part of the district, along Křižíkova, is another up-and-coming area, with lots of lovely old Art Nouveau buildings – Lýčkovo namesti is one of the prettiest squares in the city.

ARMY MUSEUM Map pp126–7

Armádní muzeum; ☎ 973 204 924; www.vhu.cz; U Památníku 2, Žižkov; admission free; 🕑 9.30am-6pm Tue-Sun; Ⓜ Florenc

On the way up Žižkov Hill you will find this grim-looking barracks of a museum, which displays a courtyard full of rusting tanks and exhibits on the history of the Czechoslovak army and resistance movement from 1918 to 1945. There is also a fascinating exhibition on the 1942 assassination of Reinhard Heydrich (see the boxed text, p115), with pride of place going to the Mercedes in which Heydrich was travelling when the attack took place.

JEWISH CEMETERY Map pp126–7

Židovské hřbitovy; Izraelská, Žižkov; admission free; 🕑 9am-5pm Sun-Thu & 9am-2pm Fri Apr-Oct, 9am-4pm Sun-Thu & 9am-2pm Fri Nov-Mar, closed on Jewish hols; Ⓜ Želivského

Franz Kafka is buried in this cemetery, which opened around 1890 when the older Jewish cemetery – now at the foot of the TV Tower (p128) – was closed. To find Kafka's grave, follow the main avenue east (signposted), turn right at row 21, then left at the wall; it's at the end of the 'block'. Fans make a pilgrimage on 3 June, the anniversary of his death.

The entrance is beside Želivského metro station; men should cover their heads (yarmulkes are available at the gate). Last admission is 30 minutes before closing.

KARLÍN STUDIOS Map pp126–7

☎ 251 511 804; www.karlinstudios.cz; Křižíkova 34; admission free; 🕑 noon-6pm Tue-Sun; Ⓜ Křižíkova

Housed in a converted factory building, this complex of artists' studios includes a public art gallery that showcases the best of Czech contemporary art, plus two small commercial galleries. This is the place to come and see what's happening at the cutting edge of art in the city.

NATIONAL MONUMENT Map pp126–7

Národní památník; ☎ 222 781 676; U Památníku 1900, Žižkov; Ⓜ Florenc

Although not, strictly speaking, a legacy of the communist era – it was completed in the 1930s – the huge monument atop Žižkov Hill is, in the minds of most Praguers over a certain age, inextricably linked with the Communist Party of Czechoslovakia, and

ŽIŽKOV & KARLÍN

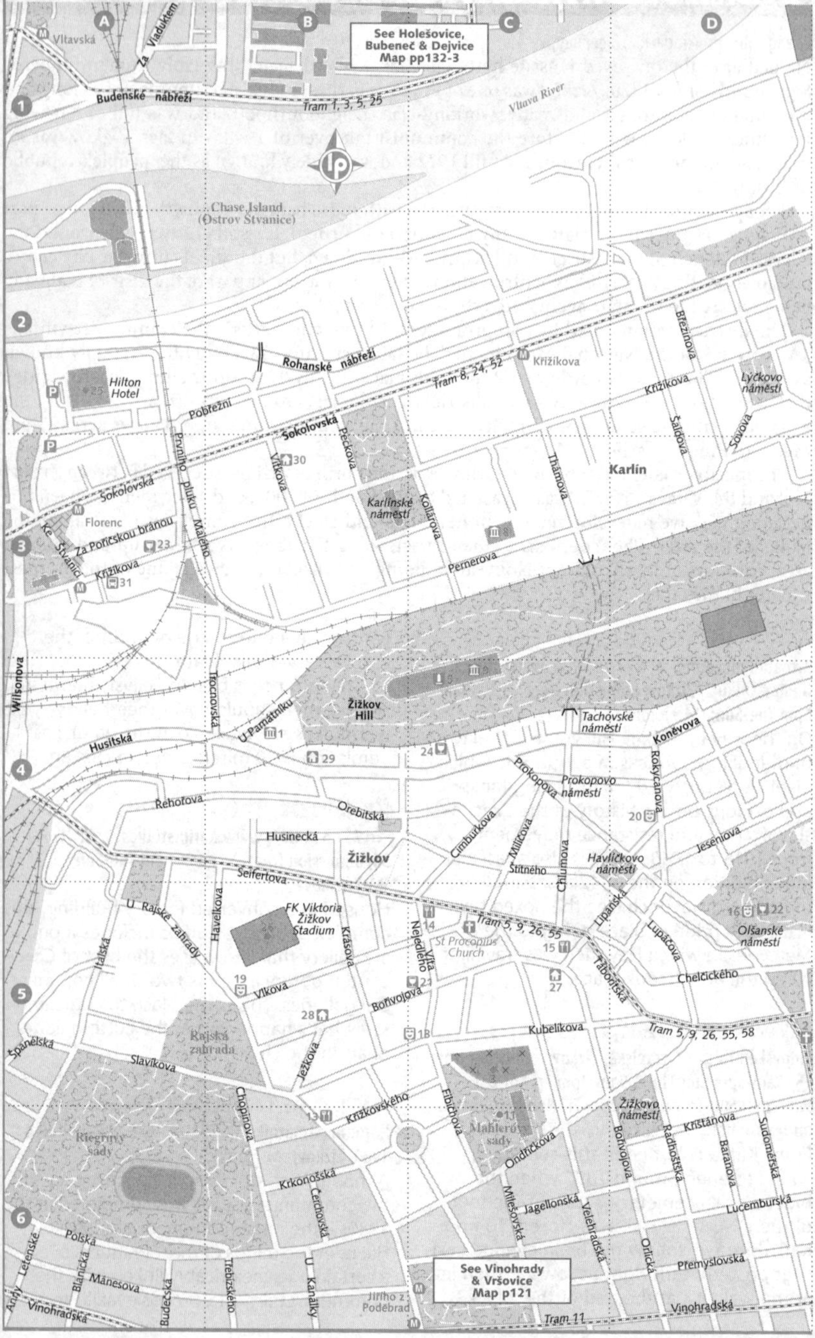

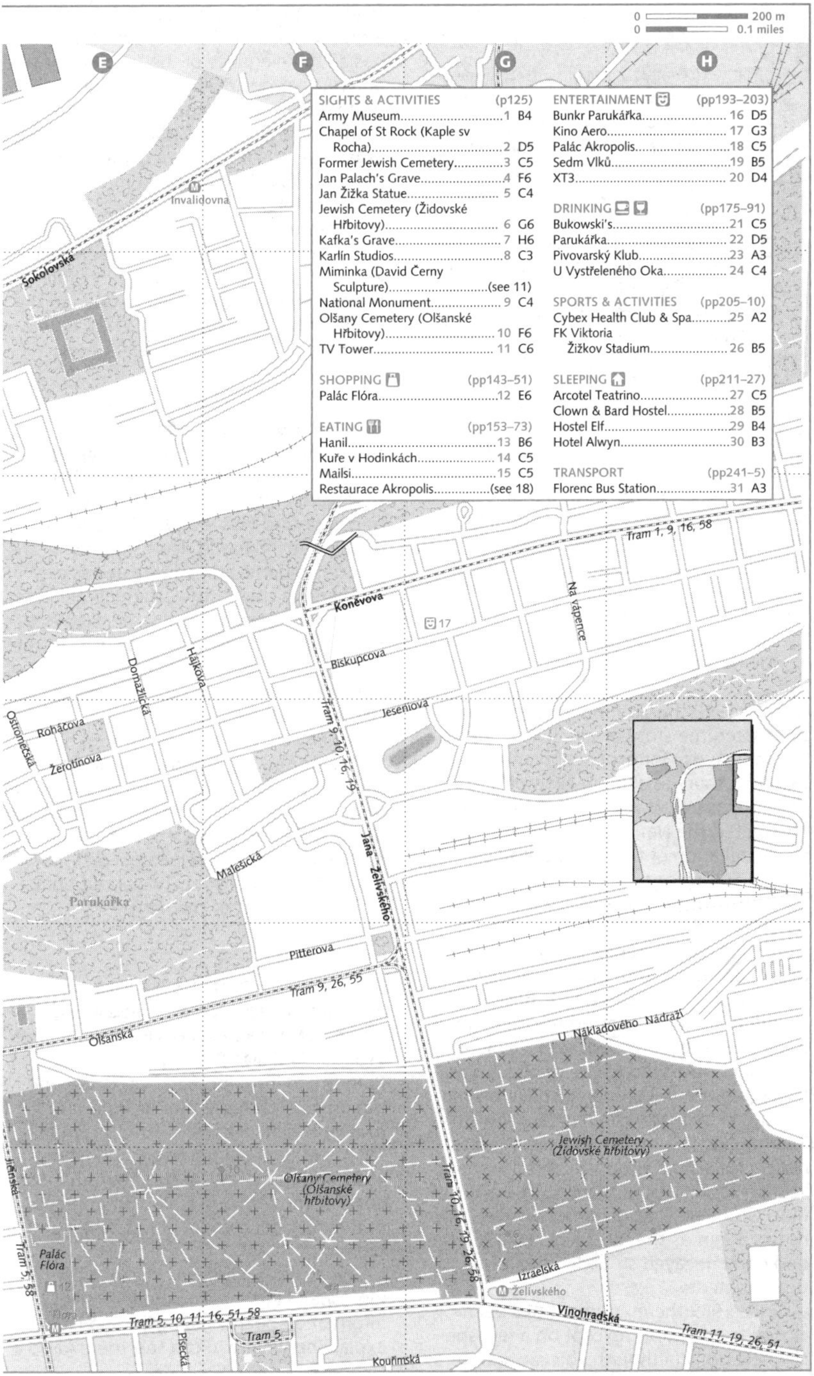
0 200 m
0 0.1 miles
E
F
G
H
Invalidovna
Sokolovská
Tram 1, 9, 16, 58
Na vápence
Koněvova
17
Biskupcova
Jeseniova
Hájkova
Domažlická
Ostromečská
Roháčova
Žerotínova
Tram 9, 10, 16, 19
Jana Želivského
Malešická
Parukářka
Pitterova
Tram 9, 26, 55
Olšanská
U Nákladového Nádraží
Jewish Cemetery
(Židovské hřbitovy)
Olšany Cemetery
(Olšanské hřbitovy)
Jičínská
Tram 10, 16, 19, 26, 58
Izraelská
Želivského
Palác Flóra
Tram 5, 58
Flóra
Tram 5, 10, 11, 16, 51, 58
Tram 5
Písecká
Kouřimská
Vinohradská
Tram 11, 19, 26, 51

JAROSLAV SEIFERT

Born into a working-class family in Žižkov, the poet and journalist Jaroslav Seifert (1901–86) is the only Czech (so far) to be awarded the Nobel Prize for Literature. Although he was originally a member of the Communist Party, he was later expelled after protesting against its increasingly 'Bolshevik tendencies' and, along with Václav Havel, was a signatory of the 1977 human rights charter, Charter 77. Hailed as a spokesman for the people of Czechoslovakia, and a standard-bearer for freedom of expression during the years of communist suppression, he was a vocal critic of the communist government; one of his best-known sayings was, 'If a writer is silent, he is lying.'

in particular with Klement Gottwald, the country's first 'worker–president'.

Designed in the 1920s as a memorial to the 15th-century Hussite commander Jan Žižka, and to the soldiers who had fought for Czechoslovak independence, it was still under construction in 1939 when the occupation of Czechoslovakia by Nazi Germany made the 'Monument to National Liberation', as it was called, seem like a sick joke.

After 1948 the Communist Party appropriated the story of Jan Žižka and the Hussites to use for propaganda purposes, extolling them as shining examples of Czech peasant power. The communists completed the National Monument with the installation of the Tomb of the Unknown Soldier and Bohumil Kafka's gargantuan bronze statue of Žižka. But they didn't stop there.

In 1953 the monument's mausoleum – originally intended to hold the remains of Tomáš Garrigue Masaryk, Czechoslovakia's founding father – received the embalmed body of the recently deceased Klement Gottwald, displayed to the public in a refrigerated glass chamber, just like his more illustrious comrade Lenin in Moscow's Red Square. It soon became a compulsory outing for school groups and busloads of visiting tourists from around the Soviet Bloc. Gottwald's morticians, however, were not as adept as the Russians – by 1962 the body had decayed so badly that it had to be cremated.

Since 1989 the monument has been closed to the public except on a few special occasions (although you can wander freely around the exterior). This is a pity; although the massive memorial building has all the elegance of the reactor house at a nuclear power station, the interior is a spectacular extravaganza of polished marble and gilt, and its memorials – Soviet as well as Czech – allow a glimpse into a period of Czech history that many would prefer to forget.

Things are looking up, though – at the time of research the National Monument was undergoing a two-year renovation project, and was scheduled to open to the public in October 2009 with a new museum and café.

OLŠANY CEMETERY Map pp126–7

Olšanské hřbitovy; Vinohradská 153, Žižkov; admission free; ⌚ 8am-7pm May-Sep, to 6pm Mar, Apr & Oct, to 5pm Nov-Feb; Ⓜ Flora

Huge and atmospheric, Prague's main burial ground was founded in 1680 to handle the increased deaths during a plague epidemic; the oldest stones can be found in the northwestern corner, near the 17th-century Chapel of St Roch (kaple sv Rocha). There are several entrances to the cemetery running along Vinohradská, east of Flora metro station, and also beside the chapel on Olšanská.

Jan Palach, the student who set himself on fire on the steps of the National Museum in January 1969 to protest the Soviet invasion (see the boxed text, p29), is buried here. To find his grave, enter the main gate (flanked by flower shops) on Vinohradská and turn right – it's about 50m along on the left of the path.

TV TOWER Map pp126–7

Televizní vysílač; ☎ 242 418 784; www.tower.cz; Mahlerovy sady 1, Žižkov; adult/child under 6/child 6-14/student 150/free/60/120Kč; ⌚ 10am-11.30pm; Ⓜ Jiřího z Poděbrad

Prague's tallest landmark – and, depending on your tastes, either its ugliest or its most futuristic feature – is the 216m-tall TV Tower, erected between 1985 and 1992. It dominates the skyline from most parts of the city, and is floodlit at night in the national colours of red, white and blue.

The viewing platforms, reached by high-speed lifts, have comprehensive information boards in English and French explaining what you can see; there's also a restaurant at 66m up. But the most bizarre thing about it is the 10 giant crawling babies with coin-slots for faces that appear to be exploring the outside of the tower – an installation called *Miminka* (Mummy) by artist David Černý (see the boxed texts, p39 and p137).

The tower is built on the site of a former Jewish cemetery (admission 20Kč; 9am-1pm Tue & Thu). The cemetery was opened after the Old Jewish Cemetery (p97) in Josefov was closed, and remained in use until 1890, when the much larger Jewish Cemetery (p125) off Vinohradská was opened.

HOLEŠOVICE, BUBENEČ & DEJVICE

Eating p169; Drinking p187; Shopping p150; Sleeping p222

Holešovice, Bubeneč and Dejvice are contiguous neighbourhoods, running east to west, north of the Old Town across the Vltava. Holešovice, the furthest east, nestles inside the big bend of the Vltava, and runs west. It's bisected by a major rail line and highway into distinct eastern and western halves. Bubeneč, in the middle and largely residential, occupies the land directly north of Old Town on the other side of Letná Park. Its defining features are two major parks, Letná Gardens (Letenské sady) and Stromovka. Dejvice, a sprawling, mostly green area to the west, is situated north of Malá Strana and Hradčany.

For decades, Holešovice was badly neglected. It was long considered the 'German' area of the city and became rundown in the decades after WWII when many of the residents left or were expelled. It didn't help that the district was chopped in two by insensitive rail and road construction. The far eastern half, built around the container ports on the Vltava, was the closest Prague had to a true slum.

All of that changed in 2002, when the Vltava flood inundated the low-level areas around the river. The flood's aftermath saw a massive injection of development funds into the neighbourhood. The district's former brewery is now being converted into luxury apartments and office complexes. High-priced condos and office towers now line the western bank of the Vltava, and clubs, restaurants and hotels are moving in. The future looks bright.

Holešovice is home to the vast exhibition grounds known as the Výstaviště (Map pp132–3). Many of the buildings were built to house the 1891 Jubilee Exhibition and are still impressive in a faded-glory kind of way. These include the Prague Pavilion and the grand, Art Nouveau Palace of Industry. Sadly, though, the Výstaviště grounds have been allowed to fall into disrepair and look a little shabby these days. There are a couple of attractions here, including the T-Mobile Arena, one of the leading concert and ice hockey venues in town, but you're not likely to want to linger long.

Bubeneč, up the hill from the western side of Holešovice, has always been a comfortable middle-class neighbourhood, and it's no different now. Anchored by two of Prague's nicest parks, the late 19th-century townhouses on both sides of central avenue Milady Horákové and to the north around Stromovka Park are in high demand. Many embassies and villas, including the spectacular residence of the US ambassador, are here.

Dejvice, further to the west, is a mix of university campuses and residential areas in the western part that merges into the leafy backstreets of Prague's embassy district in the eastern section. There's not too much to see out here, but there are some good restaurants and accommodation options.

Just north of Dejvice is the unusual 1930s villa suburb of Baba, a functionalist project designed by a team of artists and designers that aimed to provide cheap, attractive, single-family houses. The Hanspaulka suburb to its southwest was a similar project, built between 1925 and 1930. Both are now highly desirable addresses.

DIVOKÁ ŠÁRKA Map pp58–9

Evropská; 🚊 20, 26

The valley of the Šárecký potok (Šárka Creek) is one of Prague's best-known and most popular nature parks. It's named after the mythical warrior Šárka, who is said to have thrown herself off a cliff here after the death of her enemy, the handsome Ctirad – whom she either seduced and murdered (committing suicide afterwards to avoid capture), or fell in love with and failed to protect (killing herself out of grief and guilt), depending on which version of the legend you prefer. The most attractive area is nearby, among the rugged cliffs near the Džbán Reservoir. People sunbathe on the rocks, and you can swim in the Džbán Reservoir.

From there it's a 7km walk northeast down the valley on a red-marked trail to the suburb of Podbaba, where the creek empties into the Vltava River. There's a bus stop by the Vltava at Podbaba, for the trip back to the centre, or you can walk south about 1.5km on Podbabská to the northern terminus of tram 8, opposite the Hotel Crowne Plaza (opposite) in Dejvice.

ECOTECHNICAL MUSEUM Map pp132–3

Ekotechnické muzeum; ☎ 233 325 500; www.ekotechnickemuseum.cz; Papírenská 6, Bubeneč;

adult/family 80/150Kč; 10am-4.30pm Sat & Sun May-Oct; 131 from M Hradčanská

Prague's former wastewater treatment plant was built between 1895 and 1906 following a design by English architect WH Lindley. Surprisingly, as the plant was designed to service a city of 500,000 people, it remained in operation until 1967, by which time Prague had a population of over a million. Several steam-powered engines are on display and more are being repaired; there are also guided tours (included with admission) of the labyrinth of sewers beneath the building.

HOTEL CROWNE PLAZA Map pp132–3

224 393 111; www.crowneplaza.cz; Koulova 15; 8

The silhouette of this huge Stalin-era building in northern Dejvice will be familiar to anyone who has visited the Russian capital. Originally called the Hotel International, it was built in the 1950s to a design inspired by the tower of Moscow University, right down to the Soviet-style star on top of the spire (though this one is green, not red).

Nip into the gleamingly restored, marble-clad lobby bar (to the right), and take a look at the large tapestry hanging on the wall in the far left-hand corner. Entitled *Praga Regina Musicae* (Prague, Queen of Music) and created by Cyril Bouda around 1956, it shows an exaggerated aerial view of central Prague. Bang in the centre is the former Stalin Monument on Letná terása, and at the bottom edge you can spot the now-departed Soviet Tank memorial (see the boxed text, p93). For a review of the hotel see p224.

TRANSPORT: HOLEŠOVICE & BUBENEČ

Metro The Vltavská and Nádraží Holešovice metro stations on line C serve the southern and northern parts of Holešovice respectively.

Tram Lines 5, 12, 14, 15 and 17 run along Dukelských Hrdínů, the main north–south street in Holešovice, while trams 1, 8, 15, 25 and 26 run east–west on Milady Horákové, serving both Holešovice and Bubeneč.

TRANSPORT: DEJVICE

Metro Dejvická station is the northwestern terminus of line A; Hradčanská, the last stop but one, serves the southern part of the district.

Tram Lines 2, 8, 20 and 26 all pass through Vítězné náměstí in the centre of Dejvice.

KŘIŽÍK'S FOUNTAIN Map pp132–3

Křižíkova fontána; 220 103 280; www.krizikova fontana.cz; U Výstaviště 1, Holešovice; shows around 250Kč; performances hourly 8-11pm Mar-Oct; 5, 12, 14, 15, 17

Each evening from spring to autumn the musical Křižík's Fountain performs its computer-controlled light-and-water dance. Performances range from classical music such as Dvořák's *New World Symphony* to rousing works performed by Andrea Bocelli, Vangelis and Queen, and theme music from popular films. Call ahead or check the website for details of what's on. The light show is best after sunset – from May to July go for the later shows.

LAPIDÁRIUM Map pp132–3

233 375 636; U Výstaviště 1, Holešovice; adult/child 40/20Kč; noon-6pm Tue-Fri, 10am-6pm Sat & Sun; 5, 12, 14, 15, 17

An outlying branch of the National Museum and an often-overlooked gem, the Lapidárium is a repository for some 400 sculptures from the 11th to the 19th centuries. The exhibits include the Lions of Kouřim (Bohemia's oldest surviving stone sculpture), parts of the Renaissance Krocín Fountain that once stood in Old Town Square, 10 of Charles Bridge's original statues, and many other superb sculptures. See also the boxed text, p93.

LETNÁ Map pp132–3

Letná is a vast open space between Milady Horáková and the river, with a parade ground to the north and a peaceful park, the Letná Gardens (Letenské sady), in the south, offering picture-postcard views over the city and its bridges. In summer you'll find an open-air beer garden (see p187). In 1261 Přemysl Otakar II held his coronation celebrations here, and during communist times, Letná was the site of Moscow-style May Day military parades. In 1989 around 750,000 people gathered here in support of the Velvet Revolution. In 2008, the far northwestern corner of the park was torn up to build the enormous Blanka Tunnel, part of Prague's future ring-road system.

HOLEŠOVICE, BUBENEČ & DEJVICE

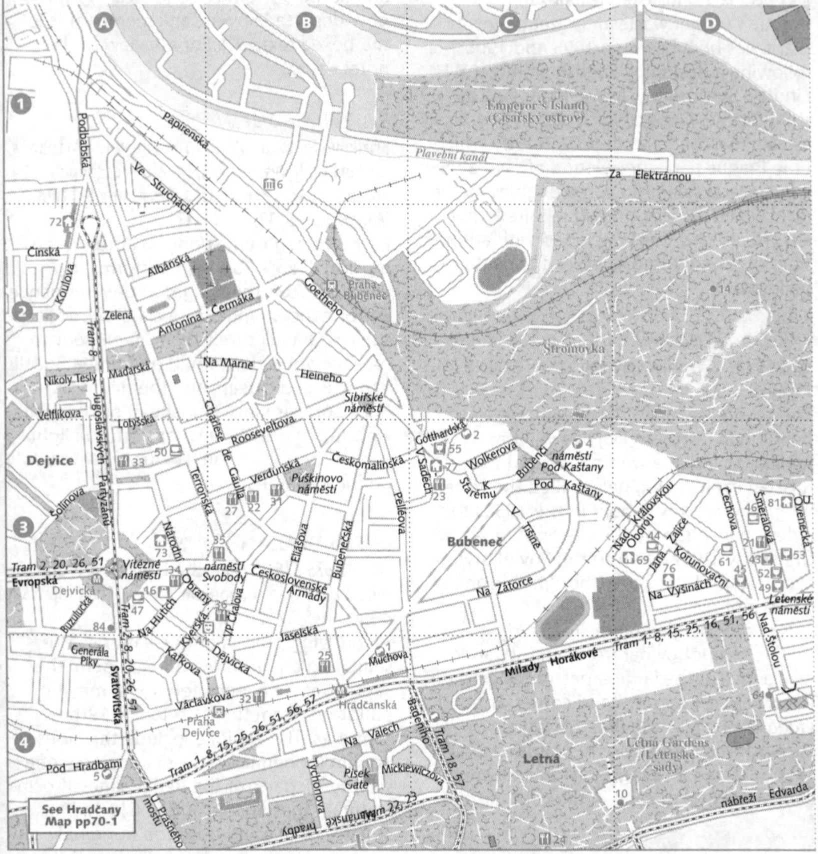

The tunnel will lead under both Letná and Stromovka parks.

In the southwestern corner is the charming, neobaroque Hanavský Pavilón (p169), built by Otto Prieser for the 1891 Jubilee Exposition.

For a walking tour through the park, see p134.

LETNÁ TERÁSA Map pp132–3

The monumental, stepped terrace overlooking the river on the southern edge of Letná Gardens dates from the mid-1950s, when a huge statue of Stalin – the world's largest – was erected here by the Communist Party of Czechoslovakia, only to be blown up in 1962 by the same sycophants when Stalin was no longer flavour of the decade (see the boxed text, p93). A giant metronome designed by artist David Černý – a symbolic reminder of the passing of time – has stood in its place since 1991.

MOŘSKÝ SVĚT Map pp132–3

☎ 220 103 275; U Výstaviště 1, Holešovice; adult/child 240/145Kč; 🕑 10am-7pm; 🚊 5, 12, 14, 15, 17

The Czech 'Sea World' has the largest water tank in the country, with a capacity of around 100,000L. Some 4500 living species of fish and sea creatures are on display, with a good and suitably scary set of sharks. The cramped interior will be disappointing if you're used to larger 'Sea World'–type amusement parks around the world. Nevertheless, it's a fun day out for little kids.

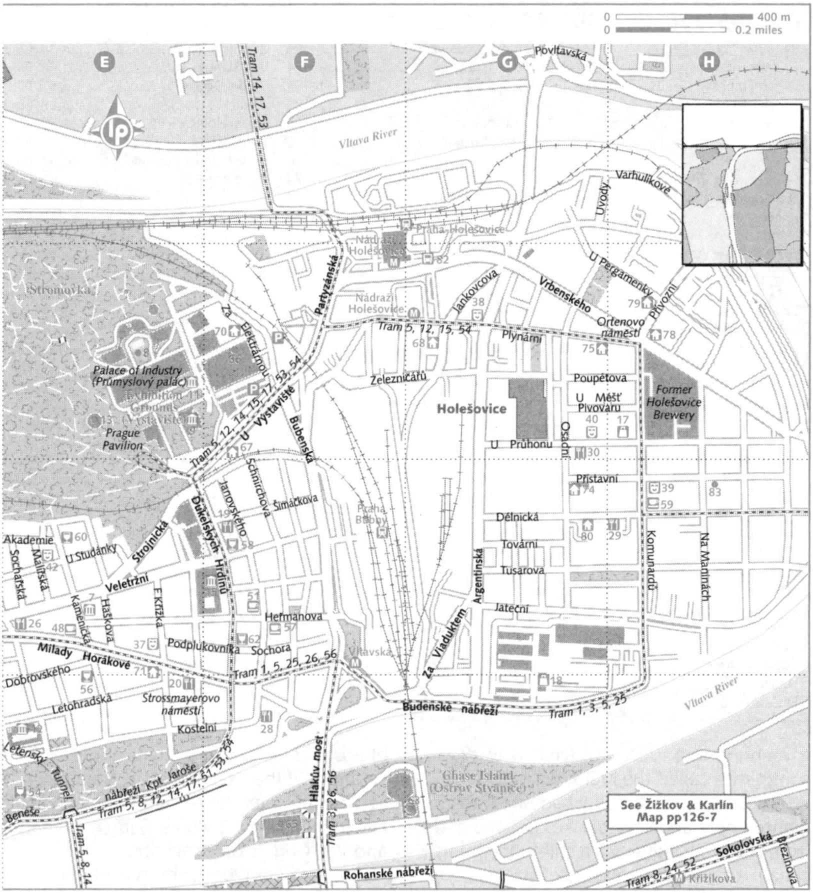

NATIONAL TECHNICAL MUSEUM

Map pp132–3

Národní technické muzeum; ☎ 220 399 111; www.ntm.cz; Kostelní 42, Holešovice; adult/child 70/30Kč; 🕑 9am-5pm Tue-Fri, 10am-6pm Sat & Sun; 🚊 1, 8, 15, 25

The museum was closed in 2008 for extensive renovations, and there was some concern that it might not reopen in time for the 2009 season. We recommend calling in advance to make sure. Before it was closed, the museum had a huge main hall chock-full of vintage trains, planes and automobiles, including 1920s and '30s Škoda and Tatra cars and even a couple of Bugattis, plus an active programme of other temporary technical exhibits aimed at machine-loving geeks and gearheads.

PRAGUE PLANETARIUM Map pp132–3

Planetárium Praha; ☎ 220 999 001; www.planetarium.cz; Královská Obora 233, Holešovice; exhibition adult/child 10/5Kč, shows 60Kč; 🕑 8.30am-noon & 1-8pm Mon-Thu, 9.30am-noon & 1-8pm Sat & Sun; 🚊 5, 12, 14, 15, 17

The planetarium in Stromovka park, just west of Výstaviště, presents various slide and video presentations in addition to the star shows. Most shows are in Czech only, but one or two of the more popular ones provide a text summary in English. There's also an astronomical exhibition in the main hall.

STROMOVKA Map pp132–3

🚊 5, 12, 14, 15, 17

Stromovka, west of Výstaviště, is Prague's largest park. In the Middle Ages it was a

HOLEŠOVICE, BUBENEČ & DEJVICE

INFORMATION

Canadian Embassy......1 B4
Dutch Embassy......2 C3
Israeli Embassy......3 C4
Russian Embassy......4 C3
Slovak Embassy......5 A4

SIGHTS & ACTIVITIES (pp130–6)

Ecotechnical Museum (Ekotechnické Muzeum)......6 B1
Hotel Crowne Plaza......(see 72)
Hunt Kastner Artworks......7 E3
Křižík's Fountain (Křižíkova Fontána)......8 E2
Lapidárium......9 E2
Létna Terása......10 D4
Mořský Svět......11 E2
National Technical Museum (Národní Technické Muzeum)......12 E4
Prague Planetarium (Planetárium Praha)......13 E2
Stromovka......14 D2
Veletržní Palace (Veletržní Palác)......15 F3

SHOPPING (pp143–51)

Antikvita......16 A3
Pivní Galerie......17 H2
Pražská Tržnice......18 G4

EATING (pp153–73)

Bohemia Bagel......19 F3
Capua......20 E4
Čínská Zahrada......21 D3
Da Emanuel......22 B3
El Gaucho......23 C3
Hanavský Pavilón......24 C4
Haveli......25 B4
Hong Kong......26 E3
Kavala......27 B3
La Crěperie......28 F4
Lucky Luciano......29 H3
Molo 22......30 G2
Na Urale......31 B3
Open-Air Market......32 B4
Pizzeria Grosseto......33 A3
Restaurant U Cedru......34 A3
Sakura......35 B3
Staročeská Krčma......36 B3

ENTERTAINMENT (pp193–203)

Bio Oko......37 E3
Cross Club......38 G2
La Fabrika......39 H3
Mecca......40 G2
Spejbl & Hurvínek Theatre......41 A3
Wakata......42 E3

DRINKING (pp175–91)

Akádemie......43 D3
Alchymista......44 D3
Andaluský Pes......45 D3
Antonie......46 D3
Artesa......47 A3
Bio Oko......(see 37)
Erhartova Cukrárna......48 E3
Fraktal......49 D3
Kabinet......50 A3
Kumbal......51 F3
La Bodega Flamenca......52 D3
Le Tram......53 D3
Letenský Zameček......54 E4
Na Slamníku......55 C3
Na Staré Kovárně......56 E4
Ouky Douky......57 F3
Postel......58 F3
První Holešovická Kavárna......59 H3
Stromoffka......60 E3
Těsně Vedle Burundi......61 D3
U sv Antoníčka......62 F3

SPORTS & ACTIVITIES (pp205–10)

Czech Lawn Tennis Club......63 G4
Půjčovna Bruslí Miami......64 D4
Štvanice Stadium......65 F4
T-Mobile Aréna......66 F2

SLEEPING (pp211–27)

A&O Hostel......67 F2
Absolut Hotel......68 G2
Art Hotel......69 D3
Expo Prague......70 F2
Hotel Belvedere......71 E3
Hotel Crowne Plaza......72 A2
Hotel Denisa......73 A3
Hotel Extol Inn......74 G3
Hotel Leon......75 G2
Hotel Letná......76 D3
Hotel Villa Schwaiger......77 C3
Plaza Alta Hotel......78 H2
Plus Prague Hostel......79 H2
Sir Toby's Hostel......80 G3
Splendid......81 D3

TRANSPORT (pp241–5)

Holešovice Bus Station......82 G2
Secco Car......83 H3
Vecar......84 A3

royal hunting preserve, which is why it's sometimes called the Královská obora (Royal Deer Park). Rudolf II had rare trees planted here and several lakes created (fed from the Vltava River via a still-functioning canal). It's now the preserve of strollers, joggers, cyclists and in-line skaters. For a walking tour through the park, see right.

VELETRŽNÍ PALACE Map pp132–3

Veletržní palác; ☎ 224 301 024; www.ngprague.cz; Dukelských Hrdinů 47, Holešovice; adult/child 200/100Kč, after 4pm 100/50Kč; 10am-6pm Tue-Sun; 5, 12, 14, 15, 17

The huge, functionalist Veletržní palác (Trade Fair Palace), built in 1928 to house trade exhibitions, is now home of the National Gallery's superb collection of 20th- and 21st-century Czech and European art.

You could easily spend an entire day here – the collection is spread over three floors of the vast, ocean-liner-like building – but if you have only an hour to spare, head for the 3rd floor (Czech Art 1900–30, and 19th- and 20th-century French Art) to see the paintings of František Kupka, pioneer of abstract art, and the art, furniture and ceramics of the Czech Cubists. The French section includes some sculpture by Rodin, a few Impressionist works, Gaugin's *Flight* and Van Gogh's *Green Wheat*.

The 1st floor (20th-century Foreign Art) includes works by Klimt, Schiele and Picasso, while the 2nd floor (Czech Art 1930 to present day) has early examples of kinetic art, some Socialist Realist stuff from the communist era and various amusing works by contemporary artists.

LETNÁ & STROMOVKA

Walking Tour

This is a long walk through some of the leafiest parts of Prague; make a half-day or even a full-day expedition out of it. Instead of taking the bus and metro from Troja back to the city centre, you can also time it so as to catch a boat trip back (see p251).

1 Stone grotto Begin at the Summer Palace (Letohrádek) at the eastern end of the Royal

Garden (Královská zahrada; p63), north of Prague Castle. A path at the southern end of the Summer Palace leads east into the neighbouring park of Chotkovy sady; in the centre of the park you'll find a little stone grotto dedicated to the historical novelist Josef Zeyer and, nearby, a park bench with a superb view over the river and Staré Město. Doing this part of the route is possible only from April to October, as the Royal Garden is closed in winter. An alternative start involves taking tram 18 to the Chotkova stop and following Gogolova east into Letná Gardens (Letenské sady). You can visit Chotkovy sady by doubling back across the bridge at the eastern end of the gardens.

2 Hanavský pavilón A footbridge at the eastern end of the gardens leads across Chotkova and into the huge Letná Gardens, crossing a broad grassy ditch lined with red-brick walls that once formed part of Prague's fortifications. Follow the main path, which bears right from the park entrance, but then detour further right to visit the Hanavský pavilón

WALK FACTS

Start Summer Palace (tram 22, 23 to Letohrádek stop)
End Troja (bus 112 to metro Nádraží Holešovice)
Distance 6km
Time Three hours
Exertion Moderate
Fuel stops Hanavský pavilón, Letná beer garden, La Crêperie

LETNÁ & STROMOVKA WALKING TOUR

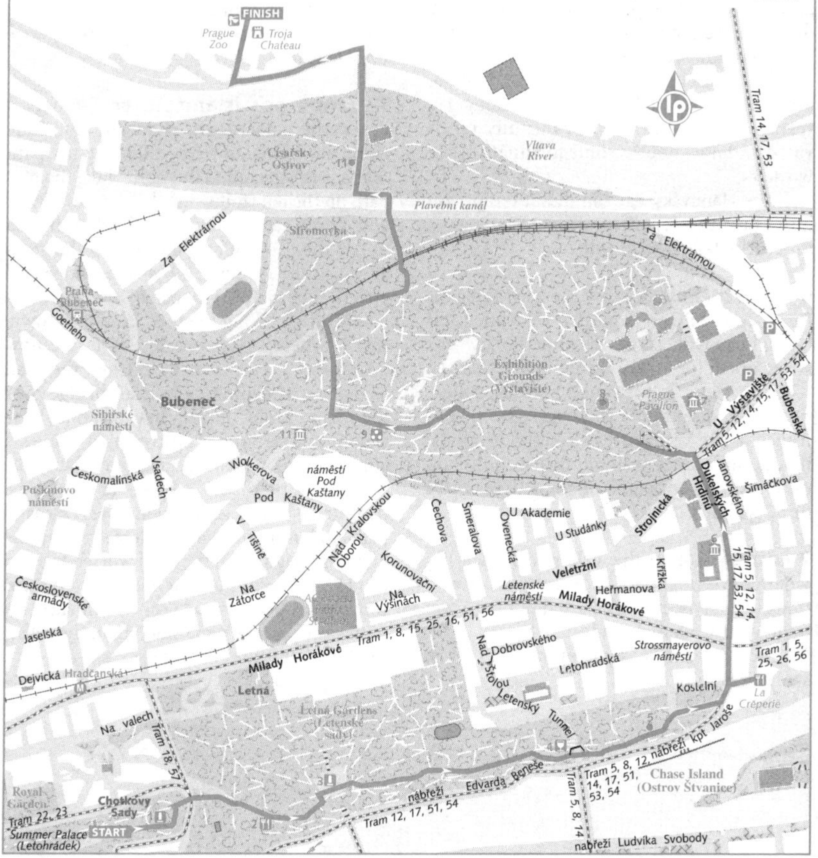

(p169), where you can enjoy a superb panorama and, perhaps, a little lunch.

3 Metronome The path continues along the top of a bluff directly above the Vltava, with great views over the river and the eastern and southern parts of the city, before arriving at a monumental stepped terrace topped by a giant, creaking metronome. Designed by artist David Černý, the metronome sits on a spot once occupied by a giant statue of Stalin (see the boxed text, p93). For more on David Černý, see the boxed texts, p39 and opposite.

4 Letná beer garden Continue east along the path at metronome level and you will eventually arrive at Letná's popular beer garden, Letenský zameček (p187), where it's almost compulsory to stop for a cold one.

5 Expo 58 Restaurant Beyond the beer garden, the path slopes down through pretty flower gardens and along an avenue of plane trees, past the futuristic Expo 58 Restaurant. Built for the Brussels World Exposition of 1958, and later re-erected here, it is no longer a restaurant but has been beautifully renovated and now houses some fortunate office workers.

If the Hanavský Pavilón didn't tempt you into a lunch stop, perhaps cosy La Crêperie (p172) on nearby Janovského will.

6 Veletržní Palace Leave the park and continue downhill on Skalecká, then turn left along busy Dukelských Hrdinů. Follow this street north for 400m – stopping to visit the Veletržní Palace (p134), Prague's premier collection of modern art, if you wish – to the entrance of the Výstaviště exhibition grounds; if you don't fancy walking this section, hop on a tram for a couple of stops (lines 5, 12 or 17 will do).

7 Lapidárium If the Veletržní Palace has whetted your appetite for cultural attractions (or maybe it's just started raining), you might like to detour into the Lapidárium (p131) for a wander among some of the city's finest sculptures.

8 Prague Planetarium Otherwise, bear left at the entrance to Výstaviště and follow the path just to the left of the terminal loop of the 5 tram, passing the dome of the Prague Planetarium (Planetárium Praha; p133) on your right as you enter the former royal hunting ground, Stromovka (p133).

9 Old restaurant Follow your nose as the path curves to the left, past people playing *boules* on the gravel verge, then bear right towards the pond. Turn left when you reach a broad main path (signposted 'Dejvice & Bubeneč'), which leads between a series of artificial lakes on the right and a once-grand but now ruined old restaurant and bandstand on the left.

10 Mistodržitelský Summer Palace Beyond this you'll see the Renaissance Mistodržitelský Summer Palace perched on a hill to the left, where Bohemian royals used to hang out on their hunting trips to Stromovka. It was remodelled in neogothic style in the early 19th century.

11 Emperor's Island At the T-junction below the palace, turn right and continue along an avenue of trees, following the path as it curves around to the right. Take the first path on the left (following the signs to 'Troja' and 'Zoo'), continue through the short tunnel under the railway line, and go up the steps ahead in the distance. Cross the bridge and go left, then right (signposted 'Zoo'; if you're planning on taking the boat back into town, this is where it leaves from). You are now on Emperor's Island (Císařský ostrov); the road leads to a sweeping pedestrian bridge over the main branch of the Vltava, with a canoe slalom course visible upstream (if there's a competition on, you can guarantee there'll be a beer tent there also). At the far end of the pedestrian bridge go left along the riverbank path, and in about 300m you'll reach a parking area; turn right, and the road will lead you to the 112 bus terminus. On one side of the bus terminus is Troja Chateau (Trojský zámek; p140), with a museum of wine-making in the cellar; on the other is the entrance to Prague Zoo (p140). Take your pick.

SMÍCHOV

Eating p172; Drinking p190; Shopping p151; Sleeping p226

Smíchov arguably deserves a reputation as Prague's most economically varied district. For years, it languished as a depressed industrial backwater that was (by some accounts) home to Prague's largest Roma community. At the same time, the hills southwest of the Anděl metro station, not far from the Barrandov film studios, had some of the city's swankiest villas. These days, those jarring contrasts are seen in the area around Anděl, which is filled with gleaming office towers, the vast Nový Smíchov shopping centre (p151), the Staropramen brewery, and some of the city's hottest boutique hotels. Just down the road, near the Smíchovské nádraží train station, the poverty and neglect sets in again.

As with the city's other riverside districts, Smíchov both suffered and benefited from the 2002 flood. Low-lying areas were submerged, but the aftermath saw a big infusion of development capital. Like Holešovice and Karlín, Smíchov is also hoping to play off its industrial chic a bit. That effort got a huge boost in 2007 when artist David Černý (see the boxed text, p39) decided to relocate his 'Meet Factory' performance art space amid the tenements and abandoned factories south of Smíchovské nádraží.

FUTURA GALLERY Map p138

☎ 251 511 804; www.futuraprojekt.cz; Holečkova 49; admission free; 🕐 11am-6pm Wed-Sun; 🚊 4, 7, 9, 10

The Futura Gallery focuses on all aspects of contemporary art, ranging from painting, photography and sculpture to video, installations and performance art. The gallery spaces, which include two floors of 'white cube' halls, a more intimate brick-vaulted cellar and a garden, host changing exhibitions by both Czech and international artists. The most notorious exhibit is in the garden, a permanent installation by David Černý (see the boxed texts, p39 and below). It consists of two huge, naked human figures, bent over at the waist with their heads buried in a blank wall. Ladders allow you to climb up and place your head – there's really no polite way to say this – up each figure's arse, where you can watch a video of Czech president Václav Klaus and the director of Prague's National Gallery spooning mush into each other's mouths. Richly metaphorical, to say the least.

MEET FACTORY Map p138

☎ 251 551 796; http://meetfactory.cz; Ke Sklárně 15; admission free; 🕐 vary by event; 🚊 12, 14, 20 stop to Lihovar

Don't come here looking for a polished art experience. For the moment, David Černý's 'Meet Factory' is very much a work in progress. The idea is to invite artists from

WEIRD ART

David Černý's sculpture is often controversial, occasionally outrageous and always amusing. Here are six of his best-known works that are permanently on view in Prague. See also the boxed text, p39.

- *Quo Vadis* (Where Are You Going; 1991) – in the garden of the German Embassy in Malá Strana (Map pp76–7). A Trabant (an East German car) on four human legs serves as a monument to the thousands of East Germans who fled the communist regime in 1989 prior to the fall of the Berlin Wall, and camped out in the embassy garden seeking political asylum. See Malá Strana Walking Tour, p85.
- *Viselec* (Hanging Out; 1997) – above Husova street in Staré Město (Map pp88–9). A bearded, bespectacled chap with a passing resemblance to Sigmund Freud, casually dangling by one hand from a pole way above the street.
- *Kun* (Horse; 1999) – in the Lucerna Palace shopping arcade, Nové Město (Map pp108–9). Amusing alternative version of the famous St Wenceslas Statue in Wenceslas Square, only this time the horse is dead.
- *Miminka* (Mummy; 2000) – on the TV Tower, Žižkov (Map pp126–7). Creepy, giant, slot-faced babies crawling all over a TV transmitter tower – something to do with consumerism and the media. We think.
- *Brownnosers* (2003) – in the Futura Gallery, Smíchov (Map p138). Stick your head up a statue's backside and watch a video of the Czech president and the director of the National Gallery feeding each other baby food.
- *Proudy* (Streams; 2004) – in the courtyard of Hergetova Cihelná, Malá Strana (Map pp76–7). Two guys pissing in a puddle (whose irregular outline, you'll notice, is actually the map outline of the Czech Republic) and spelling out famous quotations from Czech literature with their pee. (Yes, the sculpture moves! It's computer controlled.)

SMÍCHOV

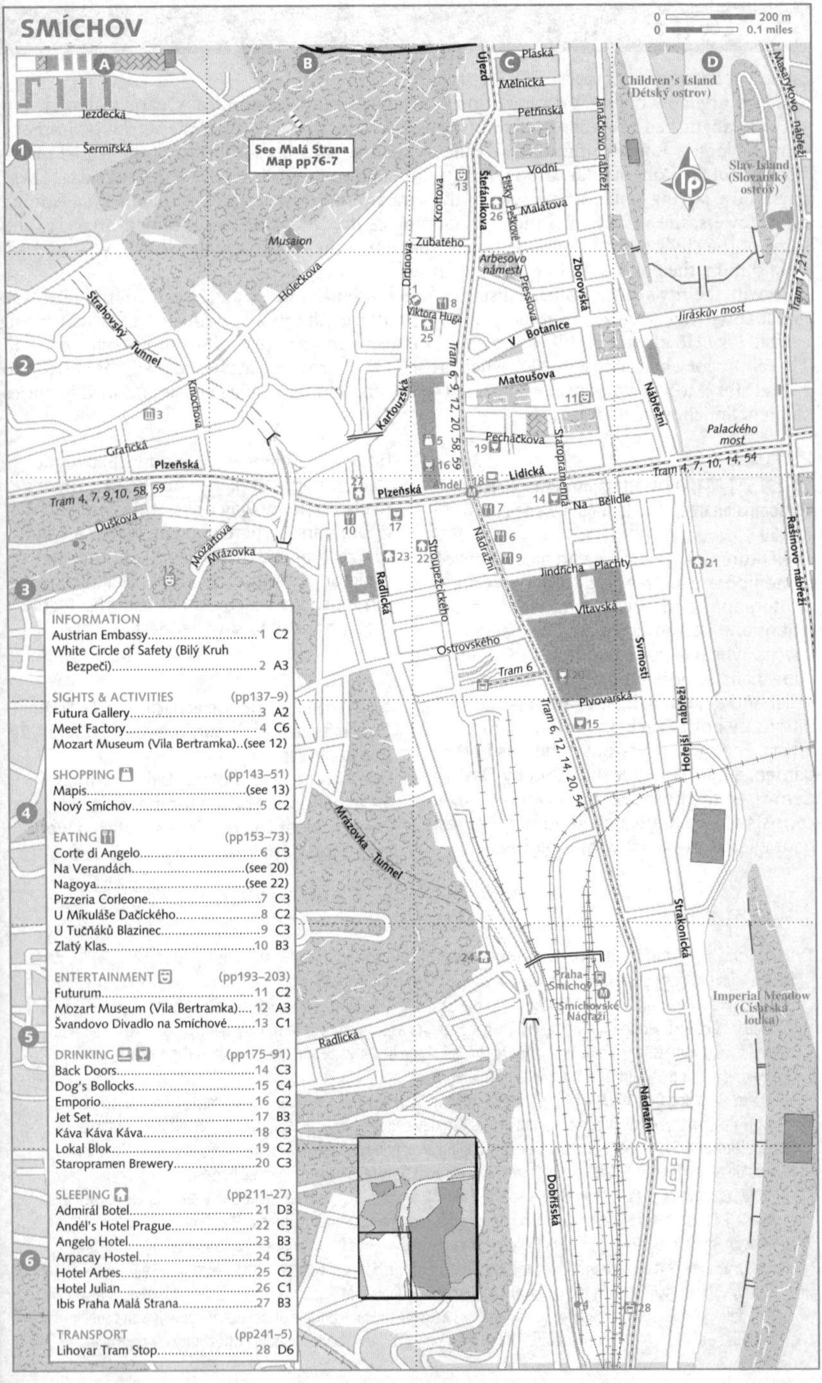

INFORMATION
- Austrian Embassy....1 C2
- White Circle of Safety (Bílý Kruh Bezpečí)....2 A3

SIGHTS & ACTIVITIES (pp137–9)
- Futura Gallery....3 A2
- Meet Factory....4 C6
- Mozart Museum (Vila Bertramka)..(see 12)

SHOPPING (pp143–51)
- Mapis....(see 13)
- Nový Smíchov....5 C2

EATING (pp153–73)
- Corte di Angelo....6 C3
- Na Verandách....(see 20)
- Nagoya....(see 22)
- Pizzeria Corleone....7 C3
- U Míkuláše Dačíckého....8 C2
- U Tučňáků Blazinec....9 C3
- Zlatý Klas....10 B3

ENTERTAINMENT (pp193–203)
- Futurum....11 C2
- Mozart Museum (Vila Bertramka)....12 A3
- Švandovo Divadlo na Smíchové....13 C1

DRINKING (pp175–91)
- Back Doors....14 C3
- Dog's Bollocks....15 C4
- Emporio....16 C2
- Jet Set....17 B3
- Káva Káva Káva....18 C3
- Lokal Blok....19 C2
- Staropramen Brewery....20 C3

SLEEPING (pp211–27)
- Admirál Botel....21 D3
- Anděl's Hotel Prague....22 C3
- Angelo Hotel....23 B3
- Arpacay Hostel....24 C5
- Hotel Arbes....25 C2
- Hotel Julian....26 C1
- Ibis Praha Malá Strana....27 B3

TRANSPORT (pp241–5)
- Lihovar Tram Stop....28 D6

TRANSPORT: SMÍCHOV

Metro Line B has stations at Anděl, in the heart of Smíchov, and at Smíchovské Nádraží in the south.
Tram Lines 4, 7, 10 and 14 rumble across Palackého most from Charles Square (Karlovo náměstí) to Smíchov; from Malá Strana take trams 12 or 20 south from Malostranské náměstí or Újezd.

around the world to live and create in this cavernous, abandoned factory south of Smíchovské nádraží. The Meet Factory also holds visual and performance art happenings, film screenings and concerts. The problem is that the group that runs it, headed by prominent local artists, is still scraping together the cash to patch the walls and install heating, so actual happenings are few and far between. Be sure to check the website before venturing this far out.

There's no easy way to get here. The best bet is to take tram 12, 14 or 20 from Smíchovské nádraží two stops to Lihovar, find the narrow gate on the right side of the road, cross five or six sets of railway tracks (be sure to look both ways!), and there it is – a crumbling greenish factory with two red fibreglass cars hanging from hooks outside, courtesy of David Černý himself.

MOZART MUSEUM Map p138

Vila Bertramka; ☎ 257 318 461; www.bertramka.com; Mozartova 169; museum admission adult/child 110/30Kč, concerts 390-450Kč; 🕑 9.30am-6pm Apr-Oct, to 5pm Nov-Mar; 🚋 4, 7, 9, 10
Mozart stayed at the elegant 17th-century Vila Bertramka during his visits to Prague in 1787 and 1791 as the guest of composer František Dušek – it was here that he finished his opera *Don Giovanni*. Today the house is a modest Mozart museum. Regular concerts are held in the salon (see p200 for more details) and in the garden (April to October only).

OUTER NEIGHBOURHOODS

Clustered around the city's historic core are the largely 20th-century suburbs of Troja, Kobylisy, Kbely, Zbraslav, Barrandov, Střešovice and Břevnov. Except to visit the Prague Zoo and Troja Chateau, few tourists venture into these outer regions and you will often have the attractions here to yourself.

PRAGUE ZOO Map pp58–9

Zoo Praha; ☎ 296 112 111; www.zoopraha.cz; U Trojského Zámku 120, Troja; adult/child/family 150/100/450Kč; 9am-7pm Jun-Aug, to 6pm Apr, May, Sep & Oct, to 5pm Mar, to 4pm Nov-Feb; 112 from M Nádraží Holešovice

Prague's attractive zoo is set in 60 hectares of wooded grounds on the banks of the Vltava River. Pride of place, at the top of the hill, goes to a herd of Przewalski's horses – the zoo's breeding programme played an important part in saving them from extinction (the zoo's logo is a Przewalski's horse) – and the Komodo dragons, which bred in captivity for the first time in 2006. Other attractions include a miniature cable car and an extensive kids' play area with adventure playground and paddling pool.

TROJA CHATEAU Map pp58–9

Trojský zámek; ☎ 283 851 614; U Trojského Zámku 1; adult/child 120/60Kč; 10am-6pm Tue-Sun Apr-Oct, to 5pm Tue-Sun Nov-Mar; 112 from M Nádraží Holešovice

Troja Chateau is a 17th-century baroque palace built for the Šternberk family, inspired by the Roman country villas seen by the architect on a visit to Italy. The sumptuously decorated palace now houses the Prague City Gallery's collection of 19th-century Czech art, a gallery of paintings of dogs and horses owned by the Bohemian aristocracy, and exhibits explaining the sculptures and frescoes that adorn the palace itself. In the cellars you'll find a small museum dedicated to the history of wine-making in the Czech lands (admission free, 20Kč per sample if you want to taste some wines). There's free admission to the palace grounds, where you can wander in the beautiful French gardens, watched over by a gang of baroque stone giants on the balustrade outside the southern door.

KOBYLISY ANTI-FASCIST RESISTANCE MEMORIAL off Map pp58–9

Památník protifašistického odboje v Kobylisích; Žernosecká; admission free; 24hr; 10, 17, 24

This grassy quadrangle of earthen embankments, ringed by trees and overlooked by apartment blocks, was once the Kobylisy Rifle Range. More than a hundred Czechs were executed here by firing squads during WWII. Today it's the site of a national memorial: a huge bronze plaque lists all the names of the dead and – such is the legacy of Nazi bureaucracy – the dates and times of their executions. Take tram 10, 17 or 24 to the terminal at Ďáblická, then walk west for 800m (about 10 minutes) along Žernosecká.

KBELY AIRCRAFT MUSEUM off Map pp58–9

Letecké muzeum Kbely; ☎ 973 207 500; Mladoboleslavská; admission free; 10am-6pm Tue-Sun May-Oct; 185 or 259 from M Českomoravská

The Kbely airfield in northeastern Prague is home to this aircraft museum, where you can have a close look at Russian MiG fighter planes and a host of exhibits on aeronautics and space flight. The impressive collection amounts to no less than 275 aircraft, including several British and American machines such as a 1931 De Havilland Tiger Moth, a Gloster Meteor jet-fighter (1950) and a McDonnell Douglas F4 Phantom (1954).

ZBRASLAV CHATEAU off Map pp58–9

Zámek Zbraslav; ☎ 257 921 638; Bartoňova 2; adult/child 80/40Kč; 10am-6pm Tue-Sun; 129, 241, 243, 255 or 360 from M Smíchovské Nádraží

Zbraslav is a small town on the western bank of the Vltava, 10km south of the centre, that was only recently incorporated into Greater Prague. As long ago as 1268 Přemysl Otakar II built a hunting lodge and a chapel here, later rebuilt as a Cistercian monastery. In 1784 it was converted into a baroque chateau that now houses the National Gallery's permanent collection of Asian art, with copies of well-known Czech sculptures in the gardens.

BARRANDOV Map pp58–9

246, 247, 248 from M Smíchovské Nádraží

The southern suburb of Barrandov, on the western bank of the Vltava River, was developed in the 1930s by Václav Havel, the father of ex-president Havel. It is famous for the Barrandov Studios, the film studios founded by Miloš Havel (the ex-president's uncle) in 1931 and increasingly popular with Hollywood producers in recent years: *Mission Impossible* (1996), *The League of Extraordinary Gentlemen* (2003), *Casino Royale* (2006) and the first two 'Chronicles of Narnia' movies (2005 and 2008) all made use of the facilities here.

The district was deliberately developed as an homage to 1920s Hollywood, with the Jazz Age architect Max Urban commissioned to create the Barrandov Terraces, an upmarket complex of Art Deco mansions, villas and apartments ranged along a bluff overlooking the Vltava River, in conscious imitation of the Hollywood Hills. Sadly, the district was 'nationalised' and neglected during the communist era and fell into disrepair; the best views of its crumbling splendour are from the opposite side of the river.

The suburb was named after the 19th-century French geologist Joachim Barrande, who studied the fossils in the contorted limestone of the Barrandov Cliffs (Barrandovské skály; Map pp58–9) – hundreds of them are on display in the National Museum.

PUBLIC TRANSPORT MUSEUM

Map pp70–1

Muzeum MHD; ☎ 296 124 900; www.dpp.cz; Patočkova 4, Střešovice; adult/child 35/20Kč; 9am-5pm Sat, Sun & hols Apr-Oct; tram 1, 2, 15, 18, 25

The museum at the Střešovice tram depot has a large collection of trams and buses, from an 1886 horse-drawn tram to present-day vehicles. It's a great place for kids as they can climb into some of the vehicles, and you can board a vintage tram (see p252) for a sightseeing tour of the city.

VILLA MÜLLER Map pp58–9

Müllerova vila; ☎ 224 312 012; www.mullerovavila.cz; Nad Hradním Vodojemem 14, Střešovice; guided tours in Czech adult/concession 300/200Kč, in English or German 400/300Kč; 9am-6pm Tue, Thu, Sat & Sun Apr-Oct, 10am-5pm Tue, Thu, Sat & Sun Nov-Mar; tram 1, 2, 18 to Ořechovka

Fans of functionalist architecture will enjoy this masterpiece of domestic design. It was built in 1930 for construction entrepreneur František Müller, and designed by the Viennese architect Adolf Loos, whose clean-cut, ultramodernist exterior contrasts with the polished wood, leather and oriental rugs of the classically decorated interior. The villa can be visited only by guided tour, which must be booked in advance; tours begin every two hours from 9am April to October, from 10am November to March.

TRANSPORT: BŘEVNOV

Tram Lines 15, 22 and 25 run along Patočkova and Bělohorská, the main drag. Tram 15 terminates at the Vypich stop; 22 and 25 continue to Bílá Hora.

TRANSPORT: TROJA

Boat Take a boat trip (see p251) from the city centre to the Troja landing.

Bus Take bus 112 from Nádraží Holešovice metro station to the end of the line. From April to September a free shuttle bus (Linka Zoo) runs on this route at weekends.

On Foot Walk from Výstaviště to Troja through Stromovka (3km).

BŘEVNOV MONASTERY Map pp58–9

Břevnovský klášter; ☎ 220 406 111; Patočková 72; gardens admission free, guided tour of church, crypt & monastery 50Kč; gardens 5.30-8am & 5-8.30pm Mon-Fri, 5.30am-8.30pm Sat & Sun, tours 10am & 2pm Sat & Sun, plus 4pm May-Sep; tram 15, 22, 25

Břevnov Monastery is the Czech Republic's oldest Benedictine monastery, founded in 993 by Boleslav II and Bishop Vojtěch Slavníkovec (later to be canonised as St Adalbert). The two men, from powerful and opposing families intent on dominating Bohemia, met at Vojtěška spring, each having had a dream that this was the place where they should found a monastery. Its name comes from *břevno* (beam), after the beam laid across the spring where they met.

The present baroque monastery building and the nearby Basilica of St Margaret (Bazilika sv Markéty) were completed in 1720 by Kristof Dientzenhofer. During the communist era the monastery housed a secret-police archive; Jan Patočka (1907–77), a leading figure of the Charter 77 movement, who died after interrogation by the secret police, is buried in the cemetery behind the monastery. In 1993 (the 1000th anniversary of the monastery's

TRANSPORT: STŘEŠOVICE

Tram Lines 1, 2 and 18 run along Střešovická, the main street.

founding) the restored 1st floor, with its fine ceiling frescoes, and the Romanesque crypt, with the original foundations and a few skeletons, were opened to the public for the first time.

The church, crypt and monastery can be be visited only by guided tour (minimum 10 people for a tour in Czech, 20 people in English or German), but at weekends you can wander the gardens at your leisure.

STAR SUMMER PALACE off Map pp58–9

Letohrádek hvězda; ☎ 235 357 938; Obora hvězda, entrances on Libocká & Bělohorská; adult/child 30/15Kč; 10am-6pm Tue-Sun May-Sep, to 5pm Tue-Sun Apr & Oct, closed Nov-Mar; 15, 22, 25

The Letohrádek hvězda is a Renaissance summer palace in the shape of a six-pointed star, built in 1556 for Archduke Ferdinand of Tyrol. It sits at the end of a long avenue through the lovely wooded park of Obora hvězda, a hunting reserve established by Ferdinand I in 1530. The palace houses a small museum about its history and an exhibit on the battle of White Mountain (see below).

From the Vypich tram stop, bear right across open parkland to the white archway in the wall; the avenue on the far side leads to the palace (a 1.5km walk from the tram).

WHITE MOUNTAIN off Map pp58–9

Bílá Hora; access from Karlovarská; 22, 25

The 381m-high White Mountain – more of a gentle hillock, actually – on the western outskirts of Prague was the site of the 1620 collapse of Protestant military forces that ended Czech independence for almost 300 years. The only reminder of the battle is a small memorial cairn located on a mound in the middle of a field, with the roof of the Star Summer Palace poking above the forest to the northeast.

Take the tram to the end of the line, then continue west past the Church of Our Lady Victorious (kostel Panny Maria Vítězná), an early-18th-century celebration of the Habsburg victory at White Mountain, and turn right; the field is visible up ahead.

V HOLEŠOVIČKÁCH Map pp58–9

10, 24

The spot in the suburb of Libeň where Reichsprotektor SS Obergruppenführer Reinhard Heydrich was assassinated (see the boxed text, p115) has changed considerably since 1942 – the tram tracks have gone and a modern road intersection has been built. It's near where the slip road exits north from V Holešovičkách to Zenklova. A small memorial was finally built here in May 2008, 66 years after the event – because the Czech paratroopers who carried out the assassination were trained in Britain, the communist regime had preferred not to remember them. At the time of research, a competition had just been launched to design a larger monument.

To get to the site, take tram 10 or 24 to the Zenklova stop (Map pp58–9) and walk south for a few minutes. The neighbouring streets, Gabčíkova and Kubišova, are named after the parachutists who carried out the attack.

The Army Museum (p125) in Žižkov has a fascinating exhibition detailing the assassination, including the actual car in which Heydrich was travelling at the time of the attack.

SHOPPING

top picks

SHOPPING

In the last decade or so Prague's shopping scene has changed beyond recognition. A massive influx of global brand names and a wave of glitzy new malls crammed with designer outlets, smart cafés and big Western brand names has left the city's main shopping streets looking very much like those of any other European capital.

Imported goods often carry Western European prices, but Czech products remain affordable for Czechs and cheap for Westerners. While tourist gift shops outside Prague – see Karlštejn (p230) or Mělník (p233) – have smaller selections, prices are significantly lower. If you're hunting for bargains, the word *'sleva'* means 'discount'.

SHOPPING AREAS

The city centre's single biggest – and most exhausting – retail zone is around Wenceslas Square (Václavské náměstí), its pavements jammed with browsing visitors and locals making beelines for their favourite stores. You can find pretty much everything here, from high fashion and music megastores to run-of-the-mill department stores and gigantic book emporia. Many of the more interesting shops are hidden away in arcades and passages, such as the Lucerna Palace (Map pp108–9).

The other main shopping drag intersects with the lower end of Wenceslas Square, comprising Na Příkopě, 28.října and Národní třída (Map pp88–9 and (Map pp108–9). Most of the big stores and malls are concentrated on Na Příkopě, with the biggest of them all – the Palladium Praha Shopping Centre (Map p106) – at its northeast end, opposite the Municipal House.

In Staré Město, the elegant avenue of Pařížská (Map pp88–9) is lined with international designer houses including Dior, Boss, Armani and Louis Vuitton, while the back streets to its east are home to boutiques operated by Czech fashion designers. In contrast, the winding lanes between the Old Town Square and Charles Bridge are thronged with tacky souvenir shops flaunting puppets, Russian dolls and 'Czech This Out' T-shirts.

In recent years many new shops have opened up outside the centre, notably in Vinohrady (Map p121), which is good for antiques and designer furniture; Smíchov (Map p138), dominated by the huge Nový Smíchov mall; and the suburb of Zličín on the far western edge of the city, which has a vast shopping centre ranged around Tesco and IKEA.

OPENING HOURS

Prague shops usually open anywhere between 8am and 10am, and close between 5pm and 7pm on Monday to Friday; major shops, departments stores and tourist businesses also open on weekends, but more local shops may be closed on Saturday afternoon and Sunday.

CONSUMER TAXES

Value-added tax (VAT, or DPH in Czech) is applied at 5% on food, hotel rooms and restaurant meals, but 22% on luxury items (including alcohol). This tax is included in the marked price and not added at the cash register.

It is possible to claim VAT refunds of up to 14% of the purchase price for purchases totalling more than 2000Kč that are made in shops displaying the 'Tax Free Shopping' sticker. They will give you a Tax Free Shopping voucher, which you then need to present to customs for validation when you leave the country (which must be within three months of the date of purchase). You can then claim your refund either at a duty-free shop in the airport (after passing through passport control) or from a cash-refund office back home (within six weeks of the purchase date). For more information, see www.globalrefund.com.

HRADČANY

ANTIQUE MUSIC INSTRUMENTS

Map pp70–1 Antiques

☎ 220 514 287; www.antiques.cz; Pohořelec 9; 9am-6pm; 22, 23

It may not get the prize for most inventive shop name, but this place is a real treasure-trove of vintage stringed instruments. You'll find an interesting stock of antique violins, violas and cellos dating from the 18th century to the mid-20th century, as well as bows, cases and other musical accessories.

In the same premises you'll find the Icon Gallery, a luminous collection of Russian and Eastern European religious icons, as well as lots of other decorative *objets d'art*, watches, porcelain and Art Nouveau glassware.

HOUPACÍ KŮŇ Map pp70–1 Toys

☎ 603 515 745; Loretánské náměstí 3; 🕑 9.30am-6.30pm; 🚊 22, 23

The 'Rocking Horse' toy shop houses a collection of carved wooden folk dolls, old 1950s wind-up tractors, toy cars and – surprise – even a couple of rocking horses. There are quality toys and art supplies you won't find anywhere else in Prague, but for a typically Czech souvenir look out for the famous and ubiquitous Little Mole character, available here in several guises.

MALÁ STRANA

VETEŠNICTVI Map pp76–7 Antiques

☎ 257 530 624; Vítezná 16; 🕑 10am-5pm Mon-Fri, 10am-noon Sat; 🚊 6, 9, 12, 20, 22, 23

This is an Aladdin's cave of second-hand goods, bric-a-brac and junk with, in all likelihood, some genuine antiques for those who know what they're looking for. There's affordable stuff for all, from communist-era lapel pins, medals, postcards, old beer mugs and toys to crystal, shot glasses, porcelain, china, pipes and spa cups, all presided over by a bust of Lenin.

SHAKESPEARE & SONS Map pp76–7 Books

☎ 257 531 894; www.shakes.cz; U Lužického Semináře 10; 🕑 11am-7pm; 🚊 12, 20, 22, 23

This is a newer and smaller branch of the famous English-language second-hand bookshop of the same name in Vinohrady (see p149).

PAVLA & OLGA Map pp76–7 Fashion

☎ 728 939 872; Vlašská 13; 🕑 2-7pm Mon-Fri, 3-7pm Sat; 🚊 12, 20, 22, 23

Sisters Pavla and Olga Michalková originally worked in the film and TV industry before setting up their own fashion label, creating a unique collection of quirky and cute hats, clothes and accessories. Past customers have included Czech supermodel Tereza Maxová, Britpop band Blur and photographer Helmut Newton. There's another branch in Staré Město (Map pp88–9; Karoliny Světlé 30; 🕑 10am-7pm).

CLOTHING SIZES

Women's clothing						
Aus/UK	8	10	12	14	16	18
Europe	36	38	40	42	44	46
Japan	5	7	9	11	13	15
USA	6	8	10	12	14	16
Women's shoes						
Aus/USA	5	6	7	8	9	10
Europe	35	36	37	38	39	40
France only	35	36	38	39	40	42
Japan	22	23	24	25	26	27
UK	3½	4½	5½	6½	7½	8½
Men's clothing						
Aus	92	96	100	104	108	112
Europe	46	48	50	52	54	56
Japan	S		M	M		L
UK/USA	35	36	37	38	39	40
Men's shirts (collar sizes)						
Aus/Japan	38	39	40	41	42	43
Europe	38	39	40	41	42	43
UK/USA	15	15½	16	16½	17	17½
Men's shoes						
Aus/UK	7	8	9	10	11	12
Europe	41	42	43	44½	46	47
Japan	26	27	27½	28	29	30
USA	7½	8½	9½	10½	11½	12½

Measurements approximate only; try before you buy.

CAPRICCIO Map pp76–7 Music

☎ 257 320 165; Újezd 15; 🕑 10am-6pm Mon-Fri; 🚊 6, 9, 12, 20

Pick up the score for Mozart's *Don Giovanni* or Dvořák's *New World Symphony* at this eclectic sheet-music shop, and hum away to yourself at the in-store café (or try it out on the in-store piano). Or you might enjoy some country music favourites – how about learning 'Rhinestone Cowboy' in Czech?

STARÉ MĚSTO

ART DECO GALERIE Map pp88–9 Antiques

☎ 224 223 076; Michalská 21; 🕑 2-7pm Mon-Fri; Ⓜ Můstek

Specialising in early-20th-century items, this shop has a wide range of 1920s and '30s stuff including clothes, handbags, jewellery, glassware and ceramics, along with knick-knacks such as the kind of cigarette case you might imagine Dorothy Parker pulling from her purse.

BRIC A BRAC Map pp88–9 Antiques

☎ 224 815 763; Týnská 7; ⌚ 10am-6pm; Ⓜ Náměstí Republiky

Hidden up a narrow lane behind the Týn church, this is a wonderfully cluttered cave of old household items and glassware and toys and apothecary jars and 1940s leather jackets and cigar boxes and typewriters and stringed instruments and… Despite the junky look of the place, the knick-knacks are surprisingly expensive; there are two 'showrooms', a small one on Týnská, and a larger one in a nearby courtyard (follow the signs), and the affable Serbian owner can give you a guided tour around every piece in his extensive collection.

ART DÉCORATIF Map pp88–9 Arts & Crafts

☎ 224 222 283; Melantrichova 5; ⌚ 10am-8pm; Ⓜ Můstek

This is a beautiful shop dealing in Czech-made reproductions of fine Art Nouveau and Art Deco glassware, jewellery and fabrics, including some stunning vases and bowls. It's also an outlet for the gorgeously delicate creations of Jarmila Plockova, granddaughter of Alfons Mucha, who uses elements of his paintings in her work.

KERAMIKA V UNGELTU
Map pp88–9 Arts & Crafts

Týn 7; ⌚ 10am-8pm; Ⓜ Náměstí Republiky

This little shop in a corner of the Týn Courtyard is a good place to look for both traditional Bohemian pottery and modern blue-and-white wares, as well as wooden toys and marionettes, at prices up to 25% lower than at many other outlets in Staré Město.

KUBISTA Map pp88–9 Arts & Crafts

☎ 224 236 378; www.kubista.cz; Ovocný trh 19; ⌚ 10am-6pm Tue-Sun; Ⓜ Náměstí Republiky

Appropriately located in the Museum of Czech Cubism (p100) in Prague's finest Cubist building, this shop specialises in limited-edition reproductions of distinctive Cubist furniture and ceramics, and designs by masters of the form such as Josef Gočár and Pavel Janák. It also has a few original pieces for serious collectors with serious cash to spend.

QUBUS Map pp88–9 Arts & Crafts

☎ 222 313 151; www.qubus.cz; Rámová 3; ⌚ 10am-6pm Mon-Fri; Ⓜ Staroměstská

This small design studio looks more impressive online than in the flesh, but Qubus – run by leading Czech designers Maxim Velčoský and Jakon Berdych – is worth a visit if you're interested in cutting-edge household accessories ranging from 'liquid lights' (lamps in the form of tear drops) to crystal wine glasses in the shape of disposable plastic cups. Whatever floats your avant-garde boat…

ANAGRAM Map pp88–9 Books

☎ 224 895 737; www.anagram.cz; Týn 4; ⌚ 10am-8pm Mon-Sat, 10am-7pm Sun; Ⓜ Náměstí Republiky

An excellent English-language bookshop, Anagram offers a vast range of fiction and nonfiction, with an especially good selection on European history, philosophy, religion, art and travel, as well as Czech works in translation and children's books. Seek out the remainders section for some bargain new books as well as second-hand offerings on various topics.

BIG BEN Map pp88–9 Books

☎ 224 826 565; www.bigbenbookshop.com; Malá Štupartská 5; ⌚ 9am-7pm Mon-Fri, 10am-6pm Sat, noon-5pm Sun; Ⓜ Náměstí Republiky

Big Ben is a small but well-stocked English-language bookshop, with shelves devoted to Czech and European history, books on Prague, travel (including Lonely Planet guides), science fiction, children's books, poetry and all the latest fiction bestsellers. There are also English-language newspapers and magazines at the counter.

BOTANICUS Map pp88–9 Cosmetics

☎ 234 677 446; www.botanicus.cz; Týn 3; ⌚ 10am-6.30pm; Ⓜ Náměstí Republiky

Prepare for olfactory overload in this always-busy outlet for natural health and beauty products. The scented soaps, herbal bath oils and shampoos, fruit cordials and handmade paper products are made using herbs and plants grown on an organic farm at Ostrá, east of Prague.

BOHÈME Map pp88–9 Fashion

☎ 224 813 840; www.boheme.cz; Dušní 8; ⌚ 11am-7pm Mon-Fri, 11am-5pm Sat; Ⓜ Staroměstská

This trendy fashion store showcases the designs of Hana Stocklassa and her associates, with collections of knitwear, leather and suede clothes for women. Sweaters, turtlenecks, suede skirts, linen blouses, knit dresses and stretch denim suits seem to be the stock in trade, and there's a range of jewellery to choose from as well.

KLARA NADEMLÝNSKÁ

Map pp88–9 Fashion

☎ **224 818 769; www.klaranademlynska.cz; Dlouhá 3; 10am-7pm Mon-Fri, 10am-6pm Sat; Ⓜ Staroměstská**

Klara Nademlýnská is one of the Czech Republic's top fashion designers, having trained in Prague and worked for almost a decade in Paris. Her clothes are characterised by clean lines, simple styling and quality materials, making for a very wearable range that covers the spectrum from swimwear to evening-wear via jeans, halter tops, colourful blouses and sharply styled suits.

TEG Map pp88–9 Fashion

☎ **222 327 358; www.timoure.cz; V Kolkovně 6; 10am-7pm Mon-Fri, 10am-5pm Sat; Ⓜ Staroměstská**

TEG (Timoure et Group) is the design team created by Alexandra Pavalová and Ivana Šafránková, two of Prague's most respected fashion designers. This boutique showcases their quarterly collections, which feature a sharp, imaginative look that adds zest and sophistication to everyday, wearable clothes.

MODERNISTA Map pp88–9 Furniture

☎ **224 241 300; www.modernista.cz; Celetná 12; 11am-7pm; Ⓜ Náměstí Republiky**

Modernista is an elegant gallery specialising in reproduction 20th-century furniture in classic styles ranging from Art Deco and Cubist to functionalist and Bauhaus. Its collection includes those sensuously curved chairs by Jindřich Halabala that are a feature of the Icon Hotel (p218) and an unusual chaise longue by Adolf Loos, a copy of the one you can see in the drawing room of the Villa Müller (p141).

ARZENAL Map pp88–9 Glassware

☎ **224 814 099; Valentinská 11; 10am-midnight; Ⓜ Staroměstská**

Arzenal is a design salon and showroom for the striking and colourful glassware of Bořek Šípek (www.boreksipek.cz), one of the Czech Republic's leading architects and designers. Unusually, it is also home to one of the city's best Thai restaurants, Siam-I-San (p162).

top picks

DESIGNER BOUTIQUES

- Bohème (opposite)
- Helena Fejková Gallery (p148)
- Pavla & Olga (p145)
- Klara Nademlýnská (left)
- TEG (left)

LE PATIO LIFESTYLE

Map pp88–9 Homewares

☎ **222 310 310; www.lepatio.cz; Dušní 8; 10am-7pm Mon-Sat, 11am-7pm Sun; Ⓜ Staroměstská**

There are lots of high-quality household accessories here, from wrought-iron chairs and lamps forged by Bohemian blacksmiths to scented wooden chests made by Indian carpenters. Plus you'll find funky earthenware plant pots, chunky crystal wine glasses in contemporary designs, and many more tempting items that you just *know* will fit into your already crammed suitcase…

FREY WILLE Map pp88–9 Jewellery

☎ **272 142 228; www.frey-wille.com; Havířská 3; 10am-7pm Mon-Sat, 10am-6pm Sun; Ⓜ Můstek**

An Austrian jewellery maker famed for its enamel work, Frey Wille produces a distinctive range of highly decorative pieces. Its traditional paisley and Egyptian designs are complemented by a range of Art Nouveau designs based on the works of Alfons Mucha.

GRANÁT TURNOV Map pp88–9 Jewellery

☎ **222 315 612; www.granat.eu; Dlouhá 28-30; 10am-6pm Mon-Sat, 10am-1pm Sun; Ⓜ Náměstí Republiky**

Part of the country's biggest jewellery chain, specialising in Bohemian garnet, with a huge range of gold and silver rings, brooches, cufflinks and necklaces featuring the small, dark blood-red stones. There's also pearl and diamond jewellery, and less expensive pieces set with the dark green semi-precious stone known in Czech as *vltavín* (moldavite).

MAXIMUM UNDERGROUND

Map pp88–9 Music

☎ **222 541 333; www.maximum.cz; Jílská 22; 11am-7pm Mon-Sat, 1-7pm Sun; Ⓜ Můstek**

On the 1st floor in an arcade just off Jílská, this place is stocked with CDs and LPs of indie, punk, hip-hop, techno and other genres. It also has a selection of new and second-hand street and club wear for those seeking that Central European grunge look.

NOVÉ MĚSTO

GALERIE ČESKÉ PLASTIKY

Map p106 Arts & Crafts

Czech Sculpture Gallery; ☎ 222 310 684; www.art-pro.cz; Revoluční 20; ⏲ 11am-7pm Mon-Sat; 🚋 5, 8, 14

This commercial gallery is a treasure house of 19th- and 20th-century and contemporary Czech sculpture, paintings, prints and photography. There are regular themed exhibitions, and all items are for sale, at prices ranging from 2000Kč to 2 million Kč.

GLOBE BOOKSTORE & CAFÉ

Map pp108–9 Books

☎ 224 934 203; www.globebookstore.cz; Pštrossova 6; ⏲ 10am-midnight; Ⓜ Karlovo Náměstí

A popular hangout for book-loving expats, the Globe is a cosy English-language bookshop with an excellent café-bar (p164) in which to peruse your purchases. There's a good range of new fiction and nonfiction, as well as a big selection of second-hand novels, newspapers, magazines and – a first for Prague – a dedicated gay, lesbian and transgender section with literature in English, German and Czech.

PALÁC KNIH NEO LUXOR

Map pp108–9 Books

☎ 221 111 364; www.neoluxor.cz; Václavské náměstí 41; ⏲ 8am-8pm Mon-Fri, 9am-7pm Sat, 10am-7pm Sun; Ⓜ Muzeum

Palác Knih Neo Luxor is Prague's biggest bookshop – head for the basement to find a wide selection of fiction and nonfiction in English, German, French and Russian, including Czech authors in translation. You'll also find internet access (1Kč per minute), a café and a good selection of international newspapers and magazines.

KANZELSBERGER Map pp108–9 Books & Maps

☎ 224 219 214; www.dumknihy.cz; Václavské náměstí 4; ⏲ 9am-8pm; Ⓜ Můstek

Housed in the tall, glass-fronted Lindt building at the foot of Wenceslas Square, Kanzelsberger has five floors of bookshelves, with a café on the 1st floor overlooking the square. You'll probably want the top floor, where there's a selection of books in English, German and French, plus hiking and city maps covering the whole of the Czech Republic.

KIWI

Map pp108–9 Books & Maps

☎ 224 948 455; www.kiwick.cz; Jungmannova 23; ⏲ 9am-6.30pm Mon-Fri, 9am-2pm Sat; Ⓜ Národní Třída

This small specialist travel bookshop stocks a huge range of maps covering not only the Czech Republic but also many other countries. It also has an extensive selection of Lonely Planet guidebooks.

HELENA FEJKOVÁ GALLERY

Map pp108–9 Fashion

☎ 224 211 514; www.helenafejkova.cz; Lucerna Pasáž, Štěpánská 61; ⏲ 10am-7pm Mon-Fri, 10am-3pm Sat; Ⓜ Muzeum

Kit yourself out in the latest Czech fashions at this *très chic* boutique and showroom. Contemporary men's and women's fashion and accessories by Prague designer Helena Fejková and others are on display, and private fashion shows can be arranged.

MANUFACTURA ABRAM KELLY

Map pp108–9 Gifts

☎ 224 233 282; www.manufactura.cz; Senovážné náměstí 16; ⏲ 9am-7pm Mon-Fri; 🚋 3, 9, 14, 24

This little workshop and studio produces handmade paper using traditional techniques, and sells it in the form of greeting cards, business cards, stationery, calligraphy, antique map prints and photographic prints.

MOSER Map pp108–9 Glassware

☎ 224 211 293; www.moser-glass.com; Na Příkopě 12; ⏲ 10am-8pm Mon-Fri, 10am-7pm Sat & Sun; Ⓜ Můstek

One of the most exclusive and highly respected of Bohemian glass makers, Moser was founded in Karlovy Vary in 1857 and is famous for its rich and flamboyant designs. The shop on Na Příkopě is worth a browse as much for the décor as for the goods – it's in a magnificently decorated, originally Gothic building called the House of the Black Rose (dům U černé růže).

BELDA JEWELLERY Map pp108–9 Jewellery

☎ 224 931 052; www.belda.cz; Mikulandská 10; 10am-6pm Mon-Thu, 10am-5pm Fri; M Národní Třída

Belda & Co is a long-established Czech firm dating from 1922. Nationalised in 1948, it was revived by the founder's son and grandson, and continues to create gold and silver jewellery of a very high standard. Its range includes its own angular, contemporary designs, as well as reproductions based on Art Nouveau designs by Alfons Mucha.

BAZAR Map pp108–9 Music

☎ 602 313 730; www.cdkrakovska.cz; Krakovská 4; 9am-7pm Mon-Fri, 10am-3pm Sat; M Muzeum

There's a vast selection of second-hand CDs, LPs and videos to browse through here at Bazar, representing a wide range of genres. Czech and Western pop jostle with jazz, blues, heavy metal, country and world music, though with most CDs costing around 300Kč to 400Kč this place is not exactly what you'd call a bargain basement.

BONTONLAND Map pp108–9 Music

☎ 224 473 080; www.bontonland.cz; Václavské náměstí 1-3; 9am-8pm Mon-Sat, 10am-7pm Sun; M Můstek

Supposedly the biggest music megastore in the Czech Republic, with pretty much everything including Western chart music, classical, jazz, dance and heavy metal, as well as an extensive collection of Czech pop. It also sells videos and DVDs, iPods and accessories, and has a large PlayStation arena and internet café.

FOTO ŠKODA Map pp108–9 Photography

☎ 222 929 029; www.fotoskoda.cz; Vodičkova 37; 8.30am-8.30pm Mon-Fri, 9am-6pm Sat; M Můstek

One of Prague's biggest camera shops, Foto Škoda stocks a wide range of digital and film cameras, video cameras, film (professional as well as amateur) and photographic accessories. It also sells used cameras, and offers a camera repair service.

JAN PAZDERA Map pp108–9 Photography

☎ 224 216 197; Vodičkova 28; 10am-6pm Mon-Sat; 3, 9, 14, 24

The friendly and knowledgeable staff members at this long-standing shop are happy to show you around their impressive stock of second-hand cameras, darkroom gear, lenses, binoculars and telescopes. Models range from the basic but unbreakable Russian-made Zenit to expensive Leicas.

BAŤA Map pp108–9 Shoes

☎ 221 088 472; www.bata.cz; Václavské náměstí 6; 9am-9pm Mon-Fri, 9am-8pm Sat, 10am-8pm Sun; M Můstek

Established by Tomáš Baťa in 1894, the Baťa footwear empire is still in family hands and is one of the Czech Republic's most successful companies. The flagship store on Wenceslas Square, built in the 1920s, is considered a masterpiece of modern architecture, and houses six floors of shoes (including international brands such as Nike, Salomon and Cat, as well as Baťa's own), handbags, luggage and leather goods.

ZERBA Map pp108–9 Toys

☎ 221 024 616; 1st fl, Černa Růže Shopping Centre, Na Příkopě 12; 9am-7pm Mon-Fri, to 6pm Sat, to 5pm Sun; M Mústek

This place is a paradise for model-railway enthusiasts of all ages, with a huge range of track and rolling stock in N- and OO-gauge, as well as a good selection of Scalextric racing sets and Matchbox model cars.

VINOHRADY & VRŠOVICE

DŮM PORCELÁNU Map p121 Arts & Crafts

☎ 221 505 320; www.dumporcelanu.cz; Jugoslávská 16, Vinohrady; 9am-7pm Mon-Fri, 9am-5pm Sat, 2-5pm Sun; M IP Pavlova

The House of Porcelain is a kind of factory outlet for the best Czech porcelain makers, including Haas & Czjzek and Thun, both based in western Bohemia. The flatware, china, blue onion pattern porcelain and other items are priced to draw in local buyers – not tourists. Prices here are a fraction what they are downtown for similar items.

SHAKESPEARE & SONS Map p121 Books

☎ 271 740 839; www.shakes.cz; Krymská 12, Vršovice; 10am-7pm; 4, 22, 23

Though its shelves groan with a formidable range of literature in English, both new and second-hand, Shakes is more than a bookshop – it's a congenial literary hangout, with a cosy café that regularly hosts poetry readings, author events and live jazz. Here you can buy magazines, such as the *New York Review of Books, Harper's* and *Atlantic Monthly,* and settle down for a read over coffee and cakes.

ORIENTÁLNÍ KOBERCE PALÁCKA

Map p121 Carpets

☎ 222 518 354; www.orientalni-koberce.cz; Vinohradská 42, Vinohrady; 10am-7pm Mon-Fri, to 2pm Sat; M Náměstí Míru

The 'Oriental Carpet Palace' is a sumptuous showroom stocked with handmade carpets, rugs and wall hangings from Iran and other Central Asian states. The colourful pieces come in all sizes and prices and in intricate traditional designs, and the knowledgeable staff will be happy to help you make an informed purchase.

PASSION CHOCOLAT

Map p121 Food & Drink

☎ 222 524 333; Italská 5, Vinohrady; 8am-midnight; M Náměstí Míru

This French-owned chocolate shop and bakery was an absolute sensation when it opened in 2007. Run by a husband and wife team – he makes the pastries – the secret is the use of high-quality Valrhona chocolate. They also do an assortment of cakes and pastries, including a highly recommended raspberry cream tarte, croissants and a few quiches and sandwiches. Eat in or take away.

KAREL VÁVRA

Map p121 Musical Instruments

☎ 222 518 114; Lublaňská 65, Vinohrady; 9am-5pm Mon-Fri; M IP Pavlova

Handmade fiddles decorate the interior of this old-fashioned violin workshop where Karel and his assistants beaver away making and repairing these instruments in time-honoured fashion. Even if you are not in search of a custom-made violin, it's worth a look just for the time-warp atmosphere.

PALÁC FLÓRA

Map pp126–7 Shopping Centre

☎ 255 741 712; www.palacflora.cz; Vinohradská 151, Vinohrady; 9am-9pm Mon-Sat, 10am-9pm Sun; M Flóra

You could be anywhere in the capitalist world in this shiny, glittering shrine to consumerism. Slick cafés share floor space with girly emporia of tiny T-shirts, sparkly make-up and globalised brand names (Hilfiger, Sergio Tacchini, Nokia, Puma, Lacoste, Guess, Diesel, Apple), a full food court, an eight-screen multiplex and an IMAX cinema that keep the crowds coming in the evenings.

VINOHRADSKÝ PAVILON

Map p121 Shopping Centre

☎ 222 097 100; www.pavilon.cz; Vinohradská 50, Vinohrady; 9.30am-9pm Mon-Sat, noon-8pm Sun; M Jiřího z Poděbrad

Housed in a lovingly restored 1902 market pavilion, this small but searingly trendy mall – completely refurbished in 2006 – has three floors of brand-name boutiques (including Tommy Hilfiger, Sergio Tacchini, La Perla), Sony electronics, jewellery, shoes and household goods. There's a very good café on the ground floor run by the Ambiente local restaurant group. Oh, and it has that obligatory adjunct to all Prague shopping malls – there's a supermarket located in the basement.

HOLEŠOVICE, BUBENEČ & DEJVICE

ANTIKVITA Map pp132–3 Antiques

☎ 233 336 601; www.antikvita.cz; Na Hutích 9, Bubeneč; 10am-5pm Mon-Fri; M Dejvická

This antique shop is a collector's delight, crammed with cases and cabinets overflowing with vintage toys, model trains, dolls, coins, medals, jewellery, clocks, watches, militaria, postcards, porcelain figures, glassware and much, much more. If you have something to sell, Antikvita holds buying sessions on Wednesday and Thursday (from 10am to noon and 2pm to 5pm).

PIVNÍ GALERIE Map pp132–3 Food & Drink

☎ 220 870 613; www.pivnigalerie.cz; U Průhonu 9, Holešovice; noon-9pm Mon-Fri; 1, 3, 5, 25

If you think that Czech beer begins and ends with Pilsner Urquell, a visit to the tasting room at Pivní Galerie (the Beer Gallery) will soon lift the scales from your eyes. Here you can sample and purchase a huge range of Bohemian and Moravian beers – more than 180 varieties from 34 different breweries – with expert advice from the owner, who speaks both English and Swedish.

PRAŽSKÁ TRŽNICE

Map pp132–3 Market

Prague Market Hall; ☎ 220 800 945; Bubenské nábřeží 306, Holešovice; 7am-6pm Mon-Fri, to 2pm Sat; 1, 3, 5, 25

Almost a suburb in itself, Prague's sprawling, slightly depressing city market includes a large open-air area selling fresh fruit, vegetables and flowers, large covered halls housing supermarkets, electrical goods and car accessories, and dozens of stalls selling everything from cheap clothes to garden gnomes. In the eastern part of the market are several antiques warehouses, some of which look like they have emptied a baroque palace or two.

SMÍCHOV

MAPIS

Map p138 Maps

☎ 257 315 459; Štefánikova 63; 9am-6.30pm Mon-Fri; 6, 9, 12, 20

Mapis is a specialist map shop with a wide selection of local, national and international maps, including hiking maps and city plans covering not just the city but also the whole of the Czech Republic.

NOVÝ SMÍCHOV

Map p138 Shopping Centre

☎ 251 511 151; www.novysmichov.eu; Plzeňská 8; 9am-9pm; M Anděl

Nový Smíchov is a vast shopping centre that occupies an area the size of several city blocks. It's an airy, well-designed space with plenty of fashion boutiques and niche-market stores – for example, you could check out Profimed, which has all the dental-care products you never knew you needed. Besides all the big brand names, there's also a large computer store, a food court, a virtual games hall, a bowling alley, a 12-screen multiplex cinema and a huge, well-stocked Tesco hypermarket.

EATING

top picks

- **Allegro** (p160)
- **Angel** (p161)
- **Da Emanuel** (p170)
- **Hanil** (p168)
- **Kampa Park** (p158)
- **Kogo** (p164)
- **Kolkovna** (p162)
- **Mozaika** (p167)
- **Oliva** (p164)
- **U Zavoje** (p161)

What's your recommendation? www.lonelyplanet.com/prague

EATING

Traditional Czech cuisine is a cardiologist's nightmare, a cholesterol-laden menu of meat, fat, salt and more meat, accompanied by high-calorie dumplings and washed down with copious quantities of beer. When it comes to food, the ultimate Czech put-down is to describe it as *neslány* or *nemaslý* ('not salty' or 'not fatty').

But if you put aside your notions of healthy eating for a few days (you're on holiday, after all – live a little!), you'll find traditional Czech food to be very tasty. The country can boast some top-notch produce, from game to fish to smoked meats to wild mushrooms, and Prague's top chefs are beginning to reinvent Czech cuisine with a lighter, more inventive touch.

Since the Czech Republic joined the EU in 2004, the steady increase in the number, quality and variety of Prague's restaurants has, if anything, accelerated. You can now enjoy a wide range of international cuisine, from Afghan to Argentinean, Korean to Cantonese, and even – miracle of miracles – expect service with a smile in many eating places.

However, don't let this kaleidoscope of cuisines blind you to the pleasures of good old-fashioned Czech grub. The city's many pubs dish up tasty pork and dumplings, often at very low prices, and a lot of the more upmarket restaurants offer gourmet versions of classic Bohemian dishes such as pork knuckle or roast duck.

CELEBRATING WITH FOOD

Christmas is the most important celebration on the Czech domestic calendar, and food and drink, as you might expect, play an important part. Christmas Eve (*Štědrý den,* or 'generous day') is a day of abstinence from meat, with people saving their appetite for the evening meal, which is traditionally *smažený kapr* (crispy, fried carp) served with *bramborový salát* (potato salad). The carp are farmed in medieval *rybníky* (fishponds) in the countryside, mostly in South Bohemia, and in December they are brought to city markets where they are sold, live, from water-filled barrels. In many homes, the Christmas carp then gets to swim around in the bathtub until it's time for the frying pan.

There is no national tradition as to what is served on Christmas Day (*vánoce*), but meat is definitely back on the menu; *pečená kachna* (roast duck), served with gravy and dumplings, is a widespread favourite. There are also Christmas cookies *(vánoční cukrovi)*, baked according to traditional family recipes, and *vánočka*, Bohemia's answer to Christmas cake, though it's actually made with bread dough, sweetened with sugar, flavoured with lemon, nutmeg, raisins and almonds, and plaited; it is usually served after the Christmas Eve dinner.

New Year's Eve *(Silvestr)* is also a big celebration. These days few people still prepare the traditional New Year's Eve dinner of *vepřový ovar* (boiled pig's head) served with grated horseradish and apple, but the day is still a big party day, with plates of *chlebičký* (small, open sandwiches), *brambůrky* (potato pancakes) and other snacks, and bottles of *šampaňské* or other sparkling wine on hand to toast the bells at midnight.

ETIQUETTE

Although the vast majority of Prague's tourist-oriented restaurants have long since adopted international manners, a dinner in a Czech home or a traditional eatery still demands traditional Czech etiquette.

To the Czech way of thinking, only barbarians would begin a meal without first saying *dobrou chut'* (the Czech equivalent of *bon appetit* – the correct response is to repeat the phrase); even the waiters in tourist restaurants will murmur *dobrou chut'* as they place the plates on your table. And the first drink of the evening is always accompanied by a toast – usually *na zdraví* (nahz-drah-*vee;* literally, 'to health') – as you clink first the tops and then the bottoms of your glasses, and finally touch the glass to the table before drinking.

It's considered bad manners to talk while eating, and especially to distract a guest while they are enjoying their food, so conversation is usually kept to a minimum while food is being consumed; the time for talk is between courses and after the meal.

SPECIALITIES

The first course of a meal is usually a hearty *polévka* (soup) – often *bramboračka* (potato

SPANISH BIRDS & MORAVIAN SPARROWS

Many Czech dishes have names that don't offer a clue as to what's in them, but certain words will give you a hint: *šavle* (sabre; something on a skewer); *tajemství* (secret; cheese inside rolled meat); *překvapení* (surprise; meat, capsicum and tomato paste rolled into a potato pancake); *kapsa* (pocket; a filling inside rolled meat); and *bašta* (bastion; meat in spicy sauce with a potato pancake).

Two strangely named dishes that are familiar to all Czechs are *Španělský ptáčky* (Spanish birds; sausage and gherkin wrapped in a slice of veal, served with rice and sauce) and *Moravský vrabec* (Moravian sparrow; a fist-sized piece of roast pork). But even Czechs may have to ask about *Meč krále Jiřího* (the sword of King George; beef and pork roasted on a skewer), *Tajemství Petra Voka* (Peter Voka's mystery; carp with sauce), *Šíp Malínských lovců* (the Malín hunter's arrow; beef, sausage, fish and vegetables on a skewer) and *Dech kopáče Ondřeje* (the breath of grave-digger Andrew; fillet of pork filled with extremely smelly Olomouc cheese).

soup), *houbová polévka* (mushroom soup) or *hovězí vývar* (beef broth). Ones worth looking out for are *cibulačka* (onion soup), a delicious, creamy concoction of caramelised onions and herbs, and *česnečka* (garlic soup), a powerfully pungent broth that is curiously addictive.

Other common appetisers include *Pražská šunka* (Prague ham), for which the capital is famous. It is cured in brine and smoked; the best stuff is *šunka od kosti* (ham off the bone).

What roast beef and Yorkshire pudding is to the English, so *vepřová pečeně s knedlíky a kyselé zelí* (roast pork with dumplings and sauerkraut) is to the Czechs; it's a dish so ubiquitous that it is often abbreviated to *vepřo-knedlo-zelo.* The pork is rubbed with salt and caraway seeds, and roasted long and slow – good roast pork should fall apart, meltingly tender, at the first touch of fork or finger.

The dumplings should be light and fluffy – *houskové knedlíky* (bread dumplings) are made from flour, yeast, egg yolk and milk, and are left to rise like bread before being cooked in boiling water and then sliced. The best *knedlíky* are homemade, but the ones you'll find in most pubs and restaurants will be factory-produced. Alternatively, you may be served *bramborové knedlíky* (potato dumplings); if you thought bread dumplings were filling, just wait until you try these stodge-bombs.

Other staples of Czech restaurant menus include *svíčková na smetaně* (slices of marinated roast beef served with a sour-cream sauce garnished with lemon and cranberries); *guláš* (a casserole of beef or pork in a tomato, onion and paprika gravy); and *vepřový řízek* (Wiener schnitzel, a thin fillet of pork coated in breadcrumbs and fried, served with potato salad or *hranolky* – French fries).

Poultry is another popular main course, either roasted or served as *kuře na paprice* (chicken in spicy paprika-cream sauce). *Kachna* (duck), *husa* (goose) and *krůta* (turkey) usually come roasted, with gravy, dumplings and sauerkraut. A few restaurants specialise in game; the most common are *jelení* (venison), *bažant* (pheasant), *zajíc* (hare) and *kanec* (boar) – fried or roasted and served in a mushroom sauce or as *guláš.*

Seafood is found only in a handful of expensive restaurants, but freshwater fish – usually *kapr* (carp) or *pstruh* (trout) – are plentiful. *Štika* (pike) and *úhoř* (eel) are found on more specialised menus. Note that the price of fish on the menu is sometimes not for the whole fish but per 100g. Ask how much the trout weighs before you order it!

The classic Czech dessert is *ovocné knedlíky* (fruit dumplings), but once again the best are to be found at domestic dinner tables rather than in restaurants. Large, round dumplings made with sweetened, flour-based dough are stuffed with berries, plums or apricots, and served drizzled with melted butter and a sprinkle of sugar.

Desserts on offer in traditional restaurants and pubs consist of *kompot* (canned/preserved fruit), either on its own or *pohár* – in a cup with *zmrzlina* (ice cream) and whipped cream. *Palačinky* or *lívance* (pancakes) are also very common. Other desserts include *jablkový závin* (apple strudel), *makový koláč* (poppy-seed cake) and *ovocné koláče* (fruit slices). For cakes and pastries it is better to go to a *kavárna* (café) or *cukrárna* (cake shop).

A typical Czech breakfast (*snídaně*) is a light affair consisting of *chléb* (bread) or *rohlík* (bread roll) with butter, cheese, jam or yogurt, washed down with tea or coffee. A hotel breakfast buffet will normally also include cereals, eggs, ham or sausage. Some Czechs eat breakfast at self-service *bufety,* which are open between 6am and 8am – these serve up soup or hot dogs, which are washed down with coffee or even beer. Some eateries serving Western-style breakfasts are noted in the boxed text (p164).

VEGETARIAN MEALS

Bezmasá jídla ('meatless dishes') are advertised on many traditional Czech menus, but some of these may be cooked in animal fat or even contain pieces of ham or bacon! If you ask, most chefs can whip up something genuinely vegetarian. Fortunately there are several good vegetarian restaurants in Prague – see the Top Picks boxed text on p169.

Useful phrases include the following:

I'm a vegetarian.	*Jsem vegetarián/ka.* (m/f)	ysem ve-ge-ta-ri-aan/-ka
I don't eat meat.	*Nejím maso.*	ne-yeem ma-so
I don't eat fish/chicken/ham.	*Nejím rybu/kuře/šunku.*	ne-yeem ri-bu/ku-rzhe/shun-ku

Some common meatless dishes:

knedlíky s vejci	kned-lee-ki s-vey-tse	fried dumplings with egg
omeleta se sýrem a bramborem	o-me-le-ta se seer-em a bram-bo-rem	cheese and potato omelette
smažené žampiony	sma-zhe-ne zham-pi-o-nee	fried mushrooms
smažený květák	sma-zhe-nee kvye-taak	fried cauliflower with egg and onion
smažený sýr	sma-zhe-nee seer	fried cheese with potatoes and tartare sauce

You can also go to a *pekárna* or *pekařství* (bakery), or to one of the French or Viennese bakeries, for *loupáčky* (like croissants but smaller and heavier). Czech bread, especially rye, is excellent and varied.

Oběd (lunch) is traditionally the main meal of the day and, except for on Sundays, it's often a hurried affair. Czechs are usually early risers, and so they may sit down to lunch as early as 11.30am, though latecomers can still find leftovers for lunch in many restaurants as late as 3pm.

Having stuffed themselves at lunchtime, for many Czechs *večeře* (dinner) is a light meal, perhaps only a platter of cold meats, cheese and pickles with bread.

PRACTICALITIES

Opening Hours

In general, lunch is served from noon to 3pm, and dinner from 6pm to 9pm. Most Prague restaurants, however, are open all day, from 10am or noon to 10pm or 11pm, allowing a laid-back approach to meal times. Cafés are usually open from 8am; see the boxed text (p164) for breakfast recommendations.

How Much?

On average, you can expect to pay around 300Kč to 600Kč per person for a meal in a midrange restaurant, not including drinks. In the more upmarket places you can double that, and in the very best restaurants the bill will be in the area of 1500Kč per person before drinks.

On the other hand, it's possible to eat well for very little. You can fill up in a pub or café for less than 200Kč per person – and that includes a glass of beer.

Unless otherwise indicated, price ranges quoted in this chapter's restaurant reviews are for main courses at dinner; prices for main courses at lunch are often cheaper.

Booking Tables

It's always a good idea to reserve a table at upmarket restaurants, especially during the high season; almost without fail the phone will be answered by someone who speaks English. That said, we have spent months researching in Prague and mostly did just fine without making any reservations at all.

Tipping

It's pretty much unheard of for Prague restaurants to include a service charge on your

PRICE GUIDE

The price guide indicates the average cost of a dinner main dish:

€€€	more than 600Kč
€€	250Kč to 600Kč
€	less than 250Kč

bill (check, though; a few do). In most tourist-area places the helpful message 'Tips Not Included', in English (hint, hint), is printed (or even hand-written, as an extra reminder) on the bill. The normal rate for tipping is 10% of the total.

Normal practice in pubs, cafés and mid-range restaurants is to round up the bill to the next 10Kč (or the next 20Kč if it's over 200Kč). The usual protocol is for the staff to hand you the bill and for you, as you hand over the money, to tell them the total amount you want to pay with the tip included.

Change is usually counted out starting with the big notes, on down to the smallest coins. If you say *děkuji* (thank you) during this process the staff will stop and assume the rest is a tip.

Self-catering

There is a wide variety of self-catering options available with *potraviny* (grocery or food shops) and supermarkets everywhere, the best-stocked and priciest being in flashy department stores near the centre. Note that some perishable supermarket food items bear a date of manufacture *(datum výroby)* plus a 'consume-within…' *(spotřebujte do…)* period, whereas others (such as long-life milk) have a stated minimum shelf-life *(minimální trvanlivost)* date, after which the freshness of the product is not guaranteed.

For supermarket supplies, head to the basement of Kotva (Map pp88–9; náměstí Republiky; 9am-8pm Mon-Fri, 9am-6pm Sat, 10am-6pm Sun; M Náměstí Republiky) or Tesco (Map pp108–9; Národní třída 26; 8am-9pm Mon-Fri, 9am-8pm Sat, 10am-8pm Sun; M Národní Třída). In Malá Strana you'll find the handy Vacek Bio-Market (Map pp76–7; Mostecká 3; 7am-10pm Mon-Sat, 10am-10pm Sun), a well-stocked minisupermarket.

The city has several open-air produce markets. The biggest one in the city centre is the tourist-oriented open-air market (Map pp88–9; Havelská; 8am-6pm) south of the Old Town Square. More authentic neighbourhood markets – mainly open in the mornings only and closed on Sundays – include the open-air market (Map pp132–3) on Dejvická, near Hradčanská metro station in Dejvice.

In Staré Město, Bakeshop Praha (Map pp88–9; Kozí 1; 7am-7pm) is a fantastic bakery that sells some of the best bread in the city, along with pastries, cakes and takeaway sandwiches, salads and quiche. Another good bakery near Old Town Square is Michelské pekářství (Map pp88–9; Dlouhá 1; 6.30am-6pm Mon-Fri, 11am-6pm Sun), which sells a wide range of freshly baked breads and freshly prepared sandwiches.

Delicatessens that are good for stocking up on picnic supplies include Fruits de France (Map pp108–9; Jindřišská 7, Nové Město; 7am-6.30pm Mon-Fri; M Můstek), which sells French wine, cheese, pastries and more. There's also Culinaria (Map pp88–9; Skořepká 9, Staré Město; 8.30am-8pm Mon-Fri, 10am-7pm Sat, noon-5pm Sun; M Národní třída), which sells handmade bread, pastries, French and Italian specialities and freshly made sandwiches.

Cellarius (Map pp108–9; Lucerna pasáž, Václavské náměstí 36, Nové Město; 9.30am-9pm Mon-Sat, 3-9pm Sun; M Můstek) is the place to head if you're looking for Czech and imported wines.

PRAGUE CASTLE & HRADČANY

Most of the restaurants in the castle district are aimed squarely at the tourist crowds, and the whole area becomes pretty quiet in the evenings after the castle closes. The following places, which are a cut above the usual tourist eateries regarding character and cuisine, are worth seeking out – Vikárka and U zlaté hrušky for Czech food with some atmosphere, Saté and Malý Buddha for authentic Asian cooking.

U ZLATÉ HRUŠKY Map pp70–1 Czech €€€

☎ 220 514 778; Nový Svět 3, Hradčany; mains 600-800Kč; 11.30am-3pm & 6.30pm-midnight; 22, 23

'At the Golden Pear' is a cosy, wood-panelled gourmets' corner, serving beautifully prepared Bohemian fish, fowl and game dishes and frequented as much by locals and visiting dignitaries as by tourists (the Czech foreign ministry is just up the road, and Margaret Thatcher once dined here). In summer get a table in its leafy *zahradní restaurace* (garden restaurant) across the street.

VIKÁRKA Map p62 International €€

☎ 233 311 962; Vikářská 39, Prague Castle; mains 200-450Kč; 11am-9pm; 22, 23

It's been a long time coming, but at last there's a decent restaurant within the castle grounds. Opened in 2006, the Vikárka inhabits a warren of beautifully restored medieval rooms, the simple Romanesque and Gothic shapes tastefully set off with splashes of bold colour and period decoration. The

FUNNY, I DON'T REMEMBER ORDERING THAT!

Keep in mind that nothing comes for free in Prague restaurants – if the waiter offers you fries with that, and you accept, you'll be charged for them. Bread, mayonnaise, mustard, vegetables...everything has a price tag. Many restaurants also have a cover charge or *couvert,* which every diner must pay regardless of what they eat and even if they eat nothing. It's not a scam; it's just the way things are done. If the menu has no prices, ask for them. Don't be intimidated by the language barrier; know exactly what you're ordering. If something's not available and the waiter suggests an alternative, ask for the price. Immediately return anything you didn't order and don't want, such as bread, butter or side dishes; don't just leave it to one side or chances are they'll appear on your bill. Most importantly, though, don't let paranoia ruin your meal. The majority of overcharging happens at tourist-oriented restaurants in the city centre. If you're not eating in Old Town Square or Wenceslas Square, or if you're at a new place run by young Czechs, you're unlikely to have any problems.

menu runs from Czech classics to steak and salmon – the goulash, *svíčkova* and roast pork knuckle are all recommended – and there's a separate kids' menu offering fish fingers, spaghetti or chicken and chips.

MALÝ BUDDHA Map pp70–1 Asian €

☎ 220 513 894; Úvoz 46, Hradčany; mains 100-250Kč; ⌚ noon-10.30pm Tue-Sun; 🚋 22, 23

Candlelight, incense and a Buddhist shrine characterise this intimate, vaulted restaurant that tries to capture the atmosphere of an oriental tearoom. The menu is a mix of Asian influences, with authentic Thai, Chinese and Vietnamese dishes, many of them vegetarian, and a drinks list that includes ginseng wine, Chinese rose liqueur and all kinds of tea. Credit cards are not accepted.

SATÉ Map pp70–1 Indonesian/Malaysian €

☎ 220 514 552; Pohořelec 3, Hradčany; mains 100-150Kč; ⌚ 11am-10pm; 🚋 22, 23

Saté is one of Prague's longest-serving Asian restaurants, a no-frills place just five minutes' walk west of the castle serving inexpensive Indonesian and Malaysian dishes such as *nasi goreng* (fried rice with veggies, prawns and egg), beef *rendang* (coconut-based curry), Javanese beefsteak and a string of tasty vegetarian dishes.

MALÁ STRANA

You'll be spoilt for choice looking for somewhere to eat in Malá Strana. The tourist crowds are swelled by hungry office workers from the district's many embassies and government offices, and this well-heeled clientele ensures that there are lots of quality restaurants offering a wide range of cuisines. Many of the best restaurants take advantage of a riverside location, or are perched on a hillside with a view over the city.

U ZLATÉ STUDNĚ Map pp76–7 International €€€

☎ 257 533 322; www.goldenwell.cz; U Zlaté Studně 4; mains 650-950Kč; ⌚ noon-11pm; Ⓜ Malostranská

Perched atop a Renaissance mansion within a champagne cork's pop of the castle, 'At the Golden Well' enjoys one of the finest settings in Prague. Weather will dictate whether you sit in the plush red-and-gold dining room, or head upstairs to the outdoor terrace – both command a stunning panorama across the red-tiled rooftops of Malá Strana. The kitchen, which has French, Mediterranean and Asian influences, conjures up dishes such as nettle soup with quail egg and garlic croutons, grilled sea bass with braised fennel and rocket, and veal tournedos with plum and almond sauce.

KAMPA PARK Map pp76–7 International €€€

☎ 257 532 685; www.kampagroup.com; Na Kampě 8b; mains 600-900Kč; ⌚ 11.30am-1am; 🚋 12, 20, 22, 23

Opened way back in 1994, Kampa Park was a pioneer of Prague's fine-dining scene and has attracted countless celebrity visitors including Mick Jagger, Johnny Depp, Lauren Bacall, Robbie Williams, and Bill and Hillary Clinton. The cuisine is as famous as the clientele, from the seared scallops with raisins and capers *beurre blanc,* to the saddle of lamb with truffle-scented potato gnocchi. There's a stylish dining room and roof terrace, but for a really romantic dinner reserve a candlelit table on the cobblestoned terrace, draped in fairy lights, right beside the river, with the lights of Charles Bridge glittering on the water.

HERGETOVA CIHELNA

Map pp76–7 International €€

☎ **800 152 672; www.cihelna.com; Cihelná 2b; mains 250-650Kč; ⌚ 11.30am-1am; Ⓜ Malostranská**

Housed in a converted18th-century *cihelná* (brickworks), this place enjoys one of Prague's hottest locations with a riverside terrace offering sweeping views of Charles Bridge and the Old Town waterfront. The menu is as sweeping as the view, ranging from Czech dishes to burgers and stir-fries, plus a new organic menu that includes crab salad with avocado and chilli, and baked sea bass with cauliflower puree and courgette fritters. Note that there are two wine lists, one reasonably priced, the other eye-poppingly expensive – we can recommend the Sonberg Rýnský Ryzlink, an excellent Moravian white.

U MALTÉZSKÝCH RYTÍŘŮ

Map pp76–7 Czech/International €€

☎ **257 530 075; www.umaltezskychrytiru.cz; Prokopská 10; mains 200-500Kč; ⌚ 1-11pm; 🚋 12, 20, 22, 23**

'At the Maltese Knights' is a cosy and romantic olde-worlde restaurant, with candlelit tables tucked into niches in the stone-and-brick Gothic vaults downstairs (the ground-floor tables are much less atmospheric). Classic Bohemian offerings include roast wild boar with rosehip sauce, and organic carp stuffed with tomato and mushroom, but there are also international dishes such as steak Chateaubriand, and a couple of vegetarian dishes; it's a popular spot, so book well ahead.

GITANES Map pp76–7 Mediterranean €€

☎ **257 530 163; www.gitanes.cz; Tržiště 7; mains 150-350Kč; ⌚ noon-midnight; 🚋 12, 20, 22, 23**

Twee meets twisted at this idiosyncratic restaurant, where a technicolour storm of floral print wallpaper and upholstery meets a gallery of weird art – check out the upside-down table on the ceiling – to create an atmosphere akin to an English tearoom designed by Salvador Dali. On acid. The food is hearty and full-on, especially the Balkan specialities – dishes such as *čevapčiči* (chargrilled spicy meatballs) and *sač* (veal and lamb roasted over an open fire) are flung out like macho, meat-eating challenges, while the paella for two could probably feed four. Lighter dishes include *smažené ančovičky* (fried white-bait), chicken risotto and a range of salads.

U MALÉ VELRYBY Map pp76–7 International €€

☎ **257 214 703; www.umalevelryby.cz; Valdštejnská 14; mains 250-320Kč; ⌚ noon-3pm & 6-11pm; Ⓜ Malostranská**

Restaurants come and go quickly in Prague's rapidly evolving dining scene, so fingers crossed that this one's still around by the time you read this. It's a tiny place – only eight tables – run by a chef–proprietor from Cork, Ireland, who gets fresh seafood flown in daily from French markets. The seared calamari with chilli, lime and ginger is meltingly tender, the seafood pie (fish and mussels topped with crispy potatoes) is tasty and filling, and the crab pasta is deliciously delicate. Other dishes include chargrilled steak with onion *tarte tatin,* and roast duck with apricot sauce.

CAFÉ DE PARIS Map pp76–7 French €€

☎ **603 160 718; www.cafedeparis.cz; Maltézské náměstí 4; mains 200-300Kč; ⌚ noon-midnight; 🚋 6, 9, 12, 20, 22, 23**

A little corner of France tucked away on a quiet square, the Café de Paris is small, straightforward and unpretentious. So is the menu – just a couple of choices, onion soup or foie gras terrine to start, followed by entrecote steak with chips, salad and a choice of sauces (they're very proud of the Café de Paris sauce, made to a 75-year-old recipe with 35 ingredients, and very nice it is too). There are also one or two daily specials, including a vegetarian alternative. The wine list offers a decent range of French wines, including a Muscadet that's good value at 390Kč a bottle.

CANTINA Map pp76–7 Mexican €€

☎ **257 317 173; www.restauracecantina.cz; Újezd 38; mains 150-300Kč; ⌚ 11.30am-midnight; 🚋 6, 9, 12, 20, 22, 23**

This homely hacienda, decked out in bleached pine and Brazilian coffee sacks, serves up the most authentic margaritas in Prague – perhaps a little light on the tequila, but nicely iced and with a good zing of fresh lime. The menu is as good as Tex-Mex gets in this town, with big portions of burrito, *chimichanga*, quesadilla and fajitas with both meat and vegetarian fillings; if the salsa isn't hot enough for you, there are bottles of chilli sauce on the table to add a bit of bite.

This place is popular, so get there early, book a table, or be prepared to wait.

EL CENTRO Map pp76–7 Spanish €€

☎ 257 533 343; Maltézské náměstí 9; mains 200-500Kč, tapas 100-300Kč; ⏰ noon-midnight; 🚊 12, 20, 22, 23

Bright colours, chunky wooden furniture and Spanish-speaking staff lend an authentic air to this classic tapas bar. Here you can nibble on snackettes of chorizo, calamari and *gambas pil-pil* (prawns in garlic) over a bottle of Rioja, or splash out on a full meal of steak, grilled chicken or paella (1100Kč for two) washed down with a jug of sangria. (We can recommend the vegetarian paella, too.)

CUKRKÁVALIMONÁDA Map pp76–7 International €

☎ 257 530 628; Lázeňská 7; mains 120-180Kč; ⏰ 9am-11pm; 🚊 12, 20, 22, 23

A cute little café-cum-restaurant that combines minimalist modern styling with Renaissance-era painted timber roof-beams, CKL offers fresh, home-made pastas, frittatas, ciabattas, salads and pancakes (sweet and savoury) by day and a slightly more sophisticated bistro menu in the evening. The coffee is excellent, the hot chocolate is to die for, and the house special elderflower drink (flavoured with mint and lemon) is crisp and refreshing. Since you ask, the name means 'sugar, coffee, lemonade' – the phrase is the Czech equivalent of 'eeny-meeny-miny-moe'.

STARÉ MĚSTO

The Old Town is littered with tourist traps, especially around Old Town Square, but there are also plenty of excellent restaurants to discover. The maze of streets leading away from Old Town Square contains many hidden gems, while the swanky strip of Pařížská boasts a more obvious string of stylish, upmarket eateries. The classic Staré Město dining room is in a brick-lined cellar – you'll soon become a connoisseur of subterranean décor.

ALLEGRO Map pp88–9 Italian €€€

☎ 221 427 000; www.fourseasons.com/prague; Veleslavínova 2a; mains 980-1300Kč; ⏰ 7am-11pm; Ⓜ Staroměstská

It's been a long time coming, but Prague finally has its first Michelin-starred restaurant. The dining room at the Four Seasons Hotel oozes understated elegance with lots of polished wood panelling and Art Deco–style glass, and boasts a terrace with stunning night-time views of the floodlit castle. A superb setting for superb food – the Italian chef turns out inspired dishes that range from steamed tiger prawns scented with jasmine tea to fillet of turbot served on fennel compote with a squid and lime broth.

CASA ARGENTINA Map pp88–9 South American €€€

☎ 222 311 512; www.lacasaargentina.cz; Dlouhá 35; mains 350-1000Kč; ⏰ 10am-2am; Ⓜ Náměstí Republiky

Prague now boasts around half a dozen South American steakhouses specialising in charcoal-grilled Argentine or Brazilian beef, but the consensus among expat diners is that the kitchen at Casa Argentina serves up the best rare steak in town. Service can be laid-back, verging on lackadaisical, and the atmosphere is idiosyncratic, to say the least, with kitschy Latin American trappings, a caged lizard, a live toucan on a perch, and a couple of professional dancers who tango among the tables. Whatever; you're only here for the beef.

V ZÁTIŠÍ Map pp88–9 International/Modern Czech €€€

☎ 222 221 155; www.vzatisi.cz; Liliová 1; mains 500-800Kč; ⏰ noon-3pm & 5.30-11pm; 🚊 17, 18

'Still Life' is one of Prague's top restaurants, famed for the quality of its cuisine (which was rewarded with a Michelin recommendation in 2007). The décor is bold and modern, with dark wood, quirky lamps and candle-holders, and bold stripes of red and orange – there's even a wall fashioned from stacked books. Of the dozen or so main courses on offer, four are seafood and two or three are vegetarian. There are also gourmet versions of traditional Czech dishes – the crispy roast duckling with red cabbage and herb dumplings is superb. There's a two-course lunch menu, including one drink (695Kč), or you can lash out on the five-course degustation menu (1595Kč; plus 895Kč extra for wines to match the dishes).

LA PROVENCE Map pp88–9 French €€€

☎ 296 826 155; www.kampagroup.com; Štupartská 9; mains 400-800Kč; ⏰ noon-midnight; Ⓜ Náměstí Republiky

With its dark-wood beams, cushion-strewn benches, dim yellow lighting and shelves crammed with cooking implements, the basement restaurant at La Provence makes a good fist of passing itself off as a French country kitchen. The menu matches the décor, ranging from terrine of foie gras to rabbit Provençal in a creamy tarragon sauce. In the evening, when candlelight and soft piano music add to the atmosphere, it's an ideal spot for a romantic *tête-à-tête*.

KHAJURAHO Map pp88–9 Indian €€

☎ 224 242 860; www.khajuraho.cz; Richtrův dům, Michalská 23; mains 450-650Kč; ⏲ noon-11pm; Ⓜ Můstek

The latest addition to Prague's growing range of Indian restaurants moves straight to the top of the chart as our favourite – a series of vaulted medieval rooms given an oriental atmosphere with Persian rugs scattered on the floor, Indian statues tucked into niches, and sequinned textiles glowing colourfully beneath glass table-tops. Service is friendly and attentive, and the food is bursting with authentic flavours – cumin, coriander, ginger, garlic and chilli – ranging from Kashmiri dishes to *handi* and South Indian specialities, with plenty of choices that will appeal to vegetarians.

LES MOULES Map pp88–9 Belgian €€

☎ 222 315 022; www.lesmoules.cz; Pařížská 19; mains 375-600Kč; ⏲ 11.30am-midnight Mon-Fri, 9am-midnight Sat & Sun; 🚊 17

This impressive, wood-panelled, Belgian-style brasserie serves up steaming pans of mussels (449Kč for a kilo) in a range of sauces, from traditional *marinière* (white wine, cream and garlic) to Thai style (lemongrass, lime and coconut milk), as well as steaks, pork ribs, *boeuf bourgignon* and lobster fresh from the *vivier* (live tank; be prepared to shell out 995Kč). The bar offers a selection of Belgian beers, including Stella Artois, Leffe and Hoegaarden on tap, and Chimay, Achel and La Trappe in bottles.

ANGEL Map pp88–9 Asian €€

☎ 773 222 422; www.angelrestaurant.cz; V Kolkovně 7; mains 325-525Kč; ⏲ 11.30am-midnight Mon-Sat, 11am-4pm Sun; Ⓜ Staroměstská

Sparkling but subtle décor in shades of champagne and chocolate, crowned with a lacy disc of fairy lights, creates a sophisticated, romantic atmosphere in this highly acclaimed new restaurant. The Asian-fusion food, with flavours and influences from Thailand, Malaysia, Indonesia and Japan and an emphasis on fresh, high-quality produce, features delectable dishes such as hot-and-sour beef (dressed with tamarind, chilli and lime with fresh coriander and mint), and seared tuna with chilli sauce, sweet potato mash and crispy seaweed.

U ZAVOJE Map pp88–9 French €€

☎ 226 006 120; www.uzavoje.cz; Havelská 25; mains 400-500Kč; ⏲ 11am-midnight; Ⓜ Můstek

This wood-panelled gourmet complex, set in a beautiful old passageway between Havelská and Kožná streets, includes a wine bar, restaurant, coffee house and delicatessen, all dedicated to fine food and French and Czech wines. The restaurant menu concentrates on fresh seasonal produce, with dishes such as artichokes stuffed with tartare of wild salmon and scallops, organic Bresse chicken with courgette lasagne, and confit of quail with asparagus purée.

DAHAB

Map pp88–9 North African/Middle Eastern €€

☎ 224 827 375; www.dahab.cz; Dlouhá 33; mains 225-500Kč; ⏲ noon-1am; 🚊 5, 8, 14

Dahab is a dimly lit North African *souq* scattered with oriental rugs and cushions where you can lounge on a divan and sip Moroccan mint tea to an oriental–jazz–ragga soundtrack. The menu ranges from baklava and other sweet snacks to more substantial couscous, *tajine* (meat and vegetable stew), lamb and chicken dishes; there are also teas from India, China and Turkey. Or just kick back with a hookah (hubble-bubble pipe); 175Kč gets you a chunk of perfumed baccy that'll last around 45 minutes.

RASOI Map pp88–9 Indian €€

☎ 222 328 400; www.rasoi.cz; Dlouhá 13; mains 200-500Kč; ⏲ 4-11pm; 🚊 5, 8, 14

Relax with a Singapore Sling in the Bombay cocktail bar, then head downstairs to this posh Indian restaurant with a refined, semi-formal atmosphere, in a cellar that's been tarted up to look like a maharajah's mansion. The cuisine is certainly good enough for royalty, though you're more likely to be sharing with an appreciative crowd of expat Brits hankering after authentic tandoori chicken, *rogan josh* and chicken *jalfrezi*.

AMBIENTE PASTA FRESCA

Map pp88–9 Italian €€

☎ 224 230 244; www.ambi.cz; Celetná 11; mains 180-480Kč; ⏰ 11am-midnight; Ⓜ Náměstí Republiky

Slick styling and service with a smile complement an extensive menu at this busy Italian restaurant. Choose from dishes such as melt-in-the-mouth *carpaccio* of beef, piquant spaghetti *aglio-olio* with chilli and crisp pancetta, and rich creamy risotto with *porcini*, along with a wide range of Italian and Czech wines. There's a long, narrow café at street level, but you'll find a more formal, intimate cellar restaurant located down below.

KOLKOVNA Map pp88–9 Czech €€

☎ 224 819 701; www.kolkovna.cz; V Kolkovně 8; mains 160-430Kč; ⏰ 11am-midnight; Ⓜ Staroměstská

Owned and operated by the Pilsner Urquell brewery, Kolkovna is a stylish, modern take on the traditional Prague beer hall, with décor by top Czech designers, and posh (but hearty) versions of classic Czech dishes such as goulash, roast duck and Moravian Sparrow (see the boxed text, p155), including the Czech favourite, pork and dumplings (the dish of the day is only 95Kč). All washed down with exquisite Urquell beer, of course.

DANICO Map pp88–9 Italian €€

☎ 222 311 807; Dlouhá 21; mains 220-420Kč; ⏰ 11am-1am; 🚊 5, 8, 14

DaNico has earned a reputation as one of the best Italian restaurants in Prague, and it's easy to see why – Italian staff, fresh produce and ingredients imported from Italy, classic Mediterranean dishes such as *carpaccio* of smoked swordfish, *linguine con vongole* (pasta with clams), *penne all'arrabiata* (pasta with tomato, basil and chilli sauce), and homemade tiramisu, a range of regional Italian wines (expensive!), and a warm, welcoming atmosphere. Bookings recommended for Friday and Saturday evenings.

SIAM-I-SAN Map pp88–9 Thai €€

☎ 224 814 099; www.arzenal.cz; Valentínská 11; mains 270-390Kč; ⏰ 10am-midnight; Ⓜ Staroměstská

This unusual little restaurant is tucked away at the back of the glassware boutique Arzenal (p147), in a colourful room created by local architect and designer Boris Šípek – it has a dramatically uplit bar, grey, orange and yellow décor, colourful print tablecloths, and arty glass objects from the neighbouring shop. Even the coffee cups have a designer touch, with an asymmetric sway reminiscent of the Dancing Building. The cuisine is authentic Thai – some of the best Thai food in Prague – with a wide range of dishes, including many vegetarian ones.

ORANGE MOON Map pp88–9 Asian €€

☎ 222 325 119; www.orangemoon.cz; Rámová 5; mains 165-365Kč; ⏰ 11.30am-11.30pm; 🚊 5, 8, 14

Buddhist statues, oriental carved-wood panels, paper lanterns and warm, sunny colours make a welcoming combination at this ever-popular Asian restaurant. The menu is mostly Thai, with authentically spicy *tom yum kai* (hot and sour chicken broth) laden with smouldering chillis, crispy *pow pyet* (spring rolls) and fragrant *kaeng phed kai* (chicken in red curry). There are also some Indonesian, Burmese and Indian dishes, and bottles of Singha beer to take the edge off that chilli burn.

CHEZ MARCEL Map pp88–9 French €€

☎ 222 315 676; Haštalská 12; mains 150-350Kč; ⏰ 8am-1am Mon-Fri, 9am-1am Sat & Sun; 🚊 5, 8, 14

There's an authentic French bistro atmosphere at this peaceful backstreet café-bar, from the blue haze of cigarette smoke hanging over the dark wood tables (though you can escape to a smoke-free room at the back) to the copies of *Le Monde* and *Le Figaro* and the *escargots* on the menu. Stick to the simple dishes – steak *au poivre*, grilled chicken, quiche lorraine, the daily specials – and you won't be disappointed. The two-course lunch for 150Kč is great value.

AMBIENTE PIZZA NUOVA

Map pp88–9 Italian €€

☎ 221 803 308; www.ambi.cz; Revoluční 1; mains 295-330Kč; ⏰ 11.30am-11.30pm; Ⓜ Náměstí Republiky

The latest idea from the Ambiente team is this cool 1st-floor space next door to the Kotva shopping centre, filled with big tables and banquettes with picture windows overlooking náměstí Republiky. For a fixed price (295Kč per person before 6pm, 328Kč after) you get an all-you-can-eat deal – either help yourself from the salad and antipasti buffet, or choose from the hot pasta dishes and pizzas offered by a band of wandering waiters (buffet and pizza-pasta combined costs 475/515Kč). Wine by the glass is around 75Kč.

ARIANA Map pp88–9 Afghan €

☎ 222 323 438; http://sweb.cz/kabulrest; Rámová 6; mains 180-250Kč; 11am-11pm; 5, 8, 14

Ariana is a welcoming little place decked out with Persian rugs and photos of Kabul, with Asian music wailing in the background. It serves a range of unusual Afghani dishes, including *ashak* (a sort of ravioli containing chopped leeks, with a rich sauce of minced lamb and yogurt), various lamb and chicken kebabs and tasty vegetarian specialities, served with light, fluffy *nan-i-dashi* (hot bread) on the side.

LEHKÁ HLAVA Map pp88–9 Vegetarian €

☎ 222 220 665; www.lehkahlava.cz; Boršov 2; mains 120-210Kč; 11.30am-11.30pm Mon-Fri, noon-11.30pm Sat & Sun; 17, 18

Tucked away down a narrow cul-de-sac, Lehká Hlava (the name means 'clear head') exists in a little world of its own. A peaceful atrium leads to two unusually decorated dining rooms, both with a vaguely psychedelic vibe – one with a rocket-shaped light fitting that projects coloured images onto the walls, the other topped by a dark blue vault pierced by twinkling stars. Both have tables lit from within, either studded with glowing glass spheres or with a radiant wood-grain effect. In the kitchen the emphasis is on healthy, freshly prepared vegetarian and vegan dishes, ranging from hummus and roast veggies to spinach burritos to a spicy oriental stir-fry that could easily feed two at lunch.

COUNTRY LIFE Map pp88–9 Vegetarian €

☎ 224 213 366; www.countrylife.cz; Melantrichova 15; mains 80-170Kč; 9am-8.30pm Mon-Thu, 9am-6pm Fri, 11am-8.30pm Sun, closed Sat; M Můstek

Prague's first-ever health-food shop opened in 1991, and is an all-vegan cafeteria and sandwich bar offering inexpensive salads, sandwiches, pizzas, vegetarian goulash, sunflower-seed burgers and soy drinks. There is plenty of seating in the rear courtyard but it can still get crowded at lunchtime, so go early or buy sandwiches to go.

BEAS VEGETARIAN DHABA

Map pp88–9 Vegetarian/Indian €

☎ 608 035 727; Týnská 19; mains 90-130Kč; 11am-7pm; M Náměstí Republiky

Tucked away in a courtyard off Týnská, this friendly, informal little restaurant offers vegetarian curries (cooked by chefs from North India), served with rice, salad, chutneys and raita; the samosas are excellent, especially with a dab of fig chutney on the side. Unusually for Prague, there's some genuine chilli heat in the food, which is tasty and good value. This is also a great place to meet Czechs of an alternative bent.

NOVÉ MĚSTO & VYŠEHRAD

The New Town has an eclectic collection of eating places, with cafés and traditional Czech pubs as well as a range of international restaurants. The main eating streets are Wenceslas Square and Na Příkopě, lined with restaurants offering cuisines that cross the world from Italy to India and Argentina to Japan; there are also lots of less obvious and more appealing eateries hidden in the back streets between Wenceslas Square and the river.

RIO'S VYŠEHRAD

Map p116 Mediterranean €€€

☎ 224 922 156; www.riorestaurant.cz; Štulcova 2; mains 300-800Kč; 10am-midnight; M Vyšehrad

Located opposite the Church of Sts Peter & Paul in the Vyšehrad fortress, this is an attractive modern restaurant set in an ancient building. There's elegant indoor dining room and an informal terrace, but the main attraction is the garden, a lovely spot for an outdoor meal in summer. The international gourmet menu includes dishes such as salad of seared tuna with Japanese pickled ginger, fillet of salmon with Pommery champagne sauce, and chargrilled Brazilian beef, plus Czech classics such as roast duck.

MIYABI Map pp108–9 Japanese €€

☎ 296 233 102; www.miyabi.cz; Navrátilova 10; mains 180-700Kč; 11.30am-11pm; 3, 9, 14

Miyabi is a relaxed, café-style Japanese restaurant with minimalist décor and modern art on the walls – a refreshing change from more formal Japanese places. There's a small sushi menu (*nigiri* sushi is 60 Kč to 120Kč a piece) and main courses that include fish and vegetable tempura (pieces of fish or vegetables dipped in batter and deep-fried), *sake no amiyaki* (salmon marinated in saki then grilled) and *karaage* (pieces of chicken marinated with ginger and soy sauce then deep-fried).

KOGO Map pp108–9 Italian €€

☎ 221 451 259; www.kogo.cz; Slovanský dům, Na Příkopě 22; pizzas 200-300Kč, mains 250-600Kč; 🕑 11am-11pm; Ⓜ Náměstí Republiky

Chic and businesslike, but also relaxed and child-friendly (highchairs provided), Kogo is a stylish restaurant serving top-notch pizza, pasta, steak and seafood – the rich, tomatoey *zuppa di pesce* (fish soup) is delicious, as is the *risotto alla pescatora* (made with squid, mussels, shrimp and octopus). There's also a good range of wines available by the glass. On summer evenings, tables filled with conversation and candlelight spill over into the leafy courtyard.

SUTERÉN Map pp108–9 International €€

☎ 224 933 657; www.suteren.cz; Masarykovo nábřeží 26; mains 345-445Kč; 🕑 11.30am-midnight Mon-Sat; 🚋 17, 21

'The Basement' is a beautiful cellar space, where modern detailing complements the old red-brick and wooden beams perfectly. Cream linen chairs, set at gleaming black tables with a single, deep-pink rose in the middle of each one, surround a circular glass bar with a colourful aquarium along one wall. The menu leans towards seafood, beef and game, with intriguing dishes such as salmon *mojito,* with the fish marinated in rum and lime juice, served with tart lime jam and sweet rum-and-mint sauce; and more traditional fare such as roast saddle of rabbit marinated in wine, vinaigrette and thyme.

OLIVA Map p116 Mediterranean €€

☎ 222 520 288; www.olivarestaurant.cz; Plavecká 4; mains 220-420Kč; 🕑 11.30am-3pm & 6pm-midnight Mon-Sat; 🚋 3, 7, 16, 17, 21

A small, friendly, family-run restaurant focusing on fresh Mediterranean cuisine, Oliva has become a victim of its own popularity. A menu of carefully prepared dishes that include rocket salad with caramelised red onion, olives, pine nuts and parmesan, roast octopus with okra and grilled peppers, and pan-fried sea bass with olive, anchovy and tomato has pulled in so many customers that on weekend evenings the waitstaff can be overwhelmed. But the food is so good that it's well worth enduring the occasional spell of slow service.

top picks

BEST BREAKFASTS

- Red Hot & Blues (Map pp88–9; ☎ 222 314 639; Jakubská 12; mains 200-500Kč; 🕑 9am-11pm; Ⓜ Náměstí Republiky) Serves a range of Western breakfasts, including pancakes and maple syrup, and a full British fry-up; the 'Home Run Special' (bacon, eggs, hash browns, pancakes and toast) will soak up the heaviest hangover, and lay a firm foundation for further debauchery. Breakfast is served to 11.30am weekdays and to 4pm on weekends.
- Kavárna Pavilón (Map p121; ☎ 222 097 201; Vinohrady Pavilón, Vinohradská 50; mains 120-260Kč; 🕑 8am-9pm Mon-Fri, 9am-9pm Sat & Sun; Ⓜ Náměstí Míru) Bright, airy café in upmarket shopping centre; offers excellent coffee and the best almond croissants in town.
- Globe Bookstore & Café (Map pp108–9; ☎ 224 934 203; Pštrossova 6; mains 120-200Kč; 🕑 10am-midnight; Ⓜ Karlovo Náměstí) Excellent brunch served 9.30am to 4pm Saturday and Sunday, including pancakes with bacon and maple syrup, freshly squeezed juices and Bloody Marys. Smaller breakfasts served till 4pm weekdays.
- Káva Káva Káva (Map pp88–9; ☎ 224 228 862; Platýz pasáž, Národní třída 37; mains 60-200Kč; 🕑 7am-10pm Mon-Fri, 9am-10pm Sat & Sun; Ⓜ Národní Třída) Has some of the best coffee in town, accompanied by bagels, croissants, cakes and pastries. Breakfast served all day.
- Café Savoy (Map pp76–7; ☎ 257 311 562; Vítězná 5, Malá Strana; mains 120-25Kč; 🕑 8am-10.30pm Mon-Fri, 9am-10.30pm Sat & Sun; 🚋 6, 9, 22, 23) Full English (including baked beans), full American (with peanut butter), or healthy breakfast with yogurt, fruit and cereal.

LEMON LEAF Map pp108–9 International €€

☎ 224 919 056; www.lemon.cz; Myslíkova 14; mains 130-300Kč; 🕑 11am-11pm Mon-Thu, 11am-12.30am Fri, 12.30pm-12.30am Sat, 12.30pm-11pm Sun; 🚋 17, 21

It's a bit off the beaten tourist path, but with its bright, high-ceiling rooms decked out with crushed-silk lampshades and Thai-style art, menus translated into English and German, and friendly smiling service, the

Lemon Leaf is certainly making an effort to pull in the visitors. And it's certainly worth a visit – the menu is mostly European, ranging from fillet of wild Scottish salmon to tournedos Rossini, but there is also a selection of excellent, authentic Thai dishes including a rich and fragrant green curry with a decent kick of chilli heat.

BRANICKÝ SKLÍPEK Map pp108–9 Czech €€

U Purkmistra; ☎ 224 237 103; Vodičkova 2; mains 100-300Kč; 9am-11pm Mon-Fri, 11am-11pm Sat & Sun; M Můstek

This is one of the few rough-and-ready, old-fashioned beer halls left in central Prague, serving meaty, good-value Czech dishes washed down with cheap beer. Menus and staff are Czech only and service can be grumpy, which puts off most tourists, but persevere – this is the real deal, serving up some of the finest pork, dumplings and sauerkraut in town (look for *purkmistrová mísa* on the menu). Nonsmokers, beware – the atmosphere is smoky enough to kipper a truckload of herring.

NA RYBÁRNĚ Map pp108–9 Fish & Seafood €€

☎ 224 918 885; Gorazdova 17; mains 100-300Kč; 9.30am-11pm; 17, 21

This unassuming little fish restaurant has been around for almost a century and has seen more than a few celebrity diners, ranging from writer Karel Čapek to ex-president Václav Havel, Rolling Stone Mick Jagger and former US secretary of state Madeleine Albright. The menu here offers everything from salmon and tuna to cuttlefish and tiger prawns, but the best dishes are the simplest and most traditional – trout with herb butter, and daily specials such as baked carp or grilled eel with lemon butter.

SIAM ORCHID Map p106 Thai €€

☎ 222 319 410; www.siamorchid.cz; Na Poříčí 21; mains 160-280Kč; 10am-10pm; 3, 8, 24, 26

The setting – a scatter of plastic tables and chairs on a 1st-floor balcony hidden up a passage beside a department store – looks none too promising, but this tiny restaurant, tucked away beside a Thai massage studio, offers some of the city's most authentic Thai cuisine. From the crisp, grease-free *po-pia thot* (spring rolls with pork and black mushrooms) and succulent *kai sa-te* (chicken satay) to the fiery *kaeng khiao wan kai* (chicken in green curry with basil), pretty much everything on the menu is a delight.

ALBIO Map p106 Vegetarian/Organic €€

☎ 222 325 414; www.albiostyl.cz; Truhlářská 20; mains 130-280Kč; 11am-10pm Mon-Sat; M Náměstí Republiky

This family-friendly, nonsmoking, whole-foods restaurant is as bright and fresh as an Alpine morning, decked out in blonde wood and rustic timber set off with salmon-pink tablecloths and seat-cushions. It sources all its food from local organic farms and operates its own bakery, shop and advice counter offering tips on organic food and healthy eating. The menu includes fish, vegetarian and vegan dishes, such as baked whole rice with oyster mushrooms, leeks and cashew nuts, and buckwheat pancakes filled with onion mash and grilled zucchini. There are also organic wines and unpasteurised beer so you can work up a healthy hangover.

U MATĚJE KOTRBY Map pp108–9 Czech €€

☎ 224 930 768; www.umatejekotrby.cz; Křemencova 17; mains 130-280Kč; noon-11pm; 6, 9, 18, 21, 22, 23

It's only 50m away from the tourist trap that is U Fleků, but this place is the real deal – an atmospheric Czech pub strewn with more bric-a-brac, musical instruments and old photos than the average antique shop and, more importantly, sporting a menu of classic Czech grub from goulash made with Pilsner Urquell to pork knuckle braised in dark beer, mustard and horseradish. There's also a range of traditional 'beer snacks' including *utopenci* (sausage pickled in vinegar), Czech cheeses with walnuts and olives, and *libová tlačenka* (pork brawn, or potted head), amusingly translated on the menu as 'home-made headcheese'.

KARAVANSERÁJ Map pp108–9 Lebanese €

☎ 224 930 390; Masarykovo nábřeží 22; mains 100-250Kč; 9am-11pm Mon-Thu, 9am-midnight Fri, noon-midnight Sat, noon-10pm Sun; 17, 21

Serving as the home base of a travellers' club, this restaurant and tearoom cultivates a ramshackle, relaxed and welcoming atmosphere, with its batik tablecloths, wicker chairs, oriental knick-knacks and library of travel guidebooks. The menu is mostly Lebanese – baba ganoush, falafel, hummus and lamb kebabs – with a couple of Indian dishes thrown in, and there's a huge range of speciality teas to choose from. It's child-friendly too, with highchairs, kids' portions and a collection of toys to play with.

U NEKLANA Map p116 Czech €

☎ 224 916 051; Neklanova 30; mains 120-225Kč; 11am-midnight; 7, 18, 24

U Neklana is a welcoming local pub nestled in the corner of one of Prague's coolest apartment buildings, a Cubist classic dating from 1915. Decked out in the cheerful red colours of the Budvar brewery, it dishes up hearty Czech fare such as potato and mushroom soup served in a scooped-out loaf of rye bread (the menu is in English and German as well as Czech), and there's a hits-of-the-'80s jukebox providing a suitably retro soundtrack.

COUNTRY LIFE Map pp108–9 Vegetarian €

☎ 224 247 280; www.countrylife.cz; Jungmannova 1; mains 60-170Kč; 9.30am-6.30pm Mon-Thu, 10am-6pm Fri, closed Sat & Sun; 3, 9, 14, 24

Country Life is a cafeteria-style health-food restaurant with all-vegan food and buffet service – load up your plate, and pay by weight (that's right! You weigh in at the till). There are only four tables at this branch, which caters mainly to the takeaway trade – if you want a better chance of a seat, head for the branch in Staré Město (p163).

PIZZERIA KMOTRA Map pp108–9 Pizza €

☎ 224 934 100; www.kmotra.cz; V Jirchářích 12; pizza 95-145Kč; 11am-midnight; M Národní Třída

One of Prague's oldest and best pizzerias, 'the Godmother' can rustle up more than two dozen varieties of pizza, from margherita to marinara, cooked in a genuine wood-fired pizza oven. Sit beside the bar upstairs, or head down to the basement where you can watch the chef slinging pizza dough in the open kitchen – both areas are non-smoking. It gets busy here after 8pm, so try to snag a table before then.

VINOHRADY & VRŠOVICE

Outside the centre, Vinohrady has Prague's largest concentration of good restaurants, and the choice is only getting better as the area moves increasingly upmarket. Most are clustered around Náměstí Míru and the long residential street, Mánesova, that parallels Vinohradská from the Muzeum to the Jiřího z Poděbrad metro stops. Vršovice picks up on the southeast corner of Vinohrady. It's not as fruitful, but has a couple of pleasant surprises, including the city's only Azerbaijani eatery.

AROMI Map p121 Italian €€

☎ 222 713 222; Mánesova 78, Vinohrady; mains 350-500Kč; noon-10pm Sun-Thu, to 11pm Fri & Sat; M Jiřího z Poděbrad or 11

Red brick, polished wood, country-style furniture and sprigs of fresh rosemary and thyme on each table create a pleasantly rustic atmosphere in this gourmet Italian restaurant. Brisk and businesslike at lunchtime, romantic in the evenings, Aromi has a reputation for authentic Italian cuisine, from the *zuppa di cannellini* (cannellini bean soup) to the *branzino al guazzetto* (sea bass baked in a sea-salt crust; seafood is a speciality).

ZAHRADA V OPEŘE Map p121 International €€

☎ 224 239 685; Legerová 75, Vinohrady; mains 280-500Kč; noon-11pm; M Muzeum or 11

This may be the best food for the money in the city, with excellently prepared Czech dishes such as *svíčková*, plus international foods inspired by South Africa and Asia, and regular sushi nights. The sophisticated contemporary décor manages to be both unstuffy and elegant at the same time. For years, the restaurant was trapped in the security cordon of US-funded Radio Free Europe/Radio Liberty next door, making it a real effort to find the front door, but the radio station was slated to move from this location by 2009.

PASTIČKA Map p121 Czech €€

☎ 222 253 228; Blanická 25 (cnr Mánesova), Vinohrady; mains 200-450Kč; 11am-10pm Mon-Fri, 5-11pm Sat & Sun; M Jiřího z Poděbrad or 11

A warm, inviting ground floor pub with a little garden out the back, Pastička is great for a beer or a meal. The décor is part 1920s Prague and part Irish pub. In the evenings, the rows of tables stretching past the bar are normally filled with students. Most come for the beer, but the mix of international and traditional Czech dishes is very good. The garden is popular with a local office crowd at lunchtime.

MOZAIKA Map p121 International €€

☎ 224 253 011; Nitranská 13, Vinohrady; mains 220-400Kč; 11.30am-11pm; M Jiřího z Poděbrad

When this stylish restaurant opened a few years back, it set new standards for both design and cooking at this price range. The menu tilts towards fusion, with entrees such as seared salmon served with a side of wasabi-infused mashed potatoes. The wine list features excellent domestic whites and reds from Moravia, and – unusual for Prague – decent wine by the glass. The sleek interior is formal enough for a business lunch and warm enough for a romantic night for two. Reservations are a must.

AMBIENTE Map p121 International €€

☎ 222 727 851; Mánesova 59, Vinohrady; mains 200-400Kč; 11am-midnight Mon-Fri, noon-midnight Sat & Sun; M Jiřího z Poděbrad or 11

'Ambiente' means atmosphere, and the warm yellow walls, banquettes, bamboo-and-basketwork chairs and rich mahogany woodwork help create a relaxing one at this flagship of the well-run Ambiente chain. The American-themed menu offers a huge range of salads (including Caesar, goat's cheese, roast veggies, avocado), tasty pasta dishes, barbecue ribs, fajitas, steaks and chicken wings, and there are excellent house wines for around 90Kč a glass.

AMIGOS Map p121 Mexican €€

☎ 222 250 594; Anny Letenské 16 (cnr Mánesova), Vinohrady; mains 200-400Kč; 11.30am-midnight; M Muzeum or 11

Amigos offers decent Mexican and South American cooking, just a short walk up Mánesova from the Muzeum metro station. There are tasty burritos, tacos, enchiladas and quesadillas, as well as steaks, hamburgers, stir-fries and big dinner salads. The atmosphere often feels more like a pub than a restaurant, and the mood can get rowdy on occasion. Fun.

OSTERIA DA CLARA Map p121 Italian €€

☎ 271 726 548; Mexická 7, Vršovice; mains 200-400Kč; 11am-11pm; M Náměstí Míru or 4, 22, 23

This relaxed Italian *trattoria* features both excellent home-made cooking and a funky, retro '70s ambience that's authentic down to the velveteen sofas by the door and the blaxploitation soundtrack wafting through the speakers. The three-course set lunch menu priced below 200Kč is excellent value. Try a simple yet delicious *zuppa di pomodoro* (tomato soup), with fresh basil on top, followed by the calamari, sautéed with courgettes, celery and spinach.

CHUDOBA Map p121 Czech €

☎ 222 250 624; Vinohradská 67, Vinohrady; mains 130-260Kč; 11am-1am Mon-Sat, 11am-midnight Sun; 11

This upscale Czech tavern–restaurant occupies a choice corner on a leafy section of Vinohradská. The customers are mostly young professionals and couples out for an after-work drink and a very good and reasonably priced Czech meal. The décor plays with the 'Olde Vinohrady' theme, with sepia-tone photos on the wall and polished wooden floors. The food is a mix of Czech and Continental, with standards like roast duck and goulash sharing the menu with pork ribs and a very hearty meat fondue. There's a sidewalk terrace in nice weather.

MASALA Map p121 International €

☎ 222 251 601; Mánesova 13, Vinohrady; mains 150-250Kč; noon-11pm Mon-Fri, 5-11pm Sat & Sun; M Muzeum or 11

Just what Prague needed: an excellent, unpretentious Indian restaurant, with all of the good food and none of the stultifying atmosphere and stiff service you normally find at Indian places here. The Indian couple who run Masala aim for what they call home-style service, meaning a relaxed presentation and good home-cooking. One minor quibble is that the food could use more spice. On a recent visit the lamb *rogan josh* had a hint of ketchup, but the meat was tender and the accompanying naan bread was just right: crispy on the edges and soft in the centre.

U DĚDKA Map p121 International €

☎ 222 522 784; Na Kozačce 12, Vinohrady; mains 150-250Kč; 10am-11pm Mon-Fri, 2pm-1am Sat; M Náměstí Míru, 4, 22, 23

This pleasantly upmarket pub–restaurant, situated near the top of Voroněžská on the border between Vinohrady and Vršovice, has a quiet, tree-covered terrace out the front. The modern décor pulls in a mix of Czech professionals, students and the occasional tourist from a nearby pension, while the menu is a blend of Czech specialities plus well-done bar food, such as chicken quesadillas and cheeseburgers. The latter are easily the best in this part of town.

CAFÉ FX Map p121 Vegetarian €

☎ 224 254 776; Bělehradská 120, Vinohrady; mains 120-240Kč; 11.30am-2am; M IP Pavlova

Café FX offers some of the best food in Prague in its price range – and it's all vegetarian. This hippy-chic restaurant at the entrance to the nightclub Radost FX (p196) – looking like a faded bordello with its draped chiffon, tasselled lampshades and distressed walls – comes up with imaginative dishes ranging from spinach ravioli stuffed with hazelnut pesto and cheese to sage and mushroom 'meatballs' with mashed potatoes and creamy mushroom sauce.

HUANG HE Map p121 Chinese €

☎ 271 746 651; Vršovická 1, Vršovice; mains 150-200Kč; 10am-11pm Mon-Fri, 2pm-1am Sat; M Náměstí Míru, 6, 7, 11, 18, 24

One of the first authentic Chinese restaurants to open in the city in the early 1990s and still one of the best, Huang He is in lower Vršovice, close to (if not actually in) Nusle. On crowded nights, the atmosphere is akin to a raucous Czech pub (a previous incarnation), and you'll be tempted, like everyone else, to wash down that spicy chicken *kung-pao* with a half-litre or two of beer. Phone ahead to reserve a table.

SEDM KRASAVIC Map p121 Azerbaijani €

☎ 267 710 777; Voroněžská 19, Vršovice; mains 150-200Kč; 10am-11pm Mon-Fri, 2pm-1am Sat; M Náměstí Míru, 4, 22, 23

Bright and cheerful, this Azerbaijani restaurant is up the street from the Czech Inn and Arco hostels. The menu is strong on *pilaf* dishes, a scrumptious mixture of fruits and ground beef, as well as kebabs and Russian-style dumplings. The daily lunch special for 85Kč is arguably the best meal deal in the neighbourhood, and there are excellent wines from Georgia on offer.

CHEERS Map p121 International €

☎ 222 513 108; cnr náměstí Míru & Belgická, Vinohrady; mains 100-200Kč; 11am-1am; M Náměstí Míru

Cheers is a modern take on the traditional Czech pub, with bright and breezy colours, lots of stainless steel and a splash or two of contemporary art. The theory behind the menu seems to be to include one favourite dish from a dozen or so cuisines around the world, so you can choose nachos or *nigiri* sushi, *carpaccio* or cheeseburgers, fresh hummus or fish and chips. There's a great range of beers available too, including Budvar, Hoegaarden and Guinness on tap.

PIZZERIA GROSSETO Map p121 Italian/Pizza €

☎ 224 252 778; Francouzská 2, Vinohrady; mains 120-180Kč; 11.30am-11pm; M Náměstí Míru

This bustling Vinohrady pizzeria, just off Náměstí Míru, serves very good pizzas, with inventive toppings such as asparagus and ricotta cheese, as well as homemade pastas and original desserts. Too often in Prague, pizzas come only with standard toppings like ham or mushrooms – but not here. The garden terrace at the back is a secluded gem and something of a local secret. To find it, walk left past the front entrance in the direction of Francouzská and through a small passageway to the right.

VEG FOOD Map p121 Vegetarian/Vegan €

☎ 721 255 253; Londýnská 35, Vinohrady; mains 100-200Kč; 11am-8pm; M Náměstí Míru or IP Pavlova

There's not much in the way of atmosphere here at Veg Food, one of the few purely vegetarian and vegan restaurants in the area. It has a simple coffee shop feel, with a scattering of plastic tables and metal chairs. But the menu holds some pleasant surprises, including lots of 'meat' dishes using tofu, such as vegetarian schnitzel and vegetarian chicken, plus plenty of Asian-inspired entrees. Nonsmoking throughout, it also offers a daily two-course lunch menu for 98Kč.

ŽIŽKOV & KARLÍN

Žižkov is more famous for its pubs than its restaurants, but there are new places springing up every year to add to the old stalwarts that have been around for ages. We haven't been able to recommend any restaurants in Karlín yet, but if you're in the area check out the Pivovarsky Klub (p186), a drinking venue that serves good traditional pub grub.

HANIL Map pp126–7 Japanese/Korean €€

☎ 222 715 867; Slavíkova 24, Žižkov; mains 300-550Kč; 11am-2.30pm & 5.30-11pm Mon-Sat, 5.30-11pm Sun; M Jiří z Poděbrad

White walls, blond-wood lattice screens, paper lanterns and polished granite tables

top picks

VEGETARIAN RESTAURANTS

- Albio (p165)
- Beas Vegetarian Dhaba (p163)
- Café FX (opposite)
- Country Life (p163)
- Lehká Hlava (p163)

create a relaxed and informal setting where a mixed crowd of businesspeople, locals and expats enjoys authentic Japanese and Korean cuisine without the fuss and formality of more expensive restaurants. Tuck into a hot bowl of tasty *bibimbap* (rice topped with meat and pickled vegetables and spiced with hot pepper paste), or order a sashimi platter – the sushi here is probably the best value in town.

MAILSI Map pp126–7 Pakistani €€

☎ 222 717 783; Lipanská 1, Žižkov; mains 200-350Kč; ⏲ noon-3pm & 6-11pm; 🚊 5, 9, 26
Mailsi was Prague's first Pakistani restaurant, and is still one of the city's best for authentic, home-style curry cuisine. The outside is inconspicuous, and it's only the qawwali music that guides you into the attractively decorated green and burgundy dining room with its tropical fishtank. Service is courteous and the food delicious, though prices have edged up in recent years – prawn and fish dishes go up to 500Kč. The *bhaji* is rather plain – just onion and potato thinly sliced, dipped in spiced flour and fried, but very light and crisp – while the *murgh dal* consists of tender chicken in a cumin-spiced lentil sauce.

KUŘE V HODINKÁCH

Map pp126–7 Czech/International €

☎ 222 734 212; www.kurevhodinkach.cz; Seifertova 26, Žižkov; mains 120-260Kč; ⏲ food served 11am-2.30pm & 6-11.30pm; 🚊 5, 9, 26
This rock music–themed pub is named after a 1972 album by Czech jazz-rock band Flamengo, which was banned by the communist authorities (it means 'Chicken in the Watch' – hey, it was the '70s, psychedelic drugs and all that…). Decked out in rock memorabilia, and with a choice of buzzing street-level bar or more intimate brick-vaulted basement, it's more upmarket than most Žižkov pubs and has a classy kitchen to match – the menu includes pasta with buttered sage and pecorino, tofu burgers, barbecued chicken wings in ginger and soy sauce, and a rich, dark and tasty goulash with bacon dumplings.

RESTAURACE AKROPOLIS

Map pp126–7 International €

☎ 296 330 913; Kubelíkova 27, Žižkov; mains 90-230Kč; ⏲ 11.30am-1am Mon-Sat; 🚊 5, 9, 26
The café in the famous Palác Akropolis club (p198) is a Žižkov institution, with its eccentric combination of marble panels, quirky metalwork light fittings and weird fishtank installations designed by local artist František Skála. The menu has a good selection of vegetarian dishes, from nachos to gnocchi, plus great garlic soup, searingly hot buffalo wings and steak tartare. Kids are welcome – you'll find toys and colouring books (though it can get a bit smoky) – and so are dogs, who can choose from their own menu of biscuits and chew toys.

HOLEŠOVICE, BUBENEČ & DEJVICE

The outlying neighbourhoods north and west of the city centre are finally coming into their own in terms of quality restaurants. Most of the better places are clustered along the residential streets around and north of the Dejvická metro station. You'll find another grouping within walking distance of Strossmayerovo náměstí. The far eastern section of Holešovice has seen a boom in property development but is still lacking in decent eateries, yet even here are there are some new names.

HANAVSKÝ PAVILÓN

Map pp132–3 Czech/International €€€

☎ 233 323 641; Letenské sady 173, Bubeneč; mains 600-900Kč; ⏲ 11am-1am, terrace to 11pm; 🚊 18
Perched on a terrace high above the river, this ornate, neobaroque pavilion dating from 1891 houses a smart restaurant with a postcard-perfect view of the Vltava bridges – from April to September you can dine on the outdoor terrace. There's a three-course set menu (from 375Kč) of Czech classics.

DA EMANUEL Map pp132–3 Italian €€€

☎ 224 312 934; Charlese De Gaulla 4, Dejvice; mains 500-700Kč; noon-11pm; M Dejvická or tram 8

This small, elegant Italian-owned place, on a quiet residential street, is one of Dejvice's true destination restaurants. The main dining room, perched romantically below an arched brick ceiling, holds around a dozen tables, each with a vase of fresh flowers and covered in white linens. Try the *tagliata con rucola* (tender slices of filet mignon sprinkled with rocket) or the mussels, served in a salty tomato sauce. Since it's small, you'll have to book in advance.

EL GAUCHO Map pp132–3 Steakhouse €€€

☎ 224 911 579; Schwaigerova 59/3, Bubeneč; mains 400-700Kč; 11am-11pm; tram 1, 8, 15, 25, 26 (stop Sparta) plus a long walk

A romantic Argentinean-style steakhouse tucked away in a valley in Bubeneč, this restaurant is part of the Hotel Villa Schwaiger, and the setting is reminiscent of a country inn. There are plenty of pasta and chicken dishes on the menu, but the focus here is on the beef. Order by the cut at prices about 100 Kč cheaper than similar steakhouses in the centre. Dine in the garden in nice weather. It's hard to find, so bring a map or take a taxi, or combine a visit with a walk through nearby Stromovka park.

RESTAURANT U CEDRU

Map pp132–3 Lebanese €€

☎ 233 342 974; Národní Obrany 27, Dejvice; mains 200-400Kč; 11am-11pm; M Dejvická

'At the Cedar' is a welcoming Lebanese restaurant with tasty *mezze* (appetisers) such as baba ganoush (smoky aubergine/eggplant and garlic puree), tabbouleh and stuffed vine leaves. Rather than agonise over the menu, you can order a spread of 10 *mezze*, which the chef will select for you – a great start to dinner, or a lunch in itself.

KAVALA Map pp132–3 Greek €€

☎ 224 325 181; Charlese De Gaulla 5, Dejvice; mains 290-350Kč; 11.30am-11.30pm; M Dejvická

If you can't get in at De Emanuel (above), try this Greek *taverna* across the street. There are the usual classics such as souvlaki and moussaka, plus a delicious seafood *mezze* (320Kč) that could easily be a meal in itself. The indoor dining room, with the sponged walls and light woods, is a little too cute – a better bet is the front garden. The Greek Society runs a small grocery next door, which is great for stocking up on fresh olives, Greek wines, authentic Greek yogurt and fresh feta.

HAVELI Map pp132–3 Indian €€

☎ 233 344 800; Dejvická 6, Dejvice; mains 250-350Kč; 11am-midnight; M Hradčanská

Indian music and a waft of incense will guide you towards this popular, authentic curry restaurant with tables split between an informal street-level bar and a cosy red-brick and whitewash cellar. The onion *bhaji* is light and crisp, the naan bread soft and buttery, and the curry dishes nicely spiced; there's a good selection of vegetarian dishes, including a very tasty *channa pindi* (chick peas and white cheese in a tangy sauce rich in cumin and fresh coriander).

ČÍNSKÁ ZAHRADA Map pp132–3 Chinese €€

☎ 233 379 656; Šmeralová 11, Bubeneč; mains 150-300Kč; 11am-11pm; tram 1, 8, 15, 25, 26

Zahrada is similar to Hong Kong (below) in that it's a largely authentic Chinese restaurant that's good enough to draw people here from around the city. In fact, it's not uncommon to see lines of Asian tourists streaming down the sidewalks, all headed here, at mealtimes. The very hot 'dry fried chicken' (pieces of chicken cooked on the bone in red pepper flake) is one of the local favourites; ask the waiter to advise. Dine on the terrace in nice weather.

HONG KONG Map pp132–3 Chinese €€

☎ 233 376 209; Letenské náměstí 5, Holešovice; mains 150-300Kč; 10.30am-11pm; tram 1, 8, 15, 25, 26

An impressively gaudy décor, with ornately carved wooden panels, an illuminated, painted-glass ceiling and red silk seat cushions, Cantonese pop music and a clientele that includes local Chinese families – it all smacks of authenticity. That extends to the mostly Cantonese menu, which, along with favourites such as dim sum, soy-sauce duck and salt-and-pepper shrimp, has such adventurous options as 'cold sliced pork tongue with soy sauce', 'chicken with strange tastes' and 'chicken with five smells'.

SAKURA Map pp132–3 Japanese €€

☎ 774 785 077; Náměstí Svobody 1, Dejvice; mains 150-300Kč; 11.30am-11pm; M Dejvická

Crown for crown, this is arguably the best sushi place in Prague. It occupies a smart

1930s functionalist building, and the open interior is a soothing blend of contemporary Japanese and Czech high modern. There's even a small play area for children. The sushi is excellent, but the rolls really stand out. The 'volcano' roll features spicy tuna; the 'crunch' roll comes lightly fried, with gently cooked salmon tucked inside.

MOLO 22 Map pp132–3 International €

☎ 220 563 348; U Průhonu 22, Holešovice; mains 150-250Kč; 8am-midnight Mon-Fri, 9am-midnight Sat & Sun; M Vltavská or 5, 12, 15

This super-slick restaurant – done out in dark panelled walls and lime green accents, just across the street from the dance club Mecca (p195) – is a sure sign that this section of Holešovice is on the way up. The menu is ambitious and eclectic, with Italian risottos and Thai curries listed alongside traditional Czech favourites such as *Svíčková na smetaně* and roast duck. Good cheesecake desserts.

STAROČESKÁ KRČMA
Map pp132–3 Czech/International €

☎ 224 321 505; VP Čkalova 15, Dejvice; mains 150-250Kč; 11am-midnight; M Hradčanská or Dejvická

A very good traditional Czech tavern, Staročeská Krčma specialises in huge portions of grilled meats, such as steaks, pork and chicken. The setting is meant to evoke an old-fashioned *koliba* (inn or country cottage), with big wooden tables, an open fireplace and stacks of wood sitting around. The pork dishes excel, while the steaks are only good. Reserve in advance, especially on weekends.

BOHEMIA BAGEL Map pp132–3 International €

☎ 220 806 541; Dukelských Hrdinů 48, Bubeneč; mains 100-200Kč; 9am-9pm; 5, 14, 15, 17

When this outlet of the local Bohemia Bagel empire opened in 2007, it was widely heralded as a sign of Holešovice's imminent rebirth. It hasn't exactly worked out that way. This remains the best all-round sandwich and light meal joint in the neighbourhood, with the usual range of bagels, breakfasts and burgers, plus seared tuna and filet mignon entrees for bigger appetites. Bohemia Bagel is only two tram stops from Nádraží Holešovice (take tram 15), making this a feasible meal option if you're waiting for a train.

NA URALE Map pp132–3 Czech €

☎ 224 326 820; Uralská 9, Dejvice; mains 100-200Kč; 11am-midnight; M Dejvická or 8

A formerly grotty Czech pub that's greatly cleaned up its act in recent years, adding some beautiful crimson walls and solid stone-tile floors. The kitchen has also had an upgrade, but the prices for well-done Czech dishes such as *guláš* and roast pork are barely higher than at a typical workers' pub. Na Urale anchors an increasingly interesting set of shops on lovely Puškinovo náměstí (Pushkin Square), which now includes both an Italian and a Japanese grocery store.

PIZZERIA GROSSETO Map pp132–3 Italian/Pizza €

☎ 233 342 694; Jugoslávských Partyzánů 8, Dejvice; mains 100-155Kč; 11.30am-11pm; M Dejvická or 8

This is a lively, friendly pizzeria with a genuine, wood-fired pizza oven that pulls in crowds of students from the nearby university campus. As well as a huge choice of tasty pizza varieties, the menu also offers salads, pastas, risotto, roast chicken, steak and grilled salmon. The main dining room, where you can watch the pizza chefs twirling their dough, is complemented by an attractive timber-decked conservatory out the back.

CAPUA Map pp132–3 Pizza €

☎ 233 382 659; Milady Horákové 9, Bubeneč; mains 100-150Kč; 11am-1am, terrace to 11pm; 1, 8, 15, 25, 26

This corner restaurant just above Strossmayerovo náměstí is widely considered the best pizza place in the neighbourhood, and even the food editor of the *Prague Post* listed it in the city's 'top four' in a 2007 pizza run-off. But in truth, it's only good, not great. The inviting interior is divided into two rooms, with nonsmokers getting the larger and nicer one to the right. The pizzas are thin-crust and follow the usual formula of Italian combinations. 'Capriccioso' is a filling mix of ham and fresh mushrooms. There's a shaded terrace out the front in nice weather.

LUCKY LUCIANO Map pp132–3 Pizza €

☎ 220 875 900; Dělnická 28, Holešovice; mains 100-150Kč; 11.30am-11pm; M Vltavská or 1, 5, 12, 14, 15, 25

You're in luck if you're staying at Sir Toby's (p225) – this little pizzeria next door serves very good pizza, as well as traditional Italian appetisers such as beef *carpaccio* and *insalata caprese*. The service is friendly, and the best part of all is the big tree-covered terrace in the front – a nice, cool spot to chill out on a hot summer day.

LA CRÊPERIE Map pp132–3 French €

☎ 220 878 040; Janovského 4, Holešovice; mains 60-140Kč; ⏰ 9am-11pm Mon-Sat, to 10pm Sun; Ⓜ Vltavská or 🚊 1, 5, 8, 12, 14, 15, 17, 25, 26

Odd place to put an authentic French crêperie, in a forgotten corner of Holešovice next to the district's massive administrative office complex. Still, if you happen to be in the area, it's worth a stop for excellent sweet and savoury open-faced crêpes called *galettes*. Everything is made to order, so you may have to wait. That's fine, since the space – fitted out like a rustic inn in Bretagne – is warm and there's usually some rousing, vintage French music piping from the speakers. The *galette complet* (ham and cheese with an egg on top) makes an excellent and filling breakfast.

SMÍCHOV

With the arrival in recent years of the Nový Smíchov shopping centre and surrounding office complexes, the area around the Anděl metro station has exploded with restaurants. Most of these, like TGI Friday's and Potrefená husa, are actually upmarket chains that cater to the lunchtime business crowd. Authentic and really decent places are harder to find. If you don't see something you like, the food court on the top floor of the shopping centre has at least a dozen more dining options.

NAGOYA Map p138 Japanese €€

☎ 251 511 724; Stroupežnického 21; mains 200-450Kč; ⏰ 11.30am-2pm & 6-11pm Mon-Sat; Ⓜ Anděl

Nagoya, hidden away down an escalator in a passage next to Anděl's Hotel (p226), is one of the few truly authentic Japanese restaurants in Prague. It has crisp, minimalist décor, with paper screens, globe lampshades and bamboo plants; most of the seating is at ordinary tables, but there are also some low tables with tatami mats if you want to take off your shoes and get the genuine Japanese dining experience. The menu ticks all the usual boxes – sushi, sashimi, teriyaki, yakitori, tempura and miso soup – but also includes *sakana,* small savoury snacks a bit like Japanese tapas, which are great if you want to try a range of flavours.

U MÍKULÁŠE DAČÍCKÉHO

Map p138 Czech €€

☎ 257 323 334; ul Victora Huga; mains 200-300Kč; ⏰ 11am-midnight; Ⓜ Anděl

An honest-to-goodness, old-fashioned *vinárna* (wine restaurant). These slightly more upmarket wine-oriented equivalents of the beer-focused *hospody* (pubs) – complete with traditional atmosphere and excellent Czech cooking – have been dying out in recent years. The owners here have gone for the 'Ye Olde Middle Ages' look, with dark woods, red tablecloths, and pictures showing the lords enjoying their wine. Reserve in advance.

NA VERANDÁCH

Map p138 International €€

☎ 257 191 200; Nádražní 84; mains 150-300Kč; ⏰ 11am-midnight Mon-Thu, to 1am Fri & Sat, to 11pm Sun; Ⓜ Anděl

Na Verandách, the combination pub–restaurant located in the Staropramen Brewery, is no longer privately run but now managed by the Staropramen-owned Potrefená husa restaurant chain. Nevertheless, it's still wildly popular with *Czuppies,* the local version of yuppies, at lunch and dinnertime. There's no shortage of quality beers (eight varieties on tap) to wash down the very good renditions of ribs, burgers, and chicken and pork dishes. In nice weather, try to snag a table on the veranda in the back.

PIZZERIA CORLEONE Map p138 Pizza €€

☎ 251 511 244; Na Bělidle 42; mains 120-280Kč; ⏰ 11am-11pm; Ⓜ Anděl

This lively neighbourhood restaurant is arguably the best pizza option in Smíchov. The wood-fired pizza oven turns out all the classics, from margherita to *moscardina,* and also allows you to choose your own toppings. The dining room shows a taste for the art of Jack Vettriano, whose paintings are reproduced in large murals. There's a nonsmoking area in the basement.

U TUČŇÁKŮ BLAZINEC

Map p138 International €

☎ 257 316 655; Nádražní 112/59; mains 140-200Kč; ⏰ 10am-3am; Ⓜ Anděl

One of the better Czech chain restaurants offers decent pizzas, steaks, sandwiches and salads, and has a nice sidewalk terrace just off the pedestrian zone near the Anděl metro station. It's not particularly authentic but an acceptable choice if you want something quick and relatively cheap. The 'penguin' *(tučňák)* part of the name refers to the NHL ice hockey team in Pittsburgh, once home to Czech star Jaromír Jágr and still a local favourite.

ZLATÝ KLAS Map p138 Czech €

☎ 251 562 539; Plzeňská 9; mains 120-200Kč; 🕑 11am-11pm Sun-Thu, 11am-1am Fri & Sat; Ⓜ Anděl

Easily the best and most tourist-friendly of the traditional Czech pubs in the immediate Anděl area, Zlatý klas offers super-fresh 'tank beer' *(tankové pivo)*, a local badge of honour, meaning the beer is served from large tanks and is free of the carbon dioxide used to pump the beer through the taps. It also offers well-done Czech grub, such as roast pork, goulash and fried breast of chicken in a kitsch but comfortable space. The service is fast and friendly.

CORTE DI ANGELO

Map p138 Pizza €

☎ 257 326 167; Nádražní 116/61; mains 120-180Kč; 🕑 11am-11pm; Ⓜ Anděl

Another decent pizza option in the Anděl area, this one goes for a kind of 'Wild West' motif. The main draws here are good thin-crust pizza from a wood-fired oven, decent starters like beef *carpaccio* and a pleasant terrace situated off the street in a small courtyard. It also operates the adjacent, street-side Caffe Gallerie, with excellent Illy espresso and a handy row of tables for people-watching.

DRINKING

top picks

- **Andaluský pes** (p189)
- **Café Savoy** (p181)
- **Caffé Kaaba** (p185)
- **Fraktal** (p187)
- **Kavárna Meduza** (p185)
- **Bodeguita del Medio** (p182)
- **Letenský zámeček** (p187)
- **Pivovarský klub** (p186)
- **U výstreleného oka** (p186)
- **U zavěšenýho kafé** (p179)

DRINKING

Bars in Prague go in and out of fashion with alarming speed, and trend-spotters are forever flocking to the latest 'in' place only to desert it as soon as it becomes mainstream. The best areas to go looking for good drinking dens include Vinohrady, Žižkov, Smíchov, Holešovice and the area south of Národní třída in Nové Město.

Most pubs serve beer snacks; some of the most popular are *utopenci* (sliced sausage pickled in vinegar with onion), *topinky* (fried toast) and, of course, the famous *Pražská šunka* (Prague ham) with gherkin. Many of the places listed here also serve more substantial meals.

If you want to avoid bumping into stag parties, stay away from Wenceslas Square, Irish and English pubs in the city centre, and the sports bars on and around Ve Smečkách in the New Town.

SPECIALITIES

Beer

The Czech lands have been famous for centuries for producing some of the finest amber nectar in the world. The earliest historical mention of beer-making and hop-growing dates back to 1088 in the founding charter of Opatovice monastery in East Bohemia. Apparently the taste of beer was quite different in those days – by today's standards it would be considered undrinkable. It was not until 1842 that a smart group of Plzeň brewers pooled their experience, installed 'modern' technology and founded a single municipal brewery, with spectacular results. Their golden lager beer, labelled Plzeňský Prazdroj (*prazdroj* is old Czech for 'the original source') or Pilsner Urquell in German is now one of the world's best, and most imitated, beers.

Even in these times of encroaching coffee culture, *pivo* (beer) remains the lifeblood of Prague. Czechs drink more beer per capita than anywhere else in the world (around 157L per head per year, easily beating both Germany and Australia), and the local *hospoda* or *pivnice* (pub or small beer hall) remains the social hub of the neighbourhood. Many people drink at least one glass of beer every day – local nicknames for beer include *tekutý chleb* (liquid bread) and *živá voda* (life-giving water) – and it's still possible to see people stopping off for a small glass of beer on their way to work in the morning.

Most Czech beers are bottom-fermented lagers, naturally brewed using Moravian malt and hand-picked hops from Žatec in northwestern Bohemia. The whole brewing and fermentation process uses only natural ingredients – water, hops, yeast and barley. As in neighbouring Germany, strict regula-

PUB ETIQUETTE

There's an etiquette to be observed if you want to sample the atmosphere in a traditional *hospoda* (pub) without drawing disapproving stares and grumbles from the regulars. First off, don't barge in and start rearranging chairs and tables – if you want to share a table or take a spare seat, ask *'je tu volno?'* (is this free?) first. It's normal practice in crowded Czech pubs to share tables with strangers. Take a beer-mat from the rack and place it in front of you, and wait for the bar staff to come to you; waving for service is guaranteed to get you ignored.

You can order without saying a single thing – it's automatically assumed that you're here for the beer. When the waiter approaches, just raise your thumb for one beer, thumb and index finger for two, etc – providing you want a 0.5L glass of the pub's main draught ale. Even just a nod will do. The waiter will keep track of your order by marking a slip of paper that stays on your table; whatever you do, don't write on it or lose it (you'll have to pay a fine if you do). As soon as the level of beer in your glass falls to within an inch of the bottom, the eagle-eyed waiter will be on his/her way with another. But never, as people often do in Britain, pour the dregs of the old glass into the new – this is considered to be deeply uncivilised behaviour.

If you don't want any more beer brought to your table, place a beer-mat on top of your glass. When you want to pay up and go, get the waiter's attention and say *'zaplatím'* (I'll pay). He or she will tot up the marks on your slip of paper, and you pay there, at the table (try to have some smallish change; handing over a 2000Kč note will prompt a display of amateur dramatics). It's normal to leave a tip (see p179).

PITHY PIVO PROVERBS

According to an old Czech saying, *kde se pivo vaří, tam se dobře daří* ('where beer is brewed, life is good'; it's one of the few that rhymes in both Czech and English). And the beer-fuelled good life has spawned a whole range of lager-related epithets.

These include, 'A fine beer may be judged with only one sip, but it's safer to be thoroughly sure'; indeed, there are many who might rewrite that opening phrase as 'A fine beer may be judged with only one glass…'

Czechs are certainly not oblivious to the effect that beer-drinking has on their bodies – a beer belly is referred to in Czech as a *pivní mozol* (literally a 'beer callus'). But they rather seem to like the effect; one of their favourite sayings is *'pivo dělá hezká těla'* (beer makes beautiful bodies).

And finally, trust the Czechs to come up with a near-nonsensical proverb extolling the virtues of their national drink – *není pivo jako pivo* (there's no beer like beer!). That one's worthy of Homer Simpson, no less.

tions prevent the use of chemicals in the beer-making process.

There are two main varieties of beer – *světlé* (light) and *tmavy* or *černé* (dark). The *světlé* is a pale amber or golden lager-style beer with a crisp, refreshing, hoppy flavour. Dark beers are sweeter and more full-bodied, with a rich, malty or fruity flavour.

Draught beers are often labelled either *dvanáctka* (12°) or *desítka* (10°). This indicator of specific gravity is known as the Balling rating, and was invented by Czech scientist Karl Josef Balling in the 19th century. One degree Balling represents 1% by weight of malt-derived sugar in the brewing liquid before fermentation. However, not all the sugar turns to alcohol, so the Balling rating gives an indication of the 'body' as well as the likely alcohol content of the finished beer – 12° is richer in flavour, as well as being stronger in alcohol, than 10°, with a slight malty sweetness that cuts the bitterness of the hops.

In 1997 Czech law adopted a new system to indicate the alcohol-by-volume (ABV) content of beer, which recognises three categories – *výcepni pivo* (less than 4.5% ABV), *ležák* (4.5% to 5.5% ABV) and *special* (more than 5.5% ABV). However, tradition dies hard, and most breweries and pubs still use the *dvanáctka* and *desítka* labels.

Czechs like their beer served at cellar temperature (around 6°C to 10°C) with a tall, creamy head (known as *pěna*, meaning foam). Americans and Australians may find it a bit warm, but this improves the flavour. Most draught beer is sold in *půl-litr* (0.5L) glasses; if you prefer a small beer, ask for a *malé pivo* (0.3L). Some bars confuse the issue by using 0.4L glasses, while others offer a German-style 1L mug known as a *tuplák*.

The world-famous Pilsner Urquell and Budvar (Budweiser) beers are brewed in the provincial towns of Plzeň (West Bohemia) and České Budějovice (South Bohemia) respectively, but Prague has its own native brews. The largest concern is Prague Breweries, which operates the Staropramen and Braník breweries in Prague, and the Ostravar brewery in Ostrava (Northern Moravia). Its brands include the traditional Staropramen lager and the newer Kelt stout and Velvet bitter, and account for around 13% of the domestic beer market.

Prague Breweries is now owned by the Belgian company InBev, the largest brewery group in the world, and Pilsner Urquell is a subsidiary of SABMiller. In fact, the Budweiser Budvar Brewery in Ceské Budějovice, which is still partly owned by the state, is the only major brewery in the country that is still 100% Czech-owned.

The takeover of the Czech Republic's breweries by multinational companies has been accompanied by a resurgence of interest in traditional beer-making, which has seen a wave of microbreweries (beer halls that brew their own beer on the premises) springing up all over the country. There are several microbreweries in Prague – see the boxed text (p179) for details.

Wine

Czech beer is, of course, world famous, and beer-heads come to Prague from all over the world to worship at the mother lode of all lagers. What is less well known is that Czech wines have improved enormously in recent years, and are well worth getting to know.

Grapes have been grown in the Czech lands since the 14th century, when Charles IV imported vines from Burgundy; their descendants are still thriving on the slopes beneath Mělnik Chateau (p233).

The standard of Czech wine has soared since the fall of communism, as small producers

BREWERY TOURS

The Staropramen Brewery in the Prague suburb of Smíchov offers tours to visitors; there are also several other breweries within reach of the capital:

- **Budweiser Budvar Brewery** (☎ 387 705 341; www.budvar.cz; cnr Pražská & K Světlé, České Budějovice; tour 100Kč; 🕑 9am-4pm) Has one-hour tours for a minimum of eight persons; must be booked in advance. České Budějovice is 160km south of Prague.
- **Pilsner Urquell Brewery** (☎ 377 062 888; www.beerworld.cz; U Prazdroje 7, Plzeň; tour 150Kč; 🕑 10am-9pm Mon-Sat, to 8pm Sun) Has one-hour guided tours (with beer tasting). Tours in English begin at 12.45pm, 2pm and 4.15pm daily; no advance booking needed. Plzeň is 80km west of Prague.
- **Staropramen Brewery** (Map p128; ☎ 257 191 402; www.staropramen.com; Nádražní 84, Smíchov; tour 100Kč; 🕑 9am-5pm) One-hour tours by appointment only; also has an excellent bar and restaurant, Na Verandách (p172).
- **Velké Popovice Brewery** (☎ 323 683 425; www.kozel.cz; Ringhofferova 1, Velké Popovice; tour 60Kč; 🕑 8am-6pm) Has 90-minute tours that can be booked for groups of 10 or more; individuals can tag along with larger groups. Velké Popovice is just 20km southeast of Prague.

have concentrated on the quality end of the market. The total area of land given over to viticulture increased from 12,000 hectares in 1989 to 19,300 hectares by 2006. The main wine-growing region in the country is South Moravia, which accounts for 96% of Czech vineyards, with the remaining 4% scattered across northern Bohemia.

Although Czech red wines – such as the South Moravian speciality, Svatovavřinecké (St Lawrence) – are mostly pretty average, Czech whites can be very good indeed. The varieties to look out for are Veltinské zelené (Grüner Veltlin), Rýnský ryzlink (riesling) and Müller-Thurgau. Tanzberg and Sonberk are both excellent winemakers.

Although not as popular as beer, *víno* (wine) is widely available in *vinárny* (wine bars), restaurants and pubs – but not in many beer halls. *Suché víno* is dry wine and *sladké* is sweet; a sign advertising *sudové vino* means that it is served straight from the barrel. If you want to sample a range of Czech wines, head for the U Zavoje (p161), Bokovka (p184) or Monarch (p183) wine bars, or go shopping at Cellarius (p157).

For about three weeks each year from the end of September to mid-October, you will see shops and street stalls selling *burčak*. This is 'young wine', freshly extracted grape juice in the early stages of fermentation. It is sweet and refreshing, more reminiscent of fruit juice than wine, but contains around 3% to 5% alcohol; beware – the stuff sneaks up on you.

Later in the year, as winter sets in and the weather gets colder, you'll notice the *svařák* stalls appearing in the streets. Short for *svařené vino* (mulled wine), *svařák* is what you would expect – red wine heated and flavoured with sugar and spices.

Spirits

Probably the most distinctive of Czech *lihoviny* (spirits) is Becherovka. Produced in the West Bohemian spa town of Karlovy Vary, famous for its 12 sulphurous, thermal springs, the bitter, herbal liqueur is famously known as the '13th spring' – a few shots will leave you feeling sprightlier than a week's worth of spa treatment. It is often served as an apéritif, and is increasingly used as an ingredient in cocktails.

The fiery and potent *slivovice* (plum brandy) is said to have originated in Moravia, where the best brands still come from. The best commercially produced *slivovice* is R Jelínek from Vizovice. Other regional spirits include *meruňkovice* (apricot brandy) and juniper-flavoured *borovička*.

The deadliest locally produced spirit is Hills Liquere absinthe from Jindřichův Hradec. While it's banned in many countries, in part because of its high alcohol content, absinthe is legal in the Czech Republic. Unfortunately, connoisseurs of absinthe consider Hills little better than highly alcoholic mouthwash.

Spirits are traditionally drunk neat and usually chilled. An exception is *grog*, a popular year-round hot drink: half rum, half hot water or tea, with a slice of lemon.

PRACTICALITIES

How Much?

Gone are the days of cheap beer. A combination of generally increasing tourist prices and a strong Czech crown have seen bar prices begin to approach those in Germany, France and even the UK.

The price of a half-litre of draught beer varies enormously, from around 25Kč to 35Kč in pubs catering mainly to local drinkers, to 90Kč and up at outdoor tables in tourist-thronged Old Town Square. Most city centre bars charge 50Kč to 80Kč.

Cocktails in the city centre range from 120Kč to 280Kč, depending on the quality of the ingredients and the fanciness of the surroundings, while good-quality Czech wine in a specialist wine bar will cost from 300Kč a bottle.

Tipping

It's customary to tip the staff in Prague pubs, bars and cafés. Normal practice is to round up the bill to the next 10Kč (or the next 20Kč if it's over 200Kč). Change is usually counted out starting with the big notes, then on down to the smallest coins. If you say *děkuji* (thank you) during this process, the bartender will stop and assume that the rest is a tip.

PRAGUE CASTLE & HRADČANY

This is a fairly quiet district, with drinking venues limited to laid-back cafés and a couple of traditional pubs.

U ZAVĚŠENÝHO KAFE Map pp70–1 Bar

☎ 605 294 595; Úvoz 6, Hradčany; 11am-midnight; 12, 20, 22, 23

This is a superb little drinking den barely five minutes' walk from the castle. Head for

SMALL IS BEAUTIFUL

While big multinational brewing companies have been busy taking over traditional Czech breweries, a growing number of enthusiasts have been setting up microbreweries that stay true to the origins of Bohemian beer, serving tasty, unpasteurised brews in atmospheric brewery pubs. Here are six in the capital:

Klášterní pivovar Strahov (Strahov Monastery Brewery; Map pp70–1; ☎ 233 353 155; Strahovské nádvoří 301, Hradčany; 10am-10pm; 22, 23) Dominated by two polished copper brewing kettles, this convivial little pub serves up two varieties of its St Norbert beer – *tmavý* (dark), a rich, tarry brew with a creamy head, and *polotmavý* (amber), a full-bodied, hoppy lager, both 59Kč per 0.4L.

Novoměstský pivovar (New Town Brewery; Map pp108–9; ☎ 224 232 448; Vodičkova 20, Nové Město; 8am-11.30pm Mon-Fri, 11.30am-11.30pm Sat, noon-10pm Sun; 3, 9, 14, 24) Like U Fleků (below), the 'New Town Brewery' has largely been taken over by coach-party invasions, but it's considerably cheaper (38Kč for 0.5L, available in both light and dark varieties), and the food is not only edible but actually rather good. If you haven't booked, you'll be lucky to get a table.

Pivovar u Bulovky (Bulovka Brewery; Map pp58–9; ☎ 284 840 650; Bulovka 17, Libeň; 11am-11pm Mon-Thu, to midnight Fri, noon-midnight Sat; 10, 15, 24, 25) Opened in 2004, this is a genuine neighbourhood bar out in the suburbs, a homely wood-panelled room with quirky metalwork, much of it home-built by the owner. The delicious house *ležák* (lager; 29Kč for 0.5L) is a yeast beer, cloudy in appearance, and crisp, citrusy and refreshing in flavour. Well worth the tram trip, but don't expect the staff to speak English!

Pivovarský Dům (Brewery House; Map pp108–9; ☎ 296 216 666; cnr Ječná & Lipová, Nové Město; 11am-11.30pm; 4, 6, 10, 16, 22, 23) While the tourists flock to U Fleků, locals gather here to sample the classic Czech lager (in light, dark and mixed varieties; 35Kč per 0.5L) that is produced on the premises, as well as wheat beer and a range of flavoured beers (including coffee, banana and cherry, 35Kč per 0.3L). The pub itself is a pleasant place to linger, decked out with polished copper vats and brewing implements and smelling faintly of malt and hops (no smoking).

U Fleků (Map pp108–9; ☎ 224 934 019; Křemencová 11, Nové Město; 9am-11pm; M Karlovo Náměstí) A festive warren of drinking and dining rooms, U Fleků is a Prague institution, though usually clogged with tour groups high on oompah music and the tavern's home-brewed, 13° black beer (59Kč for 0.4L), known as Flek. Purists grumble but go along anyway because the beer is good, though tourist prices have nudged out many locals. Beware the waiter asking if you want to try a Becherovka (Czech liqueur) – it's not a great accompaniment to beer, and it'll add 80Kč to the bill.

U Medvídků (At the Little Bear; Map pp88–9; ☎ 224 211 916; Na Perštýně 7, Staré Město; beer hall 11.30am-11pm, museum noon-10pm; M Národní Třída) The most micro of Prague's microbreweries, with a capacity of only 250L, U Medvídků started producing its own beer only in 2005, though its beer hall has been around for many years. What it lacks in size, it makes up for in strength – the dark lager produced here, marketed as X-Beer, is the strongest in the country, with an alcohol content of 11.8% (as strong as many wines). Available in bottles only (48Kč for 0.33L), it's a malty, bitter-sweet brew with a powerful punch; handle with caution! There's also Budvar on tap at 33Kč for 0.5L.

the cosy, wood-panelled back room, quirkily decorated with weird art and mechanical curiosities by local artist Kuba Krejci (all for sale), and an ancient jukebox crammed with Beatles, Stones and Czech rock. Foaming Gambrinus is only 25Kč a half-litre, and the coffee (40Kč for a cappuccino) is damn fine too.

LOBKOWICZ PALACE CAFÉ
Map p62 Café

☎ 233 312 925; Jiřská 3, Prague Castle; 10am-6pm; 22, 23

This new café housed in the 16th-century Lobkowicz Palace is the best café in the castle complex by an imperial mile. Try to grab one of the tables on the balconies at the back – the view over Malá Strana is superb, as are the café's chocolate brownies, served with a splash of mango sauce and fresh strawberries. The coffee is good too, and service is fast and friendly.

PIVNICE U ČERNÉHO VOLA
Map p62 Pub

☎ 220 513 481; Loretánské náměstí 1, Hradčany; 10am-10pm; 22, 23

Many religious people make a pilgrimage to the Loreta, but just across the road is a shrine that pulls in pilgrims of a different kind – the 'Black Ox'. This surprisingly authentic and inexpensive beer hall is visited by real-ale aficionados for its authentic atmosphere and lip-smackingly delicious draught beer, Velkopopovický Kozel (26.50Kč for 0.5L), which is brewed in a small town southeast of Prague.

MALÁ STRANA

Malá Strana is the place to go for pavement table people-watching, with lots of cafés and bars spilling out onto the streets – especially on main square Malostranské náměstí and on Nerudova, which leads up to the castle. Places here range from cute tea houses and cafés to traditional cellar-pubs and funky bars.

KLUB ÚJEZD Map pp76–7 Bar

☎ 257 316 537; Újezd 18; 2pm-4am; 6, 9, 12, 20, 22, 23

Klub Újezd is one of Prague's many 'alternative' bars, spread over three floors (DJs in the cellar, and a café upstairs) and filled with a fascinating collection of handmade furniture and fittings, original art and weird wrought-iron sculptures. Clamber onto a two-tonne bar stool in the agreeably grungy street-level bar, and sip on a beer while you watch a thick rope of herbal-scented smoke uncoil across the ceiling beside the scaly, fire-breathing sea-monster that dangles over your head. Trippy.

ST NICHOLAS CAFÉ Map pp76–7 Bar

☎ 257 530 205; Tržiště 7; noon-1am Mon-Fri, 4pm-1am Sat & Sun; 12, 20, 22, 23

Descend from the bustle of Malá Strana into this dark and atmospheric Gothic cellar, a favourite midday refuge in the heart of the tourist zone. Dimly lit alcoves, flickering candlelight and worn wooden tables make an appealing setting for a few quiet beers or a bottle of wine; later in the evening it gets busier and develops a cool, jazzy atmosphere, with live music on weekend nights.

KAFÍČKO Map pp76–7 Café

☎ 724 151 795; Míšenská 10; 10am-10pm; 12, 20, 22, 23

This smoke-free, family-friendly little café, with its cream walls, bentwood chairs, fresh flowers and arty photographs, is an unexpected setting for some of Prague's finest tea and coffee. Choose from a wide range of quality roasted beans from all over the world, and have them freshly ground and made into espresso, cappuccino or latte (40Kč to 55Kč); the espresso is served, as it should be, with a glass of water.

U ZELENÉHO ČAJE Map pp76–7 Café

☎ 257 530 027; Nerudova 19; 11am-10pm; 12, 20, 22, 23

'At the Green Tea' is a charming little olde-worlde tea house on the way up to the castle. The menu offers around a hundred different kinds of tea (45Kč to 80Kč a pot) from all over the world, ranging from classic green and black teas from China and India to fruit-flavoured teas and herbal infusions, as well as tempting cakes and tasty sandwiches.

BLUE LIGHT Map pp76–7 Cocktail Bar

☎ 257 533 126; Josefská 1; 6pm-3am; 12, 20, 22, 23

The Blue Light is an appropriately dark and atmospheric jazz cavern, as popular with locals as with tourists, where you can sip a *caipirinha* or cranberry colada as you cast an eye over the vintage jazz posters, records, old photographs and decades-worth of

GRAND CAFÉS

Prague's café society flourished from the late 19th century until the 1930s, when the city's coffee houses provided a meeting place for artists, writers, journalists, activists and political dissidents. Many fell into disrepair following WWII, but half a dozen or so have survived or been restored to their former glory.

Café Imperial (Map p106; ☎ 246 011 600; Na Poříčí 15, Nové Město; 🕒 7am-11pm; Ⓜ Náměstí Republiky) First opened in 1914, and given a complete facelift in 2007, the Imperial is a tour de force of Art Nouveau tiling – the walls and ceiling are covered in original ceramic tiles, mosaics, sculptured panels and bas-reliefs, with period light fittings and bronzes scattered about. The coffee is good, there are cocktails in the evening, and the café menu offers all-day English and American breakfasts, as well as excellent eggs Benedict.

Café Savoy (Map pp76–7; ☎ 257 311 562; Vítězná 5, Malá Strana; 🕒 8am-10.30pm Mon-Fri, 9am-10.30pm Sat & Sun; 🚋 6, 9, 22, 23) Established in 1893 and restored in 2004, the Savoy fairly glows with *belle époque* splendour, its colourful, ornately decorated ceiling decked with crystal chandeliers (grab a table on the mezzanine for a closer view) and its waiting staff dressed in matching red waistcoats and ties. Great coffee and hot chocolate, and a decent wine list too.

Grand Café Orient (Map pp88–9; ☎ 224 224 240; Ovocný trh 19, Staré Město; 🕒 9am-10pm Mon-Fri, 10am-10pm Sat & Sun; Ⓜ Náměstí Republiky) Prague's only Cubist café, the Orient was designed by Josef Gočár and is Cubist down to the smallest detail, including the lampshades and coat-hooks. It was restored and reopened in 2005, having been closed since 1920. Decent coffee and inexpensive cocktails.

Kavárna Lucerna (Map pp108–9; ☎ 224 215 495; Palác Lucerna, Štěpánská 61, Nové Město; 🕒 10am-1am Mon-Sat, to 11pm Sun; 🚋 3, 9, 14, 24) The least touristy of the cafés listed here, the Lucerna is part of an Art Nouveau shopping arcade designed by the grandfather of ex-president Václav Havel. Filled with faux marble, ornamental metalwork and glittering crystal lanterns (*lucerna* is Czech for lantern), this 1920s gem has arched windows overlooking David Cerný's famous *Horse* sculpture hanging beneath the glass-domed atrium.

Kavárna Obecní dům (Map pp88–9; ☎ 222 002 763; náměstí Republiky 5, Staré Město; 🕒 7.30am-11pm; Ⓜ Náměstí Republiky) The spectacular café in Prague's opulent Municipal House (Obecní dům) offers the opportunity to sip your cappuccino amid an orgy of Art Nouveau splendour. Also worth a look is the neat little American Bar in the basement of the building, all polished wood, stained glass and gleaming copper.

Kavárna Evropa (Map pp108–9; ☎ 224 228 117; Václavské náměstí 25, Nové Město; 🕒 9.30am-11pm; Ⓜ Můstek) The Grand Hotel Evropa sports the most atmospheric café on Wenceslas Square, a fading museum of over-the-top Art Nouveau. Sadly, it has long since become a tourist trap, with second-rate cakes and coffee and rip-off prices, but it's still well worth a quick look inside.

Kavárna Slavia (Map pp88–9; ☎ 224 220 957; Národní třída 1, Nové Město; 🕒 8am-midnight Mon-Fri, 9am-midnight Sat & Sun; Ⓜ Národní Třída) The Slavia is the most famous of Prague's old cafés, a cherrywood-and-onyx shrine to Art Deco elegance, with polished limestone-topped tables and big windows overlooking the river. It has been a celebrated literary meeting place since the early 20th century – Rainer Maria Rilke and Franz Kafka hung out here, and it was frequented by Václav Havel and other dissidents in the 1970s and '80s.

scratched graffiti that adorn the walls. The background jazz is recorded rather than live, but on a quality sound system that never overpowers your conversation.

HOSTINEC U KOCOURA Map pp76–7 Pub

☎ 257 530 107; Nerudova 2; 🕒 11am-11pm; 🚋 12, 20, 22, 23

'The Tomcat' is a long-established traditional pub, still enjoying its reputation as a former favourite of ex-president Havel, and still managing to pull in a mostly Czech crowd despite being in the heart of touristville (maybe it's the ever-present pall of cigarette smoke). It has relatively inexpensive beer for this part of town – 30Kč for 0.5L of draught Budvar, Pilsner Urquell or Bernard yeast beer.

STARÉ MĚSTO

The Old Town is tourist central, with crowded pubs and prices to match. But all you have to do is explore the maze of narrow back streets that radiate from Old Town Square to find hidden gems like Čili Bar, Duende and Literární Kavárna Řetězová.

DUENDE Map pp88–9 Bar

☎ 775 186 077; Karoliny Světlé 30; 🕒 1pm-midnight Mon-Fri, 3pm-midnight Sat, 4pm-midnight Sun; Ⓜ Národní Třída

Barely five minutes' walk from Charles Bridge but half a world away in atmosphere, this cute little bar is the opposite of touristy – a bohemian drinking den that pulls in an arty, mixed-age crowd of locals. Here you can enjoy a drink while casting an eye over the fascinating photos and quirky art that cover the wall, or listen to live guitar or violin. As well as wines and cocktails, the bar serves the excellent Bernard beer for 29Kč per 0.5L.

FRIENDS Map pp88–9 Bar

☎ 226 211 920; Bartolomějská 11; 🕒 6pm-4am; M Národní Třídá

Friends is a welcoming gay music-and-video bar serving excellent coffee, cocktails and wine. It's a good spot to sit back with a drink and check out the crowd, or join in the party spirit on assorted theme nights, which range from Czech pop music and movies to cowboy parties (see www.friends-prague.cz for listings). DJs add their own spin from 10pm Wednesday to Saturday.

KOZIČKA Map pp88–9 Bar

☎ 224 818 308; Kozí 1; 🕒 noon-4am Mon-Fri, 6pm-4am Sat, 6pm-3am Sun; M Staroměstská

The 'Little Goat' is a buzzing, red-brick basement bar decorated with cute steel goat sculptures, serving Krušovice on tap at 40Kč for 0.5L (though watch out – the bartenders will occasionally sling you a 1L *tuplák* if they think you're a tourist). It fills up later in the evening with a mostly Czech crowd, and is a very civilised setting for a late-night session.

CAFÉ CAFÉ Map pp88–9 Café

☎ 224 210 597; Rytířská 10; 🕒 10am-11pm; M Můstek

Exposed brick and aluminium ducting meet burgundy drapes, sparkly chandeliers and hot pink woodwork in this deeply trendy café, host to many a fashion launch and designer event – Fashion TV plays on the plasma screens, and half the staff look like supermodels. They must be avoiding the big fat chocolate cakes and ice cream sundaes that plump out the menu, and sticking to the excellent espressos.

EBEL COFFEE HOUSE Map pp88–9 Café

☎ 224 895 788; Týn 2; 🕒 9am-10pm; M Náměstí Republiky

If you can't face the watery instant coffee served up with your hotel breakfast, head to Ebel for a jolt of full-fat, 98-octane arabica. Munchies on offer include toasted bagels with herby cream cheese, quiches, carrot cake and chocolate brownies. Only a few minutes' walk from Old Town Square, this branch is in a top people-watching spot in a corner of the Týn courtyard; there are several other branches across the city (including one on Řetězová).

KÁVA KÁVA KÁVA Map pp88–9 Café

☎ 224 228 862; Platýz pasáž, Národní třída 37; 🕒 7am-10pm Mon-Fri, 9am-10pm Sat & Sun; M Národní Třída

Tucked away in the peaceful Platýz courtyard, this American-owned café has some of the best coffee in town – the *grande cappuccino* is big enough to bathe in – and a selection of bagels, croissants, chocolate brownies, carrot cake and other goodies. There's also internet access via desktop computers, and it's a wi-fi hotspot (you need to ask for the password). You can find a second branch in Smíchov (see p191).

LITERÁRNÍ KAVÁRNA ŘETĚZOVÁ Map pp88–9 Café

☎ 222 221 244; 🕒 noon-11pm Mon-Fri, 5-11pm Sat & Sun; 🚊 17, 21

This is the kind of place where you can imagine yourself tapping out the Great Prague Novel on your laptop with a half-finished coffee on the table beside you. It's a plain, vaulted room with battered wooden furniture, a scatter of rugs on the floor, old black-and-white photos on the wall, and the sort of quiet, relaxed atmosphere where you can read a book without feeling self-conscious. If you fancy something stronger than coffee, try the fruity, full-flavoured Bernard *kvasnicové* (yeast beer).

BAR & BOOKS Map pp88–9 Cocktail Bar

☎ 731 184 123; Týnská 19; 🕒 2pm-4am Mon-Fri, 6pm-4am Sat, to 3am Sun; M Náměstí Republiky

The walls are indeed lined with books at this branch of the famous Manhattan cocktail bar, but the well-heeled clients are more likely to be reading the labels on the vast range of single malts, bourbons, brandies and vintage ports on offer, along with Cuban and Dominican cigars. The black-waistcoated staff are unerringly polite and efficient, and mix a mean martini, margarita or champagne cocktail.

BODEGUITA DEL MEDIO Map pp88–9 Cocktail Bar

☎ 224 813 922; Kaprova 5; 🕒 10am-2am; M Staroměstská

The Prague incarnation of the Havana cocktail-bar and restaurant chain brings a whiff of Hemingway to the Old Town streets, with chunky wooden tables, ceiling fans and cigars. And, of course, classic *mojito* cocktails. The food is excellent, the cappuccinos are froth-topped caffeine bombs, and the pavement tables catch the sun at lunchtime…perfecto.

ČILI BAR Map pp88–9 Cocktail Bar

☎ 777 945 848; Kožná 8; ⏰ 5pm-2am; Ⓜ Můstek

Hidden in the crook of a narrow Old Town alley but only a few paces from Old Town Square, this tiny cocktail bar could not be further removed in atmosphere from your typical Old Town drinking place. Cramped and smoky – there are Cuban cigars for sale – with a couple of battered leather armchairs competing for space with a handful of tables and the crowd at the bar, it's friendly, relaxed and lively. Don't miss the speciality of the house – a shot of rum mixed with finely chopped red chillis.

U ZLATÉHO TYGRA Map pp88–9 Pub

☎ 222 221 111; Husova 17; ⏰ 3-11pm; Ⓜ Staroměstská

The 'Golden Tiger' is one of the few old-town drinking holes that has hung on to its soul – and its low prices (29Kč per 0.5L of Pilsner Urquell), considering its location. It was novelist Bohumil Hrabal's favourite hostelry – there are photos of him on the walls – and the place that Václav Havel took fellow president Bill Clinton in 1994 to show him a real Czech pub.

MONARCH VINNÝ SKLEP
Map pp88–9 Wine Bar

☎ 224 239 602; Na Perštýně 15; ⏰ noon-midnight Mon-Sat; Ⓜ Národní Třída

The Monarch wine cellar is one of the best places in town to get to know Czech wines. Despite its knowledgeable staff and vast selection of vintages, it manages to avoid any air of pretentiousness, and has a tempting menu of nibbles – cheeses, olives, prosciutto, salami and smoked duck – to accompany your wine, which is not as expensive as you might expect. A range of Moravian wines are available by the glass from only 39Kč.

NOVÉ MĚSTO

Nové Město, particularly the area around Wenceslas Square, is a magnet for stag parties and groups of young lads on the piss – best avoided if you're looking for a quiet drink. But there are plenty of good drinking holes, too. Check out the streets south of Národní třída near the river, where you'll find studenty cafés like Velryba and quirky wine bars like Bokovka.

JÁMA Map pp108–9 Bar

☎ 224 222 383; V Jámě 7; ⏰ 11am-1am; Ⓜ Muzeum

Jáma ('the Hollow'), southeast off Vodičkova, is a popular American expat bar with vaulted ceilings plastered with old rock gig posters ranging from Led Zep and REM to Kiss and Shania Twain. There's a leafy little beer garden out the back shaded by lime and walnut trees, smiling staff serving up Pilsner Urquell, Gambrinus and Velkopopvický Kozel on draught, and a menu that includes good burgers, steaks, ribs and chicken wings.

DOBRÁ ČAJOVNA Map pp108–9 Café

☎ 224 231 480; Václavské náměstí 14; ⏰ 10am-9.30pm Mon-Fri, 3-9.30pm Sat & Sun; Ⓜ Můstek

This tearoom, tucked up a passage off Wenceslas Square, is a little haven of incense burners, oriental rugs and comfy cushions hidden away from the heaving crowds on the nearby street. They take their tea seriously here, and you can choose from a wide range of Chinese, Indian, Sri Lankan, Japanese and Turkish leaves. There are also cakes and vegetarian snacks such as hummus and pitta bread.

KÁVOVARNA Map pp108–9 Café

☎ 296 236 233; Pasáž Lucerna, Svtěpánská 61; ⏰ 8am-midnight; Ⓜ Můstek

One of the few decent cafés in the region of Wenceslas Square, this retro-styled place has bentwood chairs and curved wooden benches in the smoky, dimly lit front room (there's a nonsmoking room beyond the bar), with exhibitions of arty black-and-white photography on the walls. The coffee is good and reasonably priced, and there's an extensive menu of flavoured and iced coffees, hot chocolates, soda and granitas.

VELRYBA Map pp108–9 Café

☎ 224 912 484; Opatovická 24; ⏰ 11am-midnight Sat-Thu, to 2am Fri; Ⓜ Národní Třída

The 'Whale' is an arty café-bar – usually quiet enough to have a real conversation – with vegetarian-friendly snacks, a smoky back room and a basement art gallery. A clientele of Czech students, local office workers and foreign backpackers attracted by the low prices keep the place jumping.

BOKOVKA Map pp108–9 Wine Bar

☎ 721 262 503; Pštrossova 8; 4pm-1am Sun-Thu, 4pm-3am Fri & Sat; M Karlovo Náměstí

Owned by a syndicate of oenophiles who include film directors Jan Hřebejk and David Ondříček, this quaint little bar is named after the movie *Sideways* (*bokovka* in Czech), which was set in the California vineyards (the bar makes an appearance in Hřebejk's 2007 film *Medvídek*). The main attraction (other than the chance of being served drinks by a famous film director – they occasionally work behind the bar) is the extensive menu of top-notch Moravian wines – we can recommend the 2004 Tanzberg Rýnský Ryzlink (390Kč a bottle).

VINOHRADY & VRŠOVICE

It may lack some of Žižkov's authentic grit, but Vinohrady is a great area for bar- and café-hopping. Check out the streets surrounding Peace Square (náměstí Míru), particularly along Americká, as well as Mánesova and those around the big park, Riegrovy sady, which has either Prague's best or second-best open-air beer garden (depending on whom you ask or where you live). With its big-screen TV, it's a popular place to gather for international sporting matches, like the World Cup.

CLUB STELLA Map p121 Bar

☎ 224 257 869; Lužická 10, Vinohrady; 8pm-5am; 4, 22, 23

Club Stella is an intimate, candlelit café-bar that seems to be the first place everyone recommends when you ask about gay and lesbian bars in Prague. There's a long narrow bar where you can just squeeze onto a bar stool, an armchair-filled lounge that looks like somebody's living room, and a welcoming crowd of locals. Ring the doorbell to get in.

POPO CAFÉ PETL Map p121 Bar

☎ 777 944 672; Italská 18, Vinohrady; 10am-1am Mon-Fri, 4pm-1am Sat & Sun; 11

A popular student dive, usually packed to the rafters and hopelessly smoky, but loads of fun at the same time. Staropramen is on tap. If that doesn't appeal, there's tons of cheap wine on offer and tables filled with drunken members of the opposite sex. It doesn't get any better.

ZVONAŘKÁ Map p121 Bar

☎ 224 251 990; Šafaříkova 1, Vinohrady; 11am-11pm Mon-Thu, noon-midnight Fri & Sat, to 11pm Sun; M IP Pavlova

Sitting at the far end of a quiet residential street where Vinohrady spills over into the Nusle valley, Zvonařká has a stylish, minimalist interior, but its biggest attraction is outdoors – a broad, tree-shaded terrace overhanging a steep hill, with expansive views across the valley to Vyšehrad, a great place for a beer on a summer evening.

RIEGROVY SADY Map p121 Beer Garden

☎ 222 717 247; Riegrovy sady, Vinohrady; noon-1am (summers only); 11 or M Jiřího z Poděbrad (plus walk)

There's a good-natured rivalry between this beer garden and the one across the river at Letná as to which one is best. The answer depends on where you live, and on summer nights the folks in Vinohrady can be counted on to come out and enforce their claim. Order drinks at the bar and carry them to one of dozens of picnic tables. The big-screen TV takes away from the atmosphere, but is a welcome addition during the Euro or World Cup football matches, when the tables are lined elbow to elbow. The easiest way to get here is from Polská, turn up Chopínova, and then enter the park across from Na Švíhance. The beer garden is 30m up the path.

BLATOUCH Map p121 Café

☎ 222 328 643; Americká 17, Vinohrady; 10am-11pm; M Náměstí Míru

When the legendary student café Blatouch shut down a couple of years ago in the Old Town, it was viewed as just another casualty of progress. The good news is that Blatouch has reopened here in Vinohrady, with the same old sign out the front and the same mix of laid-back service and good-natured student clientele. Excellent coffee is served with light eats like salads and sandwiches to go along with the ultra-relaxed vibe. Just what the neighbourhood needed.

CAFÉ CELEBRITY Map p121 Café

☎ 222 511 343; Vinohradská 40, Vinohrady; 🕑 10am-11pm; M Náměstí Míru

This gay-friendly café is part of the cluster of gay-friendly joints, including the Club Valentino, that are part of the old Radio Palác building on Vinohradská. There's nothing special here except a welcoming atmosphere, lots of good-natured people-watching, and decent coffee, beer and wine.

CAFFÉ KAABA Map p121 Café

☎ 222 254 021; Mánesova 20, Vinohrady; 🕑 8am-10pm; 🚋 11

Caffé Kaaba is a stylish little architect-designed café-bar with retro furniture and pastel-coloured décor that comes straight out of the 1959 Ideal Homes Exhibition. It serves up excellent coffee (made with freshly ground imported beans), offers an extensive list of Czech and imported wines (the house wine is only 30Kč a glass), and also has an in-house news and tobacco counter.

DOBRÁ TRAFIKA Map p121 Café

☎ 222 510 261; Korunní 42, Vinohrady; 🕑 7am-11pm; M Náměstí Míru or 🚋 10, 16

From the outside, you'd never know there was a cute little coffee shop tucked behind this tobacconist on busy Korunní. The tobacco shop is interesting in its own right – not just pipes, loose tobacco, cigars and cigarettes, but also excellent teas, sweets and gifts. It feels a bit like a step back in time. At the back there's a small room for drinking coffee and a larger garden for just hanging out. Popular with students.

KAVÁRNA MEDÚZA Map p121 Café

☎ 222 515 107; Belgická 17, Vinohrady; 🕑 10am-1am Mon-Fri, noon-1am Sat & Sun; M Náměstí Míru

The perfect Prague coffee house, Medúza is an oasis of old, worn furniture, dark wood and local artworks, with an antique sugar bowl on every table and an atmosphere that invites you to sink into a novel or indulge in a conversation on the nature of self. Coffee, tea, hot chocolate, beer, wine and even non-alcoholic cocktails are all on the menu, along with pancakes, nachos and banana splits.

KAVÁRNA ZANZIBAR Map p121 Café

☎ 222 520 315; Americká 15, Vinohrady; 🕑 8am-11pm Mon-Fri, 10am-11pm Sat & Sun; M Náměstí Míru

Zanzibar started out years ago as a *trafika*, a place to buy newspapers and tobacco products. Over the years it's evolved into a homey space that defies easy description. It's not quite a café (though coffee is probably the most popular beverage), not quite a bar (though there's beer on tap and a place to sit up front) and not quite a restaurant (though the food they serve is pretty good). Treat it as a great place to meet up for whatever mood you're in. The terrace out front is pleasant in nice weather.

NANOCAFÉ Map p121 Café

☎ 604 517 786; Kodaňská 22, Vršovice; 🕑 8am-10pm Mon-Fri, 10.30am-10pm Sat & Sun; 🚋 4, 22, 23

This tiny café on a leafy street in Vršovice is recommendable chiefly for its early opening hours (great if you're staying nearby and don't have access to morning coffee) and the fact that it serves hard-to-find Primátor *weizenbier*, a rare Czech wheat beer. It has a friendly, informal vibe and a couple of pavement tables for spending a warm summer evening.

OUT Map p121 Café

☎ 272 730 496; Korunní 104 (in the Korunni dvůr housing estate), Vinohrady; 🕑 8am-10pm Mon-Fri, 10am-10pm Sat & Sun; M Flora

It's good to know about this swanky café and chocolatier in the upscale Korunní dvůr housing estate in case you're staying in the area and need to scrounge a decent breakfast early in the morning, or just passing by and have a sudden chocolate craving. They take their cocoa seriously here – it's imported all the way from Venezuela and Trinidad. There are also decent lunches, with good homemade soups.

RYBA NA RUBY Map p121 Café

☎ 731 570 704; Mánesova 87, Vinohrady; 🕑 10am-11pm Mon-Sat; M Náměstí Jiřího z Poděbrad

Ryba na Ruby is something different for upscale Vinohrady: an ecofriendly tea and gift shop on the ground floor with a laid-back bar–club downstairs. This is a great place to stock up on things like fair-trade teas and coffees, plus organic foodstuffs like nuts, spices, cocoa, jams and oils. The below-ground club is a relaxed space for a beer or a coffee.

SAHARA CAFÉ Map p121 Café

☎ 222 514 987; náměstí Míru 6, Vinohrady; 9am-11pm; M Náměstí Míru

The beautifully minimalist Morocco-inspired interior sets a design standard that few places can match; unfortunately, the food doesn't live up to the décor. Still, if it's just a cup of coffee or a glass of wine you're after, you can hardly do flashier in this neighbourhood. The convenient location makes it a good meet-up spot for a drink before heading elsewhere.

CORNER BAR AND BISTRO Map p121 Cocktail Bar

☎ 222 724 581; Mánesova 64, Vinohrady; 5pm-3am; 11

This upmarket New York–style cocktail and cigar bar occupies a former rugby pub and couldn't be more different in terms of atmosphere. It's been given a bad rap for its cocktail prices, but the truth is they're not much higher here than elsewhere; an Apple Martini (Skyy vodka, apple pucker and lime juice) runs to 125Kč, about the same as in the city centre. There are some lighter food options like sandwiches, cheese platters and fondues. On Monday nights, women get a free cigar.

MON AMI Map p121 Pub

☎ 271 726 693; Kodaňská 47, Vršovice; 11am-11pm Mon-Fri, 1-11pm Sat & Sun; 4, 22, 23

This is actually a Balkan-themed restaurant that morphs into a standard pub in the evenings. The food is nothing to write home about; on the other hand, it can be fun on crowded evenings when everyone's in a reckless mood, and there might even be someone sitting around playing a guitar.

VINIČNÍ ALTÁN Map p121 Wine Bar

☎ 224 262 861; Havlíčkovy sady 1369, Vršovice; 11am-11pm; 6, 7, 24 (stop Otakarova plus uphill walk), 4, 22, 23 (stop Jana Masaryka plus walk)

Prague's nicest open-air wine garden claims to be its oldest as well – apparently established by Emperor Charles IV himself. Enjoy a glass of locally made white or red on a refurbished wooden gazebo overlooking the vineyards and the Nusle valley. There's no easy way to get here; try cutting through Vinohrady, following Americká and then continuing through Havlíčkovy sady. There are minimal but decent food offerings, including salads and sausages.

ŽIŽKOV & KARLÍN

Žižkov is famous for having more pubs per head of population than any other city district in Europe, and – depending on your tastes – offers the most authentic or the most terrifying pub-crawling experience in Prague. Be prepared for smoke, sticky floors, wall-to-wall noise and some heroically drunk companions.

BUKOWSKI'S Map pp126–7 Cocktail Bar

☎ 222 212 676; Bořivojova 86; 6pm-2am; 5, 9, 26

Like most of the drinking dens that are popular among Prague expats, Bukowski's – the city's latest barfly magnet – is more a cocktail dive than a cocktail bar. Named after hard-drinking American writer Charles Bukowski, it cultivates a dark and slightly debauched atmosphere – the décor is self-consciously 'interesting' (when you can see it through the smoke-befogged candlelight) – but it peddles quality cocktails and cigars, and has friendly bartenders and cool tunes.

PIVOVARSKÝ KLUB Map pp126–7 Pub

☎ 222 315 777; Křižíkova 17; 11am-11.30pm; M Florenc

This bar is to beer what the Bodleian Library is to books – the wall-to-wall shelves are lined with myriad varieties of bottled beer from all over the world, and there are six guest beers on tap (the fresh and hoppy Štěpán *ležák* and the citrusy Primátor yeast beer are both excellent). Perch on a bar stool in the street-level no-smoking area or head downstairs to the snug, smoky cellar, and order some of the pub's excellent grub to soak up the beer (authentic *guláš* with bacon dumplings for only 85Kč).

U VYSTŘELENÉHO OKA Map pp126–7 Pub

☎ 226 278 714; U Božích Bojovníků 3; 4.30pm-1am Mon-Sat; 133, 207

You've got to love a pub that has vinyl pads on the wall above the gents' urinals to rest your forehead on. 'The Shot-Out Eye' – the name pays homage to the one-eyed Hussite hero atop the hill behind the pub (see National Monument, p125) – is a bohemian (with a small 'b') hostelry with a raucous Friday night atmosphere where the cheap Pilsner Urquell (29Kč for 0.5L) pulls in a typically heterogeneous Žižkov crowd. There's no need to worry about the language barrier – everyone here speaks the international language of booze.

HOLEŠOVICE, BUBENEČ & DEJVICE

Working-class Holešovice has always had its share of old men's pubs, but only relatively recently has the neighbourhood exploded with nicer drinking options, including loads of new cafés. Most of the better places are clustered around Letenské náměstí in Bubeneč. Look particularly down the street Šmeralová. If you can't find something that suits your fancy, walk to the corner at Keramícká and then on to Čechova. There are at least a dozen bars and watering holes around here, all offering pretty much the same mix of cheapish beer and tables filled with students and local residents knocking one back.

FRAKTAL Map pp132–3 Bar

☎ 777 794 094; Šmeralová 1, Bubeneč; 11am-midnight; 1, 8, 15, 25, 26

This subterranean space under a corner house near Letenské náměstí is easily the friendliest bar this side of the Vltava. This is especially true for English speakers, as Fraktal serves as a kind of unofficial expat watering hole. It serves the Pilsner Urquell family of beers, including popular 10° Gambrinus. There's also good Mexican-style nosh for spacing beers. The only drawback is the early closing time. Last orders are at 11.30pm, and every year they seem to bring it forward another 30 minutes.

LA BODEGA FLAMENCA

Map pp132–3 Bar

☎ 233 374 075; Šmeralová 5, Bubeneč; 4pm-1am Sun-Thu, to 3am Fri & Sat; 1, 8, 15, 25, 26

La Bodega is an atmospheric, red-brick cellar, painted and plastered to look like an adobe shack. With the Latin music turned down low, the buzz of conversation and the flickering candlelight, the crowd seems a bit more reflective (well, at least compared to the crew at Fraktal next door). Most people come for the sangria or the beer, but there's also a nice selection of tapas on hand, including *tortilla español, chorizo al vino tinto* (chorizo sausage stewed in red wine) and *gambas pil-pil* (prawns in garlic and chilli). There's also live music and dance some nights.

LE TRAM Map pp132–3 Bar

☎ 233 370 359; Šmeralová 12, Bubeneč; 8pm-6am; 1, 8, 15, 25, 26

Another decent choice on the same street as La Bodega and Fraktal (and open much later). Le Tram looks like it's been furnished from a Prague public transport closing-down sale. Filled with plastic seats, benches and other accoutrements salvaged from decommissioned trams, as well as other 1970s *objets trouvés*, this pleasantly scruffy French-owned bar pulls in an international crowd with cheap beer, lively conversation and cool tunes.

STROMOFFKA Map pp132–3 Bar

☎ 737 141 997; Kamenická 54, Holešovice; 5pm-2am Mon-Sat; 1, 8, 15, 25, 26

This popular student bar, with occasional DJs and dancing downstairs, draws a local, early 20-ish crowd, but is large enough to be welcoming to newcomers. It tends to get packed out late on Fridays and Saturdays, when the lower-level bar is three-deep in drink orders and sweaty bodies are pounding out the beat behind.

LETENSKÝ ZÁMEČEK

Map pp132–3 Beer Garden

☎ 233 378 208; Letenský sady 341, Bubeneč; 11am-11pm (summer only); 1, 8, 15, 25, 26

No accounting of watering holes in the Holešovice area would be complete without a nod towards the city's best beer garden, situated at the eastern end of Letná park. If it's beer you're after, you have two choices: one, known euphemistically as 'business class', is to pull up a chair at the grill-garden restaurant towards the left, where you can get a half-litre Pilsner Urquell for around 30Kč a glass, plus pretty good pizzas and burritos. The other option – 'coach' – is to line up at the beer window and get a 28Kč half-litre in a plastic cup and sit at the picnic tables along the ridge. Though it's open only in nice weather, it's the best game in town on a warm summer evening.

ALCHYMISTA Map pp132–3 Café

☎ 233 370 359; Jana Zajívce 7, Bubeneč; 8pm-6am; 1, 8, 15, 25, 26

This old-fashioned coffee house with an adjacent art gallery is an oasis in the culturally barren neighbourhood behind Sparta stadium. Freshly ground coffees, a serious selection of teas (no Lipton in a bag here),

BEER GARDENS

On a hot summer day, what could be finer than sitting outdoors with a chilled glass of Bohemia's finest beer, admiring a view over river or city. Many of Prague's pubs have small beer gardens or courtyards, but the following summer-only spots are truly out in the open air. Opening times are weather-dependent, but are typically noon to midnight April to September; expect to pay around 25Kč to 30Kč for a half-litre for beer.

Letenský zámeček (Map pp132–3; Letenské sady, Bubeneč) A slew of rickety benches and tables spread along a dusty scarp beneath the trees at the eastern end of Letná Gardens enjoys one of the city's most stunning views, looking across the river to the spires of Staré Město, and southwest to Malá Strana. Gambrinus on tap. See p187.

Letní bar (Map pp76–7; Střelecký ostrov, Malá Strana) Basically a shack serving Budvar in plastic cups, this is the place to pick up a beer before hitting the little beach at the northern end of the island.

Občerstvení U okénka (Map p116; Soběslavova, Vyšehrad) Not a proper beer garden as such, but a collection of outdoor tables with a view over Vyšehrad Gardens – a pleasant spot for a beer on a sunny day, with bottled Braník at only 16Kč for 0.5L.

Riegrovy sady (Map p121; Riegrovy sady, Vinohrady) Perched on top of precipitous Riegrovy Park, this bustling beer garden has awesome night-time views of the castle, a big screen showing sport and the opportunity to play table football and table hockey with half of Prague. Pilsner Urquell and Gambrinus. See p184 for a full review.

Parukářka (Map pp126–7; Olšanská, Žižkov) Ramshackle wooden hut in park overlooking Žižkov, with plenty of outdoor tables and lots of sweet-smelling smoke wafting about in the evenings. Gambrinus on tap.

Petřínské terasy (Map pp76–7; Petřín, Malá Strana) Traditional country-style pub with large, outdoor wooden deck and a stunning view over the city. Pilsner Urquell on tap.

and freshly made cakes and strudels draw a mostly neighbourhood crowd. In nice weather ask to take your coffee in the back garden.

ANTONIE Map pp132–3 Café

☎ 233 374 814; Šmeralová 15, Bubeneč; 🕑 11am-10pm; 🚊 1, 8, 15, 25, 26

This bright, cheerful café is a relatively new addition to this rapidly gentrifying neighbourhood between Letenské náměstí and Stromovka Park. The café is owned by an interior design company, and the polish shows, especially in the lovely open kitchen at the back. The menu includes a delicious selection of home-made cakes and light food items like soups and sandwiches. It's popular with mothers with babies making the trek to and from the park.

ARTESA Map pp132–3 Café

☎ 224 318 625; Dejvická 33, Dejvice; 🕑 8am-9am Mon-Fri, noon-7pm Sat & Sun; Ⓜ Dejvická or 🚊 2, 8, 20, 26

Retro is big these days, and this little coffee joint, just off Vítězné náměstí, easily evokes the futuristic 1950s and '60s with its modular chairs, pinkish walls and groovy, hanging cylinder lamps. Customers run the gamut from old ladies to supermodels – all there for the very good coffee as well as cakes, sweets and rolls. The front room is nonsmoking; the back, smoking.

BIO OKO Map pp132–3 Café

☎ 233 312 148; Františka Křížka 15, Holešovice; 🕑 2-11pm; 🚊 1, 8, 15, 25, 26

The café in the repertory cinema Bio Oko (p201) is a gem. It's classically retro as befits a cinema that regularly shows arty faves from the 1950s and '60s. Serving good espresso-based drinks as well as beer and cocktails, it's a nice choice for before or after the show.

ERHARTOVA CUKRÁRNA Map pp132–3 Café

☎ 233 312 148; Milady Horákové 56, Holešovice; 🕑 10am-7pm; 🚊 1, 8, 15, 25, 26

This stylish 1930s-era café and sweet shop in a refurbished functionalist building is adjacent to the local branch of the public library. It draws a mix of mothers with strollers, students and old folks, attracted mainly by the local varieties of biscuits, doughnuts and cinnamon rolls in the glass case, and ice cream in hot weather. Nonsmoking throughout.

KABINET Map pp132–3 Café

☎ 233 326 668; Terronská 25, Dejvice; 🕑 11am-11pm Mon-Fri, 3-11pm Sat & Sun; Ⓜ Dejvická or 🚊 2, 8, 20, 26

A retro 1920s-style coffee house, slightly reminiscent of a cabaret, Kabinet is situated in a cool rondocubist building in a pleasantly residential part of Dejvice. Old cameras, posters and photographs emphasise the throwback feel. The name of the café, for Czechs, recalls early school days – a *kabinet* being a teacher's office – to add to the nostalgic feel. A perfect spot for a quiet conversation or for relaxing over a coffee and a good book.

KUMBAL Map pp132–3 Café

☎ 777 559 842; Heřmanová 12, Holešovice; 9am-8am; 1, 5, 8, 12, 14, 15, 17, 25, 26
Another stylish coffee bar in a 1930s Functionalist building that manages to be both hip and comfortable at the same time. There's good coffee and tea drinks, though not much on the menu aside from a few simple sandwiches and a daily soup (usually vegetarian). It's nonsmoking throughout, which attracts the stroller crowd in the afternoon and makes a pleasant place to linger (maybe that's why there's rarely a free table). Free wi-fi.

OUKY DOUKY Map pp132–3 Café

☎ 266 711 531; Janovského 14, Holešovice; 8am-11pm; 1, 5, 8, 12, 14, 15, 17, 25, 26
This was the original home of the Globe Bookstore & Café (née Coffeehouse) in the 1990s, and a kind of eclectic, San Francisco funkiness lingers. Today it houses a used bookstore with a worn-out selection of Czech-language books and an inviting café filled with students, housewives from the neighbourhood, a few bohemian types and a wandering expat or two. The light menu features mostly toasts, sandwiches and salads. Free wi-fi.

PRVNÍ HOLEŠOVICKÁ KAVÁRNA Map pp132–3 Café

☎ 283 871 327; Kommunardů 30, Holešovice; 8pm-6am; 1, 3, 12, 14, 25
This sterile, street-level coffee house is about as intellectual as it gets in the far eastern end of Holešovice. The name means 'First Holešovice Coffee house', but it isn't quite accurate. The old Globe Bookstore & Coffeehouse on Janovského (now Ouky Douky, above) was technically first, but this is a true survivor. Average coffee drinks, indifferent service and minimal food offerings don't seem to diminish the charm; it's packed most afternoons and evenings. Excellent original art occasionally features on the walls.

TĚSNĚ VEDLE BURUNDI Map pp132–3 Café

☎ 777 170 803; Sládkova 4, Bubeneč; 10am-10pm; 1, 8, 15, 25, 26
A curious pub–coffee house hybrid that draws a mix of intellectuals, students, ageing rockers, and garden-variety neighbourhood drinkers. It has a vaguely old-school dissident whiff about the place, making it a more satisfying spot to linger than the swish bars in the city centre. Limited food options include a couple of salads and toasts.

ANDALUSKÝ PES Map pp132–3 Cocktail Bar

☎ 773 026 584; Korunovační 4, Bubeneč; 7pm-4am; 1, 8, 15, 25, 26
'Le Chien Andalou' is an after-hours cocktail bar with retro flair. The inviting front room, sporting red-velvet bar stools and purple glitter walls, attracts a kind of Edward Hopper 'Nighthawks' crowd after Fraktal closes and the night-time crowd moves in. The back rooms have a more risqué feel, dark and crowded some nights, with faces recognisable only by the glow of their cigarettes. It tends to close early on quiet nights, so take the official opening hours with a grain of salt.

POSTEL Map pp132–3 Cocktail Bar

☎ 220 874 797; Veletržní 14, Holešovice; 5pm-2am Mon-Sat; 1, 5, 8, 12, 14, 15, 17, 25, 26
The name means 'bed', and that's obviously the goal at this flash meat-market–cocktail bar not far from Strossmayerovo náměstí. Fans of the film *Cocktail* will delight at the bartenders' juggling skills. Others will marvel at the attractive clientele. All in all, not a bad place to while away a couple of hours before, well, bed.

AKÁDEMIE Map pp132–3 Pub

☎ 233 375 236; Šmeralová 5, Bubeneč; 4pm-4am; 1, 8, 15, 25, 26
This cavernous pub has several pool tables and dartboards to amuse in case you tire of sitting around chewing the fat (quite literally given the menu options). The game of choice here is eight ball; the tables are large and well maintained. Waiters bring your beers to the table, and everything is toted up – billiards included – at the end.

Late opening hours make this a good place to wrap up.

NA SLAMNÍKU Map pp132–3 Pub

☎ 233 322 594; Wolkerova 12, Bubeneč; 🕑 11am-11pm; 🚊 1, 8, 15, 25, 26 (plus walk)

A great traditional Czech pub and beer garden dating from the 19th century, Na Slamníku is tucked away in a small valley in Bubeneč in the neighbourhood just behind the sprawling Russian embassy. There are three separate spaces: on the left side is an old-school tavern with cheap and decent Czech dishes, the right side is more a raucous pub, and in summer you can eat and drink outside under the trees. It's hard to find, so bring a map or take a taxi.

NA STARÉ KOVÁRNĚ
Map pp132–3 Pub

☎ 233 371 099; Kamenická 17, Holešovice; 🕑 11am-1am; 🚊 1, 8, 15, 25, 26

The motorcycle hanging from the ceiling sets a rakish tone for one of the most popular Czech pubs in the neighbourhood. The food is at least two notches above standard *hospoda* fare – and has even garnered raves from local critics – but honestly no-one comes here for the food. It's a shot and a beer joint in the best sense of the term.

U SV ANTONÍĆKA Map pp132–3 Pub

☎ 220 879 428; Podplukovníka Sochora 20, Holešovice; 🕑 11am-11pm; 🚊 1, 5, 8, 12, 14, 15, 17, 25, 26

A relative rarity these days close to the centre: a fully unreconstructed Czech pub and all that that entails, including cantankerous locals, an occasional hygiene issue with the glassware, layers of smoke, and toilets that will have to be buried in a nuclear landfill someday. Yet it has a certain charm. If you're curious about how things used to be, or long for a drink far from the tour coaches, this is your place. Not for the faint-hearted.

SMÍCHOV

Smíchov continues to surprise. Every year brings at least one or two new bar and café openings. Most of the action is clustered near the Anděl metro station, anchored by the enormous Nový Smíchov shopping centre. The Staropramen brewery is located near here, but alas the funky bar inside the brewery has been replaced by yet another branch of the cookie-cutter, Staropramen-owned Potrefená husa restaurant chain. The beer's still fresh, though, and brewed on-site.

BACK DOORS Map p138 Bar

☎ 257 315 827; Na Bělidle 30; 🕑 11am-1am; Ⓜ Anděl or 🚊 4, 6, 7, 9, 10, 14, 20

The owners say this funky cellar bar is inspired by similar spaces in New York and Amsterdam (though the subterranean Gothic cellar look could really only be Prague). It offers decent Czech DJs and a relaxed vibe most nights, though it can get stuffy on a crowded weekend night. If you're hungry, there's a full menu of well-done international dishes.

DOG'S BOLLOCKS
Map p138 Bar

☎ 775 736 030; Nádražní 82; 🕑 5pm-midnight Mon, 5pm-3am Tue-Sat; Ⓜ Anděl

This run-of-the-mill bar and nightspot is just down from the Staropramen brewery, and is a decent choice if you're staying in the area and don't want to go too far for your fun. In spite of the English-friendly name, it draws mostly Czech students and young professionals. Open late.

JET SET Map p138 Cocktail Bar

☎ 257 327 251; Radlická 1c; 🕑 11am-2am; Ⓜ Anděl

Smíchov's trendiest cocktail bar is a strictly black-and-white affair, with a big bar area and a large dance floor for later in the evenings when it morphs from workaday restaurant to an after-work drink place to a late-night hotspot. It's worth it if you happen to be catching a movie at a nearby multiplex, but don't make a special trip. The food, including fresh salads and sandwiches with a Mediterranean touch, is very good.

LOKAL BLOK Map p138 Pub

☎ 251 511 490; náměstí 14.října 10; 🕑 noon-1am Mon-Fri, 4pm-1am Sat & Sun; Ⓜ Anděl

The perfect Prague combination: a raucous pub and a state-of-the-art climbing wall (though presumably you're supposed to boulder before you drink and not vice versa). Most nights there's a lively crowd, fuelled by Pilsner Urquell on tap and some good Mexican eats, such as nachos and quesadillas. Highly recommended.

NA VERANDÁCH

Map p138 Pub

☎ 257 191 200; Nádražní 84; 🕑 11am-midnight Mon-Thu, to 1am Fri & Sat, to 11pm Sun; Ⓜ Anděl

This combination pub and restaurant, managed by the Potrefená husa local restaurant chain, is inside the Staropramen Brewery, and while lots of people come here to eat, it's perfectly fine to come in just for a super-fresh beer (there are seven varieties on tap). The menu is the same at other branches of Potrefená husa. It's essentially high-tone fast food: ribs, burgers, chicken breasts and the lot. Sit on the veranda in the back in nice weather, or up front by the bar on a chilly night.

EMPORIO Map p138 Café

☎ 257 329 240; Plzeňská 8 (inside the Nový Smíchov shopping centre); 🕑 10am-9pm; Ⓜ Anděl

The best of several cafés in the Nový Smíchov shopping centre is located on the second floor towards the front of the building. It serves up good espresso drinks as well as some light bites and cakes. The modern, upmarket look draws a glamour crowd taking a break from the apparently heavy demands of shopping.

KÁVA KÁVA KÁVA Map p138 Café

☎ 257 314 277; Lidická 42; mains 70-120Kč; 🕑 7am-10pm; Ⓜ Anděl

The Smíchov branch of the popular internet café in Staré Město (p180) is bigger and brighter than the original, with Etruscan orange walls, terracotta floor tiles and modern art. There's a more extensive menu too – you can snack on salads, sandwiches, quiche or nachos, or tuck into more substantial chicken gyros, Mexican chilli or home-made soup of the day.

ENTERTAINMENT

top picks

What's your recommendation? www.lonelyplanet.com/prague

ENTERTAINMENT

Across the spectrum, from ballet to blues, jazz to rock, theatre to film, there's a bewildering range of entertainment on offer in this eclectic city. Prague is now as much a European centre for jazz, rock and hip-hop as it is for classical music. The biggest draw, however, is still the Prague Spring festival of classical music and opera.

For reviews, day-by-day listings and a directory of venues, consult the 'Night & Day' section of the weekly Prague Post (www.praguepost.cz). Monthly listings booklets include *Culture in Prague* and the Czech-language *Přehled*, available from PIS offices (see p255 for contact details).

Look out for Provokátor (www.provokator.org), a free monthly magazine that is dedicated to art, music, culture and politics; the website has listings of upcoming cultural events. You can pick up the print magazine in clubs, cafés, arthouse cinemas and backpacker hostels. There is also *Metropolis*, a free weekly booklet with film, theatre and music listings, available in cinemas, pubs and clubs (it's in Czech only, but the listings are easily deciphered), and the English-language magazine Think Again (www.thinkagain.cz).

For web-based entertainment listings, check out www.prague.tv, www.heartofeurope.cz and www.pis.cz/en/prague/events.

NIGHTLIFE

If discussing Kafka over a coffee or analysing last night's hockey match over a glass of Pilsner seems too tame, Prague offers plenty of places for night owls to party on into the small hours. From traditional jazz joints in smoky cellars to innovative live music venues, cool cocktail clubs and even an underground nuclear bunker, you'll find a place worth staying up late for.

CLUBBING

Prague's club scene is nothing to rave about. With few exceptions, the city's dance clubs cater to crowds of partying teenagers and tourists weaned on MTV Europe – if you want to dance to anything other than '80s hits or happy house, you'll have to look long and hard. Prague's main strengths are its alternative music clubs, DJ bars, 'experimental' venues such as Palác Akropolis and the Roxy and places that are just plain weird, like Bunkr Parukářka.

Refreshingly, dress codes don't seem to have reached Prague yet, and it's unlikely you'll be knocked back anywhere unless you're stark naked. And there are even a few places that would probably be OK with that…

Check www.prague.tv, www.techno.cz/party or www.hip-hop.cz for up-to-date club listings (the latter two are in Czech, but you can work out what's going on).

BUNKR PARUKÁŘKA Map pp126–7

☎ 603 423 140; www.parukarka.eu; Na Kříže, Olšanské náměstí, Žižkov; admission free-50Kč; 🕑 8pm-3am Thu-Sat; 🚊 5, 9, 26

Only in Prague… A graffiti-covered steel door in the hillside at the west end of Parukářka park leads unexpectedly to a vast circular staircase that descends 15m underground into a 1950s nuclear bunker where a makeshift bar serves cheap beer in plastic glasses. This is the unlikely setting for one of Prague's most unusual clubs, a claustrophobic shrine to electropunk, industrial, psytrance-electro-acid and any other weird and wonderful avant-garde electronic music genre you can think of (winners of the most eccentric label so far are Vložte Kočku, whose music is promoted as 'psycountryemotriphoprap'). See the website for what's on when you're in town.

CROSS CLUB Map pp132–3

☎ 736 535 053; http://crossclub.cz; Plynární 23, Holešovice; admission free-100Kč; 🕑 4pm-3am; Ⓜ Nádraží Holešovice

This is an industrial club in every sense of the word: the setting in an industrial zone in Holešovice, the throbbing music (with both DJs and live acts) and the interior, an absolute must-see jumble of gadgets, shafts, cranks and pipes, many of which move and pulsate with light to the music. The programme includes occasional cabaret nights, theatre performances and art happenings. There's drinking on two levels, plus a few picnic tables outside in case it gets to be too much. It's easy to find despite the location: after exiting Nádraží Holešovice metro station, walk 100m to the east along Plynární street. You've arrived once you see the enormous industrial sculpture out the front.

FUTURUM Map p138

☎ 257 328 571; www.musicbar.cz; Zborovská 7, Smíchov; admission 100-120Kč; 7pm-2am; 7, 9, 12, 14

Futurum is a cross-fertilisation of alternative and mainstream, with a bizarre décor that looks like a cross between an Art Deco ballroom and Flash Gordon's spaceship. Midweek nights see occasional live performances of jazz and soul, indie bands and record launches, but what really pulls in the crowds is the regular Friday and Saturday night '80s and '90s Video Party, with local DJs blasting out everything from REM and Nirvana to Bon Jovi and the Village People, complete with cringe-worthy videos.

KARLOVY LÁZNĚ Map pp88–9

☎ 222 220 502; www.karlovylazne.cz; Novotného lávka 1, Staré Město; admission 100Kč; 9pm-5am; 17, 18

Self-proclaimed as 'the biggest club in middle Europe', KL is a vast, steaming hive of heaving young bodies, awash with alcohol and teenage pheromones. That said, it's a fascinating venue in a labyrinthine medieval building with old murals, mosaics and partly preserved Roman-style baths (now dance floors); a single cover charge admits you to four floors – from the Music Café (black music) on the ground floor, up through Discotheque (classic disco sounds) and Kaleidoskop ('60s, '70s and '80s revival) to Paradogs (dance, house, techno, drum 'n' bass etc).

top picks

GAY & LESBIAN PRAGUE

- Castle Steps (p215)
- Club Stella (p184)
- Friends (p182)
- Pension Arco (p221)
- Termix (p196)
- Valentino (p196)

KLUB 007 STRAHOV Map pp76–7

☎ 257 211 439; www.myspace.com/klub007strahov; Block 7, Chaloupeckého 7; admission 50-250Kč; 7.30pm-midnight Sun-Thu, 7.30pm-1am Fri & Sat; 143, 176, 217

Klub 007 is one of several grungy student clubs in the basements of the big college dormitory blocks in Strahov. The legendary 007 has been around since 1987, when it was a focus for underground music, and is now famed for its devotion to hardcore, punk, ska, ragga, jungle, ambient and other alternative sounds. On Saturday nights it hosts a regular hip-hop party.

LE CLAN Map p121

☎ 222 251 226; www.leclan.cz; Balbínova 23, Vinohrady; admission 50-160Kč; 2am-10am Wed-Sun; M Muzeum

A decadent French-accented after-party club, with DJs on two floors, lots of bars, cosy armchairs and myriad rooms stuffed with 'VSPs' (Le Clan's own acronym for Very Strange People). It's usually got a good, racy vibe.

M1 SECRET LOUNGE Map pp88–9

☎ 227 195 235; www.m1lounge.com; Masná 1, Staré Město; admission free; 7pm-3am Sun-Thu, 7pm-5am Fri & Sat; 5, 8, 14

An American-owned, industrial-chic cocktail den where polished concrete and stainless steel contrast with candlelight and plush purple sofas, M1 attracts lots of English-speaking expats, well-heeled locals and the occasional visiting celeb (absolutely no stag parties). Wednesday nights are ladies' nights, while Fridays see a regular set from US DJ Big J, a dance-floor-filling mix of R&B, house and hip-hop.

MECCA Map pp132–3

☎ 602 711 225; www.mecca.cz; U Průhonu 3, Holešovice; admission 100-300Kč (frequent free entry nights, check the website); 10pm-6am Wed-Sat; 5, 12, 15

This former warehouse in Holešovice is now 10 years old and is still one of the best of the ultrafashionable dance clubs. Its industrial red brick and right angles are softened by rounded shapes, floaty drapes and futuristic curvy couches. Mecca is a magnet for models, film stars and fashionistas, and for the legion of clubbers who come for the huge, DJ-dominated dance floor and pumping sound system.

RADOST FX Map p121

☎ 603 181 500; www.radostfx.cz; Bělehradská 120, Vinohrady; admission 100-250Kč; 🕑 10pm-6am; Ⓜ IP Pavlova

Though not quite as hot as it once was, Prague's slickest, shiniest and most self-assured club is still capable of pulling in the crowds, especially for its Thursday hip-hop night, FXbounce (www.fxbounce.com). The place has a chilled-out, bohemian atmosphere, with Moroccan boudoir–meets–Moulin Rouge décor, and there's an excellent lounge-cum–vegetarian restaurant that keeps serving into the small hours. DJs spin tunes in the ground floor gallery on Thursday, Friday and Saturday nights.

ROXY Map pp88–9

☎ 224 826 296; www.roxy.cz; Dlouhá 33, Staré Město; admission free-250Kč Fri & Sat; 🕑 7pm-midnight Mon-Thu, 7pm-6am Fri & Sat; 🚋 5, 8, 14

Set in the ramshackle shell of an Art Deco cinema (extensively restored after severe flood damage in 2002), the legendary Roxy has nurtured the more independent and innovative end of Prague's club spectrum since 1987 – this is the place to see the Czech Republic's top DJs. On the 1st floor is NoD, an 'experimental space' that stages drama, dance, performance art, cinema and live music; events here usually begin earlier in the evening before the nightclub kicks off at around midnight.

SEDM VLKŮ Map pp126–7

☎ 222 711 725; www.sedmvlku.cz; Vlkova 7, Žižkov; admission free; 🕑 5pm-3am Mon-Sat; 🚋 5, 9, 26

'Seven Wolves' is a two-level, art-studenty café–bar and club. At street level there's candlelight, friendly staff, weird wrought-iron work and funky murals, and music low enough to have a conversation; down in the darkened cellar, DJs pump out techno, breakbeat, drum 'n' bass, jungle and reggae from 9pm on Friday and Saturday nights.

TERMIX Map p121

☎ 222 710 462; www.club-termix.cz; Třebízckého 4a, Vinohrady; admission free; 🕑 8pm-5am Wed-Sun; Ⓜ Jiřího z Poděbrad

Termix is one of Prague's most popular gay and lesbian dance clubs, with an industrial–high-tech vibe (lots of shiny steel and glass and plush sofas) and a young crowd that contains as many tourists as locals. The smallish dance floor fills up fast during Thursday's best of the '80s and '90s party, when you may have to queue to get in.

VALENTINO Map p121

☎ 222 513 491; www.club-valentino.cz; Vinohradská 40, Vinohrady; admission free; 🕑 9pm-5am; Ⓜ Muzeum plus 🚋 11, or Ⓜ Náměstí Míru

Valentino bills itself as the biggest gay dance club in the Czech Republic, with DJs on two floors and theme nights that vary from the ubiquitous '80s and '90s to Oldies, Czech music and the 'Best of the Millennium'. It's located at the same address as Bordo (opposite).

WAKATA Map pp132–3

☎ 233 370 518; www.wakata.cz; Malířská 14, Bubeneč; admission free; 🕑 5pm-3am Mon-Thu, to 5am Fri & Sat, 6pm-3am Sun; 🚋 1, 8, 15, 25, 26

There's no designer chic or style statements in this small, unpretentious, laid-back DJ lounge, a house-free zone where you can enjoy inexpensive beers and cocktails among the scuffed and mismatched furniture while you bop along to a soundtrack of funk, Latin, dub, ambient, jungle, reggae or hip-hop.

XT3 Map pp126–7

☎ 222 783 463; www.xt3.cz; Rokycanova 29, Žižkov; admission free; 🕑 bar 11am-3am Mon-Fri, 2pm-3am Sat & Sun, club 6pm-3am Sun-Thu, 6pm-5am Fri & Sat; 🚋 5, 9, 26

This is the essential Žižkov club – scruffy, laid-back, eclectic and great fun. There's a lively bar at street level, all red-brick arches and wood-and-leather booths, plus a cavern-like club venue that hosts local DJs and live music (from hardcore rock to acoustic singer-songwriters).

JAZZ CLUBS

Prague has lots of good jazz clubs, many of which have been around for decades. Unless otherwise indicated, most have a cover charge of around 200Kč.

AGHARTA JAZZ CENTRUM Map pp88–9

☎ 222 211 275; www.agharta.cz; Železná 16, Staré Město; 🕑 7pm-1am, music 9pm-midnight; Ⓜ Můstek

Agharta has been staging top-notch modern Czech jazz, blues, funk and fusion since

1991, but moved into this very central Old Town venue only in 2004. A typical jazz cellar with red-brick vaults and a cosy bar and café, the centre also has a music shop (open 7pm to midnight), which sells CDs, T-shirts and coffee mugs. As well as hosting local musicians, the centre occasionally stages gigs by leading international artists.

BLUES SKLEP Map pp88–9

☎ 221 466 138; www.bluessklep.cz; Liliová 10, Staré Město; admission 100Kč; bar 7pm-2.30am, music 9pm-midnight; M Staroměstská

One of the city's newest jazz clubs, the Blues Sklep (*sklep* means 'cellar') is a typical Old Town basement with dark, Gothic-vaulted rooms that provide an atmospheric setting for regular nightly jazz sessions. Bands play anything from trad New Orleans jazz to bebop, blues, funk and soul. The icing on the cake – the bar serves excellent, competitively priced Ferdinand beer (28Kč for 0.5L).

METROPOLITAN JAZZ CLUB Map pp108–9

☎ 224 947 777; Jungmannova 14, Nové Město; 7pm-1am, music 9pm-12.30am; M Národní Třída

Regular performers the Senior Swingers sum up the atmosphere and age range at this traditional basement jazz haunt, which offers an easily digestible menu of Dixieland, ragtime and swing. The Met shows a similar preference for substance over style in its choice of décor, with a plain tiled floor, a few musical instruments and posters on the walls, and a general lack of adornment that focuses the attention on the solid, dependable, evergreen music.

REDUTA JAZZ CLUB Map pp108–9

☎ 224 933 487; www.redutajazzclub.cz; Národní třída 20, Nové Město; admission 300Kč; 9pm-3am; M Národní Třída

The Reduta is Prague's oldest jazz club, founded in 1958 during the communist era – it was here in 1994 that former US president Bill Clinton famously jammed on a new saxophone presented to him by Václav Havel. It has an intimate setting, with smartly dressed patrons squeezing into tiered seats and lounges to soak up the big-band, swing and Dixieland atmosphere. Book a few hours ahead at the box office (open from 5pm Monday to Friday and from 7pm Saturday and Sunday), or through Ticketpro.

U MALÉHO GLENA Map pp76–7

☎ 257 531 717; www.malyglen.cz; Karmelitská 23, Malá Strana; 10am-2am, music from 9.30pm Sun-Thu, from 10pm Fri & Sat; tram 12, 20, 22, 23

'Little Glen's' is a lively American-owned bar and restaurant where hard-swinging local jazz or blues bands play every night in the cramped and steamy stone-vaulted cellar. There are regular jam sessions where amateurs are welcome (as long as you're good!) – it's a small venue, so get here early if you want to see, as well as hear, the band.

USP JAZZ LOUNGE Map pp88–9

☎ 603 551 680; www.jazzlounge.cz; Michalská 9, Staré Město; admission 250Kč; 7pm-2am, music 9pm-midnight; M Můstek

Located in the basement of the Hotel U Staré Paní, this long-established jazz club caters to all levels of musical appreciation. There's a varied programme of modern jazz, soul, blues and Latin rhythms, and a nightly DJ spot from midnight onwards.

LIVE MUSIC

Prague has a high-energy live-music scene, with rock, metal, punk, electro, industrial, hip-hop and newer sounds at a score of DJ and live-music venues; most have a cover charge of around 50Kč to 200Kč. As well as the venues listed here, clubs such as Futurum, Klub 007 Strahov, Palác Akropolis and Roxy (see under Clubbing, p194) also host live rock bands.

For current listings and reviews check out the media listed at the start of this chapter, and keep an eye on flyers posted around town.

BATALION Map pp88–9

☎ 220 108 147; www.batalion.cz; 28.října 3, Staré Město; bar 24hr, music from 9pm; M Můstek

Batalion is a delightfully grungy bar with a basement music club offering anything from rock and jazz to punk and death metal performed by up-and-coming Czech bands (plus DJ-fronted dance parties on Friday and Saturday). Despite a location in the midst of the tourist hordes, it pulls in a young, mainly local crowd.

BORDO Map p121

☎ 774 039 991; www.bordo.cz; Vinohradská 40, Vinohrady; 8pm-3am Mon-Sat; M Muzeum plus tram 11 or M Náměstí Míru

A cavernous rock and experimental music club, Bordo is part of the former Radio

Palác complex on Vinohradska. The interior vaguely resembles a dance at a high school gym. Though Bordo shares an address with gay-friendly Valentino (p196), this is an all-gender, all-preference affair, with people here for the live music, which can be pretty good some nights.

LA FABRIKA Map pp132–3

www.lafabrika.cz; Komunardů 30, Holešovice; admission free-100Kč; variable depending on events; M Nádraží Holešovice plus 5, 12 or M Vltavská plus 1, 3, 5, 25

The name refers to a 'factory', but this is actually a former paint warehouse that's been converted into an experimental performance space. Depending on the night, come here to catch live music, theatre, dance or film. Summers are usually slow, but the season picks up again in autumn. Consult the website for the latest programme. The ticket office and bar open about an hour before the event starts.

LUCERNA MUSIC BAR Map pp108–9

224 217 108; http://musicbar.iquest.cz; Vodičkova 36, Nové Město; 8pm-4am; M Můstek

Nostalgia reigns supreme at this atmospheric old theatre, now looking a little dog-eared, with anything from Beatles tribute bands to mainly Czech artists playing jazz, blues, pop, rock and more on midweek nights. But the most popular event – don't ask us why – is the regular 1980s and '90s video party held every Friday and Saturday night, which pulls in huge crowds of young locals bopping along to Duran Duran and Gary Numan.

MALOSTRANSKÁ BESEDA Map pp76–7

257 532 092; Malostranské náměstí 21, Malá Strana; bar 5pm-1am, music from 8.30pm; 12, 20, 22, 23

Malá Strana's former town hall now houses a large café–bar that hosts anything from hard rock to bluegrass via jazz and folk, playing to a young, mostly Czech crowd – it packs out early, particularly on weekends. The building was closed for reconstruction at the time of research, but should be open again in summer 2009.

PALÁC AKROPOLIS Map pp126–7

296 330 911; www.palacakropolis.cz; Kubelíkova 27, Žižkov; admission free-50Kč; club 7pm-5am; 5, 9, 26

The Akropolis is a Prague institution, a labyrinthine, sticky-floored shrine to alternative music and drama. Its various performance spaces host a smorgasbord of musical and cultural events, from DJs to string quartets to Macedonian Roma bands to local rock gods to visiting talent – Marianne Faithfull, the Flaming Lips and the Strokes have all played here. DJs do their stuff in the Theatre Bar (Divadelní Bar) and Small Hall (Malá Scéna), spinning everything from house to hip-hop, and reggae to breakbeat.

RETRO MUSIC HALL Map p121

222 510 592; www.retropraha.cz; Francouzská 4, Vinohrady; admission 150-500Kč; box office 9am-7pm, shows start 8pm; M Náměstí Míru

There's been a dance club here for years, but Retro Music Hall has come into its own in the past year or two as a live venue for old rockers, niche bands and, well, 'retro' acts as diverse as Asia and Fishbone (yes, they're both apparently still touring). Consult the website for what's on when you're in town. Definitely worth checking out.

ROCK CAFÉ Map pp108–9

224 933 947; www.rockcafe.cz; Národní třída 20, Nové Město; 10am-3am Mon-Fri, 5pm-3am Sat, 5pm-1am Sun, music from 7.30pm; M Národní Třída

Not to be confused with the Hard Rock Café, this is a multilevel club next door to the Reduta Jazz Club sporting a stage for DJs and live rock bands, a funkily decorated café–bar downstairs, a cinema and an art gallery. Live bands are mostly local, ranging from nu-metal to folk rock to Doors and Sex Pistols tribute bands.

SKUTEČNOST Map p121

728 927 118; www.skutecnost.cz; Francouzská 76, Vršovice; admission free-100Kč; shows start 8pm; M Náměstí Míru plus 4, 22, 23

This experimental not-for-profit performance space just below the Czech Inn hostel hosts high-quality Czech and foreign indie bands, as well as art happenings, openings, film nights, readings and general groove-ins. Check the website to make sure something's on before venturing out here.

THE ARTS

For classical music, opera, ballet, theatre and some rock concerts – even with the most thoroughly 'sold-out' events – you can often find a

BUYING TICKETS

The 'wholesalers' with the largest agency networks are Bohemia Ticket International (BTI), FOK and Ticketpro; the others probably get their tickets from them.

Bohemia Ticket International (BTI; Map pp88–9; ☎ 224 227 832; www.ticketsbti.cz; Malé náměstí 13, Staré Město; 9am-5pm Mon-Fri, 9am-1pm Sat) BTI provides tickets for all kinds of events. There's another branch (Map pp108–9; ☎ 224 215 031; Na Příkopě 16, Nové Město; 10am-7pm Mon-Fri, 10am-5pm Sat, 10am-3pm Sun) near the Municipal House.

FOK Box Office (Map pp88–9; ☎ 222 002 336; www.fok.cz; U Obecního Domu 2, Staré Město; 10am-6pm Mon-Fri) Prague Symphony Orchestra box office, for classical concert tickets; also open for one hour before performance begins.

Ticketcentrum (Map pp88–9; ☎ 296 333 333; Rytířská 31, Staré Město; 9am-12.30pm & 1-5pm Mon-Fri) Walk-in centre for all kinds of tickets; branch of Ticketpro.

Ticketpro (Map pp108–9; ☎ 296 333 333; www.ticketpro.cz; Pasáž Lucerna, Štěpánská 61, Nové Město; 9am-1pm & 1.30-5.30pm Mon-Fri) Tickets are available here for all kinds of events. There are Ticketpro branches in PIS offices (see p255) and many other places.

Ticketstream (www.ticketstream.cz) Internet-based booking agency that covers events in Prague and all over the Czech Republic.

ticket or two on sale at the theatre's box office a half-hour or so before show time.

If you want to be sure of a seat, Prague is awash with ticket agencies (see the boxed text, above). Their advantage is convenience: most are computerised, fast and accept credit cards. Their drawback is a probable 8% to 15% mark-up.

Many venues have discounts for students and sometimes for the disabled. Most performances have a certain number of tickets set aside for foreigners. For rock and jazz clubs you can turn up at the door, but advance bookings are recommended for big names.

CLASSICAL MUSIC, OPERA & BALLET

There are half-a-dozen concerts of one kind or another almost every day during the summer, making a fine soundtrack to accompany the city's visual delights. Many of these are chamber concerts performed by aspiring musicians in the city's churches – gorgeous but chilly (take an extra layer, even on a summer day) and not always with the finest of acoustics. However, a good number of concerts, especially those promoted by people handing out flyers in the street, are second-rate, despite the premium prices that foreigners pay. If you want to be sure of quality, go for a performance by one of the city's professional orchestras.

In addition to the hours indicated here in the individual reviews, box offices are also open from 30 minutes to one hour before the start of a performance. For classical music, opera and ballet listings, check out www.heartofeurope.cz and www.czechopera.cz.

DVOŘÁK HALL Map pp88–9

Dvořákova síň; ☎ 227 059 352; www.rudolfinum.cz; náměstí Jana Palacha 1, Staré Město; tickets 200-600Kč; box office 10am-12.30pm & 1.30-6pm Mon-Fri; M Staroměstská

The Dvořák Hall in the neo-Renaissance Rudolfinum is home to the world-renowned Czech Philharmonic Orchestra (Česká filharmonie). Sit back and be impressed by some of the best classical musicians in Prague.

DVOŘÁK MUSEUM Map pp108–9

Muzeum Antonína Dvořáka; ☎ 224 918 013; Ke Karlovu 20, Nové Město; tickets 565Kč; concerts 8pm Tue & Fri Apr-Oct; M IP Pavlova

The pretty little Vila Amerika was built in 1717 as a count's immodest summer retreat. These days it's home to the Dvořák Museum (p114), and stages performances of Dvořák's vocal and instrumental works by the Original Music Theatre of Prague (www.musictheatre.cz), complete with period costume. Tickets are available through BTI (see the boxed text, above).

ESTATES THEATRE Map pp88–9

Stavovské divadlo; ☎ 224 902 322; www.narodni-divadlo.cz; Ovocný trh 1, Staré Město; tickets 100-2000Kč; box office 10am-6pm; M Můstek

The Estates Theatre (p101) is the oldest theatre in Prague, famed as the place where Mozart

OTHER CONCERT VENUES

Numerous churches and baroque palaces also serve as concert venues, staging anything from choral performances and organ recitals to string quartets, brass ensembles and occasionally full orchestras. You can get comprehensive details of these concerts from PIS offices (see p255). We've listed here a selection of the more popular venues around town.

Hradčany & Malá Strana

Basilica of St George (Bazilika sv Jiří; Map p62; náměstí U sv Jiří, Prague Castle) The Czech Republic's best-preserved Romanesque church.

Liechtenstein Palace (Lichtenštejnský palác; Map pp76–7; Malostranské náměstí, Malá Strana; tram 12, 20, 22, 23) Home to the Music Faculty of the Prague Academy of Performing Arts (Hudební fakulta AMU; www.hamu.cz).

St Nicholas Church (Kostel sv Mikuláše; Map pp76–7; Malostranská náměstí 38, Malá Strana; M Malostranská) Mozart himself tickled the ivories on the 2500-pipe organ here in 1787.

St Vitus Cathedral (Katedrála sv Víta; Map p62; 3rd Courtyard, Prague Castle, Hradčany; M Malostranská) The nave of Prague's cathedral is flooded with colour from beautiful stained-glass windows, and the acoustics are just as impressive.

Strahov Monastery (Strahovský klášter; Map pp70–1; Strahovské nádvoří 1, Hradčany; tram 22, 23) Mozart is said to have played the organ here as well.

Staré Město

Bethlehem Chapel (Betlémská kaple; Map pp88–9; Betlémské náměstí 1; tram 6, 9, 18, 21, 22, 23) This 14th-century chapel was torn down during the 18th century and painstakingly reconstructed between 1948 and 1954.

Chapel of Mirrors (Zrcadlová kaple; Map pp88–9; Klementinum, Mariánské náměstí; tram 17, 18, 53) Ornately decorated chapel dating from the 1720s.

Church of St Francis (Kostel sv Františka; Map pp88–9; Křížovnické náměstí; tram 5, 8, 14) Alongside the complex of the Convent of St Agnes.

Church of St Nicholas (Kostel sv Mikuláše; Map pp88–9; Staroměstské náměstí; M Staroměstská) Built in the 1730s by Kilian Dientzenhofer.

Convent of St Agnes (Klášter sv Anežky; Map pp88–9; U Milosrdných 17; tram 5, 8, 14) Prague's oldest surviving Gothic building.

Nové Město

National Museum (Národní muzeum; Map pp108–9; Václavské náměstí 68; M Muzeum) Chamber music and operatic duets performed on the grand staircase in the museum's main hall at 6pm most evenings.

Take care when buying tickets through people who hand out flyers in the street – some of these concerts are OK, but some may turn out to be a disappointment. Make sure you know exactly where the concert will be held – if you are told just 'the Municipal House', don't expect the magnificent Smetana Hall, as it may well be in one of the smaller concert halls.

conducted the premiere of *Don Giovanni* on 29 October 1787. A touristy version is staged here by the Opera Mozart company each summer; the rest of the year sees various opera, ballet and drama productions. The theatre is equipped for the hearing-impaired and has wheelchair access (wheelchair bookings can be made up to five days in advance); the box office is around the corner in the Kolowrat Palace.

MOZART MUSEUM Map p138

Muzeum Mozarta; ☎ 257 318 461; www.bertramka.com; Vila Bertramka, Mozartova 169, Smíchov; museum 110Kč, concert tickets 390-450Kč; tram 4, 7, 9, 10

Mozart stayed in the Vila Bertramka during his visits to Prague. It now houses a museum (p139), which serves as a charming venue for classical concerts held in the salon and garden from April to October. You can buy tickets at the museum cash desk, or through BTI or Ticketpro.

NATIONAL THEATRE Map pp108–9

Národní divadlo; ☎ 224 901 377; www.narodni-divadlo.cz; Národní třída 2, Nové Město; tickets 100-2000Kč; box office 10am-6pm; M Národní Třída

The glorious, golden-roofed centrepiece of the Czech National Revival, the much-loved National Theatre provided a stage for the re-emergence of Czech culture in the late 19th and early 20th centuries. Today you'll find traditional opera, drama and ballet by the likes of Smetana, Shakespeare and Tchaikovsky sharing the programme, alongside more modern works by composers and playwrights such as Philip Glass and John Osborne.

PRAGUE STATE OPERA Map pp108–9

Státní opera Praha; ☎ 224 227 266; www.opera.cz; Wilsonova 4, Nové Město; opera tickets 100-1200Kč, ballet tickets 100-900Kč; box office 10am-5.30pm Mon-Fri, 10am-noon & 1-5.30pm Sat & Sun; M Muzeum

The impressive neo-rococo home of the Prague State Opera provides a glorious setting for performances of opera and ballet. An annual Verdi festival takes place here in August and September, and less conventional shows, such as Leoncavallo's rarely staged version of *La Bohème,* are also performed here.

SMETANA HALL Map pp88–9

Smetanova síň; ☎ 220 002 101; www.obecnidum.cz; náměstí Republiky 5, Staré Město; tickets 250-600Kč; box office 10am-6pm; M Náměstí Republiky

Smetana Hall, centrepiece of the stunning Municipal House (Obecní dům; p99), is the city's largest concert hall with seating for 1200. This is the home venue of the Prague Symphony Orchestra (Symfonický orchestr hlavního města Prahy), and also stages performances of folk dance and music.

FILM

Prague has more than 30 cinemas, some showing first-run Western films, some showing Czech films, and including several excellent arthouse cinemas. For cinema listings check the 'Night & Day' section of the *Prague Post* or www.prague.tv.

Most films are screened in their original language with Czech subtitles *(české titulky)*, but Hollywood blockbusters are often dubbed into Czech *(dabing)*; look for the labels 'tit' or 'dab' on cinema listings. Czech-language films with English subtitles are listed as having *anglický titulky*.

BIO OKO Map pp132–3

Oko Cinema; ☎ 233 382 606; www.biooko.net; Františka Křížka 15, Holešovice; tickets 100Kč; 1, 5, 8, 12, 14, 15, 17, 25, 26

This repertory cinema shows a varied programme of underground films, selections from film festivals, documentaries, big-budget movies, and classics from around the world. Most films are shown in the original language (not necessarily English), with Czech subtitles. Check the website for the latest film showings.

KINO AERO Map pp126–7

☎ 271 771 349; www.kinoaero.cz; Biskupcova 31, Žižkov; tickets 40-100Kč; 5, 9, 10, 16, 19

The Aero is Prague's best-loved arthouse cinema, with themed programmes, retrospectives and unusual films, often in English or with English subtitles. This is the place to catch reruns of classics from *Smrt v Benátkách* (Death in Venice) to *Život Briana* (The Life of Brian). The same managers run a similar venue in the city centre, Kino Světozor (below).

KINO MAT Map pp108–9

☎ 224 915 765; www.mat.cz; Karlovo náměstí 19, Nové Město; tickets 99Kč; M Karlovo Náměstí

A former film and TV studio's private screening room (there are only 40 seats), Kino Mat is now a hip arthouse cinema where film buffs sip espressos in the celluloid-decorated downstairs bar while discussing the use of visual metaphor in *Citizen Kane*. The programme includes the latest Czech films (with English subtitles) and the latest European films (with Czech ones).

KINO SVĚTOZOR Map pp108–9

☎ 224 946 824; www.kinosvetozor.cz; Vodičkova 41, Nové Město; tickets 60-110Kč; M Můstek

The Světozor is under the same management as Kino Aero but is more central, and has the same emphasis on classic cinema

PRAGUE SPRING

First held in 1946, the Prague Spring (Pražské jaro) international music festival is the Czech Republic's best-known annual cultural event. It begins on 12 May, the anniversary of composer Bedřich Smetana's death, with a procession from his grave at Vyšehrad (p117) to the Municipal House (p99), and a performance there of his patriotic song cycle *Má vlast* (My Homeland). The festival runs until 3 June, and the beautiful concert venues are as big a drawcard as the music.

Tickets can be obtained through the official Prague Spring Box Office (Map pp88–9; ☎ 227 059 234; www.festival.cz; Náměstí Jana Palacha, Staré Město; 10am-6pm Mon-Fri) in the Rudolfinum, or from any branch of Ticketpro (see the boxed text, p199).

If you want a guaranteed seat at a Prague Spring concert try to book it by mid-March at the latest, though a few seats may still be available as late as the end of May.

and arthouse films screened in their original language – everything from *Battleship Potemkin* and *Casablanca* to *Annie Hall* and *Motorcycle Diaries*.

PALACE CINEMAS Map pp108–9

☎ 257 181 212; www.palacecinemas.cz; Slovanský dům, Na Příkopě 22, Nové Město; tickets 169Kč; M Náměstí Republiky

Housed in the posh Slovanský dům shopping centre, this is central Prague's main popcorn palace – a modern 10-screen multiplex showing first-run Hollywood films (mostly in English). There's also a 12-screen multiplex on the top floor of the huge Nový Smíchov (Map p138; Plzeňská 8, Smíchov; M Anděl) shopping centre.

THEATRE

Most Czech drama is, not surprisingly, performed in Czech, which rather diminishes its appeal to non-Czech-speakers. However, there are some English-language productions, and many predominantly visual shows at which language is not a barrier.

Prague is famous for its black-light theatre – occasionally called just 'black theatre' – a hybrid of mime, drama, dance and special effects in which live actors wearing fluorescent costumes do their thing in front of a black backdrop lit only by ultraviolet light (it's a growth industry in Prague, with at least half a dozen venues). An even older Czech tradition is puppetry, and the city has several marionette shows on offer.

CELETNÁ THEATRE Map pp88–9

Divadlo v Celetné; ☎ 222 326 843; www.divadlovceletne.cz; Celetná 17, Staré Město; tickets 160-350Kč; box office 10am-7.30pm Mon-Fri, 2-7.30pm Sat & Sun; M Náměstí Republiky

The Divadlo v Celetné, in a courtyard between Celetná and Štupartská, stages mainly Czech drama, both old and new, some foreign plays (including Shakespeare and Tom Stoppard) translated into Czech, and the occasional opera production by the students of the Prague Conservatory.

IMAGE THEATRE Map pp88–9

Divadlo Image; ☎ 222 314 448; www.imagetheatre.cz; Pařížská 4, Staré Město; tickets 480Kč; box office 9am-8pm; M Staroměstská

Founded in 1989, this company uses creative black-light theatre along with pantomime, modern dance and video – not to mention liberal doses of slapstick – to tell its stories. The staging can be very effective, but the atmosphere is often dictated by audience reaction.

LATERNA MAGIKA Map pp108–9

☎ 224 931 482; www.laterna.cz; Nova Scéna, Národní třída 4, Nové Město; tickets adult/child 680/300Kč; box office 10am-8pm Mon-Sat; M Národní Třída

Laterna Magika has been wowing audiences, both at home and abroad, ever since its first cutting-edge multimedia show caused a stir at the 1958 Brussels World Fair. Its imaginative blend of live dance, opera, music and projected images continues to pull in the crowds. Nová Scena, the futuristic glass-block building next to the National Theatre, has been home to Laterna Magika since it moved here from its birthplace in the basement of the Adria Palace in the mid-1970s. Some agencies (which charge 735Kč a ticket) may tell you it's booked out, but you can often bag a leftover seat at the box office on the day before a performance, or a no-show seat half an hour before the show starts.

MINOR THEATRE Map pp108–9

Divadlo Minor; ☎ 222 231 351; www.minor.cz; Vodičkova 6, Nové Město; tickets 80-200Kč; ⏲ box office 10am-1.30pm & 2.30-8pm Mon-Fri, 11am-6pm Sat & Sun; Ⓜ Karlovo Náměstí

Divadlo Minor is a wheelchair-accessible children's theatre that offers a fun mix of puppets, clown shows and pantomime. There are performances (in Czech) at 9.30am Monday to Friday and at 6pm or 7.30pm Tuesday to Thursday, and you can usually get a ticket at the door before the show.

NATIONAL MARIONETTE THEATRE

Map pp88–9

Národní divadlo marionet; ☎ 224 819 323; www.mozart.cz; Žatecká 1, Staré Město; tickets adult/child 590/490Kč; ⏲ box office 10am-8pm; Ⓜ Staroměstská

Loudly touted as the longest-running classical marionette show in the city – it has been performed almost continuously since 1991 – *Don Giovanni* is a life-sized puppet version of the Mozart opera that has spawned several imitations around town. Younger kids' attention might begin to wander fairly early on during this two-hour show.

REDUTA THEATRE Map pp108–9

Divadlo Reduta; ☎ 257 921 835; www.blacktheatresrnec.cz; Národní třída 20, Nové Město; tickets adult/child 590/490Kč; ⏲ box office 3-7pm Mon-Fri; Ⓜ Národní Třída

The Reduta Theatre is home to the Black Theatre of Jiří Srnec, who was a founding member of Prague's original black-light theatre back in the early 1960s. Today the company's productions include versions of *Alice in Wonderland* and *Peter Pan,* and a compilation of the best of black theatre from the early days.

SPEJBL & HURVÍNEK THEATRE

Map pp132–3

Divadlo Spejbla a Hurvínka; ☎ 224 316 784; www.spejbl-hurvinek.cz; Dejvická 38, Dejvice; tickets 50-90Kč; ⏲ box office 10am-2pm & 3-6pm Tue-Fri, 1-5pm Sat & Sun; Ⓜ Dejvická

Created in 1930 by puppeteer Josef Skupa, Spejbl and Hurvinek are the Czech marionette equivalents of Punch and Judy, although they are father and son rather than husband and wife. The shows are in the Czech language, but most can be followed whatever language you speak.

ŠVANDOVO DIVADLO NA SMÍCHOVĚ

Map p138

Šandovo Theatre in Smíchov; ☎ 257 318 666; www.svandovodivadlo.cz; Stefaníkova 57; tickets 150-300Kč; ⏲ box office 11am-7pm Mon-Fri, 5-7pm Sat & Sun; 🚋 6, 9, 12, 20

This experimental theatre space, performing Czech and international dramatic works, is unique for its commitment to staging 'English-friendly' performances, by which they mean English-language theatre or with English subtitles. It also hosts occasional live music and dance, as well as regular 'Stage Talks', unscripted discussions with noted personalities. A couple of years ago, one featured Václav Havel and Lou Reed.

TA FANTASTIKA Map pp88–9

☎ 222 221 366; www.tafantastika.cz; Karlova 8, Staré Město; tickets 350-650Kč; ⏲ box office 11am-9.30pm; Ⓜ Staroměstská

Established in New York in 1981 by Czech émigré Petr Kratochvil, Ta Fantastika moved to Prague in 1989. The theatre produces black-light theatre based on classic literature and legends such as *Alice in Wonderland, Excalibur, The Picture of Dorian Gray* and *Joan of Arc.*

THEATRE ON THE BALUSTRADE

Map pp88–9

Divadlo Na Zábradlí; ☎ 222 868 868; www.nazabradli.cz; Anenské náměstí 5, Staré Město; tickets 90-300Kč; ⏲ box office 2-4pm & 4.30-7pm Mon-Fri, 2hr before show starts Sat & Sun; 🚋 17, 18

The theatre where Václav Havel honed his skills as a playwright four decades ago is now the city's main venue for serious Czech-language drama, including works by a range of foreign playwrights translated into Czech.

SPORTS & ACTIVITIES

top picks

- **Cycling** along the Vltava (p206)
- **Hiking** in Stromovka (p206)
- **AXA Arena** (p209)
- **Stadión Eden** (p209)
- **Czech Lawn Tennis Club** (p209)
- **Divoká Šárka** (p208)
- **Cybex Health Club** (p206)

What's your recommendation? www.lonelyplanet.com/prague

SPORTS & ACTIVITIES

The Czechs have always been keen on sports and outdoor activities, and Prague's extensive green spaces – from the former royal hunting grounds of Stromovka to the riverside parks and islands strung along the Vltava – offer plenty of opportunity for exercise. Although hiking, swimming and ice hockey are the traditional favourites, recent years have seen a steady increase in the numbers of cyclists in the city as bike lanes and dedicated cycle trails have been introduced.

Golf was never a high priority during the communist era, but the emergence of a class of young professionals with money to burn has seen a growth of interest in more exclusive outdoor pursuits, including the construction of a championship golf course at Karlštejn (p230).

HEALTH & FITNESS

There has been a move away from the sweaty gyms and weight rooms of the past towards a new generation of spas and health clubs, where the goal is pampering rather than fitness. Most are associated with top-end hotels – check out http://prague.tv/prague/health/spas for a list.

GYMS & SPAS

The luxurious Cybex Health Club & Spa (Map pp126–7; ☎ 224 842 375; www.cybexprg.cz; Pobřežní 1, Nové Město; ⏲ 6am-10pm Mon-Fri, 7am-10pm Sat & Sun; Ⓜ Florenc) in the Hotel Hilton charges 900Kč for a day pass, which gives access to the gym, pool, sauna, Jacuzzi and steam room, and 1200Kč for a half-hour massage.

If you're looking for a workout, you can use the *posilovna* (weights room) at the Sportcentrum YMCA (Map p106; ☎ 224 875 811; Na Poříčí 12, Nové Město; ⏲ 6.30am-9.30pm Mon-Fri, 10am-8.30pm Sat & Sun) for 120Kč per hour. There's also the centrally located Fitness Týn (Map pp88–9; ☎ 224 808 295; Týnská 19, Staré Město; ⏲ 7am-9pm Mon-Fri, 10am-8pm Sat & Sun), which charges 95Kč (75Kč for ISIC holders) for use of the weights room, and 200Kč for a half-hour massage.

ACTIVITIES

Summer or winter, rain or shine, Prague is packed with places where you can work off the beer-and-dumpling calorie rush – from hiking and biking trails to swimming pools, skate parks and ice rinks.

HIKING

The Czech Republic is covered with a network of waymarked hiking trails, colour-coded and clearly marked on a range of excellent 1:50 000 and 1:25 000 hiking maps *(turistické mapy)*. Prague has its share of trails – the Klub Českých Turistů (Czech Hiking Club) 1:50,000 map sheet 36, *Okolí Prahy-západ* (Prague & Around, West) covers the best hiking in and around the city, including Beroun and Karlštejn.

For easy walks of an hour or two, you can head for the big parks and nature reserves – Stromovka in the north (see Walking Tour, p134), Prokopské udolí in the southwest, and Michelský les and Kunratický les in the southeast – or follow the riverbank trails north from Prague Zoo to the little ferry at Roztoky, and return to the city by train.

A more challenging day hike, which takes in a visit to Karlštejn Castle (p230), begins at the town of Beroun to the southwest of the city. From Beroun train station follow a red-marked trail east for 6km to the Monastery of St John under the Rock (Klášter sv Jan pod Skálou), situated in a spectacular limestone gorge. From here, continue on the red trail through wooded hills for another 8km to Karlštejn, where you can catch another train back to the city centre. Allow five hours from Beroun to Karlštejn.

CYCLING

Prague has a long way to go before it's a cycling town comparable with big cities in Germany, or even Vienna. Nevertheless, there's a group of hard-core cyclists at work promoting things like commuter cycling, extending bike paths and raising driver awareness. Their efforts are starting to bear fruit. Prague now has a relatively complete, if disjointed, network of bike paths – signposted in yellow – that crisscross the city centre and fan out in all directions. Recreational cyclists will probably be content just to putz around on one of the tours offered by the bike rental companies (p251). More serious cyclists should consider buying a good map, hiring a bike and hitting the outlying trails for a day or two.

Arguably the best cycling trails lead off to the north following the Vltava River in the direction of Germany. Someday, the Prague–Dresden run will be the stuff of cycling legend, but for now there are still significant gaps in the route. That said, the path northward along the river is nearly complete as far as the town of Kralupy nad Vltavou (20km from Prague; it's possible to return by rail), from where you can continue on back roads to Mělník (p233). There are plenty of bridges and ferries to take you back and forth across the river, and some really great trails leading inland along the way. From the centre of Prague, start off at Čechův most (the bridge over the Vltava by the Intercontinental Hotel), ride across the bridge and up the hill to Letná. From there, follow the signs to Stromovka and on to Prague Zoo. The riverside trail continues northward from the zoo.

Most large bookstores stock cycling maps (*cycloturisticka mapa*). One of the best is the 2008 edition Freytag & Berndt *Praha a Okoli* (Prague & Surroundings; 1:75 000), which costs about 100Kč. Another good choice for the northwestern section of the city is *Z prahy na kole, Severozapad* (Around Prague by Bike, Northwest; 1:65 000) for about 65Kč. Remember to pack water and sunscreen and always watch out for cars. Czech drivers, inexplicably, are rabidly anti-cyclist.

There are several useful websites:

Cyklojizdy (www.cyklojizdy.cz) Mostly in Czech, with an English summary – portal that organises the twice-yearly (spring and autumn) Critical Mass rides to raise cycling awareness.

Grant's Prague Bike Blog (http://praguebikeblog.blogspot.com) An American expat's weekly cycling exploits, with great ride ideas, maps and photos.

Greenways (www.pragueviennagreenways.org) Details of a 250-mile cycle trail linking Prague and Vienna.

Prague City Hall (http://doprava.praha-mesto.cz) The city's public transport portal with a nice section in English on bike trails and rules for cyclists.

Hire

City Bike (Map pp88–9; ☎ 776 180 284; www.citybike-prague.com; Králodvorská 5, Staré Město; 4/8hr 400/500Kč; 9am-7pm Apr-Oct; M Náměstí Republiky) Rental includes helmet, padlock and map.

Praha Bike (Map pp88–9; ☎ 732 388 880; www.prahabike.cz; Dlouhá 24, Staré Město; 4/8hr 380/520Kč; 9am-7pm 15 Mar-15 Nov; 5, 8, 14) Hires out good, new bikes with lock, helmet and map, plus free luggage storage. Also offers student discounts and group bike tours (also see p251).

GOLF

The Czech Republic is one of the undiscovered gems of European golf, with new, high-quality courses springing up all over the place – the country has gone from having three 18-hole courses in 1990 to no fewer than 70 in 2008. There are a couple of nine-hole courses within the city boundary, but the nearest championship course is at Karlštejn. For more information, see www.czechgolfguide.com.

GOLF CLUB PRAHA Map pp58–9

☎ 257 216 584; www.gcp.cz; Plzeňská 401/2, Motol; green fees (nine holes) Mon-Fri 400-500Kč, Sat, Sun & hols 600Kč; 7am-dusk; 7, 9, 10

Duffers will be happy to know that Prague has a nine-hole golf course, complete with driving range and chipping and putting greens, behind the Hotel Golf in the western suburbs; you can hire a set of clubs for 500Kč. Take tram 7, 9 or 10 west to the Hotel Golf stop, and follow the trail across the course to the clubhouse.

GOLF & COUNTRY CLUB off map pp58–9

☎ 244 460 435; www.hodkovicky.cz; Vltavanů 982, Hodkovičky; green fees (nine holes) Mon-Fri 600Kč, Sat & Sun 800Kč, driving range per 50 balls 100Kč; golf course 8am-7pm, driving range 7am-9pm; 3, 17, 21

Way out on the southern edge of the city, this place also offers a nine-hole course, a driving range and chipping and putting greens. Take tram 3, 17 or 21 south to the Černý kůň stop, and walk west towards the river on V Náklích for 100m (follow the signs for Hostel Boathouse), then turn down the first right immediately after passing under the railway bridge.

KARLŠTEJN GOLF COURSE

☎ 311 604 999; www.karlstejn-golf.cz; Běleč 272, Líteň; green fees Mon-Fri 2000Kč, Sat, Sun & hols 3000Kč; 7am-9pm May-Aug, 8am-7pm Sep, 8am-6pm Apr & Oct

The closest 18-hole facility to Prague is this prestigious championship course overlooking Karlštejn Castle (p230), southwest of the city. It's 4km south of Karlštejn village, on the southern side of the Berounka River.

RUNNING

The Prague International Marathon (Pražský mezinárodní maraton; ☎ 224 919 209; www.pim.cz; Záhořanského 3, 120 00 Praha 2), established in 1989, is held annually in mid- to late May. It's considered to be one of the world's top 10 city marathons, and attracted 4517 entrants in 2008. There's also a half-marathon, held in late March. If you'd like to compete, you can register online or obtain entry forms from the website. The registration fee is €60.

SKATING

With ice hockey probably the country's most popular spectator sport, it's no surprise that the Czechs are skate-mad. In winter, when the mercury drops below zero, sections of parks are sprayed with water and turned into makeshift ice rinks. In summer, ice skates are replaced with inline skates and street hockey takes over, while the park trails and riverside cycle tracks are taken over by whole families of rollerbladers.

PŮJČOVNA BRUSLÍ MIAMI Map pp132–3

Miami Skate Rental; ☎ 731 281 571; Nad Štolou 1, Holešovice; skate rental per hr 80Kč; 9am-9pm May-Sep, noon-9pm Oct, 2-8pm Apr; 1, 8, 15, 25, 26

A great way to spend a summer's day: you can rent inline skates from this place (they speak a bit of English), which is close to the National Technical Museum, then head off to explore the extensive skating trails in Letná Gardens before enjoying a cold one at the Letná beer garden (p187).

ŠTVANICE STADIUM Map pp132–3

Zimní stadión Štvanice; ☎ 233 378 327; Ostrov Štvanice 1125, Holešovice; adult/child under 7yr 70/20Kč; public skating 2.30-4pm Mon & Wed, 3-5pm Tue, Thu & Fri; 3, 26

This is the oldest ice-hockey stadium in Central Europe – Czechoslovakia's first ice-hockey match on artificial ice was played here in 1931. It provides public skating sessions as well as hosting ice-hockey and roller-hockey games in season. Skate hire costs 80Kč.

SWIMMING

DIVOKÁ ŠÁRKA Map pp58–9

Evropská; 20, 26

Prague summers can be hot, and at weekends many locals escape the heat by heading for the open-air swimming at Divoká Šárka (also see p130). There's a large lake with a sandy beach and grassy area for sunbathing, plus volleyball and table tennis facilities (admission 70Kč). Further down the valley you'll find a stream-fed open-air swimming pool (admission 50Kč); both lake and pool can be a bit chilly, even in high summer.

PODOLÍ SWIMMING POOL Map pp58–9

Plavecký stadión Podolí; ☎ 241 433 952; Podolská 74, Podolí; admission per 1½/3hr 80/125Kč, child under 13yr half-price; 6am-9.45pm; 3, 16, 17, 21

There are more swimming and tanning opportunities at this huge swimming complex with Olympic-sized pools, both indoor and outdoor, and plenty of sunbathing space (best to bring footwear for the grotty showers, though). To get there, take the tram to the Kublov stop; from there it's a further five-minute walk south.

SPECTATOR SPORT

Those widescreen TVs perched ubiquitously on pub walls and newsstands groaning under the weight of sports magazines give the game away: the Czechs are avid sports fans. From soccer to ice hockey, rarely a weekend goes by without some sporting showdown providing fertile ground for an in-depth, post-match analysis – in the pub, of course.

FOOTBALL

Football is a national passion in the Czech Republic. The national team performs well in international competitions, having won the European Championship in 1976 (as Czechoslovakia), and reached the final in 1996 and the semifinal in 2004. Sadly, it crashed out in the first round of the 2006 World Cup in Germany, but bounced back to be ranked sixth in the world by FIFA in the run-up to Euro 2008, a ranking that seemed over-optimistic when the Czechs failed to reach the quarter-finals. Home international matches are played at Slavia Praha's brand new, 21,000-seat Stadión Eden in eastern Prague, which opened in May 2008.

Prague's two big football clubs, SK Slavia Praha and AC Sparta Praha, are both leading contenders in the national *fotbal* (football) league. Two other Prague-based teams – FC Bohemians (Map pp58–9; ☎ 271 721 459; www.bohemians1905.cz; Vršovická 31, Vinohrady; 🚋 4, 22) and FK Viktoria Žižkov (Map pp126–7; ☎ 221 423 427; www.fkvz.cz; Seifertova, Žižkov; 🚋 5, 9, 26) – attract fervent local support. The season runs from August to December and February to June, and matches are mostly played on Wednesday, Saturday and Sunday afternoons.

AXA ARENA Map pp132–3

☎ 296 111 400; www.sparta.cz; Milady Horákové 98, Bubeneč; 🚋 1, 8, 15, 25, 26

The all-seater AXA Arena, with a capacity of 20,854, is the home ground of Sparta Praha – winners of the Czech football league in 2001, 2003, 2005 and 2007, and of the Czech National Cup in 2004, 2006 and 2007. The club was founded in 1893.

STADIÓN EDEN Map pp58–9

Stadión Eden; ☎ 257 213 290; www.slavia.cz; www.stadioneden.cz; Vladivostocká, Vršovice; 🚋 6, 7, 22, 23, 24

This brand-new stadium is home to SK Slavia Praha, founded in 1892 – one of the oldest sporting clubs in continental Europe and an honorary member of England's Football Association. Czech National Cup winner in 1997, 1999 and 2002, Slavia holds an unusual record – the design of its distinctive red-and-white strip has remained unchanged since 1896.

ICE HOCKEY

It's a toss-up whether football or ice hockey inspires more passion in the hearts of Prague sports fans, but hockey probably wins. The Czech national team has been rampant in the last decade, winning the World Championship three years running (1999 to 2001) and taking the title again in 2005; it reached the final in 2006 but lost to Sweden. It also won Olympic gold in 1998 by defeating the mighty Russians in the final.

Prague's two big hockey teams are HC Sparta Praha and HC Slavia Praha, both of which compete in the 14-team national league. Promising young players are often lured away by the promise of big money in North America's National Hockey League, and there is a sizeable Czech contingent in the NHL.

Sparta plays at the huge, modern T-Mobile Aréna at Výstaviště in Holešovice, and Slavia Praha at O2 Arena; games are fast and furious, and the atmosphere can be electrifying – it's well worth making the effort to see a game. The season runs from September to early April.

O2 ARENA Map pp58–9

☎ 266 212 111; www.sazkaarena.com, www.hc-slavia.cz; Ocelařská 2, Vysočany; Ⓜ Českomoravská

The O2 Arena is Prague's biggest multipurpose venue, and home rink of HC Slavia Praha, Czech Extraliga champions in 2008. It can accommodate up to 18,000 spectators, and is used to host sporting events, rock concerts, exhibitions and other major events as well as hockey games.

T-MOBILE ARÉNA Map pp132–3

☎ 266 727 443; www.hcsparta.cz; Za Elektrámou 419, Výstaviště, Holešovice; 🚋 5, 12, 14, 15, 17

You can see HC Sparta Praha – Czech Extraliga champions 2006 and 2007 – play at the 13,000-capacity T-Mobile Aréna beside the Exhibition Grounds in Holešovice.

TENNIS

Tennis is another sport in which the Czechs have excelled, having produced world-class players such as Jan Kodeš, Ivan Lendl, Petr Korda, Hana Mandlikova, Jana Novotna, Cyril Suk and up-and-coming star Nicole Vaidisova. Plus, of course, very probably the finest female tennis player ever, Martina Navratilova.

In May the 8000-seat centre court at the Czech Lawn Tennis Club on Štvanice Island hosts the Prague Open (www.pragueopen.cz), a WTA competition that was established in 2001 in the hope of luring international tennis talent back to the Czech capital (Prague no longer hosts the Czech Open, which is now held at Prostějov). In 2005 the Prague Open was joined by a women's WTA tournament, which runs concurrently.

CZECH LAWN TENNIS CLUB Map pp132–3

Český Lawn-Tennis Klub; ☎ 222 316 317; www.cltk.cz; Ostrov Štvanice 38, Holešovice; match tickets 100-150Kč; 🚋 3, 26

Founded in 1893, this is the oldest and most prestigious tennis club in the country (despite the name, all its courts are clay!), and it was here that Ivan Lendl and Martina Navratilova learned their craft.

HORSE RACING

PRAGUE RACECOURSE off map pp58–9

Velká Chuchle závodiště Praha; ☎ 257 941 431; www.velka-chuchle.cz; Radotínská 69, Velká Chuchle; adult/child under 18yr 100Kč/free; 🚌 129, 172, 243, 244, 255

If you fancy a flutter on the ponies, check out the *dostihy* (horse racing) scene at this racecourse on the southern edge of the city. There are races run every Sunday from April to October – check the website for more information and the full racing calendar. You can get to the racecourse by taking the bus from Smíchovské Nádraží metro station.

SLEEPING

top picks

- **Absolut Hotel** (p224)
- **Angelo Hotel** (p226)
- **Castle Steps** (p215)
- **Czech Inn** (p221)
- **Hotel Aria** (p215)
- **Hotel Josef** (p217)
- **Hotel U Zlaté Studné** (p215)
- **Icon Hotel** (p218)
- **Mandarin Oriental** (p215)

SLEEPING

A 2007 headline in the *Mlada Fronta Dnes* newspaper said it all – 'More hotels than streets'. According to the article, there were 286 named streets in the Prague 1 postal district (the city centre, including Staré Město and Malá Strana), and no fewer than 320 hotels.

Prague today offers a wide range of accommodation options, from cosy, romantic hotels set in historic town houses to luxurious international chain hotels, and from budget hostels and pensions to a new generation of sharply styled boutique hotels. However, it is no longer the bargain it was back in the 1990s – hotel rates have increased sharply and along with the strong Czech crown have put accommodation prices on a par with many cities in Western Europe.

The last five years has seen a huge boom in hotel building in Prague, especially in the four- and five-star sector. The Hotel Josef led the way for boutique hotels in 2002, though it took a few more years before the design hotel concept really began to take off in Prague, with a flurry of new places opening from 2005 on, notably the Yasmin and the Icon.

Luxury hotels are also beginning to pop up all over the place – the long-established Four Seasons in Staré Město and the much newer Mandarin Oriental in Malá Strana are soon to be joined in 2009 by offerings from Kempinksi, Rocco Forte and Le Méridien, among others.

However, there is still a dearth of decent budget to midrange accommodation – it's very hard to find a good double room for less than 3000Kč (around £100/€125) unless you're prepared to stay in a backpacker hostel.

The oversupply at the top end of the market has resulted in falling occupancy rates in luxury hotels – in mid-2008 sales were down 20% on the previous year. Many places are dropping their prices in an attempt to attract business, so it's well worth shopping around and looking for special offers or even asking for discounts.

An increasing number of Prague hotels provide specially adapted rooms and facilities for wheelchair users; we have noted these facilities in the individual listings.

Accommodation listings in this book are broken down first by neighbourhood, then by budget, from most to least expensive.

LONGER-TERM RENTALS

More and more travellers are discovering the pleasures of renting an apartment in Prague. Before you scoff at the idea, consider that the extra cost of a very basic self-catering flat near the centre means minimal transport costs, access to cheap local food, and the freedom to come and go as you like.

Many Prague agencies will find a flat for you (see the boxed text, opposite). Typical rates for a modern two-person apartment with living room–bedroom, bathroom, TV and kitchenette range from around 1500Kč per night for a place in the outer suburbs, to around 3000Kč for a flat near Old Town Square; longer stays can knock the price down to as little as 20,000Kč for a month in a two-person flat in Žižkov. All short-term rental apartments are fully furnished and serviced, meaning that utilities (gas, water, electricity) and bed linen are included in the price, and staff will clean up and change the beds at least weekly.

The real estate section of the weekly Prague Post (www.praguepost.cz) newspaper also lists agencies and private individuals with apartments to rent by the month.

RESERVATIONS

Booking your accommodation in advance is strongly recommended (especially if you want to stay in or near the centre), and there are dozens of agencies that will help you find a place to stay; some are better than others. The places listed in the boxed text (opposite) are reliable, and even if you turn up in peak period without a booking, these agencies should be able to find you a bed.

Hotels usually require you to check out on the day of departure between 10am and noon. As to check-in times, there are no hard-and-fast rules, but if you're going to arrive late in the evening, it's best to mention this when you book your room.

ROOM RATES

A double room in a midrange hotel in central Prague will cost around 4000Kč in high

ACCOMMODATION AGENCIES

- Alfa Tourist Service (Map pp108–9; ☎ 224 230 037; www.alfatourist.cz; Opletalova 38, Nové Město; ⌚ 9am-5pm Mon-Fri) Can provide accommodation in student hostels, pensions, hotels and private rooms.
- Apartments.cz (Map pp88–9; ☎ 224 990 990; www.apartments.cz; Divadelní 24, Staré Město; ⌚ 8am-8pm) Long-established specialist in holiday apartments near the city centre.
- AVE Travel (Map pp108–9; ☎ 251 551 011 or 224 223 226; www.avetravel.cz; Praha hlavní nádraží, Nové Město; ⌚ 6am-11pm) Convenient offices at the airport, main train station and Praha-Holešovice train station. The branch at the main train station specialises in finding last-minute accommodation.
- Happy House Rentals (Map pp108–9; ☎ 224 946 890; www.happyhouserentals.com; Jungmannova 30, Nové Město; ⌚ 8am-6pm Mon-Fri) Specialises in rental apartments, both short-term and long-term.
- Hostel.cz (☎ 415 658 580; www.hostel.cz) Website database of around 60 hostels and cheap pensions, with a secure online booking system.
- Mary's Travel & Tourist Service (Map p121; ☎ 222 253 510; www.marys.cz; Italská 31, Vinohrady; ⌚ 9am-9pm) Friendly, efficient agency offering private rooms, hostels, pensions, apartments and hotels in all price ranges in Prague and surrounding areas.
- Prague Apartments (☎ 604 168 756; www.prague-apartment.com) Web-based service with range of comfortable, IKEA-furnished flats. Availability of apartments displayed online.
- Stop City (Map p121; ☎ 222 521 233; www.stopcity.com; Vinohradská 24, Vinohrady; ⌚ 9am-9pm Apr-Oct, 10am-8pm Nov-Mar) Specialises in apartments, private rooms and pensions in the city centre, Vinohrady and Žižkov areas.

season; outside the centre, this might fall to around 3000Kč. Top-range hotels cost from 4000Kč and up, with the best luxury hotels charging 6000Kč and more. The budget options listed in this chapter charge 2000Kč or less for a double room. Note that some midrange and top-end hotels quote rates in euros, and a few quote in US dollars. At these hotels you can pay cash in Czech crowns if you like, but the price will depend on the exchange rate on the day you settle the bill.

The rates quoted in this chapter are for the high season, which generally covers April to June, September and October, and the Christmas–New Year holidays. July and August are midseason, and the rest of the year is low season, when rates can drop by 30% or 40%.

Even high-season rates can be inflated by up to 15% on certain dates, notably at New Year, Easter, during the Prague Spring festival, and at weekends (Thursday to Sunday) in May, June and September. On the other hand, you can often find much lower rates from January to March and there are often good internet booking deals from June to August.

Most hostel, pension and budget-hotel rates do not include breakfast; most midrange and top-end hotel rates do.

PRICE GUIDE

The categories used in this chapter indicate the cost per night of a standard double room in high season.

€€€	more than 4000Kč (more than €160)
€€	2000Kč to 4000Kč (€80 to €160)
€	less than 2000Kč (less than €80)

HRADČANY

Hradčany is the place to stay if you're looking for peace and quiet. You'll be within a short walk of the castle, but when the crowds ebb away at the end of the day the streets are almost deserted.

ROMANTIK HOTEL U RAKA

Map pp70–1 Hotel €€€

☎ 220 511 100; www.romantikhotel-uraka.cz; Černínská 10; s/d from 4000/4500Kč; 🚊 22, 23

Concealed in a manicured rock garden in a quiet corner of Hradčany, the historic Hotel U Raka is an atmospheric, late-18th-century timber cottage with just six elegant, low-ceilinged doubles, complete with timber beams, wooden floors and red-brick fireplaces. With its cosy bedrooms, attentive staff, artistic décor and farmhouse kitchen-style breakfast room, it's ideal for a romantic getaway, and the castle is less than 10 minutes' walk away. Be sure to book at least a few months ahead.

NEAR THE AIRPORT

The following places all lie at the western edge of the city and are the best options for staying within easy reach of the airport.

Hotel Elegant (off Map pp58–9; ☎ 235 300 521; www.hotelelegant.cz; Ruzyňská 197, Ruzyně; s/d 2790/3300Kč; 🚌 225; 🅿) A stylish 1930s functionalist building that has been converted into a boutique hotel. Only five minutes from the airport by car, or seven minutes on bus 225; get off at the Ruzyňská škola stop.

Hotel Tranzit (off Map pp58–9; ☎ 236 161 111; www.hoteltranzit.cz; Aviatická; s/d from 2875/3125Kč; 🚌 100, 119, 179; 🅿 💻) Modern hotel with bright, attractive rooms just five minutes' walk from the airport terminal, with some wheelchair-accessible rooms.

Pension Větrný Mlyn (off Map pp58–9; ☎ 235 301 686; www.pensionmlyn.cz; Ruzyňská 3/96, Ruzyně; s/d 1000/1600Kč; 🚌 225; 🅿 💻) The 'Windmill' is a friendly, family-run pension where all rooms have TV and en suite shower. Free wi-fi. Across the street from Hotel Elegant (see above).

Ramada Airport Hotel (off Map pp58–9; ☎ 220 111 250; www.hotel-ramada-airport.info; Terminal Jih, K Letišti 25a, Ruzyně; r from 2500Kč; 🅿) The Ramada is at the southern terminal of Ruzyně airport, four stops on bus 100, 119, 179 or 225 from the main terminal.

DOMUS HENRICI

Map pp70–1 Hotel €€€

☎ 220 511 369; www.domus-henrici.cz; Loretánská 11; s/d 3875/4250Kč; 🚋 22, 23; 💻

This historic building in a quiet corner of Hradčany is intentionally nondescript out front, hinting that peace and privacy are top priorities here. There are eight spacious and stylish rooms, half with private fax, scanner/copier and internet access (via an ethernet port), and all with polished wood floors, large bathrooms, comfy beds and fluffy bathrobes. Service is impeccable, and there's an attractive guest lounge as well as a sunny outdoor terrace with gorgeous views over the city. Free internet and wi-fi in the hotel lobby.

HOTEL U KRÁLE KARLA

Map pp70–1 Hotel €€

☎ 257 531 211; www.romantichotels.cz; Úvoz 4; s/d 3500/4000Kč; 🚋 12, 20 22, 23; 🅿

The 'King Charles' is a cosy, romantic hotel set in a lovely, 'baroquefied' Gothic building, with rooms set on landings around an impressive central atrium with a stained-glass ceiling. The atmosphere here leans towards a sort of medieval–fairytale look, with studded wood-and-leather antique furniture, painted timber ceilings, murals, stained-glass windows and statues of old Czech kings and queens. The rooms are filled with dark polished-wood furniture, Persian rugs, swagged velvet drapes and ostentatious fireplaces – charming, if you like that sort of thing. The bathrooms, however, though reasonably sized, are beige and forgettable. There's also a restaurant on site with room service and a sauna for guest use. The hotel vies with Hotel Neruda for the title of closest hotel to the castle; it's just a few minutes' walk to the main gate.

RESIDENCE MONASTERY

Map pp70–1 Hotel €€

☎ 233 090 200; www.avehotels.cz/prague/monastery.html; Strahovské nádvoří 13; s/d 2475/2900Kč; 🚋 22, 23; 🅿 💻

Ancient meets modern at this small hotel in the peaceful courtyard of Strahov Monastery, where the only noise likely to disturb you is the occasional tolling of a church bell. The 12 quirkily shaped rooms in this 17th-century building have been given a bright, IKEA-style modern makeover with polished wood floors, plain white walls hung with photos of Prague, and a splash of colour from the bedspread and sofa. (Two of the rooms are also wheelchair-accessible.) And it's all just a five-minute walk away from the castle. There's also free wi-fi.

MALÁ STRANA

Lots of Malá Strana's lovely old Renaissance and baroque buildings have been converted into hotels and apartments, making this a good district to stay in if you're looking for a romantic atmosphere. You'll also be within walking distance of Charles Bridge and surrounded by lots of good restaurants and bars.

MANDARIN ORIENTAL

Map pp76–7 Boutique Hotel €€€

☎ 233 088 888; www.mandarinoriental.com/prague; Nebovidská 1; r from 6200Kč, ste from 16,750Kč; 🚊 12, 20, 22, 23; 💻

One of Prague's most talked about new hotels, the Mandarin occupies the converted premises of a 17th-century Dominican monastery. The main talking point – other than the celeb guest list, which ranges from Madonna to the Dalai Lama – is the sumptuous hotel spa, built inside a Renaissance chapel with the remains of a 14th-century church preserved beneath a glass floor, but the rooms are pretty special too. The interiors were designed by the same team who did the Burj Al Arab in Dubai. Some have antique parquet floors, some have vaulted ceilings, others are completely modern; the most appealing are the garden rooms dotted around the old cloister gardens.

HOTEL ARIA Map pp76–7 Boutique Hotel €€€

☎ 225 334 111; www.aria.cz; Tržiště 9; d from 5750Kč; 🚊 12, 20, 22, 23; P 💻

The Aria offers five-star luxury with a musical theme – each of the four floors is dedicated to a musical genre (jazz, opera, classical and contemporary), and each room celebrates a particular artist or musician and contains a selection of their music that you can enjoy on the in-room hi-fi system. Service is professional and efficient, and the rooms are furnished with crisp bed linen, plump continental quilts, Molton Brown toiletries and complimentary chocolates. Other facilities include a music and movie library, screening room, fitness centre and steam room. The location is very central, a few minutes' walk from Charles Bridge, and just around the corner from a major tram stop.

HOTEL U ZLATÉ STUDNĚ

Map pp76–7 Hotel €€€

☎ 257 011 213; www.zlatastudna.cz; U Zlaté Studně 4; d from 4875Kč, ste from 10,625Kč; M Malostranská; 💻

'At the Golden Well' is one of Malá Strana's hidden secrets, tucked away at the end of a cobbled cul-de-sac – a Renaissance house that once belonged to Emperor Rudolf II (and was once inhabited by astronomer Tycho Brahe), with an unbeatable location perched on the southern slope of the castle hill. The rooms (five twins, 12 doubles and three luxury suites) are quiet and spacious, with polished wood floors, reproduction period furniture, and blue-and-white bathrooms with underfloor heating and whirlpool baths; many have views over the Palace Gardens below. The hotel has an excellent restaurant (p158) and a terrace with superb outlook over the city.

HOTEL NERUDA

Map pp76–7 Boutique Hotel €€

☎ 257 535 557; www.hotelneruda.cz; Nerudova 44; s/d from 3125/3625Kč; 🚊 12, 20, 22, 23; 💻

Set in a tastefully renovated Gothic house dating from 1348 and extending into the neighbouring building, the Neruda offers a refreshingly modern and stylish alternative to the sometimes-tacky so-called 'historic' hotels, which are all too common in Malá Strana. The décor is chic and minimalist in shades of chocolate and cream, with a lovely glass-roofed atrium that houses the hotel café, and a sunny roof terrace. The comfortable bedrooms share the modern, minimalist décor and are mostly reasonably sized, but be aware that some of the rooms in the top of the building are a bit on the cramped side – ask for one on the 1st or 2nd floor. The staff are friendly and unfailingly helpful, and the breakfasts are excellent (and served until 11am if you fancy a long lie-in).

PENSION DIENTZENHOFER Map pp76–7

Pension €€

☎ 257 311 319; www.dientzenhofer.cz; Nosticova 2; s/d 2700/3600Kč; 🚊 12, 20, 22, 23

Take a room in this homely pension and you're rubbing shoulders with famous figures from the past – this lovely old 16th-century house was once the home of the Dientzenhofer family of architects who designed many of Prague's most famous baroque landmarks (see p48). Set in a peaceful park but only five minutes' walk from Charles Bridge, the house has seven plain but comfortable rooms and a couple of good-value suites that sleep up to five. The owner is friendly and helpful, and will even collect you from the airport.

CASTLE STEPS Map pp76–7 Apartments €€

☎ 257 216 337; www.castlesteps.com; Nerudova 7; r 1750-2625, apt 2625-4375Kč; 🚊 12, 20, 22, 23; 💻

The name applies to a collection of private rooms and apartments spread across several buildings on Nerudova and further uphill on Úvoz. Management is laid-back, helpful, gay-friendly and decidedly informal – don't expect porters and room service! (By the way, there are no lifts either.) The various 16th- and 17th-century buildings have been converted into apartments and suites sleeping from two to eight, and offer remarkable value in a great location. All have been beautifully renovated and equipped to a high standard, and are furnished with antiques, oil paintings and pot plants. There is free internet access at the reception office at Nerudova 7 (ring the doorbell labelled Castle Steps).

CHARLES BRIDGE B&B

Map pp76–7 Pension €€

☎ 257 218 103; www.charlesbridgebb.com; Dražického náměstí; s/d 2200/2500Kč, apt 3300-3500Kč; 🚊 12, 20, 22, 23; P 💻

Location, location, location – those three little words that mean so much when it comes to property. It would be hard to beat this quaint little pension for location – any closer to Charles Bridge and you'd be on it. The rooms are nothing to write home about, with cheap beds and plain décor tastefully brightened up with colourful curtains, dried flowers and a painting or two; for families, there are two apartments with kitchen facilities. There's free internet access at reception and wi-fi in the rooms; the parking space outside must be booked in advance.

STARÉ MĚSTO

Staré Město offers a wide range of accommodation, from backpacker hostels to some of the city's most luxurious hotels, with everything in between. Be aware that a lot of pensions and midrange hotels have been squeezed into historic old buildings with no room for a lift – be prepared for a bit of stair climbing.

PERLA HOTEL Map pp88–9 Boutique Hotel €€€

☎ 221 667 777; www.perlahotel.cz; Perlová 1; s/d 4250/4750Kč; M Můstek

The 'Pearl' on Pearl Street is typical of the brand of slinky, appealing designer hotels that are beginning to appear all over central Prague. Here the designer has picked a – surprise, surprise – pearl motif that extends from the giant pearls that form the reception desk to the silky, lustrous bedspreads and huge screen prints on the bedroom walls. The rooms are on the small side, but the décor is sleek and modern with muted colours offset by bright-red lacquered chairs and glossy black-tiled bathrooms. The whole building is wheelchair accessible, and one room is specially designed for wheelchair users.

HOTEL ANTIK Map pp88–9 Hotel €€

☎ 222 322 288; www.hotelantik.cz; Dlouhá 22; s/d 3590/3990Kč; M Náměstí Republiky

As the name suggests, this place has a passion for bric-a-brac, with an antique shop on the ground floor and various pieces scattered elsewhere throughout the building. The location is ideal, right in the heart of the Old Town and close to lots of good restaurants and bars. The cosy rooms have been thoroughly modernised and are perfectly comfortable though a little lacking in character – ask for one with a balcony overlooking the garden, to avoid any noise from night-time revellers in the street. Breakfast is served in the lovely garden courtyard out the back.

APOSTOLIC RESIDENCE

Map pp88–9 Apartments €€

☎ 221 632 222; www.apostolic.cz; Staroměstské náměstí 25; s/d from 3725/3975Kč, apt from 6000Kč; M Staroměstská; 💻

This lovely old building on Old Town Square has been converted into a luxury hotel with 30 large, well-appointed rooms filled with heavy antique furniture and rugs, paintings, wooden floors and chandeliers. Some have the additional charm of painted wooden-beamed ceilings. The attic apartment (sleeps four), with its spiral staircase and massive timber beams, is our favourite. The unique selling point, though, is its location – you can hang out your window and watch the Astronomical Clock do its thing. You'll pay extra for a room with a view of Old Town Square, but for this level of quality, it's still reasonable value compared to many top-end hotels around town.

SAVIC HOTEL Map pp88–9 Hotel €€

☎ 226 201 910; www.hotelsavic.cz; Jilská 7; s/d 3725/3975Kč; M Národní Třída; 💻

From the complimentary glass of wine when you arrive to the comfy king-size beds, the Savic certainly knows how to make you feel welcome. Housed in the former monastery of St Giles, the hotel is bursting with character and full of delightful period details including old stone fireplaces, beautiful painted timber ceilings and fragments of frescoes. The bedrooms are furnished in antique style with parquet floors, dark wooden furniture, wingback armchairs and plush sofas, while the bathrooms are lined with polished marble. And it's barely two minutes' walk from the Astronomical Clock on Old Town Square.

HOTEL JOSEF Map pp88–9 Boutique Hotel €€

☎ 221 700 111; www.hoteljosef.cz; Rybná 20; r from 3725Kč; Ⓜ Náměstí Republiky; Ⓟ ⊠ 💻

Designed by London-based Czech architect Eva Jiřičná, the Josef is one of Prague's most stylish contemporary hotels. As soon as you step through the doors into the stark, white, minimalist lobby with its glass spiral staircase you get the impression that it's designed to impress you with how exceedingly cool and trendy it all is. But it's tastefully done, and staff are welcoming and helpful. The minimalist design is continued in the bedrooms, where things are kept clean and simple with plenty of subtle neutral tones in the bed linen and furniture. The glass-walled en suites are especially attractive, boasting extra-large 'rainfall' shower heads and modish glass bowl basins. There are two wheelchair-accessible rooms and a stylish bar and business lounge.

U ZELENÉHO VĚNCE

Map pp88–9 Pension €€

☎ 222 220 178; www.uzv.cz; Řetězová 10; s/d 2900/3400Kč; Ⓜ Staroměstká

Located on a quiet side street, but only a few minutes' stroll from Old Town Square, the Green Garland is a surprisingly peaceful and rustic retreat right in the heart of the city. Set in a restored 14th-century building, it takes its name from the house-sign above the door. The bedrooms vary in size – some cramped and some relatively spacious – but all are spotlessly clean and simply but appealingly decorated, with exposed medieval roof beams in the attic rooms, and the English-speaking owner is unfailingly polite and helpful.

RESIDENCE KAROLINA

Map pp88–9 Apartments €€

☎ 224 990 990; www.residence-karolina.com; Karoliny Světlé 4; 2-/4-person apt from 3050/4975Kč; 🚊 6, 9, 19, 21, 22, 23; 💻

We're going to have to invent a new category of accommodation – boutique apartments – to cover this array of 20 beautifully furnished flats. Offering one- or two-bedroom options, all apartments have spacious seating areas with comfy sofas and flat-screen TVs, sleek modern kitchens and dining areas. The location is good too, set back on a quiet street but close to a major tram stop, across the street from the National Theatre, and just two blocks from the Tesco supermarket for your self-catering supplies. There's a daily maid service, elevator, and cable or wi-fi broadband in all apartments.

HOTEL U MEDVÍDKŮ

Map pp88–9 Pension €€

☎ 224 211 916; www.umedvidku.cz; Na Perštýně 7; s/d/tr 2300/3500/4500Kč; Ⓜ Národní Třída

Cosy and centrally located, 'At the Little Bear' is a traditional beer hall (see the boxed text, p179) on the southern edge of the Old Town, about 10 minutes' walk from Old Town Square. The rooms have polished hardwood floors and dark wooden furniture, with good-sized bathrooms (and good water pressure in the showers). Some of the 1st-floor rooms have Renaissance painted wooden ceilings, and a few are almost big enough to be called a suite (the 'historic' rooms, which have a bit of character, cost 10% more than the ordinary ones, which have less atmosphere but are similar in size). For a romantic splurge, choose one of the attic rooms – No 33 is the best in the house, spacious and atmospheric, with a big pine bed and huge exposed roof beams.

OLD PRAGUE HOSTEL

Map pp88–9 Hostel €

☎ 224 829 058; www.oldpraguehostel.com; Benediktská 2; dm from 375Kč, s/d 1000/1200Kč; Ⓜ Náměstí Republiky; ⊠ 💻

Cheerful and welcoming with colourful home-made murals brightening the walls, this is one of Prague's most appealing and sociable hostels, with a good mix of people from backpackers to families. Facilities are good, with lockers in the dorms, free breakfast and nonsmoking rooms, though the mattresses on the bunks are a bit on the thin side. The staff are very helpful (there's 24-hour reception) and the location could hardly be more central, just five minutes' walk east of Old Town Square and two minutes from tram and metro. There are two PCs with free internet access (often busy) and wi-fi throughout the hostel.

NOVÉ MĚSTO & VYŠEHRAD

Although there are one or two grand old luxury hotels here, Nové Město's accommodation is mostly in modern chain hotels and upgraded 1930s establishments. What they might lack in historical atmosphere and romantic appeal they make up for in spaciousness and facilities. Those on Wenceslas Square are right in the thick of things, but there are quiet corners to be found as well, especially in southern Nové Město (ie Charles Square and its surrounds).

HOTEL YASMIN

Map pp108–9 Boutique Hotel €€€

☎ 234 100 100; www.hotel-yasmin.cz; Politických Vězňů 12, Nové Město; r from 6500Kč; Ⓜ Můstek; Ⓟ ⊠ 💻

This designer hotel, a block east of Wenceslas Square, is very cutting edge, a blend of Space Age and organic. The public areas are covered in motifs in the shape of jasmine blossoms (from small white petals on the black granite floors to giant leaf prints on the walls), and decorated with birch-twig arrangements and chrome balls. (We're not sure what the orange, furry sculptures in the breakfast room are meant to be – triffids?) The spacious bedrooms have a neutral palette of white, beige and tan, the clean lines set off by plants, flowers or a curved edge; the bathrooms are in black tile and chrome. The hotel is entirely nonsmoking.

ICON HOTEL

Map pp108–9 Boutique Hotel €€€

☎ 221 634 100; www.iconhotel.eu; V Jámě 6, Nové Město; r from 6250Kč; 🚊 3, 9, 14, 24; 💻

Staff clothes by Diesel, computers by Apple, beds by Hästens – pretty much everything in this gorgeous boutique hotel has a designer stamp on it. Plugged by *Condé Nast Traveller* in its 2008 Hot List, the Icon's sleekly minimalist rooms are enlivened with a splash of imperial purple from the silky bedspreads, while the curvy, reproduction Art Deco armchairs are supplied by Modernista (p147). High-tech touches include iPod docks, Skype phones and fingerprint-activated safes, and there are broadband ports in all rooms plus free wi-fi in the public spaces. And if your muscles are aching after a hard day's sightseeing, the hotel also boasts one of Prague's best Thai massage studios.

RADISSON SAS ALCRON HOTEL

Map pp108–9 Hotel €€€

☎ 222 820 000; www.radissonsas.com; Štěpánská 40, Nové Město; r from 4000Kč; Ⓜ Můstek; Ⓟ 💻

Located just a few minutes' walk from Wenceslas Square, the five-star Radisson is the modern reincarnation of the 1930s Alcron Hotel, long favoured by celebrities and diplomats. Many of the original Art Deco marble-and-glass fittings have been preserved, including in the beautiful La Rotonde restaurant, and the 211 rooms have been far more tastefully renovated than in many other refurbished Prague hotels. The rooms have pleasant soft furnishings, retro prints and chic marble bathrooms, while mod cons such as free wi-fi access, video games and minibars add to the comfort and convenience. There are also wheelchair-accessible rooms for disabled guests.

HOTEL UNION

Map p116 Hotel €€

☎ 261 214 812; www.hotelunion.cz; Ostrčilovo náměstí 4, Vyšehrad; s/d from 2900/3750Kč; 🚊 7, 16, 24; Ⓟ 💻

A grand old hotel from 1906, it was nationalised by the communists in 1958 and returned to the former owner's grandson in 1991. It's still family run, and the staff take great pride in looking after their guests properly. Comfortably renovated, with a few period touches left intact, the hotel is at the foot of the hill below Vyšehrad fortress; Charles Bridge is just 10 minutes away on tram 18. Bedrooms are plain but pleasant, and the double glazing helps to cut down on street noise; ask for one of the deluxe corner rooms (from 4500Kč a double), which are huge and have bay windows with a view of either Vyšehrad or distant Prague Castle. Free wi-fi.

HOTEL 16 U SV KATEŘINY

Map p106 Hotel €€

☎ 224 920 636; www.hotel16.cz; Kateřinská 16, Nové Město; s/d 2900/3700Kč; Ⓜ Karlovo Náměstí; Ⓟ 💻

Near the Botanic Gardens and about five minutes' walk from Karlovo Náměstí metro station, 'St Catherine Hotel' is a friendly, family-run little place with just 14 rooms, tucked away in a very quiet corner of town where you're more likely to hear birdsong than traffic. The rooms vary in size and are simply but smartly furnished; the best, at the back, have views onto the peaceful terraced garden. Buffet breakfast is included in the price, and the hotel is fitted with a lift.

SUITEHOME RESIDENCE

Map pp108–9 Hotel Apartments €€

☎ 222 230 833; www.suitehome.cz; Příčná 2, Nové Město; 2-person ste from 3375Kč; M Karlovo Náměstí; 💻

Straddling the divide between apartment and hotel, this place offers the space and convenience of a suite with private bathroom and kitchen along with hotel facilities such as reception desk, daily maid service and breakfast room. It's a good choice for families or groups of friends, with suites for up to six persons; the rooms are pleasantly old-fashioned, and some on the upper floors have good views towards the castle. There's a lift, though it's a bit on the small side – important, as the building has five floors. There's also free wi-fi.

PENZIÓN U ŠUTERŮ

Map pp108–9 Pension €€

☎ 224 948 235; www.u-suteru.cz; Palackého 4, Nové Město; s/d 2390/3190Kč; 🚋 3, 9, 14, 24 or M Můstek; 💻

A block west of Wenceslas Square, this small side-street pension (10 rooms) is very central but away from the worst of the city-centre noise. With their polished wooden floors and plain wooden furniture, the bedrooms have a certain rustic charm; it's worth paying a little extra for one of the deluxe doubles (3590Kč), which have a bit more character. Breakfast is served in the Gothic basement, which doubles as a decent restaurant in the evenings.

MISS SOPHIE'S Map pp108–9 Hostel €

☎ 296 303 530; www.miss-sophies.com; Melounova 3, Nové Město; dm 520Kč, s/d from 1650/1890Kč, apt from 2300Kč; M IP Pavlova; ⊠ 💻

This hostel in a converted apartment building on the southern edge of the New Town makes a pleasant change from the usual characterless backpacker hive. There's a touch of contemporary style here, with oak-veneer floors and stark, minimalist décor – the main motif is 'distressed' concrete, along with neutral colours and black metal-framed beds. The place is famous for its 'designer' showers, with autographed glass screens and huge 'rainfall' shower heads. There is a very cool lounge in the basement, with red-brick vaults and black leather sofas, and reception (open 24 hours) is staffed by a young, multilingual crew who are always eager to help.

HOSTEL U MELOUNU

Map p106 Hostel €

☎ 224 918 322; www.hostelumelounu.cz; Ke Karlovu 7, Nové Město; dm 400Kč, s/d 990/1600Kč; M IP Pavlova; P 💻

One of the prettier hostels in town, 'At the Watermelon' is set in a historic building on a quiet back street, a short walk from Vinohrady's restaurants and bars (it's a 10-minute walk south of IP Pavlova metro station). The rooms are all on the ground floor and range from basic dorms to self-contained apartments radiating off a large central garden, giving the place a peaceful, cottage-y feel. Dorms, sleeping between six and 10 people in bunk beds, are the basic, functional spaces you would expect, but they are spotlessly clean and have lockers, and there's the added attraction of that peaceful, sunny garden complete with barbecue. Free wi-fi.

VINOHRADY & VRŠOVICE

Vinohrady is a great place to stay. Not only is it relatively close to the centre, with good metro connections from Náměstí Míru and Jiřího z Poděbrad stations, but also there are lots of nice places to stroll and stop for a beer or bite to eat. Vršovice is a little further out, and not quite as conveniently connected. Nevertheless, prices are lower here and some attractive new properties have recently opened.

LE PALAIS HOTEL Map p121 Hotel €€€

☎ 234 634 111; www.palaishotel.cz; U Zvonařky 1, Vinohrady; s/d €350/370, ste from €680; 🚋 6, 11; P ⊠ 💻

Le Palais is housed in a gorgeous *belle époque* building dating from the end of the 19th century that was once home to Czech artist Luděk Marold (1865–98; his former apartment is now rooms 407 to 412). It has been beautifully restored, complete with original floor mosaics, period fireplaces, marble staircases, wrought-iron balustrades, frescoes, painted ceilings and delicate stuccowork. The luxury bedrooms are decorated in warm shades of yellow, pink and ochre, while the various suites – some located in the corner tower, some with a south-facing balcony – make the most of the hotel's superb location perched on top of a bluff with views of Vyšehrad fortress.

HOTEL SIEBER
Map p121 Boutique Hotel €€€

☎ 224 250 025; www.sieber.cz; Slezská 55, Vinohrady; s/d/ste 4480/4780/5480Kč; Ⓜ Jiřího z Poděbrad; ☒ 💻

Popular with business travellers, the Sieber is a small luxury hotel with 13 rooms and seven suites, set in a grand 19th-century apartment building. Stylish décor and attentive service are accompanied by thoughtful little touches such as bathrobes and fresh flowers. The building dates from 1889 and has been restored to its former grandeur after suffering years of neglect under the communist regime, and the rooms are decorated in restful, neutral tones (lots of cream and light wood). Service can't be faulted, and staff are courteous and very helpful. Rates are frequently discounted on its website.

ORION Map p121 Hotel Apartments €€

☎ 222 521 706; www.okhotels.cz; Americká 9, Vinohrady; 2-person/4-person apt 2590/3590Kč; Ⓜ Náměstí Míru; Ⓟ ☒ 💻

A good-value hotel in an upmarket section of Vinohrady, within easy walking distance of Náměstí Míru and Havlíčkovy sady park. All 26 apartments are equipped with a small kitchen, including fridge and coffee maker. Several apartments have multiple rooms and can accommodate small groups. There's also a Finnish sauna on the premises. Ask to see a couple of rooms if possible, since they are all slightly different. Some come with hardwood floors, others with carpets. Free wi-fi throughout.

AMETYST Map p121 Boutique Hotel €€

☎ 222 921 921; www.hotelametyst.cz; Jana Masaryka 11, Vinohrady; s/d from €110/120; Ⓜ Náměstí Míru; Ⓟ ☒ 💻

The polished Ametyst straddles the line between boutique and hotel, with just enough style points in the lobby (nice retro flagstone) and the rooms (hardwood floors, arty lamps and flat-screen TVs) to put it in the boutique camp. All the rooms have air-conditioning, LAN connections for the PC, and tubs and hair dryers in the bathroom. There's a cosy coffee bar off the lobby and dozens of places to relax within easy walking distance in one of the nicest parts of leafy Vinohrady.

HOTEL LUNÍK Map p121 Hotel €€

☎ 224 253 974; www.hotel-lunik.cz; Londýnská 50, Vinohrady; s/d from 2000/2900Kč; Ⓜ Náměstí Míru or IP Pavlova; Ⓟ ☒ 💻

Clean, attractive and smallish, Hotel Luník is on a quiet residential street a block from Peace Square and between the Náměstí Míru and IP Pavlova metro stations. There's been a hotel here since the 1920s, and the lobby and public areas exude a quiet sophistication. The rooms are homey and slightly old-fashioned, with attractive green-tiled baths. There's free internet access in the rooms via LAN connection and a couple of terminals off the lobby. The friendly receptionist is willing to negotiate room rates on slow nights.

HOTEL ANNA Map p121 Hotel €€

☎ 222 513 111; www.hotelanna.cz; Budečská 17, Vinohrady; s/d from €70/90, ste from €100; Ⓜ Náměstí Míru; Ⓟ ☒ 💻

Hotel Anna is small and friendly, with helpful and knowledgeable staff who speak both English and German. The late-19th-century building retains many of its Art Nouveau features, and the bedrooms are bright and cheerful with floral bedspreads and arty black-and-white photos of Prague buildings on the walls. There are two small suites on the top floor, one of which has a great view towards the castle. The hotel is tucked away on a quiet back street but close to the metro and lots of good restaurants and bars; you can walk to the top end of Wenceslas Square in 10 minutes. Check the website for special offers.

HOTEL CLARIS Map p121 Hotel €€

☎ 242 446 111; www.hotel-claris.cz; Slezská 26, Vinohrady; s/d from €70/90; Ⓜ Náměstí Míru; Ⓟ ☒ 💻

The sister hotel to the Anna (above) and nearly identical in terms of price and facilities. Though it's on a busier street than the

Anna and lacks a bit of the charming neighbourhood feel, the furnishings are brighter and more cheerful. Either is an excellent pick if you're looking for a simple hotel and don't need a lot of facilities.

CZECH INN Map p121 Hostel/Hotel €

☎ 267 267 600; www.czech-inn.com; Francouzská 21, Vršovice; dm 430-495Kč, s/d 1320/1540Kč, en suite d/apt from 1870/2090Kč, 3-room apt 4400Kč; M Náměstí Míru plus 4, 22, 23; P

The Czech Inn calls itself a hostel, but 'luxury boutique' wouldn't be out of place. Everything seems sculpted by an industrial designer on Ian Schrager's payroll, from the handcrafted iron beds to the swish brushed-steel flooring and minimalist square sinks – right out of a German design catalogue. The Czech Inn offers a variety of accommodation, from standard hostel dorm rooms to good-value private doubles (with or without attached bath), and one-, two- or three-room apartments. The fifth-floor apartments come with a shared rooftop terrace and sleep up to eight. A bank of internet terminals in the lobby and an adjoining bar–café round out the charms.

HOLIDAY HOME Map p121 Pension €

☎ 222 512 710; www.holidayhome.cz; Americká 37, Vinohrady; s/d from 1500/1850Kč; M Náměstí Míru; P

This simple family-owned and -operated pension offers good value in one of the city's nicest residential neighbourhoods. Don't expect anything fancy in spite of the elegant town-house setting. The rooms are small and bare bones, with tiny beds. On the other hand, the location is ideal and the friendly owners will take good care of you from the moment you arrive. Free wi-fi throughout the hotel and an internet café next door.

PENZION MÁNES Map p121 Pension €

☎ 222 252 180; www.penzionmanes.cz; Mánesova 46, Vinohrady; s/d from 1500/2000Kč; M Jiřího z Poděbrad;

It's bare-bones accommodation here, but a great price given the location on handsome Mánesova, close to some good bars, restaurants and clubs. There are few facilities, but rooms (some with a courtyard view) are comfortable and quiet, and staff are friendly.

PENSION BEETLE Map p121 Pension €

☎ 222 515 093; www.beetle-tour.cz; Šmilovského 10, Vinohrady; d from 1800Kč, ste from 3000Kč; 4, 22, 23; P

The Beetle occupies a lovely 1910 apartment building in a leafy back street, far from the tourist throng. The cheaper rooms are plain but functional, while the larger rooms and 'suites' (like two-room apartments) are more stylishly decorated and furnished, with antique and stripped pine furniture, and equipped with bedside lamps, minibar, table and chairs. A continental breakfast, with all the coffee you can drink, is included in the price.

PENSION ARCO

Map p121 Pension/Apartments €

☎ 271 740 734; www.arco-guesthouse.cz; Voroněžská 21, Vršovice; d/apt from €54; 4, 22, 23;

The Arco is a gay-friendly pension and café–bar offering clean, comfortably furnished pension rooms, as well as several two- to four-person apartments in nearby buildings. The apartments are good value – bright and clean with laminate floors and IKEA furniture, and close to a tramline that will take you all the way to the castle, while Vinohrady's restaurants, pubs and clubs are just a few blocks away.

ŽIŽKOV & KARLÍN

If you're looking for somewhere inexpensive but not far from the city centre, then Žižkov and Karlín are your best bet. The slightly run-down air of these districts puts a lot of people off, but they are as safe as anywhere else in the city and only a couple of tram stops from Staré Město. Unfortunately a lot of the accommodation here is pretty mediocre, but things are improving all the time – Žižkov is sure to sprout some cool designer hotels in the next few years as rising property prices in neighbouring Vinohrady force developers to look elsewhere.

HOTEL ALWYN

Map pp126–7 Boutique Hotel €€

☎ 222 334 200; www.hotelalwyn.cz; Vítkova 26, Karlín; s/d from 3000/3500Kč; 8, 24;

The Alwyn is the first of what will probably be many designer hotels to appear in the up-and-coming district of Karlín. Set on a quiet side street only a few tram stops east

WORTH A DETOUR

Travellers rave about Hostel Boathouse (off Map pp58–9; ☎ 241 770 051; www.hostelboathouse.com; Lodnická 1, Braník; dm 350-420Kč; 🚋 3, 17, 21; P 💻), a friendly, popular hostel with a peaceful riverbank setting a few miles south of the city centre, run by the vivacious and unstinting crew of Věra and Helena. Accommodation is in three- to nine-bed rooms, with separate bathroom facilities for men and women, and there's a sunny, outdoor deck in front. A continental breakfast is provided free (you can get a cooked breakfast for 50Kč) and extras available include bike and boat hire, a minishop and laundry service. Take tram 3, 17 or 21 to the Černý kůň stop, and follow the hostel signs west to the river (it's a five-minute walk).

of Staré Město, the hotel sports deliciously modern décor in shades of chocolate brown, beige and burnt orange, with lots of polished wood and Deco-style sofas in the cocktail bar, and super-comfortable Hästens beds in the rooms. It's designed for both business and pleasure, with broadband ports and free wi-fi, conference room, fitness centre, sauna and massage centre.

ARCOTEL TEATRINO

Map pp126–7 Hotel €€

☎ 221 422 111; www.arcotel.at; Bořivojova 53, Žižkov; r from 3125Kč; 🚋 5, 9, 26; 💻

The design of some boutique hotels could be described as theatrical, but there can't be too many that were actually designed as a theatre. Dating from 1910, the Art Nouveau building that houses this Austrian-run hotel was originally a cultural centre, Žižkov's equivalent of the Municipal House (p99) – guests here can enjoy an excellent buffet breakfast in what was originally the theatre auditorium. The rooms are plain and modern, but the public areas are filled with beautiful period features, from wrought-iron railings to stained glass windows.

CLOWN & BARD HOSTEL

Map pp126–7 Hostel €

☎ 222 716 453; www.clownandbard.com; Bořivojova 102, Žižkov; dm 300-380Kč, d 1000Kč, tw/tr 1400/2100Kč; 🚋 5, 9, 26; P 💻

Set in the heart of Žižkov's pub district, the Clown & Bard is a full-on party place – don't come here looking for peace and quiet. This ever-popular hostel has a café (with free, vegetarian, all-you-can-eat breakfast from 9am to 2pm), a lively bar, friendly, knowledgeable staff and good tours. As well as dorms and doubles, there are two- or three-person rooms with en-suite bathroom. The party crowd gravitates towards the thumping basement bar that stays open till midnight and features regular live acts and DJ nights. Rooms are fairly basic, but clean and perfectly comfortable. There are four computers offering free internet access, and free wi-fi.

HOSTEL ELF Map pp126–7 Hostel €

☎ 222 540 963; www.hostelelf.com; Husitská 11, Žižkov; dm 340-370Kč, s/d 1230/1460Kč; M Florenc; 💻

Young, hip and sociable, Hostel Elf welcomes a steady stream of party-hearty backpackers from across the globe to its well-maintained dorms, and many end up staying longer than they originally planned. The dorms, sleeping up to 11 people, are immaculately clean and brightly decorated with graffiti art or the odd mural. There's a little beer-garden terrace and cosy lounge, with free tea and coffee and cheap beer, and Žižkov with its many pubs is right on the doorstep; the downside is the noisy train line that runs close by. The hostel is less than 10 minutes' walk from Florenc bus station.

HOLEŠOVICE, BUBENEČ & DEJVICE

Don't choose a hotel in the neighbourhoods of Holešovice, Bubeneč or Dejvice if you require niceties like a window view on Prague Castle or the ability to tumble from your hotel door onto the cobblestones of Malá Strana. While these neighbourhoods have their attractive areas too, for the most part they are ordinary workaday parts of Prague. On the plus side, the rates tend to be more reasonable than in the centre, and your bargaining power at the reception desk is greater because the demand for rooms is lower. Also, Dejvice and Bubeneč are easy to reach from the airport, and the properties around the Nádraží Holešovice train station are convenient if you're arriving there from Vienna, Budapest or Berlin (many international trains stop there). There's also a direct bus connection, the Airport Express/AE, between the airport and Nádraží Holešovice. Metro and tram connections to the centre are generally very good.

HOTEL PRAHA Map pp58–9 Hotel €€€

☎ 224 341 111; www.htlpraha.cz; Sušická 20, Dejvice; d €290; taxi; P ⊠ 💻

The Hotel Praha is one of Prague's more interesting hotels. Hidden away on a hill in Dejvice, surrounded by several hectares of private grounds that were once protected by an electric fence, it's a luxury complex that was built in 1981 for the Communist Party elite. The public areas of the hotel are an intriguing mix of 1970s futuristic (sweeping curves and stainless steel) and 1950s Soviet splendour (polished marble and cut-glass chandeliers). The bedrooms are very spacious, with all the luxury you'd expect from a five-star establishment, and many are accessible to wheelchair users. But the hotel's biggest drawcard is the fact that each of its 124 rooms has its own private balcony – the entire southern face of the hotel is a sloping grandstand of stacked balconies, all draped with greenery and commanding a superb view of Prague Castle. Before 1989, such Soviet-era stalwarts as Nicolae Ceauşescu, Erich Honecker and Eduard Shevardnadze all hung their hats here; in recent years, the clientele has shifted from heads of state to Hollywood, with stars such as Tom Cruise, Johnny Depp, Alanis Morissette, Kris Kristofferson and Paul Simon ringing room service in the small hours.

HOTEL BELVEDERE
Map pp132–3 Hotel €€

☎ 220 106 111; www.europehotels.cz; Milady Horákové 19, Holešovice; s/d from 2700/3600Kč; 🚊 1, 8, 15, 25, 26; P ⊠

The Belvedere is an old communist-era hotel that has been completely refurbished, and now provides good-value accommodation within easy reach of the city centre. The standard rooms are nothing special, but they're comfortable and spotlessly clean. The 'executive' rooms (4200Kč in season) on the 2nd floor are much more spacious, with soundproofed windows, smart crimson drapes and bedspreads, and huge, white, marble-lined bathrooms. Check the website for occasional steep discounts, especially in mid-summer. The large breakfast room has a slightly institutional feel, but the food is good and there's plenty of it. There's a tram stop right outside the front door, and it's only five minutes to Náměstí Republiky metro station on tram 8.

ART HOTEL Map pp132–3 Boutique Hotel €€

☎ 233 101 331; www.arthotel.cz; Nad Královskou Oborou 53, Bubeneč; s/d from €120/140; 🚊 1, 8, 15, 25, 26; P ⊠ 💻

There are lots of word-of-mouth recommendations for this small hotel hidden away in the peaceful embassy district. It has sleek modern styling with a display of contemporary Czech art in the lobby and art photography on the walls of the bedrooms. Room 203 is the best in the house, with a balcony and a view of the sunset; rooms 104 and 106 also have balconies. It may look out of the way on the map, but it's only a few minutes' walk from a tram (8) that will take you to the city centre in about 10 minutes.

PLAZA ALTA HOTEL
Map pp132–3 Hotel €€

☎ 220 407 011; www.plazahotelalta.com; Ortenovo náměstí 22, Holešovice; s/d from €109/129; M Nádraží Holešovice or 🚊 12, 15; P ⊠ 💻

The snazziest hotel in this part of town draws a mostly business clientele and travellers looking for a full-service property within easy reach (one tram stop) of Nádraží Holešovice. The hotel had a complete makeover in 2007, giving the rooms a cleaner look, with thicker mattresses and bold, striped bedspreads. All the rooms have air-conditioning and minibars, and free wi-fi is available throughout.

SPLENDID Map pp132–3 Hotel €€

☎ 233 375 940; www.hotelsplendid.cz; Ovenecká 33, Bubeneč; s/d 2000/2700Kč; 🚊 1, 8, 15, 25, 26; ⊠ 💻

This hotel-cum-guesthouse, occupying a town house on a beautiful residential street next to Stromovka Park, dates from well before the Velvet Revolution, and there is still a slight communist whiff in the air. Maybe it's the '70s-style black-leatherette stools in the hotel bar or the ultra-spartan rooms, with their tiny, narrow beds and thin mattresses (communists apparently never slept together in the same bed). The Splendid is actually crying out for a thorough upgrade. On the other hand, it's clean and quiet, and the location is superb if you're looking for something green and outside the tourist throng. Note that parking is restricted to residents only. The only internet option is a public terminal near the reception.

HOTEL CROWNE PLAZA

Map pp132–3 Hotel €€

☎ 296 537 111; www.crowneplaza.cz; Koulova 15, Dejvice; d from €110; 8; P

Originally called the Hotel International, this place was built in the 1950s in the style of Moscow University, complete with Soviet star atop the tower. Now modernised, it is comfortable and quiet, tucked away at the end of tram 8. Come here for the décor rather than anything else – although the rooms here are standard chain-hotel style, with all the necessities but not too many luxuries, the building itself is really something special, covered in polished marble, bas-reliefs and frescoes of the noble worker. The deluxe rooms, on the 9th floor and above, are more spacious and have good views over the city.

HOTEL VILLA SCHWAIGER

Map pp132–3 Boutique Hotel €€

☎ 233 320 271; www.villaschwaiger.com; Schwaigerova 59/3, Bubeneč; s/d from €90/110; taxi or 1, 8, 15, 25, 26 (plus long walk); P

This elegant, colonial-style villa in a quiet valley in Bubeneč feels a world away from the bustle of Old Town Square. Great care has gone into designing the 22 rooms, including one – No 102 – done up in 'Chinese' style, with dark hardwoods, dramatic crimson fabrics and Chinese prints on the wall. The 'Zen' bath is done in brushed metal with a simple porcelain basin. Guests can relax in the back garden, take the hotel's bikes out for a spin in nearby Stromovka, or relax in the private sauna. The public areas are stunning, with white woods, marble floors and comfortable wicker furniture. Free wi-fi access throughout. The hotel is tricky to find, so it's best to take a taxi (at least for the first visit).

EXPO PRAGUE

Map pp132–3 Hotel €€

☎ 266 712 470; www.expoprag.cz; Za Elektrárnou 3, Holešovice; s/d from 1800/2600Kč; 5, 12, 14, 15, 17; P

Medium-sized and modern, this hotel was built in the mid-1990s to accommodate trade fair delegations at the nearby Výstaviště fairgrounds. It lacks atmosphere but would do in a pinch if the nearby (and better) **Absolut Hotel** (below) is not available. It's just one tram stop from the Nádraží Holešovice train station and close to the sports and concert venue Sportovní hala. The rooms are decorated in a bland, contemporary, chain-hotel style, but they're clean, and also have air-conditioning, minibars and safes. Free wi-fi throughout.

ABSOLUT HOTEL

Map pp132–3 Boutique Hotel €€

☎ 222 541 406; www.absoluthotel.cz; Jablonského 639/4, Holešovice; s/d from €89/99; M Nádraží Holešovice; P

A highly recommended, eye-catching boutique hotel (without the boutique price tag), Absolut is located across the street from the Nádraží Holešovice train and metro stations. While the neighbourhood wouldn't win a beauty contest, the hotel compensates with a list of amenities almost unheard of at this price point, including big, beautifully designed rooms with exposed brickwork, huge modern baths (many rooms have both a shower and a tub), air-conditioning, an excellent in-house restaurant, free wi-fi, a massage and wellness centre next door, and free parking. The friendly receptionist is willing to cut rates if you happen to arrive on a slow night.

HOTEL DENISA

Map pp132–3 Pension/Hotel €€

☎ 224 318 969; Narodní Obrany 33, Dejvice; s/d from €50/90; M Dejvická; P

This small, family-run hotel in a turn-of-the-century apartment building on a quiet side street was undergoing a massive renovation in 2008. The changes are hoped to give the plain rooms a much-needed upgrade, with nicer beds, thicker mattresses and updated baths. The location is great, just a few minutes' walk to the Dejvická metro station and convenient to the airport. The neighbourhood itself is wonderful for strolling, with lots of cafés and restaurants. At the time of research, there was no in-room internet, but free public terminals were on hand for guests.

HOTEL EXTOL INN Map pp132–3 Hotel €

☎ 220 876 541; www.extolinn.cz; Přístavní 2, Holešovice; s/d from 1050/1800Kč; 🚊 1, 3, 5, 25; P ⊠ 💻

The bright, modern Extol Inn provides budget accommodation in an up-and-coming neighbourhood within easy reach of the city centre. The cheapest rooms (on the upper floors) are basic, no-frills affairs with shared bathrooms. These are often occupied by groups of high-schoolers, so if you value your peace and quiet it might be worth paying a bit extra for the more expensive three-star rooms (doubles from 2350Kč), which have private bathroom, TV, minibar and free use of the hotel sauna and spa. There's a public internet terminal in the lobby. The hotel is entirely nonsmoking and wheelchair-accessible. There's a tram stop 100m away, from which it's a 10-minute ride to the city centre.

HOTEL LEON Map pp132–3 Hostel/Hotel €

☎ 220 941 351; www.leonhotel.eu; Ortenovo náměstí 26, Holešovice; s/d from 1100/1700Kč; M Nádraží Holešovice or 🚊 5, 12; P ⊠ 💻

The Hotel Leon advertises itself as something between a hostel and a small hotel. In truth, it's actually much nicer than a standard hostel and not much more expensive (especially if you share a three- or four-bed room). The rooms are basic, with no TV or much of anything else, but are quiet and clean, with adjoining bathrooms. If noise is an issue, ask for a quieter room overlooking the back garden. There's a common room for TV and a shared computer for internet access. It's one tram stop from the Nádraží Holešovice train and metro station.

SIR TOBY'S HOSTEL

Map pp132–3 Hostel €

☎ 246 032 610; www.sirtobys.com; Dělnická 24, Holešovice; dm 360-470Kč, s/d 1150/1600Kč; 🚊 1, 3, 5, 25; P ⊠ 💻

Set in a quiet, nicely refurbished apartment building with spacious kitchen and common room, and run by friendly, cheerful staff, Sir Toby's is only 10 minutes north of the city centre by tram. The dorms have between four and eight bunks, and the bigger dorms are some of the cheapest in Prague. The private rooms, meanwhile, are fitted with metal-framed single beds. All rooms are light, clean and spacious, but don't expect anything fancy. The mattresses are a little on the thin side, but all sheets and blankets are provided at no extra cost. There's a communal kitchen for self-caterers to do their thing, a lounge and a relaxing little garden where you can sit back and chat.

PLUS PRAGUE HOSTEL

Map pp132–3 Hostel €

☎ 220 510 046; www.plusprague.com; Přívozní 1, Holešovice; dm 320Kč, s/d 800/1600Kč; M Nádraží Holešovice; P ⊠ 💻

The cheerful Plus Prague Hostel is one tram stop from Nádraží Holešovice (take any tram heading left as you exit the station). Cheap rates, clean rooms with en-suite bathrooms, friendly staff, free wi-fi *and* an indoor swimming pool and sauna make this a special place. The staff hold special game nights at the in-house bar and conduct regular pub-crawls for the guests. It also offers four-, six- and eight-bed 'girls only' dorm rooms.

HOTEL LETNÁ Map pp132–3 Pension Hotel €

☎ 233 374 763; www.prague-hotel-letna.com; Na Výšinách 8, Bubeneč; s/d from €50/60; 🚊 1, 8, 15, 25, 26; P ⊠ 💻

Pleasant and family-owned, Hotel Letná is in a late-19th-century apartment block on a quiet residential street not far from Sparta Stadium, near Letenské náměstí. There are few facilities on hand, but the rooms are quiet and clean, most with tubs as well as showers, hair-dryers and minibars. It's about five minutes by foot to the tram stop, from where it's 10 minutes to the centre. Check the website for occasional special offers.

A&O HOSTEL

Map pp132–3 Hostel €

☎ 220 870 252; www.aohostels.com; U Výstaviště 1/262, Holešovice; dm €14, s/d €21/42; M Nádraží Holešovice; ⊠ 💻

This clean, well-maintained hostel is in a converted apartment building across the street and a short walk down from the Nádraží Holešovice train and metro stations. The rooms are plain with wooden floors and white walls, lending a slightly institutional feel (think small hospital). There are a couple of computers in the lobby to check email and some snacks to buy at the reception desk, but not much else to distract you. The rates fluctuate dramatically from day to day, depending on demand. Book in advance to lock in a lower rate.

SMÍCHOV

A few years ago, the idea of staying in Smíchov would have been laughable, but the area has gone upmarket and now boasts some of the city's nicest hotels. While Smíchov is not within easy walking distance of the centre (despite what hotel brochures might imply), the metro connection from Anděl is excellent and puts you at Můstek, at the foot of Wenceslas Square, in about 10 minutes.

ADMIRÁL BOTEL Map p138 Hotel €€

☎ 257 321 302; www.admiral-botel.cz; Hořejší nábřeží 57; s/d 2980/3130Kč; Ⓜ Anděl; Ⓟ
If you've ever harboured a desire to sleep in a ship's cabin but would rather do without the seasickness, then climb aboard the Admiral, a permanently berthed riverboat floating quietly off the west bank of the Vltava. The reception area, with its plush leather seating and polished wood and brass, has a smart nautical feel, with narrow corridors leading towards the rooms. These cabins are what you might expect: simple, compact and functional rather than luxurious, with tiny en-suite shower rooms. Rooms facing the river have an attractive outlook, and you can feed the swans from your window. The 'botel' recently added free wi-fi throughout.

ANGELO HOTEL Map p138 Boutique Hotel €€€

☎ 234 801 111; www.angelohotel.com; Radlická 1g; s/d from €245/265; Ⓜ Anděl; Ⓟ ⊠ 💻
The Angelo is the brighter, more-extravagant cousin of Anděl's (below). It has the same slick lobby presentation and high-tech room décor, but instead of the Anděl's muted whites, the Angelo is a riot of rich colour. Both are owned and operated by the same Austrian group, Vienna International, and there's not much difference between the two in terms of price or service. It all boils down to personal taste. The hotels are situated back to back, so if you can't get into one, try around the corner.

ANDĚL'S HOTEL PRAGUE

Map p138 Boutique Hotel €€€

☎ 296 889 688; www.andelshotel.com; Stroupežnického 21; s/d from €235/255; Ⓜ Anděl; Ⓟ ⊠ 💻
This sleek designer hotel, all stark contemporary style in white with black and red accents, has floor-to-ceiling windows, DVD and CD players, internet access and modern abstract art in every room, while the bathrooms are a wonderland of polished chrome and frosted glass. Superior 'club rooms' come with pleasurable perks such as bathrobes and slippers, newspapers delivered to your room and free room-service breakfast. The website offers packages with significant discounts from the rack rate.

HOTEL ARBES

Map p138 Hotel €€

☎ 233 107 522; www.hotelarbes.cz; Viktora Huga 3; s/d from 2300/2800Kč; Ⓜ Anděl; Ⓟ ⊠ 💻
Clean, quiet and excellent value, the Arbes is a down-to-earth tonic to Anděl's (left) and Angelo (left). Viktora Huga is a quiet street, about two blocks from the Anděl metro station and the Nový Smíchov shopping centre, with excellent connections to the centre. The hotel is family-owned and friendly, and the rooms are basic, with modern furnishings and clean bathrooms. Ask for a courtyard room if noise is an issue. There's a public computer near the lobby to check email. There's limited street parking, but paid parking nearby.

HOTEL JULIAN

Map p138 Hotel €€

☎ 257 311 144; www.julian.cz; Elišky Peškové 11; s/d from €118/128; 🚊 6, 9, 12, 20; Ⓟ ⊠ 💻
A deservedly popular small hotel with helpful staff and a quiet location just south of Malá Strana. The smart, well-kept bedrooms are decorated with relaxing pastel shades and pine-topped furniture, and the public areas include a clubbish drawing room with a library, comfy armchairs and an open fire; smokers get their breakfast here (served till 11am at weekends), and the main breakfast room is smoke-free. If you're travelling with kids or in a group, there is a family room (two adults and two children) and three suites (sleeping three to six adults), and there's one wheelchair-accessible room.

IBIS PRAHA MALÁ STRANA

Map p138 Hotel €€

☎ 221 701 700; www.hotelibis.cz.com; Plzeňská 14; s/d from €98/98; Ⓜ Anděl; Ⓟ ⊠ 💻

Never mind that it's nowhere near Malá Strana (but hey, a nice try by the marketing department) – Smíchov's IBIS hotel is a great addition to the neighbourhood, offering a little of the splash of Anděl's (opposite) and Angelo (opposite), but at less than half the price. The rooms are stripped down, pretty much standard-issue, but they have air-conditioning and free wi-fi. The building's aggressively modern style actually looks rather good amid the futuristic boxes found around the area of the Anděl metro station. It's also an easy walk to public transport and the shopping centre.

ARPACAY HOSTEL Map p138 Hostel €

☎ 251 552 297; www.arpacayhostel.com; Radlická 76; dm 390Kč, s/d 1300/1300Kč; Ⓜ Smíchovské Nádraží or 🚋 6; Ⓟ ⊠ 💻

This clean, colourful hostel is near Smíchovské nádraží train station and is the best cheap accommodation in the immediate vicinity. Though it's not within walking distance of the centre as the website says, it's not a bad trip with tram 6 or metro line B from the train station. The relatively remote location keeps prices a little lower here than at competing hostels, and forces management to offer things like free wi-fi throughout.

EXCURSIONS

EXCURSIONS

The Central Bohemian countryside, most of it within an hour's train or bus ride from Prague, is rich in rural landscapes, medieval towns and historic sights. This chapter lists a selection of day trips and potential overnight visits that can be made easily using public transport. At the top of the list are photogenic Karlštejn Castle, the appealing silver-mining town of Kutná Hora and the harrowing former concentration camp, Terezín.

CASTLES & CHATEAUX

Central Bohemia is rich in castles and chateaux, the former country seats of kings and aristocrats. Popular castles include Karlštejn (right), a fairytale fortress built to house Charles IV's royal treasury; Konopiště (p232), the country retreat of the ill-fated Archduke Franz Ferdinand, whose assassination kicked off WWI; and the Lobkowicz family's chateau at Mělník (p233), with its tiny but historic vineyard overlooking the confluence of the Labe and Vltava Rivers.

MEDIEVAL TOWNS

There are many interesting medieval towns in the region surrounding Prague, offering an escape from the crowds that churn through the capital's narrow streets. Litoměřice (p236) has a picture-postcard town square lined with lovely Gothic and Renaissance houses, while the tiny old town of Mělník (p233) has peaceful back-streets and a stunning view over the Bohemian countryside. Most impressive of all is Kutná Hora (p237), with its lovely cathedral, baroque statues and hilltop setting.

MONUMENTS

The region to the north of Prague contains two deeply moving monuments to the suffering of the Czech people in WWII – the village of Lidice (p234), destroyed by the Nazis as an act of vengeance for the assassination of Reichsprotektor Reinhard Heydrich, and Terezín (p234), a former concentration camp through which 150,000 Czech Jews passed on their way to the gas chambers.

OUT OF THE ORDINARY

There are several sights around Prague that are decidedly out of the ordinary. The Trophy Corridor and Chamois Room in Konopiště Chateau (p232), crammed with the antlers, skulls and stuffed heads of thousands of animals, stand as bizarre witness to the hunting obsession of Archduke Franz Ferdinand, while Kutná Hora's Czech Silver Museum (p237) offers the chance to don a miner's helmet and lamp and explore the claustrophobic tunnels of a medieval silver mine beneath the town. Most extraordinary of all is the Sedlec Ossuary (p238) at Kutná Hora, where the bones of 40,000 people have been fashioned into a series of weird and wonderful decorations.

KARLŠTEJN

Karlštejn Castle (☎ 274 008 154; www.hradkarlstejn.cz; Karlštejn; 🕑 9am-6pm Tue-Sun Jul & Aug, to 5pm Tue-Sun May, Jun & Sep, to 4pm Tue-Sun Apr & Oct, closed Feb; see website for opening times in Nov-Jan & Mar), rising above the village of Karlštejn 30km southwest of Prague, is in such good shape these days that it wouldn't look out of place on Disneyworld's Main St. The crowds come in theme-park proportions as well (it's best to book ahead for the guided tours), but the peaceful surrounding countryside offers views of Karlštejn's stunning exterior that rival anything you'll see on the inside.

Perched high on a crag that overlooks the Berounka River, this cluster of turrets, high walls and looming towers is as immaculately maintained as it is powerfully evocative. It's rightly one of the top attractions of the Czech Republic, and the only drawback is its overwhelming popularity: in the summer months it is literally mobbed with visitors, ice-cream vendors and souvenir stalls.

Karlštejn was born of a grand pedigree, starting life in 1348 as a hideaway for the crown jewels

TRANSPORT: KARLŠTEJN

Distance from Prague 30km

Direction Southwest

Travel time One hour

Train Trains to Beroun from Praha-Smíchov stop at Karlštejn (42Kč, 33 minutes, hourly).

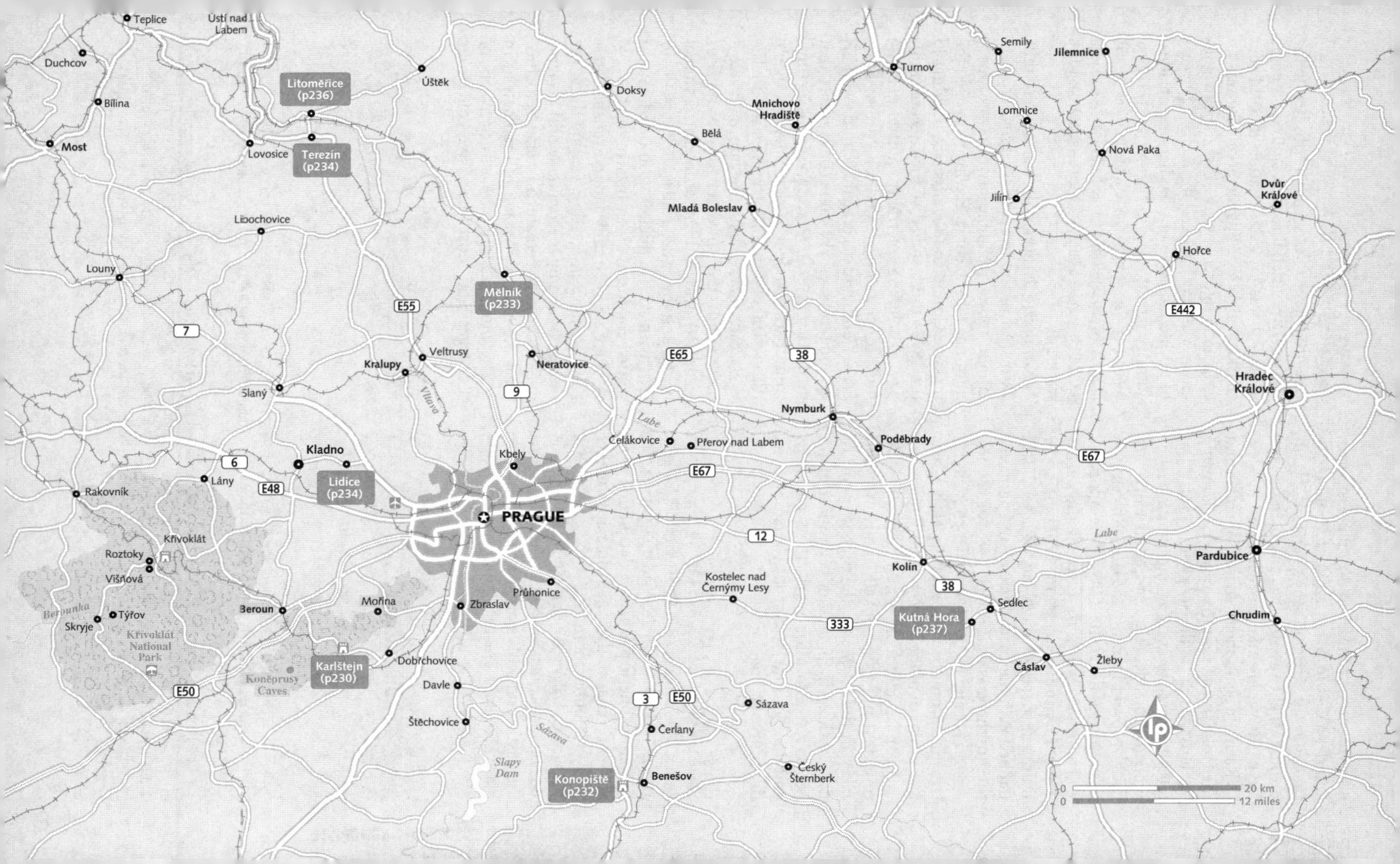
Teplice
Ústí nad Labem
Duchcov
Bílina
Most
Litoměřice (p236)
Terezín (p234)
Lovosice
Úštěk
Doksy
Bělá
Mnichovo Hradiště
Turnov
Semily
Jilemnice
Lomnice
Nová Paka
Jilín
Dvůr Králové
Mladá Boleslav
Libochovice
Louny
Hořce
Mělník (p233)
E55
7
E442
E65
38
Veltrusy
Kralupy
Neratovice
Slaný
9
Vltava
Hradec Králové
Nymburk
Labe
Kladno
Poděbrady
Čelákovice
Přerov nad Labem
Kbely
6
E67
Lány
Lidice (p234)
E48
Rakovník
PRAGUE
12
Křivoklát
Roztoky
Višňová
Mořina
Berounka
Beroun
Týřov
Skryje
Křivoklát National Park
Zbraslav
Průhonice
Kostelec nad Černými Lesy
Kolín
Pardubice
Sedlec
333
Kutná Hora (p237)
Chrudim
Karlštejn (p230)
Dobřichovice
Koněprusy Caves
E50
Davle
3
Sázava
Čerľany
Štěchovice
Čáslav
Žleby
Český Šternberk
Slapy Dam
Konopiště (p232)
Benešov
0 20 km
0 12 miles

and treasury of the Holy Roman Emperor, Charles IV. Run by an appointed burgrave, the castle was surrounded by a network of land-owning knight-vassals, who came to the castle's aid whenever enemies moved against it.

Karlštejn again sheltered the Bohemian and the Holy Roman Empire crown jewels during the Hussite wars of the early 15th century, but fell into disrepair as its defences became outmoded. Considerable restoration work, not least by Josef Mocker in the late 19th century, has returned the castle to its former glory.

There are two tours through the castle. Tour I (adult/concession 220/120Kč, 50 minutes) passes through the Knight's Hall, still daubed with the coats-of-arms and names of the knight-vassals, Charles IV's Bedchamber, the Audience Hall and the Jewel House, which includes treasures from the Chapel of the Holy Cross and a replica of the St Wenceslas Crown.

Tour II (adult/concession 300/150Kč, 70 minutes) must be booked in advance and takes in the Great Tower, the highest point of the castle, which includes a museum on Mocker's restoration work, the Marian Tower and the exquisite Chapel of the Holy Cross, with its decorative ceiling.

EATING & SLEEPING

Pension & Restaurant U Janů (☎ 311 681 210; info@ujanu.cz; d/apt 1000/1200Kč) On the road up to the castle, this atmospheric place has a decent dollop of authentic charm; there are three apartments and one double room.

Penzión U královny Dagmar (☎ 311 681 614; www.penziondagmara.cz; d/tr/apt 800/1000/1200Kč) Closer to the castle and with similar prices, this slick place has all the creature comforts and a top-notch eatery.

KONOPIŠTĚ

Archduke Franz Ferdinand d'Este, heir to the Austro-Hungarian throne, is famous for being dead – it was his assassination in 1914 that sparked off WWI. But the archduke was an enigmatic figure who avoided the intrigues of the Vienna court and for the last 20 years of his life hid away in what became his ideal country retreat, Konopiště Chateau (☎ 317 721 366; Benešov; 9am-5pm Tue-Sun May-Aug, 9am-4pm Tue-Fri, to 5pm Sat & Sun Sep, 9am-3pm Tue-Fri, to 4pm Sat & Sun Apr & Oct, 9am-3pm Sat & Sun Nov; closed Dec-Mar & noon-1pm year-round).

Konopiště, lying amid extensive grounds 2km west of the town of Benešov, is a testament to the archduke's twin obsessions – hunting and St George. Having renovated the massive Gothic and Renaissance building in the 1890s and installed all the latest technology – including electricity, central heating, flush toilets, showers and a luxurious lift – Franz Ferdinand decorated his home with his hunting trophies. His game books record that he shot about 300,000 creatures in his lifetime, from foxes and deer to elephants and tigers. About 100,000 animal trophies adorn the walls, each marked with the date and place it met its end – the crowded Trophy Corridor (Tour I and III), with a forest of mounted animal heads, and the antler-clad Chamois Room (Tour III), with its 'chandelier' fashioned from a stuffed condor, are truly bizarre sights.

There are three guided tours available. Tour III is the most interesting, visiting the private apartments used by the archduke and his family, which have remained unchanged since the state took possession of the chateau in 1921. Tour II takes in the Great Armoury, one of the largest and most impressive collections

TRANSPORT: KONOPIŠTĚ

Distance from Prague 50km

Direction South

Travel time 1¼ hours

Bus There are buses from Prague's Roztyly metro station to Benešov (39Kč, 40 minutes, twice hourly) – their final destination is usually Pelhřimov or Jihlava. There are also buses to Benešov from Prague's Florenc bus station (48Kč, 40 minutes, eight daily).

Train There are frequent direct trains from Prague's Hlavní Nádraží to Benešov u Prahy (66Kč, 1¼ hours, hourly). Konopiště is 2km west of Benešov. Local bus 2 (8Kč, six minutes, hourly) runs from a stop on Dukelská, 400m north of the train station (turn left out of the station, take first right on Tyršova and then first left) to the castle car park. If you'd rather walk, turn left out of the train station, go left across the bridge over the railway, and follow Konopištská street west for 2km.

in Europe. Tour I and Tour II in English are adult/child 190/110Kč; Tour III in English is 300/200Kč.

The archduke's collection of art and artefacts relating to St George is no less impressive, amounting to 3750 items, many of which are on show in the St George Museum (Muzeum sv Jiří; adult/child 30/15Kč; same as chateau) beneath the terrace at the front of the castle.

EATING & SLEEPING

Hostinec U zlaté hvězdy (☎ 317 723 921; Masarykovo náměstí 2, Benešov; mains 90-180Kč; 10am-10pm Mon-Thu, to 11pm Fri & Sat, 11am-10pm Sun) Enjoy Bohemian pub grub at this snug, central *pivnice* (beer hall).

Hotel Atlas (☎ 317 724 771; www.hotel-atlas.cz; Tyršova 2063, Benešov; s/d from 840/980Kč) This place is bland and functional, but the rooms are spotless and comfortable. Benešov is located just 2km east of the Konopiště Chateau.

Hotel Nová Myslivna (☎ 317 722 496; www.e-stranka.cz/novamyslivna; Konopiště; r from 375Kč per person; P) The sweeping angular roof of this chalet-style hotel clashes somewhat with the softer lines of the castle, but the hotel's location by the Konopiště Chateau car park is unbeatable.

MĚLNÍK

Mělník, an hour's drive north of Prague, sprawls over a rocky promontory surrounded by the flat sweep of the central Bohemian plain. Staunchly Hussite in its sympathies, the town was flattened by Swedish troops in the Thirty Years' War, but the castle was rebuilt as a prettier, less threatening chateau and the centre retains a strong historical identity. Modernity has caught up with the town's trailing edge, bringing a clutch of factories to its outskirts, but views from the castle side are untouched and Mělník remains a good place for a spot of wine-tasting – the town is the focus of Bohemia's modest wine-growing region.

The Renaissance Mělník Chateau (Zámek Mělník; ☎ 315 622 121; adult/concession 80/60Kč; 10am-5pm) was acquired by the Lobkowicz family in 1739; the family opened it to the public in 1990. You can wander through the former living quarters, which are crowded with a rich collection of baroque furniture and 17th- and 18th-century paintings, on a self-guided tour with English text. Additional rooms have changing exhibits of modern works and a fabulous collection of 17th-century maps and engravings detailing Europe's great cities. A separate tour descends to the 14th-century wine cellars, where you can taste the chateau's wines; a shop in the courtyard sells the chateau's own label. Wine-tasting sessions cost from 70Kč to 200Kč.

TRANSPORT: MĚLNÍK

Distance from Prague 30km

Direction North

Travel time One hour

Bus On weekdays, buses run to Mělník (44Kč, 45 minutes, every 30 minutes) from stop 10 in the bus station outside Praha-Holešovice train station; buy your ticket from the driver (one-way only, no return tickets).

Next to the chateau is the 15th-century Gothic Church of Sts Peter & Paul (kostel sv Petra a Pavla), with its baroque furnishings and tower. Remnants of its Romanesque predecessor have been incorporated into the rear of the building. The old crypt is now an ossuary (kostnice; adult/child 30/15Kč; 9.30am-12.30pm & 1.15-4pm Tue-Fri, 10am-12.30pm & 1.15-4pm Sat & Sun), packed with the bones of some 10,000 people dug up to make room for 16th-century plague victims, arranged in macabre patterns. This crypt is much more visceral – and claustrophobic – than the ossuary at Sedlec (see p238): the floor is of beaten earth and you are literally rubbing shoulders with the stacked bones.

The path between chateau and church leads to a terrace with superb views across the river and the central Bohemian countryside. The steep slopes beneath the terrace are planted with vines – supposedly descendants of the first vines to be introduced to Bohemia, by Charles IV, back in the 14th century.

INFORMATION

Tourist Information Centre (☎ 315 627 503; infocentrum@melnik.cz; náměstí Míru 11; 9am-5pm May-Sep, Mon-Fri only Oct-Apr) Sells maps and historical guides, and can help with accommodation.

EATING & DRINKING

Restaurace sv Václav (☎ 315 622 126; Svatováclavská 22; mains 120-230Kč; 11am-11pm) Dark wood décor, cigar humidors, red leather seats and an outdoor terrace that's a lunchtime suntrap conspire to make this one of Mělník's most appealing restaurants.

Kavárna ve Věží (☎ 315 621 954; ulice 5.května; 🕒 8am-10pm Mon-Thu, 8am-11pm Fri, 2-11pm Sat, 2-10pm Sun) Set in the medieval tower of the Prague Gate, this atmospheric café and art gallery spreads across three floors linked by creaking wooden stairs, and served by an ingenious dumb waiter: write your order on the note pad, ding the bell, and the tray goes down, returning a few moments later with your order. Choose from a wide range of freshly ground coffees and exotic teas, local wines, beer and *medovina* (mead).

SLEEPING

Hotel U Rytířů (☎ 315 621 440; www.urytiru.cz; Svatováclavská 17; d 1900-2500Kč) Located conveniently right next to the castle, this opulent little place has plush, apartment-style rooms with all the trimmings and a garden restaurant (mains 100-250Kč; 🕒 8am-11pm).

Penzión Centrum (☎ 315 625 585; penzioncentrum@seznam.cz; Seiferta 13; s/d incl breakfast 1000/1300Kč) This reasonably central place (it's just two blocks south of náměstí Míru) has modest but comfortable rooms. Look for the bright yellow façade.

LIDICE, TEREZÍN & LITOMĚŘICE

The Bohemian countryside to the north of Prague contains two villages that provide a sobering reminder of the horrors inflicted on the Czech people during WWII. If you're driving, Lidice and Terezín can be combined in one day; if you want to spend the night, head for the attractive town of Litoměřice, 3km north of Terezín. Using public transport, you'll have to choose; it's only practical to do one or the other in a single day.

LIDICE

When British-trained Czechoslovak paratroops assassinated Reichsprotektor Reinhard Heydrich in June 1942 (see the boxed text, p115), the Nazis took a savage revenge. Picking the mining and foundry village of Lidice, 18km northwest of Prague, apparently at random, they proceeded on 10 June 1942 to obliterate it from the face of the earth. All its men were shot, the women and the older children were shipped to the Ravensbrück concentration camp, and the younger children were farmed out to German foster homes. The village was then systematically burned and bulldozed so that no trace remained. Of its 500 inhabitants, 192 men, 60 women and 88 children eventually died. The atrocity caused shock around the world and triggered a campaign to preserve the village's memory. The site is now a green field, eloquent in its silence, dotted with a few memorials and the reconstructed foundations of a farm where most of the men were murdered.

TRANSPORT: LIDICE

Distance from Prague 18km
Direction Northwest
Travel time 30 minutes
Bus Buses from Prague to Lidice (25Kč, 30 minutes, hourly) depart from the bus stop on Evropa, opposite the Hotel Diplomat, just west of Dejvická metro station.

The onsite Muzeum Lidice (www.lidice-memorial.cz; Lidice; adult/concession 80/40Kč; 🕒 9am-6pm Apr-Oct, to 5pm Mar, to 4pm Nov-Feb) recreates the village in photographs, text and an emotive multimedia exhibition, and also screens chilling SS film footage of its destruction.

TEREZÍN

A massive bulwark of stone and earth, the fortress of Terezín (Theresienstadt in German) was built in 1780 by Emperor Joseph II with a single purpose in mind: to keep the enemy out. Ironically, it is more notorious for keeping people in – it served as a political prison in the later days of the Habsburg Empire. Gavrilo Princip, the assassin who killed Archduke Franz Ferdinand in 1914, was incarcerated here during WWI, and when the Germans took control during WWII the fortress became a grim holding pen for Jews bound for the extermination camps. In contrast to the colourful, baroque face of many Czech towns, Terezín is a stark but profoundly evocative monument to a darker aspect of Europe's past.

The bleakest phase of Terezín's history began in 1940 when the Gestapo established a prison in the Lesser Fortress. Evicting the inhabitants from the Main Fortress the following year, the Nazis transformed the town into a transit camp through which some 150,000 people eventually passed en route to the death camps. For most, conditions were

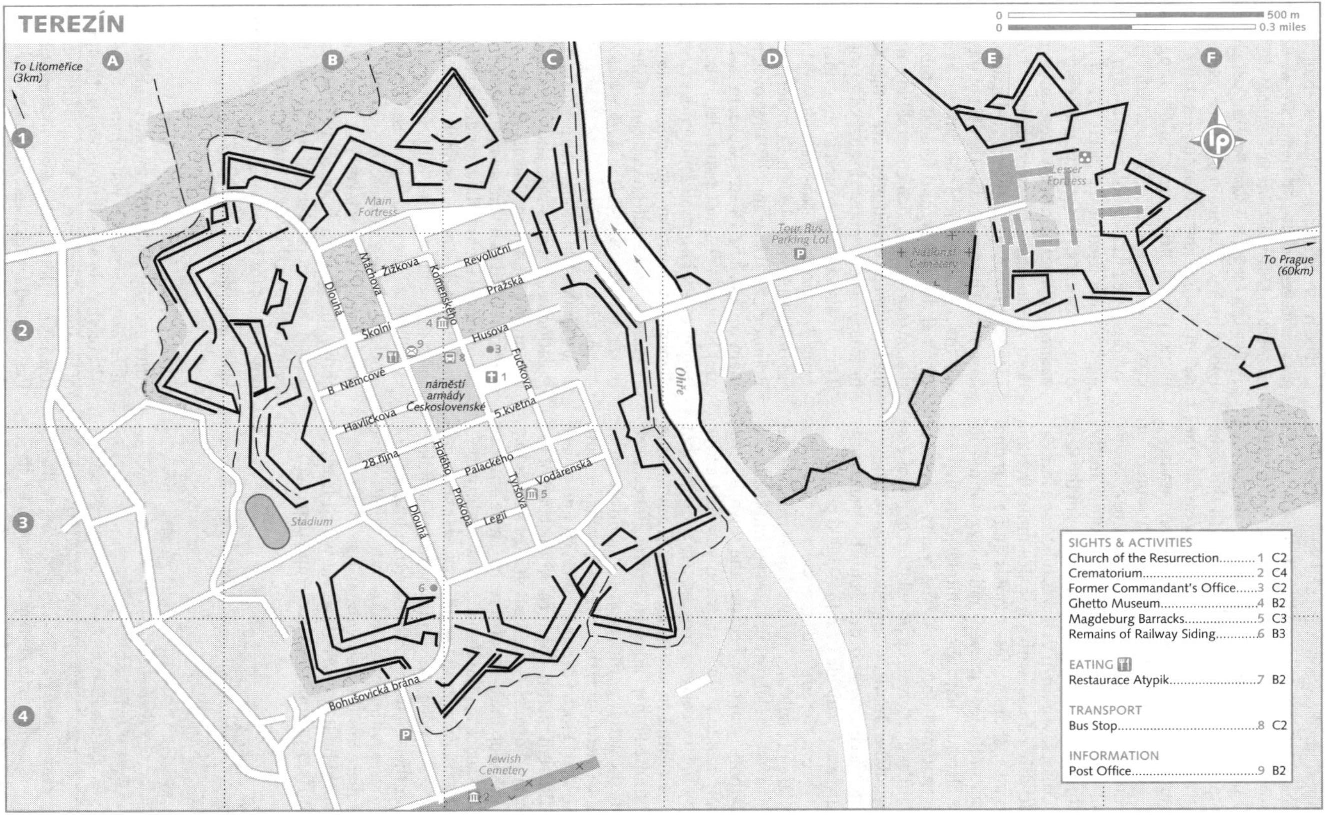
TEREZÍN
0 500 m
0 0.3 miles
A
B
C
D
E
F
1
2
3
4
To Litoměřice (3km)
To Prague (60km)
Main Fortress
Lesser Fortress
Tour Bus Parking Lot
National Cemetery
Ohře
Stadium
Jewish Cemetery
Dlouhá
Máchova
Žižkova
Komenského
Revoluční
Pražská
Školní
Husova
Fučíkova
B. Němcové
náměstí armády Československé
5.května
Havlíčkova
28.října
Hollého
Palackého
Vodárenská
Prokopa
Tyršova
Legií
Bohušovická brána
SIGHTS & ACTIVITIES
Church of the Resurrection....1 C2
Crematorium....2 C4
Former Commandant's Office....3 C2
Ghetto Museum....4 B2
Magdeburg Barracks....5 C3
Remains of Railway Siding....6 B3
EATING
Restaurace Atypik....7 B2
TRANSPORT
Bus Stop....8 C2
INFORMATION
Post Office....9 B2

appalling. Between April and September 1942 the ghetto's population increased from 12,968 to 58,491, leaving each prisoner with only 1.65 sq m of space and causing disease and starvation on a terrifying scale. In the same period, there was a 15-fold increase in the number of deaths within the prison walls.

Terezín later became the centrepiece of one of the Nazis' more extraordinary coups of public relations. Official visitors to the fortress, including representatives of the Red Cross, saw a town that was billed as a kind of Jewish 'refuge', with a Jewish administration, banks, shops, cafés, schools and a thriving cultural life – it even had a jazz band – in a charade that twice completely fooled international observers. The reality was a relentlessly increasing population of prisoners, regular trains departing for the gas chambers of Auschwitz, and the death by starvation, disease or suicide of some 35,000 people.

From the ground, the sheer scale of the maze of walls and moats that surrounds the Main Fortress (Hlavní pevnost) is impossible to fathom – mainly because the town is actually inside it. In fact, when you first arrive by bus or car you may be left thinking that the central square looks no different from a hundred other old town centres. Take a peek at the aerial photograph in the Museum of the Ghetto, or wander past the walls en route to the Lesser Fortress, however, and a very different picture emerges. At the heart of the Main Fortress is the neat grid of streets that makes up the town of Terezín. There's little to look at except the chunky, 19th-century Church of the Resurrection, the arcaded former Commandant's office, the neoclassical administrative buildings on the square and the surrounding grid of houses with their awful secrets. South of the square are the anonymous remains of a railway siding, built by prisoners, via which loads of further prisoners arrived – and departed.

TRANSPORT: TEREZÍN & LITOMĚŘICE

Distance from Prague 60km (to Terezín)
Direction North
Travel time 1½ hours
Bus Direct buses from Prague to Litoměřice (64Kč, one hour, hourly), stopping at Terezín, depart from the bus station outside Praha-Holešovice train station. There are also frequent buses between Litoměřice bus station and Terezín (9Kč, 10 minutes, at least hourly).

The main sight here is the absorbing Ghetto Museum (Muzeum ghetta; ☎ 416 782 576; www.pamatnik-terezin.cz; Komenského, Terezín; adult/child 160/130Kč; 9am-6pm Apr-Oct, to 5.30pm Nov-Mar), which has two branches. The main branch explores the rise of Nazism and life in the Terezín ghetto, using period bric-a-brac to startling and evocative effect. Erected in the 19th century to house the local school, the museum building was later used by the Nazis to accommodate the camp's 10- to 15-year-old boys. The haunting images painted by these children still decorate the walls. A newer branch is housed in the former Magdeburg Barracks (Magdeburská kasárna), which served as the seat of the Jewish 'town council'. Here you can visit a reconstructed dormitory, and look at exhibits on the extraordinarily rich cultural life – music, theatre, fine arts and literature – that somehow flourished against this backdrop of fear. There is also a small exhibit in the grim Crematorium (Krematorium; 10am-6pm Sun-Fri Apr-Oct, to 4pm Sun-Fri Nov-Mar) in the Jewish Cemetery just off Bohušovická brána, about 750m south of the main square. The Ghetto Museum has good multilingual self-guide pamphlets, a large selection of books for sale, and guides (some of them ghetto survivors) to offer assistance.

You can take a self-guided tour of the Lesser Fortress (Malá pevnost; ☎ 416 782 576; www.pamatnik-terezin.cz; Terezín; adult/child 160/130Kč; 8am-6pm Apr-Oct, to 4.30pm Nov-Mar) through the prison barracks, isolation cells, workshops and morgues, past execution grounds and former mass graves. It would be hard to invent a more menacing location, and it is only while wandering through the seemingly endless tunnels beneath the walls that you begin to fully appreciate the vast dimensions of the fortress. The Nazis' mocking concentration camp slogan, *Arbeit Macht Frei* ('Work Makes You Free'), hangs above the gate. In front of the fortress is a National Cemetery, established in 1945 for those exhumed from the Nazis' mass graves. A combined ticket for both the Ghetto Museum and Lesser Fortress is 200/150Kč.

LITOMĚŘICE

After gritting your teeth through the horrors of Terezín, Litoměřice is your chance to exhale. Although only a few kilometres to the north of the infamous fortress, this quaint riverside town is a million miles away in atmosphere. Pastel-hued façades and intricate gables jostle for dominance on the main square, and the town's lively bars and restaurants play host to some vibrant after-hours action. Once stridently Hussite, much of the Gothic face of Litoměřice was levelled during the Thirty Years' War (1618–48), and today the town's unassuming castle plays second fiddle to a clutch of effete Renaissance houses and impressive churches (many by esteemed 18th-century architect Ottavio Broggio).

Dominating Mírové náměstí, the town's attractive main square, is the Gothic tower of All Saints Church (kostel Všech svatých), built in the 13th century and 'Broggio-ised' in 1718. Beside it, with multiple gables, pointy arches and a copper-topped tower, is the handsome, Gothic Old Town Hall (Stará radnice), which includes a small town museum. Most striking is the 1560 Renaissance House at the Black Eagle (dům U černého orla), covered in *sgraffito* biblical scenes and housing the Hotel Salva Guarda. A few doors down is the present town hall, in the 1539 House at the Chalice (dům U kalicha), featuring a massive Hussite chalice on the roof. This building also houses the tourist information office. The thin slice of baroque wedding cake at the uphill end of the square is the House of Ottavio Broggio.

Along Michalská at the southwest corner of the square you'll find another house where Broggio left his mark, the excellent North Bohemia Fine Arts Gallery (Severo česká galerie výtvarného umění; ☎ 416 732 382; Michalská 7, Litoměřice; adult/concession 32/16Kč; 9am-noon & 1-6pm Tue-Sun Apr-Sep, 9am-5pm Tue-Sun Oct-Mar) with the priceless Renaissance panels of the Litoměřice Altarpiece.

Turn left at the end of Michalská and follow Domská towards grassy, tree-lined Domské náměstí on Cathedral Hill, passing pretty St Wenceslas Church (kostel sv Václav), a true baroque gem, along a side street to the right. At the top of the hill is the town's oldest church, St Stephen Cathedral (Chrám sv Štěpán), dating from the 11th century.

Go through the arch to the left of the cathedral and descend a steep, cobbled lane called Máchova. At the foot of the hill turn left then take the first right, up the zigzag steps to the old town walls. You can follow the walls to the right as far as the next street, Jezuitská, where a left turn leads back to the square.

INFORMATION

Litoměřice Tourist Information Office (☎ 416 732 440; www.litomerice.cz; Mírové náměstí 15, Litoměřice; 8am-6pm Mon-Fri, 8am-5.30pm Sat, 9.30am-4pm Sun May-Sep, 8am-5pm Mon & Wed, 8am-4.15pm Tue & Thu, 8am-4pm Fri, 8-11am Sat Oct-Apr)

EATING

Bašta Steakhouse (☎ 608 437 783; Mezibraní 5, Litoměřice; mains 100-500Kč; 11am-midnight) Housed in a former bastion in the old city walls opposite the train station, this lively restaurant boasts a charcoal grill that turns out everything from buffalo wings to thick T-bone steaks.

Restaurace Atypik (☎ 416 782 780; Máchova 91, Terezín; mains 70-120Kč; 11am-10pm) Atypik by name but rather typical by nature, this bustling place offers all the predictable local favourites, with an emphasis on stodge and unapologetic meatiness.

SLEEPING

Hotel Salva Guarda (☎ 416 732 506; www.salva-guarda.cz; Mírové náměstí 12, Litoměřice; s/d from 1220/1750Kč; P) Litoměřice's top hotel is set in the lovely Renaissance House at the Black Eagle; it also has the best restaurant on the square.

Pension Prislin (☎ 416 735 833; www.prislin.cz; Na Kocandě 12, Litoměřice; s/d 750/1260Kč; P) A view across the river and breakfast in the garden are good reasons for choosing the family-friendly Prislin. It's five minutes' walk east of the town square, along the main road.

U svatého Václava (☎ 416 737 500; www.upfront.cz/penzion; Svatováclavská 12, Litoměřice; s/d 800/1200Kč) Tucked away in the shadow of St Wenceslas Church, this pretty villa houses a tip-top pension with sauna, well-equipped rooms and a homely apron-toting owner who whips up a fine breakfast.

KUTNÁ HORA

Now dwarfed by 21st-century Prague, Kutná Hora once marched in step with the capital and, with a little help from fate, might even have stolen its crown as the heart and soul of Bohemia. Enriched by the silver ore that ran in veins through the surrounding hills, the medieval city once enjoyed explosive growth, becoming the seat of Wenceslas II's royal mint in 1308 and the residence of Wenceslas IV just under 100 years later. The silver *groschen* that were minted here at that time represented the hard currency of Central Europe. But while boom time Kutná Hora was Prague's undisputed understudy, the town tripped out of history when the silver mines began to splutter and run dry in the 16th century, its demise hastened by the Thirty Years' War and finally certified by a devastating fire in 1770. While the capital continued to expand, its sister city largely vanished from sight.

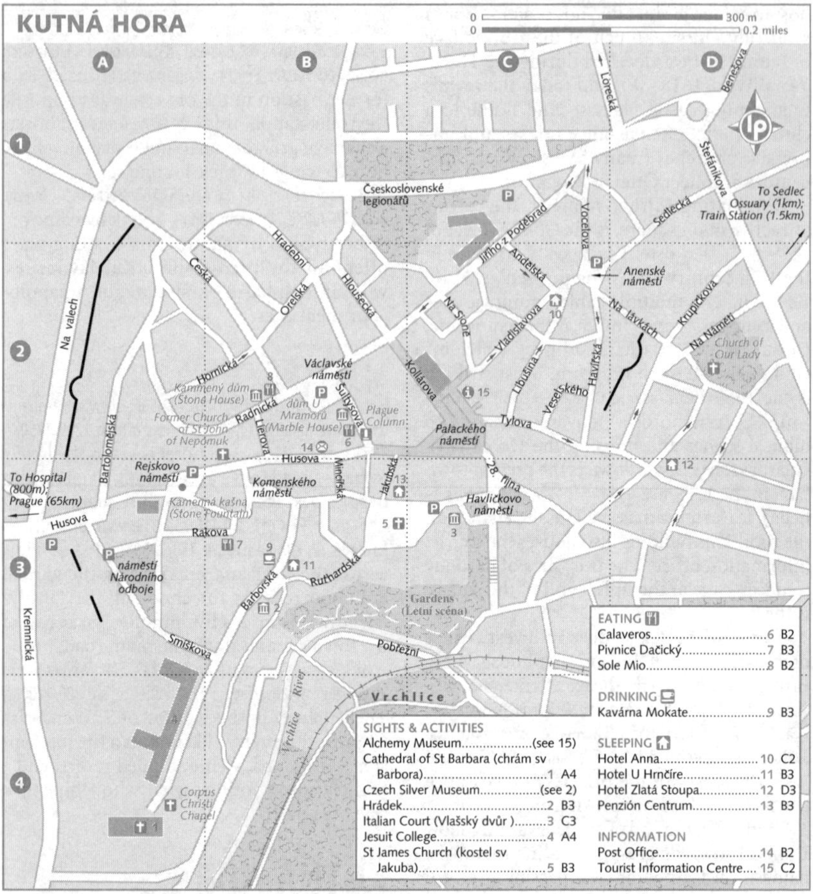

But that's not to say everyone has forgotten about it. Kutná Hora today is an A-list tourist attraction – it was added to Unesco's World Heritage List in 1996 – luring visitors with a smorgasbord of historic sights and more than a touch of nostalgic whimsy. Standing on the ramparts surrounding the mighty Cathedral of St Barbara, looking out across rooftops eerily reminiscent of Prague's Malá Strana, it's all too easy to indulge in spot of melancholic what-might-have-been.

If you arrive by train, a natural first stop is the remarkable 'bone church' of the **Sedlec Ossuary** (Kostnice; ☎ 327 561 143; www.kostnice.cz; Zámecká 127; adult/concession 50/30Kč; 🕑 8am-6pm Apr-Sep, 9am-noon & 1-5pm Mar & Oct, 9am-noon & 1-4pm Nov-Feb), an 800m walk south from Kutná Hora's main train station. When the Schwarzenberg family purchased Sedlec monastery in 1870 they allowed a local woodcarver to get creative with the bones that had been piled in the crypt for centuries. But this was no piddling little heap of bones: it was the remains of no fewer than 40,000 people. The result was spectacular – garlands of skulls and femurs are strung from the vaulted ceiling like Addams Family Christmas decorations, while in the centre dangles a vast chandelier containing at least one of each bone in the human body. Four giant pyramids of stacked bones squat in each of the corner chapels, and crosses, chalices and monstrances of bone adorn the altar. There's even a Schwarzenberg coat-of-arms made from bones – note the crow pecking the eyes from the Turk's head, a grisly motif of the Schwarzenberg family.

From Sedlec it's a 1.5m walk (or five-minute bus ride) into central Kutná Hora. Palackého náměstí, the main square, is unremarkable; the most interesting part of the old town lies to its south. But first, take a look at the Alchemy Museum (☎ 327 511 259; Palackého náměstí 377; adult/concession 50/30Kč; ⏲ 10am-5pm Apr-Oct, to 4pm Nov-Mar), in the same building as the information centre, complete with basement laboratory, Gothic chapel and mad-scientist curator.

From the upper end of the square a narrow lane called Jakubská leads directly to the huge St James Church (kostel sv Jakuba; 1330). Just east of the church lies the Italian Court (Vlašský dvůr; ☎ 327 512 873; Havlíčkovo náměstí 552; adult/concession 100/60Kč; ⏲ 9am-6pm Apr-Sep, 10am-5pm Mar & Oct, 10am-4pm Nov-Feb), the former Royal Mint – it got its name from the master craftsmen from Florence brought in by Wenceslas II to kick-start the business, and who began stamping silver coins here in 1300. The oldest remaining part, the niches in the courtyard (now bricked up), were minters' workshops. The original treasury rooms hold an exhibit on coins and minting. The guided tour (with English text) is worth taking for a look at the few historical rooms open to the public, notably a 15th-century Audience Hall with two impressive 19th-century murals depicting the election of Vladislav Jagiello as king of Bohemia in 1471 (the angry man in white is Matthias Corvinus, the loser), and the Decree of Kutná Hora being proclaimed by Wenceslas IV and Jan Hus in 1409.

From the southern side of St James Church, a narrow cobbled lane (Ruthardská) leads down and then up to the Hrádek (Little Castle). Originally part of the town's fortifications, it was rebuilt in the 15th century as the residence of Jan Smíšek, administrator of the royal mines, who grew rich from silver he illegally mined right under the building. It now houses the Czech Silver Museum (České muzeum stříbra; ☎ 327 512 159; adult/concession 60/30Kč; ⏲ 10am-6pm Jul & Aug, 9am-6pm May, Jun & Sep, 9am-5pm Apr & Oct; closed Nov-Mar & Mon year-round). The exhibits celebrate the mines that made Kutná Hora wealthy, including a huge wooden device once used to lift loads weighing as much as 1000kg from the 200m-deep shafts. You can even don a miner's helmet and lamp and join a 45-minute guided tour (adult/child 110/70Kč) through 500m of medieval mine shafts beneath the town.

Just beyond the Hrádek is the 17th-century former Jesuit College, fronted by a terrace with a row of 13 baroque statues of saints, an arrangement inspired by the statues on Prague's Charles Bridge. All are related to the Jesuits and/or the town; the second statue – the woman holding a chalice, with a stone tower at her side – is St Barbara, the patron saint of miners and therefore of Kutná Hora.

At the far end of the terrace is Kutná Hora's greatest monument, the Gothic Cathedral of St Barbara (Chrám sv Barbora; ☎ 776 393 938; adult/concession 50/30Kč; ⏲ 9am-5.30pm Tue-Sun May-Sep, 10am-4pm Tue-Sun Oct-Apr). Rivalling Prague's St Vitus in size and magnificence, its soaring nave culminates in elegant, six-petalled ribbed vaulting. Work was started in 1380, interrupted during the Hussite Wars and abandoned in 1558 when the silver began to run out. It was finally completed in neogothic style at the end of the 19th century. The ambulatory chapels preserve some original 15th-century frescoes, some of them showing miners at work. Take a walk around the outside of the church, too; the terrace at the east end enjoys the finest view in town.

TRANSPORT: KUTNÁ HORA

Distance from Prague 65km

Direction East

Travel time 1½ hours

Train There are direct trains from Prague's main train station to Kutná Hora Hlavní Nádraží (129Kč return, 55 minutes, seven daily).

Bus There are about six direct buses a day, on weekdays only, from stop 2 at Prague's Florenc bus station to Kutná Hora (62Kc, 1¼ hours).

INFORMATION

Tourist Information Centre (☎ 327 512 378; www.kh.cz; Palackého náměstí 377; ⏲ 9am-6pm Apr-Oct, 9am-5pm Mon-Fri, 10am-4pm Sat & Sun Nov-Mar) Books accommodation, rents bicycles and offers internet access (per min 1Kč, minimum 15Kč).

EATING & DRINKING

Calaveros (☎ 327 513 810; Šultysova 173; mains 100-200Kč; ⏲ 11am-11pm Mon-Sat, to 10pm Sun) This lively (but smoky) Mexican restaurant in the Marble House may not win a golden sombrero for authenticity, but it's not bad for Central Bohemia – the salsa is fresh and the *chimichangas* are tasty.

Sole Mio (☎ 327 515 505; Česká 184; mains 90-120Kč; ⏲ 11am-10pm Sun-Thu, to 11pm Fri & Sat) Choose from 40 varieties of pizza at this homely little restaurant decorated with – surprise, surprise, considering the name – lots of suns.

Pivnice Dačický (☎ 327 512 248; Rakova 8; mains 110-300Kč; 🕒 11am-11pm) Get some froth on your moustache at this old-fashioned, wood-panelled Bohemian beer hall, where you can dine on dumplings and choose from five different draught beers, including Pilsner Urquell, Budvar and Primátor yeast beer.

Kavárna Mokate (Barborská 37; 🕒 8am-10pm Mon-Fri, 10am-10pm Sat, 10am-8pm Sun) This cosy little café, with ancient earthenware floor tiles, timber beams, mismatched furniture and oriental rugs dishes up a wide range of freshly ground coffees and exotic teas, as well as iced tea and coffee in summer.

SLEEPING

Hotel Anna (☎ 327 311 014; hotel.anna@seznam.cz; Vladislavova 372; s/d 930/1350Kč; P) Offers comfortable, modern rooms with shower, TV and breakfast in a lovely old building with an atmospheric stone-vaulted cellar restaurant.

Hotel Zlatá Stoupa (☎ 327 511 540; zlatastoupa@iol.cz; Tylova 426; s/d from 1220/1980Kč; P) If you feel like spoiling yourself, the most luxurious place in town is the elegantly furnished 'Golden Mount'. We like a hotel room where the minibar contains full-size bottles of wine.

Penzión Centrum (☎ 327 514 218; www.sweb.cz/penzion_centrum; Jakubská 57; d/tr 1000/1400Kč; P) Tucked away in a quiet, flower-bedecked courtyard off Kutná Hora's main drag, this place offers snug rooms and a sunny garden.

Hotel U Hrnčíře (☎ 327 512 113; hotel.hrncir@tiscali.cz; Barborská 24; d 750-2000Kč) This beautifully ornate pink townhouse has five stylish double rooms (rate depends on season and facilities) and a delightful garden terrace out back.

TRANSPORT

Prague sits right at the heart of Europe, and is well served by air, road and rail routes. The city itself has an excellent integrated public transport system with frequent tram, metro and bus services, though the historic central neighbourhoods are small enough to cover easily on foot.

THINGS CHANGE...

The information in this chapter is particularly vulnerable to change. Check directly with the airline or a travel agent to make sure you understand how a fare (and ticket you may buy) works and be aware of the security requirements for international travel. Shop carefully. The details given in this chapter should be regarded as pointers and are not a substitute for your own careful, up-to-date research.

AIR

Airport

Prague-Ruzyně Airport (Letiště Praha-Ruzyně; off Map pp58–9; flight information ☎ 220 113 314; www.csl.cz), 17km west of the city centre, is the hub for the national carrier Czech Airlines (ČSA; Map p106; ☎ 239 007 007; www.csa.cz; V Celnici 5, Nové Město), which operates direct flights to Prague from many European cities, including London, Dublin, Paris, Rome and Amsterdam, and also from New York and Toronto.

Prague's airport has two international terminals. Terminal 1 is for flights to/from non-Schengen countries (including the UK, Ireland and countries outside Europe), and Terminal 2 is for flights to/from Schengen Zone countries (most EU nations plus Switzerland, Iceland and Norway).

In both terminals the arrival and departure halls are next to each other on the same level. The arrival halls have exchange counters, ATMs, accommodation and car-hire agencies, public-transport information desks, taxi services and 24-hour left-luggage counters (per piece per day 100Kč). The departure halls have restaurants and bars, information offices, airline offices, an exchange counter and travel agencies. Once you're through security, there are shops, restaurants, bars, internet access and wi-fi.

There's a post office (🕑 8am-6pm Mon-Fri, to 1pm Sat) in the administrative centre on the far side of the Europort Shopping Centre opposite the arrival hall of Terminal 1.

BICYCLE

Prague is not the best city for getting around by bike. Traffic is heavy, tram tracks can be dangerous and there are lots of hills and

CLIMATE CHANGE & TRAVEL

Climate change is a serious threat to the ecosystems that humans rely upon, and air travel is the fastest-growing contributor to the problem. Lonely Planet regards travel, overall, as a global benefit, but believes we all have a responsibility to limit our personal impact on global warming.

Flying & Climate Change

Pretty much every form of motor transport generates CO_2 (the main cause of human-induced climate change) but planes are far and away the worst offenders, not just because of the sheer distances they allow us to travel, but also because they release greenhouse gases high into the atmosphere. The statistics are frightening: two people taking a return flight between Europe and the US will contribute as much to climate change as an average household's gas and electricity consumption over a whole year.

Carbon Offset Schemes

Climatecare.org and other websites use 'carbon calculators' that allow jetsetters to offset the greenhouse gases they are responsible for with contributions to energy-saving projects and other climate-friendly initiatives in the developing world – including projects in India, Honduras, Kazakhstan and Uganda.

Lonely Planet, together with Rough Guides and other concerned partners in the travel industry, supports the carbon offset scheme run by climatecare.org. Lonely Planet offsets all of its staff and author travel.

For more information check out our website: www.lonelyplanet.com.

GETTING INTO TOWN

To get into town, buy a transfer ticket (26Kč) from the public transport (Dopravní podnik; DPP) desk in Arrivals and take bus 119 (20 minutes, every 10 minutes, 4am to midnight) to the end of the line (Dejvická), then continue by metro into the city centre (another 10 to 15 minutes; no new ticket needed). Note that you'll also need a half-fare (13Kč) ticket for your bag or suitcase if it's larger than 25cm x 45cm x 70cm. If you're heading to the western part of the city, take bus 100, which goes to Zličín metro station.

Alternatively, take a Cedaz minibus (☎ 221 111 111; www.cedaz.cz) from outside Arrivals to the Czech Airlines office (Map p106), near náměstí Republiky (120Kč, 20 minutes, every 30 minutes 5.30am to 9.30pm); buy a ticket from the driver. You can also opt to get off earlier at the Dejvická metro stop (90Kč) instead. Or you can get a Cedaz minibus direct to your hotel or any other address in the city centre (480Kč for one to four people, 960Kč for five to eight) – book and pay at the Cedaz desk in the Arrivals hall. Prague Airport Shuttle (☎ 602 395 421; www.prague-airport-shuttle.cz) and SmartShuttle (☎ 728 40 40 40; www.smartshuttle.cz) operate similar services.

Airport Cars (☎ 14014, 222 333 222) operate a 24-hour taxi service, charging around 550 to 600Kč to get to the centre of Prague. Drivers usually speak some English and accept Visa credit cards.

cobbled streets. That said, the popularity of cycling is steadily increasing and the city now has about 260km of signposted cycle routes.

Bikes must be equipped with a bell, mudguards, a white reflector and white light up front, a red reflector and flashing red light at the rear, and reflectors on pedals – if not, you can be fined up to 1000Kč. Cyclists up to the age of 15 must wear helmets.

If you're at least 12 years old you can take your bicycle on the metro, but you must place it near the last door of the rear carriage, and only two bikes are allowed per train. Bikes are not permitted if the carriage is full, or if there's already a pram in the carriage.

For more information on cycling and bike hire, see p206.

BOAT

See p251 for details of river transport between Prague city centre and Troja (for Prague Zoo and Troja Chateau; see p140).

BUS

Prague has two main bus stations. All international and long-distance domestic buses (and many regional services) use Florenc bus station (ÚAN Praha Florenc; Map pp126–7; Křižíkova 4, Karlín), while regional buses to the northeastern Czech Republic (including Mělník, see p233) depart from Holešovice bus station (AN Praha Holešovice; Map pp132–3; Vrbenského, Holešovice).

International bus operators include Touring Bohemia/Eurolines (☎ 224 218 680; www.bei.cz) and Student Agency (☎ 800 100 300; www.studentagency.cz); both have offices at Florenc bus station.

You can find local and regional bus timetable info in English at www.vlak-bus.cz and ☎ 900 144 444. On these services you buy your ticket from the driver as you board. For details of city bus services see Public Transport, opposite.

CAR & MOTORCYCLE

Driving in Prague is no fun, especially in the narrow, winding streets of the city centre. Trying to find your way around – or to park legally – while coping with trams, buses, other drivers, cyclists and pedestrians can make you wish you'd left the car at home.

Prague Information Service (see p255) publishes a *Transport Guide* with many useful tips for drivers, including emergency breakdown services, where to find car-repair shops (by make) and all-important parking tips.

Driving

Traffic in the Czech Republic drives on the right. In Prague you may overtake a tram only on the right, and only if it's in motion. You must stop behind any tram taking on or letting off passengers where there's no passenger island. A tram has the right of way when making any signalled turn across your path.

In case of an accident the police should be contacted immediately if repairs are likely to cost over 20,000Kč or if there is an injury. Even if damage is slight, it's a good idea to report the accident as the police will issue an insurance report that will help avoid problems when you take the car out of the country or return it to the rental company.

For emergency breakdowns, the ÚAMK (Central Automobile & Motorcycle Club; Map pp58–9; ☎ 261

104 333; www.uamk.cz; Na Strži 9, Nusle) provides nationwide assistance 24 hours a day – call ☎ 1230 for breakdown assistance (or ☎ +420 21230 if calling from a non-Czech mobile phone). ÚAMK has agreements with national motoring organisations across the world through its affiliations with the Alliance Internationale de Tourisme and the Fédération Internationale de l'Automobile. If you are a member of any of these, ÚAMK will help you on roughly the same terms as your own organisation would. If not, you must pay for all services.

Hire

The major international car-hire chains all have airport pick-up points as well as offices in the city centre. Their rates begin at around 1600/9000Kč per day/week for a Škoda Fabia, including unlimited mileage, collision-damage waiver and value-added tax (VAT; 'DPH' in Czech). There's a 650Kč surcharge to pick up your vehicle from the airport, but delivery to hotels in central Prague is free.

Small local companies such as Secco, Vecar and West Car Praha offer much better rates, but are less likely to have fluent English-speaking staff – it's easier to book through their websites than by phone. Typical rates for a Škoda Fabia are around 800Kč a day, including unlimited mileage, collision-damage waiver and VAT.

A-Rent Car/Thrifty (Map pp108–9; ☎ 224 233 265; www.arentcar.cz; Washingtonova 9, Nové Město; Ⓜ Muzeum)

Avis (Map p106; ☎ 810 777 810; www.avis.cz; Klimentská 46, Nové Město; 🚊 5, 8, 14)

CS-Czechocar (Map p116; ☎ 261 222 079; www.czechocar.cz; Congress Centre, 5.května 65, Vyšehrad; Ⓜ Vyšehrad)

Europcar (Map pp88–9; ☎ 224 810 515; www.europcar.cz; Pařížská 28, Staré Město; 🚊 17)

Hertz (Map pp108–9; ☎ 225 345 000; www.hertz.cz; Karlovo náměstí 15, Nové Město; Ⓜ Karlovo Náměstí)

Secco Car (Map pp132–3; ☎ 220 802 361; www.seccocar.cz; Přístavní 39, Holešovice; 🚊 1, 3, 12, 15, 25)

Vecar (Map pp132–3; ☎ 224 314 361; www.vecar.cz; Svatovítská 7, Dejvice; Ⓜ Dejvická)

West Car Praha (Map pp58–9; ☎ 235 365 307; www.westcarpraha.cz, in Czech; Veleslavínská 17, Veleslavín; 🚊 20, 26)

Parking

Parking in most of Prague is regulated with colour-coded zones. Blue zones are for residents only; visitors can park in orange zones (40Kč per hour, maximum stay two hours) or green zones (30Kč per hour, up to six hours). You pay at a parking meter, effective 8am to 6pm weekdays (they accept both Czech crowns and euros). Traffic inspectors are always keen to hand out fines, clamp wheels or tow away vehicles. Parking in one-way streets is normally allowed only on the right-hand side.

There are several car parks at the edges of Staré Město, as well as Park-and-Ride car parks around the outer city (most are marked on city maps), close to metro stations.

PUBLIC TRANSPORT

Prague's excellent public transport system combines tram, metro and bus services. It's operated by Dopravní podnik hlavního město Prahy (DPP; ☎ 800 19 18 17; www.dpp.cz), which has information desks at Ruzyně airport (7am to 10pm) and in four metro stations – Muzeum (7am to 9pm), Můstek, Anděl and Nádraží Holešovice (all 7am to 6pm) – where you can get tickets, directions, a multilingual transport-system map, a map of night services *(noční provoz)* and a detailed English-language guide to the whole system.

On metro trains and newer trams and buses, an electronic display shows the route number and the name of the next stop, and a recorded voice announces each station or stop. As the train, tram or bus pulls away, the announcer says *Příští stanice*... (The next station is...) or *Příští zastávka*... (The next stop is...), perhaps noting that it's a *přestupní stanice* (transfer station). At metro stations, signs point you towards the *výstup* (exit) or to a *přestup* (transfer to another line).

The metro's operating hours are from 5am to midnight. There are three lines: line A runs from the northwestern side of the city at Dejvická to the east at Skalka; line B runs from the southwest at Zličín to the northeast at Černý Most; and line C runs from the north at Letňany to the southeast at Háje. Line A intersects line C at Muzeum, line B intersects line C at Florenc and line A intersects line B at Můstek.

After the metro closes, night trams (51 to 58) and buses (501 to 512) still rumble across the city about every 40 minutes through the night (only 26Kč tickets are valid on these services). If you're planning a late evening, find out if one of these lines passes near where you're staying.

Tickets

You need to buy a ticket before you board a bus, tram or metro. Tickets are sold from machines at metro stations and tram stops, at newsstands, Trafiky snack shops, PNS newspaper kiosks, hotels, PIS tourist information offices (see p255), metro station ticket offices and DPP information offices. Tickets are valid on tram, metro, bus and the Petřín funicular.

A transfer ticket *(přestupní jízdenka)* costs 26/13Kč per adult/child aged six to 15 years; kids under six ride free. You'll also need a 13Kč ticket for each large suitcase or backpack if it's larger than 25cm x 45cm x 70cm. Validate (punch) your ticket by sticking it in the little yellow machine in the metro station lobby or on the bus or tram the first time you board; this stamps the time and date on it. Once validated, transfer tickets remain valid for 75 minutes; within this time period you can make unlimited transfers between all types of public transport (you don't need to punch the ticket again).

There's also a short-hop 18/9Kč ticket, valid for 20 minutes on buses and trams, or for up to five metro stations. No transfers are allowed with these (except between metro lines), and they're not valid on the Petřín funicular or on night trams (51 to 58) or buses (501 to 512).

You can also buy tickets valid for 24 hours (100Kč) and three/five days (330/500Kč); the latter two include one adult and one child aged six to 15 years. Again, these must be validated on first use only; if a ticket is stamped twice, it becomes invalid. With these tickets, you don't need to pay an extra fare for your luggage.

Being caught without a valid ticket entails a 500Kč on-the-spot fine (100Kč for not having a luggage ticket). The plain-clothes inspectors travel incognito, but will show a red-and-gold metal badge when they ask for your ticket. A few may demand a higher fine from foreigners and pocket the difference, so insist on a receipt *(doklad)* before paying.

TAXI

Prague City Council has cracked down on the city's notoriously dishonest taxi drivers by installing a network of taxi stands with red-and-yellow signs quoting the correct fares between various parts of the city. The official rate for licensed cabs is 40Kč flag fall plus 28Kč per kilometre and 6Kč per minute while waiting. On this basis, any trip within the city centre – say, from Wenceslas Square to Malá Strana – should cost around 170Kč. A trip to the suburbs should be around 400Kč to 500Kč, and to the airport between 550Kč and 600Kč. Journeys outside Prague are not regulated; negotiate a fare before you get in.

However, hailing a taxi on the street – at least in a tourist zone – still holds the risk of an inflated fare. The usual tactic is to quote a 'maximum' fare for a given destination, then drive around long enough to ensure that the meter clocks up the quoted maximum.

You're much better off calling a radio-taxi than flagging one down, as they're better regulated and more responsible. From our experience the following companies have honest drivers (most of whom speak a little English) and offer 24-hour services.

AAA Radio Taxi (☎ 14014; www.aaaradiotaxi.cz)

Airport Cars (☎ 220 113 892; www.airport-cars.cz)

City Taxi (☎ 257 257 257; www.citytaxi.cz)

ProfiTaxi (☎ 844 700 800; www.profitaxi.cz)

TRAIN

The railway system is operated by recently privatised České dráhy (ČD; Czech Railways; www.cd.cz). Timetable information is available online at www.vlak-bus.cz.

Arriving in Prague by Train

Most international trains arrive at Praha hlavní nádraží (Prague Main Station; Map pp108–9). Some stop only at Praha-Holešovice (Map pp132–3) in the north of the city (including some trains from Berlin, Vienna and Budapest), or Praha-Smíchov (Map pp58–9) in the south; all three stations have their own metro stops. Masarykovo nádraží (Map p106), two blocks north of the main train station, is the main domestic rail terminus. (Note: Praha hlavní nádraží is undergoing a major redevelopment until 2009; during this period the layout of the station may be changed.)

On arriving at Praha hlavní nádraží, the underpass from the platforms leads you to level 3 of the four-level station complex; turn left here to find the AVE accommodation agency (see the boxed text, p213). Continue down a short flight of stairs to level 2, the main concourse, where you'll find the PIS Tourist Information Booth (⌚ 9am-7pm Mon-Fri, to 5pm Sat & Sun) beside the metro entrance at the southern (left) end.

Ramps to either side of the ticket counters in the main concourse lead down to level 1, with a 24-hour left-luggage office (úschovna; per

YOU'RE GOING WHERE?

Although most staff at the international ticket counters in Prague's main train station speak at least some English, those selling domestic tickets rarely do. In order to speed up the process of buying a ticket, and to avoid misunderstandings, it's often easier to write down what you want on a piece of paper and hand it to the clerk (this works for bus tickets, too).

Write it down like this:

- *od:* departure station, eg PRAHA
- *do:* destination station, eg KARLŠTEJN
- *čas:* departure time using 24-hour clock
- *datum:* date, eg for 2.30pm on 20 May, write '14.30h. 20/05'. Or just *dnes* (today)
- *osoby:* number of passengers
- *jednosměrný* (one way) or *zpáteční* (return).

If you're making a reservation on an EC or IC train, you may also want to specify *1. třídá* or *2. třídá* (1st or 2nd class), and whether you want an *okno* (window) or *chodba* (aisle) seat.

One-way domestic train tickets for distances of more than 50km are valid for 24 hours from time of purchase, but for distances under 50km only until 6am the next day. Note that domestic return tickets (about 10% more expensive than singles) are only valid for 48 hours from time of purchase – if you plan to be away for more than two days, buy two one-way tickets instead.

bag per day 15 or 30Kč) and luggage lockers (60Kč) that accept 5Kč, 10Kč and 20Kč coins.

There are four metro station entrances in the concourse – the two nearer the stairs from level 3 lead to the northbound platform (direction Letňany), the two nearer the exits are southbound (direction Haje). Public transport tickets and information are available at the DPP booths beside the southbound metro entrances. There are taxi ranks at either end of the concourse. To find the nearest tram stop (for trams 5, 9 and 26), exit the main concourse and turn right; the stop is at the far end of the park.

Try not to arrive in the middle of the night – the station closes from 12.40am to 3.40am, and the surrounding area is a magnet for pickpockets and drunks.

Leaving Prague by Train

You can buy international train tickets in advance from train stations and ČD Travel (Map p106; ☎ 972 233 930; V Celnici 6, Nové Město) and Čedok (Map pp108–9; ☎ 221 447 242; www.cedok.com; Na Příkopě 18, Nové Město) travel agencies.

At Prague's main train station, you can get information on international services at the ČD info centre at the south end of the main concourse, and from ticket windows 2 to 8 (usually only one of them – look for a sign advertising information in English). Full printed timetables are displayed on level 3; timetable information is available online at www.vlak.cz.

The big display board on the main concourse lists departures with columns marked *druh vlaku* (type of train – EC for international, IC for domestic, etc), *čislo vlaku* (train number), *cilová stanice* (final destination), *směr* (via), *odjezd* (departure time) and *našt* (platform number). To make sure you're on the correct train, confirm that its number (displayed on a panel on the side of the carriage) matches the train number of the service you want.

You can buy domestic tickets *(vnitrostátní jízdenky)* at the odd-numbered ticket windows (marked with an A) to the left of the departures board on the main concourse; for international advance reservations *(mezínárodní rezervace)* go to windows 2 to 8 (marked B), and for international tickets *(mezínárodní jízdenky)* go to windows 12 to 24 (marked C) to the right.

DIRECTORY

BUSINESS HOURS

Shops tend to open from 8.30am to 5pm or 6pm Monday to Friday, and 8.30am to noon or 1pm on Saturday. Department stores close at 8pm Monday to Friday, and at 6pm on Saturday and Sunday. Touristy shops in central Prague are open later at night and all day Saturday and Sunday.

Banks generally open 8am to 4.30pm Monday to Friday. The city's main post office opens 7am to 8pm every day, while other post offices open 8am to 6pm or 7pm Monday to Friday and until noon on Saturday. Restaurants tend to open between 10am and 11pm (cafés generally open around 8am), while bars usually open 11am to midnight (though some in the city centre stay open till 3am or 4am).

Most museums and galleries open from 9am or 10am to 5pm or 6pm year-round. Many are closed on Monday and on the first working day after a holiday. Some of Prague's bigger churches are open similar hours.

Castles, chateaux and other historic monuments outside the city are open May to September, from 8am or 9am to 5pm or 6pm, except for a lunch break, daily except Monday and the first working day after a holiday. Most shut down from November to March, with some limited to weekends in October and April. If you plan to take a guided tour, remember that ticket offices close an hour or so before the official closing time, depending on the length of the tour.

CHILDREN

Czechs are very family oriented, and there are plenty of activities for children around the city. An increasing number of Prague restaurants cater specifically for children, with play areas and so on, and many offer a children's menu *(dětský jídelníček);* even if they don't, they can usually provide smaller portions for a lower price.

For outdoor activities take a walk around Prague Zoo (p140) – if possible, go there by boat (p251) – or hire inline skates at Letná Gardens (p208). Petřín (p84) is a beautiful park on a hill where parents and kids alike can take a break from sightseeing, and climb up the Petřín Lookout Tower for terrific views over Prague. For an even higher viewpoint, go to the TV Tower (p128) in Žižkov.

March is the time of the St Matthew Fair (p16), when Holešovice's exhibition grounds are full of fairground rides, shooting galleries and candy floss; in summer there are rowing and paddle boats for hire along the Vltava River as well as river cruises and boat tours (p251).

At weekends and on holidays between April and mid-November, vintage tram cars trundle along a special sightseeing route, line 91, around the city centre (see p252 for more information). And don't miss the changing of the guard at Prague Castle (see p61 for details) – but get into position before the crowds do, or the kids won't see a thing.

Museums of possible interest to children include the Toy Museum (p67), though, frustratingly, its many displays are hands off; the Public Transport Museum (p141), where kids can climb on the vintage trams and buses; and the Aircraft Museum (p140), where they can see Russian MiG fighter planes up close.

There are safe, fenced playgrounds by the entrance to Petřín park on náměstí Kinských (Map pp76–7); at the northern end of Kampa island (Map pp76–7); on Children's Island (p82); at the southern end of Slav Island (p113); and on Vlašská, just west of the German embassy (Map pp76–7).

For more information and inspiration on how to make travelling with children as hassle-free as possible, check out Lonely Planet's *Travel with Children* by Cathy Lanigan. Also see the Top Picks boxed text, p113.

Babysitting

The Prague Information Service (Pražská informační služba, PIS; ☎ 12444 or 221 714 444 in English & German; www.prague-info.cz) usually has a list of babysitting *(hlídaní dětí)* agencies, and most top-end hotels provide a babysitting service; rates are generally around 150Kč per hour. Prague Family (☎ 224 224 044; www.praguefamily.cz) is an agency that can provide English-speaking babysitters.

CLIMATE

Prague has warm, occasionally showery summers and cold, often snowy winters with generally changeable conditions. A typical day in Prague from June to August sees the mercury

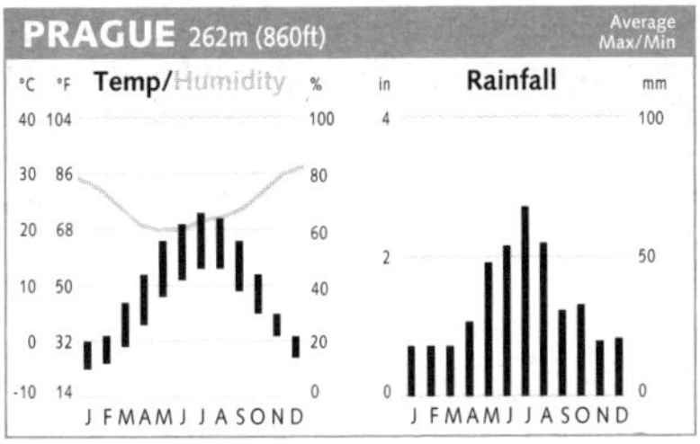

range from about 12°C to 22°C. Temperatures from December to February push below freezing. Wide variations are common, sometimes surpassing 35°C in summer and -20°C in winter. The summer's long, sunny, hot spells tend to be broken by sudden, heavy thunderstorms. In general, May and September enjoy the most pleasant weather.

See p16 for advice on the best time to visit.

COURSES

Places offering Czech language courses:

Institute for Language & Preparatory Studies (Ústav jazykové a odborné přípravý; Map p116; ☎ 224 990 420; www.ujop.cuni.cz; Vratislavova 10, Vyšehrad; Ⓜ Vyšehrad) ÚJOP runs six-week Czech language courses for foreigners. No prior knowledge of the Czech language is required. The course fee is €610, not including accommodation. You can also opt for individual lessons (45 minutes) at 550Kč each. Further details and an application form are available on the website.

London School of Modern Languages (Map pp58–9; ☎ 226 096 140; www.londonschool.cz; Podolská 54, Podolí; 🚋 3, 16, 17, 21) Offers Czech courses for both individuals and companies, including specialised Czech language courses for business, law or IT. Individual tuition costs from 350Kč for a 45-minute lesson.

CUSTOMS REGULATIONS

Travelling between the Czech Republic and other EU countries, you can import/export 800 cigarettes, 400 cigarillos, 200 cigars, 1kg of smoking tobacco, 10L of spirits, 20L of fortified wine (eg port or sherry), 90L of wine and 110L of beer, provided the goods are for personal use only (each country sets its own guide levels; these figures are minimums).

Travellers from outside the EU can import or export, duty-free, a maximum of 200 cigarettes *or* 100 cigarillos *or* 50 cigars *or* 250g of tobacco; 2L of still table wine; 1L of spirits *or* 2L of fortified wine, sparkling wine or liqueurs; 60mL of perfume; 250mL of eau de toilette; and €175 worth of all other goods (including gifts and souvenirs). Anything over this limit must be declared to customs officers. People under 17 do not get the alcohol and tobacco allowances.

Any goods you buy in the Czech Republic can be taken to any other EU country without paying additional VAT. If you are resident outside the EU, you may be able to reclaim VAT on your purchases (see p144). You're not permitted to export genuine antiques.

There is no limit to the amount of Czech or foreign currency that can be taken in or out of the country, but amounts exceeding 500,000Kč must be declared.

DISCOUNT CARDS

The Prague Card is a combined admission card and public-transport pass. The admission card is valid for one year, but the transport ticket is valid only for 48 hours, allowing unlimited travel on metro, trams and buses. The card provides free entry to around a dozen city sights, including the Loreta, the TV Tower and the Vyšehrad Casemates, plus discounts of up to 50% at others including the Museum of Communism. However, it does not include major attractions such as Prague Castle, the Church of St Nicholas in Malá Strana and the Prague Jewish Museum.

The pass costs 860Kč (or €32.50 if bought via the internet), and can be purchased from the EuroAgentur desk at Prague Airport, the **Prague Card Change Office** (Map pp108–9; Vodičkova 34, Nové Město; 🕒 9am-6pm Mon-Fri) and online at www.praguecard.info.

ELECTRICITY

Electricity in Prague is 230V, 50Hz AC. Outlets have the standard European socket with two small round holes and a protruding earth (ground) pin. If you have a different plug, bring an adaptor (see www.kropla.com for info). North American 110V appliances will also need a transformer if they don't have built-in voltage adjustment.

EMBASSIES & CONSULATES

Australia (Map p106; ☎ 296 578 350; www.dfat.gov.au/missions/countries/cz.html; 6th fl, Klimentská 10, Nové Město) Honorary consulate for emergency assistance only (eg a stolen passport); the nearest Australian embassy is in Vienna.

Austria (Map p138; ☎ 257 090 511; www.austria.cz, in German & Czech; Viktora Huga 10, Smíchov)

Canada (Map pp132–3; ☎ 272 101 800; www.canada.cz; Muchova 6, Bubeneč)

France (Map pp76–7; ☎ 251 171 711; www.france.cz, in French & Czech; Velkopřerovské náměstí 2, Malá Strana)

Germany (Map pp76–7; ☎ 257 113 111; www.deutschland.cz, in German & Czech; Vlašská 19, Malá Strana)

Ireland (Map pp76–7; ☎ 257 530 061; www.embassyofireland.cz; Tržiště 13, Malá Strana)

Israel (Map pp132–3; ☎ 233 097 500; http://prague.mfa.gov.il; Badeniho 2, Bubeneč)

Netherlands (Map pp132–3; ☎ 233 015 200; www.netherlandsembassy.cz; Gotthardská 6/27, Bubeneč)

New Zealand (Map p121; ☎ 222 514 672; egermayer@nzconsul.cz; Dykova 19, Vinohrady) Honorary consulate providing emergency assistance only (eg stolen passport); the nearest NZ embassy is in Berlin.

Poland Embassy (Map pp76–7; ☎ 257 099 500; www.prague.polemb.net; Valdštejnská 8, Malá Strana); Consular Department (Map pp58–9; ☎ 224 228 722; konspol@mbox.vol.cz; V úžlabině 14, Strašnice) Come here for visas.

Russia (Map pp132–3; ☎ 233 374 100; www.czech.mid.ru; Pod Kaštany 1, Bubeneč)

Slovakia (Map pp132–3; ☎ 233 113 051; www.slovakemb.cz, in Slovak; Pod Hradbami 1, Dejvice)

South Africa (Map p121; ☎ 267 311 114; saprague@terminal.cz; Ruská 65, Vršovice)

UK (Map pp76–7; ☎ 257 402 111; www.britain.cz; Thunovská 14, Malá Strana)

USA (Map pp76–7; ☎ 257 022 000; www.usembassy.cz; Tržiště 15, Malá Strana)

EMERGENCY

Ambulance (☎ 155)

Breakdown Assistance for Motorists (ÚAMK; ☎ 1230)

EU-wide emergency hotline (☎ 112)

Fire (☎ 150)

Municipal Police (☎ 156)

State Police (☎ 158)

GAY & LESBIAN TRAVELLERS

Homosexuality is legal in the Czech Republic (the age of consent is 15), but Czechs are not accustomed to seeing same-sex couples showing affection to each other in public; it's best to be discreet. However, Prague is the most liberal place in the country, and has a lively gay scene, with most gay bars and clubs concentrated in the city centre and in the districts of Vinohrady and Žižkov.

The bimonthly gay guide and contact magazine *Amigo* has a few pages in English, but the Gay Guide Prague (http://prague.gayguide.net) is the most useful source of information. See also the boxed text (p195) for gay-friendly venues and accommodation options.

HOLIDAYS

Banks, offices, department stores and some shops will be closed on public holidays. Restaurants, museums and tourist attractions tend to stay open. See also p16.

New Year's Day 1 January

Easter Monday March/April

Labour Day 1 May

Liberation Day 8 May

Sts Cyril & Methodius Day 5 July

Jan Hus Day 6 July

Czech Statehood Day 28 September

Republic Day 28 October

Struggle for Freedom & Democracy Day 17 November

Christmas Eve (Generous Day) 24 December

Christmas Day 25 December

St Stephen's Day 26 December

INTERNET ACCESS

Many hotels now offer wi-fi connections for guests, though you'll probably have to ask reception for a password. If not, you should be able to log on from your hotel room for the cost of a local call by registering with an internet roaming service such as MaGlobe (www.maglobe.com), which has access numbers for Prague. Most midrange and top-end hotels have telephone jacks, usually US standard (RJ-11), which you can plug your modem cable into, or ethernet ports for sharing the hotel's broadband connection. If you plan to use the phone line, buy a line tester – a gadget that goes between your computer and the phone jack – so that you don't inadvertently fry your modem. For more information on travelling with a laptop check out www.kropla.com.

For those without a laptop, Prague has dozens of internet cafés. Conveniently located ones include the following:

Bohemia Bagel (Map pp88–9; ☎ 224 812 560; www.bohemiabagel.cz; Masná 2, Staré Město; per min 1.50Kč; 🕒 7am-midnight; Ⓜ Náměstí Republiky)

Globe Bookstore & Café (Map pp108–9; ☎ 224 934 203; www.globebookstore.cz; Pštrossova 6, Nové Město;

WI-FI ACCESS

You can search for wi-fi hotspots in Prague (and around the world) at www.jiwire.com. More and more cafés and bars in Prague are advertising free wi-fi for paying customers, but in our experience around half the places boasting this service don't actually have a functioning internet connection ('Sorry, it's not working today'); if it's important, make sure you can connect before buying a drink! We have found the following places, along with the branches of Starbucks on Malostranské náměstí and in the Palladium shopping mall, to have reliable, free wi-fi connections:

- Café Café (p182)
- Café Savoy (p181)
- Caffe Kaaba (p185)
- Grand Café Orient (p181)
- Káva Káva Káva (p182) Need to ask for password.

per min 1Kč; 🕑 10am-midnight; Ⓜ Karlovo Náměstí) No minimum. Also has wi-fi and ethernet ports so you can connect your own laptop (same price; cables provided, 50Kč deposit).

Internet Centre (Map pp88–9; Rytířská 18, Staré Město; per min 1.60Kč; 🕑 9am-11pm Mon-Fri, 10am-9pm Sat, 11am-9pm Sun; Ⓜ Můstek) At the back of Au Gourmand café; 25Kč minimum, low-cost international phone calls.

Pl@neta (Map p121; ☎ 267 311 182; Vinohradská 102, Vinohrady; per min 0.44-0.88Kč; 🕑 8am-11pm; Ⓜ Jiřího z Poděbrad) Cheapest place in town, with lowest rates before 10am and after 8pm Monday to Friday, all day Saturday and Sunday; 5Kč minimum.

Spika (Map pp88–9; ☎ 224 211 521; http://netcafe.spika.cz; Dlážděná 4, Nové Město; per 15min Mon-Fri 20Kč, Sat & Sun 16Kč; 🕑 8am-midnight; Ⓜ Náměstí Republiky)

LEGAL MATTERS

If you find yourself under arrest for any reason whatsoever, you are entitled to call your embassy (see p247 for listings). Note that it is technically illegal not to carry some form of identification (normally your passport). If you can't prove your identity, police have the right to detain you for up to 48 hours. Some older police officers retain a communist-era mistrust of foreigners; younger officers are easier to deal with, but almost none speak fluent English.

Penalties for dealing in drugs are harsh and it's unlikely that your embassy can do much to help if you are caught, but new laws passed in 2008 have decriminalised the possession of 'a small amount' of drugs, defined as fewer than 20 joints or a gram of hashish.

Drink-driving is strictly illegal; there is a zero blood-alcohol limit for drivers. Traffic fines are generally paid on the spot (ask for a receipt). A smoking ban levies a 1000Kč on-the-spot fine for smoking in public places, including hospitals, libraries, railway stations and public transport – and even at bus and tram stops, even though they are in the open air – but not in restaurants, bars and clubs.

WHEN YOU'RE LEGAL

The following minimum legal ages apply in the Czech Republic:

- Drinking alcohol – 18 years
- Driving – 18 years
- Heterosexual/homosexual sex – 15 years
- Smoking – 16 years
- Marriage – 18 years
- Voting – 18 years

MAPS

City maps are available at newsagents, bookshops and travel agencies. A detailed plan of the city centre and inner suburbs is Kartografie Praha's *Praha – plán města* (1:10,000). It includes public transport and parking information, an index, a metro map, plans of the castle and Charles Bridge, and a brief description of the major historical sites.

Lonely Planet's plastic-coated *Prague* city map is handy and hard-wearing, and has sections covering central Prague, Prague Castle, greater Prague, the Prague metro and the region around Prague, and an index of streets and sights.

The Prague Information Service (Pražská informační služba, PIS; ☎ 12444 or 221 714 444 in English & German; www.prague-info.cz) stocks a free English-language pamphlet called *Welcome to the Czech Republic*, which is produced by the Ministry of Interior. It features a map of the historical centre, transport routes in the centre, and information such as emergency phone numbers and embassy addresses.

If you are staying in Prague for a significant amount of time, Kartografie Praha's pocket atlas *Praha – plán města – standard* (1:20,000), covering all of Prague, is invaluable.

A public-transport map showing all day and night services (metro, tram and bus) is available from any of the public information offices of Dopravní podnik Praha (DPP; see p243), the city transport department.

MEDICAL SERVICES

Emergency medical treatment and nonhospital first aid are free for all visitors to the Czech Republic. If you have a serious medical emergency (eg suspected heart attack), call ☎ 112 (English- and German-speaking operators are available).

Citizens of EU countries can obtain a European Health Insurance Card (EHIC); this entitles you to free state-provided medical treatment in the Czech Republic (see www.cmu.cz/languages/en.htm for information on using the card in the Czech Republic). Non-EU citizens must pay for treatment, and at least some of the fee must be paid upfront. Everyone has to pay for prescribed medications.

Clinics

American Dental Associates (Map p106; ☎ 221 181 121; www.americandental.cz; 2nd fl Atrium, Stará Celnice Bldg, V Celnici 4, Nové Město; Ⓜ Náměstí Republiky) Entirely English-speaking.

Canadian Medical Care (Map pp58–9; ☎ 235 360 133, after hours 724 300 301; www.cmcpraha.cz; Veleslavínská 1, Veleslavín; 🕒 8am-6pm Mon-Fri, to 8pm Tue & Thu; 🚋 20, 26 from Ⓜ Dejvická) A pricey but professional private clinic with English-speaking doctors; an initial consultation will cost from 1500Kč to 2500Kč.

Polyclinic at Národní (Poliklinika na Národní; Map pp88–9; ☎ 222 075 120, 24hr emergencies 720 427 634; www.poliklinika.narodni.cz; Národní 9, Nové Město; 🕒 8.30am-5pm Mon-Fri; Ⓜ Národní Třída) A central clinic with staff who speak English, German, French and Russian. Expect to pay around 600Kč to 1200Kč for an initial consultation.

Emergency Rooms

Na Homolce Hospital (Map pp58–9; ☎ 257 271 111; www.homolka.cz; 5th fl, Foreign Pavilion, Roentgenova 2, Motol; 🚌 167 from Ⓜ Anděl) The best hospital in Prague, equipped and staffed to Western standards, with staff who speak English, French, German and Spanish.

Pharmacies

There are plenty of pharmacies *(lékárna)* in Prague, and most city districts have one that stays open 24 hours. In Nové Město you'll find it at the **district clinic** (Map pp108–9; ☎ 224 946 982; Palackého 5, Nové Město; 🕒 7am-7pm Mon-Fri, 8am-noon Sat; Ⓜ Národní Třída). In Vinohrady go to **Lékárna U sv Ludmily** (Map p121; ☎ 222 513 396; Belgická 37, Vinohrady; 🕒 7am-7pm Mon-Fri, 8am-noon Sat; Ⓜ Náměstí Míru).

For emergency service after hours, ring the bell – you'll see a red button with a sign *zvonek lékárna* (pharmacy bell) and/or *první pomoc* (first aid). Some prescription medicines may not be available, so it's wise to bring enough for your trip.

MONEY

The Czech crown (Koruna česká, or Kč) is divided into 100 heller or *haléřů* (h). Banknotes come in denominations of 50, 100, 200, 500, 1000, 2000 and 5000Kč; coins are of 50h and one, two, five, 10, 20 and 50Kč.

Keep small change handy for use in public toilets and tram-ticket machines, and try to keep some small-denomination notes for shops, cafés and bars – getting change for the 2000Kč notes that ATMs often spit out can be a problem.

See the inside front cover of this guidebook for the exchange-rates table.

Changing Money

The easiest, cheapest way to carry money is in the form of a debit card from your bank, which you can use to withdraw cash either from an ATM *(bankomat)* or over the counter in a bank. Using an ATM will result in your home bank charging a fee (usually 1.5% to 2.5%), but you'll get a good exchange rate and provided you make withdrawals of at least a couple of thousand crowns at a time, you'll pay less than the assorted commissions on travellers cheques. Check with your bank about transaction fees and withdrawal limits.

Travellers cheques are not much use here, as they are not accepted by shops and restaurants and can be exchanged only at banks and currency exchange counters.

The main Czech banks – Komerční banka, Česká spořitelna, Československá obchodní banka (ČSOB) and Živnostenská banka – are the best places to change cash. They charge 2% commission with a 50Kč minimum (but always check, as commissions can vary from branch to branch). They will also provide a cash advance on Visa or MasterCard without commission.

Hotels charge about 5% to 8% commission, while Čedok travel agencies and post offices charge 2% – similar rates to the banks. Note that Scottish and Northern Irish banknotes are almost impossible to change, and where they are accepted you'll get a worse exchange rate than for Bank of England notes.

Try to avoid the many private exchange booths *(směnárna)* in the main tourist areas. They lure you in with attractive-looking exchange rates that turn out to be 'sell' *(prodej* or *prodajáme)* rates; if you want to change foreign currency into Czech crowns, the 'buy' *(nákup)* rate applies. There is also an even worse rate for transactions under a certain amount, typically around €500. Check the rates carefully, and ask exactly how much you will get before parting with any money.

NEWSPAPERS & MAGAZINES

The kiosks on Wenceslas Square, Na Příkopě and náměstí Republiky, and the Relay newsagencies in central metro stations, sell a wide range of international newspapers and magazines, including British papers such as the *Times*, *Independent* and *Guardian* (international edition), which are available on the day of publication.

See p53 for information about local newspapers.

ORGANISED TOURS

Pragotur (see p252) and various private companies operating from kiosks along Na Příkopě offer three-hour city bus tours for around 650Kč per person. They're OK if your time is short, but the castle and other sights get so crowded that you often can't enjoy the tour; we suggest one of our self-guided walking tours instead. There are also some excellent specialist tours on offer.

Bicycle

City Bike (Map pp88–9; ☎ 776 180 284; www.citybike-prague.com; Králodvorská 5, Staré Město; 9am-7pm Apr-Oct; M Náměstí Republiky) has 2½-hour guided tours costing 490Kc, departing at 11am, 2pm and 5pm May to September, and 11am and 2pm April and October. Tours take in the Old Town, the Vltava River and Letná park, and include a stop at a riverside pub.

Praha Bike (Map pp88–9; ☎ 732 388 880; www.prahabike.cz; Dlouhá 24, Staré Město; 2hr tour 420Kč; 9am-7pm; M Náměstí Republiky) offers a 2½-hour guided cycling tour through the city or an easy evening pedal through the parks (490Kč). Tours depart at 2.30pm mid-March to October and also at 11.30am and 5.30pm May to September. Trips outside the city can also be arranged. Helmets and locks are provided, and bikes are available for private rental (see p207).

AVE Travel (Map pp108–9; ☎ 251 551 011; www.bicycle-tours.cz) operates a full-day guided bicycle tour from Prague to Karlštejn Castle (p230) for 1500Kč per person, including bike hire, lunch at Karlštejn and a train ticket back to the city. It also offers bike trips to Konopiště (p232) and one-week tours through the Czech countryside.

Boat

Evropská Vodní Doprava (EVD; Map pp88–9; ☎ 224 810 030; www.evd.cz; Čechův most, Staré Město; 17) operates large cruise boats based at the quay beside Čechův most (Bohemia Bridge), and offers a one-hour return cruise departing hourly from 10am to 6pm (220/110Kč per adult/child); a two-hour return cruise including lunch and live music, departing at noon (690/380Kč per adult/child); a two-hour return cruise to Vyšehrad (420/350Kč), departing at 3.30pm; and a three-hour evening return cruise with dinner and music (790/500Kč), departing at 7pm. All cruises run year-round.

Prague Venice (Map pp88–9; ☎ 603 819 947; www.prague-venice.cz; Platnéřská 4, Staré Město; adult/child 290/145Kč; 10.30am-11pm Jul & Aug, to 8pm Mar-Jun, Sep & Oct, to 6pm Nov-Feb; 17) operates entertaining 45-minute cruises in small boats under the hidden arches of Charles Bridge and along the Čertovka millstream in Kampa. Boats depart every 15 minutes from jetties beneath the eastern end of Charles Bridge (entrance next to the Charles Bridge Museum; Map pp88–9), at the western end of Platnéřská, on the Čertovka stream in Malá Strana (Map pp76–7), and at the western end of Mánesův most (Mánes Bridge; Map pp76–7), near Malostranská metro station.

From April to October, Prague Passenger Shipping (Pražská paroplavební společnost, PPS; Map pp108–9; ☎ 224 930 017; www.paroplavba.cz; Rašínovo nábřeží 2, Nové Město; M Karlovo Náměstí) runs cruises along the Vltava, departing from the central quay on Rašínovo nábřeží. Most photogenic is a one-hour jaunt taking in the National Theatre, Štrelecký island and Vyšehrad, departing at 11am, 2pm, 4pm, 5pm and 6pm April to September (adult/child 190/90Kč).

At 9am on Saturday and Sunday from May to mid-September, a boat goes 37km south (upstream) through a wild, green landscape to the Slapy Dam at Třebrenice. This fine, all-day escape costs 340/170Kč return, arriving back in the city at 6.30pm.

Boats making the 1¼-hour trip to Troja (near the zoo; 140/70Kč one way) depart at 8.30am on weekdays in May and June only, at 9.30am, 12.30pm and 3.30pm daily May to mid-September, and at weekends and holidays in April and from mid-September to the end of October. Returning boats depart from Troja at 11am, 2pm and 5pm.

Bus & Tram

Nostalgic Tram No 91 (☎ 233 343 349; www.dpp.cz; Muzeum MHD [Public Transport Museum], Patočkova 4, Střešovice; adult/child 25/10Kč; departs hourly noon-5.30pm Sat, Sun & hols Apr–mid-Nov) offers vintage tram cars dating from 1908 to 1924, which trundle along a special route, starting at the Public Transport Museum (Map pp70–1) and going via stops at Prague Castle, Malostranské náměstí, the National Theatre, Wenceslas Square, náměstí Republiky and Štefánikův most to finish at Výstaviště. You can get on and off at any stop, and buy tickets on board; ordinary public transport tickets and passes are not valid on this line.

A whole range of outings is offered by Prague Sightseeing Tours (☎ 222 314 661; www.pstours.cz) – look for the yellow kiosk near the metro entrance on náměstí Republiky (Map pp88–9). The two-hour 'Informative Prague' bus tour (adult/child 410/280Kč, departing 11am and 1.30pm from April to October) takes in all of Prague's important historical sites, and the 'Grand City' tour (660/330Kč, departing 9.30am and 2pm April to October) combines a bus tour of the main sites with a walk through Prague Castle.

Jewish Interest

Precious Legacy Tours (Map pp88–9; ☎ 222 321 954; www.legacytours.net; Kaprova 13, Staré Město; per person 630Kč; tours begin 10.30am Sun-Fri, also at 2pm by arrangement) offers guided tours of places of interest to Jewish visitors, including a three-hour walking tour of Prague's Josefov district (the fee includes admission to four synagogues, but not the Staronová Synagogue – this is 200Kč extra). There's also a daily six-hour excursion to Terezín (1160Kč per person; departs 10am); for more information on Terezín, see p234. Customised, private tours can be arranged for €50 an hour for two people.

Wittmann Tours (Map p121; ☎ 222 252 472; www.wittmann-tours.com; Mánesova 8, Vinohrady) offers a three-hour walking tour of Josefov (850Kč per person) that begins at 9.30am Monday, Wednesday and Friday from May to October. Wittmann also runs seven-hour day trips to Terezín (p234) for 1150/1000Kč per adult/student. In our opinion, the Wittmann tours are better than the Precious Legacy ones as they feel less rushed and more personal.

Personal Guides

An affiliate of the Prague Information Service (PIS), Pragotur (Map pp88–9; ☎ 236 002 562; guides@pis.cz; Old Town Hall, Staroměstské náměstí 1; 3hr tour per person 1000Kč, per 2 persons 1200Kč plus 300Kč per additional person; 9am-6pm Mon-Fri, to 4pm Sat & Sun) can arrange personal guides fluent in all major European languages. The desk is in the PIS office in the Old Town Hall.

Vintage Car

A couple of businesses offer tours around the city in vintage Czech cars dating from the late 1920s and early 1930s. There are pick-up points at various city centre locations; tours depart as available, or whenever you ask, if it's quiet. Tours last about 40 minutes.

3 Veterans (☎ 603 521 700; www.3veterani.cz; 1-2 persons 950Kč, 3-4 persons 1300Kč; 9am-6pm) has a small fleet of Praga Piccolos and early Škodas, all from the early 1930s. Pick-up points in Staré Město are on Rytířská, in Malé náměstí, and at the junction of Pařížská and Staroměstské náměstí; and on Malostranské náměstí in Malá Strana.

With Old Timer History Trip (☎ 776 829 897; www.historytrip.cz; 1-2 persons 950Kč, 3-6 persons 1300Kč; 9am-6pm Apr-Nov) you can rattle along the city's cobblestone streets in a 1928 Praga Piccolo or a larger 1929 Praga Alfa. Pick-up points in Staré Město are in Malé náměstí, on Karlova and on Malostranská náměstí in Malá Strana. There's also a two-hour night-time tour (from 1890Kč).

Walking

The corner of Old Town Square outside the Old Town Hall is usually clogged with dozens of people touting for business as walking guides; quality varies, but the best are listed here. Most operators don't have an office – you can join a walk by just turning up at the starting point and paying your money, though it's best to phone ahead to be sure of a place.

Most walks begin at the Astronomical Clock (Map pp88–9).

Lots of travellers have recommended George's Guided Walks (☎ 607 820 158; www.praguemaster.com/george), whose intimate, personalised tours include a four-hour History Walk (up to four persons 2200Kč; if you have been to Prague before, he'll take you off the beaten track); a two-hour Iron Curtain Walk (up to four persons 1400Kč); and a five-hour pub crawl, including dinner in a Czech pub (1400Kč per person). George will meet you at your hotel, or anywhere else that's convenient.

Prague Walks (☎ 222 322 309; www.praguewalks.com; per person 300-1000Kč) runs interesting jaunts with themes such as Prague architecture, Žižkov pubs and the Velvet Revolution. Meet at the Astronomical Clock (Map pp88–9), or you can arrange to be met at your hotel.

POST

The main post office (Map pp108–9; ☎ 221 131 111; www.cpost.cz; Jindřišská 14, Nové Město; 2am-midnight; M Můstek), just off Wenceslas Square, uses an automatic queuing system. Take a ticket from one of the machines in the entrance corridors – press button No 1 for stamps, letters and parcels, or No 4 for Express Mail Service (EMS). Then watch the display boards in the main hall – when your ticket number appears (flashing), go to the desk number shown. Most of the city's other post offices open from 8am to 6pm or 7pm Monday to Friday and until noon Saturday.

The Czech postal service (Česká Pošta) is fairly efficient. Anything you can't afford to lose, however, should go by registered mail *(doporučený dopis)* or by EMS. A postcard or letter up to 20g costs 17Kč to other European countries and 18Kč for destinations outside Europe. A 2kg parcel by EMS costs 900Kč to Europe, 1200Kč to North America and 1600Kč to Australia. You can buy stamps from street vendors and newspaper kiosks as well as from post offices.

You can pick up poste-restante mail *(výdej listovních zásilek)* at desk Nos 1 and 2 (at the far left) in the main post office from 7am to 8pm Monday to Friday and until noon Saturday. Mail should be addressed to Poste Restante, Hlavní pošta, Jindřišská 14, 110 00 Praha 1, Czech Republic. You must present your passport to claim mail (check under your first name, too). Mail is held for one month.

If you need a professional courier service, DHL (Map pp108–9; ☎ 800 103 000; www.dhl.cz; Václavské náměstí 47, Nové Město; 8am-6.30pm Mon-Fri, 9am-3pm Sat) has a convenient office just off Wenceslas Square, with English-speaking staff.

RADIO

Radio Prague (www.radio.cz; 92.6MHz FM) broadcasts 15-minute-long programmes in English covering Czech news, culture and current affairs at 7.07pm Monday to Thursday. The city's best alternative music station is Radio 1 (91.9MHz FM), though commercial-free Radio Wave (100.7MHz FM), which broadcasts an English-language breakfast show on Fridays, gives it a good run for its money.

The BBC World Service (www.bbc.co.uk/worldservice) broadcasts both English-language and Czech news and cultural programmes locally on 101.1MHz FM, from 11am to 1pm and 4pm to 8am.

SAFETY

Although Prague is as safe as any European capital, the huge influx of money to the city has spawned an epidemic of petty crime. Where tourists are concerned, this mainly means pickpockets. The prime trouble spots are Prague Castle (especially at the changing of the guard), Charles Bridge, Old Town Square (in the crowd watching the Astronomical Clock), the entrance to the Old Jewish Cemetery, Wenceslas Square, the main train station, in the metro (watch your backpack on escalators) and on trams (notably on the crowded lines 9, 22 and 23).

There's no need to be paranoid, but keep valuables well out of reach, and be alert in crowds and on public transport. A classic ruse involves someone asking directions and thrusting a map under your nose, or a woman with a baby hassling you for money – anything to distract your attention – while accomplices delve into your bags and pockets.

Lost or Stolen Belongings

If your passport, wallet or other valuables have been stolen, report the loss to any police station within 24 hours. The easiest place is the Praha I police station (Map pp108–9; Jungmannovo náměstí 9; 24hr), near the foot of Wenceslas Square. Tell them what language you speak, and they'll give you a standard crime report form *(Policejní zpráva)* to fill out, which they will stamp and return (this is for insurance purposes only; the crime will almost certainly not be investigated). Unless you speak Czech, forget about phoning the police, as you will rarely get through to an English speaker. Once you have a crime report, you can apply to the consular department of your embassy for a replacement passport.

Do likewise if you have lost your passport, wallet or other valuables. For anything except travel documents, you might get lucky at the city's lost & found office (ztráty a nálezy; Map pp88–9; ☎ 224 235 085; Karoliny Světlé 5; 8am-noon & 12.30-5.30pm Mon & Wed, to 4pm Tue & Thu, to 2pm Fri; 6, 9, 18, 22, 23). There's another lost & found office (☎ 220 114 283; 24hr) at the airport.

Racism

You may be surprised at the level of casual prejudice directed against the Roma, whom people are quick to blame for the city's problems. Overt hostility towards visitors is rare, though there have been some assaults by skinheads on dark-skinned people.

Scams

Beware of men who claim to be plain-clothes police officers investigating counterfeiting or illegal moneychanging. They approach tourists and ask to see their money, which is returned after being examined. When you check your wallet you'll find that a substantial amount of money has been taken. No genuine police officer has the right to inspect your money.

Another ploy involves a 'lost tourist' asking for directions (usually in halting English). Once you have been in conversation for a few minutes, two of the tourist's 'friends' interrupt, claiming to be plain-clothes policemen and accusing you of changing money illegally. They will demand to see your wallet and passport, but if you hand them over they are likely to run off with them.

TELEPHONE

All Czech phone numbers have nine digits – you have to dial all nine for any call, local or long distance (there are no area codes). All land-line numbers in Prague begin with a 2; mobile numbers begin with a 6 or 7. See the inside front cover for useful phone numbers and codes.

There are payphones all over town that can be used to make local, long-distance and international calls. Coin-operated phones accept only 2Kč, 5Kč, 10Kč and 20Kč coins; a more common and convenient alternative is a prepaid calling card, which allows you to make domestic and international calls from any phone or payphone in the Czech Republic.

You can also make international calls from the telephone bureau at the main post office (to the left inside the right-hand entrance) – you simply pay a deposit and make your call in a soundproof booth, where a little meter ticks off the rate.

The telephone bureau has directories for Prague and other major cities. You can also look up business phone numbers online at www.zlatestranky.cz.

Mobile Phones

The Czech Republic uses GSM 900 (now 3G compatible), which is the same as the rest of Europe, Australia and New Zealand but is not compatible with the North American GSM 1900 or the totally different system in Japan. Some North Americans, however, have dual-band GSM 1900/900 phones that do work here; check with your service provider about using your mobile abroad, and beware of calls being routed internationally (which is very expensive for a 'local' call). The main mobile networks in Prague are Telefonica/02 (www.cz.o2.com), T-Mobile (www.t-mobile.cz) and Vodafone (www.vodafone.cz).

If your mobile phone is unlocked, you can buy a Czech SIM card from any mobile phone shop for around 450Kč (including 300Kč of calling credit) and make local calls at local rates (3Kč to 9Kč a minute). In this case, of course, you can't use your existing mobile number.

Phonecards

Local prepaid cards include Smartcall (www.smartcall.cz) and Karta X Plus – you can buy them from hotels, newspaper kiosks and tourist information offices for 300Kč to 1000Kč. To use one, follow the instructions on the card – dial the access number, then the PIN code beneath the scratch-away panel, then the number you want to call (including any international code). Rates from Prague to the UK, USA and Australia with Smartcall are around 6.6Kč to 10Kč a minute; the more expensive the card, the better the rate.

TIME

The Czech Republic is on Central European Time, ie GMT/UTC plus one hour. Clocks are set to daylight-saving time in summer, that is, forward one hour on the last weekend in March and back one hour on the last weekend in October. Czechs use the 24-hour clock.

TOILETS

Public toilets are free in state-run museums, galleries and concert halls. Elsewhere, such as in train, bus and metro stations, public toilets are staffed by attendants who charge 5Kč to 10Kč for admission. Most places are clean and well kept. Men's are marked *muži* or *páni*, and women's *ženy* or *dámy*.

In the main tourist areas, there are public toilets in Prague Castle; opposite the tram stop on Malostranské náměstí; next to the Goltz-Kinský Palace on Old Town Square; on Templova, just off Celetná close to the Powder Gate; on Uhelný trh in the Old Town; and next to the Laterna Magika on Národní třída.

TOURIST INFORMATION

The Prague Information Service (Pražská informační služba, PIS; ☎ 12444 or 221 714 444 in English & German; www.prague-info.cz) is the main provider of tourist information: it has good maps and detailed brochures (including accommodation options and historical monuments), all free. PIS also sells public transport tickets.

There are four PIS offices:

Main train station (Praha hlavní nádraží; Map pp108–9; Wilsonova 2, Nové Město; 9am-7pm Mon-Fri, 9am-4pm Sat & Sun Apr-Oct, 9am-6pm Mon-Fri, 9am-4pm Sat & Sun Nov-Mar)

Malá Strana Bridge Tower (Map pp76–7; Charles Bridge; 10am-6pm Apr-Oct)

Old Town Hall (Map pp88–9; Staroměstské náměstí 5, Staré Město; 9am-7pm Apr-Oct, 9am-6pm Nov-Mar)

Rytířská (Map pp88–9; Rytířská 31, Staré Město; 9am-7pm Apr-Oct, 9am-6pm Nov-Mar)

Overseas Offices

Czech Tourism (www.czechtourism.com) offices around the world provide information about tourism, culture and business in the Czech Republic.

Austria (☎ 01-533 21933; Herrengasse 17, 1010 Vienna)

France (☎ 01 53 73 00 22; rue Bonaparte 18, 75006 Paris)

Germany (☎ 030-204 4770; Friedrichstrasse 206, 10969 Berlin-Kreuzberg)

Netherlands (☎ 020-575 3014; Strawinskylaan 517, 1077 XX Amsterdam)

Poland (☎ 022-629 2916; Al. Róż 16, 00-556 Warsaw)

UK (☎ 020-7631 0427, brochure requests 09063-640641; 13 Harley St, London W1G 9QG)

USA (☎ 212-288 0830; 1109 Madison Ave, New York, NY 10028)

TRAVELLERS WITH DISABILITIES

Increasing, but still limited, attention is being paid to facilities for people with disabilities in Prague. Wheelchair ramps are becoming more common, especially at major street intersections, in newer shopping malls and in top-end hotels (in the Sleeping chapter we identify hotels with facilities for wheelchair users). For people who are blind or vision-impaired, most pedestrian crossings in central Prague have a sound signal to indicate when it's safe to cross. McDonald's and KFC entrances and toilets are wheelchair-friendly.

Much of Prague Castle is wheelchair-accessible, but the cobbled streets, narrow pavements and steep hills of the surrounding Hradčany and Malá Strana districts are not. The Estates Theatre (p199) is equipped for the hearing-impaired, while the Convent of St Agnes (p95) has a ground-floor presentation of medieval sculptures with explanatory text in Braille; these venues and several other theatres are wheelchair-accessible. The monthly what's-on booklet *Přehled* – which is published by PIS in Czech only – indicates venues with wheelchair access. We also note lifts and other accessibility factors in individual listings.

Few buses and no trams have wheelchair access; special wheelchair-accessible buses operate Monday to Friday on bus lines 1 and 3, including between Florenc bus station and náměstí Republiky, and between Holešovice train station and náměstí Republiky (visit the website at www.dpp.cz for more information).

Prague's main train station (Praha hlavní nádraží), Praha-Holešovice train station and a handful of metro stations (Hlavní Nádraží, Hůrka, Luka, Lužiny, Nádraží Holešovice, Stodůlky and Zličín) have self-operating lifts. Other metro stations (Chodov, Dejvická, Florenc C line, Háje, IP Pavlova, Opatov, Pankrác, Roztyly and Skalka) have modified lifts that can be used with the help of station staff. Czech Railways (ČD) claims that every large station in the country has wheelchair ramps and lifts, but in fact the service is poor.

When flying, travellers with special needs should inform the airline of their requirements when booking, and again when reconfirming, and again when checking in. Most international airports (including Prague's) have ramps, lifts and wheelchair-accessible toilets and telephones. Aircraft toilets, on the other hand, present problems for wheelchair users, who should discuss this early on with the airline and/or their doctor.

Some useful organisations include the following:

Czech Blind United (Sjednocená organizace nevidomých a slabozrakých v ČR; Map pp108–9; ☎ 221 462 146; www.braillnet.cz; Krakovská 21, Nové Město) Represents the vision-impaired; provides information but no services.

Prague Wheelchair Users Organisation (Pražská organizace vozíčkářů; Map pp88–9; ☎ 224 827 210; www.pov.cz, in Czech; Benediktská 6, Staré Město) Can organise a guide and transportation at about half the cost of a taxi, and has a CD-ROM guide to barrier-free Prague in Czech, English and German.

VISAS

Everyone is required to have a valid passport (or ID card for EU citizens) to enter the Czech Republic. Citizens of EU and EEA (Europe Economic Area) countries do not need a visa for any type of visit. Citizens of Australia, Canada, Israel, Japan, New Zealand and the USA can stay for up to 90 days without a visa; other nationalities can check their visa requirements on www.czech.cz (click on the Tourism link). Visas are not available at border crossings or at Prague's Ruzyně airport; you'll be refused entry if you need one and arrive without one.

Non-EU citizens who want to stay in the Czech Republic for more than 90 days must apply for a long-term visa, employment visa or residency permit; get details from your nearest Czech embassy, and apply at least four months in advance.

The Czech Republic became part of the Schengen Zone in December 2007; visitors who need a visa can apply for a Schengen Visa, which will allow them to visit other countries in the zone (see http://europa.eu for details). Visa regulations change from time to time, so check www.czech.cz.

WOMEN TRAVELLERS

Walking alone on the street is as safe – or as dangerous – as in most large European cities. Avoid the park in front of Prague's main train station after dark, and be aware that the area around the intersection of Wenceslas Square and Na Příkopě is effectively a red-light district at night. The city has developed a burgeoning sex industry, with strip clubs, lap-dancing clubs, brothels and street workers all in evidence, and British stag parties stumbling drunkenly through the streets around Wenceslas Square at weekends.

There are few services for women such as help-lines and refuge or rape crisis centres. The main organisation in Prague is the **White Circle of Safety** (Bílý kruh bezpečí; Map p138; ☎ 257 317 110; www.bkb.cz; Duškova 20, Smíchov), which provides help and counselling to victims of crime and violence.

WORK

Unemployment in Prague is low – around 3.5% in 2007 – and although there are job opportunities for foreigners in English teaching, IT, finance, real estate and management firms, competition for jobs is fierce and finding one is increasingly difficult.

EU citizens do not need a work permit to work in the Czech Republic; non-EU citizens do, however. You might be able to find short- or long-term employment teaching English (or other languages) at the numerous language schools in Prague. Alternatively, you might look for jobs with the city's many expat-run restaurants, hostels and bars. Possibilities also exist in foreign-owned businesses. Investment banking, real estate, IT and management firms in particular need experienced staff and often employ non-Czech speakers, but the odds of getting such a job are better if you apply from home rather than waiting until you are in Prague.

You can research the employment market on websites such as www.jobs.cz, www.expats.cz and www.prague.tv, and look for jobs in the classified-ad section of the **Prague Post** (www.praguepost.cz).

Business Contacts

Czech Chamber of Commerce (☎ 296 646 112; www.komora.cz; Freyova 27, Vysočany, 190 00 Prague)

Prague Convention Bureau (☎ 224 235 159; www.pragueconvention.cz; Rytířská 26, Staré Město, 110 00 Prague)

LANGUAGE

Czech *(čeština)* is the main language spoken in the Czech Republic. It belongs to the West Slavonic group of Indo-European languages, along with Slovak, Polish and Lusatian.

It's true – anyone can speak another language. Don't worry if you haven't studied languages before or that you studied a language at school for years and can't remember any of it. It doesn't even matter if you failed English grammar. After all, that's never affected your ability to speak English! And this is the key to picking up a language in another country. You just need to start speaking.

Learn a few key phrases before you go. Write them on pieces of paper and stick them on the fridge, by the bed or even on the computer – anywhere that you'll see them often.

You'll find that locals appreciate travellers trying their language, no matter how muddled you may think you sound. So don't just stand there, say something! If you want to learn more Czech than we've included here, pick up a copy of Lonely Planet's comprehensive but user-friendly *Czech Phrasebook*. For a more concise language guide, look for Lonely Planet's *Small Talk Eastern Europe*.

PRONUNCIATION

It's not easy to learn Czech pronunciation, and you may have to learn a few new linguistic tricks to do so. It is, however, spelt the way it's spoken, and once you become familiar with the sounds, it's easy to read. Stress is usually on the first syllable.

Vowels

Vowels have long and short variants; they have the same pronunciation, but the long vowels are simply held for longer. The long vowels are indicated by an acute accent. The following approximations reflect British pronunciation:

a	as the 'u' in 'cut'
á	as the 'a' in 'father'
e	as in 'bet'
é	as the word 'air'
ě	as the 'ye' in 'yet'
i/y	as the 'i' in 'bit'
í/ý	as the 'i' in 'marine'
o	as in 'pot'
ó	as the 'aw' in 'saw'
u	as in 'pull'
ú/ů	as the 'oo' in 'zoo'

Diphthongs

aj	as the 'i' in 'ice'
áj	as the word 'eye'
au	as the 'ow' in 'how'
ej	as the 'ay' in 'day'
ij/yj	short; as 'iy'
íj/ýj	longer version of ij/yj
oj	as the 'oi' in 'void'
ou	as the 'o' in 'note', though each vowel is more strongly pronounced than in English
uj	as the 'u' in 'pull', followed by the 'y' in 'year'
ůj	longer version of uj

Consonants

c	as the 'ts' in 'lets'
č	as the 'ch' in 'chew'
ch	like 'ch' in Scottish *loch*
j	as the 'y' in 'year'
r	a rolled 'r' (at the tip of the tongue)
ř	no English equivalent; a rolled 'rzh' sound, as in the composer, Dvořák
š	as the 'sh' in 'ship'
ž	a 'zh' sound, as the 's' in 'treasure'
ď, ľ, ť	very soft palatal sounds, ie consonants followed by a momentary contact between the tongue and the hard palate, as if followed by 'y' (like the 'ny' in canyon). The same applies to d, n and t when followed by i, í or ě.

All other consonants are similar to their English counterparts, although the letters k, p and t are unaspirated, meaning they are pronounced with no audible puff of breath after them.

SOCIAL

Greetings & Civilities

Hello/Good day.
Dobrý den. (polite)
Ahoj. (informal)
Goodbye.
Na shledanou. (polite)
Ahoj/Čau. (informal)
Yes.
Ano/Jo. (polite/informal)
No.
Ne.
May I? (asking permission)
Dovolte mi?
Sorry/Excuse me. (apologising or seeking assistance)
Promiňte.
Could you help me, please?
Prosím, můžete mi pomoci?
Please.
Prosím.
Thank you (very much).
(Mockrát) děkuji.
You're welcome. (as in 'don't mention it')
Není zač.
Good morning.
Dobré jitro/ráno.
Good afternoon.
Dobré odpoledne.
Good evening.
Dobrý večer.
How are you?
Jak se máte?
Well, thanks.
Děkuji, dobře.

Going Out

What's there to do in the evenings?
Kam se tady dá večer jít?
What's on tonight?
Co je dnes večer na programu?
In the entertainment guide.
V kulturním programu.

I feel like going to a/an/the ...
Mám chuť jít ...

bar	do baru
café	do kavárny
cinema	do kina
nightclub	do noční podnik
opera	na operu
restaurant	do restaurace
theatre	do divadla

Do you know a good restaurant?
Znáš nejakou dobrou restauraci?

Are there any good nightclubs?
Jsou tady nějaké dobré noční podniky?

Language Difficulties

Do you speak English?
Mluvíte anglicky?
I understand.
Rozumím.
I don't understand.
Nerozumím.
Could you write it down, please?
Můžete mi to napsat, prosím?

PRACTICAL

Directions

Do you have a local map?	Máte mapu okolí?
Where is ...?	Kde je ...?
Go straight ahead.	Jděte přímo.
Turn left.	Zatočte vlevo.
Turn right.	Zatočte vpravo.
behind	za
in front of	před
far	daleko
near	blízko
opposite	naproti

Numbers

It's quite common for Czechs to say the numbers 21 to 99 in reverse; for example, *dvacet jedna* (21) becomes *jedna dvacet*.

0	nula
1	jedna
2	dva
3	tři
4	čtyři
5	pět
6	šest
7	sedm
8	osm
9	devět
10	deset
11	jedenáct
12	dvanáct
13	třináct
14	čtrnáct
15	patnáct
16	šestnáct
17	sedmnáct
18	osmnáct
19	devatenáct
20	dvacet
21	dvacet jedna
22	dvacet dva

23	dvacet tři
30	třicet
40	čtyřicet
50	padesát
60	šedesát
70	sedmdesát
80	osmdesát
90	devadesát
100	sto
1000	tisíc

Banking

Where's a/the ...?
Kde je ...?

ATM	bankomat
bank	banka
exchange office	směnárna

I want to change (a) ...
Chtěl/a bych vyměnit ... (m/f)

cash/money	peníze
(travellers) cheque	(cestovní) šek

What time does the bank open?
V kolik hodin otevírá banka?

Post Office

Where's a/the post office?
Kde je pošta?

I want to buy ...
Rád/a bych koupil/a ... (m/f)

postcards	pohlednice
stamps	známky

I want to send a ...
Chtěl/a bych poslat ... (m/f)

letter	dopis
parcel	balík
postcard	pohled

Phones & Mobiles

Where's the nearest public phone?
Kde je nejbližší veřejný telefon?
Could I please use the telephone?
Mohu si zatelefonovat?
I want to call ...
Chci zavolat ...
I want to make a long-distance call to ...
Chtěl/a bych volat do ... (m/f)
I want to make a reverse-charge/collect call.
Chtěl/a bych zavolat na účet volaného. (m/f)
I want to buy a phonecard.
Chtěl/a bych koupit telefonní karta. (m/f)

Internet

Is there a local internet café?
Je tady internet kavárna? (m/f)
I'd like to get internet access.
Chtěl/a bych se připojit na internet. (m/f)
I'd like to check my email.
Chtěl/a bych si skontrolovat můj email. (m/f)

Paperwork

name	jméno
address	adresa
date of birth	datum narození
place of birth	místo narození
age	věk
sex	pohlaví
nationality	národnost
passport number	číslo pasu
visa	vizum
driving licence	řidičský průkaz

Question Words

Who?	Kdo?
What?	Co?
When?	Kdy?
Where?	Kde?
How?	Jak?

Shopping & Services

Where's (a/the) ...?
Kde je ...?
I'm looking for (a/the) ...
Hledám ...

art gallery	uměleckou galérii
city centre	centrum
embassy	velvyslanectví
main square	hlavní náměstí
market	tržiště
museum	muzeum
public toilet	veřejné záchody
tourist office	turistická informační kancelář

What time does it open/close?
V kolik hodin otevírají/zavírají?

Signs

Kouření Zakázáno	No Smoking
Otevřeno	Open
Umývárny/Toalety	Toilets
Páni/Muži	Men
Dámy/Ženy	Women

Vchod	Entrance
Vstup Zakázán	No Entry
Východ	Exit
Zákaz	Prohibited
Zavřeno	Closed

Time & Dates

What time is it?	Kolik je hodin?
in the morning	ráno
in the afternoon	odpoledne
in the evening	večer
today	dnes
now	teď
yesterday	včera
tomorrow	zítra
next week	příští týden
Monday	pondělí
Tuesday	úterý
Wednesday	steda
Thursday	čtvrtek
Friday	pátek
Saturday	sobota
Sunday	neděle
January	leden
February	únor
March	březen
April	duben
May	květen
June	červen
July	červenec
August	srpen
September	září
October	říjen
November	listopad
December	prosinec

Dates in Museums

year	rok
century	století
millennia	milénium/tisíciletí
beginning of ...	začátek ...
first half of ...	první polovina ...
middle of ...	polovina ...
second half of ...	druhá polovina ...
end of ...	konec ...

Transport

What time does the train/bus leave?
V kolik hodin odjíždí vlak/autobus?
What time does the train/bus arrive?
V kolik hodin přijíždí vlak/autobus?
Excuse me, where is the ticket office?
Prosím, kde je pokladna?
I want to go to ...
Chci jet do ...
I'd like ...
Rád/a bych ... (m/f)

a one-way ticket	jednosměrnou jízdenku
a return ticket	zpáteční jízdenku
two tickets	dvě jízdenky

FOOD

For more detailed information on food and dining out, see p156 for vegetarian-specific phrases.

Can you recommend a ...?
Můžete doporučit ...?

café	kavárnu
pub	hospodu
restaurant	restauraci

I'd like ..., please.
Chtěl/Chtěla bych ..., prosím. (m/f)
a table for (five)
stůl pro (pět)
the nonsmoking section
nekuřáckou místnost
the smoking section
kuřáckou místnost

Is service included in the bill?
Je to včetně obsluhy?
What's the local speciality?
Co je místní specialita?
What would you recommend?
Co byste doporučil/doporučila? (m/f)
Cheers!
Na zdraví!

I'd like (the) ..., please.
Chtěl/Chtěla bych ..., prosím. (m/f)

bill	účet
drink list	nápojový lístek
menu	jídelní lístek
that dish	ten pokrm

I'm allergic to ...
Mám alergii na ...

dairy produce	mléčné výrobky
gluten	lepek
nuts	ořechy
seafood	plody moře

snack	občerstvení
breakfast	snídaně
lunch	oběd
dinner	večeře

COMMON DISHES

bramborový salát – potato salad – mayonnaise-based with yogurt, diced potatoes, carrots, peas, dill pickles, onions & corn

chlebíčky – open sandwiches on French bread, with cold meat, eggs, cheese, or mayonnaise salads like lobster, fish, potato or ham and peas

ďábelská topinka – a piquant toast with meat and cheese

guláš – thick, spicy stew, usually made with beef & potatoes, sometimes with venison or mushrooms

hranolky – French fries (hot chips)

krokety – deep-fried mashed potato balls; croquettes

kuře na paprice – chicken boiled in spicy paprika cream sauce

míchaná vejce s klobásou – scrambled eggs with sausage

opékané brambory – roasted potatoes

párek v rohlíku – hot dog

Pražská šunka – Prague ham – ham pickled in brine & spices & smoked over a beechwood fire

ruská vejce – hard-boiled egg, potato and salami, with mayonnaise

salát – salad

sendvič – sandwich

smažené žampiony – fried mushrooms

smažený květák – fried cauliflower in breadcrumbs

smažený sýr – fried cheese in breadcrumbs

smažený vepřový řízek – fried pork schnitzel

šopský salát – lettuce, tomato, onion & cheese salad

vejce se slaninou – bacon & eggs

FOOD GLOSSARY

ananas	pineapple
arašídy	peanuts
banán	banana
brambor	potato
brokolice	broccoli
česnek	garlic
chléb	bread
cibule	onion
citrón	lemon
čokoláda	chocolate
cuketa	zucchini (courgette)
cukr	sugar
dort	cake
dýně	pumpkin
fazole	bean
hlávkový	lettuce
hořčice	mustard
houba	mushroom
hovězí	beef
hrášek	peas
hruška	pear
jablko	apple
jahoda	strawberry
jehněčí	lamb
jogurt	yogurt
kapusta	cabbage
kari	curry
knedlíky	dumplings
krůta	turkey
kukuřice	corn
kuře	chicken
květák	cauliflower
kyselá smetana	sour cream
lilek	eggplant (aubergine)
losos	salmon
majonéza	mayonnaise
malina	raspberry
mandle	almond
máslo	butter
maso	meat
med	honey
mrkev	carrot
ocet	vinegar
okurka	cucumber or dill pickle
olej	oil
omáčka	sauce
omeleta	omelette
ořechy	nuts
ovoce	fruit
palačinka	crepe (pancake)
paprika	capsicum (bell pepper)
pečivo	bread rolls
pepř	black pepper
plody moře	seafood
polévka	soup
pomeranč	orange
pstruh	trout
rajče	tomato
rozinky	raisins (sultanas)
ryba	fish
rýže	rice
salám	salami
skopové	mutton
slanina	bacon
sleď	herring
šlehačka	whipped cream
smetana	cream
sójová omáčka	soy sauce
sójové mléko	soy milk
sójový tvaroh	tofu
špenát	spinach
sůl	salt
šunka	ham
svíčková	sirloin
sýr	cheese
tatarská omáčka	tartar sauce
telecí	veal
těstovina	pasta
tuňák	tuna
tvaroh	cottage cheese
ústřice	oyster
vanilka	vanilla

vařený	boiled
vejce	eggs
vepřové	pork
zelenina	vegetables
zelí	cabbage, sauerkraut
zmrzlina	ice cream

METHODS OF PREPARATION

čerstvý	fresh
fritovaný	deep-fried
grilovaný	broiled
horký	hot
krvavý	rare (of meat)
míchaný	mixed
na roštu	grilled
pečený	roasted
propečený	well-done (of meat)
se sýrem	with cheese
sladký	sweet
smažený	fried
středně propečený	medium rare (of meat)
studený	cold
teplý	warm
uzený	smoked
zmrzlí	frozen

DRINKS

čaj	tea
káva	coffee
limonáda	lemonade
mléko	milk
nealkoholický nápoj	soft drink
neperlivá voda	still water
odstředěné mléko	skim milk
perlivá minerálka	carbonated mineral water
pivo	beer
pomerančový džus	orange juice
slivovice	plum brandy
víno	wine
voda	water
bez kofeinu	decaffeinated
bez ledu	without ice
s citrónem	with lemon
s ledem	with ice
s mlékem	with milk
se smetanou	with cream

EMERGENCIES

Help!
Pomoc!
It's an emergency!
To je naléhavý případ!
Could you please help me?
Prosím, můžete mi pomoci?
Call an ambulance/a doctor/the police!
Zavolejte sanitku/doktora/policii!
Where's the police station?
Kde je policejní stanice?

HEALTH

Where's the ...?
Kde je ...?

chemist/pharmacy	lékárna
dentist	zubař
doctor	doktor
hospital	nemocnice

I need a doctor who speaks English.
Potřebuji lékaře, který mluví anglicky.
I'm sick.
Jsem nemocný/nemocná. (m/f)
I have a headache.
Bolí mě hlava.

I have (a) ...
Mám ...

diarrhoea	průjem
fever	horečku

GLOSSARY

You may encounter these terms and abbreviations while in Prague. For more on food terms see p261.

autobus – bus

bankomat(y) – ATM(s)

čajovná – teahouse
ČD – Czech Railways, the state railway company
Čedok – the former state tour operator and travel agency, now privatised
chrám – cathedral
ČSA – Czech Airlines, the national carrier
ČSAD – Czech Automobile Transport, the state-run bus company
ČSSD – Social Democratic Party
cukrárna – cake shop

divadlo – theatre
doklad – receipt or document; see also *potvrzení*
dům – house or building

galérie – gallery, arcade

hlavní nádraží (hl nád) – main train station
hora – hill, mountain
hospoda – pub
hostinec – pub
hrad – castle
hřbitov – cemetery

jízdenka – ticket

kaple – chapel
katedralá – cathedral
kavárna – café or coffee shop
Kč (Koruna česká) – Czech crown
kino – cinema
knihkupectví – bookshop
kolky – duty stamps, for payment at certain government offices, such as for a visa extension; sold at post offices and elsewhere
kostel – church
koupelna – bathroom
kreditní karta – credit card
KSČM – Czech Communist Party

lékárna – pharmacy

město – town
most – bridge
muzeum – museum

nábřeží (nábř) – embankment
nádraží – station
náměstí (nám) – square
národní – national

ODS – Civic Democratic Party
ostrov – island

palác – palace
pasáž – passage, shopping arcade
pekárna – bakery
penzión – pension
pěší zóna – pedestrian zone
pivnice – small beer hall
pivo – beer
pivovar – brewery
pokoj – room
potraviny – grocery or food shop
potvrzení – receipt or confirmation; see also *doklad*
Praha – Prague
provozní doba – business hours, opening times
přestup – transfer or connection

restaurace – restaurant

sad(y) – garden(s), park(s), orchard(s)
samoobsluha – self-service, minimarket
sleva – discount
stanice – train stop or station
sv (svatý) – Saint

třída (tř) – avenue

ulice (ul) – street
ulička (ul) – lane

Velvet Divorce – separation of Czechoslovakia into fully independent Czech and Slovak republics in 1993
Velvet Revolution (Sametová revoluce) – bloodless overthrow of Czechoslovakia's communist regime in 1989
věž – tower
vinárna – wine bar
vlak – train
výdej listovních zásilek – poste restante mail

zahrada – gardens, park
zámek – chateau
zastávka – bus, tram or train stop

BEHIND THE SCENES

THIS BOOK

This 8th edition of *Prague* was researched and written by Neil Wilson and Mark Baker. Neil also wrote the 5th, 6th and 7th editions and contributed to the 4th edition. This guidebook was commissioned in Lonely Planet's London office, and produced by the following:

Commissioning Editors Fiona Buchan, Emma Gilmour

Coordinating Editor Ali Lemer

Coordinating Cartographer Csanad Csutoros

Coordinating Layout Designer Jacqueline McLeod

Managing Editor Sasha Baskett

Managing Cartographer Mark Griffiths

Managing Layout Designer Laura Jane

Assisting Editors Susie Ashworth, Cathryn Game

Assisting Cartographers Valentina Kremenchutskaya, Anthony Phelan, James Regan, Peter Shields

Assisting Layout Designers Jim Hsu, Katherine Marsh

Cover Designer Pepi Bluck

Project Managers Chris Girdler, Craig Kilburn

Language Content Coordinator Quentin Frayne

Thanks to Fayette Fox, Charity Mackinnon, Jelena Milosevic, Wayne Murphy, Trent Paton

Cover photographs Charles Bridge, Bibikow Walter/Jon Arnold Images (top); Cavelike interior of Dutá Hlava restaurant at Klub Architektů, Bethlehem Square, Richard Nebesky/LPI (bottom).

Internal photographs p4 (#2) Charles Bridge, Prague, Czech Republic © Jon Arnold Images. All other photographs by Lonely Planet Images and by Richard Nebesky except: p5 (#4) John Elk III; p2 Christer Fredriksson; p3 Izzet Keribar; p5 (#5) Ali Lemer; p6 (#1), p12 (#4) Doug McKinlay; p10 (#2) Martin Moos; p10 (#1) Jonathan Smith.

THANKS

NEIL WILSON

Many thanks to the usual gang, especially Carol Downie, Brendan Bolland and Richard Nebesky, and also to the unusual gang at Bukowski's. And a big thank-you to coauthor Mark for making this edition so much fun to research.

MARK BAKER

I would like to thank my three interview subjects, Camille Hunt, Anna Siskova and Iva Pekárková, for their time, and also my coauthor Neil for helping me to learn the ropes at Lonely Planet as a first-time author.

THE LONELY PLANET STORY

Fresh from an epic journey across Europe, Asia and Australia in 1972, Tony and Maureen Wheeler sat at their kitchen table stapling together notes. The first Lonely Planet guidebook, *Across Asia on the Cheap*, was born.

Travellers snapped up the guides. Inspired by their success, the Wheelers began publishing books to Southeast Asia, India and beyond. Demand was prodigious, and the Wheelers expanded the business rapidly to keep up. Over the years, Lonely Planet extended its coverage to every country and into the virtual world via lonelyplanet.com and the Thorn Tree message board.

As Lonely Planet became a globally loved brand, Tony and Maureen received several offers for the company. But it wasn't until 2007 that they found a partner whom they trusted to remain true to the company's principles of travelling widely, treading lightly and giving sustainably. In October of that year, BBC Worldwide acquired a 75% share in the company, pledging to uphold Lonely Planet's commitment to independent travel, trustworthy advice and editorial independence.

Today, Lonely Planet has offices in Melbourne, London and Oakland, with over 500 staff members and 300 authors. Tony and Maureen are still actively involved with Lonely Planet. They're travelling more often than ever, and they're devoting their spare time to charitable projects. And the company is still driven by the philosophy of *Across Asia on the Cheap*: 'All you've got to do is decide to go and the hardest part is over. So go!'

OUR READERS

Many thanks to the travellers who used the last edition and wrote to us with helpful hints, useful advice and interesting anecdotes:

Mayumi Abe, Sandie Feinman Antar, Janelle Aurisch, Mike Ballestrin, Samuel Baumgartner, George Beran, Amelie Böcher, Jeremy Burton, Jane Carter, Veronika Cihulkova, Tamara Cocco, Graham Courtenay, Margaret Dickson, Craig Eychner, Jonathan Franklin, Ruben Garcia, Andrea Giacchino, Helen Goldhawk, Lynne Grabar, Carmel Harrison, Anke Joosens, Paul Kail, Marjan Knossenburg, David Larsen, Beth Lasser, Warren Lee, Dave Leurquin, Peter Mair, Hannah Marder, Peggy Meyer, Richard Moss, Chris Piper, Sue Roden, Andrew Rogers, George Rothschild, Mike Rudling, Zihni Saglam, Elaine Santos, Flora Seul-Jacklein, Jørgen Simonsen, Phillip Simpson, Carol Smitham, Rebecca Spence, Karsten Staehr, Sharon Styve, Istvan Szucs, Patricia Wagenhuber, Yvonne Warners, Raymond Yee, Tierney Young.

ACKNOWLEDGMENTS

Many thanks to Northwestern University Press for the use of their content.

SEND US YOUR FEEDBACK

We love to hear from travellers – your comments keep us on our toes and help make our books better. Our well-travelled team reads every word on what you loved or loathed about this book. Although we cannot reply individually to postal submissions, we always guarantee that your feedback goes straight to the appropriate authors, in time for the next edition. Each person who sends us information is thanked in the next edition – and the most useful submissions are rewarded with a free book.

To send us your updates – and find out about Lonely Planet events, newsletters and travel news – visit our award-winning website: lonelyplanet.com/contact.

Note: We may edit, reproduce and incorporate your comments in Lonely Planet products such as guidebooks, websites and digital products, so let us know if you don't want your comments reproduced or your name acknowledged. For a copy of our privacy policy visit lonelyplanet.com/privacy.

Notes

Notes

Notes

Notes

Notes

Notes

Notes

INDEX

See also separate indexes for:

000 map pages
000 photographs

INDEX

000 map pages
000 photographs

BRIDGES

BREWERIES

BUILDINGS & STRUCTURES

000 map pages
000 photographs

CASTLES & PALACES

CEMETERIES

CHURCHES & CATHEDRALS

GRAVES

HOUSES

ISLANDS

JEWISH INTEREST

HOSTELS

HOTEL APARTMENTS

HOTELS

MONASTERIES

PENSIONS

WHEELCHAIR-ACCESSIBLE

SPORTS & ACTIVITIES

BICYCLE HIRE

FOOTBALL

GOLF

GYMS

HORSE RACING

ICE HOCKEY

MASSAGE

ROLLER HOCKEY

RUNNING

SKATING

SPAS

SWIMMING

TENNIS

TOP PICKS

000 map pages
000 photographs

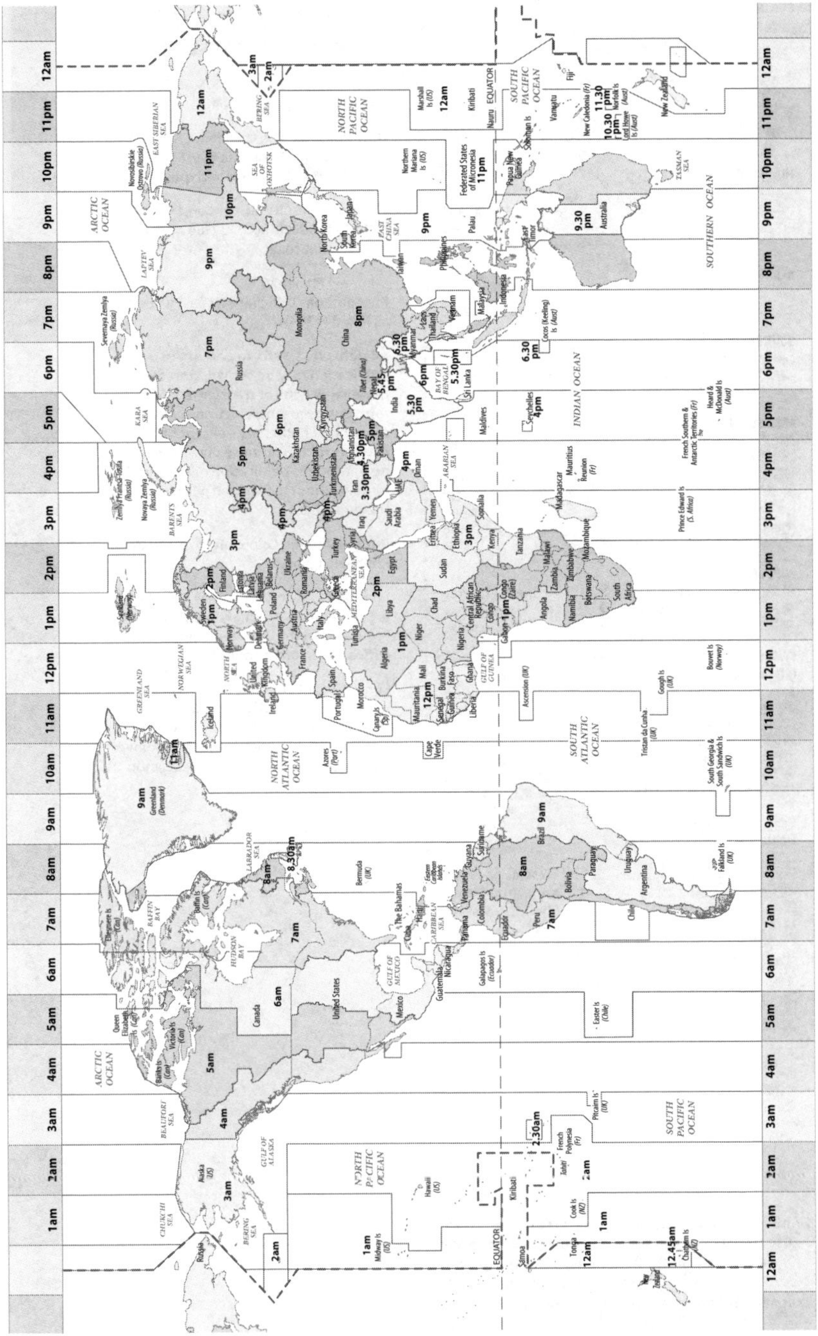
12am
11pm
10pm
9pm
8pm
7pm
6pm
5pm
4pm
3pm
2pm
1pm
12pm
11am
10am
9am
8am
7am
6am
5am
4am
3am
2am
1am
12am
ARCTIC OCEAN
EAST SIBERIAN SEA
LAPTEV SEA
KARA SEA
BARENTS SEA
GREENLAND SEA
NORWEGIAN SEA
NORTH SEA
BERING SEA
SEA OF OKHOTSK
EAST CHINA SEA
NORTH PACIFIC OCEAN
SOUTH PACIFIC OCEAN
TASMAN SEA
SOUTHERN OCEAN
INDIAN OCEAN
BAY OF BENGAL
ARABIAN SEA
MEDITERRANEAN SEA
GULF OF GUINEA
NORTH ATLANTIC OCEAN
SOUTH ATLANTIC OCEAN
LABRADOR SEA
BAFFIN BAY
HUDSON BAY
GULF OF MEXICO
CARIBBEAN SEA
BEAUFORT SEA
GULF OF ALASKA
CHUKCHI SEA
EQUATOR
Novosibirskie Ostrovo (Russia)
Severnaya Zemlya (Russia)
Zemlya Frantsa-Iosifa (Russia)
Novaya Zemlya (Russia)
Svalbard (Norway)
Russia
Mongolia
China
Tibet (China)
North Korea
South Korea
Japan
Taiwan
Philippines
Vietnam
Laos
Thailand
Myanmar
Malaysia
Indonesia
East Timor
Palau
Papua New Guinea
Solomon Is
Vanuatu
Fiji
New Caledonia (Fr)
Norfolk Is (Aust)
Lord Howe Is (Aust)
New Zealand
Australia
Marshall Is (US)
Kiribati
Nauru
Northern Mariana Is (US)
Federated States of Micronesia
Cocos (Keeling) Is (Aust)
Sri Lanka
Maldives
Seychelles
Mauritius
Reunion (Fr)
Madagascar
Heard & McDonald Is (Aust)
French Southern & Antarctic Territories (Fr)
Prince Edward Is (S. Africa)
India
Nepal
Pakistan
Afghanistan
Kazakhstan
Kyrgyzstan
Uzbekistan
Turkmenistan
Iran
Iraq
Saudi Arabia
Oman
UAE
Yemen
Somalia
Ethiopia
Eritrea
Kenya
Tanzania
Malawi
Mozambique
Zimbabwe
Zambia
Botswana
Namibia
South Africa
Angola
Congo (Zaire)
Congo
Gabon
Central African Republic
Sudan
Chad
Egypt
Libya
Niger
Nigeria
Algeria
Tunisia
Mali
Burkina Faso
Ghana
Liberia
Guinea
Senegal
Mauritania
Morocco
Canary Is (Sp)
Cape Verde
Azores (Port)
Ascension (UK)
Gough Is (UK)
Bouvet Is (Norway)
Tristan da Cunha (UK)
South Georgia & South Sandwich Is (UK)
Syria
Turkey
Greece
Italy
Ukraine
Belarus
Romania
Poland
Austria
Germany
Denmark
France
Spain
Portugal
Ireland
United Kingdom
Norway
Sweden
Finland
Estonia
Latvia
Lithuania
Iceland
Greenland (Denmark)
Ellesmere Is (Can)
Baffin Is (Can)
Queen Elizabeth Is (Can)
Victoria Is (Can)
Banks Is (Can)
Canada
Alaska (US)
United States
Mexico
Bermuda (UK)
The Bahamas
Cuba
Haiti
Eastern Caribbean Islands
Guatemala
Nicaragua
Panama
Colombia
Venezuela
Guyana
Suriname
Ecuador
Peru
Brazil
Bolivia
Paraguay
Uruguay
Chile
Argentina
Falkland Is (UK)
Galapagos Is (Ecuador)
Easter Is (Chile)
Pitcairn Is (UK)
French Polynesia (Fr)
Tahiti
Cook Is (NZ)
Hawaii (US)
Midway Is (US)
Samoa
Tonga
Chatham Is (NZ)
3am
2am
12am
11pm
10pm
9pm
9.30 pm
10.30 pm
11.30 pm
8pm
7pm
6.30 pm
6pm
5.45 pm
5.30 pm
5.30pm
6.30 pm
5pm
4.30pm
4pm
3.30pm
3pm
2pm
1pm
12pm
11am
9am
8am
8.30am
7am
6am
5am
4am
3am
2.30am
2am
1am
12am
12.45am

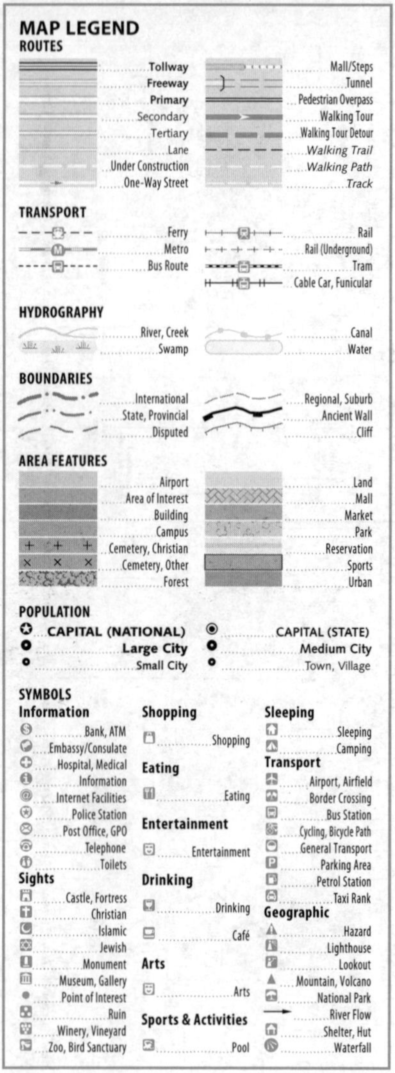

Published by Lonely Planet Publications Pty Ltd
ABN 36 005 607 983

Australia Head Office, Locked Bag 1, Footscray, Victoria 3011, ☎03 8379 8000, fax 03 8379 8111, talk2us@lonelyplanet.com.au

USA 150 Linden St, Oakland, CA 94607, ☎510 250 6400, toll free 800 275 8555, fax 510 893 8572, info@lonelyplanet.com

UK 2nd fl, 186 City Rd, London, EC1V 2NT, ☎020 7106 2100, fax 020 7106 2101, go@lonelyplanet.co.uk

Printed through Colorcraft Ltd, Hong Kong.
Printed in China.